国外动植物检验检疫法律法规系列丛书

东盟十国动植物检疫法规汇编

本书编委会　编

中国质检出版社
中国标准出版社
北　京

图书在版编目(CIP)数据

东盟十国动植物检疫法规汇编/本书编委会编. —北京：中国质检出版社，2014.12
ISBN 978-7-5026-3979-2

Ⅰ.①东… Ⅱ.①本… Ⅲ.①进出境动植物检疫法—汇编—东南亚国家联盟 Ⅳ.①D933.021

中国版本图书馆CIP数据核字（2014）第025754号

中国质检出版社
中国标准出版社 出版发行
北京市朝阳区和平里西街甲2号（100029）
北京市西城区三里河北街16号（100045）
网址：www.spc.net.cn
总编室：(010)64275323 发行中心：(010)51780235
读者服务部：(010)68523946
中国标准出版社秦皇岛印刷厂印刷
各地新华书店经销
*
开本 880×1230 1/16 印张 44.25 字数 1235千字
2014年12月第一版 2014年12月第一次印刷
*
定价 **220.00** 元

《国外动植物检验检疫法律法规系列丛书》
编 审 委 员 会

《东盟十国动植物检疫法规汇编》

编辑委员会

前　言

东南亚国家联盟（Association of Southeast Asia Nations），简称东盟（ASEAN），是东南亚十国成立的联盟组织，成立于1967年。2010年1月1日，随着中国－东盟自由贸易区正式全面启动，中国与东南亚各国经贸关系飞速发展。双边贸易额由2003年的782亿美元迅速攀升至2012年的4001亿美元，年均增长22%。作为世界第三大自由贸易区，中国－东盟自由贸易区的建成对东南亚乃至整个亚洲的经济产生着积极而深远的影响。

农产品贸易是中国－东盟自由贸易区建设的重要内容和最先开放领域，自由贸易区的建立对农产品贸易有巨大的促进作用，促进双边贸易朝着发挥各自优势的方向发展。中国和东盟在许多农产品上具有互补性，例如我国从东盟进口水果和蔬菜、糖和植物油等农产品，增加小麦等粮食作物向东盟的出口。这种贸易互补提高了资源配置的效率，为农产品提供更多的动力和机会。

了解东盟各国动植物检验检疫法律法规对于农产品顺利出口非常必要。由于社会、政治和经济发展程度不同，东盟各国动植物检验检疫法规体系存在较大差异，再加上语言方面的障碍，使得各利益相关方在收集和掌握东盟各国动植物检疫法律法规方面存在较大困难。为此，国家质量监督检验检疫总局动植物检疫监管司专门成立了“东盟各国动植物检验检疫法规协作组”，由质检总局标准法规研究中心主持，广西、云南两个地方出入境检验检疫局参与，系统地收集、整理、翻译和出版东盟国家动植物检验检疫法规。

《东盟十国动植物检疫法规汇编》一书涵盖了菲律宾、马来西亚、印度尼西亚等10个国家的动植物检疫相关法规40余部，均为截至到2014年的最新版本。在编译过程中，参与人员兢兢业业，尽量使内容更忠于原文本，以求译文能够较为准确地反映出原法律文本的实际含义。同时，考虑到法律文本的严肃性，对于译文，我们附有相应的原文。如对译文有异议，请参照原文。

由于各国法律体系各异，加之任务重、时间紧，在汇编内容的收集、取舍等方面难免存在一些问题；由于水平有限，译文也难免存在不妥和错漏之处，恳望读者指正。

作　者

2014年10月于北京

目　录

菲律宾

柬埔寨

马来西亚

缅　甸

泰　国

文　莱

新加坡

印度尼西亚

越　南

老　挝

菲律宾

菲律宾植物检疫法

（第 1433 号总统令）

1978 年，颁布植物检疫法是为进一步提高和加强植物产业局的植物检疫服务，修订和完善现有植物检疫法。

鉴于：

因植物性有害生物危害农作物而引起的经济损失已经日趋严重；

利用控制国内外植物和植物产品扩散来防止植物有害生物的传入定殖及扩散蔓延，这是防控植物性有害生物比较经济实用的手段；

现代交通工具和进出口贸易加速了植物和植物产品迅速广泛流通，因此也增加了植物性有害生物的入侵；

植物检疫是一项基础的必要的预防性措施，它是阻止危害农作物的植物性有害生物进入我国的第一防线；

1922 年颁布的第 3027 号法令，名为“为了保护菲律宾岛内的农业免受国外植物性有害生物和疾病的危害，将已传入我国的有害生物和疾病所致的危害减至最小而进一步控制国内植物材料的法令”，及 1930 年 12 月 26 日颁布的第 3767 号法令，名为“为保护我国农业及其相关产业，控制活体动物进入菲律宾岛内（包括昆虫、鸟类、虾蟹贝类、蝙蝠、软体动物、爬行动物、哺乳动物及其他不属于第 3639 号法令第 4 章中规定的‘国内动物’范围内的动物）的法令”，这两部法令中的某些条款已不适应保护我国的农业的需要，迫切需要及时修正更新；

菲律宾植物检疫的规定和条例必须适应其他国家的相关法律并遵循国际粮农组织——联合国植物保护公约（菲律宾是签署国之一）中的条款；

通过制定相应法律和条例，提供所需的资源和设备，以及奖励植物检疫官来提高和加强植物产业局的植物检疫服务质量，从而实现上述的目标；

我——菲律宾总统 Ferdinand E. Marcos，以议会赋予我的权利特此批准以下法令和规定。

第 1 节

此法令名为“1978 年植物检疫法”。

第 2 节　术语定义

以下术语用于该法令时的含义如下：

a. **人**　任何自然人或法人如法人团体、合伙企业、社团、协会、商号、公司和其他法律实体。

b. **局长**　指植物产业局局长。

c. **植物检疫官员**　指由植物产业局局长任命或指派的人。

d. **国家**　指任何独立的政治单位或君主制的国家、地区、殖民地、政治和领土上的从属国。

e. **运输工具**　包括任何类型的船或其他人工发明的能够用于海陆空的运输装置。

f. **植物**　指活的植物及其某个部位，包括种子、插条、砧木、球茎和鳞茎、接穗、叶片、根、幼芽和其他繁殖材料。

g. **植物产品**　指所有来自植物的产品，无论是天然状态或是已加工的状态，它们可能隐匿植物性有害生物。

h. **潜在的动物性有害生物**　由某种动物构成，这些动物容易成为农作物的有害生物如昆虫、猴子、啮齿动物、蝙蝠、雀科动物、兔子、蜗牛和其他可能危害农作物的动物。

i. **包装材料**　包括树叶、稻草、树皮和其他用于包装并有可能隐匿植物性有害生物的植物材料。

j. **植物性有害生物**　任何能够对植物及其产品造成危害的或潜在危害的植物、动物、病原物。

k. **检疫规定**　用于执行本总统令的由植物产业局局长实施颁布的行政条例。

l. **商品处理**　任何应用于植物、植物产品和其他有可能隐匿植物性有害生物的处理方法，其目的是消灭由植物性有害生物引起的感染和传染。

m. **入境口岸**　指进行国内和国外贸易的港口，它包括第一口岸和第二口岸。

n. **进口**　据本法令第三节和第四节所述，进口是指把国外的商品输入国内用于栽培、消费、加工、驯化或其他目的。

o. **过境植物/植物产品**　植物、植物产品从国内任何一个口岸入境但不卸货。

p. **出口**　根据本法令第3、4、6节所述，出口是指把本地的商品输出到国外。

q. **植物检疫证书**　植物健康证书。

第3节　植物和植物产品的进口

凡进口或引入菲律宾的植物、植物产品、可能隐匿植物有害生物的植物性土壤包装材料和植物性有害生物的传染源或介质，都必须严格遵守由农业部秘书长委任的局长颁布的检疫法律、规定和条例。

第4节　潜在的动物性有害生物的进口

禁止进口可能成为农作物有害生物或危害农作物的某些动物，如此类动物的限量进口有其正当理由，则凭主管部门的书面批准可以进口。

第5节　过境商品

这里所指的商品是本法令第3、4节中规定的商品和船载货物中的植物性食品或有植物包装的食品，此类商品在过境时需由植物检疫官在港口指定相关人员对商品进行消毒处理。

第6节　植物和植物产品的出口

如进口国需要，植物产业局局长和植物检疫官应对可能隐匿植物性有害生物的植物、植物产品及其他相关材料进行检验和签发植物检疫证书。

第7节　植物/植物产品、潜在的动物性有害生物及其他物品的检验

为实现本法提出的目标，植物产业局局长因对本法第3、4、5、6节中所指的商品进行检验并采取必要的植物检疫措施。

第8节　植物和植物产品的境内检疫

为防止菲律宾境内某地危险性植物性有害生物的扩散，植物产业局局长和植物检疫官员应对植物和植物产品进行检验，必要时采取相应措施并签发检疫证书，证书中必须注明其调运地点。为防止植物性有害生物的蔓延，必要时，局长可以限制某植物和植物产品在国内的调运。

第9节　植物检疫官的指派和委任

局长可以指派或专门委任植物检疫官代表他本人执行和实施本法的各项条款，专门的委任须以书

面形式下达。

第 10 节 植物检疫官的权力和职责

a. 对所有的运输工具、船员或乘客的行李和进境邮件实施检疫，以确定是否存在植物、植物产品和其他可能隐匿植物性有害生物的材料以及潜在的动物性有害生物。

b. 可以进入所有植物、植物产品和其他可能隐匿植物性有害生物的材料贮存场所、生长地进行检疫或鉴定。

c. 为确保本法得到有效实施，可采取必要的措施检查进口的植物、植物产品和其他可能隐匿植物性有害生物的材料以及潜在的动物有害生物。

d. 若进口国有要求，可对出口植物、植物产品以及其他有关材料实施检疫、管理、必要的处理以及签发植物检疫证书。

e. 没收和销毁或拒绝进口禁止进境的植物、植物产品和潜在的动物性有害生物以及禁止在国内调运的植物和植物产品；对禁止出口的植物产品不予签发植物检疫证书。

f. 履行赋予的其他有关职责。

植物检疫官在执行上述权力和职责时，具有警察部门同等权力。

第 11 节 免责条款

所有货物贮存费、滞留费、运费、劳务费和检验检疫延期费、货物处理费以及邮寄费由进出口商、货主或有关当事人承担。植物产业局或其授权代表对因执行本法规定所引起的货物损害不承担责任。

第 12 节 进出口方的责任

本法第 3、4、6 节中所指的进出口商品在登记入舱前，进口方、出口方或其委托代表须向局长出具一份声明，其中应包括收货人/发货人的姓名、地址、商品的用途、种类、性质、数量、原产地、货物装卸的时间、地点、装运货物的运输工具的注册号等。

第 13 节 运输工具的入境和消毒

国际和国内运输工具的所有人、经营或代理人须向口岸植物检疫官出具出入境通知和进出货物清单及其他相关资料。在出境前，上述运输工具的代理人须在植物检疫官的指导下对交通工具进行清洁消毒。

第 14 节 收费

在对第 3、4、6 节中所指的商品进行植物检疫、签发植物检疫证书、进口许可证、货物处理等时，将收取一定的管理费用，局长将就收费标准制定相关法规和条例。上述收费应设立国家植物检疫基金，以便合理使用，且应遵守政府的审计制度。

所有政府部门、国有公司或国家控股公司的进出口货物、经注册登记的赈灾组织或由社会服务发展部批准成立的慈善机构的捐赠物、外国大使和享有总统豁免的人员，国家经济发展局是为发展经济而提出的，可免交上述植物检疫费，但货物处理费除外。

第 15 节 加班

植物检疫官、熏蒸人员和辅助人员的加班、加餐、交通补贴、住宿补贴及其他开支应由当事人支付，补贴标准应经植物产业局局长提出由农业部秘书处划定。

第 16 节　协助单位

必要时，植物产业局局长可组织政府部门（包括军事、非军事、国家和当地部门）实施植物检疫条例并向其宣传与该条例相关信息。

第 17 节　制定特别检疫规定和条例的权力

由农业部秘书处委任的植物产业局局长有权根据执行本法各条款的需要而制定特别植物检疫规定和条例。

第 18 节　植物检疫局

为执行好本法各规定，植物检疫局由以下各部分组成：

a. 植物产业局局长	主席
b. 海关委托人或代表	成员
c. 菲律宾口岸局主管或代表	成员
d. 检疫局局长或代表	成员
e. 动物产业局局长或代表	成员
f. 国家经济发展局代表	成员
g. 菲律宾中央银行代表	成员
h. 菲律宾椰子局负责人及代表	成员
i. 林业局局长或代表	成员
j. 植物产业局法律顾问	成员
k. 进出口商会代表	成员
l. 植物产业局农作物保护处负责人	成员
m. 邮政局局长或代表	成员
n. 植物产业局植物检疫处负责人	秘书

第 19 节　植物检疫局的职责

植物检疫局是协助植物产业局局长为有效执行和修订本法而制定相应法规和条例的顾问机构。

第 20 节　植物检疫局会议

植物检疫局应每季度召开一次会议，必要时可召开特别会议，但特别会议每年不得超过四次。植物检疫局各与会人员每参加一次会议可获 200 菲律宾元。

第 21 节　法定人数

植物检疫局多数成员都具备法定人数。

第 22 节　植物检疫局的专款专用

每年有 300,00 菲律宾元经费用于植物检疫局各项开支，上述经费除外如有额外经费将纳入植物检疫专项基金。

第 23 节　罚则

根据法院的判决，对违反本法规定或伪造、变更、涂改、毁损根据本法签发的任何文件的任何个人、公司和企业处以 20,000 菲律宾元以下的罚金或监禁，或监禁并处罚金。

第 24 节　附则

本法规定生效之前，其他法律继续有效。

第 25 节　废除条款

所有与本法规定相抵触的法律、规定和条例均以本法为准或予以废除。

第 26 节　生效

本法经批准后生效。

1978 年 6 月 10 日签发于马尼拉

Plant Quarantine

(Presidential Decree No. 1433)

Promulgating the plant quarantine law of 1978, thereby revising and consolidating existing plant quarantine laws to further improve and strengthen the plant quarantine service of the bureau of plant industry

WHEREAS, economic losses due to injury on agricultural crops brought about by plant pests have become increasingly significant;

WHEREAS, the prevention of introduction, incursion, establishment and subsequent spread of plant pests by regulating the international and domestic movements of plants and plant products, is considered more practical and economical than any other method of plant pest control;

WHEREAS, modern means of transportation and handling of imports and exports have favored the expeditious and extensive movements of plants and plant products, thereby, increasing the risk of plant pest introduction and/or incursion;

WHEREAS, plant quarantine is basically and essentially a preventive measure, it being the actual frontline defense against the introduction or incursion into the country of plant pests which are destructive to our agricultural crops;

WHEREAS, some of the provisions of Act No. 3027 dated March 8, 1922, entitled "an act to protect the agricultural industries of the philippine islands from injurious plant pests and diseases existing in foreign countries and further to regulate the domestic movement of plant materials in order to minimize the injury from pests and diseases already introduced. " and act no. 3767, dated november 26, 1930, entitled " an act regulating the importation, bringing or introduction into the philippine islands of living animals, such as insects, birds, crustaceans, bats, mollusks, reptiles, mammals, and other animals, not falling within the scope of the term 'domestic animals' as provided and defined in section four of act numbered thirty - six hundred and thirty - nine, in order to protect the agricultural industries of this country and for other purposes" are no longer relevant and applicable to the protection of plant industries of this country, and therefore, require urgent and immediate modification and updating;

WHEREAS, the Plant Quarantine rules and regulations of the Philippines must be compatible with those of other countries and with the provisions of the Food and Agriculture Organization - International Plant Protection Convention of the United Nations to which the Philippines is a signatory;

WHEREAS, the attainment of the foregoing objectives requires the necessary improvement and strengthening of the Plant Quarantine Services of the Bureau of Plant Industry by providing adequate laws; regulations; resources and facilities; and incentives to Plant Quarantine Officers.

NOW, therefore, I, Ferdinand E. Marcos, President of the Philippines, by virtue of the powers vested in me by the Constitution do hereby decree and order the following:

Section 1 This Decree shall be known as the "Plant Quarantine Decree of 1978" .

Section 2 **Definition of Terms.** —The following terms used in this Decree shall mean as follows:

a. Person any natural or juridical person such as corporation, partnerships, societies, associations, firms, companies and other legal entities.

b. Director the Director of Plant Industry.

c. Plant Quarantine Officer any person so appointed and/or designated by the Director of Plant Industry.

d. Country any independent political unit or sovereign nation, territory, colony and political or territorial subdivision.

e. Carrier includes every sort of craft or other artificial contrivance used, capable of being used as a means of transportation in land, water or air.

f. Plants shall comprise living plants and parts thereof, including seeds, cuttings, rhizomes, bulbs and corms, grafts, leaves, roots, scions and others that are capable of propagation.

g. Plant Products shall mean products derived from plants, either in their natural state or in manufactured or processed form and are capable of harboring plant pests.

h. Potential Animal Pest shall comprise certain species of animals that are liable to become agricultural crop pests such as insects, monkeys, rodents, bats, finches, rabbits, snails and other forms of animal life capable of causing injury to agricultural crops.

i. Packing Materials include leaves, straw, bark and other plant materials used as wrapping, packing, or covering and are capable of harboring plant pets.

j. Plant Pest any form of plant or animal life, or any pathogenic agent, injurious or potentially injurious to plants and/or plant products.

k. Quarantine Orders shall mean those Administrative Orders promulgated and issued by the Director of Plant Industry to implement the provisions of this Decree.

l. Commodity Treatment any form of treatment applied to plants, plant products, and other materials capable of harboring plant pests, for the purpose of destroying or eliminating any infection/infestation caused by plant pests.

m. Port of Entry is a port open to both foreign and domestic trade. The term includes principal ports of entry and subports of entry.

n. Importation is the act of bringing into the country foreign commodities mentioned under Section 3 and 4 of this Decree for planting, consumption, manufacturing, domestication or for any other purpose.

o. Plants/Plant Products in Transit shall refer to plants/plant products brought into any port in the country but are not intended for landing at the said port.

p. Exportation is the act of transporting commodities mentioned under Sections 3, 4, and 6 hereof, from a local port to a foreign port.

q. Phytosanitary Certification shall mean plant health certification.

Section 3 Importation of plants and plant products. —The importation and/or introduction into the Philippines of plants, plant products, soil packing materials of plant origin capable of harboring plant pests and are a source or medium of infection/infestation of plant pests, *is hereby restricted* subject to such quarantine orders, rules and regulations as may be promulgated, from time to time, by the Director with the approval of the Secretary of Agriculture.

Section 4 Importation of potential animal pests. —The importation of certain species of animals which are liable to become agricultural crop pests and are capable of causing injury to agricultural crops, is hereby prohibited. However, importation in limited quantities for a justifiable purpose and upon a written permit from the Director of Plant Industry, may be allowed.

Section 5 Commodities in transit. —Commodities mentioned under Section 3 and 4 of this Decree, as well as, food provisions of plant origin and plant ornaments on board carriers, that are in transit shall be required of a clearance from the Plant Quarantine Officers assigned at the port concerned.

Section 6　Exportation of Plants and plant products. —The Director and/or the Plant Quarantine Officers shall cause the inspection and phytosanitary certification of all plants, plant products and other related materials capable of harboring plant pests, if the importing country so requires.

Section 7　Inspection of plants/plant products, potential animal pests, and other materials. —The Director shall cause the appropriate inspection, of the commodities mentioned in Sections 3, 4, 5 and 6 and to apply the necessary plant quarantine measures in order to attain the objectives of this Decree.

Section 8　Domestic Quarantine of plants and plant products. —In order to prevent and arrest the spread to other areas, of injurious plant pests existing in certain localities within the Philippines, the Director, and/or the Plant Quarantine Officers shall cause the inspection; treatment, if necessary; and certification of plants and plant products involved in the movement from one locality to another within the country.

In cases where it is necessary to contain plant pest (s) the Director may limit the movement of certain plants and/or plant products.

Section 9　Appointment and/or designation of Plant Quarantine Officers. —The Director shall cause the appointment and/or special designation of Plant Quarantine Officers, who shall act as his representatives, in implementing and enforcing the provisions of this Decree. Provided, however, that such special designation shall be in written form.

Section 10　Powers and Duties of Plant Quarantine Officers. —To inspect all carriers, crew/passenger luggages and incoming mails, in order to determine the presence of plants, plant products, and other materials capable of harboring plant pests, as well as, potential animal pests.

a. To enter into and inspect any and all areas where plants, plant products, and other materials capable of harboring plant pests are landed, stored, and/or grown.

b. To examine imported plants, plant products, and other materials capable of harboring plant pests as well as potential animal pests and to administer necessary measures to ensure effective implementation of the provisions of this Decree.

c. To inspect; administer treatment, if necessary; and issue phytosanitary certificates on plants, plant products, and other related materials intended for export, if the importing country so requires.

d. To confiscate and destroy or refuse entry of plants, plant products and potential animal pests involved in prohibited importations, as well as prohibited plants and plant products involved in domestic movement, and to deny phytosanitary certification of plants and plant products which exportation is, likewise, prohibited.

e. To perform such other related duties which maybe assigned to him, from time to time.

In the exercise of the powers and duties herein vested to Plant Quarantine Officers, they are hereby given police power and authority.

Section 11　Non-liability clause. —All charges for storage, demurrage, cartage, labor and delays incident to inspection, cost of disinfection or disinfestation and other post – entry requirements shall be the responsibility of the importer or the exporter, as the case may be. Provided, that the Bureau of Plant Industry and/or its authorized representative shall not be held liable for damages to the commodity in the course of the implementation of the provisions of this Decree.

Section 12　Duties of the Importer and Exporter. —The importers, exporters, or their authorized representatives shall submit a declaration to the Director of Plant Industry or his authorized representative at, or before the time of entry/embarkation of commodities mentioned under Sections 3, 4 and 6 hereof, for importation/exportation. Such declaration shall indicate the name and address of the consignor/consignee; the purpose; kind, nature and quantity of said commodities; the country or locality where the same was grown; place and date of unloading or embarkation, and the registered name of carrier carrying the consignment.

Section 13 Entrance and Clearance of Carriers. —The owner, operator, agent or master of carriers flying international and/or domestic routes are hereby required to serve a notice of arrival and departure and to provide inward and outward cargo manifests and other declarations of said carriers to the Plant Quarantine Officer at the port. Prior to departure, the agent or master of said carrier must secure a clearance from the Plant Quarantine Officer thereat.

The Collector of Customs or his authorized agents shall, require the owner, agent or master of carrier to submit a copy of the certificate of Plant Quarantine Clearance as a pre – requisite to the issuance of the Customs Clearance.

Section 14 Collection of fees. —The Director shall promulgate rules and regulations governing the collection of nominal regulatory fees for inspection, certification, import permits, commodity treatment and other, on commodities mentioned under Section 3, 4 and 6. Provided, that said collections shall constitute the Revolving Fund of the National Plant Quarantine Service; to augment the existing appropriations therefor, subject to government accounting and auditing regulations. Provided, however, that importations and exportations of all government agencies; government owned or controlled corporations; donations to and for the account of any duly registered relief – organizations; or any charitable institution certified by the Department of Social Services and Development; embassies of foreign governments; and those that maybe declared by the President, upon the recommendation of the National Economic and Development Authority, in the interest of economic development, are exempted from payment of such fees excluding, however, the expenses incurred in commodity treatment.

Section 15 Overtime Services. —The services of Plant Quarantine Officers, fumigators and helpers performed outside office hours and reimbursement of meal, transportation, lodging and other incidental expenses shall be chargeable to party or parties served at rates to be prescribed by the Secretary of Agriculture upon recommendation of the Director.

Section 16 Cooperating Agencies. —The Director may, when necessary, call upon other government agencies (military, civil, national or local) in the implementation of plant quarantine regulations and dissemination of information to the general public.

Section 17 Authority to promulgate Special Quarantine Orders, Rules and Regulations. —The Director, with the approval of the Secretary of Agriculture, is hereby authorized to promulgate such Special Quarantine Orders, rules and regulations to implement the provisions of this Decree.

Section 18 The Plant Quarantine Board. —For the purpose of carrying out the provisions of this Decree, a Plant Quarantine Board is hereby created composed of the following:

a. The Director of Plant Industry	Chairman
b. Commissioner of Customs or representative	Member
c. General Manager or representative of Philippine Ports Authority	Member
d. Director, Bureau of Quarantine or representative	Member
e. Director, Bureau of Animal Industry or representative	Member
f. Representative from the National Economic and Development Authority	Member
g. Representative from the Central Bank of the Philippines	Member
h. Administrator or representative of the Philippine Coconut Authority	Member
i. Director of Foresty or representative	Member
j. Bureau of Plant Industry, Legal Officer	Member
k. Representative from the Importers' and Exporters' Confederation	Member
l. Chief, Crop Protection Division, Bureau of Plant Industry	Member

m. Postmaster – General or representative — Member

n. Chief, Plant Quarantine Section, Bureau of Plant Industry — Secretary

Section 19 Duties of the Board. —The Plant Quarantine Board shall be the advisory body to assist the Director of Plant Industry in formulating orders, rules and regulations for the effective implementation of the revisions of this Decree.

Section 20 Board Meeting. —The Board shall meet once every quarter, or may call special meetings when necessary, provided, that such special meetings shall not be held more than four (4) times annually. The members of the Board shall receive a per diem of Two Hundred Pesos (P200) each per meeting.

Section 21 Quorum. —A majority of the members of the Board shall constitute a quorum.

Section 22 Appropriation of the Plant Quarantine Board. —The sum of P300,000 annually is, hereby appropriated for the expenses of the Plant Quarantine Board. Provided, that any unexpected amount of the said sum shall be reverted to the Plant Quarantine Revolving Fund.

Section 23 Penalty Clause. —Any person, company or corporation who violates the provisions of this Decree, or forges, counterfeits, alters, defaces and destroys any document issued by virtue of this Decree shall be fined not more than Twenty Thousand Pesos (P20,000) or by imprisonment from prison correctional to prison mayor, or both, at the discretion of the Court.

Section 24 Separability Clause. —If any of the provisions of this Decree shall be invalid, the remainder shall be operative.

Section 25 Repealing Clause. —All laws, rules and regulations inconsistent with the provisions of this Decree are, hereby superseded or revoked accordingly.

Section 26 Effectivity. —This Decree shall take effect immediately upon approval.

Done in the City of Manila, this 10th day of June,
Nineteen Hundred and Seventy – Eight.

农业部植物产业局检疫管理条例第1号

（1981年系列）

主题：执行总统令1433号的规定和条例，名为“1978年植物检疫法”，为进一步提高和加强植物产业局的植物检疫服务，对现有植物检疫法的修正和完善。

根据1978年6月10日总统令17节的条款，植物产业局长颁布了以下的规定和条例，作为有关信息和指南。

第1章 术语定义

以下术语用于该行政规定时的含义如下：

a. **人** 任何自然人或法人如法人团体、合伙企业、社团、协会、商号、公司和其他法律实体。

b. **局长** 指植物产业局局长。

c. **植物检疫官员** 指由植物产业局局长任命或指派的人。

d. **国家** 指任何独立的政治单位或君主制的国家、地区、殖民地、政治和领土上的从属国。

e. **运输工具** 包括任何类型的船或其他人工发明的能够用于海陆空的运输装置。

f. **植物** 指活的植物及其某个部位，包括种子、插条、根茎、种球和谷粒、接穗、叶片、根、幼芽和其他繁殖材料。

g. **植物产品** 指所有来自植物的产品，无论是天然状态或是已加工的状态，它们可能隐匿植物有害生物。

h. **潜在的动物性有害生物** 由某种动物构成，这些动物容易成为农作物的有害生物如昆虫、猴子、啮齿动物、蝙蝠、雀科动物、兔子、蜗牛和其他可能危害农作物的动物。

i. **包装材料** 包括树叶、稻草、树皮和其他用于包装并有可能隐匿植物有害生物的植物材料。

j. **植物有害生物** 任何能够对植物及其产品造成危害的或潜在危害的植物、动物、病原物。

k. **检疫规定** 用于执行第1433号总统令的由植物产业局长颁布的行政规定。

l. **商品处理** 任何应用于植物、植物产品和其他有可能隐匿植物有害生物的处理方法，其目的是消灭由植物有害生物引起的感染和传染。

m. **入境口岸** 指进行国内和国外贸易的港口，它包括第一口岸和第二口岸。

n. **进口** 根据1433令第3节和第4节所述，进口是指把国外的商品输入国内用于栽培、消费、加工、驯化或其他目的。

o. **过境植物/植物产品** 植物、植物产品从国内任何一个口岸入境但不卸货。

p. **出口** 根据1433令第3、4、6节所述，出口是指把本地的商品输出到国外。

q. **植物检疫证书** 植物健康证书。

第2章 植物、植物产品和有可能隐匿植物有害生物的其他材料的进口

第1节 植物、植物产品和有可能隐匿植物有害生物的其他材料、可能是传染源和有毒杂草传入的介质的进口必须受植物检疫的限制，在没有得到检疫官员授权情况下，货物不得从到达地转移，应当及时接受检疫检查以确定货物的植物卫生状况。

被证实无检疫性病害的货物，在遵循植物检疫机构的要求下，海关及与进口有关的港务局可以放

行给进口商或其法人代表。

感染植物有害生物的进口植物、植物产品和其他材料应当接受商品处理或销毁或退货，其费用由进口商承担。

当获知原产国存在危险性的植物有害生物时（不论是产地还是途经地），并且这些有害生物的存在还未被确定，那么这些植物、植物产品无论是否已受感染，其使用和从运输工具上卸下应当受到限制。

第2节 要求“进口许可证”的植物、植物产品和其他材料：进口下列材料应有植物产业局局长签发的进口许可证。

- 活植物；
- 苗木，包括其他用于繁殖材料的营养部分；
- 用于栽种的种子和坚果；
- 根据特殊的检疫规定，已宣布为禁止或限制进口的新鲜水果、蔬菜和其他植物产品，已知它们是某些植物有害生物的寄主或它们来自受限制地区的；
- 纯培养的真菌、细菌、病毒、线虫和其他植物致病材料；
- 蘑菇（包括菌丝）；
- 作为豆料根瘤菌种的藻类、根瘤菌；
- 用于分离生物体的土壤和植物材料；
- 其他植物。

植物产业局局长可以根据国家利益的需要许可进口上述材料。

第3节 申请进口许可证：任何想进口在第2节里列举的材料的个人应当向植物产业局局长递交一份“进口许可证申请”（BPI“Q”格式No.1），申请经批准后，签发一式四份的“进口许可证”（BPI“Q”格式“No.2）。

许可证原件由申请许可方呈送给入境口岸的植物检疫官员，副本1由申请许可方交原出口国的承运人，按照许可证里的条件来指导运输，副本2交入境口岸海关，副本3同申请一同归档。

在进口许可证签发之前，植物产业局局长可要求申请许可方提供相当于进口材料发票价值的保证金（不低于100比索）来确保进口人遵守许可证上提出的条件。

第4节 由申请许可方在货物到达最终目的地和装运的通知：要求具有“进口许可证”的材料到达口岸进，申请许可方或承运人应立刻通知入境口岸植物检疫官员（BPI“Q”格式No.3），说明进口许可证序列号，运输工具名称，到达日期，货物原产国，承运人姓名，进口商地址和姓名，进口材料的种类、特性和数量。在这些材料经检验完毕，从到达地被搬运之前，按照BPI格式的要求，进口商应指明运输方式和路线，最终收货人的姓名和地址和最终目的地的准确位置。

第5节 吊销进口许可证：当进境物是第2节中列出的材料时，并且它们来自的国家有以下任何一种情形时，将吊销进口许可证，对再次申请许可证也不会批准。

a. 植物产业局发现或证实货物出口国的检验和证明书不详实的；

b. 申请许可方未按第四节的要求发出通知的；

c. 错误通知的；

d. 错误申报货物的；

e. 违反进口许可证中规定的植物检疫条款的。

第6节 不需要进口许可证的材料：进口以下材料可以不需要“进口许可证”而进口，但是在货物放行前必须接受检验检疫和规定的商品处理。

a. “植物产品”如水果、蔬菜和准备用于食物和动物饲料的冷冻贮藏过的植物产品，还有那些不在植物检疫限制和禁止范围内的用于深加工的植物产品；

b. 不带土壤、泥沙的干的、无菌的、有毒的植物标本和样品；

c. 不在检疫限制/禁止范围内的船员或旅客随身携带或邮寄的10株以内的植物；

d. 不带土壤、泥沙的鲜花和花束。

第7节 植物、植物产品和可能隐匿植物有害生物的检验/鉴定。

进口商进口的植物、植物产品无论是天然状态还是加工状态，只要可能隐匿植物有害生物，就应向进境口岸植物检疫官员及时提交“检验申请”（BPI“Q”格式No.4），除有其他规定外，进境物按照10%~15%的比例随机接受检验。

所有的植物、植物产品和其他材料经检验未发现植物有害生物，且与申请检验表上所申请的进口植物品名一致时便可放行，进口商或法人代表应付规定的植物检疫费用。

发现进境物带有植物有害生物时，应进行规定的商品处理，或退回原产国或在入境口岸销毁，有关费用由进口商承担。

第8节 进口商提交植物检疫证书或植物健康证书。植物、植物产品或其他可能隐匿植物有害生物的材料，进口时必须具有由原产国的植物检疫部门或相应的技术部门签发的植物检疫证书或植物健康证书，指明在这些进境物中不带植物有害生物。

没有植物检疫部门的国家，检验检疫证书由进口商或营运商以保证书的形式完成，保证书必须在原产国经过公证，保证书保证：进口的植物材料不是来自植物有害生物流行的地区；它们的贮存地不受害虫或植物病原菌的污染；在货物装运前的除害处理和运输条件必须符合菲律宾植检部门的要求。

在上面由运营商呈送的植物卫生证书或保证书不得排除第7节规定的对进口植物、植物产品和其他可能隐匿植物有害生物的材料的检验检疫和处理。

第9节 进口的植物、植物产品和其他可能隐匿植物有害生物的材料到达时，没有植物卫生证书或没有第8节所述相当于植物卫生证书的文件：对于没有植物卫生证书和相当于植物卫生证书文件的进口植物、植物产品和其他相关材料到达后，应当100%检验，如有必要则进行处理、邮寄物检疫观察或其他检疫安全措施。

进口的植物、植物产品和其他旅客随身携带的材料或以邮件方式限量入境的货物没有植物检疫证书的，应当100%检验；如果没有植物检疫证书又没有保证书或声明的，必要时可采取其他检疫措施。

第10节 商品处理：为了消除进口植物、植物产品所携带或其他可能隐匿植物有害生物引起的侵染，这些植物、植物产品应当接受熏蒸、消毒和其他方式的商品处理作为进境和放行的条件，由此产生的费用由进口商承担。

第11节 植物、植物产品和其他来自土壤、泥沙的进口的材料：所有进口的植物、植物产品和其他相关的材料包括包装材料、容器都不得带有土壤、泥沙和其他可能隐匿植物有害生物的类似材料，所有植物的根、根茎、块茎等必须彻底清洗干净，并且具有原产国官方正式的证明证书。如果泥沙、土壤要用于包装种球等，那它们必须按照菲律宾植物产业局的处理方法经过消毒或采取安全措施，这一过程也必须由原产国官方证实。

使用过的汽车、挖土机、容器车进入菲律宾也将接受植物检验检疫以确保它们不带土壤、泥沙，如果发现它们带有上述禁止进境的材料，那么就必须进行消毒处理或彻底清洗，所产生的费用由进口商或货主承担。

第12节 包装材料的审批：用于包装进境植物、植物产品和其他限制的类似材料必须由入境口岸的植物检疫官员进行检验检疫以确保使用的安全性。用于任何进境物的包装材料不得包括稻草、糠壳、可可叶片、甘蔗叶片、竹子叶片、麦秆、绿草、杂草和根据特别检疫法可能会被禁止进口的其他类似材料。

所有与进境物有关的禁止进口的包装材料应当在植物检疫部门的监控下转移并销毁，由此产生的费用由进口商承担。

销毁禁止进境包装物的收费标准：10千克以下收费10比索，每增加1千克收费20分。

第13节 进境后的检疫要求：入境后的植物、植物产品可能被扣留作为进境后的检疫留验，在此期间这些货物必须完全满足不带外来有害生物的植物检疫条件。植物产业局局长可以通过正式协议向一些研究机构如植物育种研究所、菲律宾大学、国际水稻研究所等寻求协助以确保这些植物不带外来有害生物。

第 14 节 在检疫期内的植物、植物产品和其他材料：所有被植物检疫官员标记过的在检疫期内的包装植物、植物产品和其他材料的包装、木箱、纸箱等不得在没有得到植物检疫官员的书面许可就从进境口岸转移或卸货，也不能交给进口商，如果入境口岸的其他官方文件允许这批货物从关税区运仓库或其他地点，那么在起运前应得到植物检疫官员的批准。

第 15 节 通过邮寄进境的植物、植物产品和其他有可能隐匿植物有害生物的材料：通过邮寄进境的植物、植物产品和其他有可能隐匿植物有害生物的材料由在场检疫官员根据邮局官员的通知检验，这些材料应与从海关入境的材料同等对待，植物检疫检验应有货主、邮局官员或海关官员在场。

第 3 章 潜在动物性有害生物的进口

第 1 节 禁止进口可危害农业作物或可能成为农作物有害生物的某些动物，如：昆虫、鸟类、猴子、啮齿动物、蝙蝠、雀类、兔、蜗牛及其他种类的动物。如此类动物的限量进口有其合理目的，则凭主管部门的书面批准可以进口。

第 2 节 申请潜在动物性有害生物的“进口许可”：任何进口或携带第 1 节所述的活动物进入本国的人必须首先向植物主管部门提交检疫申请（BPI “Q” 格式 No. 5）。经植物产业局局长（BPI）的批准，签发一份“进口许可证”（BPI “Q” 格式 No. 6），副本四份。许可证持有人应将正本提交给指定入境港口的植物检疫官；将第二副本交原产国发运人，以便按许可证所规定的相关条件给发运人提供指导；第三副本由植物产业局局长（BPI）交入境港口岸海关征收员；第四副本与申请表一同归档；第五副本交菲律宾港务局。

但是，在签发“进口许可”前，进口货物符合规定的条件的，植物产业局局长可要求申请人支付相当于拟进口活动物估计发票金额的保证金，但该保证金不得低于 100 比索（P100）。

第 3 节 进口申请人进口动物到港及最终目的地的通知：自动物到港时，进口申请人或货物引进人应按 BPI “Q” 格式 No. 7 的要求，正式通知入境口岸的植物检疫官，说明许可证号码、签发日期、进口动物的种类和数量、载运工具注册名称、原产国、收货人的名称和地址及最终目的地。

第 4 节 吊销“进口许可证”：当进口申请人或货物引进人违反许可证规定的条款和条件错误提供或不完全提供进口有关的信息，可吊销已签发的“进口许可证”并拒绝第一节所述动物的再次进口申请。

第 5 节 潜在动物性有害生物的检疫检验及鉴定：在货物到达时或到达前，进口或携带活动物进入本国家内的任何人应向入境口岸的植物检疫官提交一份要求进口动物检验的正式申请表（BPI “Q” 格式 No. 8）。如受本章约束的进口动物不得带有饲料或有滋生或受植物有害生物感染的物品，或含有害杂草。当发现这类杂草已滋生或被“植物有害生物”感染时，应执行必要的检疫措施。

第 6 节 无“进口许可证”的潜在动物性有害生物：对无“证”到港的，经植物检疫不符合本章规定而予以放行的应当扣留。在对“潜在动物性有害生物”检疫放行前，为留档及强制执行制约该进口的某些条件，进口或携带活动物进入本国家内的任何人需由植物主管部门签发的符合本章要求的“进口许可证”。如植物检疫官员认为，该类动物的进口及放行有害于菲律宾农业利益时，应责令将该货物销毁或退回到原产国。在上述两种情况下，有关费用应由进口商承担。

在货物经过植物检疫部门检验前，任何人、以任何方式或任何手段转移或运走任何进口的“潜在的动物性有害生物”，包括动物产品及饲料从登陆地点运走均属非法行为。

第 4 章 商品的运输

第 1 节 货物的直接运输：植物、植物产品和其他可能隐匿植物有害生物的有关材料，以及潜在的动物性有害生物包括随运的动物饲料，根据直接运输方案，承运人从外国港口装载出口货物到菲律宾的任何港口而不卸载的，应当接受植物检验检疫，以评估与运输有关的植物检疫风险。如果结果表明此批货物受植物检疫性有害生物的污染，那么为了防止船上的植物有害生物的传入，应当采取适当的安全措施。

第 2 节 货物的间接运输：植物、植物产品和其他有可能隐匿植物有害生物的有关材料以及潜在的动物性有害生物包括随运的动物饲料，根据间接运输方案货物要从运输工具上卸下，在港口拆包或要重新包装，在转移到其他的运输工具上运往目的地国或其他地方，这种情况也视为进口货物到菲律宾，必须按本法第 2 章第 7 节的规定接受植物检疫和消毒处理。

第 3 节 转口物检疫证书的签发：如果目的地国要求有转口植物检疫证书，则第四章第 1 节、第 2 节所述的货物应有转口植物检疫证书（BPI“Q”格式 No. 9），货物原产国的植物检疫证书将作为出具转口植物检疫证书的依据，货物在菲律宾停留期间所接受的货物处理和其他检疫措施须在转口植物检疫证书中注明。

第 4 节 货主、经营人或运输货物代理的责任：进口属于植物检疫机构必须检疫货物的，货主、经营人或代理运输人有责任在货物到达进境口岸时将货物到达的事实及有关货物的详细情况立即通知植物检疫官员进行检疫，所有植物检验所产生的费用和运输工具清洁的费用由货主、经营人或运输代理人负担。

第 5 章 植物、植物产品和其他有可能隐匿有害生物材料的出口

第 1 节 只要进口国或国际公约要求植物检疫证书或植物健康证书，出口植物，植物产品和其他可能隐匿植物有害生物的材料的检疫都必须由植物产业局植物检疫所来实施。

第 2 节 填写检验申请：出口植物、植物产品和其他材料的出口商应及时向植物检疫机构递交一份正式的填写好的“检验申请”，格式 No. 10。装运货物口岸的官员，有由经授权代理银行签发的官方出口声明的副本和其他植物检疫所要求的文件，为了保证有足够的时间进行检验、商品处理和出具植物检疫证书，所有的单证必须在装载货物 48 小时之前递交完毕。

第 3 节 检验检疫：为了确定出口商品的卫生状况，需要出具植物检疫证书的出口商品，将由植物检疫官员指定检验地点接受随机的检验检疫，检疫官员将随机抽取具有代表性的样品作为室内检测材料，经检验未发现带有有害生物的商品将签发植物检疫证书。为了消除有害生物的感染，发现带有有害生物的商品将进行规定的处理，或不出具证书退给出口商。只要发现货物隐匿植物有害生物，或商品中混有受植物有害生物感染的其他材料时，将不会签发植物检疫证书，当出口货物是进口国禁止进口的货物时，所签发的植物检疫证书将作废。

第 4 节 允许用于出口货物的包装和填充材料：所有用于出口植物、植物产品和其他有关材料的植物性或泥沙、土壤包装和填充材料必须接受植物检疫官员的检验，以证实它们的安全性和可接受性。出口货物包装和填充材料的使用应当根据进口国的检疫规定来决定。

第 6 章 疫 区

第 1 节 疫区的公告：一旦证实了危险性植物有害生物在菲律宾的某个地区存在或可能存在，植物产业局局长将根据特殊植物检疫规定发布公告，宣布该地区、省或岛屿为疫区。公告内容包括疫区的地理界限、检疫关注的有害生物、寄主和其他相关的信息。

第 2 节 疫区申报通知：当证实在某地存在检疫性植物有害生物时，植物产业局局长将向以下部门发出正式通知：农业部长、省长、政府领导人和对此关注的私人机构，特别是发现有害生物存在地的地方农业部部长。通知包括有害生物的可能寄主，一旦接到通知，省长或其他机构的领导人应当立即通知他们的下属机构。市长和市级机构下属单位的领导人应当向疫区的居民发布通告，一般通知的复印件粘贴在市政局醒目的地方，经证实无误的副本送植物产业局局长，公共信息部应植物产业局局长的请求应当协助发布有关该植物检疫措施的信息。

第3节 地方农业部部长的职责：一旦某地被确立为官方的疫区，那么疫区所在地地方农业部部长有职责制定和实施控制感染和除害措施以防止植物有害生物的扩散的计划，植物产业局局长应向地方农业部部长提供在疫区制定并实施植物保护措施计划的技术指导。

第4节 来自疫区的植物及其产品在国内调运的检验和签发证书：所有准备运出疫区的植物、植物产品和其他可能传播植物检疫性有害生物的寄主材料等将接受严格的检验和商品处理，货主执行该检疫措施的情况应得到官方证实，如符合《特别检疫行政法》的规定，则由植物产业局的植物检疫官员签发准运证。一旦货物到达目的地，货主将准运证递交给目的地的植物检疫官员，由他来验证货物与所递交的文件是否相符合。

第5节 为执行本章规定，必要时植物产业局局长可根据1433总统令第10节委任疫区所在地地方农业部部长和其他直属下属官员来作为植物检疫官员。上述职权只能在公告的疫区行使且不得与《特别检疫法》相抵触。

第6节 所有运输公司，无论是空运、陆运或海运都必须配合植物产业局局长或他的官方代表，严格执行本章规定，不得允许或接受可能扩散植物有害生物的寄主材料调运往非疫区。

第7节 根据植物检疫结果与本章规定和其他《特别检疫法》相抵触的任何已知为植物有害生物寄主的货物，包括植物有害生物及其寄主，均由植物产业局局长或其授权的代表扣留并视情况立即退回原产地或彻底销毁或进行处理。

因退回、销毁处理及其他检疫措施所发生的费用由货主或收货人承担。

第7章　运输工具的入境和清洁消毒

第1节 进行国际贸易船只的检验和清洁消毒按照如下程序操作：

a. 递交货轮“到达通知”：

当往返于国际贸易航线上的货轮将停泊在菲律宾任何一个入境口岸时，货轮所有人、经营人或代理人应当递交轮船“到达通知”给第一入境口岸的植物检疫官员，通知必须在抵港前24小时递交。

b. 轮船和货物的检验检疫与鉴定当轮船停泊在菲律宾入境口岸时，为了确定船上货物的类别包括船上配备的食物、植物性家具，轮船应当接受检验。轮船代理人或所有人要向植物检疫官员提供一份航行日志、舱单，船上乘务员、旅客的行李申报、包裹清单、备用品清单、动植物清单和植物检疫官员可能需要的其他轮船文件和信息。

c. 来自或途径植物检疫限制区或“自由港”的轮船应当执行更严格的植物检疫措施，包括轮船警戒，监管船上检疫性食物的使用和处理，同时也防止某些商品或补给的非法登陆以及防止根据本法或本法以后颁布的法律而控制、禁止的货物进口。

d. 当货轮来自植物检疫限制区或领土时，轮船上装有新鲜水果、蔬菜和其他植物产品的贮存仓将被封存，当要使用这些食物时，货主或船上的负责人要递交一份正式的请求给植物检疫官员，根据许可可以打开贮存舱，对货物进行处理，也可在受监督的情况下使用货物。当取出上述水果、蔬菜时，应在监督下重新封存贮存舱。

e. 采自非限制区的新鲜水果、蔬菜和其他植物产品，经检疫认为不带有检疫性植物有害生物时，可在轮船上使用或消费而不受任何检疫要求的限制。

f. 为了防止乘客、游客带有检疫性的商品登陆，客轮或游轮停靠菲律宾港口时，必须接受适当的检疫监管。

g. 装载有小麦、玉米、高粱、大豆和其他植物产品的货轮在卸货时同样也要接受检疫监管，如有必要的话，这些货物首先必须在船上接受熏蒸或其他形式的商品处理，所产生的费用（检疫处理费）由货主或经营人承担。

h. 停泊在菲律宾港口的船只要求进行植物检疫清关。如果船只停靠在菲律宾的某港口，此港口植物、植物产品的调运受限制时，那么就要要求船只进行植物检疫清关。一份货物清单的复印件，一份乘客或乘务组成员所带植物、植物产品的清单将递交给植物检疫官员。接到上述文件后，检疫官员对货物和船只进行检疫，只要符合植物检疫法律和规定，将签发“植物检疫清关证书”（BPI“Q”格式No. 13），此证书作为海关清单的前提条件。

第 2 节 往返于国际贸易航线上的飞机的检验和检验清关遵循如下程序：

a. 来自国外的飞机，航空公司或代理人在飞机降落后应当向植物检疫官员提交一份航行路线图、乘客清单、货物清单和其他所需文件。

b. 所有降落在菲律宾机场的飞机应当接受植物检疫官员的检查。所有受植物检疫禁止或限制的食物或其他材料将被封存，如果要使用这些物品，必须向植物检疫官员递交一份正式的请求，在其监控下使用和处理物品。

第 3 节 往返于国内贸易航线上的轮船的检验和检疫消毒。

a. 停靠在菲律宾所有港口的来自疫区或途径疫区的船只都应当接受植物检疫官员的检验和消毒。船舶所有人、代理人应当向植物检疫官员提交一分国内货物清单、包裹清单和其他有关文件。

b. 所有从疫区港口起航的国内船只必须具有“国内植物检疫消毒证书”，当船只停靠在别的港口时交给植物检疫官员。

第 4 节 往返于国内贸易航线上的飞机的检验和消毒，须遵循以下程序：

a. 停靠在菲律宾所有港口的来自疫区或途径疫区的飞机都应当接受植物检疫官员的检验和消毒。航空公司应当向植物检疫官员提交一份国内货物清单和其他实施检疫有关的文件。

b. 所有从国内疫区机场起飞的国内飞机应当具有“国内植物检疫消毒证书”（BPI“Q”格式No. 14），当飞机在下一个机场着陆时交给植物检疫官员。

第 5 节 对运输工具上垃圾处理的检疫控制：禁止在菲律宾领土或水域内运输工具上私自处理厨房废料和垃圾，垃圾和厨房废料应当保存在船上的密封容器内，任何打算在菲律宾境内处理垃圾的船舶应当向当班的植物检疫官员递交一份正式申请，在检疫官员监控下，按植物检疫官员指定的方法和场所处理这些垃圾和废料。

第 8 章 植物检疫费用

第 1 节 下列条款规定：国家针对进/出境植物、植物产品、其他植物材料及可隐匿植物有害生物、动物病的其他货物进行植物检疫、出具证书、进口许可、检疫处理等必须收取的规定费用，所征收的费用应建立国家植物检疫业务循环基金。

a. 进口许可证收费：

（a-1）植物、植物产品的进口许可证进口本法第二章第 1 节规定的植物、植物产品和其他材料，每份许可证收取 P5；

（a-2）进口潜在动物性有害生物的进口许可证。进口本法第三章第 1 节所述的危害农作物的潜在的动物性有害生物的，每份许可证收取 P50。

b. 检验和鉴定费：

（b-1）进口 10 株以下活植物最低收费为 P5，每增加 1 株加收 P0. 50，盆栽活植物每盆收费 P5；

（b-2）出口活植物的检疫鉴定，10 株以下最低收费为 P2，每增加 1 株加收 P0. 20，盆栽植物每盆收费 P2；

（b-3）进口种子、切条、块根、球茎、接穗和其他繁殖材料按净重每吨收费 P2；

（b-4）进口植物产品和其他可能隐匿植物有害生物的材料用于消费或加工的，按净重每吨收费 P1；

（b-5）出口植物产品 P1/吨；

（b-6）进口潜在动物性有害生物 10 个以下最低收费 P10，超过 10 个的部分每增加1 个加收 P1。

c. 货物处理费：对进出口和国内的植物、植物产品和其他材料或商品的熏蒸、消毒和其他处理，包括清洁，支付的处理费用根据工作量、材料消耗及植物产业局所提供的设备情况来确定，如前述处理由当事人自己完成，则不收取费用。

d. 进境邮寄物的检疫收费：对进口材料（植物、植物产品、潜在动物性有害生物）的保管应处于进境后的检疫观察的状态，费用的多少视植物产业局所花费的工作量和提供材料的情况而定。

e. 禁止进境物和禁运品的销毁费用：销毁没收的禁运品或禁止进境物低于20千克的，进口商至少应向植物产业局支付P20。如果没收的禁运品或禁止进境物数量很小，也可不收销毁费用。

f. 免交前述植物检疫费：所有政府机构、国有公司或国有控股公司的进出口货物、向经注册登记的赈灾组织或由社会服务发展部批准成立的慈善机构的捐赠物、外国政府的大使以及享有总统豁免的人员、由国家经济发展局为发展经济而提出的，可以免交前述植物检疫费，但货物处理费和植物检疫人员的加班费除外。

第9章　加　　班

第1节　以下条款规定有关加班费。植物产业局植物检疫人员对植物、植物产品和其他可能隐匿植物有害生物的材料、潜在的动物性有害生物、木板等的检验处理、鉴定、审批文件和其他检疫措施以及国际国内贸易航线上船舶的检验监管和其他需采取的植物检疫措施以及为当事人提供信息和所有有关的指导。

a. 加班时间：

（a－1）加班时间是指从正常工作时间结束后即从下午5点至下一个工作日凌晨8点之间的时间，包括中午12点至下午1点，夏日制时间的下午12点30分至下午1点30分的午休时间，星期六、星期日和节假日的加班时间是指从星期下午5点的正常工作时间结束开始最迟至下一个工作日凌晨8点为止，除非加班能迅速结束；

（a－2）加班费：植物产业局的植物检疫官员、熏蒸人员、工人和辅助人员的加班费由货主支付，植物检疫官员和熏蒸人员的加班费为P9/小时，工人或辅助人员的加班费为P7/小时；

（a－3）加班的计算：植物检验检疫人员的加班时间从船舶到达前、检疫开始前、对植物、植物产品等的货物处理开始前2小时至工作结束后的1小时计算。但如果植物检疫官员的加班场所在官方机构所在地以外的小港口或其他地方，则加班时间从执行植物检疫任务开始前的2小时至完成工作的最后1小时计算，植物检疫官员的实际支出的交通费、住宿费另付。

如果船舶迟延到港或由于进口没有按时到达，使得检验或货物处理不能按预定时间进行，则植物检疫人员的等待时间应当计算为加班时间。

b. 误餐补贴：加班的植物检疫人员的误餐补贴为每餐P14，而不管就餐时间是否在加班期间之中。但在加班时间当事人如果能够提供满意的膳食，则可以免收误餐补贴。

进餐时间如下：

早餐：上午6：00～8：00

午餐：中午12：00～下午1：00

晚餐：晚上6：00～8：00

c. 交通补贴

（c－1）在马尼拉和其他城市交通补贴为每人每次P14；

（c－2）在省内的交通补贴以当地通常的补贴为标准或者是参照付给其他类似服务的政府机构人员的补贴标准；

（c－3）当检疫官员外出检疫需要使用交通工具时，可以租用交通工具，由此所产生的费用由货主按发票支付。

d. 住宿补贴：被派往官方机构所在地以外的地方执行检疫任务的植物检疫局的植物检疫人员需要在外住宿时，可以按照当地的标准获得住宿补贴。但每夜最高不得超过P50，货主可以根据通常贯例或合同向植物检疫人员提供报酬而获得特别服务。

第 10 章　植物检疫官员的权利和义务

第 1 节　为实现本法之目的，植物产业局植物检疫官员有如下权利和义务：

a. 对所有的运输工具、船员或乘客的行李和进境邮件实施检验，以确定是否存在植物、植物产品和其他可能隐匿植物有害生物的材料以及潜在的动物性有害生物。

b. 可以进入所有植物、植物产品和其他可能隐匿植物有害生物的材料的贮存场所、生长地进行检验或鉴定。

c. 为确保本法得到有效实施，可采取必要的措施检查进口的植物、植物产品和其他可能隐匿植物有害生物的材料以及潜在的动物性有害生物。

d. 对出口植物、植物产品以及其他有关材料实施检验、管理、必要的处理以及签发植物检疫证书。

e. 没收和销毁或拒绝进口禁止进境的植物、植物产品和潜在的动物性有害生物以及禁止在国内调运的植物和植物产品；对禁止出口的植物和植物产品不予签发植物检疫证书。

f. 履行赋予的其他有关职责。

g. 根据 1433 号总统令的第 10 节的规定，植物检疫官员在履行其职权时，赋予警察的权利。

第 11 章　协 作 单 位

第 1 节　在贯彻执行本法规定的过程中，植物产业局局长或其授权代表可以要求或号召下列政府机构和人员提供协助（根据 1433 号总统令第 16 节的规定）：

a. 海关；

b. 菲律宾港务局；

c. 检疫局；

d. 邮局；

e. 动物产业局；

f. 菲律宾警察局；

g. 菲律宾空军；

h. 菲律宾海岸警卫队；

i. 民航管理局；

j. 菲律宾中央银行；

k. 移民局；

l. 菲律宾椰子权威机构；

m. 林业局；

n. 省长；

o. 市长；

p. 地方警察局；

q. 贸易部长；

r. 菲律宾出口理事会；

s. 国家经济和发展机构；

t. 可协助执行本法规定的其他政府结构；

u. 其他政府部门颁布的有关进出口植物和植物产品的规定和条例不得排除本法的适用。

第 12 章　免 责 条 款

第 1 节　所有货物贮存费、滞留费、运费、劳务费和检疫检验延期费、货物处理费以及邮寄费由进出口商、货主或有关当事人承担。植物产业局或其授权代表对因执行本法规定所引起的货物损害不承担责任。

第13章 处　罚

根据法院的裁判，对违反本法规定或者伪造、变造、涂改、毁损根据本法签发的任何文件的任何个人、公司和企业处以P20 000以下的罚金或监禁或者监禁并处罚金。

第14章 附　则

本法规定生效之前，其他有关法律继续有效。

第15章 废除条款

所有与本法规定相抵触的行政法、规定和条例均以本法为准或予以废除。

第16章 生　效

本法经批准和发布后生效。

Ministry of Agriculture Bureau of plant industry quarantine administrative order No. 1

(Series of 1981)

Subject: Rules and Regulations to Implement Presidential Decree No. 1433, Entitled "Promulgating The Plant Quarantine Law of 1978. Thereby Revising And Consolidating Existing Plant Quarantine Laws to Further Improve and Strengthen The Plant Quarantine Service of The Bureau of Plant Industry."

Pursuant to the provisions of Section 17 of Presidential Decree No. 1433, dated June 10, 1978, the Director of Plant Industry hereby promulgates the following rules and regulations for the information and guidance of all concerned.

Rule I Definition of terms

The following terms when used in this Administrative Order shall mean as follows:

a. Person any natural or juridical person such as corporations, partnerships, societies, associations, firms, companies and other legal entities.

b. Director The Director of Plant Industry.

c. Plant Quarantine Officer any person so appointed and/or designated by the Director of Plant Industry.

d. Country any independent political unit or sovereign nation, territory, colony, and political or territorial subdivision.

e. Carrier includes every sort of craft or other artificial contrivance used, or capable of being used as a means of transportation on land, water or air.

f. Plants shall comprise living plants and parts thereof, including seeds, cuttings, rhizomes, bulbs and corms, grafts, leaves, roots, scions and others that are capable of propagation.

g. Plant Products shall mean products derived from plants, either in their natural state or in manufactured or processed form and are capable of harboring plant pests.

h. Potential Animal Pest shall comprise certain species of animals that are liable to become agricultural crop pests such as insects, monkeys, rodents, bats, finches, rabbits, mails and other forms of animal life capable of causing injury to agricultural crops.

i. Packing Materials include leaves, straw, bark and other plant materials used as wrapping, packing, or covering and are capable of harboring plant pests.

j. Plant Pest any form of plant or animal life, or any pathogenic agent, injurious or potentially injurious to plants and/or plant products.

k. Quarantine Orders shall mean those Administrative Orders promulgated and issued by the Director of Plant Industry to implement the provisions of this Decree.

l. Commodity Treatment any form of treatment applied to plants, plant products and other material capable of harboring plant pests, for the purpose of destroying or eliminating any infection/infestation caused by plant pests.

m. Port of Entry is a port open to both foreign and domestic trade. The term includes principal ports of entry and subports of entry.

n. Importation is the act of bringing into the country foreign commodities mentioned under Sections 3 and 4 of the Decree for planting, consumption, manufacturing, domestication or for any other purpose.

o. Plants/Plant Products in Transit shall refer to plants/plant products brought into any port in the country but are not intended for landing at the said port.

p. Exportation is the act of transporting commodities mentioned under Sections 3, 4 and 6 hereof, from a local port to a foreign port.

q. Phytosanitary Certification shall mean plant health certification.

Rule Ⅱ Importation of plants, plant products and other materials capable of harboring plant pests

SEC. 1 The importation of plants, plant products and other materials capable of harboring plant pests or which may be a source of infection/infestation or a medium for the introduction of noxious weeds are subject to certain quarantine restrictions and shall not be removed or transferred from the place of landing unless authorized by the Plant Quarantine officer assigned at the port of entry. Such consignments shall promptly be subjected to quarantine inspection or verification to determine their phytosanitary condition.

Importations that have been verified to be free from maladies of quarantine significance shall be released to the importer or to his authorized representative upon compliance with the requirements of the Plant Quarantine Service, Bureau of Customs and Philippine Ports Authority relative to such importations and/or shipment.

Imported plants, plant products and other materials found infected/ infested with plant pests shall be subjected to a prescribed commodity treatment, or destroyed or returned to the country of origin at the expense of the importer.

The discharge from the carrier or even the use therein of certain classes or genera of plants and plant products is restricted, whether visibly infested/ infected or not, when information has been received that dangerous plant pests exists in the countries of origin (including not only where the materials were produced but also where they had been transhipped or gone through) and the presence of such plant pests cannot be readily and economically determined.

SEC. 2 Plants, Plant Products and Other Materials which a "Permit to Import" is required. — The following materials, as a condition of their entry, must be covered by a "Permit to Import" issued by the Director of Plant Industry.

- Living plants.
- Nursery stocks, including vegetative parts thereof used as propagating materials.
- Seeds and nuts for planting.
- Fresh fruits, vegetables and other plant products which have been declared as prohibited/restricted imports under Special Quarantine Orders by virtue of their being known hosts of certain plant pests, or because they originate from restricted areas.
- Pure cultures of fungi, bacteria, virus, nematode and other phytopathogenic materials.
- Mushroom cultures including spawn.
- Algae cultures, rhizobial cultures as legume inoculants.
- Soil and plant material for isolation of organism.

- Other plant cultures.

The importation of the abovementioned materials may be allowed under "permit" subject to such reasonable conditions that the Director of Plant Industry may impose in the national interest.

SEC. 3 Application for "Permit to Import". —Any person who desires to import the materials enumerated in Section 2 hereof, shall submit an "Application for Permit to Import" (BPI "Q" Form No. 1), to the Director of Plant Industry. Upon approval by the Director of such application, a "permit to import" (BPI "Q" Form No. 2) shall be issued in quadruplicate. The original shall be given to the Permittee for presentation to the Plant Quarantine Officer at the Port of Entry; the duplicate shall be sent to the shipper in the country of origin by the Permittee for their guidance relative to the terms and conditions imposed in the "permit"; the triplicate shall be furnished to the Collector of Customs at the Port of Entry, and the fourth copy shall be filed with the application.

Provided, however, that before the issuance of the "Permit to Import", the Director of Plant Industry may require the "permittee" to file a bond in the mount equal to estimated invoice cost of the materials to be imported, but in no case shall it be less than One hundred Pesos (P100) to ensure compliance with the conditions in the "permit".

SEC. 4 Notice of Arrival and Shipment to Final Destination by the Permittee. —Upon arrival of the materials for which a "Permit to Import" is required, the Permittee or person bringing them into the country shall immediately notify the Plant Quarantine Officer at the Port of Entry (BPI "Q" Form No. 3) stating the serial number of the "permit", name of carrier, date of arrival, the country of origin, name of shipper, name and address of the importer, the kind, character and quantity of material imported. After the materials have been inspected and before removing them from the place of landing, the importer shall also indicate in the said BPI Form the type and route of transport, the completed name and address of the ultimate consignee and the exact location of the final place of destination.

SEC. 5 Revocation of Permit to Import. —Permits may be revoked and further permits refused for the importation of materials mentioned in Section 2 hereof, from any country where:

a. inspection and certification have been found and/or verified by the Bureau of Plant Industry to be merely superficial;

b. failure of the "Permittee" to give the "notice" required in Section 4 hereof;

c. false "notice" has been given;

d. shipment has been misdeclared; and

e. violation of the plant quarantine rule: and regulations and conditions imposed in the permit.

SEC. 6 Materials for which "Permit to Import" is not required—the following materials may be imported or brought into the country without the necessity of "permit" subject however to plant quarantine inspection/verification and/or to a prescribed commodity, treatment before being released:

a. "Plant Products" such as fruits, vegetables and stored products intended for food or animal feed - purposes, or those for processing or manufacturing and when not governed by any plant quarantine restriction/prohibition.

b. Properly dried or sterilized, or poisoned botanical specimens or herbaria when free from soil, sand or earth.

c. "Plants" in crew and/or passenger hand baggage or by mail, for ten (10) pieces and when not governed by any quarantine restrictions/ prohibitions.

d. Fresh flowers, bouquets, etc. when free from soil, sand or earth.

SEC. 7 Inspection/Verification of Plants, Plant Products and Other Materials Capable of Harboring Plant

Pests. —Any "person" who desires to import or bring into the country plants and plant products either in their natural state, or in manufactured or processed form but are still capable of Harboring plant pests, shall submit to the BPI – Plant Quarantine Officer at the port of entry a duly accomplished "Application for Inspection" (BPI "Q" Form No. 4). Except as otherwise provided, such importations shall be subjected to 10% ~ 15% random inspection.

All plants, plant products and other materials found to be substantially free from plant pests and verified to be same materials applied for shall be released to the importer or via authorized representatives, upon payment of prescribed Plant Quarantine Fees and Charges.

Importations found infested or infected by plant pests shall either be subjected to a prescribed commodity treatment or rammed to the country of origin or destroyed at the Port of Entry and all fees, charges and other expenses relative to such quarantine action shall be borne by the importer.

SEC. 8 Submission of Phytosanitary or Plant Health Certificate by the Importer. —Importation of plants, plant products and other materials capable of harboring plant pests must be accompanied by a Phytosanitary or Health Certificate issued by the Plant Quarantine Service or its equivalent technical entity in the country of origin stating among others that the materials are free from "plant pests" .

In countries where the government does not maintain Plant Quarantine and/or Phytosanitary Certification Service, the Certificate of Inspection required in this Section must be accomplished by the exporter or shipper concerned in an affidavit form duly subscribed and sworn to by him before a person legally authorized to administer oath in the country of origin. Such documents shall contain among others, a statement to the effect that the materials shipped to the Philippines did not originate from an area where "plant pests" are prevalent; that they have not been kept or stored in places infested by injurious insects or infected by disease pathogens; and that whatever commodity treatment and/or other pre – shipment conditions required by the BPI Plant Quarantine Service had been satisfied prior to the leading of the shipment.

The presentation of the "Phytosanitary Certificate" or sworn statement by the shipper mentioned in the preceding subsection shall not preclude quarantine inspection/verification or treatment of the imported plants, plant products and other materials capable of harboring "plant pests" as provided in Section 7 hereof.

SEC. 9 Imported Plants, Plant Products and Other Materials Capable of Harboring "Plant Pests" Arriving without the Required "Phytosanitary Certificate" or its Equivalent Documents. —Imported "Plants", "Plant Products" and other related materials in commercial quantity arriving without the required "phytosanitary certificate" or its equivalent document mentioned in Section 8 hereof, may be subjected to 100% inspection and if deemed necessary, to "Commodity Treatment", and/or held under "post entry quarantine observation" and/or subjected to other quarantine safeguard measures.

Imported "plants", "plant products" and other materials in passenger baggage or mail in limited quantity arriving without the required Phytosanitary Certificate shall be subjected to 100% inspection and to such other plant quarantine action as may be deemed necessary; provided however, that the requirement of submitting an affidavit or sworn statement promising the surrender of the Phytosanitary Certificate may be waived.

SEC. 10 Commodity Treatment. —For the purpose of destroying or eliminating any infection or infestation caused by plant pests in or amongst such imported plants, plant products and such other related materials which are capable of harboring such plant pests, the Plant Quarantine Officer may, as a condition of its entry and release, subject said plants, plant products and other related materials to fumigation, disinfection or other forms of commodity treatment, as is necessary. Prodded, that expenses incurred on account of such treatments shall be charged to the importer thereof.

SEC. 11 Freedom of Imported Plants, Plant Products and Other Related Materials from Soil. Sand or earth. —All imported plants, plant products and other related materials, including their packing or containers must be free from soil, sand, earth and other similar materials which could harbor "plant pests". All plant roots, rhizomes, tubers, etc. must be washed thoroughly to free them from sand, soft, or earth, and must be so certified by the duly authorized officer of the country of origin. Provided, that sand, soil or earth, may be employed for the packing of bulbs, corms, etc. when they have been Sterilized or rendered safe in accordance with the methods of treatment prescribed by the Bureau of Plant Industry and this fact is so certified by the authorities concerned from the country of origin.

Used vehicles, earth moving equipment as well as container vans brought into the country shall be subjected to plant quarantine inspection to determine that they are free from soil, sand or earth and those found contaminated with the abovementioned prohibited materials shall be required to be disinfected or washed and cleaned thoroughly. All expenses incurred in connection with the implementation of this requirement shall be borne by the importer or owner thereof.

SEC. 12 Approval of Packing Materials. —Packing materials employed in the importation of plants, plant products and such other restricted materials shall be inspected or verified by the Plant Quarantine Officer at the Port of Entry to ensure safety for such use. Packing materials used in any importation must not include rice straw, rice chaffs, coconut leaves, sugar cane leaves, bamboo leaves; wheat straw, grasses or weeds, and such other materials which may hereafter be declared prohibited under Special Quarantine Orders.

All prohibited packing materials associated in any importation shall be removed and destroyed under Plant Quarantine supervision and control and all incidental expenses to be incurred in such undertakings shall be borne by the importer.

For the destruction of prohibited packing materials, a fee of Ten Pesos (P10) for the first ten kilos or fraction thereof and twenty centavos (P 0.20) for every kilo thereafter shall be imposed on the importer or owner of such importation.

SEC 13 Post Entry Quarantine Requirements. —Imported "plants" and "plant products" may be placed under post entry quarantine observation during such period as may be determined by the Plant Quarantine Office in order to fully satisfy the requirements of being freed from exotic "plant pests" in or amongst the imported materials which may not be detectable at the time of inspection. The Director of Plant Industry may seek assistance, through formal agreements, from such other research institutions such as The Institute of Plant Breeding, University of the Philippines at Los Bafios, International Rice Research Institute, etc. in order to fully ascertain or establish that such plants are free from exotic "plant pests".

SEC. 14 Plants, Plant Products and Other Materials Held Under Quarantine. —Any package, case, box or parcel containing plants, plant products and such other materials so marked by the Plant Quarantine Officer as being held subject to quarantine inspection and clearance (Held Under Quarantine), shall not be removed or transferred from the place of landing nor released to the importer without the written approval and the sanction of the Plant Quarantine Officer. Provided, that official covering document issued by the other Port Authorities allowing transfer of such cargoes to bonded warehouses, container yards and other places outside the Customs zone shall first be coursed to the Plant Quarantine Officer for notation and/or approval before actual transfer commences.

SEC. 15 Imported Plants, Plant Products and Other Materials Capable of Harboring "Plant Pests" Arriving through the Post Office. —The importation of plants, plant products and other related materials capable of harboring plant pests, through the mail services shall be inspected by the Plant Quarantine Officer upon notification of the presence of such materials by the Postal Service officials. Such materials shall be treated like those coming through the Customs' House. Plant Quarantine Inspection shall be made in the presence of the consignee, a Postal Official and/or Customs Officials.

Rule Ⅲ　Importation of potential animal pests

SEC 1　The importation of certain species of animals such as insects, birds, monkeys, rodents, bats, finches, rabbits, snails and other forms of animal life that are capable of causing injury to agricultural crops or are liable to become agricultural crop pests, is hereby prohibited. Provided, however, the importation of such animal in limited quantity for a justifiable purpose may be allowed upon a written permit from the Director.

SEC. 2　Application for "Permit to Import" Potential Animal Pests. – Any person who desires to import or bring into the country live animals mentioned in Section 1 hereof must first file an application with the Director of Plant Industry (BPI "Q" Form No. 5) . Upon approval by the Director of Plant Industry, a "permit to import" (BPI "Q" Form No. 6) shall be issued in quadruplicates. The original copy shall be given to the permittee for presentation to the Plant Quarantine Officer at the designated port of entry; the duplicate shall be sent by the permittee to the shipper in the country of origin for their guidance relative to the conditions embodied in the permit; the third copy shall be sent to Collector of Customs at the port of entry by the Bureau of Plant industry; the fourth copy shall be filed with the application; and fifth copy for the Philippine Ports Authority.

Before the issuance of the "permit to import" however, the Director, to ensure compliance with the conditions imposed therein, may require the Permittee to file a bond in the amount equal to the estimated invoice cost of the live animals proposed to be imported, but in no case shall such bond be less than One Hundred Pesos (P100).

SEC. 3　Notices of Arrival and Final Destination of the Imported Animals by the importer – Permitee. – Immediately upon the arrival of the animals, the importer – permittee or the person bringing in the consignment shall formally notify the Plant Quarantine Officer at the Port of Entry upon BPI "Q" Form No. 7, indicating therein the Permit number and date of issue, the kind and quantity of the animals imported, the registered name of the carrier, the country of origin, the name and address of the consignee and the final destination.

SEC. 4　Revocation of "Permit to Import" – "Permit to Import" previously issued may be revoked and further permit refused for the importation of animals mentioned in Section 1 hereof when the perrnittee or the person bringing in the consignment has violated the terms and conditions embodied in the permit; or when the permittee had given false or incomplete information relative to the importation.

SEC. 5　Quarantine Inspection and/or Verification of Potential Animal Pests. – Any person who imports or brings into the country live animals shall submit a duly accomplished application for inspection of imported animals, upon (BPI "Q" Form No. 8), on or before the arrival of the shipment to the Plant Quarantine Officer at the Port of Entry. All such imported animals shall be inspected/verified as to their kind and quantity and condition.

Provided, further, that imported animals governed by this Rule must not be accompanied by feeds or animal effects that are infested/infected by plant pests or containing noxious weeds. In case such feeds axe found to be infested/infected by "plant pests", the required quarantine action shall be administered.

SEC. 6　Potential Animal Pests Arriving Without "Permit" . – The release from plant quarantine of animals failing within the purview of this Rule, arriving without "Permit" shall be withheld. For record purposes and for the imposition of certain requirements governing such importations, the importer or the person bringing in such animals shall be required to secure from the Director of Plant Industry the "permit to import" required in this Rule before the release of the "potential animal pests" from quarantine is effected. However, if the Plant Quarantine Officer believes that the entry and release of such animals might be detrimental to the best interest of Philippine agriculture, such shall be ordered destroyed or returned to the country of origin. In either case, the cost shall be borne by the importer.

It shall be unlawful for anyone in any manner or by any means to remove or carry away any imported "potential animal pests", including the animal effects and feeds from the place of landing before the same shall have been passed upon by the Plane Quarantine Service.

Rule Ⅳ Commodities in transit

SEC. 1 Direct Transit Cargo. – Cargoes of "plants", "plant products" and other related materials capable of harboring plant pests, as well as "potential animal pests" including the accompanying animal feedstuffs, on a direct transit scheme whereby the carrier laden with exports of a foreign country berths in any port of the Philippines without breaking bulk (without unloading), shall be subjected to quarantine inspection/verification for the purpose of evaluating the quarantine risk that may be associated with such in – transit cargo. If the inspection reveals positive signs of infection/infestation by "plant pests" of plant quarantine significance, proper safeguard measures shall be instituted to preclude the entry into the country of the plant pests that are present in the shipment.

SEC. 2 Indirect Transit Cargo. – In the case of cargoes of "plants", "plant products" and other related materials capable of harboring plant pests, as well as "potential animal pests", including the accompanying animal feedstuffs, on an indirect transit scheme, in which the goods are discharged from the carrier and which may be unpacked or repacked in the port and/or transferred to another carrier for reshipment to the country of destination or reconsigned elsewhere, the same shall be considered as an importation into the philippines and shall be subject to plant quarantine inspection and/or treatment as presort – bed in Section 7 Rule II of this Administrative Order.

SEC. 3 Issuance of phytosanitary Certification for Re – export. – Phytosanitary (Re – export) Certificate (BPI "Q" Form No. 9) shall be issued to cover the transit shipments mentioned in Sections 1 and 2 of Rule IV if the country of destination requires such certificate. The original phytosanitary certificate issued by the country of origin shall be used as a basis' for the issuance of the said plant health certificate. The commodity treatment and other quarantine actions instituted on the transit cargo during its stay in the Philippines shall be written in the Phytosanitary (Re – export) Certificate.

SEC. 4 Responsibility of the Owner Operator or Agent of Carriers Laden with In – Transit Cargo. – It shall be the duty of the owner, operator or agent of carriers bringing in of laden with in – transit cargo that are subject to Plant Quarantine to notify promptly the Plant Quarantine Officer at the port of entry about the arrival and particulars of such in – transit cargo and all expenses relative to the quarantine inspection and clearance of such shipments shall be borne by the owner, operator and/or agent of the Carrier.

Rule V Exportation of plants, plant products and other materlals capable of harboring pests

SEC. 1 The plant quarantine inspection and certification of plants, plant products and other material capable of harboring plant pests intended for exportation shall be conducted by the BPI Plant Quarantine Service whenever the Phytosanitary or Plant Health Certificate is required by the importing country or by an International Convention Agreement (Section 1, Rule III, Rules and Regulations, P. D. 930 and Section 6, P. D. 1433).

SEC. 2 Filing of Application for Inspection. Exportation of plants, plant products and other materials for export shall submit a duly accomplished "Application for Inspection" upon (BPI "Q" Form No. 10) to the Plant Quarantine. Officer at the port of loading together with a certified true copy of the Official Export Declaration issued by the Authorized Agent Bank, as well as other documents which the Plant Quarantine Officer may require at least forty - eight (48) hours prior to the time of loading in order to allocate ample time for the required inspection and/or the conduct of commodity treatment, as well as for the preparation of the Phytosanitary Certificate.

SEC. 3 Inspection and Phytosanitary, Certification. - Export commodities, for which a Phytosanitary Certificate's required shall be subjected to random inspection in a place to be designated by the Plant Quarantine officer, in order to determine their sanitary condition. Representative samples may be taken at random by the Plant Quarantine Officer for examination or for testing. Commodities that are found to be substantially free from plant pests shall be officially certified and issued the "Phytosanitary Certificate" (BPI "Q" Form No. 11). However, those manifesting the presence of plant pests shall either be subjected to a prescribed commodity treatment in order to eliminate the infection or infestation, as the case may be, or shall be returned to the exporter without certification. Under no circumstance shall a "Phytosanitary Certificate" be issued to shipments which have been found to harbor "plant pests" or which have been taken From or mixed with other materials that are diseased or infested with "plant pests." The issuance of phytosanitary certificate shall likewise be denied to exports intended to a country to which their entry is absolutely prohibited.

SEC. 4 Approval of Packing or Filling Materials Employed in Exports. - All packing or filling materials of plant origin or soil, and or earth employed in the exportation of plants, plant products and other related materials shall be verified by the Plant Quarantine officer in order to evaluate their safety and acceptability for such use. The approval of the packing or filling materials associated with exports shall be based on the quarantine regulations of the importing country.

Rule Ⅵ Areas declared under quarantine

SEC. 1 Declaration of Quarantine Area. - The Director of Plant Industry, upon confirmation of the existence or suspected presence of dangerous "plant pest" in any place in the Philippines shall declare such localities, provinces, or island as a "quarantine area" through the promulgation of a Special Quarantine Order, containing among others, the geographical boundaries of the quarantined area, the "plant pest" under quarantine consideration, the host materials, and other pertinent information.

SEC. 2 Notice of Declaration of Quarantine. - Whenever a certain plant pest of quarantine significance has been verified to exist in a certain locality, the Director of Plant Industry shall send a formal notification through the Ministry of Agriculture, the Governor of the province and the Heads of other government and private agencies concerned, particularly the Regional Director of the Ministry of Agriculture in the Region declaring such locality: under quarantine which notification shall include the probable hosts of the "plant pests" under quarantine consideration. Upon receipt of the notification, the Provincial Governor and/or Heads of other agencies shall immediately inform their subordinate offices of the notification from the Director of Plant Industry. The Municipal Mayor and/or the Heads of subordinate agencies/office at the Municipal level shall then issue a general written notification to the inhabitants of the locality. Copies of the general notification shall be posted in conspicuous places in the Municipality and a certified copy of the said "Notice" shall be sent to the Director of Plant Industry. The Ministry of Public Information, upon request of the Director of Plant Industry, shall assist to the distribution of information regarding this plant quarantine action.

SEC. 3 Duties of the Regional Director (Ministry of Agriculture). - The moment a Municipality or portion thereof, or an area has been declared officially as a "quarantine area", it shall be the duty and responsibility of the Regional Director (Ministry of Agriculture) in the region concerned to formulate and carry out control containment and eradication measures as are necessary to prevent the spread of such quarantinable plant pests. In formulating and carrying out such crop protection measures within the area under quarantine, the Director of

Plant Industry shall provide technical supervision to the Regional Director (Ministry of Agriculture).

SEC. 4 Inspection and Issuance of Certificate on Internal Movements of Plant/Plant Products Coming from Areas under Quarantine. – All plants, plant products, other probable host materials and other media for spreading of the plant pest under plant quarantine consideration, intended for shipment to places outside the area under quarantine shall be subjected to rigid inspection and/or commodity treatment. Such quarantine action conducted thereon shall be officially certified to have been complied with by the owner the, thereof in accordance with the requirements of the Special Quarantine Administrative Order governing the same and a "Permit to Transport" (BPI "Q" Form No. 12) shall be issued by the BPI Plant Quarantine Officer to accompany the shipment. Upon arrival of the shipment at the point of destination the owner shall submit the "Permit to Transport" to the BPI Plant Quarantine Officer assigned thereat who shall check or verify the shipment against the document submitted.

SEC. 5 In order to carry out the provisions of this Rule, the Director of Plant Industry shall, if deemed necessary, deputize/designate as Plant Quarantine Officers the Regional Director of the Ministry of Agriculture in the Region concerned and such other subordinate officials of the Ministry of Agriculture within the area under quarantine thereby vesting them the powers and duties of Such Plant Quarantine Officer in accordance with the provisions of Section 10 of P. D. 1433in the area concerned. Provided, that said deputization shall only be applicable within the area declared under quarantine and for as long as the same Special Quarantine Order is in effect.

SEC. 6 All transportation companies either land, water or air shall cooperate with the Director of Plant Industry or his duly authorized representatives in the strict enforcement of the provisions of this Rule by not allowing or accepting shipments of known host materials which are capable of spreading the "plant pest" to other places or areas where the pest is not yet known to exist.

SEC. 7 Any shipment of the known host materials of the "plant pest" under plant quarantine consideration made in contravention of the provisions of this Rule and other Special Quarantine Orders covering specific "plant pests" and their hosts, shall be seized by the Director of Plant Industry or by his authorized representatives and shall either be returned immediately to the place of origin or completely destroyed or treated, whichever is appropriate. Provided, that the cost of the return, or the destruction or treatment or other quarantine action that may be conducted thereon, shall be borne by the owner or consignee.

Rule Ⅶ Entrance and clearance of carriers

SEC. 1 Inspection and Clearance of Vessels Engaged in the International Trade shall be governed by the following procedures:

a. Submission of "Notices of Arrival" of Vessels. The owner, operator or agent of vessel plying the international trade routes, desiring to call at any Philippine Port of Entry shall serve "Notices of Arrival" of their subject vessels to the Plant Quarantine Officer at the initial port of entry within the country thereafter that the vessel may desire to call, at least twenty four (24) hours before the estimated time of arrival of the vessels at the port.

b. Quarantine Inspection/Verification of Vessels and Cargoes. Vessels calling at Philippine Ports of Entry shall be boarded and inspected upon arrival thereat by the Plant Quarantine Officer for the purpose of determining the cargoes laden on board, including the ship's food provisions and plant furnishings. For this purpose, the ship's Agent or Master of the vessel shall furnish the Plant Quarantine Officer with a copy each of the Voyage Itinerary, Inward Cargo Manifest, Baggage Declarations of disembarking crew or passengers, Parcel List, Stores List, Plant and Animal List and such other ship's document and/or information that the Plant Quarantine Officer may require.

c. Vessels coming from or passing through plant quarantine restricted areas or "open ports" ("free ports") shall be subjected to more rigid plant quarantine action including guarding of the vessel and/or supervision on use and disposal of quarantinable food provisions on board the vessel, as well as prevent the unlawful landing of certain commodities or provisions the importation of which are controlled, prohibited or banned under this Order or under such other Orders that may hereafter be promulgated.

d. The storage chambers of vessels mentioned in sub – section hereof which contain fresh fruits, vegetables and other plant products shall be sealed if and. when such provisions originate from plant quarantine restricted areas or territories. Provided, however, that when the vessel desires to utilize such restricted provision for the consumption of the crew members and passengers, the master or any responsible officer on board shall submit a formal request on the matter to the Plant Quarantine Officer. Upon submission and approval of such request said storage chamber shall be opened and disposal of said provisions or parts thereof shall be under the supervision of the Plant Quarantine Officer on board the vessel. Provided, further that after withdrawal of such provisions, the said storage chambers shall be resealed under similar supervision.

e. The utilization or consumption of fresh fruits, vegetables and other plant products originating from non – restricted areas shall be allowed on board the vessel without the imposition of any quarantine restriction, provided, they are verified upon inspection to be substantially free from "plant pests" of plant quarantine significance.

f. Passenger liners or tourist vessels shall be placed under appropriate quarantine supervision and control while berthed by any Philippine port to preclude the unauthorized landing or loading of quarantinable materials or commodities by the passengers, tourists and other parties.

g. Vessels with cargoes of wheat, corn, sorghum, soybean and other plant products shall likewise be subjected to quarantine supervision and control during the cargo discharging operations, and if deemed necessary, such bulk cargo shall first be subjected to fumigation or to other forms of commodity treatment on board the vessel or in the receiving barges as the case may be. Provided, however, that the cost and charges to be incurred in such quarantine inspection and/or treatment shall be borne by the owner of such cargo or by the operator or silent of the vessel it being incidental to the business in which they are engaged.

h. Plant Quarantine clearance on vessels calling at all Philippine Ports shall be required. Provided, however, that in case such vessels call at local Philippine Ports, where movements of plants and plant materials is restricted, such plant quarantine clearance shall be required of the vessels from such restricted ports. A copy each of the Outward Cargo Manifest and the list of plants and plant products brought on board by the members of the crew or passengers shall be furnished to the Plant Quarantine Officer. Upon receipt of the aforementioned ship's document, and after a satisfactory assessment of the vessel's compliance with the Plant Quarantine Laws and Rules. a "Plant Quarantine Clearance" (BPI "Q" Form No. 13) shall be issued as a pre-requisite for the issuance of the Customs Clearance (Section 13, P. D. 1433).

SEC. 2 Inspection and Clearance of Aircrafts Plying the Intentional Trade Routes shall be governed by the following procedures:

a. Airline companies or the authorized agents of private aircrafts coming from a foreign country and calling at any airport in the Philippines shall furnish the Plant Quarantine Officer with a copy of the aircraft's itinerary general declaration, passenger manifest, cargo manifest and other documents which the Plant Quarantine Officer may require.

b. All such aircrafts shall be inspected upon arrival in any airport in the Philippines by the Plant Quarantine Officer and all food provisions and other materials covered by quarantine prohibition or restriction shall be sealed. Provided, however, that should the aircraft desire to utilize such provisions, a formal request on the matter shall be submitted to the Plant Quarantine Officer who shall supervise the use and disposal thereof.

SEC. 3 Inspection and Clearance of Vessels Plying the Domestic Trade Routes shall be governed by the following procedures:

a. All vessels coming from or passing through declared quarantine area shall be inspected and cleared by the Plant Quarantine Officers at all ports of call in the Philippines. It shall be the duty of the Owner, Agent or Master of such vessel to furnish the Plant Quarantine Officer with a copy each of the Domestic Cargo Manifest, Parcel List and other shipping document which the Plant Quarantine Officer may require.

b. All domestic vessels departing from a port within a quarantined area shall be required to secure a "Domestic Plant Quarantine Clearance" (BPI "Q" Form No. 14) which shall be sumbitted to the Plant Quarantine Officer in all ports.

SEC. 4 Inspection and Clearance of Aircrafts Plying the Domestic Trade Route shall be governed by the following procedures:

a. All aircrafts coming from an airport within a declared plant quarantine area shall be inspected and cleared by the Plant Quarantine Officers in every part of call. It shall be the duty of the airline company to furnish the Plant Quarantine Officers with a copy of the Domestic Cargo Manifest and other documents relevant to quarantine enforcements.

b. All aircrafts departing from a domestic airport within a quarantined area shall be required to secure a "Domestic Plant Quarantine Clearance" for submission to the Plant Quarantine Officer at the next airport of call.

SEC. 5 Quarantine Control over Garbage Disposal by Carriers. – The unauthorized disposal of kitchen waste and garbage by carriers within the territory or waters of the Philippines is prohibited. Garbage and kitchen wastes shall always be kept on board the carrier in covered containers or receptacles. Should any carrier desire to dispose off her garbage while within Philippine territory, a formal request to that effect shall be submitted to the Plant Quarantine Officer on duty thereat, who shall supervise the disposal thereof in such manner and at such place designated for the purpose.

Rule Ⅷ Plant quarantine prescribed regulatory fees and charges

SEC. 1 The following rules and regulations are hereby promulgated to govern the imposition and collation of nominal plant quarantine regulatory fees and charges for the inspection, certification, issuance of permit to import, commodity treatment, etc. on imported/exported plants, plant products, other materials and commodities' capable of harboring plant pests, potential animal pests, and others, and such collections shall constitute the Revolving Fund of the National Plant Quarantine Service.

a. Fees for the Issuance of "Permit to Import"

(a – 1) "Permit to Import Plants and Plant Products", For every "permit" issued for the importation of plants, plant products and other materials enumerated in Section 1 of Rule II of the Administrative Order, a fee of Five Pesos (P5) shall be collected.

(a – 2) "Permit to Import" Potential Animal Pests. – For every "permit" issued for the importation of live animals which are considered as potential pests to agricultural crops, as enumerated in Section I of Rule Ⅲ of this Administrative Order, a fee of Fifty Pesos (P50) shall be collected.

b. Inspection and Certification Fees:

(b – 1) For the inspection of imported living plants, a minimum charge of Five Pesos (P5) for a shipment of ten (10) plants or less shall be imposed and every plant thereafter, an additional Fifty Centavos (P0.50) each shall be collected; Provided, that in the case of small living plants in community pots or similar packaging or container, a fee of Five Pesos (P5) on every community pot shall be levied.

(b－2) For the phytosanitary certification of living plants for export, a minimum charge of Two Pesos (P2) for a shipment of ten (10) plants or less shall be imposed, and for every plant thereafter, an additional Twenty Centavos (P0.20) each shall be collected. Provided that in the case of small living plants in community pots or similar packaging or container, a fee of Two Pesos (P2) on every community pot shall be levied;

(b－3) For the inspection of imported seeds, cuttings, rhizomes, bulbs, corns, grafts, scions and other materials capable of propagation, a fee of Two Pesos (P2.00) per metric ton or fraction of the net weight shall be collected.

(b－4) For the inspection of imported "plant products" and other materials capable of harboring "plant pests" intended for consumption, for processing or manufacturing purposes, a fee of One Peso (P1) per metric ton or fraction of the net weight thereof shall be collected.

(b－5) For the inspection and phytosanitary certification of "plant products" and other materials for export, a fee of One Peso (P1) per metric ton or fraction of the net weight thereof shall be collected.

(b－6) For the inspection and clearance of imported "potential animal pests", an inspection fee of Ten Pesos (P10.00) shall be charged on the first one to ten animals, and for any additional head thereof, a fee of One Peso (P1.00) shall be imposed.

c. Commodity Treatment Charges. – For the fumigation, disinfection and other treatments, including cleansing, conducted on imported/exported/ domestic plants, plant products and other materials or commodities, the charges shall be based on the prevailing cost of labor and material/consumed thereto and furnished by the Bureau of Plant Industry. Provided, that the imposition of treatment charges shall be waived if the fumigant, disinfectant and other materials are supplied by the party or parties concerned.

d. Post Entry Quarantine Charge. For the care and/or maintenance of imported materials (plants, plant products, potential animal pest, etc.) being held under post entry quarantine observation, the fees and charges shall be based on the prevailing cost of labor and materials furnished by the Bureau of Plant Industry.

e. Fees for the Destruction of Prohibited or Contraband Materials. For the destruction of confiscated contraband and/or prohibited imported materials, the importer shall be required to pay the Bureau of Plant Industry a minimum destruction fee of Twenty Pesos (P20.00) for the first twenty kilos or fraction thereafter. Provided, that in the case of small quantities of confiscated contrabands or prohibited materials, the imposition of destruction fee may be waived.

f. Exemption from the Payment of Plant Quarantine Prescribed Fees and Charges. The importation and exportations of all government agencies, government owned or controlled corporations, donations to and for the account of any duly registered Relief Organizations or any Charitable Institutions as certified to by the Ministry of Social Services and Development, embassies of foreign governments, and those that may be declared by the President, upon the recommendation of the National Economic and Development Authority in the interest of economic development, shall be exempted from payments of Plant Quarantine prescribed fees and charges, excluding however the expenses incurred in commodity treatments and overtime services of Plant Quarantine personnel.

Rule Ⅸ Overtime services

SEC. 1 The following rules and regulations are hereby promulgated to govern the rate of payment of overtime services, transportation allowances and lodging of the BPI Plant Quarantine personnel in connection with the inspection treatment, certification, documentation and other prescribed quarantine actions on imported/exported/domestically moved plants, plant products and other materials or commodities capable of harboring "plant pests", potential animal pests; boarding and/or inspection or guarding of carriers plying the international and domestic trade routes, and others that may hereinafter require plant quarantine action, chargeable to the party of parties served, for the information and guidance of all concerned.

a. Prescribed Overtime Hours:

(a-1) Overtime service shall commence at the end of the regular office hours; that is from 5: 00 o'clock in the afternoon up to 8: 00 o'clock in the morning of the following working day including the noon interval between 12: 00 noon to 1: 00 PM and 12: 30 PM to 1: 30 PM (Summer Session). During Saturdays, Sundays and Holidays, the overtime period shall begin from the termination of the regular office hours at 5: 00 PM on Friday and to terminate not later than 8: 00 AM of the following working day unless the service is terminated sooner.

(a-2) Rate of Overtime Charges: Services of BPI Plant Quarantine Officers, Fumigators, laborers and helpers performed outside the official working hours shall be paid by the party or parties served at the rate of Nine Pesos (P9) per hour for Plant Quarantine Officers and Fumigators, and Seven Pesos (P7) per hour for laborers and/or helpers.

(a-3) Computation of Overtime Services: The overtime rendered by the BPI Plant Quarantine Personnel shall be computed, commencing at two (2) hours before the arrival at the carrier or before the start of the inspection or commodity treatment to be conducted on plants, plant products, etc., and until the end of an hour after the work is finished. Provided, however, that the overtime services of Plant Quarantine Officers rendered outside their officials stations, in outports, subports, or other places, shall commence at two (2) hours before the start of plant quarantine undertaking and until the end of an hour within which the work is finished, without prejudice to the payment of actual and necessary traveling expenses or lodging allowance incurred by the Plant Quarantine Officer.

In case of delay in the arrival of carriers or failure on the part of importers, exporters and other parties concerned to adhere with the scheduled time alloted for the inspection or commodity treatment of their commodities, the waiting time or standby hours of the Plant Quarantine personnel shall be included in the computation of overtime services rendered.

b. Meal Allowance: Plant Quarantine personnel rendering overtime services shall be entitled to claim meal allowances at the rate of Fourteen Pesos (P14) per meal, whenever such overtime work coincides with meal time. Provided, however, that when the party or parties served are willing to provide satisfactory meals during the overtime periods this privilege shall be waived.

The Meal periods are as follows

Breakfast	6: 00A. M. -8: 00 A. M
Lunch	12: 00 Noon-1: 00 P. M
Supper	6: 00 P. M-8: 00 P. M

c. Transportation Allowance:

(c-1) For trips inside the Greater Manila area and other Metropolitan areas or cities, there shall be fixed rate of Fourteen pesos (P14) per one way for transportation allowance.

(c-2) For trips in the provinces, the transportation allowance shall be paid in accordance with the prevailing rate in the locality or the rate being paid to the personnel of other government agencies rendering similar services.

(c-3) In case of extreme necessity or where the interest of the service demands, the Plant Quarantine Officer may be allowed to hire such conveyance as is necessary in the course of performing his functions or meeting the demands of the service. In such case, that parties served shall reimburse the Plant Quarantine Officer the cost of hiring such conveyance which cost shall be supported with the corresponding receipt.

d. Lodging Allowances: BPI Plant Quarantine Personnel assigned to accomplish a quarantine mission and/or function in a place outside their official stations shall be allowed to claim lodging allowances, when such overnight stay is necessary, at the rates prevailing in the locality. Provided that, however, such shall not exceed Fifty Pesos (P50). Provided fuller that the party or parties served shall have the option to request remuneration of the extra services of the Plant Quarantine personnel on flat rate or contractual basis.

Rule X Powers and duties of the plant quarantine officer

SEC. 1 For purposes of this Administrative Order, BPI Plant Quarantine Officers shall have the following powers and duties:

a. To inspect all carriers, crew/passenger baggages and incoming mails, in order to determine the presence of plants, plant products and other materials capable of harboring plant pests, as well as potential animal pests.

b. To enter into and conduct inspection/verification of any and all areas where plants, plant products, and other materials capable of harboring plant pests are landed, stored and/or grown.

c. To examine imported plants/plant products, and other materials capable of harboring plant pests as well as potential animal pests and to administer necessary measures to insure effective implementation of the provisions of this Administrative Order.

d. To inspect, administer treatment if necessary and issue phytosanitary certification on plants, plant products and other related materials intended for export.

e. To confiscate and destiny or refuse entry of plants, plant products and potential animal pests involved in prohibited importations as well as prohibited plant and plant products involved in domestic movement and to deny phytosanitary certification of plants and plant products which exportation is, likewise, prohibited.

f. To perform such related duties which may be assigned to him, from time to time.

g. As provided, in Section 10 of P. D. No. 1433, Plant Quarantine Officers, in the exercise of their powers and duties, are given police power and authority.

Rule XI Cooperating agencies

SEC. 1 In the implementation/enforcement of the provisions of this Administrative Order, the Director of Plant Industry and/or his authorize representative may request or call for the assistance of the following government offices/agencies (Section 16, P. D. No. 1433).

a. The Bureau of Customs
b. The Philippine Ports Authority
c. The Bureau of Quarantine
d. The Bureau of Posts
e. The Bureau of Animal Industry
f. The Philippine Constabulary
g. The Philippine Airforce
h. The Philippine Coast Guard
i. The Civil Aeronatucs Administration
j. The Central Bank of the Philippines
k. The Bureau of Immigration
l. The Philippine Coconut Authority
m. The Bureau of Forestry
n. The Provincial Governors

o. The Municipal Mayors

p. The Local Police Agencies

q. The Ministry of Trade

r. The Philippine Export Council

s. The National Economic and Development Authority

t. Other government offices/agencies which could provide assistance in the implementation of the provisions of this Administrative Order,

u. Nothing in this Order shall preclude compliance with applicable rules and regulations promulgated by other agencies of the government regarding the importation and exportation of plants and plant products.

Rule XII Non – liability clause

SEC. 1 All charges for storage, demurrage, cartage, labor and delays incidental to quarantine inspection, cost of commodity treatments and other post – entry requirements shall be the responsibility of the importer, exporter, owner, or the parties concerned. Provided, that the Bureau of Plant Industry and/or its authorized representatives shall not be held liable for damage to the commodity in the course of the implementation of the provisions of this Administrative Order.

Rule XIII Penalty clause

Any person, company, or corporation who violates the provisions of this Administrative Order, or forges, counterfeits, alter, defaces and destroys any document issued by virtue of this Administrative Order shall be fined not more than Twenty Thousand Pesos (P20 000) or by imprisonment from prison correctional to prison mayor, or both, at the discretion of the court.

Rule XIV Separability clause

If any of the provisions of this Administrative Order shall be held invalid, the remainder shall be operative.

Rule XV Repealing clause

All Administrative Orders, Rules and Regulations inconsistent with the provisions of this Administrative Order are hereby superseded and/or revoked accordingly.

Rule XVI Effectivity

This Administrative Order shall take effect upon its approval and after appropriate publications.

(SGD.) **MANUEL Q. LIM, JR.**
Officer – in – Charge
Ministry of Agriculture
RECOMMENDING APPROVAL:
(SGD.) DOMINGO F. PANGANIBAN
Director of Plant Industry

国际贸易中木质包装材料管理指南

（植物产业局检疫管理条例　2004 年系列）

根据第 1433 号总统令第 17 条规定，植物产业局长兹将涉及的所有相关信息及指引性的规则与规定予以公布。

术语定义

商品　一种为出售或其他目的而进行运输的植物、植物产品或者其他物品（联合国粮农组织，1990 年；植物检疫措施临时委员会 2001 年修订）。

垫舱物料　用以固定或支撑一种商品，但并不与该商品相连接的木质包装材料（联合国粮农组织，1990 年；国际植物检疫措施标准 2002 年第 15 号出版物修订）。

熏蒸　用任一种化学试剂完全或主要以气态接触商品的处理方法（联合国粮农组织，1990 年；联合国粮农组织 1995 年修订）。

标识/加施标识　某个施加于任一种受到管制的物品，以证明其植物检疫状态且得到国际性认可的官方印章或印记（国际植物检疫措施标准 2002 年第 15 号出版物）。

植物检疫措施　其目的在于阻止检疫性有害生物的引进以及/或者传播，或者对受到管制的非检疫性有害生物的经济影响加以限制的任何立法、规定或官方程序（联合国粮农组织，1995 年；国际植物保护公约 1997 年修订；入侵物种纲要，2001 年）。

检疫性有害生物　对被其危及到的相关地区具有潜在的经济影响，但并未在该处存在，或者虽然存在，却并未广泛分布，并且已受到官方控制的任一种有害生物（联合国粮农组织，1990 年；联合国粮农组织，1995 年修订；国际植物保护公约，1997 年）。

原木　并未经过加工或者处理的木材（国际植物检疫措施标准 2002 年第 15 号出版物）。

细木　根据《商品名称及编码协调制度》（《协调制度》或 HS），被认为其厚度等于或小于 6mm。

处理　得到官方授权的，将有害生物杀死或清除，抑或使有害生物无法繁殖的相关流程（联合国粮农组织，1990 年；联合国粮农组织 1995 年修订；国际植物检疫措施标准 2002 年第 15 号出版物）。

胶合板材木芯　高温处理胶合板层生产的副产品，构成经过剥皮加工的圆木的木芯。

木质包装材料　用以支撑、保护或运输任一商品（包括其垫舱物料）的木材或木材产品（不包括纸质产品）（国际植物检疫措施标准 2002 年第 15 号出版物）。

1. 基本原理

植物检疫措施临时委员会（ICPM）于 2002 年 3 月 15 日批准了《国际贸易当中所涉及的木质包装材料管理指南》（ISPM15）。该批准是在《国际植物保护公约》确定了由未经加工的原木所制成的木质包装材料（WPM）可导致窃蠹科 Anobiidae、长蠹科 Bostrichidae、吉丁甲科 Buprestidae、天牛科 Cerambycidae、象鼻虫科 Curculionidae、等翅目 Isoptera、粉蠹科 Lyctidae、拟天牛科 Oedemeridae、小蠹科 Scolyitidae 和树蜂科 Siridae 以及松材线虫 *Bursaphelenchus xylophilus* 等多种有害生物的引入与扩散而出台的。

社会各界对贸易中涉及的木质包装进行管制的需要已经有了认识，因为木质包装材料有害生物的引入是一个世界性的问题。通常的情况是，木质包装材料往往被再利用、修复或再加工，木质包装材料的真正原产地很难界定，所以其植物检疫状况无法查明。

这一点反映了《国际植物检疫措施标准》第 15 号：《国际贸易当中所涉及的木质包装材料管理指

南》中所确立的监管指导方针。

2. 涵盖范围

本指导方针适用于包括下列各项在内的针叶及非针叶木质包装材料：货盘、垫舱物料、板条箱、衬层、圆形箱、承载板、托盘环、滑动垫木。

本规定并不包括完全由木质产品构成的木质包装材料，如使用胶水、热能及压力或者这些方法的结合等加工方法而生产的胶合板、刨花板、定向刨花板或薄板（贴面板）等，上述材料应被视为进行了充分加工，已将涉及到原木的风险予以排除。

胶合板材木芯、锯屑、木丝与刨花，以及切成片的原木等木质包装材料可能不会造成有害生物的引入，除有可用的相关技术依据以外，不应对其进行管制。

3. 执行措施（仅适用于菲律宾）

3.1 处理设施/服务供应商的认证

认证标准

适用于熏蒸公司

3.1.1 持有由肥料与杀虫剂监管当局（FPA）颁发的熏蒸执照

3.1.2 应至少具有下列的设备及安全装置/仪器：

- 空气循环器；
- 排气扇；
- 蒸发器（在需要时）；
- 分布管/发生器；
- 瓦斯监测管/装置；
- 探测泵；
- 配套呼吸装置（在必要情况下）；
- 全面罩；
- 安全带与吊带（梯子等）；
- 经植物产业局批准的标识设备；
- 沙粒疏通器；
- 柏油帆布/防霉纸；
- 急救药箱；
- 其他可能必要的物件。

3.1.3 通过由植物产业局授权的任一官员进行监督的实际（熏蒸）测试。

适用于热处理公司

3.1.4 应至少具有下列的设备/仪器：

- 数量充足的温度探针（最少5个传感探头/室）；
- 热处理室；
- 温度与数据记录器；
- 其他可能必要的物件。

3.1.5 通过由植物产业局授权的任一官员进行监督的实际（热处理）测试

熏蒸公司/设施认证步骤

Ⅰ. 熏蒸公司应向植物产业局申请进行认证；

Ⅱ. 提供下列文件的原件及复印件：FPA 执照、DTI/SEC 注册、市长许可及 TIN 编号以供评测；

Ⅲ. 植物产业局的植物检疫机构应对熏蒸公司的相关设施及设备进行检查、评测；

Ⅳ. 开展实际的熏蒸测试；

Ⅴ. 植物检疫机构负责人在植物产业局局长做出最终审批之前提出推荐意见；

Ⅵ. 颁发的《认证证书》应附有指定代号。

热处理公司认证步骤

Ⅰ. 熏蒸公司应向植物产业局提出申请;

Ⅱ. 提交下列文件:FPA 执照、DTI/SEC 注册、市长许可及 TIN 编号以供评测;

Ⅲ. 植物产业局的植物检疫机构应对热处理公司的相关设施及设备进行检查、评测;

Ⅳ. 开展实际的热处理测试;

Ⅴ. 植物检疫机构负责人在植物产业局局长做出最终审批之前提出推荐意见;

Ⅵ. 颁发的《认证证书》应附有指定代号。

监测/报告

要求获得认证的、进行相关处理的公司/服务供应商每周向植物产业局提交以下信息:

Ⅰ. 所处理的木质包装材料的数量以及其预计重量;

Ⅱ. 所使用的木质包装材料的数量以及其目的地;

Ⅲ. 所应用的处理的类型;

Ⅳ. 使用过木质包装材料的公司/出口商。

3.2　处理

- 处理应仅由经过认证的处理公司/服务供应商开展;
- 对木质包装材料的处理对于执行国际植物检疫措施标准第 15 号的所有国家均具有强制性;
- 相关处理**应在**植物检疫官员/检查员现场监督的情况下进行;
- 应由参与处理的植物检疫官员制作附有植物检疫机构批准代号的相关处理报告,并予以签署确认;
- 植物检疫机构批准代号应与木质包装材料标标识上所显示的代号相匹配;
- 经过回收、重新制造或修理的木质包装材料应进行**重新验证、重新标识**。任何之前的标识均应予以适当地移除。上述材料的所有部件均应进行处理。

3.2.1　溴甲烷熏蒸

- 溴甲烷(MB)熏蒸——该处理方式应以 **MB** 标识的形式予以标明,并达到木质包装材料的 **MB** 熏蒸处理的最低标准。
- **其最低温度不应低于 10℃,最短熏蒸时间不应少于 16 小时。**

温度	剂量率	最低浓度(g/m^3)			
		0.5 小时	2 小时	4 小时	16 小时
21℃或以上	48	36	24	17	14
16℃或以上	56	42	28	20	17
11℃或以上	64	48	32	22	19

3.2.2　热处理

- 木质包装材料应按照所要求的特定时间温度计划表的规定进行处理,即**最低木芯温度达到 56℃并至少持续 30 分钟**。
- 在热处理标识上应使用 HT 标记(**HT mark**)对所进行的处理予以标明。

3.2.3 《国际植物保护公约》在将来所可能规定的其他可选用的处理方法。

3.3　建议做出的标识(仅适用于菲律宾的木质包装材料)

在经批准的相关措施范围内,木质包装材料应使用喷漆加施经批准做出的标识。相关标识应在木质包装材料上至少两(2)个相对面上列出。

经批准做出的标识应符合下述要求:

- 尺寸——不超过 3 英寸 ×4 英寸；
- 颜色为绿色；
- 使用喷漆；
- 以相关模型为准；
- 易于辨认；
- 永久性和不可转移；
- **放置在可见的位置，位于两个相对面上；**
- 在所做标识当中应有 **MB**（溴甲烷）或 **HT**（热处理）标识，以标明所应用的处理的类型。

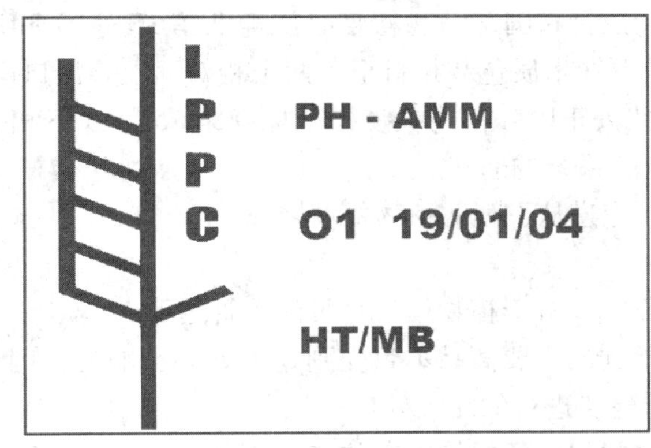

编号系统

PHAMM0119/01/04

PH – ISO 国家代码

AMM – 公司

01 – 批次

19/01/2004 – 熏蒸日期

植物产业局身为国家植物保护组织，应具有其自身的标识代码，并在必要情况下予以使用。

3.4 对不合规情况的处罚

1. 相关处理作业的**不合规情况**涉及下列各项：

Ⅰ. 使用不当/标识不当；

Ⅱ. 因未能进行相关处理导致进口国不予接受；

Ⅲ. 未提交相关报告；

Ⅳ. 在进行处理前未告知植物检疫官员。

2. 首次违反

- 书面训诫

3. 第二次违反

- 撤销认证

出 口

1. 所有使用了木质包装材料的运货商或出口商均应在出口之前、在进行相关处理至少 72 小时之前申请并填写一张木质包装材料的申请表格（为植物检疫官员的计划实施留出时间）。

2. 对于尚未执行国际植物检疫措施标准第 15 号的目的地，直至相关目的地决定执行该标准时为止，相关检查应被视为已达到充分程度。

3. 经过处理的木质包装材料应在处理后进行适当保护，以避免再次污染/再次感染。

4. 所有的木质包装材料均应含有经批准的标识，以标明处理的日期、代号及所运用处理的类型。

5. 对木质包装材料的处理应仅由**经植物产业局认证的处理公司/服务供应商**来完成。

6. 对木质包装材料的处理应在植物检疫官员现场监督的情况下完成。

7. 在成功完成一次相关处理后，应加施经批准的标识。

进口（到达菲律宾各港口）

1. 所有的进口商均应在货物到达至少 24 小时前为木质包装材料所附随的所有商品申请进行检查/清关。

2. 一旦到达，木质包装材料则应由植物检疫官员进行检查、清关。

3. 所有的转口货物均应在其最终目的地港口进行检查/清关。

4. **所有的木质包装材料均应具有国际植物检疫措施标准第 15 号项下所规定的、所要求/批准的最少标识**。所加施的标识应被放置在木质包装材料至少两个相对面上。出口国可采用其自身的标识系统/方式，前提是采用的系统/方式处于国际植物检疫措施标准第 15 号项下相关参数的范围内，且菲律宾应在首次装运之前得到关于上述系统的通知。

5. 如发生下列情形的，则应遵从下列的植物检疫措施：

如不带批准标识的

- 相关商品必须暂停操作，并置于植物检疫官员的监管之下。
- 如木质包装材料所涉及到的主要商品不致受到相关处理影响的，则立即进行处理，否则要求将该商品进行剥离，并立即进行建议进行的相关处理。
- **任何不合规的木质包装材料必须始终被存放在一个可有效确保有害生物不会进入环境中的密闭容器内。不合规木质包装材料的存放区域必须同已经过加工的其他的国内的木质商品、材料相隔离开来。**
- **如不合规木质包装材料已埋存的，其应被埋入地表下至少 3 米深之处。木材必须埋藏在无法将该材料重新发掘出的场址处。木材在埋藏坑中不得外露。**
- 如无法进行可靠的处理或埋放的，则应将木质包装材料立即予以销毁。
- 应由植物检疫官员制作不合规情况报告，并立即向原产国的国家植物保护组织提交，副本抄送植物检疫机构及进口商。

具有批准标识，但发现有活的检疫性有害生物的

- 相关商品应立即与木质包装材料一并在植物检疫官员的监管之下接受相关处理，相关费用则由进口商承担。
- 或者将整批托运货物退还发送人/原产国，相关费用则由进口商承担。
- 植物检疫官员应制作不合规情况报告，并立即向原产国的国家植物保护组织提交，相关副本抄送植物检疫机构及进口商。

涉及木质包装材料的非农业性商品

1. 所有的进口商均应在货物到达至少 24 小时前为木质包装材料所附随的所有商品申请进行检查/清关。

2. 一旦到达，木质包装材料应接受检查。

3. 所有的转口货物均应在其最终目的地港口进行检查/清关。

4. 所有的木质包装材料均应具有所要求/批准做出的标识。

5. 如发生下列情形的，则应遵从下列的植物检疫措施：

如不带批准标识的

- 相关商品必须暂停操作，并置于植物检疫官员的监管之下。
- 如木质包装材料所涉及到的商品不致受到相关处理影响的，则应立即在港口区域进行所建议的相关处理。

● 如相关处理需要在特定场地或经加工方可完成，不合规的木质包装材料则必须放置在密闭的容器内并直接运送至将进行处置或加工的场地处。

● 任何不合规的木质包装材料必须始终被存放在一个可有效确保有害生物不会进入环境中的密闭容器内。不合规木质包装材料的存放区域必须同已经过加工的其他的国内的木质商品、材料相隔离开来。

● 如无法进行可靠处理的，则应将木质包装材料立即予以销毁。

● 植物检疫官员应制作不合规情况报告，并立即向原产国的国家植物保护组织提交，相关副本抄送植物检疫机构及进口商。

具有批准标识，但发现有存活的检疫性有害生物的

● 相关商品应立即与木质包装材料一并在植物检疫官员的监管之下接受相关处理，相关费用则由进口商承担。

● 或者将整批托运货物退还发送人/原产国，相关费用则由进口商承担。

● 植物检疫官员应编制不合规情况报告，并立即向原产国的国家植物保护组织提交，相关副本抄送植物检疫机构及进口商。

对于并未执行国际植物检疫措施标准 15 号的出口国

对于并无木质包装材料标示系统的相关国家，则其应被要求在截至 2005 年 6 月 1 日前做到遵从必要的标识规则。

从 2005 年 1 月 1 日至 2005 年 6 月 1 日的整个执行期间，应要求所有不具批准标记的木质包装材料出具植物检疫证书。该植物检疫证书应述明所规定的相关处理已在其原产国进行。

本命令应予立即发布，并应自 2005 年 1 月 1 日起生效。

CLARITO · M · BARROW，CESOIV
助理局长
植物产业局负责官员
2004 年 10 月 21 日

Guidelines for regulating wood packaging material involved in international trade

(BPI quarantine administrative order Series of 2004)

Pursuant to the provisions of Section 17 of the Presidential Decree No. 1433, the Director of Plant Industry hereby promulgates the following rules and regulations for the information and guidance of all concerned.

Definition of Terms

Commodity A type of plant, plant product, or other article being moved for trade of other purpose (FAO, 1990; revised ICPM, 2001)

Dunnage Wood packaging material used to secure or support a commodity but which does not remain associated with the commodity (FAO, 1990; revised ISPM Pub. No. 15, 2002)

Fumigation treatment with a chemical agent that reaches the commodity wholly or primarily in a gaseous state (FAO, 1990; revised FAO, 1995)

Mark/Marking an official stamp or brand, internationally recognized, and applied to a regulated article to attest its phytosanitary status (ISPM Pub. No. 15, 2002)

Phytosanitary measure Any legislation, regulation or official procedure having the purpose to prevent the introduction and or spread of quarantine pests, or to limit the economic impact of regulated non – quarantine pests (FAO, 1995; revised IPPC, 1997; ISC, 2001)

Quarantine pest A pest of potential economic importance to the area endangered thereby and not yet present there, or present but not widely distributed and being officially controlled (FAO, 1990; revised FAO, 1995; IPPC 1997)

Raw wood Wood, which has not undergone processing, or treatment (ISPM Pub. No. 15, 2002)

Thin wood considered to be 6mm thickness or less according to the Customs Harmonized Commodity Description and Coding System (the Harmonized System or HS)

Treatment Officially authorized procedure for the killing or removal of pests or rendering pests infertile (FAO, 1990; revised FAO, 1995; ISPM Pub. No. 15, 2002)

Veneer peeler cores By product of veneer production involving high temperatures and comprising the center of a log remaining after the peeling process.

Wood packaging Wood or wood products (excluding paper products) used material (WPM) in supporting, protecting or carrying a commodity (Includes dunnage) (ISPM Pub. No. 15, 2002)

1. Rationale

The Interim Commission on Phytosanitary Measures (ICPM) approved the "Guidelines for Regulating Wood Packaging Material in International Trade (ISPM 15)" on 15 March 2002. The approval is brought about after the IPPC determined that the worldwide movement of Wood Packaging Material (WPM) made of unprocessed raw wood is a pathway for the introduction and spread of a variety of pests belonging to the family, Anobiidae, Bostrichidae, Buprestidae, Cerambycidae, Curculionidae, Isoptera. Lyctidae, Oededmeridae, Scolyitidae and Siridae for insects, and *Bursaphelenchus xylophilus*, a nematode.

The need to regulate was realized because the introduction of pests linked to WPM is a worldwide problem.

More often than not, WPM's are often re – used, recycled or re – manufactured, true origin cannot be determined and phytosanitary status cannot be ascertained.

This reflects the established regulatory guideline in International Standard for Phytosanitary Measures No. 15: Guidelines for Regulating Wood Packaging Materials in International Trade.

2. Coverage

This guidelines are for coniferous and non – coniferous Wood Packaging Materials which includes the following: pallets, dunnage, crating, packing blocks, drums cases, load boards, pallet collars, skids.

This regulation does not cover WPM's made wholly of wood – based products such as plywood, particle board, oriented strand board or veneer that have been created using glue, heat and pressure or a combination thereof should be considered sufficiently processed to have eliminated the risk associated with the raw wood

Wood packaging material such as veneer peeler cores, sawdust, wood wool, and shavings, and raw wood cut into thin pieces may not be pathways for introduction of quarantine pests and will not be regulated unless the technical bases are available.

3. Measures for Implementation (For Philippines only)

3.1 Accreditation of Treatment Facilities/ Service Providers

Criteria for Accreditation

For Fumigation Companies

3.1.1 Licensed by the Fertilizer and Pesticide Authority (FPA) for fumigators

3.1.2 Should have at least the following equipment and safety devices/apparatus:

- Air Circulator
- Exhaust Fan
- Evaporator (as necessary)
- Distributor hose/applicator
- Gas Monitoring tubes/ devices
- Detector pump
- SCBA (as necessary)
- Full face mask
- Safety belts and harnesses (ladder, etc.)
- Marking equipment approved by BPI
- Sand snakes
- Tarpaulin/P. E. sheet
- First aid kit
- Others as may be necessary

3.1.3 Pass the actual (fumigation) test to be supervised by an officer authorized by BPI.

For Heat Treatment Companies

3.1.4 Should have at least the following equipment/apparatus:

- Sufficient number of temperature probes (minimum of 5 sensor probes/chamber)
- Heat treatment chamber
- Temperature and Data Logger
- Others as may be necessary

3.1.5 Pass the actual (heat treatment) test to be supervised by an officer authorized by BPI.

Steps for Accreditation for Fumigation Companies/ Facilities

Ⅰ. Fumigation companies should apply for accreditation to the BPI.

Ⅱ. Present the original and photocopy of the following documents: FPA license, DTI/SEC Registration, Mayors Permit and TIN number for evaluation.

Ⅲ. BPI – PQS shall inspect and evaluate the facilities and equipment of the fumigation company.

Ⅳ. Conduct actual fumigation test.

Ⅴ. Recommendation by the PQS Chief prior to the final approval of the BPI Director.

Ⅵ. Certificate of Accreditation shall be issued with the assigned code.

Steps for Accreditation for Heat Treatment Companies

Ⅰ. Heat Treatment companies should apply to the BPI.

Ⅱ. Present the following documents: FPA license, DTI/SEC Registration, Mayors Permit and TIN number for evaluation.

Ⅲ. BPI – PQS shall inspect and evaluate the facilities and equipment of the heat treatment company.

Ⅳ. Conduct actual heat treatment test.

Ⅴ. Recommendation by the PQS Chief prior to the final approval of the BPI Director.

Ⅵ. Certificate of Accreditation shall be issued with the assigned code.

Monitoring/ Reporting

The accredited company/ service provider conducting treatment is required to submit to BPI the following information on a weekly basis:

Ⅰ. Number of WPM treated and estimated weight.

Ⅱ. Number of WPM used and its destination.

Ⅲ. Kind of treatment applied.

Ⅳ. Company/ Exporter who used the WPM.

3.2 Treatments

- Treatment should be done only by accredited treatment companies/ service provider.
- Treatment of WPM is mandatory to all countries implementing ISPM 15.
- Treatment **should be done** in the presence of a Plant Quarantine Officer/inspector.
- Treatment report with approved PQS codes shall be prepared and signed by the attending PQO.
- Approved PQS codes should match to the codes displayed on the markings of the WPM.
- Recycled, remanufactured or repaired wood packaging material should be **re – certified** and **remarked.** Any traces of the previous marks should be properly removed. All components of such material should be treated.

3.2.1 Methyl Bromide Fumigation

1. Methyl Bromide (MB) fumigation – treatment should be indicated by **MB** mark, following the minimum standard for MB fumigation treatment for wood packaging material.

2. The minimum temperature should not be less than 10℃ and the minimum exposure time should be 16 hours.

Temperature	Dosage rate	Minimum concentration (g/m^3)			
		0.5hrs	2hrs	4hrs	16hrs
21℃ or above	48	36	24	17	14
16℃ or above	56	42	28	20	17
11℃ or above	64	48	32	22	19

3.2.2 Heat treatment

1. Wood packaging material should be treated in accordance with the specific time temperature schedule required to meet the **minimum wood core temperature of 56℃ for a minimum of 30 minutes.**

2. Treatment should be indicated by **HT mark**.

3.2.3 Other alternative treatment method as may be prescribed by the IPPC in the future.

3.3 Recommended Marking (For Philippine WPM only)

Wood packaging materials subjected to the approved measures should display the approved marking using spray paint. The marking should be placed on at least two (2) opposite sides of the WPM.

Approved Marking Should Be:

- SIZE – should not be more than 3″×4″
- GREEN in color
- Spray painted
- According to the model
- Legible
- Permanent and non – transferable
- **Placed in a visible location, in two opposing side**
- **MB** (methyl bromide) or **HT** (heat treatment) mark should appear on the marking to indicate the kind of treatment applied

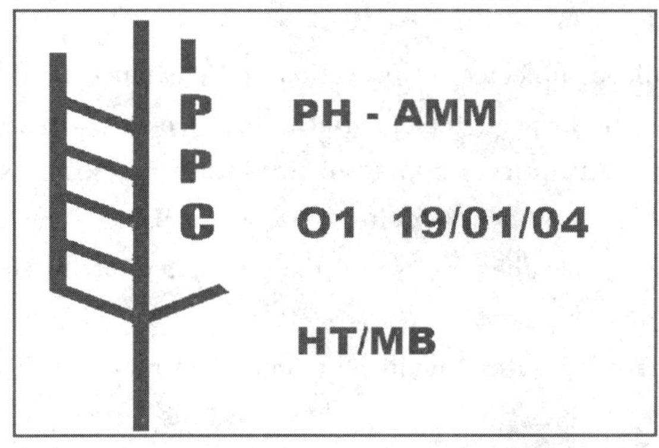

System of Coding

PHAMM 01 19/01/04

PH – ISO Country Code

AMM – Company

01 – Batch

19/01/2004 – Date of Fumigation

The Bureau of Plant Industry being the NPPO shall have its own code for marking and will be used whenever necessary.

3.4 Sanctions for non – compliance

1. **Non – compliance** of the treatment covers the following:

Ⅰ. Misuse/ improper marking

Ⅱ. Non – acceptance of the importing country due to treatment failure

Ⅲ. Non – submission of reports

Ⅳ. Failure to inform the PQO prior to treatment

2. First offense

- Reprimand in writing

3. Second offense

- Revoked accreditation

Export

1. All shippers or exporters using WPM should apply and accomplish an application form for WPM prior to exportation at least 72 hours before treatment (to give time for PQO scheduling)

2. For destinations that does not yet implement ISPM 15, inspection should be deemed sufficient until the destinations decides to implement the standard

3. Treated WPM's should be properly secured after treatment to avoid recontamination/re – infestation

4. All WPM's should bear the APPROVED MARK indicating the date of the treatment, code and the kind of treatment used.

5. Treatment of WPM's should be done only by **accredited treatment companies/ service providers of BPI.**

6. Treatment of WPM's should be done in the presence of a PQO.

7. Approved marking should be placed after a successful completion of the treatment

Import (Arriving at Philippine Ports)

1. All importers should apply for inspection/clearance at least 24 hours prior to arrival of cargo for all commodities accompanied with WPM

2. Upon arrival, WPM shall be subjected to inspection and clearance by PQ Officer.

3. All trans – shipment shall be inspected/cleared at the final port of destination

4. **All WPM should have the required/approved minimum marking as prescribed under ISPM 15.** The marking should be placed on at least two opposite sides of the WPM. The exporting country may adopt its own system/manner of marking provided they are within the parameters of ISPM 15 and the Philippines is notified of such system prior to the first shipment.

5. The following Phytosanitary Measures should be followed in the event of the following situations:

Without approved marking

- Commodity must be put on hold and shall be under guard by PQ Officer

- Should the main commodity with the WPM will not be affected by treatment, conduct treatment at once, if not, stripping off the commodity will be required, recommended treatment will be conducted immediately.

- **Any non – compliant wood packaging materials must be at all times stored in a closed container that is effective in ensuring that pests may not be allowed to enter the environment. Storage areas of non – compliant wood packaging materials must be isolated from other domestic wood commodities, materials that have already undergone processing.**

- **If the non – compliant wood packaging material is buried, it should be buried at a minimum depth of 3 meters below the surface of the ground. The wood must be buried at a site where – re – excavation of the material will not occur. Woods must not be left exposed within the burial pit.**

- If treatment or burying is not readily available, WPM should be destroyed immediately.

- Non – compliance report shall be prepared by the PQO to be submitted immediately to the NPPO of the country of origin, copy furnished the PQS and importer

With approved marking but with live quarantine pest found

- Commodity together with the WPM should be subjected to treatment at once under the direct supervision of Plant Quarantine Officer at the importer's expense.

- or the whole consignment returned to sender/country of origin at the importer's expense.
- Non – compliance report shall be prepared by the PQO to be submitted immediately to the NPPO of the country of origin, copy furnished the PQS and importer

Non – Agricultural Commodities with WPM

1. All importers should apply for inspection/clearance at least 24 hours prior to arrival of cargo for all commodities accompanied with WPM.
2. Upon arrival, WPM shall be subjected to inspection.
3. All trans – shipment shall be inspected/cleared at the final port of destination.
4. All WPM should bear the required/approved marking.
5. The following Phytosanitary Measures should be followed in the event of the following situations:

Without approved marking

- Commodity must be put on hold and shall be under guard by PQ Officer
- Should the commodity with the WPM will not be affected by treatment, conduct recommended treatment at once at the port area.
- **Should the treatment be done to a specified site or processing, the non – compliant wood packaging material must be moved in a closed container directly to the site at which disposal or processing is going to take place.**
- **Any non – compliant wood packaging materials must be at all times stored in a closed container that is effective in ensuring that pests may not be allowed to enter the environment. Storage areas of non – compliant wood packaging materials must be isolated from other domestic wood commodities, materials that have already undergone processing.**
- If treatment is not readily available, WPM should be destroyed immediately
- Non – compliance report shall be prepared by the PQO to be submitted immediately to the NPPO of the country of origin, copy furnished the PQS and importer

With approved marking but with live quarantine pest found

- Commodity together with the WPM should be subjected to treatment at once under the direct supervision of Plant Quarantine Officer at the importer's expense.
- or the whole consignment returned to sender/country of origin at the importer's expense.
- Non – compliance report shall be prepared by the PQO to be submitted immediately to the NPPO of the country of origin, copy furnished the PQS and importer

For Exporting Countries Not Yet Implementing ISPM 15

For those countries without system of marking WPM, they shall be given until June 1, 2005 to comply with the necessary marking.

From January 1,2005 until the full implementation in June 1,2005, a Phytosanitary Certificate will be required for all WPM lacking the approved mark. The Phytosanitary Certificate shall state that the prescribed treatment is carried out at the country of origin.

This order shall be published immediately and will take effect January 1,2005.

CLARITO M. BARRON, CESO IV
Assistant Director
Officer In – charge, BPI
October 21, 2004

关于进出口经辐照的植物、植物产品及辐照处理法规

（植物产业局检疫管理条例　第2号　2008年系列）

鉴于：

菲律宾是《国际植物保护公约》（IPPC）的成员，该国际条约旨在阻止植物及植物产品中有害生物的传播与引入，以及促进对其加以控制的适当措施。

IPPC的各缔约方采用了国际植物检疫措施标准（ISPM），后者为世界贸易组织（WTO）各成员方通过《实施卫生与植物卫生措施协定》（SPS协定）而承认为各植物检疫措施基准的相关标准、指导方针与建议。

2003年IPPC的植物检疫措施临时委员会（ICPM）批准了第18号ISPM，后者就对受管制有害生物或物品使用电离辐射作为植物检疫处理手段的特定程序提供了技术指导。

植物产业局（BPI）作为国家植物保护组织（NPPO），负责植物检疫工作中评价、采纳和使用辐照作为植物检疫措施。在必要时，植物产业局（BPI）应与其他的国家性或国际性监管机构，如在管制使用钴－60及铯－137等放射性来源的辐照设施方面拥有强制性权力的菲律宾核研究院（PNRI），以及在管制使用电子束及X光线等电子、电气设备所发射辐射的辐照设备方面拥有强制性权力的卫生设备与技术局（BHDT）等进行合作。

辐照处理逐渐在国际上被接受为一种检疫处理手段，可在检疫方面为植物与植物产品提供有效的灭害/消毒方法。

据此，根据第1433号总统令第17条相关条文，植物产业局局长发布本命令，对受辐射植物及植物产品的进口、出口及境内运送，以及将辐照作为植物检疫处理措施进行管理。

一　般　规　定

第1条　术语与定义缩写

以下术语用于本行政规定时的含义如下：

吸收剂量　　单位质量的特定货物吸收的辐射能量（单位：戈瑞）

商品　　为贸易或其他用途被调运的一种植物、植物产品或其他物品。

货物　　从一个国家运往另一个国家，并当有要求时在同一植物检疫证书中注明的一定数量的植物、植物产品和/或其他物品（货物可由一种、多种或数批组成）。

国内运送　　相关商品在国境内从一个地点运送至另一个地点。

剂量绘图　　使用剂量仪在具体场点对装载过程进行吸收剂量分布的测量。

剂量仪　　在辐射时可显示仪表某些特性定量变化的一种仪表，可使用适当的分析仪器和技术与某种材料中的吸收剂量相关。

剂量测定　　用于确定吸收剂量的一种方法，包含剂量仪、计量仪器及其有关的参考标准和该方法的使用程序。

效果（处理）　　按预定处理方法能达到的明确、可测量、可重复的效果。

出口　　将相关商品从任一本地港口运输至任一国外港口的行为。

戈瑞（Gy）　　吸收剂量单位，1Gy相当于每千克吸收1焦耳。

千戈瑞（kGy）　吸收剂量单位，等于1000戈瑞（Gy）。

进口　将用于种植、消费、制造、驯养或其他任何用途的外国商品引入至国内的行为。

检查　对植物、植物产品或其他限定物进行官方的直观检查以确定是否存在有害生物和/或是否符合植物检疫法规。

电离辐射　带电离子和电磁波经过初级或次级过程的相互物理作用产生离子的辐照。

辐照　用任何一种电离辐射进行处理。

批次　货物的组成部分，其成份和产地可证实的单一商品单位。

最低吸收剂量　处理装载物中局部最低吸收剂量（D_{min}）。

非目标检疫性有害生物　已经照射而被杀死的、具有未知检疫重要性的任一有害生物。

有害生物　对植物或植物产品有害的植物、动物或病原体的种、株（品）系或生物型。

植物检疫出证　应用植物检疫程序签发植物检疫证书。

植物产品　未经加工的植物源性材料（包括谷物），和虽经加工但因其天然性质或加工的工艺而仍有可能造成有害生物传入和扩散风险的产品。

植物　活的植物及其组织，包括种子和种质。

目标检疫性有害生物　可经施用所允许的剂量而予以杀灭的，具有检疫重要性的任一有害生物。

处理　旨在杀灭、灭活或消除有害生物、或使有害生物不育或丧失活力的官方程序。

缩写：

BPI　植物产业局

BHDT　卫生设备与技术局

IPPC　《国际植物保护公约》

ISPM　国际植物检疫措施标准

NPPO　国家植物保护组织

PNRI　菲律宾核研究院

PQS　植物检疫机构

第2条　覆盖范围

本条例覆盖范围为（a）受辐照活体植物及其相关部分，植物产品或来源于植物的未经加工材料，以及其性质或对其的加工可能造成有害生物引入与扩散风险的半成品植物产品或制造产品的进口、出口及境内运送，以及（b）作为植物检疫处理方式的辐照的使用。

执　行　规　则

第3条　辐照机构的批准

辐照机构应在其运用于植物检疫相关处理之前由其所在国的NPPO予以批准。此点包括本国及国外相关机构的进口、出口与本地贸易。

A. 审批要求

1. 本地机构

a. 文件要求

ⅰ. 填写完毕的申请表格

ⅱ. 证券交易委员会（SEC）注册文件或贸易与工业部（DTI）营业许可证的副本，以其中适用者为准

ⅲ. 市长许可的副本

ⅳ. 公司/机构相关概况

ⅴ. 税务登记号（TIN）以及（可用的）最近的所得税申报表（ITR）

ⅵ. 该处理机构所在地址图

ⅶ. 由 PNRI（适用于使用钴－60 及铯－137 等放射性来源的情况）或 BHDT（适用于使用由电子束或 X 光线等电力产生的辐射的情况）所颁发的执照

ⅷ. 成文的《标准操作流程》，其中应对该处理机构的系统及相关流程进行详细描述，包括所有的相关商品搬运、处理及处理后保护流程

ⅸ. 可能经由该机构处理的商品列表

b. 已通过由 BPI 授权官员开展的机构检查

c. 已通过应在 BPI 授权官员监管下进行的实际机构测试

d. 由所有有关官员拟定并签署的机构合规协议

e. 可能被视为必要的其他相关要求

2. 外国机构

a. 由该机构所在地的 NPPO 批准的意向书

b. 由该机构所在地的 NPPO 批准的相关证明

c. 菲律宾对该机构做出的验证与最终审批

B. 机构批准流程

1. 本地机构

a. 有意向的本地机构/公司应向 BPI 提交一项关于机构批准的申请

b. 应提交上述相关要求的原件及复印件

c. 有意向的本地机构/公司应请求植物产业局的植物检疫机构对本机构开展检查与测试

d. 由授权的植物检疫官员/检查员对相关处理机构进行检查、评测并开展实际测试

e. 该植物检疫官员/检查员应向植物检疫机构的负责人提交一项关于所检查机构及其实际测试结果的报告

f. 签署《机构合规协议》。该协议应在相关公司/机构与 BPI 之间达成，并应包括下列内容：

- BPI 对该机构的审批；
- BPI 所管理的监测项目；
- 相关审计条文，包括突击查访；
- 对该处理机构相关记录以及相关文档的自由获取；以及
- 在有不合规情况下应采取的纠偏措施。

g. PQS 负责人在 BPI 局长最终审批之前做出相关建议

h. 颁发的《批准证书》应附上所分配的编号

2. 外国机构

对于外国机构，该机构所在国的 NPPO 应向 BPI 签发其对该机构申请的批准。BPI 应在必要情况下对该申请进行审核、评估，并应在必要时对该机构进行实际查访，以便进行核证与最终审批。

C. 相关处理

作为植物检疫措施使用的辐照应能阻止限定性有害生物的进入或扩散。这一点可通过在目标有害生物当中造成特定的反应效果来实现，比如：杀灭、防止成功发育（如不出现成虫）、不能繁殖（如不育），或灭活等方面。

电离辐射可通过放射性同位素（钴－60 或铯－137 产生的伽马射线）、由机器来源生成的电子（最高为 10 兆电子伏）以及 X 射线机器（最高为 5 兆电子伏）来生成。

针对任一特定商品的处理剂量必须通过在菲律宾及其他各贸易伙伴方之间达成双边协议，在符合科学的基础上予以确定。对于本地贸易，NPPO 则应针对可能在将来进行扩张的特定目标有害生物发布并采用相应的指导方针。

下列为相关处理要求：

- 所处理商品应仅在相关剂量测定确认已达到其最低剂量时方可予以认证、放行。
- 可允许对托运货物进行重新处理，但应以其最高吸收剂量在其进口国所允许的限额内的为条件。
- 相关处理仅应由经植物产业局批准的机构进行。
- 相关处理仅应在植物检疫官员/检查员在场的情况下进行。
- 剂量率、处理时间、温度、湿度及通风条件等应在开展相关处理时予以详细考虑。

D. 剂量测定

1. 校准

- 剂量测定系统的所有要素均应以相关国际剂量标准为准。
- BPI 应对剂量测定系统的运行进行测评。

2. 剂量绘图

- 剂量绘图应按相关的成文标准操作流程来完成。
- 剂量绘图的制作应完全地反应照射室内及相关商品的剂量分布特征，并证明相关处理始终符合所定义、所控制条件下予以规定的相关要求。
- 应就不完全（部分填充）装载、首次及最后一次负载（适用于连续辐照）制作独立的剂量绘图，以确定其吸收剂量的分布是否与常规装载存在明显差异，并对处理作出相应调整。

3. 常规剂量测定

- 作为验证程序的一部分，应确保对任一托运货物均进行一次精确的吸收剂量测量，以对处理效果进行确定与监测。
- 所要求的相关测量的数量、地点及频率等均应根据特定的设备、程序、商品、相关标准及植物检疫要求而做出规定。
- 应对剂量仪进行验证，以对其在各种变量，如光照、温度、湿度、存储时间，以及所要求分析的类型与时间安排的效果之下的稳定性状况进行测评。

E. 包装与贴标

1. 包装

为避免在辐照后造成感染，应将相关商品包装于可提供防止再次感染的有效隔离的材料内。包装应符合进口国 NPPO 的相关要求。容器的尺寸与形状应在某种程度上根据辐照机构的相关操作特点如产品运输系统及辐照来源来确定，因为后两者可影响到容器内的剂量分布情况。

2. 贴标

包装/箱盒应至少以下列的辨认特征进行标识，以便能对各处理批次进行识别和追踪：

- 产品名称及数量
- 处理机构代号
- 包装机构的识别号及所在地
- 处理机构识别号及所有地
- 种植者/生产地区代码
- 处理批次的编号
- 所规定的相关处理
- 包装日期
- 处理日期
- 雷地亚符号（可选）

所有的包装均应标识“**经辐射处理**”或“**经照射处理**”。

F. 验证

应通过对机构相关处理记录的监测与审计，包括直接对相关处理的稽查来对相关处理机构及程序的充分性进行验证。验证应达到可充分而及时地检测并纠正相关不足的程度。

G. 处理机构的文件制作

BPI 负责对处理机构的相关记录与文件制作进行监测，并确保该记录可供各相关方查阅。

1. 相关流程的文件制作

成文的流程有助于确保相关商品得到与所要求方式一致的处理。任一书面的流程应至少述及下列内容：

- 相关处理之前、之中及之后的托运货物处理流程；
- 在相关处理期间相关商品的定位与配置；
- 各关键程序参数及对其进行监测的方式；
- 剂量测定；
- 相关处理失败或关键处理程序出现问题时采取的应急措施和纠偏行动；
- 被拒收批次货物的处置流程；
- 贴标、记录保存及文档制作的相关要求。

2. 机构相关记录及可追溯性

处理机构的营运人应保存相关记录，并应在必要时向 BPI 提供记录以供后者审查；记录应保存至少一年。可能要求的记录包括：

——最小及最大的（目标值及测量值）吸收剂量；

——相关客户的名称及其详情；

——处理的商品名称；

——处理目的；

——批次尺寸、体积及标识，包括相关物品或包装的数量；

——处理日期；

——发现的与处理规格要求的任何偏差。

第 4 条　出口商及包装机构的认证

所有欲出口受照射植物与植物产品的出口商均应按下列的相关要求及流程，向距其最近的植物产业局的植物检疫机构（BPI－PQS）办事处申请进行认证：

A. 认证要求

1. 文件要求

ⅰ. 填写完毕的申请表格

ⅱ. 证券交易委员会（SEC）注册文件或贸易与工业部（DTI）营业许可证的副本，以其中适用者为准

ⅲ. 市长许可的副本

ⅳ. 公司/机构相关概况

ⅴ. 税务登记号（TIN）以及（可用的）最近的所得税申报表（ITR）

ⅵ. 该处理机构所在地址图

2. 包装工厂的标准操作流程

3. 其他相关要求

B. 认证流程

1. 所有有意向的出口商均应按上述的相关要求，向距其最近的植物产业局的植物检疫机构申请进行认证。

2. BPI 应对该申请进行验证，在有必要的情况下植物检疫机构应开展一次涉及植物检疫法律法规的面谈。

3. 各利益相关的出口商均应就其包装机构的检查向 BPI－PQS 提出申请。

4. 应由任一经适当授权的植物检疫官员/检查员对相关包装工厂机构进行检查、测评。

- 该包装工厂机构应具有良好的条件；
- 包装工厂（包括其周边场所）应保持卫生并喷洒杀虫剂，以防止有害生物进入；
- 包装工厂在任何的开口处必须配备有罗网（小于 1.6×1.6mm），以防止有害生物进入；
- 包装必须拥有充足的清洗用水源；
- 包装者在包装工厂内应戴上发网；
- 包装工厂应具有充足的照明。

5. 该植物检疫官员/检查员应向植物检疫机构的负责人提交一份关于所检查的包装工厂的报告。

6. PQS 负责人向 BPI 局长提出最终审批的相关建议。

7. 完成上述相关要求后，BPI－PQS 则将颁发一项附有所分配编号的《认证证明》。

8. 任何经认证的出口商违反《植物检疫法》、本协议书相关规章制度的，均将被从认证出口商名单中移除，其《认证证明》则将被撤销。仅当在彻底的植物检疫调查的基础上采取的所有纠偏措施得到遵从时，才有可能进行重新认证。

第 5 条　机构的暂停运营与恢复运营

A. 暂停运营

下列为暂停运营的依据：

1. 出口商/包装机构

- 任一包装工厂机构不符合所设定的相关标准的
- 篡改/更改《植物检疫证书》的
- 篡改/更改用于出口的相关包装或箱盒的标签的
- 植物检疫官员在审计过程中检测出问题的
- 未能就包装机构以及可能会对出口造成实质性影响的营运流程发生的变更告知 BPI－PQS 的
- 在植物检疫官员不在场的情况下进行相关商品包装的

2. 处理机构

- 相关处理机构多次（两次）不符合所设定的相关标准与规定的，将导致该机构暂停运营。
- 植物检疫官员在审计过程中检测出问题的。
- 在植物检疫官员不在场的情况下进行相关处理的。
- 未能就该机构以及可能会对该处理程序的任何层面造成实质性影响的营运流程发生的变更告知 BPI－PQS 的。

B. 机构的恢复营运

包装工厂及处理机构在已做出相关矫正措施之后方允许恢复营运。

C. 恢复营运的流程

1. 该包装/处理机构应向 BPI 申请恢复营运。
2. BPI 应对该请求进行审查、评测。
3. BPI 应对该机构进行查访（包装工厂及/或处理机构）并开展检查。
4. BPI 应对处理机构进行实际性的测试（校准、剂量绘图及常规剂量测定等）以进行认证。
5. BPI 批准恢复营运。

第 6 条　检查与植物检疫出证

A. 出口检查

1. 包装工厂机构

a. 应指定一位 BPI 的植物检疫官员到包装区域对相关包装程序进行检查。

b. 该 BPI 植物检疫官员应就所有纸板箱已得到适当包装、封合与贴标做出验证。

c. 该 BPI 植物检疫官员应依据与任一贸易伙伴方议定的协议，对所详细规定的样品规格开展检查。

2. 辐照机构

a. 所处理的相关商品应与未处理的相关商品分离开来。

b. 所处理的相关商品应在仓库中保护起来，以防止有未经处理的商品混入及重新感染有害生物。

c. 应由 BPI 完成相关文档验证，以对其完整性、准确性进行核查，并将其作为验证相关处理的依据。

d. 所处理的相关商品应进行适当贴标，并且必须在放行前做适当的标记。

B. 植物检疫出证

一旦遵从相关要求，BPI 则应颁发由任一被授权为代表的植物检疫官员签署的《植物检疫证明》。

C. 进口检查

进口检查应按非律宾与相关出口国之间所达成的双边协议而开展，并将下列各项考虑在内：

- 目标有害生物
- 非目标有害生物
- 相关处理效果的验证

1. 所有的出口商均应至少在相关托运货物到达的 24 小时前，就经照射处理的所有相关商品申请进行检查/清关。

2. 一旦到达，相关商品则应接受由植物检疫官员/检查员进行的检查与清关。

3. 所有的装运货物均应具有适当的标签/标记。

4. 在下列情况下，应采取下列各措施：

在死亡率并非为所要求的反应效果时，检测到目标有害生物

- 不应将检测到存活阶段的目标有害生物视为是将导致出现不合规情况的处理失败，但相关处理系统完整性不足的除外。
- 可对存活的目标有害生物开展实验室或其他的相关分析，以对处理效果进行验证。

在死亡率为所要求的反应效果时，检测到目标有害生物

- 在运输时间较短的情况下，可能会发现有存活阶段的有害生物，但通常情况下不应拒收相关托运货物，但已超过确定死亡时间的除外。

检测到除目标有害生物以外的其他有害生物

- 应对所造成的风险及已采取的适当措施进行测评，并将对非目标有害生物进行处理的效果考虑在内。
- BPI 可采取对相关托运货物予以扣留，以及采取任何适当的行动。

D. 违规情况及紧急行动的通知

如 BPI 已识别出对所详细规定的植物检疫要求不符合的情况，则应立即通知相关出口国的 NPPO。此点意在使相关出口国能有一次对明显违规的情况进行调查，并在必要情况下做出矫正的机会。下列内容可能会被视为是重大的违规：

- 未能遵从相关文件要求的，包括：

a. 无相关植物检疫证书

b. 未经验证的、对相关植物检疫证书的变更或涂擦

c. 相关植物检疫证书的信息严重不足

d. 相关植物检疫证书不实

- 托运被禁止的货物

- 有证据表明所规定的相关处理失败
- 其他重大的不符规定情况

相关通知应包含有 ISPM 第 13 号《违规和紧急行动通知准则》中所述明的相关信息。

为避免反复发生不合规情况，相关出口国应对各重大的不合规情况进行调查，以确定其可能的肇因。一旦有所请求的，则应向 BPI 提供该调查的相关结果。

菲律宾可能依据相关托运货物当前的植物检疫状况，对其采取相关紧急行动。

附 录

相关双边性协议及其详细流程（比如《营运工作计划》及相关官方格式）应构成本条例的一部分。

法 律 制 裁

在遵从关于受辐照植物及植物产品、作为植物检疫处理手段的辐照的运用的各规章制度方面的任何不到位，或者对本管理条例任何条文的任何违反，均应构成经适当通知后实施罚款、暂停运营或撤销认证的依据。

废 止 条 款

所有与本条例不相符合的、现有的规章制度均应兹此相应地予以修订、撤销或废止。

效 力

本条例应在其于任一国家级报纸或综合性通告当中公布十五（15）日后生效。

植物产业局局长 JOEL S. RUDINAS，CESOIV
核准人 ARTHUR C. YAP 部长
2008 年 8 月 8 日

Rules and regulations for the importation, exporation and domestic movement of irradiated plants and plant products and the use of irradiation as phytosanitry treatment

(BPI quarantine administrative order NO. 02)

(Series of 2008)

WHEREAS, the Philippines is a member of the International Plant Protection Convention (IPPC), an international treaty securing action to prevent the spread and introduction of pests of plants and plant products, and to promote appropriate measure for their control.

WHEREAS, contracting parties of the IPPC adopts international standards for Phytosanitary Measure (ISPMs) which are standards, guidelines and recommendations recognized as the basis for phytosanitary measures by World Trade Organization (WTO) members under the agreement on the application of sanitary and phytosanitary (SPS Agreement).

WHEREAS, in 2003 the Interim Commission on Phytosanitary Measure (ICPM) of he IPPC approved ISPM NO. 18, providing technical guidance on the specific procedures for the application of ionizing radiation as a phytosanitary treatment for regulated pest or articles.

WHEREAS, the Bureau of Plant Industry (BPI), being the National Plant Protection Organization (NPPO), is responsible for the phytosanitary aspects of evaluation, adoption and use of irradiation as a phytosanitary measure, and to the extent necessary, should cooperate with other national of international regulatory agencies such as the Philippine Nuclear Research Institute (PNRI) which has the mandate to regulate irradiation facilities using radioactive sources such as cobalt – 60 and cesium – 137 and the Bureau of Health Devices and Technology (BHDT) which has the mandate to regulate irradiation facilities using radiation emitted by electronic and electrical devices such as electron beam and X – ray.

WHERWAS, irradiation is increasingly accepted internationally as a quarantine treatment, providing effective means of disinfesting/disinfecting plants and plant products for quarantine purposes.

NOW, THEREFORE, pursuant to the provisions of Section 17 of the Presidential Decree NO. 1433, the Director of Bureau of Plant Industry hereby issue this Order governing the importation, exportation and domestic movement of irradiated plants and plant products and the use of irradiation as phytosanitary treatment.

General provisions

Sections 1
Definition of Terms and Abbreviations

The following terms when used in this administrative order shall means as follows:

Absorbed dose Quantity of radiation energy absorbed per unit of mass of a specified target. the SI unit is gray (Gy).

Commodity A type of plant, plant product, or other article being moved for trade of other purpose.

Consignment A quantity of plant, plant products and/or other articles being moved from one country to anther and covered, when required, by a single phytosanitary certificate.

Domestic movement Movement of commodity from one locality to another within the country.

Dose mapping Measurement of the absorbed dose distribution within a process load through the use of dosimeters placed at specific locations within the process load.

Dosimeter A device that, when irradiated exhibits a quantifiable change in some property of the device which can be related to the absorbed dose in a given material using appropriate analytical instrumentation and techniques.

Dosimetry A system used for determining absorbed dose, consisting of dosimeters, measurement instrument and their associated reference standards, and procedures for the system's use.

Efficacy A defined, measurable and reproducible effect by a prescribed treatment.

Exprotation The act of transporting commodities from a local port to a foreign port.

Gray (Gy) Unit of absorbed dose where 1 gray (Gy) is equivalent to the absorption of 1 joule per kilogram.

Kilo Gray (kGy) Unit of absorbed dose which is equivalent to 1,000 gray (Gy)

Importation The act of bringing into the country foreign commdities for planting, consumption, manufacturing, domestication or for any other purpose.

Inspection Official visual examination of plants, pant products or other regulated articles to determine if pests are present and/or to determine compliance which phytosanitary regulation.

Ionizing radiation Charged particles and electromagnetic waves that as a result of physical interaction create ions by either primary or secondary processed.

Irradiation Treatment with any type of ionizing radiation.

Lot A number of units of a single commodity, identifiable by its homogeneity of composition, origin, etc., forming part of a consignment.

Minimum Absorbed dose the localized minimum absorbed dose (D_{min}) within the process load.

Non – Target Quarantine Pest A pest of quarantine importance that is not known be neutralized by the irradiation.

Pest Any species, strain or biotype of plant, animal or pathogenic agent injurious to plant and plant products.

Phytosanitary certification Use of phytosanitary procedures leading to the issuance of a phytosanitary certificate.

Plant products Unmanufactured material of plant origin (including grain) and those manufactured products that, by their nature of that of their processing, may create a risk for the introduction and spread of pests.

Plants Living plants and parts thereof, including seeds and germplasm.

Target Quarantine Pest A pest of quarantine significance that will be neutralized by the approved dose.

Treatment Official procedure for the killing, inactivation of removal of pests, or for rendering pests infertile of for devitalization.

Abbreviations:

BPI	Bureau of Plant Industry
BHDT	Bureau of Health Devices and Technology
IPPC	International Plant Protection Convention
ISPM	International Standard for Phytosanitary Measures
NPPO	National Plant Protection Organization

PNRI Philippine Nuclear Research Institute

PQS Plant Quarantine Service

Section 2
Coverage

This order covers the (a) importation, exportation and domestic movement of irradiated living plants, and parts thereof, plant products of unmanufactured material of plant origin and semi - processed plant products of manufactured products that, by their nature or that of their processing, may create a risk for the introduction and spread of pests, and (b) the use of irradiation as a phytosaniary treatment.

Implementation rule

Section 3
Irradiation facility approval

Irradiation facility should be approved by the NPPO in the country where the facility is located prior to applying phytosanitary treatments. It covers both local and foreign facility, both for import, export and local trade.

A. Requirements for Approval

1. Local facility

a. Documentary requirements

ⅰ. Duly accomplished application form

ⅱ. Copy of security and exchange commission (SEC) Registration or Department of trade and industry (DTI) business permit, whichever is applicable.

ⅲ. Copy of mayor's permit.

ⅳ. Company/facility profile.

ⅴ. Tax Identification Number (TIN) and latest income tax return (ITR) where applicable.

ⅵ. Location map of the treatment facility.

ⅶ. License form PNRI (if using radioactive source such as cobalt - 60 and cesium - 137) or BHDT (if using electrically generated radiation such as electron beam of X - ray).

ⅷ. Documented standard operating procedures describing in detail the treatment facility system and procedures including all processes from handling, treatment, and post treatment safeguarding of commodity

ⅸ. List of probable commodities to be treated at the facility.

b. passed the facility inspection conducted by a BPI authorized officer.

c. passed the actual facility testing to be supervised by a BPI authorized officer.

d. facility compliance agreement completed and signed by all appropriate officials.

e. other requirements that maybe deemed necessary.

2. Foreign Facility

a. Letter of intent for facility approval from the NPPO where the facility is located.

b. Certificate of approval by the NPPO of the country where the facility is located.

c. Philippine verification of facility and final approval.

B. Procedure for Facility Approval

1. Lacal facility

a. Interested local facility / company should file an application for facility approval to the BPI.

b. Original and photocopy of the above - mentioned requirements should be presented

c. Interested local facility/company should request for facility inspection and testing at the BPI – PQS.

d. A duly authorized plant Quarantine officer/inspector shall inspected and evaluate the treatment facility and shall conduct actual testing.

e. The plant quarantine officer/inspector shall submit a report of the inspected facility and the result of the actual testing conducted to the chief of the plant quarantine service.

f. Signing of facility compliance agreement. the agreement shall be concluded between the company/facility and the BPI which shall include the following:

- BPI's approval of the facility;
- Monitoring programme administered by BPI;
- Audit provisions including unannounced visits;
- Free access to documentation and record of the treatment facility;
- Corrective action to be taken in cases of non – compliance.

g. Recommendation by the PQS Chief prior to the final approval of the BPI Director.

h. Certificate of Approval shall be issued with the assigned code.

2. Foreign Facility

For foreign facility, the NPPO of the country where the facility is located shall endorse the application for facility approval to the BPI. The BPI shall review and evaluate the application and if necessary shall conduct an actual visit of the facility for verification and final approval.

C. Treatment

The use of irradiation as a phytosanitary measure shall prevent the introduction of spread of regulated pest. This may be realized by achieving certain responses in the targeted pest (s) such as: mortality, preventing successful development (e. g. non – emergence of adults), inability to reproduce (e. g. sterility), or inactivation.

Ionizing radiation may be provided by radioactive isotopes (gamma rays from cobalt – 60 or cesium – 137), electrons generated from machine sources (up to 10 MeV) and X – ray machine (up to 5 MeV).

Treatment dose for a specific commodity must be determined based on science through bilateral agreement between Philippines and its trading partner. For local trade, the NPPO shall issue and adopt guidelines for specific target pest that may be developed in the future.

The following are treatment requirements:

- Treated commodities shall be certified and released only after dosimetry measurements confirm that the Dmin was met.
- Re – treatment of consignments may be allowed, provided that the maximum absorbed dose is within the limits allowed by the importing country.
- Treatment shall be done only by facilities approved by the bureau of plant industry.
- Treatment shall be done in the presence of a plant quarantine officer/inspector.
- Dose rate, treatment time, temperature, humidity, and ventilation should be carefully considered when conducting treatments.

D. Dosimetry

1. Calibration

- All components of the dosimetry system shall be in accordance with international dosimetry standards.
- BPI shall assess performance of the dosimetry system.

2. Dose mapping

- Dose mapping shall be done in accordance with documented standard operating procedures.
- Dose mapping shall be conducted to fully characterize the dose distribution within the irradiation chambers

and commodity, and demonstrate that the treatment consistently meets the prescribed requirements under defined and controlled conditions.

■ Independent dose mapping shall by done for incomplete as well as first and last process loads (for continuous irradiation) to determine if the absorbed - dose distribution is significantly different from a routine load and to adjust the treatment accordingly.

3. Routine Dosimetry

■ As part of the verification process, an accurate measurement of absorbed dose in a consignment should be ensured to determine and monitor treatment efficacy.

■ The required number, location and frequency of the measurements should be prescribed based on the specific equipment, processes, commodities, relevant standards and phytosanitary requirements.

■ Dosimeters verification shall be carried out to evaluate for stability against the effects of variables such as light, temperature, humidity, storage time, and the type and timing of analyses required.

E. Packaging and Labeling

1. Packaging

In order to avoid infestation after irradiation, commodities should be packed in materials that provide an effective barrier to re - infestation. Packaging shall conform to the requirements of the NPPO of the importing country. The size and shape of containers are determined, in part, by the operating characteristics of the irradiation facility. These characteristic include the product transport systems and the irradiation source, as they affect the dose distribution with in the container.

2. Labeling

Packages/boxes shall be marked with at least the following identifying features to allow identification of treatment lots and trace - back:

■ Name of product and quantity

■ Treatment facility code

■ Packing facility identification number and location

■ Treatment facility identification number and location

■ Grower/production area code

■ Treatment lot numbers

■ Prescribed treatment

■ Date of packing

■ Treatment date

■ Radura symbol (optional)

All packages should be labeled "***treated with radiation***" or "***treated by irradiation***".

F. Verification

Adequacy of treatment facilities and facilities and processes shall by verified through monitoring and audit of facility treatment records that include, direct treatment oversight. The level of oversight should be sufficient to detect and correct deficiencies promptly.

G. Documentation by the treatment facility

BPI shall be responsible for monitoring records and documentation of the treatment facility and ensuring that are available to concerned parties.

1. Documentation of procedures

Documented procedures help ensure that commodities are consistently treated as required. At a minimum, an agreed written procedure should address the following:

■ consignment handling procedure before, during and after treatment;

■ orientation and configuration of the commodity during treatment;

■ critical process parameters and the means for their monitoring;

■ dosimetry;

■ contingency plans and corrective actions to be taken in the event of treatment failure or problem with critical treatment processes;

■ procedures for handling rejected lots;

■ labeling recordkeeping, and documentation requirements.

2. Facility records and traceability

Treatment facility operators shall keep records which shall be available to BPI for review when necessary and shall be kept for at least one year. Records that maybe required include:

—Minimum and maximum absorbed doses (target and measured);

—Name of clients and their detail;

—Commodity treated;

—Purpose of treatment;

—Lot size volume and identification including number of articles or packages;

—Date of treatment;

—Any observed deviation from treatment specification.

Section 4

Accreditation of exporter and packing facility

All exporters intending to export irradiated plants and plant products shall apply for accreditation at the nearest bureau of plant industry – plant quarantine service (BPI – PQS) office with the following requirements and procedure:

A. Requirements for Accreditation

1. Documentary for accreditation

i. Duly accomplished application form

ii. Copy of security and exchange commission (SEC) registration or department of trade and industry (DTI) business permit, whichever is applicable

iii. Copy of mayor's permit

iv. Company/facility profile

v. Taxi Identification Number (TIN) and latest income tax return (ITR) where applicable

vi. Location map of the packing facility

2. Standard operating procedure of the packing house

3. Other requirements that maybe deemed necessary

B. Procedure for Accreditation

1. All interested exporters shall file an application for accreditation to the nearest BPI – PQS with the above – mentioned requirements.

2. BPI shall validate the application and whenever necessary, the BPI – PQS shall conduct an interview which shall cover plant quarantine law and rules and regulations.

3. Interested exporters should request for packing facility inspection to BPI – PQS.

4. A duly authorized plant quarantine officer/inspector shall inspect and evaluate the packing house facility.

■ Packing house facility should be in good condition;

■ Packing house should by hygienically maintained and sprayed with insecticides; To include surrounding premises so as to exclude the entry of pests;

■ Packing house must be equipped with net (less than 1. 6x1. 6mm) for any opening to prevent entry of pests;

■ Packing house must have sufficient water supply for cleaning;

■ Packing should wear hairnets within the packing house;

■ Packing house should have sufficient lighting.

5. The plant quarantine officer/inspector shall submit a report of the inspected packing house facility to the chief of the plant quarantine service.

6. Recommendation by the chief PQS for final approval of the BPIDIRECTOR.

7. Upon completion of the abovementioned requirements, BPI – PQS will issue a certificate of accreditation with assigned code.

8. Any accredited exporter who violates the Plant Quarantine Law, rules and regulations of this protocol will be delisted as an accredited exporter and its Certificate of Accreditation shall be revoked. Re – accreditation shall only be possible upon compliance of all corrective measures based on through plant quarantine investigation.

Section 5

Suspension and Reinstatement of Facility

A. suspension

The following are the grounds for suspension:

1. Exporter / Packing facility

■ Non compliance with the set standards for a packing house facility;

■ Tampering/alteration of the phytosanitary certificate;

■ Tampering/alterations of labels of the packages or boxes intended for export;

■ Problems detected by the plant Quarantine Officer during audit;

■ Failure to inform the BPI – PQS of the changes made in the packing facility and in the operational procedures that may substantially affect the export;

■ Packing of commodity without the presence of the Plant Quarantine Officer.

2. Treatment Facility

■ Repeated non – compliance (twice) of treatment facilities with the set standards and regulations shall result to suspension of the facility;

■ Problems detected by the plant quarantine officer during officer;

■ Conduct of treatment without the presence of the Plant Quarantine Officer;

■ Failure to inform the BPI – PQS of the changes made in the facility and in the operational procedures that may substantially affect any aspect of the treatment process.

B. Re – instatement of Facility

Re – instatement of the packing house and treatment facility shall only be granted when corrective measures have been undertaken.

C. Procedure for Re – instatement

1. The packing/treatment facility shall request for re – instatement to the BPI.

2. BPI shall review and evaluate the request.

3. BPI shall visit the facility (packinghouse and/or treatment facility) and conduct inspection

4. BPI shall conduct actual testing of the treatment facility (calibration, dose mapping and routine dosimetry) for certification.

5. Approval of BPI for re - instatement.

Section 6
Inspection and Phytosanitary Certification

A. Export Inspection

1. Packinghouse Facility

a. A BPI Plant quarantine officer shall be assigned to inspect the packing process at the packing area.

b. BPI plant quarantine officer shall verify that all cartons are properly packed, sealed and labeled.

c. The BPI plant quarantine officer shall carry out inspection on specified sample size based on protocol agreed with a trading partner.

2. Irradiation Facility

a. Treated commodities shall be separated from non - treated commodities.

b. Treated commodities shall be safeguarded in holding rooms to prevent unauthorized entry and re - infestation.

c. Documentation verification shall be done by the BPI to check for completeness and accuracy as the basis for certifying the treatment.

d. Treated commodities shall be properly labeled and must bear the appropriate markings prior to release.

B. Phytosanitary Certification

BPI shall issue phytosanitary certificate signed by a deputized plant quarantine officer upon compliance with the requirements.

C. Import Inspection

Import inspection shall be carried out in accordance with bilateral agreement between Philippines and the exporting country taking in consideration the following:

■ Target pest/s

■ Non - target pest

■ Verification of efficacy of the treatment

1. All importers should apply for inspection/clearance at least 24 hours prior to arrival of the consignment for all commodities treated with irradiation

2. Upon arrival, commodities shall be subjected to inspection and clearance by the plant quarantine officer/inspector.

3. All shipment should have the proper label/markings.

4. The following measures shall be followed in the event of the following situation:

Detection of target pest(s) when mortality is not the required response

■ Detection of live stages of target pests should not be considered treatment failure resulting in non - compliance, unless the integrity of the treatment system is inadequate.

■ Laboratory of other analyses may be performed on surviving target pest(s) to verify treatment efficacy.

Detection of target pest(s) when mortality is the required response

■ Live target pests maybe found when transport times are short, but should not normally result in consignment refusal, unless the established mortality time has been exceeded.

Detection of pests other than target pest(s)

■ Should be assessed for risk posed and appropriate measures done, taking into consideration the effect of treatment on the non - target pest(s)

■ Consignment maybe detained and any appropriate action may be taken by the BPI.

D. Notification of Non – Compliance and Emergency Actions

The BPI should immediately notify the NPPO of the exporting country if they have identified non – compliance with specified phytosanitary requirements. This is to give the exporting country an opportunity to investigate instances of apparent non – compliance, and correct as necessary. The following maybe considered as significant failures:

- Failure to comply with documentary requirements, including:

a. Absence of phytosanitary certificates.

b. Uncertified alterations or erasures to phytosanitary certificates.

c. Serious deficiencies in information on phytosanitary certificates.

d. Fraudulent phytosaniary certificates.

- Prohibited consignment
- Evidence of failure of specified treatments
- And other significant failures.

Notification should include information as stipulated in ISPM No. 13 "*guidelings for the notification of non – compliance and emergency action*".

For non – compliance, the exporting country should investigate significant instances of non – compliance to determine the possible cause with a view to avoid recurrence. upon request, the result of the investigation should be provided to the BPI.

Emergency actions maybe undertaken by the Philippines based on the current phytosanitary situation of the consignment.

Appendices

Bilateral agreements and detailed procedure (eg. operational work plan and official form) shall form part of this order.

Legal sanctions

Any deficiencies in complying with the rules and regulations for the movement of irradiated plans and plant products and the use of irradiation as phytosanitary treatment or any violations of any provisions of this administrative order shall be ground for the imposition of fines, suspension or revocation of the accreditation after due notice.

Repealing clause

All existing rules and regulations inconsistent with this order are hereby modified, revoked or repealed accordingly.

Effectivity

This order shall take effect fifteen (15) days after its publication in a national newspaper of general circulation.

JOEL S. RUDINAS, CESO IV
BPI DIRECTOR
APPROVED:
ARTHUR C. YAP
Secretary
08 August 2008

向菲律宾出口肉及肉类品的进境前措施

（菲律宾农业部2006年第16号行政令）

（2006年10月13日发布）

鉴于：

家畜家禽业国际性贸易的不断增进，加剧了动物疾病及食源性疾病在各国家之间的相互传播，其相关产品对菲律宾国内产业和经济造成了负面影响。

对于政府来说最重要的是保护其边境及领地，防止进口携带疫病病原的、受污染的或变质的肉及肉类品，避免由此可能引起的动物疫病的进入、繁殖和传播，以此来保护消费者的健康和生命，并保证家畜、家禽以及相关产业的正常运行。

世界贸易组织（WTO）多边贸易体制的规定，特别是卫生及植物卫生措施（SPS）、贸易技术壁垒协议（TBT）的实施协议，强调和保证了一个国家制定适当措施以保护人类和动物健康或防止欺诈的权利，其实施方式不得构成对国际贸易的变相限制。

农业部门（DA）在认可和采用国际规定，指导方针和建议时：（a）在动物健康和人畜共患病方面，参考国际兽疫局（OIE）陆生动物卫生法典的规范要求；（b）在食品安全方面，遵守食品法典委员会的规定。

菲律宾共和国法案（RA）第9296号规定，亦称为菲律宾肉类检疫法，在卫生管理方面提供了一个全面的指导方针，涉及肉类及肉类品的管理、加工、分配、销售及贸易流通各个环节。

菲律宾共和国法案9296号第34节规定：向菲律宾出口肉及肉类品的出口商必须是获得菲律宾主管当局认可的国外肉类企业（FMEs）；在产品出口前，其产地或原产国家必须接受菲律宾农业部（DA）的进口风险分析（IRA）。

农业部2005年第26号行政令，亦称为关于菲律宾进口肉及肉类品的修订规则、条例及标准，其规定：进境前管理措施（PBMs）是国家风险管理办法（RMMs/RMP）不可或缺的组成部分，以达到适当保护水平（ALOP）；农业部2005年第26号行政令第XV－B部分规定：将对现存的向菲律宾出口肉及肉类品的出口商的认可状况进行重新审定和评估。

RA第9296号规定第35部分和农业部门农业部2005年26号行政令第V部分规定：FMEs必须是经过出口国的国家主管当局（NCA）验证和检查，并获得菲律宾农业部认可合格，才有资格向菲律宾出口肉及肉类品。

本着透明和公正的原则，并保证出口到菲律宾的肉及肉类品不会危及消费者的健康和安全以及对当地的畜禽产业造成威胁。因此，我们有必要制定一套完善的规章、条例和程序实施肉类或肉类品的进境前管理，特别是用来规范对相关的管理。

为此，国家农业部部长经法律授权颁布此项关于管理向菲律宾出口肉及肉类品FMEs的进境前措施的行政命令。

第一章 术语定义

1 认证 是指DA给予一个国家或FME向菲律宾出口肉类或肉类品的特别授权。其授权是依据一系列规则、条例、建议和标准对出口国政府的兽医服务体系、动物卫生、监督或检测系统、肉品检查系统和FME现行状况进行正当评价、确认、现场检查和进口风险分析后才颁发的。

2 获认证FME 是指通过菲律宾NCA查验评估并符合菲律宾进口肉类或肉类制品要求的国外

肉类企业。

3 申请国 指为获得向菲律宾出口肉或肉类品资格而申请国家认证或企业个别认证的国家。

4 申请费 指由申请国必须支付的与申请项目相关的处理和管理费用。

5 审计 是一项系统的和功能性的独立检查，以确定项目行为和相关结果是否符合计划目标。包括（但不仅限于此）对养殖厂、实验室、政府、企业和 FMEs 的现场查验和评估，以确定其是否符合标准以及 DA 依据相关国际标准指定的条例要求。开展审计的一般注意事项见附表 A1。

6 FME 认证证书（CFMEA） 是指由农业部部长签发的具有法律文件，证明该 FME 已经满足 DA 相关要求并获准向菲律宾出口肉和肉制品。

7 体系认证证书（CSA） 是指由农业部长签发的具有法律效应的文件，证明该出口国已经满足 DA 相关要求并获准向菲律宾出口肉和肉制品。

8 食品法典委员会 指由 WTO 认可的负责制定食品标准、规程、指南和建议用以保护消费者健康和保证食品贸易业务公平的一个国际性组织。规范也指由委员会基于食品标准及相关文件制定和采用，并为 WTO 所承认涉及食物质量安全的基准标准。

9 农业部考察组（DAIM） 是指由部长任命的技术专家小组，服务于边境控制、动物卫生和肉类查验。

10 DAIM 报告 是指 DAIM 完成对 FMEs 和出口国相关体系的现场考察后以及完成进口风险分析（IRA）后作出的书面报告文件。报告内容包括经过科学和技术考察得出的相关信息、数据、支持性文件以及相关建议。整个评审过程中的所有支持性文件，包括开展 IRA 和 PBMs/RMMs 的结果都是报告不可或缺的组成部分。

11 国外肉类企业（FMES） 指从事食用动物屠宰和分割、加工、切片、包装和存放肉及肉类品的国外企业，该企业获得 NVA 认证并可以向菲律宾出口肉及肉类品。

12 危害分析与关键控制点（HACCP） 指由食品法典委员会颁布的“HACCP 应用体系和指导方针”。

13 进口风险分析（IRA） 是指借助国际性组织建立的风险分析技术，基于对人类、动植物安全或健康的考虑，对进口商品进行风险评估。

14 个体 FME 指在没有获得体系认证国家中申请获得认可的 FME。

15 检查和审计基金 是指收集自申请费而成立的基金，基金应存放在 NMIS 信托管理机构并设立特别帐目，其只能用于检查和审计相关的活动。

16 肉 指动物源性的可食用的新鲜的或冷冻胴体或部分，包括动物下水等。

17 肉类品 是指物理已经发生改变或经过蒸煮、晒干，腌制或熏制的肉类。

18 国家主管当局（NCA） 是指管辖全国的国家兽医管理局，负责贯彻执行各项动物卫生实施措施。这些措施是基于国际兽疫局陆地动物卫生法和肉及肉类品质量和安全管理措施来制定的。

19 国际兽疫局（OIE） 是指由 WTO 建立的负责任制订动物卫生标准、指南和建议的国际公认组织。

20 代表性 FME 指的是由 DA 在由 NCA 提供的某一国家申请体系认证的 FMEs 清单中随机挑选一个 FME。DAIM 将对其进行实地考察和评审，这个 FME 将作为一个对其他的 FMEs 具有示范性的例子。所有从提交了申请表和其他资料的申请国中抽取的 FMEs 都会由 DA 进行评审。

21 风险管理政策（RMP） 是指 DA 依据 OIE 和规范标准以及其他科学标准采纳和应用的整个风险管理办法（RMMS），这是国家要达到适当保护水平所必需的。DA 所要求的各项此类措施都归属于整个 RMP，能保证国家对境外疾病的传入、定殖和扩散以及受污染的进口肉类或肉制品加以适当控制。RMP 及各项措施的作用范围涉及能原产国、海关监管区和后补手续区或核实 SPS 控制结果，采用形式包括（不仅限于）：文件要求、相关证书、屠宰和加工标准、包装和标签要求、运输和处理条件、销售和广告以及分发要求、风险传达措施以及疾病和污染物控制措施。

22 体系认证国家 是指在动物和公共卫生的检测、监督、检查和控制等方面均符合向菲律宾出口肉及肉类品要求并获得认证的国家。

第二章 适用范围和限制

本法规和实施条例适用于拟向菲律宾出口获得 HACCP（或同等标准）认证的国家或 FME。

第三章 认 证 要 求

1. 拟向菲律宾出口的申请国必须是 OIE 成员国。

2. 申请国可申请体系认证或个体 FME 认证。

3. 申请国 NCA 作为 DA 的联络对象，其负责签注和证实递交到 DA 所有文件的真实性。

4. 申请体系认证的国家应提交本命令附件 A 提及的相关文件资料，并提供一份出口 FMEs 名单，以供 DA 从中挑选出有代表性 FME 的进行实地考察和确认。

5. 已具有认证资格的国家，通过其 NCA，送交一份将出口肉及肉类品到菲律宾的 FMEs 名单。这些 FMEs 不会被实地考察，但须完成并提交一份附件 B 的文件到 DA，以供参考和监督。FME 认证证书（CFMEA）应在出口肉及肉类品到菲律宾前签发。

6. 个体 FME 的申请国应提交本命令附件 A 提及的相关文件资料和拟向菲律宾出口肉及肉类品的 FME 名单，并按附件 B 要求提交上述 FMEs 资料。

7. 所有的规定文件应用英语完成。

第四章 申请手续和初步评审

1. 寻求国家体系认证或个体 FME 认证的国家应提交一份意向和申请书给菲律宾农业部部长。信封书写如下：

THE SECRETARY

Department of Agriculture

Elliptical Road, Diliman, Quezon City 1101, Republic of the Philippines

2. 意向和申请书中应同时附上一份如附件 A 的调查表。寻求个体 FMEs 认证的国家还需附上如附件 B 的调查表。

3. 附件 A 调查表上的声明可通过附加相关信息和材料来证实。所提交的材料应完整，以避免延误评审进程。

4. 所有申请材料必须通过申请国 NCA 递交。

5. DA 应该对申请和调查表中的相关材料进行初步评审。

6. 在初审中，DA 可能会要求申请国提供其他一些相关资料对现有的资料和调查表进行补充。

7. 对申请国的初步评审将在所有必要条件齐备之后的 6 个月内完成。

8. DA 会通知申请国初审结果以及需要查证和确认的内容。申请国将被分为符合体系认证资格或个体 FME 认证资格两类。

9. 获得体系认证资格的申请国，应在经过 DA 查证和确认范围内的为 DAIM 提出计划和行程。申请国也应支付申请费和 DA 安排的对现场查验和评审等活动的费用。

第五章 现场查验和评审

1. 农业部部长将任命 DAIM 组成成员。DAIM 将负责资料审核，选择申请体系认证中的代表性 FME 或申请个体 FME 认证的个体 FME，以及进行现场查验和其他与 IRA 相关的行动。

2. DAIM 职能不仅限于边境控制、动物卫生和肉类查验，还有以下使命：

a. 准备 IRA 计方案；

b. 推行现场查验和文件审查；

c. 在完成 IRA、现场查验和文件审查等工作后 30 天内，准备好 DAIM 报告并提交至认证审查委员会（ARB）。

d. 从事其他与认证相关的评审活动。

3. 申请国 NCA 应保证在 DAIM 考察期间提供最大限度的帮助，以便在日程内完成相关活动。

4. 对于没有获得体系认证资格国家的个体 FMES 的评估，将基于其提交的调查表、申请国 NCA 签署的补充材料、DAIM 实地考察结论以及 IRA 总结进行。

第六章　认证审查机构（ARB）

1. 组建好的 ARB 将对 DAIM 报告（如条款 1. 10 所定义的）进行审查，并向部长提出针对申请认证对象的适当建议。

2. ARB 的组成：

主席，农业部副部长；副主席，由主席指定的成员；代表成员：

a. 国家肉品检验服务部（NMIS）

b. 动物产业办公室（BIA）

c. 畜牧业发展委员会（LDC）

d. 农业和渔业产品标准办公室（BAFPS）

e. DA 政策研究中心（（DA－PRS）

f. DA 法律办公室

第七章　认证的签发和维持

1. DA 为申请国出具体系认证（CSA）证书。

2. DA 为获得认证体系国家的 FMEs 发放 CFMEA。

3. 为完成所有的要求后的个体 FMEs 发放 CFMEA。

4. CSA 或 CFMEA 被发放后认证将得到有效实施，已获得认证的国家和 FME 在遵守 AO 相关规定的条件下，其资格将被延续。

5. 不管是获得体系认证国家或是个体 FME，如果每年不能提供一份年度动物卫生状况报告，食品安全问题报告包括召回产品以及肉类出口企业清单的，将取消或暂停出口。

第八章　暂停或取消认证资格

如有以下情况的，DA 将暂停或取消其资格：

1. 认证国家违反菲律宾相关法律规定和 DA 宣布其行为可能危害菲律宾民众和植物卫生的；

2. 认证国家或 FME 未能符合审计要求的；

3. 出口国发生突法事件，可能危及菲律宾民众和动物健康的（例如爆发动物疫情和重大人畜共患病）；

4. 出口国货物抵达菲律宾境内由于存在严重的食品安全和公共卫生问题而一再拒绝交货的；

5. 多次严重误导或欺骗消费者；

6. 进口产品多次显示输出国家存在严重的检验或监控问题；

7. 多次出现可纠正的错误（如商标错误，文件失实等）；

8. NCA 方面没有遵守 DA 规定的义务。

第九章　资 金 审 查

1. 检查和审计费用应由 DA 和申请国或个体 FME 申请者来分担。

2. 所有与认证相关的活动资金应开设帐户并存入依据共和国法案 9296 号文件第 47 部分规定设立的 NIMIS 发展信托基金。

3. 在政府财政和审计的法律法规的管理下，这些资金将用于支付相关认证和审核出口国家的经营活动。

4. 如果申请国家需要进行额外的现场或后续审查，可与 DA 约定补缴费用。

第十章　出口肉及肉类品的复审和审计

1. 在本命令施行之前向菲律宾出口肉及肉类品的 FMEs 或国家，应接受根据本命令规定的标准和程序进行的复审和审计。本年内仍未达到本命令要求的 FMEs 或国家，将暂停相关出口业务。

2. 经批准认证后的 FMEs 或是国家，将接受两年的按认证要求进行的审计，以后每隔三年审计一次。审计也可能视具体情况（如动物卫生和食品安全状况）提前进行。

3. 审计频次可视个体 FMEs 具体情况而改变。

第十一章　撤 销 法 规

所有与此命令相违背的现行法规和规章，将进行修正、撤销或废除。

第十二章　可分离性条款

特此声明，本命令各条款具有独立性，如果其中一个或多个条款违反宪法规定，其他条款的效力不受影响。

第十三章　有　效　性

本命令在两种全国发行的报纸上公布 15 日后生效。

2006 年 11 月 16 日　奎松市

附件 A

认证调查表
动物和兽医公共卫生资料

（由出口国国家主管当局填写）

申请国：________________________

1. 基本资料

地址：与肉及肉类品查验和卫生有关的国家兽医当局的主站点和推广办事处地址，包括主站点和推广办事处官员以及各官方代表的管辖区域。检验肉及肉类品的 NCA 核心实验室和推广肉品实验室地址以及其属地。

2. 立法

列出与菲律宾肉及肉类品查验和卫生法律条款相似的国家立法名称，包括与当地公共卫生有关的法律规定，并提供上述法律规定的复印件。

第一部分：动物卫生项目

1. 兽医服务体系的组织和结构

a. 国家兽医服务体系组织结构图，包括人员的数量和职位；

b. 下属地方（州或省）的兽医服务组织结构图，包括人员的数量和职位；

c. 其他相关的提供兽医服务人员。

2. 全国人力资源资料

a. 兽医

ⅰ. 总数：

1. 该国已注册的兽医；
2. 已毕业仍未注册的兽医。

ⅱ. 人数：

1. 国家和地方的专职兽医；
2. 国家和地方的兼职兽医；
3. 私营兽医，经 NCA 授权可行使官方兽医职能（例如制订认证的标准、责任或权限等）。

ⅲ. 动物卫生：

按照地域，专业能力划分的专职兽医人数（适用于区分不同专业领域的人员，如实验室工作、行政工作以及进出口工作等）：

1. 国家和地方的专职兽医；
2. 国家和地方的兼职兽医；
3. 私人雇佣的兽医。

ⅳ. 兽医公共卫生：

专职从事肉类检验的兽医人数（适用于区分参与检验工作、实验室工作及其他相关职能的人员的类别和数量）：

1. 国家和地方的专职兽医；
2. 国家和地方的兼职兽医；
3. 私人雇佣的兽医。

ⅴ. 兽医的相关比例数量：

1. 总人口中的兽医比例；

2. 在该地区内，农场的牲畜存栏总数所对应的兽医比例；

3. 在该地区内，畜牧场数量所对应的兽医比例。

ⅵ. 兽医教育：

1. 兽医学校的数量；

2. 兽医学习的时间（以年为单位）；

3. 国际认可的兽医学位（在合适的情况下）；

b. 大学毕业（非兽医专业）并服务于和可利用于国家兽医体系的人员（包括生物学、生物统计学、经济学、工程师、律师和其他学科的毕业生等）的分类信息。

c. 为兽医体系服务的技术助理。

ⅶ. 动物卫生：

1. 按地域划分，大部分涉及的牲畜农场的数量；

按地域划分，兽医部门中服务于农场的兽医官的数量和比例；

教育和培训详细资料。

3. 财务管理信息

a. 现在和过去两个会计年度内财政总预算拨给兽医部门的经费；

b. 预算的来源、分配和数额；

c. 为兽医部门组成计划和业务活动分配款项的比例；

d. 国家公共部门分配总额比例的预算（这个数据可能有必要与其他国家作比较评估，其中应考虑到该国背景，畜牧部门对国民经济和动物健康状况的重要性）；

e. 按实际贡献的大小，畜牧业在国内生产总值的比例。

4. 行政部门详细资料

a. 大致的国家官方兽医服务行政中心（国家和地方）驻地的数量和分布状态；

b. 对全国及地方基地的兽医部门的通讯系统。

c. 运送

ⅰ. 兽医部门主要的运送类型和数量的详细资料；

ⅱ. 兽医部门次要的运送方式的详细资料。

5. 实验室服务

a. 诊断实验室（主要从事实验室诊断）

ⅰ. 简要描述政府兽医部门，尤其是其相关的兽医实验室部门的组织结构和作用。

ⅱ. 该国现有兽医诊断实验室的数量：

1. 官方实验室；

2. 政府认可的私营实验室，其职责是支持官方或官方认可的动物疫情监测、公共卫生检测和进出口商品检测。

ⅲ. 简要叙述私营实验室的认可程序和标准。

ⅳ. 官方兽医实验室配备的人力和财政资源，包括员工人数、研究生和本科生的资力以及学习的深造机会。

ⅴ. 针对农场牲畜（包括家禽）主要疫病的诊断方法。

ⅵ. 与外部实验室合作的详细资料，包括国际参考实验室以及递交特定数量样本的详细资料。

ⅶ. 关于兽医实验室内部质量监控和评估（或验证）的详细运作情况。

ⅷ. 最近公布的官方兽医实验室报告，包括已接受样本情况和国外动物疫情调查的详细资料。

ⅸ. 对提供的样品贮藏和复苏程序和结果的详细资料。

ⅹ. 由政府或私人组织（如果可用）对实验室部门进行审查的独立报告。

xi. 兽医官方实验室的服务策略和操作计划（如果可用）。

b. 研究实验室（主要从事研究的实验室）

i. 该国现有兽医科研所的数量：

1. 官方实验室；
2. 从事与动物卫生和兽医公共卫生直接相关研究的私营实验室，包括动物物种的研究。

ii. 简述政府对兽医科研所配备的人力和财政资源。

iii. 已经公布的政府资助的兽医学研究项目。

iv. 官方兽医研究实验室的年度报告。

6. 实际作用和立法支持

a. 动物健康和兽医公共卫生

i. 对有关法例（国家或地方）执行情况和充分性的评价，主要包括：

1. 在国家边境的动物和兽医公共卫生控制；
2. 地方性动物疫情的控制，包括人畜共患病；
3. 对外来疫情，包括人畜共患病的紧急控制；
4. 对已注册并使用的兽医制剂（包括疫苗）的监控。

7. 对兽医服务体系执法能力的评估

a. **进出口检验**

i. 评价相关国家的完备和执行情况，如：

1. 与进出口的动物、动物遗传物质、动物产品、动物饲料和其他须经兽医检验的产品相关的动物卫生和兽医公共卫生控制；
2. 有关生物体进口、使用和生物安全防护的动物卫生控制，这些生物体能传播动物疫病和致病物质；
3. 对进口兽用生物制品包括疫苗的动物卫生监控；
4. 给予兽医部门的行政权力，以便实施产品检验和为进行兽医控制而注册厂家（如果上述的其他立法没有提及此项权力的话）；
5. 文件和遵守。

ii. 对兽医服务体系执法能力的评估。

b. **动物卫生控制**

i. 从兽医部门监控和管理或合作的任何国家动物疾病报告系统得来的报告说明和取样参考数据。

ii. 从其他组织监控和管理的其他国家动物疾病报告系统得来的报告说明和取样参考数据，这些数据和结果是申请国兽医部门可利用的。

iii. 提供目前官方控制计划的相关数据，其中包括：

1. 流行病学的监测项目；
2. 经正式批准的对特殊疫情的控制管理或扑灭计划。

iv. 对于应对动物疫情紧急情况的准备和计划的相关详细资料。

v. 近几年的动物疫情情况。

1. 过去的 10 年国家或界定地区对动物疫情的扑灭。
2. 在过去的 10 年，动物疫病的发病率一直控制在较低水平。
3. 在过去的 10 年，本国或地区出现的动物疫情。
4. 在过去 10 年，新出现的传染病。
5. 在过去多年，动物疫病的患病率有所增加。

8. OIE 的成员

如果申请国家是一个 OIE 的成员国和其作为成员国的简史。

第二部分：兽医公共卫生项目

1. 国家主管部门（NCA）控制体系

a. 管理结构

ⅰ. 提供负责肉类检验和肉类卫生 NCA 的详细资料，包括主要负责人的主要职责和相关的详细资料；

ⅱ. 描述 NCA 的构成并制表列出从国家到地方的组织结构。注明每个办公地点的地址。

ⅲ. 注明谁是 NCA 的主管，说明 NCA 与其他相关政府机构的联系。

b. NCA 的独立性

ⅰ. 确保 NCA 独立性的程序。

ⅱ. NCA 与业内人士、消费者团体以及其他私人机构之间存在的联系。

ⅲ. NCA 拥有调查和强制执法的权力。

c. 资源

ⅰ. 财政

1. 简要说明 NCA 运作的预算（包括那些由政府提供的和其他来源）

ⅱ. 工作人员

1. 由 NCA 直接雇佣的为检验出口肉及肉类品和国内消费品的官方兽医总数。

2. 由 NCA 直接雇佣的为检验出口肉及肉类品和国内消费品的非官方检验员总数。

3. 国家肉类实验室及其推广实验室的工作人员总数及其具体职能。

4. 地方肉类实验室的工作人员总数及其具体职能。

d. 人员管理

ⅰ. 适用于对政府官员在工作职责之外的个人或职业行为管理的规则。

ⅱ. 肉品检验人员的纪律守则。

e. 招聘和培训

ⅰ. 兽医资格的最低要求。

ⅱ. 非兽医肉类检验员的最低要求。

ⅲ. 对新招募的和正式的兽医或非兽医肉类检验员的最初和继续职业培训项目，还包括深造计划。

f. 执法权力

ⅰ. 对不遵守现行法律法规的，可强制执行或进行制裁。

ⅱ. NCA 有权要求肉类工厂提供所需的数据和资料。

g. 控制方案

ⅰ. 对于由 NCA 操作的食品安全控制项目，说明用以鉴定或区分其优先次序的各种正式文书形式。解释如何在监控程序下进行规范的定期复审。

h. 文件的管理

i. 提供详细的正式的监控计划书面材料和有记录的范例结果，什么行为影响到这些结果？

2. 证书

a. 说明证书的印制、储存、维护和分配系统，包括负责实体。

b. 说明证书的完成流程（附流程图）。

c. 提供经认可的官方权威，并获授权能签署出口商品卫生证书的管理人员名单。

d. 修改和废除已签署证书的流程（附流程图）和经授权的签字人。

3. 进口货物管理

这部分涉及到来自第三国进口商品的控制管理

a. 说明对进口肉及肉类品的常规管理（立法、被认可的国家和肉品加工厂、发放进口许可证、公共卫生保障、合格证明书、进口检验等)。

b. 说明对进口肉类和肉类产品在入境时,应进行检验的种类和周期。

c. 简要说明在边境口岸负责对进口产品进行检验的官方人员的职位和责任。

d. 当发现有非法进口产品危害到公共卫生安全,可根据法律和实际情况采取的有力措施。

4. 实验室部门

a. 说明 NCA 实验室部门的管理结构(包括组织结构)。

b. 如果实验室被一个国际机构进行认证认可的,请具体说明。

c. 如果由授权的私人实验室完成实验室检验的,请作说明。

d. 说明与国际参考实验室的任何关联。

e. 实验室对食品卫生的检测项目和检验结果报告的详细资料(如微生物、药物残留等)。

f. 说明实验室可操作的成熟检测方法。

g. 提供现行的实验室内部质量管理体系(例如 ISO、GLP 等)的详细资料。

h. 说明实验室工作人员的资历和学历。

i. 就实验室工作人员的职责和作用所给予的培训项目。

5. 食品安全标准

a. 提供国家肉类安全和质量保证系统计划的详细资料,包括该项目的计划文件及其结果。

b. 提供 NCA 对肉类企业进行检验的周期和自然调整的监控。

c. 说明对肉类企业通过、延迟和撤销认证/注册的程序。说明公布/通告已注册肉类企业的名单的程序,注明公布地点。

d. 为食品从业员进行体检的周期/标准以及员工的具体健康状况。

e. 说明肉类企业工作人员需要执行的质量保证管理体系,包括 NCA 的职能。

f. 说明产品的可追溯性制度。

g. 说明产品召回的安置制度。

h. 说明屠宰后肉类必须盖上的官方卫生标志,并且在肉类包装的标签上必须标出肉及肉类品是由已注册或被认证过的肉类生产企业生产的。对其复制品(产品标志,印刷标签等)进行控制,以防止未经授权的使用。

i. 在已注册的出口肉及肉类品的肉类生产企业中,提供除了供人食用产品类别外产品的分类详细资料(如宠物食品、用作饲料生产等)。

6. HACCP(或同等国际标准)认证

a. 说明肉类生产企业采纳的 NCA 相关规定的符合肉品安全和品质保证体系。

b. 说明 NCA 的审核制度,以确保有效地执行该计划。

7. 残留计划

a. 提供一份用于控制农业或工业化学物残留和兽药残留的法规的复印件,提供各个残留的容许量和退回项目的清单。

b. 说明对用作饲料农作物使用杀虫剂和除草剂的批准体系。包括经认可的化学药品清单。

8. 地方兽医管理局(州或省)

a. 说明涵盖了整个供应零售贸易的肉类检验及肉类卫生控制水平,对于这些职责安排是否有相应立法。

b. 详细说明国家兽医管理局对地方兽医管理局的监督管理系统/组织。

附件 A1.

申请体系认证和个体 FME 认证的一般注意事项

1. 声明申请国家畜家禽、其他驯养的和野生的动物的健康状况，考虑外来动物疫病是否会危害菲律宾人类和动物的健康。

2. 对于可报告的动物疫病信息，申请国应有系统而及时的境内上报机制。

3. 该国对动物疫病进行预防和控制的规章和政策。

4. 该国兽医服务体系和权力结构。

5. 国家有足够的法律规则来管制边境、动物健康、食品安全、食品质量和兽医公共卫生。

6. 国家确保可以执行和遵守这些规定的保证书，并随后进行声明。

7. 现存的国家管理边境、动物健康、食品安全、食品质量和兽医公共卫生的制度，以确保各机构和管理部门遵守与肉及肉类品相关的法规规定和国家对进口产品的要求。

8. 该国主管部门（NCA）发放所必须的证书的可靠性。

9. 出口到菲律宾的肉及肉类品的动物来源。

10. 外国肉类企业（FME）获得食品法典委员会的建议和申请 HACCP 体系认证或其他国际公认的同等标准认证。

11. 该国 NCA 对出口肉类的 FME 的认证或分类。

12. NCA 在 FME 就准备和处理出口到菲律宾的肉及肉类品进行监管，并在兽医的直接监督下由兽医或检验员进行检验。

13. 对一个 FME 始终维持单一的检验和卫生处理制度，并分开出口企业和非出口企业。

14. 符合菲律宾肉类检查法的规定（RA9296），并符合与向菲律宾出口肉及肉类品相关的菲律宾食品法规。

15. 对于附件 A 和附件 B 上文件所列内容要求完整而真实。FME 细节着重于其物质结构和建立符合出口企业卫生操作守则相关标准的操作程序。

16. 积极与国家的 NCA 合作，并遵守本号菲律宾行政令规定的进口肉及肉类品的要求。

17. 申请国作为出口国资格的评估和确认，无论是体系认证还是个体 FME 认证都应基于完成提交调查表及有关的证明文件、其他相关资料、现场考察和进口风险分析并由 DA 来执行。

附件 B

认证调查表
关于国外肉类企业的资料

（由 FME 申请者以英文填写）

（A）FME 的详细资料

1. FME 名称：
2. 地址：
3. 工厂注册号：
4. 创建时间：
5. 占地总面积：
6. 建筑总面积：
7. 产品类型：
8. 计划出口到菲律宾产品：
9. 家畜/家禽/其他动物的来源：

* 列出供屠宰/加工的动物来源国；
* 是公司自己或是契约收购的；
* 简单说明 FME 的动物货源营销计划与办法。

10. FME 出口记录：

出口国家的明细表、批准时间、被批准出口产品的类型、首次出口的时间、最近的出口日期。随附最近一次出口到各个国家的兽医卫生证书的复印件。

11. 声明 FME 使用服务性设备或公司专用设备进行生产。

（B）FME 的选址和规划

1. 说明 FME 坐落的范围

* 附上一张位置图清楚地显示 FME 周围的环境。
* 附上一张全国地图，以展示 FME 坐落的乡镇或城市。

2. FME 的规划图

* 以彩色箭头在规划图上标示以下内容。
* 不同的操作空间。
* 人员的入口和出口。
* 步骤和产品流向。

3. 使用和设计的材料

简要说明：

* 地板；
* 墙壁；
* 天花和上层构造；
* 照明；
* 通风系统；
* 进入屠宰/加工区时洗脚或类似消毒的地方。

（C）供水/冰

1. 水源
2. 氯化物残留；（有或无）* 如果有，说明 PPM 水平的含量。

3. 细菌学检验：

＊方法；

＊周期；

＊有效记录：(有/无)

4. 工厂内的制冰机：(有/无)

＊如果有，机器的生产情况，说明蓄冷能力；

＊如果没有，说明用冰来源。

(D) 人力资源

1. 工作人员资料

FME 所雇佣的职工人数、学历以及专业、技术和普通工人的姓名等。

2. 体检和继往史

员工体检并证明其适合在食品部门工作，

员工在企业雇佣前进行体检？(是/否)

工人的年度健康检查和记录：(是/否)

有用的员工病历？(是/否)

3. 制服 /服装：

统一制服：(是/否)

统一靴子：(是/否)

统一手套和口罩：(是/否)

衣物洗烫（工厂内或合约定点）：

(E) 屠宰场所

1. 设备

配上使用设备的清单（型号、品牌和制造商）。

2. 屠宰程序

＊随附家畜/家禽/其他动物的屠宰程序流程图：

＊简要说明步骤：

＊流程速度：

3. 食品安全程序

拟出口菲律宾的，已获得 HACCP 认证的（或等同国际标准）产品清单

是否依据 HACCP 的理念（或等同国际标准）：(是/否)

如果是，随附 HACCP（或等同国际标准）的计划

是否进行厂检或提供实验室检测

如果是厂检，附上工厂和检验的项目：附上操作手册的副本，取样和检验程序，产品和原料退回/通过的标准：

4. 简要说明产品回收与跟踪制度

5. 简要说明卫生标准操作程序（SSOP）

指定的个人（姓名）执行和维护 SSOP 的活动

6. 日常工作

每日轮班次数；

每班的屠宰量（公吨）；

每周工作天数；

7. 生产量

年屠宰/生产量（公吨）：

8. 肉品检验
由政府或公司进行
检验员的人数、资格和培训；
检验员轮班次数；
检验程序，附上检验记录的副本。
9. 剔骨/分割室
温控特点：（有/无），如果有，温度多少
生产能力
10. 储存设施简要说明
包装/罐头制造材料
干燥剂成分
化学药品、消毒剂和其他清洁剂（附上一份最近的记录）
11. 冷却器/冷藏库
数量、类型（静态、通风或强风吹干，使用氨或氟里昂制冷等）、容量；
12. 简要说明垃圾处理和冷却程序
13. 废物处理/处置
不合格产品的运输处理系统
废物处理/处置系统
污水处理/处置系统
指定的处理地点
日常处理废物和多余产品的周期
14. 简要说明有害物控制系统

（F）工厂福利/洗涤物品

简要讲述

- 员工食堂
- 厕所
- 储物柜
- 客房收费
- 淋浴设施
- 为熄灯和厕所冲水设置的非手动操作
- 处理毛巾及手的消毒剂

（G）照片、录像带、录音带、说明书、年度报告和其他有利于FME认证的相关资料

可连同这份问卷一起提交。

（H）企业宣言

我声明上述资料是真实和可靠的
指定提交资料的人员（姓名）
签署姓名日期并盖章

（I）由国家主管部门查证

我已核实以上由该公司提交的资料是真实和正确的。
指定核实以上资料的兽医官（姓名）
NCA的签署和盖章

FME的申请表和完成的调查表（附件B）**必须由出口国的国家主管部门提交**

Pre – Border measures for the export of meat and meat products to the Philippines

(October 13, 2006
Administrative Order
No. 16 Series of 2006)

WHEREAS, the spread of animal diseases and food – bome diseases among countries that continues as a consequence of increased global and inter – country trade of livestock and poultry and their products causes negative impacts on the domestic industry and economy.

WHEREAS, it is a paramount objective of the government to protect its borders and territories from the entry, establishment and spread of animal diseases that may be introduced by the importation of disease – carrying, contaminated, and/or adulterated meat and/or meat products, which endanger the safety/health and lives of the consuming public and which could bring potentially serious economic consequences to the livestock, poultry and related industries;

WHEREAS, the multilateral framework of rules and disciplines on International trade under the World Trade Organization (WTO) particularly the *Agreement on the Application of Sanitary and Phytosanitary Measures (SPS) and the Agreement of Technical Barriers to Trade (TBT)* reaffirm and guarantee the right of a country to institute appropriate measures as it deems necessary for the protection of human and animal health/life, or the prevention of deceptive practices, at the levels it considers appropriate, subject to the requirement that they are not applied in a manner that would constitute as a disguised restriction to trade;

WHEREAS, the Department of Agriculture (DA) recognizes and adopts international standards, guidelines and recommendation for (a) animal health and zoonoses prescribed under the Terrestrial Animal Health Code of the Office International Des Epizooties (OIE); and (b) food safety prescribed by the Codex Alimentarius Commission;

WHEREAS, Republic Act (RA) No. 9296 otherwise known as the Meat Inspection Code of the Philippines provides the general guidelines governing the sanitary regulations in handling, processing, distribution, marketing and trading of meat and meat products.

WHEREAS, Section 34 of RA 9296 provides that an exporter to the Philippines is required to secure accreditation of its Foreign Meat Establishment (FMEs) and to subject its relevant region/s and/or country to the DA's import risk analysis (IRA) before the export of meat and meat products to the Philippines can be commenced.

WHEREAS, the DA Administrative Order (AO) No. 26, Series of 2005, otherwise known as the *Revised Rules, Regulations, and Standards Governing the Importation of Meat and Meat Products into the Philippines* provides that pre – border measures (PBMs) are integral part of the country's risk management measures/policy (RMMs/RMP) to achieve the country's appropriate level of the protection (ALOP);

WHEREAS, Section XV – B of AO 26, Series of 2005 provides that existing exporters of meat and/or meat products to the country shall be subject to review and assessment of their accreditation status.

WHEREAS, Section 35 of RA 9296 and Section V of DA AO 26, Series of 2005, mandate that only those FMEs recognized by, or under the inspection of the National Competent Authority (NCA) of the exporting country are qualified for DA accreditation to export to the Philippines;

WHEREAS, in the interest of transparency and clarity while ensuring that meat and meat products exported to the Philippines do not pose a threat to the health and safety of the consuming public and the domestic livestock and poultry industry, there is a need to issue a comprehensive set of rules, regulations and procedures governing pre – border measures particularly on the accreditation of FMEs that may be allowed to export meat and meat products to the Philippines;

NOW, THEREFORE, I, DOMINGO F. PANGANIBAN, Secretary of Agriculture, by the powers vested upon me by law do hereby issue this Order prescribing specific Pre – Border Measures governing the accreditation of Foreign Meat Establishments to export meat and meat products to the Philippines.

Section I
Definition of terms

1 **Accreditation** refers to the privilege granted by the DA to a country or FME to export its meat and meat products to the Philippines after due evaluation, validation, on – site inspection and conduct of import risk analysis based on a set of rules, regulations, recommendations, and standards to determine the soundness of the veterinary services, animal health, surveillance/monitoring system and the meat inspection system of the government and the status of features of the FMEs.

2 **Accredited FME** refers to a foreign meat establishment that has been assessed by the NCA of the Philippines and have been found to meet the requirements to export meat and meat products to the Philippines.

3 **Applicant country** refers to a foreign country applying for accreditation either system or for individual FME accreditation to export meat and meat products to the Philippines.

4 **Application fee** refers to the fee to be paid by applicant countries to cover processing and administrative expenses of their application.

5 **Audit** is a systematic and functionality independent examination to determine whether activities and related results comply with planned objectives including, but not limited to, on – site inspection and evaluation of livestock farms, laboratories, government establishment, FMEs to ascertain conformity to the standards and compliance to regulations set by the DA in accordance with the international standards. General onsiderations during the conduct of audit is stated in ANNEX A1.

6 **Certificate of FME Accreditation** (CFMEA) refers to the legal instrument issued by the Secretary of Agriculture declaring and notifying the public that a particular FME has been accredited to export meat and meat products to the Philippines and has satisfied all the requirements set by the DA.

7 **Certificate of System Accreditation** (CSA) refers to the legal instrument issued by the Secretary of Agriculture declaring and notifying the public that a particular country has been accredited by the DA as source of meat and/or meat products to the Philippines processed from its NCA accredited and guaranteed FMEs.

8 **Codex Alimentarius Commission** refers to the international organization recognized by the WTO for establishing food standards, codes of practice, guidelines and recommendations aimed at protecting consumer health and ensuring fair food trade practices. Codex also refers to food standards and related texts elaborated and adopted by the Commission, which are recognized by the WTO as benchmark standards in relation to food quality and safety.

9 **DA Inspection Mission** (DAIM) refers to the team of technical experts designated by the Secretary on border control, animal health and meat inspection.

10 **DAIM Report** refers to the written document prepared by the DAIM upon completion of on – site inspection of FMEs and a country's system and of the IRA, which contains the relevant information, data and sup-

porting documents referring to the scientific and technical findings including its recommendations. Integral to this report are all supporting documents relevant throughout the accreditation process including those resulting from the IRA undertaken and the prescribed PBMs/RMMs.

11 **Foreign Meat Establishment** (FMEs) refers to facilities in a foreign country engaged in slaughtering and dressing of food animals, and processing, cutting, packing and storing of meat and meat products, and are duly licensed by the NCA of that country to export meat and meat products.

12 **Hazard Analysis and Critical Control Point** (HACCP) refers to the "HACCP System and Guidelines for its Application" issued by the Codex Alimentarius Commission [CAC/RCP 1 – 1969, Rev. 3 (1997)].

13 **Import Risk Analysis** (IRA) refers to the assessment of the risks of importation based on the risks to human, animal, plant life or health, taking into account risk assessment techniques developed by international organizations.

14 **Individual FME** refers to an applicant FME in a country which is not a system accredited.

15 **Inspection and Audit Fund** refers to the fund collected from fees paid by the applicant relative to their application for accreditation to export meat and meat products to the Philippines, which shall be deposited in the NMIS Trust Fund as a special account for the sole purpose of expending on activities relevant to accreditation and audit.

16 **Meat** refers to the fresh, chilled or frozen edible carcass or parts thereof including offal derived from food animals.

17 **Meat Product** refers to meat, which has been subjected to physical change and/or treatment such as cooking, drying, brining or smoking.

18 **National Competent Authority** (NCA) refers to the national veterinary authority having jurisdiction over the whole country for implementing the animal health measures based on OIE Terrestrial Animal Health Code and/or meat and meat products quality and safety measures based on Codex standards.

19 **Office International des Epizooties** (OIE) refers to the international organization recognized by the WTO as the responsible body for establishing the animal health standards, guidelines and recommendations.

20 **Representative FME** refers to an FME which has been randomly selected by the DA from among the list of FMEs submitted by the NCA of a country applying for system accreditation. It shall serve as an example of export FMEs in the applicant country for inspection and evaluation for physical structure and operations during on – site visits of the DAIM. The total number of selected representative FMEs to be visited shall be based on the DA's evaluation on the submitted questionnaire and other available information not necessarily provided by the applicant country.

21 **Risk Management Policy** (RMP) refers to the overall risk management measures (RMMS) being applied by DA based on OIE and Codex standards and other sciencebased standards, which are deemed necessary to achieve the country's appropriate level of protection. Each measure required by DA herein is an integral part of the whole RMP, which guarantees protection of the country from the entry, establishment and spread of foreign diseases and contaminations associated with the importation of meat and/or meat products into the country. The RMP includes all measures which have the effect or verifying SPS controls as the country of origin, the country's customs areas, and postentry areas, which take the form of, but not limited to, documentation requirements, certifications by appropriate bodies, slaughtering and processing standards, packing and labeling requirements, transportation and handling conditions, marketing, advertising, distribution requirement, risk communication measures, and disease and contamination control measures.

22 **System Accredited Country** a country whose standards and system of monitoring, surveillance, inspection and control for animal and public health have been assessed by the NCA of the Philippines and have

been found to meet the requirements to export meat and meat products to the Philippines.

Section Ⅱ
Scope and limitations

This set of rules and regulations shall apply to a country or FME that intends to export HACCP (or equivalent standard) certified meat and meat products to the Philippines.

Section Ⅲ
Requirements for accreditation

1. The applicant country intending to export to the Philippines must be an OIE member.

2. The applicant country may apply either for a *SYSTEM ACCREDITATION or INDIVIDUAL FME ACCREDITATION*.

3. The NCA of the applicant country shall serve as the counterpart contact agency of the DA. It shall be responsible for endorsing and certifying the veracity of all documentary requirements submitted to the DA.

4. Applicant country for system accreditation shall submit documentary requirements referred to in this AO as the questionnaire on Information on Animal and Veterinary Public Health (ANNEX A) and a list of exporting FMEs from which the DA shall select representatives for inclusion in the on – site visits and validation.

5. A country that would qualify for system accreditation shall, through its NCA, submit the list of FMEs interested to export meat and meat products to the Philippines. These FMEs will not be subjected to on – site visits but shall be required to submit an accomplished ANNEX B for DA's reference and monitoring. Certificate of FME Accreditation (CFMEA) shall be issued prior to any exportation of meat and meat products to the Philippines.

6. Applicant countries seeking individual FME accreditation shall submit documentary requirements referred to in this AO as the questionnaire on Information on Animal and Veterinary Public Health (ANNEX A) and a list of exporting FMEs intending to export meat and meat products to the Philippines together with accomplished questionnaire on information on the Foreign Meat Establishment (ANNEX B) of the said FMEs.

7. All documentary requirements shall be accomplished in English.

Section Ⅳ
Application procedures and preliminary evaluation

1. The applicant country seeking either system accreditation or individual FME accreditation shall submit a letter of intent and application to the Secretary of the Department of Agriculture. The letter shall be addressed to:

THE SECRETARY
Department of Agriculture
Elliptical Road, Diliman,
Quezon City 1101
Republic of the Philippines

2. The letter of intent and application shall be accompanied by an accomplished ANNEX A questionnaire for all applicant countries. Applicant countries seeking accreditation for individual FMEs are further required to submit accomplished ANNEX B questionnaires of the FMEs wishing to export meat and meat products to the Philippines.

3. Additional information and materials may be attached to the questionnaire (ANNEX A) to support claims and statements made. Complete information must be provided to avoid delays in the processing.

4. All applications shall be coursed through the NCA of the applicant country.

5. The DA shall make a preliminary evaluation of the application and the information provided in the questionnaires.

6. In the conduct of the preliminary evaluation, the DA may require the applicant country to submit other pertinent information that may be needed apart from what have been already provided in the application and in the questionnaires.

7. Preliminary evaluation of the applicant country shall be completed within six (6) months provided all the necessary requirements are complied with.

8. The DA shall notify the applicant country of the results of the preliminary evaluation and the areas of interest for verification and validation of the DA. The applicant country shall be classified as either qualified for System Accreditation or individual FME Accreditation.

9. Application country deemed qualified for system accreditation shall now propose and itinerary for the DAIM based on the areas of interest for verification and validation identified by DA. The applicant country shall also pay the application fee and shall coordinate with the DA regarding cost sharing arrangements on the on – site verification and validation activities.

Section V
On – Site inspection and validation

1. The Secretary of Agriculture shall designate the members of DAIM team, which shall undertake the validation of documents, select the representative FME in the case of system accreditation or individual FME in the case of individual FME accreditation, the conduct of on – site inspection and other activities related to the IRA.

2. The DAIM shall be composed of but not limited to technical experts on border control, animal health and meat inspection. It shall have the following mandate;

a. Prepare the IRA design;

b. Conduct the on – site inspection and document validation;

c. Prepare and submit the DAIM Report to Accreditation Review Board (ARB) within 30 days from the completion of IRA, on – site inspection and validation;

and

d. Undertake other activities relevant to the accreditation

3. The NCA of the applicant country shall extend full cooperation with the DAIM during the inspection by ensuring, among others, that the DA approved itinerary including the activities relevant thereto, are duly completed.

4. Individual FMEs from countries that do not qualify for system accreditation shall be evaluated based on the submitted questionnaire and additional information endorsed by the NCA of that country and findings of the DAIM during on – site visit and summary of IRA.

Section Ⅵ
The accreditation review body (ARB)

1. The ARB shall be created and tasked to review the DAIM Report as defined in Section 1. 10 and recommend to the Secretary the appropriate action on the application for accreditation.

2. The ARB shall be composed of the following

Chairperson DA Undersecretary

Vice – Chair Designated by the Chair from the members

Members Representatives:

a.) National Meat Inspection Service (NMIS)

b.) Bureau of Animal Industry (BAI)

c.) Livestock Development Council (LDC)

d.) Bureau of Agriculture and Fisheries Products Standards (BAFPS)

e.) DA Policy Research Service (DA – PRS)

f.) DA – Legal Office

Section Ⅶ
Issuance and maintenance of accreditation

1. The DA shall issue a Certificate of System Accreditation (CSA) to a country

2. The DA shall issue CFMEA to FMEs under System Accredited Country.

3. CFMEA can only be issued to individual FMEs after all the requirements are complied with.

4. The accreditation shall be effective upon the issuance of the CSA or CFMEA and shall continue to be in effect provided the accredited country and FME conform to the provision of this AO.

5. The NCA of all exporting countries regardless of accreditation status as system or individual shall submit a copy to the DA of its annual animal health status report, food safety concerns to include product recalls and current list of meat establishments licensed to export including the list of those that were delisted or suspended.

Section Ⅷ
Suspension and/or cancellation of accreditation

The accreditation shall be suspended and/or cancelled by DA if:

1. the accredited country violates relevant provisions of Philippine laws and DA issuances that pose risk to human, and plant health in the Philippines;

2. the accredited country / FME fails to meet audit requirements;

3. Emergency situations in the exporting countries that may pose risk to human and animal health in the Philippines (e. g. outbreaks of zoonoses and important notifiable diseases);

4. Repeated rejection of consignments upon arrival due to evidence of serious food safety or public health issues in the exporting country;

5. Repeated occasions of serious misrepresentation or consumer fraud;

6. Repeated evidence of a serious failure in the inspection or control system in the exporting country reflected in the imported products;

7. There are evidence of repeated failures of correctable nature (e. g. labeling errors, misrepresentation of documents etc); and

8. Failure or lack of interest on the part of the NCA to comply with commitments with the DA.

Section Ⅸ
Inspection and audit fund

1. The inspection and audit expenses shall be shared by the DA and the applicant country and/or individual FME applicant.

2. All amounts collected relative to accreditation activities shall be deposited in the account of the NIMIS Development Trust Fund created under Section 47 of RA 9296.

3. The funds are to be disbursed for the purpose of undertaking the activities pertinent to accreditation and

audit of exporting countries, subject to government accounting and auditing rules and regulations.

4. Supplemental fees may be required subject to the mutual agreement of the DA and the applicant country if additional on – site or follow – up inspection is required.

Section X
Review and audit of exporters of meat and meat products

1. FMEs or countries, which have been exporting meat and/or meat products to the Philippines prior to the issuance of this AO, shall be subject to review and audit following the standards and procedures prescribed under this regulation. Failure of FMEs or countries to comply with this one (1) year from the approval of this AO shall lead to suspension of export.

2. FMEs or countries accredited after the issuance of this AO shall be audited two years from the approval of the accreditation and every three years thereafter. Audits can be done earlier as may be warranted by circumstances e. g. animal health and food safety conditions.

3. The frequency of audit may be modified in accordance with the history of compliance of the individual FMEs.

Section XI
Repealing clause

All existing rules and regulations, which are inconsistent with this Order, are thereby modified, revoked or repealed accordingly.

Section XII
Separability clause

The provisions of this Order are hereby declared to be separable and in the event one or more of such provisions are held unconstitutional, the validity of the other provisions shall not be affected thereby

Section XIII
Effectivity

This order shall take effect 15 days after its publication in two (2) newspapers of national circulation.

Done in the City of Quezon, this 16the day of October in the year of the Lord, 2006

DOMINGO F. PANGANIBAN

Secretary

DR. MINDA S. MANANTAN

OIC, Office of the Executive Director

National Meat Inspection Service

DR. DAVINIO P. CATBAGAN

OIC, Office of the Director

Bureau of Animal Industry

DOMINGO F. PANGANIBAN

DR. MINDA S. MANANTAN

DR. DAVINIO P. CATBAGAN

Annex A

Accreditation Questionnaire
Information on Animal and Veterinary Public Health

(To be filled up by the National Competent Authority of the Exporting Country)

Applicant Country: ____________________

1. General Information

Geographical issues:

Site of the main and extension offices of the national veterinary authority on all matters pertaining to meat and meat product inspection and hygiene. Include the territorial jurisdiction of the main and extension offices and their respective official representative. Site of the main and extension meat laboratories of the NCA involved in the analysis of meat and meat product samples and include the territorial jurisdiction.

2. Legislation:

Give the title of the national legislation considered providing equivalence to meat and meat product inspection and hygiene of the Philippines. Include also local legislation pertaining to public health. Copies of the above should be provided.

PART Ⅰ: Animal Health Program

1. Organization and Structure of Veterinary Services

a. National Veterinary Services Organizational chart including number of personnel and positions

b. Sub – national (State or Provincial) Veterinary Services Organizational charts including number of personnel and positions

c. Other providers of Veterinary Services Description of any linkage with other providers of Veterinary Services.

2. National Information on Human Resources

a. Veterinarians

ⅰ. Total numbers of:

1. Veterinarians registered in the country.

2. Graduate veterinarians (of other veterinary schools) who are not included in the above list.

ⅱ. Numbers of:

1. Full time government veterinarian; national and sub – national

2. Part time government veterinarians; national and sub – national

3. Private veterinarians authorized by the NCA to perform official veterinary functions (Describe accreditation standards, responsibilities and/or limitation applying to these private veterinarians.)

ⅲ. Animal health:

Numbers associated with farm livestock sector on the majority time basis in a veterinary capacity, by geographical area (Show categories and numbers to differentiate staff involved in field service, laboratory, administration, import/export and other functions, as applicable):

1. Full time government veterinarians: national and sub – national

2. Part time government veterinarians: national and sub – national

3. Privately employed veterinarians.

ⅳ. Veterinary public health:

Numbers employed in meat inspection on a majority time basis, by commodity (Show categories and numbers to differentiate staff involved in inspection, laboratory and other functions, as applicable):

1. Full time government veterinarians: national and subnational
2. Part time government veterinarians: national and subnational
3. Privately employed veterinarians.

ⅴ. Numbers of veterinarians relative to certain national indices:

1. Per total human population
2. Per farm livestock population, by geographical area;
3. Per livestock – farming unit, by geographical area.

ⅵ. Veterinary education:

1. Number of veterinary schools;
2. Length of veterinary course (years);
3. International recognition of veterinary degree (if applicable)

b. Graduate staff (non – veterinarian)

Details to be provided by category (including biologists, biometricians, economists, engineers, lawyers, others science graduates and others) on numbers within national Veterinary Services and available to national Veterinary Services.

c. Technical assistants employed by the Veterinary Services

ⅰ. Animal health:

1. Numbers involved with farm livestock on a majority time basis: by geographical area;

Proportional to numbers of field Veterinary Officers in the Veterinary Services, by geographical area.

Education/training details

3. Financial Management Information

a. Total budgetary allocations to the Veterinary Services for the current and past two fiscal years:

b. Sources of the budgetary allocations and amount

c. Proportional allocations of the amounts in 3. a for operational activities and for the program components of Veterinary Services.

d. Total allocation proportionate of national public sector budget (this data may be necessary for comparative assessment with other countries, which should take into account the context of the importance of the livestock sector to the national economy and of the animal health status of the country)

e. Actual and proportional contribution of animal production to gross domestic products.

4. Administration Details

a. Accommodation

Summary of the numbers and distribution of official administrative centers of the Veterinary Services (national and sub – national) in the country;

b. Communications

Summary of the forms of communication systems available to the Veterinary Services on a nation – wide and local area bases.

c. Transport

ⅰ. Itemized numbers of types of functional transport available on a fulltime basis for the Veterinary Services. In addition provide details of transport means available part – time.

5. Laboratory Services

a. Diagnostic laboratories (laboratories engaged primarily in diagnosis)

ⅰ. Descriptive summary of the organizational structure and role of the government veterinary laboratory service in particular its relevance to the Veterinary Services.

ⅱ. Numbers of veterinary diagnostic laboratories operating in the country

1. government operated laboratories;

2. private laboratories accredited by government for the purposes of supporting official or officially – endorsed animal health control or public health testing and monitoring programs and import/export testing.

ⅲ. Descriptive summary of accreditation procedures and standards for private laboratories.

ⅳ. Human and financial resources allocated to the government veterinary laboratories, including staff numbers, graduate and postgraduate qualifications and opportunities for further training.

ⅴ. List of diagnostics methodologies available against major diseases of farm livestock (including poultry).

ⅵ. Details of collaboration with external laboratories including international reference laboratories and details on numbers of samples submitted.

ⅶ. Details of quality control and assessment (or validation) programs operating within the veterinary laboratory services.

ⅷ. Recent published reports of the official veterinary laboratory service which should include details of specimens received and foreign animals disease investigations made.

ⅸ. Details of procedures for storage and retrieval of information on specimen submission and results.

ⅹ. Reports of independent reviews of the laboratory services conducted by government or private organizations (if available)

ⅺ. Strategic and operational plans for the official veterinary laboratory service (if available)

b. Research Laboratories (laboratories engaged primarily in research)

ⅰ. Numbers of veterinary research laboratories operating in the country:

1. government operated laboratories;

2. private laboratories involved in full time research directly related to animal health and veterinary public health matters involving production animal species.

ⅱ. Summary of human and financial resources allocated by government to veterinary research.

ⅲ. Published programs of future government sponsored veterinary research.

ⅳ. Annual reports of the government research laboratories.

6. Functional Capabilities and Legislative Support

a. Animal health and veterinary public health

ⅰ. Assessment of the adequacy and implementation of relevant legislation (national or sub – national) concerting the following:

1. animal and veterinary public health controls at national frontiers;

2. control of endemic animal diseases, including zoonoses;

3. emergency powers for control of exotic disease outbreak; including zoonoses;

4. registration and use of veterinary pharmaceutical products including vaccines.

7. Assessment of Ability of Veterinary Services to Enforce Legislation

a. Export and Import Inspection

ⅰ. Assessment of the adequacy and implementation of relevant national legislation concerning:

1. Animal health and veterinary public health controls of the export and import of animals, anima genetic material, animal products, animal feedstuffs and other products subject to veterinary inspection;

2. Animal health controls of the importation, use and biocontainment of organisms which are etiological

agents of animal diseases, and of pathological materials.

3. Animal health controls of importation of veterinary biological products including vaccines.

4. Administrative powers available to Veterinary Services for inspection and registration of facilities for veterinary control purposes (if not included under other legislation mentioned above);

5. Documentation and compliance.

ii. Assessment of ability of Veterinary Services to enforce legislation.

b. Animal Health Controls

i. Description of and sample reference data from any national animal disease reporting system controlled and operated or coordinated by the Veterinary Services.

ii. Description of and sample reference data from other national animal disease reporting systems controlled and operated by other organizations which make data and results available to Veterinary Services.

iii. Description and relevant data of current official control programs including

1. epidemiological surveillance of monitoring programs;

2. officially approved industry – administered control or eradication programs for specific diseases.

iv. Description and relevant details of animal disease emergency preparedness and response plans.

v. Recent history of animals disease status.

1. animal diseases eradicated nationally or from defined sub – national zones in the last ten years.

2. animal diseases of which the prevalence has been controlled to a low level in the last ten years.

3. animal diseases introduced to the country or to previously free sub – national regions in the last ten years.

4. emerging diseases in the last ten years;

5. animal diseases of which the prevalence has increased in the last then years.

8. Membership of the OIE

State if the applicant country is a member of the OIE and brief history of its membership

PART Ⅱ: Veterinary Public Health Program

1. National Competent Authority (NCA) Control Systems

a. Management Structures

i. Give the details of the NCA (for meat inspection and meat hygiene) to include main responsibilities and contact details of the key officials.

ii. Describe the structure of the NCA and provide and organizational chart from the national to sub – national. Indicate the address of each office.

iii. Indicate to whom the head of the NCA report to. Describe the linkages of the NCA with other related government agencies.

b. Independence of the NCA

i. Procedure to ensure the independence of the NCA.

ii. Links existing between the NCA and the industry, consumer groups and other private bodies.

iii. Powers of investigation and enforcement given to the NCA

c. Resources

i. Financial

1. indicate the budget for the operation of the NCA (include those provided by the government and other sources).

ⅱ. Personnel

1. Give the total number of official veterinarians employed directly by the NCA for the inspection of meat and meat products for export and domestic consumption.

2. Give the total number of official non – veterinary meat inspectors employed directly by the NCA for the inspection of meat and meat products for export and domestic consumption including the education requirements for these inspectors.

3. Give the total number of personnel in the national meat laboratories and its extension laboratories and their specific functions.

4. Give the numbers of sub – national meat laboratories, their functions and personnel

d. Personnel Conduct

ⅰ. Rules that apply to the private/professional conduct of government officials outside their official duties.

ⅱ. Code of discipline for Meat Inspection Officers.

e. Recruitment and training

ⅰ. Give the minimum qualifications/requirements for veterinarians.

ⅱ. Give the minimum qualifications/requirements for non – veterinary meat inspectors.

ⅲ. Give the details of the initial and continuing training programs for newly recruited and regular veterinary and non – veterinary meat inspectors in relation to their duties and functions. Include also the continued professional development

f. Enforcement powers

ⅰ. Indicate powers of enforcement and sanctions in the event of noncompliance with existing rules and regulations.

ⅱ. Indicate the power of NCA to require data or information from a particular meat establishment.

g. Control programs

ⅰ. Describe any formal written system for the identification and prioritization of food safety controls operated by the NCA. Explain how regular reviews are undertaken of the control program

h. documentation of controls

i. Provide details of written official control programs and provide examples of documented results. What actions are taken in response to these results?

2. Certification

a. Describe the system of printing, storage, maintaining and distribution of certificates to include the entity responsible for it.

b. Describe the procedure for the completion of certificates (attach flow chart).

c. Provide the lists of authorized controlling officer signatories for health certificates and who are authorized to sign/issue health certificates for export.

d. Procedure in the recall and amendment of signed certificates (attach flow chart) and the authorized signatory.

3. Import Controls

This section relates to control of operation over imports from a third country

a. Describe the general controls over the import of meat and meat products (legislation, approved countries and meat plant establishments, issuance of import permits, public health guarantees, certification, post – import testing, etc.).

b. Describe the type and frequency of checks carried out on imports of meat and meat products at the point of entry.

c. Indicate the status and responsibility of the officer in charge of import controls at the border inspection posts.

d. Describe the action available under legislation and actually taken when an illegal import is detected that is related to public health safety.

4. Laboratory Services

a. Describe the management structure of the NCA laboratory service (include the organizational structure).

b. State if the laboratory is certified by an international body. If yes, specify.

c. Indicate if it accredits private laboratories of perform laboratory testing.

d. Give the describe any links with international reference laboratories.

e. Give details of the type of tests undertaken by the laboratories in respect to food hygiene with the test results reported (e. g. Microbial, residue, etc.)

f. Describe the laboratory participation in the conduct of proficiency testing

g. Give details of internal quality management systems (e. g. ISO GLP etc.) that exist in the laboratory.

h. Describe qualification and academic credential of laboratory staff.

i. Give training programs for laboratory staff in relation to their duties and functions.

5. Food Safety Standards

a. Give details of the national meat safety and quality assurance program. Documentation of this program and its result should be provided.

b. Give the frequency of visit/inspection and nature of regulatory controls of the NCA over the operation of meat establishments.

c. Describe the procedures for the granting, suspension and withdrawal of accreditation/ registration for meat establishments. Describe the notification/ communication procedures in the issuance of the registration list of meat establishments. Where are these published?

d. Give the frequency/standard of medical check – up of food handlers and how the health status of the employees is addressed.

e. Describe if any, the quality assurance management system that meat establishment operators are required to implement and include the role of the NCA.

f. Describe the product traceability system.

g. Describe the product recall system in placed.

h. Describe the required labeling official health mark used on carcasses, and labels of packaged meat, to indicate that the meat and meat products were prepared in registered or accredited meat establishment. Its reproduction (manufacture of stamps, printing of labels) and control to prevent unauthorized use.

i. Provide details of categories of products other than that passed for human consumption, in establishments registered for export for meat and meat products. (e. g. for pet food, for rendering for feed manufacture, etc.)

6. HACCP (or equivalent international standard) Program

a. Describe the system that firmly establishes the NCA's requirement pertaining to the adoption of a meat safety and quality assurance program by meat establishments.

b. Describe the NCA's audit system to ensure the effective enforcement of the program.

7. Residue Plan

a. Provide a copy of regulations used in the control of agricultural/industrial chemical residues and veterinary drugs, providing the list of respective tolerances and withdrawal program.

b. Describe system of approving use of pesticides and herbicides for crops used as animal feeds. Include a list of the approved chemicals.

8. Sub – National Veterinary Authority (State or Province)

a. Describe levels of control over meat inspection and meat hygiene to cover the whole range of supply to retail trade. Is there legislation attendant to the functional arrangement.

b. Describe in detail supervisory authority of national veterinary authority over sub – national control systems/organizations.

Annex A1

General Considerations in System and Individual FME Accreditation

1. The state of health of livestock poultry, other domestic animals and wildlife in a country, taking into consideration exotic animal diseases which will endanger human and animal health in the Philippines.

2. The regularity and rapidity of the information supplied by the country relating to the existence of reportable animal diseases in its territory.

3. The regulations and policies of a country on the prevention and control of animal diseases.

4. The structure of veterinary services and their powers in a country.

5. The country adequacy of legislations governing controls on border, animal health, food safety, food quality and veterinary public health.

6. The guarantee, which a country can offer with respect to the implementation and compliance with the provisions of the regulations, referred to in the succeeding statement.

7. The existence of a national system of controls on border, animal health, food safety, food quality and veterinary public health to ensure the organization and administration compliance of meat and meat products with the provisions of relevant legislations and of import requirements in a country.

8. Reliance of certificates required and issued by the National Competent Authority (NCA) of a country.

9. Sources of animals where meat and meat products are derived for export to the Philippines.

10. The foreign meat establishment (FME) adoption of the recommendations of Codex and application of HACCP or other internationally accepted standards of equivalence.

11. Accreditation/classification of the FME as a meat export facility by the NCA of a country.

12. Supervision and control of the NCA in the FME on the preparation and handling of meat and meat products to be exported to the Philippines, inspection carried out by veterinarians or inspectors under direct supervision of veterinarians.

13. Maintenance of a single system of inspection and sanitation throughout the FME and the separation of export establishment from a non – export establishment.

14. Compliance to the provisions of the Meat Inspection Code of the Philippines (RA 9296) and other relevant food regulations in force in the Philippines reflected in the meat and meat products to be exported to the Philippines.

15. Completeness and veracity of documentary requirements referred to as questionnaires for information on the: 1. Animal and Veterinary Public Health (ANNEX A) and 2. Applicant FME (ANNEX B). The FME details focusing on the physical structure and the operation of such an establishment in meeting the criteria in the Code of Hygienic Practice for export establishment.

16. Willingness and cooperation of the NCA of a country to comply and commit to the meat and meat products import requirements of the Philippines stipulated in this AO.

17. Evaluation and validation of an applicant country qualification as an exporting country whether for SYSTEM ACCREDITATION or INDIVIDUAL FME

ACCREDITATION shall based on the submitted accomplished questionnaires and supporting documents, other available information, on – site visits and import risk analysis to be conducted by the DA.

Annex B

Accreditaiton Questionnaire
Information on the Foreign Meat Establishment

(To be filled up by the applicant FME and information must be written in English)

(A) Particulars of the FME

1. Name of the FME:
2. Address:
3. Establishment Number:
4. Year Constructed:
5. Total Land Area:
6. Total Building Area:
7. Types of Products Manufactured:
8. Products Intended for Export to the Philippines:
9. Source of Livestock/Poultry/Other Animals:

- List part of the country from where animals are sourced for slaughter/processing
- Whether company owned or contracted
- Brief description of the animal sourcing marketing plan and policy of the FME

10. FME exportation record:

- List the countries, dates of approval, types of products approved for export, year of first export, dates of most recent exports. Attach copy of Veterinary Health Certificate that accompanied latest shipment to each country.

11. State whether FME is a service facility or used exclusively by the company

(B) Location and layout of the FME

1. Description of the Area where FME is located

- Attach a location plan to show clearly the surroundings where the FME is located.
- Attach a country map to show the town or city where the FME is located

2. Layout Plan of FME

- Attach layout plan (s) showing the following in color indicated by arrows
- rooms for different operations.
- Entrance and exit of personnel.
- Process and product flow

3. Materials Used and Design

Describe briefly:

- Floor,
- Walls;
- Ceilings and superstructures;
- Lighting;
- Ventilation system;
- Footbaths or similar disinfection areas for entrance into slaughter/processing areas.

(C) Water Supply/ICE

1. Source of Water

2. Chiorination; (YES/NO)

If yes, state level in ppm

3. Bacteriological Examination:

- Method;
- Frequency;
- Records availability: (YES/NO)

4. Ice making machine in the premises: (YES/NO)

If YES, state capacity of machine, describe the ice storage and its capacity

If NO, but using ice, state information on the source

(D) Manpower

1. Staff information

List the number, qualifications and names of professional, technical, general workers, etc employed by the FME.

2. Medical Examination and History

Are employees medically examined and certified fit to work in a food preparation establishment prior to employment? (YES/NO)

Annual health check and records for workers: (YES/NO)

Medical record of employees available? (YES/NO)

3. Uniforms/attire

Uniforms: (YES/NO)

Boots: (YES/NO)

Gloves and facemasks: (YES/NO)

Laundry (in - plant or contracted):

(E) Slaughtering premises

1. Equipment

Attach list of equipment (types, brand and manufacturer) used.

2. Slaughtering Procedures

- Attach process flow chart of livestock/poultry/other animals slaughtered:
- Brief description of process
- Line speed:

3. Food safety programs

List of HACCP (or equivalent international standard) Certified Products intended for export to the Philippines

Whether based on HACCP concepts (or equivalent international standard): (YES/NO)

If YES, attach HACCP (or equivalent international standard) Plan

State whether testing done in - house or provided by a service laboratory

If in - house, list the facilities and tests:

Attach copy of manual

Sampling and testing procedures

Criteria for rejection/acceptance of products and raw materials:

4. Product Recall and Traceability System

Brief description

5. Sanitation Standards Operating Procedures (SSOP)

Brief description

Name and designation of individuals implementing and maintaining SSOP activities

6. Daily Throughout

- Number of shifts;
- Slaughter capacity (Tonnes) per shifts;
- Number of working days per week;

7. Capacity

Total annual slaughter/production capacity (tonnes):

8. Meat Inspection

- By government or company
- Total number of inspectors, qualification and training;
- Number of inspectors per shift;
- Inspection Procedures; Attach copy of the inspection record

9. Boning/Cutting Room

- Temperature control features: (YES/NO)

If YES, temperature

- Production capacity

10. Storage Facilities

- Brief description
- For packing/canning materials
- For dry ingredients
- For chemicals, disinfectants and other cleaning agents

(Attach copy of the latest record)

11. Chillers/Freezers

Number, type (static, air, blast, etc/ammonia or Freon), capacity;

12. Offal Handling and Cooling Procedures

Brief Description

13. Waste Treatment/Disposal

- System of delivery of inedible/condemned products for treatment
- System of waste treatment/disposal
- System of effluent treatment/disposal
- Designated disposal area/center
- Daily frequency of disposal for waste and affluent

14. Pest Control System

Brief Description

(F) Welfare/Washing facilities

Brief description

- Staff canteen (s)

- Toilets
- Lockers
- Charging rooms
- Shower facilities
- Hands free operated features for taps and toilet flush
- Disposal towels and hand disinfectant

(G) Photographs, video, tapes, brochures, annual reports and other relevant information on the fme to support

information provided may be submitted together with this questionnaire.

(H) Declaration by establishment

I declare that the information given above is true and correct

Name and designation of person who submitted above information

Signature and Company Stamp Date

(I) Verification by the national competent authority

I have verified the above information given by the company and certified that they are true and correct.

Name and designation of veterinarian who verified above information

Signature and Official Stamp of NCA Date

The FME application and accomplished questionnaire (ANNEX B) must be submitted through the National Competent Authority of the exporting country.

菲律宾的肉类及肉制品进口管理条例

（菲律宾农业部2005年第26号行政令）

2005年8月31日

鉴于，近期爆发了一些高度传染性疾病。如禽流感或鸟类流感的爆发在短期内迅速蔓延至亚洲和北美洲多个国家，并声称有许多人和禽类被感染。

鉴于，牛海绵状脑病（疯牛病）在欧亚大陆爆发流行，现已传播至北美洲。由于违反良好农业操作规范行为（如将被感染的骨头和内脏粉碎后掺入饲料）的存在就可能导致该病通过污染肉类或肉制品传播给人类，因此检疫该病具有重要的国际检疫价值和公共卫生意义。

鉴于，存在通过非法或不正当渠道进口肉类或肉制品行为，这不仅违背了国家关于消费品安全和质量标准的法律、法规和规章制度以及动物检疫措施的要求，也严重威胁着人类和动物的生命健康。

鉴于，政府的首要目标是保护国家的进口防线，防止因进口携带疾病或已被污染或者次等的肉类及肉制品而导致动物疾病的传入、产生和传播，从而威胁到公众的生活健康和生命安全以及可能带来的对家畜、家禽和相关产业的严重经济后果。

基于此，政府有责任颁布一套全面有力且透明的法规条例以管理肉类和肉制品的进口，在不降低进出口肉类和肉制品的质量安全和现有产业发展的情况下促进贸易活动。

世界贸易组织（以下使用英文简称WTO）关于应用卫生和植物卫生措施（以下使用英文简称SPS）的协议重申了契约国有制定适当措施来保护人与动物健康和生命的权利，并认为这不属于贸易限制。

为此，国家农业部部长经法律授权颁布该项肉类和肉制品进口管理条例。

第一章　术语定义

第一条　下述术语、词和词组的使用解释如下：

1. 认可　指农业部根据特定项目标准对企业和生产设施是否适合从事特定行业进行的合格评估活动。

2. 认可进口商　指由农业部授权的可对进口肉类和肉制品进行自行使用、处理、批发和零售的自然人或法人。

3. 食品规范委员会　指由WTO认可的负责制定食品标准、规程、指南和建议用以保护消费者健康和保证食品贸易业务公平的国际组织。规范也指由委员会基于食品标准及相关文件制定和采用的WTO所承认的涉及食物质量安全的标准。

4. 原产国　指肉类和/或肉制品的来源国家。当产品在另一国家经加工处理并改变其自然状态后，那么处理该产品的国家则被认为是原产国。相反，当产品在某国只进行了极为轻微的加工或使产品发生极为轻微的物理学变化，如重新包装或重贴商标，产品的原始来源国则被认为是原产国。

5. 声明　指任何用以说明或提示产品产地、营养成分、自然属性、加工方法、构成或其他相关品质的表述。

6. 有效期　指基于规范或其他国际公认标准，或者由生产商或相关政府权威机构规定的确保产品安全和能被接受的最后日期。

7. 保质期（保证最好品质）　指在特定环境下，产品不再适于销售或者不再符合农业部基于规范、其他国际公认标准所制定质量要求的最早日期。这些质量要求是由出口国生产商或者政府当局制定的。

8. 外国肉类生产商　指农业部认可的境外国家从事食用动物屠宰、分割和肉/肉制品分割、加工、包装和存放的并由国家兽医管理局认可的出口肉类和肉制品的生产商。

9. 信誉良好的外国肉类生产商　指由农业部认可的对菲律宾出口或供货的已有一定年数的已建立良好信誉的肉类或肉制品的出口商或供应商。其出口产品合格并连续通过农业部检查和实验室测试。

10. 信誉良好的进口商　指经农业部认可的有权进行肉类处理、分销和储存（例如冷库和处理厂）并遵守农业部对肉类和肉制品的规定条例进口肉类或肉制品的合法进口商。

11. 国际兽医证书　指由原产国国家兽医管理局颁发的证明货物符合菲律宾兽医检疫和卫生要求的兽医检疫证书。出口到菲律宾的肉类及肉制品在装运前须获得菲律宾畜牧局签发的兽医检疫许可证，许可证中明确了对货物的兽医检疫和卫生要求。

12. 标识　指加工厂的名称、代码、产品批次等。

13. 肉　指家畜屠宰后新鲜的，冷藏的或冰冻的可食部分：在菲律宾法律允许范围内的黄牛、水牛、猪、家禽、山羊、绵羊、马和其他食用动物，但国际贸易协议里关于保护濒危野生动物的规定中所指的海洋动物和濒临绝种的物种除外（《濒临绝种野生动植物国际贸易公约》）。

14. 肉制品　指经过了如煮、烘干、盐渍、腌制或烟熏等物理处理的肉。

15. 国家兽医管理局　指按国际兽疫局标准执行保障动物健康的措施和/或按食品规范委员会标准保障肉制品质量和安全措施的国家兽医权威机构。

16. 新产品供应商　指农业部认可的有资格向菲律宾出口肉及肉制品的外国肉类供应商，但其供应可信度尚未建立。

17. 国际兽疫局　指由 WTO 认可的负责建立动物兽医健康标准、指南和建议的国际组织。

18. 兽医检疫许可证（VQC）　一次性使用政策是指对一船/航班装载的肉/肉制品的兽医检疫许可证只能有效使用一次。使用过的进口检疫许可证应标注“已使用”字样，以避免重复使用。

19. 入境口岸　依照海关定义。

20. 检验口岸　由国家肉品检验局批准或指定的在某入境港一公里半径之内的对货物在国内销售之前进行采样和检验的场所。

21. 风险管理办法/政策　指由农业部根据国际兽疫局和食品规范委员会的标准制定的整体风险管理措施，是使整体水平达到国家的适当的/可接受的生产水平的必要措施。农业部在此制定的每项措施是风险管理办法/政策的重要组成，用以避免由于携带疾病的肉和肉制品的输入而导致的国外疫情的传入。

风险管理办法/政策包括所有在原产国、海关监管区和入境后监管区采取多种的有效控制措施，包括：文件要求、主管机构证明、包装和标记的要求、运输和管理情况、营销、广告、销售要求、交流风险措施、疾病和感染控制等措施。

22. 卫生和植物卫生措施　是指（1）保护人或动物生命免受食品中的添加剂、污染物、毒素或病原微生物危害的措施；（2）保护人类免受动植物所携带疾病危害的措施；（3）保护动植物免受害虫、疾病或病原微生物危害的措施；（4）预防或减少国家因进口导致病虫害传播而造成损害的措施。

卫生和植物卫生措施同样保护森林和野生植物以及鱼和野生动物的健康。

23. 兽医检疫许可证/SPS 清关单　指货物进口前畜牧局签发的文书。兽医检疫清关单的签发基于以下信息（1）肉类/肉制品来源于非疫区；（2）认可的进口商和外国肉类生产商（出口商）信誉良好。兽医检疫许可证也规定将由进口商、出口商和国家兽医局在原产国观察的作为进口的条件和风险管理必要措施。

24. 兽医检疫、肉类检验和实验室证明　指在由国家畜牧局的兽医检疫官员和国家肉品检验局检验官员签发给海关（副本提供给畜牧局和进口商）用于通关的证书，证明该批肉类/肉制品接受并通过了兽医检疫、肉类检验和/或实验室分析和清关。

第二章 适 用 范 围

第一条 附件 1 中，符合第一章第一条 13 和 14 规定的肉类和/或肉制品在本规定所辖之列。

第二条 所有进口到菲律宾的肉类/肉制品，将在指定海关监管区域卸货后，直接销售、重新打包、重贴标签/商标的、加工、生产、销售、流通、再出口都在本法规所管辖之列。

第三条 因转运进入菲律宾的肉类/肉制品不在本规定所管辖之列。

第三章 兽医检疫许可证的申请和签发

第一条 在肉类/肉制品从原产国进口之前，认可进口商（第一章第一条（二）所指）首先应取得由畜牧局颁发的兽医检疫许可证。此证书必须经农业部根据进口商和国外肉类生产商的情况进行的检查和修订。

第二条 认可进口商（申请人）应做到以下下几点：

1. 递交一份完整的申请书（见附件 2），其中须说明进口货物的性质，并注明肉类/肉制品仍在生产国，未装船或空运；
2. 递交相关的发票；
3. 向畜牧局支付必要的申请费用。

第三条 兽医检疫许可证的申请、办理和领取都应由企业的总裁/执行总裁/总经理或其全权代表办理。

第四条 畜牧局和国家肉品检验局协商后符合以下条件的将签发兽医检疫许可证：

1. 在动物生长相关区域、地区或原产国（包括动物饲养、生产、屠宰、加工、包装、装罐、装货/装载以及船运或空运路线过程中），均未发生相关疫病、病虫害及未受到污染。
2. 国外肉类生产商具备第一章第一条 9 中所定义的“良好信誉”；
3. 认可进口商具备第一章第一条 10 中所定义的“良好信誉”；
4. 具备了适当的国际兽疫局和食品规范委员会规定的针对进口肉类/肉制品的风险处理条件。
5. 其他必要因素和与 SPS 相关因素。

第五条 基于以上考虑，畜牧局将在收到完整申请文件后的 5 个工作日内作出批准或不批准的决定。已正式签发的兽医检疫许可证应有畜牧局局长的署名和畜牧局的印章。

第六条 兽医检疫许可证签发后，进口商应立刻将其复印件（即电子拷贝，传真）提供给出口商，原产国国家兽医局基于此签发的证明产品健康和安全的国际兽医证书。

第七条 没有延期的兽医检疫许可证自签发之日起，有效期为 60 天。在这期间，肉类/肉制品需从原产国输出（以提货单上所示日期为准）。如果装运期超过了有效期为非法装运，予以没收并根据第十章进行相应的处理。

第八条 兽医检疫许可证不能转借，只供当事人使用。

第九条 如本章第三条所述，只有进口企业的总裁/执行总裁/总经理或全权代理人才有权接收已批准的兽医检疫许可证。

第十条 如第一章第一条 18 所述，每次进口货物将严格按照兽医检疫许可证一次性使用政策执行，所以兽医检疫许可证只能用于相关的货物装运。任何违反规定的货物装运都是非法的，根据第十章进行相应的处理。此外，如果进口行为违反了行政规定，根据第十一章所述的罚责给予罚款。

第十一条 对已经离开港口的货物不再签发兽医检疫许可证，与事实不符的申报将导致兽医检疫许可证失效和进口货物违法，并根据第十章进行相应的处理。

第四章 个人和非商业进口

若持有有效的兽医检疫许可证和国际兽医证书，个人或非商业性质的消费方可以进口新鲜的、冷藏的和未煮过的肉制品。

第五章　一般性要求和条件

第一条　外国肉类生产商（第一章第一条 8 和 9 所指）只有经产品出口国的国家兽医管理机构所认可的，才可以将产品出口菲律宾，如果是经由出口国地方、省级、地方性兽医管理机构认可的不被菲律宾农业部所认可。

第二条　只有认可进口商（如第一章第一条 2 所指）可以因进口肉类/肉制品而申请兽医检疫许可证，并从国外肉类生产商处进口商品。

第三条　认可进口商应该确保，在肉类/肉制品装船发往菲律宾之前，它的原产国出口商接收到兽医检疫许可证副本（即电子拷贝，传真）。

第四条　注册进口商应该确保，货物的发货日期（在提单上反映的日期）不早于兽医检疫许可证的签发日期。

第五条　在整个出口过程中，出口肉类/肉制品的容器必须保持密闭。事实上进口的肉产品或肉制品在到达菲律宾之前，会被换船或经过起运港以外的其他口岸，如果原始的封印没有残破，那么兽医检疫许可证和国际兽医证书仍然有效。

第六章　附加措施、贸易的临时进口禁令与解禁

第一条　在紧急状态期间，农业部将在现行法律许可范围内行使其权力，颁布临时进口禁令，保证从相关区域/地区进口相应的肉类/肉制品不会对人和动物的健康或生命造成威胁。在一项进口禁令颁布的时候，农业部将：

1. 暂停相关应用方面的兽医检疫许可证的签发；
2. 取消/撤回已签发的相关的兽医检疫许可证；
3. 扣留相关货物；
4. 没收所有相关的货物，并根据第十章的规定进行处理。

第二条　紧急状态包括以下情形：

1. 爆发国际兽疫局规定的法定传染病；
2. 有污染物事件发生或存在污染威胁（如二噁英污染）；
3. 农业部规定的其他对公众健康和安全有危害的情况发生。

第三条　在进口禁令施行过程中，农业部应考虑到：

1. 国际兽疫局、世界卫生组织和/或食品规范委员会的建议；
2. 出口国依据既有信息制定的风险管理和通讯措施有可能不充分；
3. 产品原产国或疾病相关的部分国家、污染物或其他涉及公众健康和安全的其他病例；
4. 农业部基于既有信息所作的任何风险评估结论；
5. 有必要施行禁令的其他情况。

第四条　临时进口禁令的撤销应该基于以下考虑：

1. 国际兽疫局、世界卫生组织和/或食品规范委员会的建议；
2. 由出口国制定的管理风险和交流措施是充分的；
3. 农业部根据既有信息所作的任何风险评估；
4. 确保进口恢复的其他考虑。

第五条　在本章第二条提到的紧急状况，不一定要求马上采取对肉类/肉制品的禁令，农业部可以制定额外的/附加的措施来区分常规的措施、标准及要求，来确保可能来自发生紧急状况的地区或国家肉类/肉制品的安全和卫生。

第七章 包装和标签要求

认可进口商应保证货物遵照以下包装和标签要求：

第一条 包装材料和容器等直接与肉类/肉制品接触的东西必须符合食品规范委员会规定的食品等级质量标准或由农业部制订的等效标准。

第二条 所有用于包装进口肉类/肉制品的木质材料均依照第15号《国际植物检疫措施标准》进行过处理。

第三条 所有食品添加剂/食品防腐剂需要在适当的位置贴上合适的标签加以说明。

第四条 包装上必须至少标注有如下内容：

1. 出口商的注册名称或产品的商标名称；
2. 出口商的企业名称和地址；
3. 来源国家；
4. 标识；
5. 产品性状说明和成分列表；
6. 利用十进制法进行计算（用公制法表示）的净含量，重量以及数量；
7. 生产日期和包装日期；
8. 保质期或有效期；
9. 操作和存贮说明。

第五条 在进口肉类/肉制品各包装盒上的标签必须用英语或菲律宾语书写，同时文本的各个字符不应该是少于2.5mm（用于预先印制或盖印）和5mm（用于钢印或手写体）。

第八章 口岸查验、清关和放行程序

第一条 必须严格执行肉类或肉制品货物的边境查验。确保有兽医及时参与肉品检查和清关的整个过程并及时办结清关手续，进口商或收货人或其代理须向兽医检疫办公室递交第八章第三条3中规定的与发货有关的所有必需文件。

第二条 肉类/肉制品到达入境口岸（第一章第一条19所指）时，需要接受农业部规定的兽医检查以及相关文件的验证和评估。只有完成这些必须的手续和清关，海关才可以放行。

第三条 在入境口岸，兽医检疫办公室将：

1. 核实和评估进口商和代理人提供的兽医检疫许可证（原件）、国际兽医证书（原件）、提货单/航运收据和装箱单的真实性、有效性和准确性；
2. 对货物进行兽医检疫查验和文件验证；
3. 重新封装运载肉类/肉制品的容器；
4. 签署《兽医检疫/肉类检验和实验室证明 》（见附件3）并且在海关进口通关文件副本上加印“INSPECTED AND PASSED FOR TRANSFER TO NMIS ACCREDITED COLD STORAGE”（“已检疫并可转入国家肉品检验局认可的冷库”）；
5. 为支付给农业部的必须查验费用并开具发票；
6. 按照要求签署《兽医检疫、肉检查和实验室证明》。

第四条 在货物调动到任一农业部认可的冷藏设备/仓库/口岸待检时，国家肉品检验局将：

1. 在24小时内立即选定和派遣一位查验员对肉品进行检验；
2. 检查和核实《兽医检疫、肉检查和实验室证明》和畜牧局的印章完整性；
3. 完成检验和/或实验室分析；

时限	供货商/产品的情况
1 天检验	达到第一章第一条 1 要求的有良好信誉的外国肉类生产商
5 天（检验和实验室分析）	• 第一章第一条 15 所指的新产品供应商 • 被农业部从“信誉良好的外国肉类生产商”名单中除名的外国肉类生产商； • 当某地发生第六章第二条所指紧急状态时，来自/转载/途经该地的货物。

4. 如果国家肉品检验局检验和/或实验室分析的结果合格，畜牧局兽医检疫办公室将签发《兽医检疫、肉检查和实验室证明》；

5. 将完整的《兽医检疫、肉检查和实验室证明》（原件）给海关（复本提供给畜牧局和进口商），海关据此对相关进口文件作最后清查。进口文件最后的清查不影响进口商运发货物。

第九章　入境卫生要求

所有进口的肉类/肉制品应该严格按照菲律宾农业部有关肉及肉制品安全条例及规则进行检验，以保证产品质量与其描述的一致性以及依照 Republic Act 9296（即菲律宾肉类检验规程）的可追溯性。

第十章　没收和处置

第一条　没有兽医检疫许可证的进口肉类/肉制品将禁止放行或进境（即卸货前）和出境，如果通过其他任何方式入境的，为保护公共卫生和人/畜健康，将对扣留这些产品并销毁。

第二条　对于进口肉类和/及肉制品存在的违规行为，如果该行为危及国家风险管理体系（第一章第一条 20 所指）的完整性或直接侵害健康和安全，货物将被没收。

1. 在入境口岸，海关根据检验报告，如有以下情况将没收进口的产品：

（1）货物包装封识残损；

（2）无合法的兽医检疫许可证；

（3）没有输出国国家兽医管理局出具的国际兽医证书；

（4）经证实进口货物体积/数量超出兽医检疫许可证和国际兽医证书上标注的 3%；体积/数量超过允许限度的，应当予以没收；

（5）货物源自未注册国外肉类生产商；

（6）动物屠宰地不是农业部批准的地区、区域或国家；

（7）虚报、编造和滥用商标的肉类/肉制品；

（8）肉类/肉制品必须在保质期内运抵；

（9）货物标签与第七章第四条 1 ~ 9 所述不一致或者是缺少任何一项规定必须标签的内容；

（10）货物被查出感染国际兽疫局公布的 A、B 类疾病；

（11）其他故意违规行为，包括收货人/进口商拒绝接受货物相关文件。

2. 在冷库/仓库/查验口岸，海关根据国家肉品检验局检验员提供的检验报告，如有以下情况将没收进口的产品：

（1）检验员检验前畜牧局封印破损或者丢失。

（2）在不具备《兽医检疫、肉检查和实验室证明》的情况下，部分或者整批货物被使用、处理、销售或者分配。

（3）货物被查出携带病原体。

（4）货物含任一种危害公共卫生的有毒或有害物质。

（5）货物被发现添加了任一种的毒性或有害物质，但允许添加的：a）食品添加剂；b）色素；c）污染物的含量低于允许值的情况除外。

（6）货物整体或者局部存在受污染、腐烂现象，含杂质，以及其他不适合人食用的情况。

（7）与肉及肉制品直接接触的包装材料中含有任何可能危害身体健康的物质。

（8）其他危害人/畜健康和生命安全的情况。

（9）其他故意违规行为，包括收货人/进口商拒绝接受货物相关文件。

3. 海关和农业部将共同没收和销毁本章符合第二条1规定的货物。

4. 进口商/收货人将负担本章第二条1和2中的罚没和销毁的相关费用。不仅限于销毁、存放和人工费用。

5. 国外肉类生产商出现的违反行为将作为取消其出口资格的依据。

第十一章　扣押和整改

第一条　进口肉类及肉制品没有按照第七章第三条1~9中相关规定加贴标签，将被查封，扣留在农业部管辖的入境口岸或者是通过农业部认证的冷库。若存在编造、滥用商标、虚报和其他蓄意行为，将同第十章中的情况一样被没收和销毁。

第二条　收货人必须严格遵守农业部相关要求进行整改，即便如此，整改的货物不能违反第十章第二条中的任何规定，否则将进行相应的查封和处理。

第十二章　处　　罚

第一条　货物违反第三章（第一条~第九条）、第七章（第一条~第四条）、第三章（第十一条）的均被视为违反了本法规，相关的罚款由发货人/委托人/进口商承担。

第二条　违法者将按照 Republic Act No. 7394 Article 19（Penalty），Chapter I，Title II 处罚，即1992年4月13日颁布的菲律宾消费者法案，如果是走私的则按照《关税及海关法》3601节处理。

第三条　政府官员/雇员不得有直接或间接触犯或违反本法规相关规定的行为，尤其是（不仅限于）第三章（第四、五、九条）和第八章（第二、三、四条）的规定。违规者要根据反渎职法追究其行政或刑事责任。政府官员/雇员同样还应该遵守政府的其他法律、规章制度、行为守则和道德标准。

第十三章　撤 销 条 款

第一条　所有与此条例不一致的规则和章程应依据本法规进行修正、撤销或重申。

第二条　规定了菲律宾进口肉类和肉类制的规则、章程、指南和标准的16号部令（2000年4月）、39号部令（2000年10月）、56号部令（2000年12月）同时废止。

第十四章　分离性条款

此法令的条款是可分离的，一个或者一些条款违反宪法的，其他条款不会受影响。

第十五章　暂时性条款

第一条　此法规生效前已从产地发货的肉类和/或肉类制品按39号部令和56号部令执行。

第二条　所有现有的进口商和出口商都将被考察并评估其信誉度。为此，农业部发布进口商和出口商的考核评估的补充条例、规则和章程。这些规定将在两份全国发行的报纸上发布后的15天后生效。

附件 1

本规定第二章所指的肉和肉制品名单

序 号	内 容
02.01	新鲜或冷藏的牛肉
02.02	冷冻的牛肉
02.03	新鲜、冷藏或冷冻的猪肉
02.04	新鲜、冷藏或冷冻的绵羊或山羊肉
02.05	新鲜、冷藏或冷冻的马，驴、骡肉
02.06	新鲜、冷藏或冷冻的牛、猪、绵羊、山羊、马、驴、骡可食用的内脏
02.07	新鲜、冷藏或冷冻的可食内脏，及 01.05 中所指的家禽
02.08	新鲜、冷藏或冷冻的其他肉类和可食用的内脏
02.09	新鲜、冷藏或冷冻的没被提取的猪油脂和家禽油脂
02.10	盐渍、烘干、烟熏的肉和可食的内脏，肉和可食的内脏的粉末
15.02	在 15.03 中所指的（未经加工）牛、绵羊和山羊油脂
16.01	香肠和类似产品；肉、内脏或血液；及其制品
16.02	其他精加工的或腌制的肉、内脏或血液

根据 TCCP 2003 年发表的《商品名称及编码协调制度》。

附件 2

农业部畜牧局国家兽医检进口兽医检疫清关单申请表

<table>
<tr><td colspan="3">进口商：完成和递交一个证明复印件和价格表/销售发票给国家兽医检疫所、畜牧局</td></tr>
<tr><td>1. 进口商名称和地址</td><td colspan="2">2. 国外肉类生产企业/出口商的名称和地址</td></tr>
<tr><td>电话/传真号</td><td colspan="2">国外肉类生产商认证号：</td></tr>
<tr><td>3. 装货口岸（若有）</td><td colspan="2">4. 原产国</td></tr>
<tr><td>5. 方式运输</td><td colspan="2">6. 菲律宾入境港</td></tr>
<tr><td>项目</td><td>种类</td><td>数量</td></tr>
<tr><td colspan="2">7. 交付时的冷库的名称和地址</td><td>8. 进口商的畜牧局认证号码</td></tr>
</table>

1. 我声明这些产品符合菲律宾国家检疫要求，正如在 VQC 里面专门为输入品或其他农业部条例及其他相关的规则。
2. 我声明在向菲律宾输入肉及肉产品时遵守所有应用于食品的农业部规则、条例、及其他相关的农业部规则、条例。
3. 我声明在填写申请表时，这些将要被出口的肉或肉产品仍然在生产国，尚未装运。
4. 我声明此处我所提供的信息真实准确。

________________　　　　________________

日　期　　　　　　　　进口商签名

<table>
<tr><td>公　　证

</td></tr>
</table>

按照农业部 2005 年______号令，不能出具畜牧局签发的有效的检疫清关单的肉类/肉制品不得入境。

附件 3

证书号：____________________

____
日 期

兽医检疫/肉类检验/实验室证书

兹证明下述装运货物已经检验：

以下由畜牧局填写：

收货人	
货物	
VQC 号码	
国际兽医证书号码	
原产国	
体积	
集装箱数量	
集装箱编号	
到达港	
到货日期	
国家肉品检验局放行日期	

以下由国家肉品检验局填写：

认可冷藏室/仓库	
入库时间	
检验和抽样时间	
检疫处理时间	
通关时间	

进一步保证输入品符合国家肉类检疫部门的所有要求，业经国家肉类检疫部门检验或实验室分析，确定这些进口食品适合于人类消费。海关凭此准予放行。

____________________ ____________________

畜牧局兽医检疫官/检验员 NMIS 肉品控制官/ 肉品检验员

Revised rules, regulations, and standards governing the importation of meat and meat products into the Philippines

(31 August 2005
Administrative Order No. 26)
(Series of 2005)

WHEREAS, recent outbreaks of highly communicable diseases, e. g. , Avian Influenza or "Bird Flu" that spread across countries in Asia and North America over a short period of time, have claimed a number of human lives and poultry populations;

WHEREAS, Bovine Spongiform Encephalopathy or "Mad Cow Disease" has spread across continents from Europe to Asia and now in North America and has remained a major international quarantine importance and public safety concern because of violations on Good Agricultural Practice (GAP) (e. g. milling into feeds infected bone and offal) thus its possible transmission to uman beings due to entry of contaminated meat and/or meat products;

WHEREAS, violation of the country's laws, rules and regulations on consumer product safety and quality standards and animal quarantine measures through illegal entry of meat and meat products as well as non-compliance thereof poses serious threat to human and animal health/life;

WHEREAS, it is a paramount objective of the government to protect its borders and territories from the entry, establishment and spread of animal disease that may be introduced by the importation of disease-carrying, contaminated, and/or adulterated meat and/or meat products, which endanger the lives and safety/health of the consuming public and which could bring potentially serious economic consequences to the livestock, poultry and related industries;

WHEREAS, in order to effectively address the above, it is the responsibility of the government to issue a comprehensive, strengthened and transparent set of rules, regulations and standards governing the importation of meat and meat products to facilitate trade without compromising the safety and quality of imported meat and meat products and the viability of existing industries;

WHEREAS, the World Trade Organization (WTO) Agreement on the Application of Sanitary and Phytosanitary Measures (SPS) reaffirms the right of a country to institute appropriate measures as it deems necessary to protect human and animal health/life, provided they are not undertaken to restrict trade;

NOW, THEREFORE, I, DOMINGO F. PANGANIBAN,

Secretary of the Department of

Agriculture (DA), in accordance with the powers vested in me by law, do hereby issue this Administrative Order (AO) governing the importation of meat and meat products into the Philippines;

Section I
Definition of terms

The following terms, words and phrases herein used shall be construed as follows:

A. Accreditation refers to the authority of DA to evaluate firms and establishments based on a set of criteria with the objective of providing eligibility to conduct/undertake specified activities;

B. Accredited Importer refers to any natural or juridical person accredited by DA as eligible importer of meat and/or meat products for its own use, processing, wholesale and/or retail distribution.

C. Codex Alimentarius Commission (CODEX) refers to the international organization recognized by the WTO as the responsible body for establishing food standards, codes of practice, guidelines and recommendations aimed at protecting consumer health and ensuring fair food trade practices. Codex also refers to food standards and related texts elaborated and adopted by the Commission, which is recognized by the WTO as benchmark standards in relation to food quality and safety.

D. Country of Origin refers to the country source of meat and/or meat products being exported. When a product undergoes processing in another country which changes its nature, the country in which processing is performed shall be considered to be the country of origin for purposes of labeling. Conversely, when such product undergoes only minimal processing/physical change e. g. re – packing or re – branding in another country, the country of origin refers to the source of the original product.

E. Claim refers to any representation, which states, suggests or implies that a product has particular qualities relating to its origin, nutritional properties, nature, processing, compositionor any other quality.

F. Date of Expiration refers to the latest date of which safety and/or acceptability of a productcan still be assured, based on Codex or other internationally accepted standards, or as determined by the manufacturer or the appropriate government authority.

G. Date of Minimum Durability ("best before") refers to the earliest date under specified conditions beyond which a product is no longer marketable and cannot meet the quality required by DA which is based from either Codex or other internationally accepted standards for which claims have been based by manufacturer or the government authority of the exporting country.

H. Foreign Meat Establishment (FME) refers to a DA – accredited facility in a foreign country engaged in slaughtering and dressing of food animals, and processing, cutting, packing and storing of meat and meat products, and recognized by the NVA to export meat and meat products.

I. FME in "Good Standing" refers to DA – accredited FME which has established its credibility as sound exporter/supplier of a specified meat or meat product because in the course of its exportations of these to the Philippines over a number of years and/or shipments, this specific product has satisfactory and consistently passed DA inspection and laboratory analysis.

J. Importer in "Good Standing" refers to a consignee whose accreditation as a legitimate importer of meat and/or meat products into the Philippines has been determined by DA to be still within the terms within which this accreditation was based with respect to its meat handling, distribution, and storage facilities (e. g. cold storage and processing plant) and compliance with applicable DA rules and regulations on meat and meat products.

K. International Veterinary Certificate (IVC) refers to the certificate issued by the NVA at the country of origin attesting that, among others, the shipment conforms to the specific veterinary/SPS requirements of the Philippines as prescribed in the Veterinary Quarantine Clearance (VQC) issued by the Bureau of Animal Industry (BAI) prior to shipment.

L. Lot Identification refers to the name and identification firm number of the plant/factory and the serial number of the specified quantity of commodity produced from this plant/factory that is essentially subjected to the same production conditions on a specified timeframe.

M. Meat refers to the fresh, chilled or frozen edible part of carcass, including offal derived from, but not limited to cattle, buffalo, pig, poultry, goat, sheep, horse and other food animals under Philippine laws but excluding marine animals and prohibited animals under the Convention on International Trade in Endangered Species of Wild Fauna and Flora (CITES)

N. Meat Product refers to meat, which has been subjected to physical change and/or treatment such as cooking, drying, salting, brining or smoking.

O. National Veterinary Administration (NVA) refers to the national veterinary controlling authority having jurisdiction over the whole country for implementing the animal health measures based on OIE Animal Health Code and/or meat products quality and safety measures based on Codex Standards.

P. New Product Supplier (NPS) refers to DA – accredited FME which has yet to establish its credibility as safe/sound supplier/exporter of a specified meat or meat product into the Philippines as required.

Q. Office International des Epizooties (OIE) refers to the international organization recognized by the WTO as the responsible body for establishing the animal veterinary health standards, guidelines and recommendations.

R. One Shipment Per VQC Policy – refers to the 'one – time' validity and use of the VQC of imported meat and/or meat products boarded/loaded only to one vessel or aircraft. A used VQC shall be marked/stamped "USED" to avoid recycling.

S. Port of Entry as defined under the Customs and Tariff Code and the Bureau of Customs (BOC).

T. Port of Inspection an establishment authorized or designated by NMIS within a certain kilometer radius from the port of entry, wherein inspection and collection of samples are being conducted prior to its release for domestic distribution.

U. Risk Management Measures/Policy (RMP) refers to the overall risk management measures being applied by DA based on OIE and Codex standards, which are deemed necessary to achieve the country's appropriate/acceptable level of production (ALOP). Each measure required by DA herein is an integral part of the whole RMP which guarantees protection of the country from the entry, establishment and spread of foreign diseases and contaminations associated with the importation of meat and/or meat products into the country. The RMP includes all measures which have the effect of verifying controls at the country of origin, the country's customs areas, and post – entry areas, which take the form of, but not limited to, documentation requirements, certifications by appropriate bodies, packing and labeling requirements, transportation and handling conditions, marketing, advertising, and distribution requirements, risk communication measures, and disease and contamination control measures.

V. Sanitary and Phytosanitary (SPS) Measures defined as measures applied (a) to protect human or animal life from risks arising from additives, contaminants, toxins or disease – causing organisms in their food; (b) to protect human life from plant – or animal – carried diseases; (c) to protect animal or plant life from pests, diseases, or disease – causing organisms; and (d) to prevent or limit other damage to a country from the entry, establishment or spread of pests.

This also includes SPS measures taken to protect the health of fish and wild fauna, as well as of forests and wild flora.

W. Veterinary Quarantine Clearance (VQC)/SPS Clearance refers to the document being issued by the Bureau of Animal Industry (BAI) prior to importation indicating that based on readily available information: (a) the source/s of meat and/or meat products are free from relevant diseases/contaminations; and (b) the accreditations of both the importer and the FME (exporter) are in 'good standing'. The VQC also prescribes the conditions and risk management measures necessary in the conduct of importation that are to be observed by the importer, exporter, and the NVA at the country of origin.

X. Veterinary Quarantine and Meat Inspection and Laboratory Certificate (VQMILC) refers to the certificate issued by the BAI Veterinary Quarantine Officer (DAVQO) and the National Meat Inspection Service (NMIS) Inspector to the BOC (copy furnish BAI and the importer) for customs processing, which certifies that the shipment of meat and/or meat products have been subjected to and passed veterinary quarantine documentation and meat inspection, and/or laboratory analysis and clearance.

Section Ⅱ
Scope

A. Only meat and/or meat products referred to in Annex "A" as defined in Section I (M) and (N) are covered by this Order.

B. All importation of meat and/or meat products into the Philippines destined to be unloaded into the customs territories for direct consumption, repacking and relabeling/rebranding, processing and manufacturing, marketing and distribution and/or re-export are covered by this Order.

C. Transshipped meat and/or meat products into the Philippines are not covered by this Order.

Section Ⅲ
Application for and issuance of VQC/SPS clearance

A. Prior to the importation of meat and/or meat products from the country of origin, an accredited importer as defined in Section I (B) shall first secure a VQC/SPS Clearance from BAI. This provision shall be subject to review and modification by the DA depending on the compliance performance of importers and FMEs.

B. The accredited importer (applicant) shall:

1. Submit a duly accomplished application form to input (attached as Annex "B") indicating and certifying the nature of the import application and a disclosure that the meat and/or meat products are still at the country of origin and have not been boarded yet to a vessel/aircraft;

2. Submit the relevant pro-forma invoice; and

3. Pay the necessary application fee/s to BAI.

C. The application, processing, and receipt of VQC shall only be undertaken by the president/CEO/general manager of the firm or through its authorized representative/s.

D. The BAI in consultation with NMIS as appropriate shall issue VQC upon determination of the following:

1. The absence of relevant diseases, pests, and/or contaminations at the relevant area/region/country of origin in/from which live animals are being domesticated, produced, slaughtered, processed, packed, canned, loaded/boarded, and transported including the route/s of the vessel/aircraft in which imported meat and meat products might be carried;

2. The FME is in 'good standing' as defined in Section I (I);

3. The accredited importer is in 'good standing' as defined in Section I (J);

4. The appropriate and specific risk management conditions relevant to the importation of specific meat and/or meat products based on OIE and Codex; and

5. Other factors necessary and pertinent to SPS concerns.

E. Based on above considerations, BAI shall approve/disapprove the application within 5 working days from the receipt of complete application documents. The approval VQC shall contain the BAI seal and the signature of the BAI Director.

F. Upon issuance of VQC, the accredited importer shall immediately provide the exporter with a copy (i. e. electronic copy, facsimile) of the approved VQC, which shall be the basis for health and safety for the issuance of IVC by the NVA at the country of origin.

G. The VQC is valid for 60 days without extension from the date of issuance, within which meat and/or meat products are to be shipped out from the country to origin as indicated in the bill of lading of airway bill. Shipment made beyond the validity period shall render such shipment illegal and therefore shall be confiscated and disposed of in accordance with Section X herein.

H. The VQC is not transferable and therefore shall only be used by the consignee for whom this was issued.

I. Only the president/CEO/general manager of the importing firm and its authorized representatives are allowed to receive the approved VQC as provided in Section III (C).

J. The one Shipment/BILL OF LADING – Per VQC Policy as defined in Section I (R) shall be strictly adhered to in the conduct of importation, such that a VQC can only be used relative to the shipment described therein. Any shipment made in violation of this provision shall render the same unlawful and subject the shipment to the disposition prescribed under Section X; furthermore the importation shall be deemed a violation of the herein Administrative Order subject to the Penalty Provisions as contained in Section XI hereunder.

K. No VQC shall be issued after the shipment has left the port of origin and any misrepresentation of such fact shall render the VQC invalid and the importation illegal and subject to Section X hereof.

Section Ⅳ
Personal and non – commercial importation

Importation of fresh, frozen and uncooked meat products for personal and non – commercial consumption shall not be allowed unless covered by a valid VQC and IVC.

Section Ⅴ
General requirements and conditions

A. Only FMEs as defined in Section I (H and I) recognized by the National Veterinary Administration of the exporting country are allowed to export into the Philippines. Recognition extended by the local, provincial, and/or regional veterinary administrations/authorities at the country of origin is not recognized by DA.

B. Only accredited importers as defined in Section I (B) are allowed to file an application for VQC for the importation of meat and meat products and to import from FMEs.

C. The accredited importer shall ensure that its exporter at the country of origin has received a copy (i. e. electronic copy, facsimile) of the approved VQC/SPS Clearance prior to the shipment/boarding of meat and/or meat products to the Philippines.

D. The accredited importer shall ensure that the date of shipment of goods (as reflected in the Bill of Lading/Airway Bill) is not earlier than the date of the issuance of VQC.

E. The seal of the container of imported meat and/or meat products must be maintained throughout the chain of importation. The fact that an imported meat or meat product is transshipped or made to pass through other ports other than original port of origin before arriving in the Philippines shall not invalidate the VQC and IVC, unless the original seal has been broken.

Section Ⅵ
Additional measure, temporary import ban and resumption of trade

A. During emergency cases/situations, DA shall exercise its authority and powers under existing laws in the 'timely' imposition of a temporary import ban on the importation of relevant meat and/or meat products from relevant areas/regions/countries to ensure human and animal health/life are secured and protected. In the promulgation of an import ban, DA shall:

1. Suspend the issuance of VQC for relevant applications;

2. Cancel/revoke all relevant VQCs issued;

3. Suspend all relevant shipments; and

4. Confiscate all relevant shipments and dispose these shipments in accordance with Section X;

B. Emergency cases/situations include the following:

1. Outbreak of any relevant OIE notifiable disease;

2. Danger/occurrence of contamination (e. g. , dioxin contamination); and/or

3. Other cases important to public health and safety as determine by DA.

C. In the imposition of any import ban, DA shall consider the following:

1. The recommendations of OIE, World Health Organization (WHO), and/or Codex;

2. The risk management and communication measures undertaken by the exporting government are not sufficient as may be determined through readily available information;

3. The importance as to the presence in the source country or part of the country of the relevant diseases, contaminations and/or other cases important to public health and safety;

4. The results of any risk assessment undertaken by DA based on readily available information; and/or

5. Other circumstances which warrant the imposition of a ban.

D. The temporary import ban shall be lifted based on the following considerations;

1. The recommendations or OIE, World Health Organizations, and/or Codex;

2. The risk management and communication measures undertaken by the exporting government are already sufficient.

3. The results of any risk assessment undertaken by DA based on readily available information;

4. Other considerations that warrant the resumption of importation.

E. In cases of emergency situations referred to in Section VI (B) which do not necessarily require immediate banning of meat and/or meat products, DA may institute extra/additional measure/s apart from the regular measures, standards and requirements necessary to ensure the safety and wholesomeness of any meat and/or meat products that may be imported from the relevant area/region/country where such emergency cases occur.

Section VII
Packing and labeling requirements

The accredited importer shall ensure that the shipment comply with the following packing and labeling requirements;

A. The packing materials and containers in direct contact with the meat and/or meat products must be of food grade quality based on the standards set by Codex or equivalent standards as may be determined by DA.

B. All wood packaging materials of imported meat/meat products shall be treated in accordance with the International Standards on Phyto sanitary Measures NO. 15 (ISPM No. 15) .

C. All food additives/preservatives shall be declared in the label as appropriate/applicable.

D. The packaging must meet the minimum labeling requirement as follows:

1. Registered trade name of the exporter or brand name of the product;

2. Business name and address of the exporter;

3. Country origin;

4. Lot identification;

5. Product description and list of ingredients;

6. Net quantity of contents, in terms of weight, measure of numerical count rounded to the nearest tenths (expressed in METRIC SYSTEM);

7. Date of manufacture and packaging;

8. Date of minimum durability ("best before") or expiration date; and

9. Handling and storage instructions

E. The label on each box/packaging of the imported meat and/or meat products must be written in English or Filipino and each character of the text should not be less than 2.5 mm (for preprinted or stamped) and 5 mm (for stenciled or hand painted).

Section Ⅷ
Border control inspection and clearance and release procedures

A. Border control shall be conducted strictly for all shipments of meat and/or meat products. To ensure timely initiation and completion of veterinary and meat inspection and clearance, the importer/consignee or his/her authorized representative shall submit to the Veterinary Quarantine Office (VQO) all the required documents of these mandatory pertinent to the shipment as prescribed in Section VIII (C. 1).

B. Upon arrival of any shipment of meat and/or meat products at the port of entry as defined in Section I (S), this shall be subjected to documentary verification and evaluation, veterinary inspection by DA. Only upon completion of these mandatory activities and clearances shall the BOC release the shipment.

C. At the port of entry, the VQO shall:

1. Verify and evaluate the authenticity, validity and accuracy of VQC (original), IVC (original), Bill of Lading/Airway Bill and Packing List submitted by the importer/consignee;

2. Subject the shipment to veterinary quarantine inspection and further documentation;

3. Reseal the container van/s carrying the meat and/or meat products;

4. Issue and sign the Veterinary Quarantine and Meat Inspection and Laboratory Certificate (VQMILC) (attached as Annex "C") and stamp "INSPECTED AND PASSED FOR TRANSFER TO NMIS ACCREDITED COLD STORAGE" on the authentic copy of the BOC import documents/entries;

5. Issue official receipt for the payment of necessary DA inspection fees; and

6. Endorse the original VQMILC and the shipment to NMIS for meat inspection and/or laboratory analysis, as required;

D. Upon transfer of the shipment to any DA - accredited cold storage facility/warehouse/port of inspection, NMIS shall;

1. Immediately designate and dispatch an NMIS Inspector and conduct meat inspection within 24 hours;

2. Check and verify the integrity of the VQMILC and BAI seal.

3. Complete the inspection and/or laboratory analysis within:

Duration Supplier/Product/Situation

1. One (1) - day (inspection)

- FME in "Good Standing" as defined in Section I (1)

2. five (5) - day (inspection and laboratory analysis)

- New Product Supplier (NPS) as defined in Section I (P)
- When an FME is delisted as an FME in "Good Standing" by DA; or When there are any of the emer-

gency cases referred to in Section VI (B) herein at the source or port/s of transshipment/routes of the shipment

4. Sign the VQMILC that was endorsed by BAI VQO if the NMIS inspection and/or laboratory test results are satisfactory; and

5. Give the completed VQMILC (original) to the BOC (copy furnish BAI and the importer), which shall then be the basis of the BOC for the final liquidation of the importation documents. The final liquidation of the importation documents does not preclude the importer from utilizing the shipment.

Section IX
Post – Border sanitary conditions

All imported meat and/or meat products shall be subject to further relevant DA meat and meat products safety rules and regulations to ensure the consistency of quality and safety of the products and their traceability pursuant to Republic Act 9296, otherwise known as the Meat Inspection Code of the Philippines.

Section X
Confiscation and disposition

A. Imported meat and/or meat products without VQC shall be refused admission or entry (i. e. while still in the vessel prior to unloading) and exported. If for any reason whatsoever these products were able to gain entry into the customs territory, the same shall be seized and destroyed at the expense of the importer to protect public health and the local animal population.

B. Imported meat and/or meat products shall be confiscated when any of the violations below is committed, as any of these violations is deemed as compromising the integrity of the country's Risk Management Measures/Policy (RMP) as defined in Section I (U) and/or directly posing serious health and safety risks.

B. 1. At the port of entry, the BOC upon the recommendation of the quarantine officer, shall confiscate the imported products if:

a. The seal of the container of the shipment has been broken

b. The shipment lacks a valid VQC.

c. The shipment has no IVC issued by NVA at the country of origin.

d. The volume/quantity of goods imported exceeds the volume indicated in the approved

VQC and IVC by more than three (3) per item; provided that only the volume/quantity which exceeds the allowable limit shall be confiscated.

e. The shipment is not sourced from accredited FME.

f. The animals slaughtered are not from DA approved area, region, or country.

g. False claims, misrepresentation, and misbranding as may be evidenced by mislabeling of meat and/or meat products.

h. The meat and/or meat products have arrived beyond the "date of minimum durability" / expiration date.

i. The shipment has been labeled not in conformity with Section VII (C) (1 to 9) or absence of any of these labeling requirements;

j. The shipment is found to be infected by any OIE lists A and/or B disease.

k. Other deliberate violations of the provisions of this Order including refusal of the consignee/importer to access/secure pertinent documents relevant to the shipment.

B. 2. At the cold storage/warehouse/port of inspection, the BOC upon the recommendation of the NMIS inspector, shall confiscate the imported products if:

a. The BAI seal is broken/removed not by NMIS inspector.

b. Part of, or the entire shipment is utilized, processed, marketed and/or distributed without VQMILC.

c. The shipment is found to be carrying any disease – causing organism.

d. The shipment contains any toxic or deleterious substance, which may render it injurious to health.

e. The shipment contain any added toxic or deleterious substance other than allowed (a) food additives, and (b) color additives (c) contaminants at levels beyond the prescribed/established tolerance.

f. The shipment consists, in whole or part, of any filthy, putrid, rotten, decomposed substance or foreign matter, or otherwise unfit for human consumption.

g. The container or packaging materials in direct contact with the meat and/or meat

products are found to be composed of, in whole or part, of any poisonous or deleterious substance, which render the contents injurious to health.

h. Other violations that pose risks to human and animal health/life.

i. Other deliberate violations of the provisions of this Order including refusal on the consignee/importer to access/secure pertinent documents relevant to the shipment.

C. Shipment in violation of Section X (B. 1) shall be confiscated and destroyed jointly by BOC and DA.

D. The importer/consignee shall bear the expenses to be incurred in the confiscation and disposition of the shipment in view of Section X (A and B). These expenses include but are not limited to the destruction, storage, and labor.

E. Violations committed at the country of origin by FMEs shall be used as a basis for possible cancellation of their accreditation.

Section XI
Seizure and modification

A. Imported meat and/or meat products shall be seized and held in abeyance at the port of entry under the supervision of DA or at any DA accredited cold storage facility when the shipment of meat and/or products is inappropriately labeled based on the requirements in Section VII (C) (1 to 9).

Provided that such violation does not constitute misrepresentation, misbranding, false claims and other deliberate acts. Otherwise, such shipment shall be confiscated and disposed of in accordance with Section X.

B. The release and utilization of such shipment are dependent on the consignee's compliance to further measures on modification that shall be required by DA, provided, however, that such shipment held in abeyance does not violate any of the provisions in Section X (B). Otherwise, such shipment shall be confiscated and disposed of accordingly.

Section XII
Penalty provisions

A. Non – compliance with Sections III (A to I), Sections VII (A to D), shipments in contravention of Section III (K), is deemed violations of this Administrative Order, with the responsible shipper/consignor/importer subject to the application of these penalty provisions.

B. Violators of the provisions of this Order shall be penalized under Article 19 (Penalty), Chapter I, Title II, of Republic Act No. 7394 otherwise known as the Consumer Act of the Philippines issued 13 April 1992 and/or in cases of fraudulent/unlawful importation, under Section 3601 of the Tariff and Customs Code.

C. Public officials/employees who shall directly or indirectly participate in the commission of an offense or any act resulting in the violation of the provision (s) of this Administrative Order, specifically, but not limited to violation of Sections III (D, E and I) and Sections VIII (B, C and D) shall be held administratively and/or criminally liable under the Anti - graft Law, Civil Service Law, Rules and Regulations and the Code of Conduct and Ethical Standards for Public Officials and Employees.

Section XIII
Repealing clause

A. All existing rules and regulations, which are inconsistent with this Order, are hereby modified, revoked or repeated accordingly.

B. This Order repeals AO 16 (April 200), AO 39 (October 2000), AO 56 (December 2000) which provide the rules, regulations, guidelines and standards governing the importation of meat and meat products into the Philippines.

Section XIV
Separability clause

The provisions of this Order are hereby declared to be separable and in the event one or more of such provisions are held unconstitutional, the validity of the other provisions shall not be affected thereby.

Section XV
Transitory provisions

A. All in - transit shipments of meat and/or meat products which are shipped out from the country of origin prior to the effectivity of this Order shall be subjected to provisions of AO 39 and AO 56.

B. All existing importers and exporters shall be subject to review and assessment of their accreditation status. For this purpose, DA shall be issuing supplementary guidelines, rules and regulations on the accreditation of both the importer and exporters.

This Order shall take effect 15 days after publication in two (2) newspaper of national circulation.

Done in the City of Quezon, this 31st day of August in the year of the Lord, 2005.

Annex "A" of DA Administrative Order No. ________

Series of 2005

Annex "A"

LIST OF MEAT AND MEAT PRODUCTS REFERRED TO IN

Section II OF DA AO NO. ________, SERIES OF 2005

Heading No. Description

02.01 Meat of bovine animals, fresh or chilled

02.02 Meat of bovine animals, frozen

02.03 Meat of swine, fresh, chilled or frozen

02.04 Meat of sheep or goats, fresh, chilled or frozen

02.05 Meat of horses, asses, mules or hinnies, fresh, chilled or frozen

02.06 Edible offal of bovine animals, swine, sheep, goats, horses, asses, mules or hinnies, fresh, chilled or frozen

02.07 Meat of edible offal, of poultry of heading no. 01.05 fresh, chilled or frozen

02.08 Other meat and edible meat offal, fresh, chilled, or frozen

02.09 Pig fat, free of lean meat, and poultry fat, not rendered or otherwise extracted, fresh, chilled and frozen

02.10 Meat and edible meat offal, salted in brine, dried or smoked, edible flours and meals of meat and meat offal

15.02 Fat of bovine animals, sheep and goats other those of heading no. 15.03 (not processed)

16.01 Sausages and similar products; of meat, meat offal or blood; food preparations based on these

16.02 Other prepared or preserved meat, meat offal or

blood Based on the Harmonized Commodity Description and Coding System, Tariff and Customs Code of the Philippines (TCCP) issued in 2003.

Bureau of Animal Industry
National Veterinary Quarantine Services
Diliman, Quezon City

Annex “B” of DA AO No. ________

Series of 2005

Application for veterinary quarantine clearance to import

INSTRUCTION TO IMPORTER: Complete and submit one notarized copy and Pro Forma Invoice/Sales Agreement to National Veterinary Quarantine Services, Bureau of Animal Industry

1. NAME AND ADDRESS OF IMPORTER	2. NAME AND ADDRESS OF EXPORTER/FOREIGN MEAT ESTABLISHMENT	
TELEPHONE/FAX NUMBER	FOREIGN MEAT ESTABLISHMENT NO.	
3. PORT OF LOADING (IF AVAILABLE)	4. COUNTRY OF ORIGIN	
5. MODE OF TRANSPORTATION	6. PHILIPPINES PORT OF ENTRY	
ITEM	DESCRIPTION	QUANTITY
7. NAME AND ADDRESS OF COLD STORAGE WHERE DELIVERY WILL BE MADE		8. BAI ACCREDITATION NO. OF IMPORTER

1. I declare that these products will be used in accordance with all Philippines quarantine requirements as may be specified in the VQC to be issued for the importation and other DA rules and regulations relevant thereto.

2. I subscribe and declare to follow all the applicable provisions of the DA rules, regulations, standards, on the importation of meat and meat products into the Country and other DA rules and regulations relevant thereto.

3. I declare that at the time of the filing of this application, the meat and/or meat products that are to be imported are still in the country of origin and have not yet boarded in a vessel/aircraft.

4. I declare that the information I have provided herein are true and accurate to the best of my knowledge and belief.

________ ________

DATE SIGNED SIGNATURE OF IMPORTER

SPACE FOR NOTARIZATION

As per DA Admin Order No. ________ Series of 2005, no meat and meat products may be imported without a valid Quarantine Clearance issued by the Bureau of Animal Industry.

Republic of the Philippines

Department of Agriculture

Office of the Secretary

Elliptical Road, Diliman, Quezon City,

Philippines

Annex "C" of the DA AO ________,

series of 2005

VQMILC No. ________

____

Date

Veterinary quarantine and meat inspection and laboratory certificate

This is to certify that the undersigned had inspected the shipment described below:

Under BAI:

Consignee:	
Commodity:	
VQC No. :	
IVC No. :	
Country of origin:	
Volume:	
Number of containers:	
Container No/s. :	
Port of arrival:	
Date of arrival:	
Date of Release to NMIS:	

Under NMIS:

Accredited cold storage/warehouse:	
Date of arrival in cold storage/warehouse:	
Date of inspection and sampling:	
Date of clearance:	
Date of release to BOC:	

This further certifies that said importation complied with all the requirements of the National Meat Inspection Service (NMIS), Bureau of Animal Industry (BAI) and had been subjected to inspection and/or laboratory analysis by the National Meat Inspection Service and found to be fit for human consumption. This document serves as the basis of the Bureau of Customs (BOC) for the final release of the import documents to the Consignee.

________________ ________________

BAI Veterinary Quarantine NMIS Meat Control Officer/Officer/Inspector Meat Inspector

柬埔寨

柬埔寨植物检疫法

（柬埔寨皇家政府第 15 号次法令）

第一章　总　　则

第一条　本次法令目的是为了保护农业生产和生物多样性，防止检疫性和危险性有害生物通过各种运输工具传入、传出国境以及在国内传播蔓延。

第二条　所有携带或运输的植物检疫物进出或过境柬埔寨国境都必须经过检疫和植物检疫处理。

第三条　农林渔业部是植物检疫主管部门，作物和农业土地改良局是植物检疫职权的执行机构。

第四条　本次法令中重要术语的定义

a. **有害生物**　包括动物界（人类除外）和植物界及病原菌所有物种，无论是否活体，在任一发育阶段能伤害、损害、毁坏及寄生在植物或植物产品内的，都称为有害生物。本次法令狭义上不只限于造成植物病害的昆虫、蜘蛛、老鼠、田鼠、蜗牛、鸟和杂草。

b. **植物检疫性有害生物（PQP）**　是指对植物有危险的（潜在经济重要性），尚未在柬埔寨王国发生，或虽已发生但分布未广，仍需要控制的所有有害生物。

c. **植物检疫**　包括调查研究、观察、检查和取样、分析和鉴定植物检疫物以确定其感染状况。

d. **危险性有害生物**　是指引起或能造成重大经济损失或对植物资源和环境造成严重破坏的有害生物。

e. **受侵染**　指携带或感染任何有害生物。

f. **过境运输**　指货物和运输工具从柬埔寨王国领土过境，其起点和终点不在柬埔寨境内，这个过程只是整个运输过程一部分，“过境运输”可包括或不包括转载、仓库贮存、拆散运输或改变运输方式。

g. **土壤**　是指可以种植植物的任何土壤或矿物质和有机物自然形成的混合物。

h. **疫区**　是发生一种或几种已公布的植物检疫性有害生物（PQP）或危险性有害生物（DP）的区域。

i. **货物**　指通过商业或其他目的流通的材料，包括植物、植物部分、植物产品、种子或种子材料。

j. **传染源**　是发生一种或几种已公布的植物检疫性有害生物（PQP）或危险性（DP）有害生物的地点。

k. **植物产品**　是指未加工、半加工和已加工的植物源性材料，其本身或加工过程能产生有害生物传入扩散的风险。

l. **人造植物源性材料**　是指未加工、半加工和已加工的植物源性材料其本身或加工过程能给有害生物的传入扩散带来风险。这些产品不包括以罐或瓶装的材料，以及不能产生传播有害生物风险的材料。

m. **植物检疫**　指植物或植物产品健康控制，即预防、处理或根除有害生物。

n. **植物检疫官（PSO）**　指受命执行植物检疫的人。

o. **植物**　指植物界的所有物种。无论是否存活，在任何生长发育期、整株或部分，此定义包括但不只限于植物的种子、谷物、块茎、球茎、鳞茎、根、茎、枝条、砧木、芽条、压条、插条、吸根、根茎、叶、花和果实，用铁罐、锡罐、玻璃瓶密封进境的果脯和蔬菜除外。

p. **植物检疫要求**　指任何国家的植物检疫当局为了防止有害生物通过各种进境途径在本国传入扩散所提出的要求，该要求符合《国际植物保护公约》（1951 年）的规定。

q. **植物检疫证书（PC）**　是指货物从原产国出口前，植物检疫局经检疫后，依照 1951 年《国际植物保护公约》规定的模式所签发的国际上公认的证书。所有须进行植物检疫的进口、出口和转口货物都要求有植物检疫证书。

r. **转口植物检疫证书（PCR）**　是指货物原产地不在该国，在出口到第三国前，该国植物检疫局经检疫后，依照 1951 年《国际植物保护公约》规定的模式所签发的国际公认的证书。所有非原产地、正在转载的、或贮入仓库的、或分散运输的、或改变运输方式的、或在第三国进行植物检疫处理的、须进行植物检疫的非直接进出口和过境的货物都要求出具植物检疫证书。

s. **植物检疫处理**　包括对货物进行挑选、除虫、再加工、净化、封存、退回原产地或销毁。

t. **有益生物**　指通过侵染、寄生、捕食植物有害生物而有益于植物生长发育的生物，此定义包括但不只限于昆虫、蜘蛛、线虫、真菌、细菌、病毒和其他微生物。这些有益生物侵入其他对植物生长发育有害的生物表面和内部，如重寄生物和昆虫病原微生物。

u. **植物检疫局（PQA）**　指负责植物检疫的权力机构，从中央到植物检疫站有明确的组织机构。该局指的是农林渔业部（MAFF）作物和农业土地改良局（DAALI）管辖的植物保护和植物检疫部门，植物检疫局（PQA）与履行《植物保护公约》（IPPC－1951）的其他国家植物检疫局保持长期紧密的合作，并负责与其协调工作。

v. **感染状况**　是植物检疫物携带或感染有害生物的程度和特征。

第二章　植物检疫

第五条　农林渔业部应派出植物检疫和动物卫生官员在柬埔寨皇家政府次法令规定的国际检查站、国际边境检查站、双边边境检查站、地区边境检查站和海上边境检查站按照他们的职责实施检疫。

农林渔业部应在皇家政府批准的火车站、陆地口岸、内河港和空港设立植物检疫和动物卫生检查站。

如果柬埔寨王国某地发生植物检疫性或危险性有害生物疫情，农林渔业部应在该地建立过渡性的植物检疫站以控制疫情，并通过植物检疫处理来扑灭疫情，当疫情扑灭后，农林渔业部应撤除所有的过渡性植物检疫站。

为了确保检疫效果植物检疫站应配备技术设备。

植物检疫站应设在便于物资运输的场所。

第六条　应按照每个国家的检疫要求实施植物检疫。

第七条　植物检疫物是：

未确认无有害生物的植物、植物的部分、植物产品及农产品。

包装材料或木箱、木托盘或任何运输和贮存工具。

土壤、附在植物根部或植物部分的土壤。

活的或死的有害生物及有益生物。

任何其他非植物源性但仍可给有害生物提供栖息环境的物品。

植物检疫物名单由农林渔业部部长、商业部部长、工业矿产和能源部部长和卫生部部长组成的 PRAEAS 共同制定。

第八条　任何人运输植物检疫物，必须执行以下程序：

正确申报材料；

获得植物检疫证书；

用好的包装材料来包装并绑紧以避免在运输过程中泄漏或散落。

按照植物检疫局指定的地点或方式来贮存和运输；

如果以非指定的地点或方式运输、贮存、装货，须向植物检疫局申请批准。

第九条 在货物抵达柬埔寨入境口岸或出境口岸前，货主应就近向植物检疫站申报并给予植物检疫提供便利，植物检疫应在接到申请后24小时内完成。

货物出口前10天，货主应向植物检疫局申请并给予检疫提供便利，在这段时间内植物检疫局应完成植物检疫和检疫处理。

第十条 任何不符合进口国植物检疫要求的植物检疫物，货主应进行植物检疫处理，处理费用由货主支付。

第十一条 任何自然人或法人发现以下情况，应通知就近的植物检疫局：

a. 装载任何植物检疫物的帆船、机动船、轮船以及其他远洋轮船，因发生故障抛锚而漂进柬埔寨领海的。

b. 飞机在柬埔寨王国领土投掷上述材料的。

第十二条 货主发现或者得知他/她的货物受到检疫性有害生物危害的，应立即采取措施进行控制，如果货主没有能力控制，应向植物检疫局申请进行检疫处理。

第十三条 为避免运输交通拥堵，当口岸发生有害生物时，植物检疫官员应立即采取有效措施进行控制和扑灭。

如果上述措施没有效果，植物检疫局应停止其运输、装卸直至有害生物完全根除。

第十四条 任何自然人或法人申请植物检疫应支付植物检疫费，如果要求对货物进行处理以控制有害生物的，须支付有害生物控制费，这些费用应由植物检疫当局上缴国库。

植物检疫费和有害生物处理费征收标准应由农林渔业部部长和财经部部长组成的PROKAS签发决定。

第十五条 对在口岸检查站处理进出口、转运植物检疫物时，各相关部门间的合作规定如下：

1. 检查站负责人及有关机构应与植物检疫官员合作，进行预防和植物检疫处理。

2. 植物检疫应与海关查验和商品检验同时进行。

第十六条 在执行检疫时，植物检疫官员应着农业部（MAFF）规定的制服并佩带植物检疫局的徽章。

植物检疫局的制服、徽章和印章由其他的次法令决定。

为了有效地、透明地、非歧视性在全国地执行本次法令，农林渔业部应按照植物检疫和其他规章的程序建立PRACAS。

第十七条 所有的PRACAS或其他与植物检疫检疫有关的法规应通过国家信息系统公布。

第三章 国内植物检疫

第十八条 如果在柬埔寨王国某地发现检疫性或危险性有害生物传染源，农林渔业部应宣布该地为疫区，并立即采取措施进行控制。

禁止该地货物出口、进口或过境，直到农林渔业部部长签发新的公告为止。

第十九条 以研究目的从疫区带来的植物检疫性有害生物或危险性有害生物标本，须经植物检疫局批准。

第四章 进境植物检疫和监控

第二十条 对进境植物检疫物的检疫应根据柬埔寨禁止入境的植物检疫性和危险性有害生物名录来进行。

柬埔寨王国禁止入境的植物检疫性和危险性有害生物名录由PRACAS决定，农林渔业部部长签署。必要时，农林渔业部部长应依法修订植物检疫性和危险性有害生物名录，在公布后30天生效。但发生严重疫情可能对农业和生物多样性造成巨大损失的紧急情况下，在公布后24小时生效。

第二十一条 植物检疫物进入柬埔寨王国时，货主应遵守以下植物检疫要求：

1. 植物检疫物必须附有输出国植物检疫局以1951年《国际植物保护公约》所规定的模式签发的植物证书。

2. 植物检疫物不得带有柬埔寨王国规定的检疫性有害生物和其他危险性有害生物，如有上述有害生物危害，在进境前须进行植物检疫处理。

第二十二条 进境植物检疫物的检疫程序如下：

1. 进境植物的自然人或法人在货物到达前10天应通知植物检疫站。

2. 在抵达第一进境口岸时，植物检疫物的货主必须申报并申请检疫，植物检疫站应在指定的地点进行检疫。

申报、检疫和检疫处理依照本次法令第九、十、十四条执行。退回或者销毁植物检疫物必须经过合法的程序。

运载植物检疫物的运输工具到达柬埔寨水域，货主应就近向植物检疫站申请检疫，经植物检疫局检疫并批准运输工具才能靠岸。

第二十三条 植物检疫局在植物检疫物进入柬埔寨王国境内后，依法发出检疫通知，并监督货物的运输、储存、销售和使用，如果某地发生检疫性或危险性有害生物，植物检疫局应立即采取有效措施进行控制和根除。

第五章 出境植物检疫

第二十四条 出境植物检疫物应根据商业合同、协议、协定和其他有关进口国植物检疫要求的文件实施检疫。

第二十五条 出境植物检疫物的要求如下：

出口植物检疫物的所有者应向植物检疫局申请检疫并签发植物检疫证书。

植物检疫物必须符合商业合同、协议、协定和其他有关文件规定的输入国植物检疫条件。

第二十六条 出口植物检疫物的检疫手续应符合本次法令第九条、第十条、第十四条规定的条件。

第六章 过境植物检疫

第二十七条 植物检疫物经过柬埔寨王国领土必须：

附有输出国签发的植物检疫证书，包装完好，并用容器装载，避免运输过程中泄漏或溢出，运输工具不得带有能在过境运输途中传播的植物检疫性或危险性有害生物。

第二十八条 过境植物检疫手续如下：

货主在货物抵达入境口岸和出境口岸前通知最近的植物检疫站。

植物检疫局必须检查运输工具和表层货物，核对输出国签发的植物检疫证书，同时要保持运输畅通。

第二十九条 如果植物检疫物不符合本次法令第二十七条规定的条件，植物检疫局应在入境口岸进行检疫处理才允许继续运输。

如果运输过程中发生事故和包装材料破损，可能造成植物检疫物扩散，货主应立即向最近的植物检疫局或地方政府申报，植物检疫局应立即进行植物检疫处理，签发植物检疫证书再出口，并允许继续运输。

第七章 植物检疫官员职责

第三十条 植物检疫官员的权利如下：

对仓库、工厂、农业生产区或农场的运输工具和植物检疫物实施植物检疫和检疫处理。对违反规定的案件准备递交法庭的有关记录和报告。

上述资产的所有者应允许植物检疫官员检查他们的材料，并配合提供有关资料。

第三十一条 地方官员或地方政府应按照植物检疫局的要求予以配合。

第八章 处 罚

第三十二条 如果有以下违禁行为的植物检疫物，不准进出口或转运：

不符合本次法令第八条植物检疫程序规定的（第八条第四点或第30条第1款除外）；

不符合输入国植物检疫要求的，或不按本次法令第十条规定进行植物检疫处理的；

不符合本次法令第二十一、二十六或第二十八条规定的；

第三十三条 按照《产品及服务质量与安全法管理法》第七章第六十二条规定处以罚款：

不符合本次法令第八条第四款植物检疫程序规定的；

违反本次法令第十三条第二款、第十八条第二款、第二十二条第二款或第三款的。

第三十四条 屡次违反本次法令第十三条第二款、第十八条第二款、第二十二条第二款或第三款的，将加倍处罚，不包括触犯刑法。

如果其违法行为造成植物检疫性或危险性有害生物传播，违反者应按照农林渔业部的评估支付根除所需费用。

第三十五条 按照《产品及服务的质量与安全管理法》第七章第六十三条规定进行罚款：

a. 设置条件，致使本次法令第三条所述植物检疫官员不能履行其职责的；

b. 拒绝出示相关文件、出示虚假文件、混淆运输植物检疫物的；

c. 未经批准，组织运输植物检疫所没收的植物检疫物的；

d. 避开植物检疫检查站运输植物检疫物，以逃避植物检疫的。

第三十六条 不交纳罚金的，他/她将被移送法庭处理。

奖励官员的奖励及其所需费用由农林渔业部部长和财政部部长的PRACAS阐释。

第九章 最后条款

第三十七条 1983年10月8日签发的次法令98 GnRk《关于进出境植物产品检疫》及其他与本次法令相矛盾的条款将废止。

第三十八条 部长委员会的部长、农林渔业部部长、执行本次法令的有关各部和政府的部长和大臣。

金边，2003年3月13日

首 相

Phytosanitary Law

(No. : 15 OR NOR KROR. BOR KOR Sub – Decree on)

Chapter Ⅰ General provisions

Article 1 This Sub – Decree aims to prevent the introduction of quarantine and dangerous pests into the territory, the spread from one to another within territory or to other countries through any means of transportation in order to protect the agriculture production and bio – diversity.

Article 2 All plant quarantine materials bringing or transporting into, exit from or transit in the territory of the Kingdom of Cambodia shall be inspected and followed the Phytosanitary Treatment.

Article 3 Ministry of Agriculture, Forestry and Fisheries is responsible for implementation of plant quarantine which has Plant Quarantine Authority of Department of Agronomy and Agricultural Land Improvement is implementing agency.

Article 4 Under this Sub – Decree, the definition and interpretation of important glossaries are:

a. Pest includes any member of the animal kingdom (other than *Homo sapiens*) or plant kingdom or pathogenic agent, whether dead or alive, which could in any stage of development injure, damage, destroy or be parasitic upon any plant or plant products. Such an expression also includes for the limited purposes of this Sub – decree, but is not restricted to, insects, arachnids, rats, moles, snails, birds, organisms causing plant diseases and weeds.

b. Plant Quarantine Pest (PQP) means any pest of plants dangerous (potential economic importance) to plant but not yet in existence in the Kingdom of Cambodia, and even those in existence but not widely spread yet that need to be controlled.

c. Phytosanitary Inspection includes researching, investigating, observing, checking and sampling, analyzing and identifying plant quarantine materials to determine its infection status.

d. Dangerous Pest (DP) is pest causing or being able to cause large economical damage or seriously destroy plant resource and environment.

e. Infested means bearing or containing any pest.

f. Transit transport means transit of goods and means of transport across the territory of the Kingdom of Cambodia when the passage is only a portion of a complete journey beginning and terminating beyond the frontier of the Kingdom of Cambodia across whose territory the traffic passes; transit transport may or may not include transshipment, warehousing, breaking bulk or change in the mode of transport.

g. Soil means any earth, ground or naturally occurring mixture of mineral and organic material in which plants may be grown.

h. Epidemic Area is zone of existing one or several species of published plant quarantine (PQP) or dangerous pests (DP).

i. Goods include plants or part of plant, plant products, seed or seed materials, which is being moved for commercial or other purposes.

j. Epidemic Nest is place, where one or several species of published plant quarantine or dangerous pest are existed.

k. Plant products mean unprocessed, semi – processed or processed material of plant origin that, by their nature or that of their processing, may create a risk for the introduction and spread of pests.

l. Manufactured materials of plant origin means unprocessed, semi – processed or processed material of plant origin that, by their nature or that of their processing, may create a risk for the introduction and spread of pests. These products are not include the material, packaged in can or bottle and may be not created a risk for spreading the pests.

m. Phytosanitary of or for plant or plant – product health especially. the prevention, treatment or removal of pests.

n. Phytosanitary Officer (PSO) refers to any person appointed for phytosanitary inspection.

o. Plant means all members of the plant kingdom, whether living or dead, at any stage of growth or development, any part or parts of such, but not preserved fruits or vegetables imported in hermetically sealed cans, tins, bottles or other containers. Such an expression also included, but is not restricted to, seed, grain, tuber, corm, bulb, root, stem, branch, stock, bud wood, cutting, layer, slip, sucker, rhizome, leaf, flower and fruits of plants.

p. Phytosanitary Requirement means the requirement of plant quarantine authority of any country to prevent against the spread of pest into the country by means of importing activities. This requirement is in accordance with the International Plant Protection Convention – 1951.

q. Phytosanitary Certificate (PC) refers to an internationally accepted certificate issued by the Plant Quarantine Authority after due phytosanitary inspection of goods prior to export from country origin in accordance with the model prescribed in the 1951 International Plant Protection Convention. A PC is required for importation, exportation and transit of all goods objected to plant quarantine.

r. Phytosanitary Certificate for Re – export (PCR) refers to an internationally accepted certificate issued by the Plant Quarantine Authority after due phytosanitary inspection of goods not riginally in that country prior to export to the third country. A PCR is in accordance with the model prescribed in the 1951 International Plant Protection Convention. A PCR is required for non – direct importation or exportation of or transit of all goods objected to plant quarantine which is not original, is being transshipped or warehoused or broken bulk or changed in the mode of transport or taken phytosanitary treatment in the second country.

s. Phytosanitary Treatment includes selecting, eliminating, re – processing, and cleaning, decontaminating, retaining, returning back to the place of origin or destroying plant quarantine materials.

t. Beneficial organism means an organism which benefit plant growth and development by infecting, parasitizing or predating on plant pests. Such an expression includes, but is not restricted to, insects, arachnids, nematodes, fungi, bacteria, viruses and other microbial organisms. These beneficial organisms are known to carry on or in them other undesirable organisms (e. g. hyper parasitoids and entomopathogenic organisms) detrimental to plant growth and development.

u. Plant Quarantine Authority (PQA) means an authority in charged in phytosanitary inspection and has clearly organizational structure from the Central level to the plant quarantine stations. This authority refers to Plant Protection and Phytosanitary Inspection Office (PP&PSO) under supervise of Department of Agronomy and Agricultural Land Improvement (DAALI) of Ministry of Agriculture Forestry and Fisheries (MAFF). The PQA have coordinated it work and permanently and closely cooperation with Plant Quarantine Authority of other countries, which are implementing the IPPC – 1951.

v. Infection Status is level and character of plant quarantine materials bearing or containing with pests.

Chapter Ⅱ Phytosanitary inspection

Article 5 Ministry of Agriculture Forestry and Fisheries shall nominate Phytosanitary and animal – sanitary Officers to implement the inspection following their duties in international check points, international border – check points, bilateral border – check points, regional border – check points and sea border – check ports throughout the Kingdom of Cambodia, where are stated by the Royal Government Sub – Decree.

Ministry of Agriculture Forestry and Fisheries shall set up Phytosanitary and animal – sanitary inspection check points at train station, dry – port and domestic ports and airports, where permitted by the Royal Government.

In case epidemic of plant quarantine pest or dangerous pest in any area of the Kingdom of Cambodia, Ministry of Agriculture Forestry and Fisheries shall be setting up transitional phytosanitary inspection check points in the place is needed to control epidemic and apply plant quarantine treatment for eliminating the problem. When epidemic has been eliminated Ministry of Agriculture Forestry and Fisheries shall be breaking up all those transitional phytosanitary inspection check points.

Phytosanitary inspection check points shall be equipped with technical apparatus in order to insure the effectiveness of inspection.

Phytosanitary inspection check points shall be situated at the place, where are convenient for the transportation of material.

Article 6 Phytosanitary inspection shall be implemented following phytosanitary requirement of each country.

Article 7 Plant quarantine materials are:

Plants, parts of plant, plant products, and agricultural products that are not certified free of pests;

Packaging material or wooden boxes, palettes or any means of transport and storage;

Soil or soil attached to root or part of plant;

Live or dead pests or beneficial organisms;

Any other items that may not be of plant origin but yet may provide a habitat for pests. List of plant quarantine materials shall define by Pracas of Minister of Agriculture Forestry and Fisheries, Minister of Commerce, Minister of Industry Mine and Energy, and Minister of Health.

Article 8 Any person, who is transporting any plant quarantine material, shall carry out the following procedures:

Proper declares the material;

Obtains a phytosanitary certificate;

Packs the materials in good package and tightly fasten to avoid leakage or spillage of materials while being transported;

Stores or transports the materials in the place or through the way designated by the Plant Quarantine Authority.

In case of transport, store or load the materials in place or through the way other than designated, shall requests the permission from Plant Quarantine Authority.

Article 9 Before the arrival of goods to the points of entry to or exit from Cambodia, the owner shall announce to the nearest phytosanitary check point and shall make good convenient for phytosanitary inspection. The phytosanitary inspection shall be completed within 24 hours after receiving the notification.

Within 10 days prior the export of the materials, the owner shall apply to Plant Quarantine Authority and shall make good convenient for the phytosanitary inspection.

Within this period of time the Plant Quarantine Authority shall complete phytosanitary inspection and treatment.

Article 10 For any plant quarantine materials, which are not complied with the phytosanitary requirement of importing country, the owner shall follows the phytosanitary treatment.

The expense for phytosanitary treatment shall be paid by the material owner.

Article 11 Any physical or juridical person shall inform to the nearest Plant Quarantine Authority, when he/she has seen:

a. A sail boat, a motor - driven boat, a ship or any other sea - going vessel loading any plant quarantine materials, which has broken down and has drifted into the maritime territory of the Kingdom of Cambodia.

b. A plane drops any material as described above into the territory of the Kingdom of Cambodia.

Article 12 The owner of plant quarantine materials shall immediately take measure to control, when he/she sees or knows that his or her material has damaged by plant quarantine pests. If owner has no ability to control them, he/ she shall requests to Plant Quarantine Authority to take phytosanitary treatment.

Article 13 If pests invade any check point, phytosanitary officer shall take adequate and appropriate measure to control and eliminate them immediately, in order to avoid the transportation stack.

If above measure is not effected, Plant Quarantine Authority shall stop transportation, loading or unloading materials until the pest have fully eliminated.

Article 14 Any physical or juridical person who requests a phytosanitary inspection shall pay a fee called *a* phytosanitary inspection fee. If requests for the treatment of the consignment to control pests - a pest control fee. These payments shall be deposited to the national budget through Plant Quarantine Authority.

Phytosanitary inspection fee and pest control fee shall be issue by PROKAS of Minister of Agriculture, Forestry and Fisheries and Minister of Economic and Finance.

Article 15 The cooperation between organizations dealing with import, export, Transit of plant quarantine materials in all check points is defined as follows:

1. The chief of check point, and other involved organization shall cooperate with plant quarantine officer to prevent and conduct phytosanitary treatment.

2. Phytosanitary inspection shall make at one time with Customs and Camcontrol.

Article 16 During operation the plant quarantine officer shall ware the uniform together with badges of Plant Quarantine Authority and accompanied by the mission order issued by MAFF.

The uniform, badges and stamp of plant quarantine authority will be determined by other Sub - Decree.

Ministry of Agriculture Forestry and Fisheries shall develop the PRACAS on procedure of plant quarantine inspection and other regulations for implementing this subdecree effectively, transparently and with non - discrimination in whole country.

Article 17 All PRACAS or other regulations that concerned with plant quarantine inspection shall be published through National Information System.

Chapter Ⅲ Domestic plant quarantine

Article 18 In the case of finding the Epidemic nest of plant quarantine pest or dangerous pest in any location in the Kingdom of Cambodia, the Ministry of Agriculture Forestry and Fisheries shall declare as an epidemic area and shall take measure to control them immediately.

The exportation, importation or transit of goods shall be prohibited until the new declaration issued by Minister of Agriculture Forestry and Fisheries.

Article 19 The bringing of plant quarantine pests or dangerous pest samples from epidemic area for research purpose shall be permitted by Plant Quarantine Authority.

Chapter Ⅳ Plant quarantine for import and monitoring

Article 20 The inspection of import of plant quarantine materials shall be conducted based on the list of plant quarantine and dangerous pests prohibited to entry into the Kingdom of Cambodia.

The list of plant quarantine and dangerous pests prohibited to entry into the Kingdom of Cambodia shall be determined by PRACAS issued by Minister of Agriculture Forestry and Fisheries. Minister of Agriculture Forestry and Fisheries shall be lawful to alter the list of plant quarantine and dangerous pests prohibited to entry into the Kingdom of Cambodia, if needed. This alteration shall be effected thirty days (30 days) after the date of publication. However, in an emergency when a very serious epidemic that could cause enormous damage to the agriculture and bio – diversity, such alteration shall take effect within twenty four hours (24 hours) after publication.

Article 21 The owner plant quarantine materials importing into the Kingdom of Cambodia shall respect to phytosanitary condition as follows:

1. The materials must be accompanied with a plant quarantine certificate issued by Plant Quarantine Authority of country – exporter in model stipulated in International Plant Protection Convention 1951.

2. The materials must be free from plant quarantine pests and other dangerous pests of the Kingdom of Cambodia. In case of materials has damaged by the above pests, the phytosanitary treatment shall be took place prior importing.

Article 22 Inspection formalities of imported plant quarantine materials are as follows:

1. Any physical or juridical person who import plant shall informs to the plant quarantine check point ten days (10 days) before arrival of materials.

2. In arrival to the first point of border's entry, owner of plant quarantine materials must declare and apply for inspection. The plant quarantine check point shall indicate concretely the proper place for plant quarantine inspection.

The declaration, inspection, and phytosanitary treatment are carried out in compliance with Art. 9, 10, and 14 of this sub – decree. It shall be lawful procedure in case of sending back to exporting country or destroying the plant quarantine materials. When mean of transport of plant quarantine materials arrives at Cambodia territorial water, the owner shall declare to the nearest plant quarantine check point for inspection. The mean of transport could ashore only after phytosanitary inspection and getting the permission from Plant Quarantine Authority.

Article 23 The plant quarantine authority is empowered to inspect advice and monitor the transportation, stock, distribution and use of plant quarantine materials since they are brought into the territory of the Kingdom of Cambodia. In case of plant quarantine or dangerous pests invade any places, plant quarantine authority shall take adequate and appropriate measure to control and eliminate them immediately.

Chapter V Plant quarantine for export

Article 24 The inspection of exporting plant quarantine materials shall be conducted based on conditions prescribed in Commercial Contract, Agreement, Convention and other documents concerning phytosanitary conditions of country – importer.

Article 25 The condition for exporting plant quarantine material is as follows:

1. The owner of exported plant quarantine materials shall requests to Plant Quarantine Authority for inspection and issuing the phytosanitary certificate.

2. The Plant Quarantine materials must be in compliance with phytosanitary condition of country – importer which prescribed in commercial contract, agreement, convention and other concerned documents.

Article 26 The inspection formalities of exporting plant quarantine materials shall be conducted in compliance with condition prescribed in the Article 9, Article 10 and Article 14 of this sub – decree.

Chapter Ⅵ Plant quarantine for transits

Article 27 Plant quarantine materials bringing in transits through territory of the kingdom of Cambodia must be:

accompanied with a phytosatary certificate issued by country – exporter, Pack the materials in good package and load in container, which could avoid leakage or spillage the materials while being transported, The mean of transport must be free from plant quarantine or dangerous pests, which could be spread out along the way of transit.

Article 28 Phytosanitary inspection formalities for transit are as follows:

Owner must informs to the nearest plant quarantine check point before their materials are reached to point of entry to and exit from Plant Quarantine Authority must inspect the means of transport and observe outer of mass of materials, examine the phytosanitary certificate issued by country exporter and must facilitate the transportation to be continued respectively.

Article 29 The Plant Quarantine Authority shall conduct the phytosanitary treatment at point of entry before permitting the transportation to be continued; in case of the plant quarantine materials are not in compliance with the conditions prescribed in Article 27 of this Sub – Degree.

In case of accident while transporting and the packaging materials are broken that are likely to spread out the plant quarantine materials, the owner shall immediately declare to the nearest Plant Quarantine Authority or local Authority. The Plant Quarantine Authority shall immediately conduct Phytosanitary Treatment, issue the phytosanitary certificate for re – export and allow the transportation to be continued.

Charter Ⅶ Authority of plant quarantine officer

Article 30 The Plant Quarantine officer has authorized as follows:

Conduct the phytosanitary inspection and treatment on mean of transport and plant quarantine materials in storage, factories, agricultural production area or farms.

Prepare the record and report on violation for submitting to the court.

The owner of the above asset shall permit the plant quarantine officer to inspect their materials and shall cooperate in providing information.

Article 31 Local Governor or Authorities shall provide their forces to cooperate with Plant Quarantine Authority, according to their request.

Chapter Ⅷ Penalty provision

Article 32 It shall not allow to import, export or transit transport of plant quarantine materials which commits any of the following wrongful acts:

Fails to plant quarantine procedure prescribed in Article 8, excluded point 4 or Article 30 paragraph 1 of this Sub – Decree,

Not complied with the phytosanitary requirement of importing country or not follows the phytosanitary treatment, prescribed in Article 10 of this Sub – Decree.

Not follows the conditions prescribed in Article 21, 26 or 28 of this Sub – decree.

Article 33 It shall be fined assisting to Article 62, charter 7 of Law on the Management of Quality and Safety of Products and Services to any person, who:

Fails to plant quarantine procedure prescribed in Article 8, point 4 of this Sub – Decree,

Violates to Article 13 paragraph 2 or Article 18 paragraph 2 or Article 19 or Article 22 paragraph 2 or 3 of this Sub – Decree.

Article 34 Any person who repeats the same kind of wrongful act prescribed in Article 18 paragraph 2 or Article 19 or Article 22 paragraph 3 of this Sub – Decree, shall be fined in double, excluding the criminal fault.

In case of wrongful act were distributed the plant quarantine or dangerous pests, the failed person should paid for the elimination the above problems according to the estimation by Minister of Agriculture Forestry and Fisheries.

Article 35 It shall be fined assisting to Article 63, charter 7 of Law on the Management of Quality and Safety of Products and Services to any person, who:

a. Make any condition, that Phytosanitary officer as mentioned in Article 3 of this Sub – decree can not implement their duties.

b. Denise to show related document or want to give not true information or to make confuse on transportation plant quarantine material;

c. Organize by not permission of plant quarantine material that has temporary confiscate by phytosanitary inspection;

d. Transport plant quarantine material to escape from plant quarantine check points in purpose avoiding phytosanitary inspection.

Article 36 Any person who rules out the fine, his/ her fault shall be submitted to a competent court of law.

The rewarded to encourage the officer and the expenditure for this mission will be defined by PRACAS of Minister of Agriculture Forestry and Fisheries and Minister of Economic and Finance.

Chapter Ⅸ Final provision

Article 37 Sub – Decree 98 GnRk, dated 08 October 1983 on phytosanitary inspection on importing and exporting plant product and other previous provisions which are contradictory to this Sub – Decree shall be repealed.

Article 38 Minister of minister's council; Minister of Ministry of Agriculture Forestry and Fisheries; Ministers and Secretaries of State of all Ministries and Authorities concerned shall implements this Sub – Decree upon signing.

Phnom Penh, 13 March 2003

Prime Minister

柬埔寨动物和动物产品卫生检疫法

（2002 年 6 月 11 日起草 柬埔寨皇家政府制定）

第一章 总 则

第一条 目的 在动物生产和运输过程中使用本法，使用兽医监测手段，在国内外运输动物及动物产品时预防疾病在动物及动物产品和人类之间相互传播，保障动物和人民健康。

第二条 重要条款的使用及上下条款间的关系由附件解释。

第三条 农林渔业部对动物及动物产品的卫生检疫负责，三部委授权动物健康和生产局具体实施。

第四条 所有柬埔寨王国出口或境内运输的产品必须申请检疫并遵循兽医监测准则。

第二章 动物和动物产品的卫生检疫

第五条 农林渔业部必须在铁路、口岸、陆路口岸、空港、国境线及所有需要的地方设置卫生检疫点。

所有检疫点必须配备充足的设施装备以确保动物和动物产品卫生检疫的有效实施，所有检疫点接受动物健康和生产局的直接监督。

第六条 农林渔业部要在第五条所说的地点设立检疫点。

第七条 动物和动物产品的卫生检疫必须遵守各国家的相应法律。

第八条 卫生检疫包括的对象：所有品种的动物、动物产品及饲料、动物运输工具、运输场地和生产的原材料及设备。

第九条 接受动物和动物产品卫生检疫的物主应符合以下法定程序：

——准备合适的货物清单；

——获得卫生许可证；

——向卫生检疫部门提供运输许可证；

——确保运输及运输场地、包装材料和设备的质量、安全和卫生状况达标；

——货物的运输和保管需在卫生检疫部门指定地点；

——为卫生检疫部门采样提供方便；

——货物不能按时运输时需预先得到卫生检疫部门的许可。

第十条 货物进出口需提前 15 天向卫生检疫部门提出检疫申请。

货物一旦到达检疫站，货主需通知检疫部门实施检查确认，货主需在货物到达边境检疫站之前提前通知，以方便检疫部门实施检查。

第十一条 所有因动物和动物产品提出卫生检疫申请的个人或法人需交纳相应税费，税费由动物健康和生产负责部门收缴后上缴国家财政。税费的制定由国家农林渔业部宣布的条例决定。

第十二条 以下代表或法人有权向就近的卫生检疫部门发出通知：

a. 装载需检疫的动物或动物产品的船、舟、艇等，因漏水或抛锚而进入柬埔寨王国境内；

b. 装载有需检疫货物的飞机在柬埔寨王国境内坠毁。

第十三条 动物和动物产品卫生检疫人员执行任务时需穿着农林渔业部门认可的统一的制服、佩带证明身份的标志、携带有效证件。

农林渔业部应该制定出其他的条例和细则对制服、身份证明标志及检疫程序的细节作出规定，确保此法能在柬埔寨境内有效、透明、公正的实施。

第三章 国内动物和动物产品的卫生检疫

第十四条 柬埔寨王国内发现疾病病原体或疾病在一定地区的流行，农林渔业部委负责宣布疫区、提供处理方法。期间，所有相关动物的买卖、相关动物和动物产品的进出口及经过境内的运输必须禁止，直到农林渔业部出台新的条例。

第十五条 a. 要求动物健康状况良好，不来自或经过疫区，按照动物健康和生产管理部门的建议进行免疫；

b. 动物的生产和饲养应按后面的相应规定讲究科学，遵守卫生原则；

c. 运输完成后，动物生产设备、场地、材料等需消毒处理。

第十六条 农林渔业部应制定条例对国内动物和动物产品的卫生检疫程序作出规定。

第四章 进口动物和动物产品的卫生检疫

第十七条 进口动物和动物产品的卫生检疫程序如下：

——所有进口动物、动物产品和饲料的业主和法人需在货物到达前 5 天通知检疫部门；

——在货物到达边境检疫站时业主向检疫部门提出检疫申请。动物和动物产品卫生检疫站要求具备相应的技术以实施检疫处理；

受卫生检疫管理的货物业主，如通过水陆运输，一旦货物抵达柬埔寨王国港口，需就近向卫生检疫站报告并申请检疫。只有经过卫生检疫站检疫处理并得到许可的船只才允许在港口停留。

第十八条 检查应参照后面的传染病名录，尤其是禁止进口的有传染病的动物和动物产品名录。

传染病情名录由农林渔业部出台其他的条理和细则规定。农林渔业部保留名录的制定权，制定后的条款在公布后 30 天内生效。在必要或紧急情况，爆发疫情时，制定公布后24 小时生效。

第十九条 所有运输动物和动物产品进入柬埔寨王国的个人和法人应遵守以下条款：

——应得到出口国的卫生检疫许可证；

——应遵守本法的第九条（除了第六款）、第十条、第十一条。

第二十条 对于所有不符合相关贸易条款、MOU、议会及其他柬埔寨王国法规或者没有相应许可证的动物及动物产品，动物及动物产品卫生检疫部门应实施以下处理：

——遣返回原产地；

——改变物品用途；

——转移动物及动物产品到动物及动物产品卫生检疫部门指定的地点；

——将动物隔离在指定的检疫地点，进行检查、确诊、治疗、免疫或消毒；

——销毁。

关于遣返或销毁的处理由农林渔业部负责。

关于治疗、免疫、消毒、留养或销毁的费用，由物主或其代理支付全部照看费用及服务等其他费用。

第五章 动物及动物产品的出口卫生检疫

第二十一条 出口的物品应经过本法令第十五条所规定的全部兽医卫生检疫技术检查。

第二十二条 从柬埔寨王国出口的全部货物应在原产地或动物隔离检疫场所进行卫生检疫处理。

货物应符合贸易协议、MOU 中的条款及相应出口国要求的惯例。

第二十三条 任何从事动物或动物产品出口贸易的个人或法人代表应遵守本法令第九条、第十条、第十一条的规定。

第二十四条 当出口卫生检疫要求检疫的货物被发现有传染病症状时，当地动物及动物产品卫生检疫站应临时停止兽医检测，并立即向动物健康和生产局报告，请求农林渔业部的鉴定。

第六章 动物和动物产品的过境卫生检疫

第二十五条 所有运输动物和动物产品从柬埔寨王国过境的个人或法人代表应遵守以下条款：

——应得到出口国家的卫生许可证；

——应遵守本法令第九条（除了第六款）；

——不允许拆开安全封条；

——运输过程不允许造成传染原对运输路程的污染。

第二十六条 动物和动物产品的过境卫生检疫程序如下：

——在货物到达或离开边境检疫站时，货主应提前通知检疫点的卫生检疫部门；

——动物及动物产品卫生检疫部门应检查装载动物产品的交通工具的外观、动物健康和输出国的许可证，并为货物的及时过境提供方便。

第二十七条 不符合贸易协议、MOU、议会及其他动物及动物产品卫生检疫法令条款规定的货物按照本法令第二十条规定处理。

凡是即将到达国境的货物在运输中发生损伤、包装泄露或者对动物造成伤害的情况，货主应立即向卫生检疫当局、公社，当地政府或最近的部门报告。动物及动物产品卫生检疫部门应实施检查和兽医检测。

第七章 动物及动物产品卫生检疫部门的权利和职责

第二十八条 动物及动物产品卫生检疫部门的权利和职责如下：

——在仓库、工厂或检疫站对所有列入卫生检疫对象的动物和动物产品进行卫生检查和兽医手段的检测；

——文件管理、记录案例并在需要时向法庭提交文件及案例记录。

以上提及的固定资产所有者或管理者应认可动物及动物产品卫生检疫部门检查，必要时协助提供相关信息。

第二十九条 农林渔业部应出台其他的规定和细则明确动物及动物健康和生产管理局在案例处理时的权利和职责。

公社及政府管理部门和军队应按卫生检疫部门的要求给予配合，完成动物和动物产品的卫生检查工作。

第八章 处 罚

第三十一条 任何人违反本法令第九条第一款、第三款、第五款、第六款、第七款规定，处以货物价值总额的1% ~2% 罚款，若是重犯，罚款加倍。

第三十二条 任何人违反本法令第九条第四款，第十一条，处以货物价值总额的3% ~5% 罚款，若是重犯，罚款加倍。

第三十三条 任何人违反本法令第九条第二款，第十九条第一款，第二十五条第一款，处以货物价值总额的10% ~15% 罚款，若是重犯，罚款加倍。

第三十四条 任何人违反本法令第十四条第二点，处以货物价值总额的15% ~20% 罚款，并加应用本法令第二十条规定处置；若是重犯，罚款加倍。

第三十五条 拒交罚款的将上交法庭处理。罚款所得资金70% 上缴国家财政，其余30% 用于奖励有突出贡献的个人及其他公务开支。

第三十六条 若因动物及动物产品卫生检疫部门官员在货物检查中玩忽职守，将给予行政处罚。

凡造成动物损害或引起疾病传播的，将按相应法律追究责任。

第三十七条 任何逃税、逃避罚款、明知故犯、骄傲自满或者滥用职权满足个人兴趣爱好的人将受到刑法处治。

第九章 附 则

第三十八条 1988 年 7 月 29 日发布的 14/ANK 号关于动物及动物产品卫生检疫的法令及其他相关条款与本法令相抵触的同时废止。

第三十九条 自签发之日起，国务院总理、农林渔业部各部长、秘书、各级政府均应依照本法行事。

Sub – Decree on sanitary inspection of animal and animal products the royal government of cambodia

KINGDOM OF CAMBODIA Nation Religion King

DRAFT (Draft dated 11 June 2002)

Chapter Ⅰ: General provisions

Article 1: This Sub – decree aims at preventing the spread of animal diseases in order to the animal health and public health with the implementation of veterinary measure on the movement of animal and animal products from a region to others, in the country, from the country, transit, or within the country through all disease transmission means from animal or animal products to animal, human or from human to animal.

Article 2: The important terms used and the context of this Sub – decree shall explain in the Annex of this Sub – decree.

Article 3: The Ministry of Agriculture, Forestry and Fisheries has a responsible obligation to implement the animal and animal products sanitary control with its delegation of authority to Department of Animal Health and Production for implementing the animal and animal products sanitary inspection.

Article 4: All exports or transport of the products objected to sanitary inspection into, from and transit in the Kingdom of Cambodia shall request for inspection and shall obey to all veterinary measures.

Chapter Ⅱ: The sanitary inspection of animal and animal products

Article 5: The Ministry of Agriculture, forestry and fisheries shall establish the sanitary check point for animal and animal products in railway station, port, dry port, airport, international border, and in other places as necessary.

The checkpoint of sanitary inspection for animal and animal products shall be equipped with adequate technical equipment in order to ensure its effective operation for animal and animal products inspection.

The checkpoint of sanitary inspection for animal and animal products shall be under the direct supervision of the Department of Animal Health and Production.

Article 6: The Ministry of Agriculture, Forestry and Fisheries shall establish the animal quarantine at the places mentioning in Article 5.

Article 7: The sanitary inspection of animal and animal products shall be processed following the sanitary conditions for animal and animal products of each country.

Article 8: Goods objected to the sanitary inspection consist:

—All animal species;

—Animal products and animal feed;

—Mean of transport, premises, animal production equipment and processing materials and equipment.

Article 9: The owner of good objected to the sanitary inspection for animal and animal products shall subject to the following legal process:

—Prepare an appropriate invoice of good;

—Obtain the sanitary certificate;

—Shall present the transportation permit to the sanitary inspection officer;

—Shall ensuring the quality, safety, and sanitary status of transport and premises, packaging materials and equipment;

—Shall transport and place the goods at places assigned by the sanitary inspection officer;

—Shall facilitate the sanitary inspector officer for collecting samples;

—Shall in advance seek the permission from the sanitary inspection officer in case good is transported not within the date specified.

Article 10: Within 15 days prior good exported imported, the owner shall submit the request application for sanitary inspection.

When good arrives at the international checkpoint, the owner shall inform to the checkpoint for inspection and verification.

Prior to arrival of good at the border checkpoint, the owner shall inform to the sanitary inspection unit and shall facilitate the inspection.

Article 11: Any person or legal person who make the request for sanitary inspection for animal and animal products shall pay the animal and animal products sanitary duty. This duty fee shall be payable to the national treasure via the animal health and production authority. The duty fee of animal and animal products shall be decided by the Prakas of the Ministry of Agriculture, Forestry and Fisheries.

Article 12: The representative or legal person has the right to inform to the closest sanitary authority in case he/she witnesses:

a. Ship, canoe, boat or other transportation means in which loading the goods subjected to the animal and animal product sanitary inspection, leak or broken down pushing into the territory of the Kingdom of Cambodia;

b. Good subjected to the sanitary inspection in the air plane crashing in the territory of the Kingdom of Cambodia.

Article 13: During operation, the authority of animal and animal products sanitary inspection shall dress the uniform, identification sign and hold the mission permit issued by the Ministry of Agriculture, Forestry and Fisheries.

The ministry of Agriculture, Forestry and Fisheries shall issue Prakas on the uniform, identification sign and sanitary inspection procedures, including other Prakas or Guidelines in order to implement this Sub - decree effectively, transparency and no discrimination through out the Kingdom of Cambodia.

Chapter Ⅲ: The domestical sanitary inspection of animal and animal products

Article 14: When there is disease antigen source or spreading of disease in a region of the Kingdom of Cambodia, the Ministry of Agriculture, Forestry and Fisheries shall declare the epidemic region and provide immediate measure.

The purchase and sale of animal and transport of animal and animal products into, from or transit that region shall be temporarily prohibited until there is new Prakas of the Ministry of Agriculture, forestry and Fisheries.

Article 15

a. Animal shall have good health, taking from non - epidemic area or having not taken via epidemic area and receiving the vaccination following the recommendation of the authority of animal health and production;

b. Animal products and animal feed shall be appropriately packed following technical and sanitary guidelines;

c. Means of transport, animal production equipment, premises, or processing materials shall be disinfected prior and after transported.

Article 16: The procedures of domestic sanitary inspection of animal and animal products shall be specified by the Prakas of the Ministry of Agriculture, forestry and Fisheries.

Chapter Ⅳ: The import sanitary inspection of animal and animal products

Article 17: The procedures of import sanitary inspection of animal and animal products shall mention as the followings:

—The owner or legal person who imports animal, animal products and animal feed shall inform to the inspection authority for at least 5 days prior arrival of good;

—Upon the arrival of good at the border checkpoint, the owner of good objected to inspection shall report and request for inspection. The sanitary inspection checkpoint for animal and animal products shall acquire appropriate technical requirement for processing inspection.

The owner of goods subjected to the sanitary inspection, transported by waterway, once the goods arrive the port of the Kingdom of Cambodia shall report to the closest sanitary inspection checkpoint and request for inspection. The mean of transport is allowed to stand by at the port only it is permitted from the sanitary inspection checkpoint after the inspection was processed.

Article 18: The inspection on imported goods objected to the sanitary inspection of animal and animal products shall be implemented following the infectious disease list. Prohibit the importation of animal or animal products that contain infectious disease agents specified in the infectious disease list.

The infectious disease list shall be declared by Prakas of the Ministry of Agriculture, Forestry and Fisheries. The Ministry of Agriculture, Forestry and Fisheries reserve its right for editing the list of infectious disease as necessary. The change/editing shall be effective after its publicity within 30 days. In a necessary case and emergency when there is a disease outbreak the editing shall decline its limits to 24 hours effective after its publicity.

Article 19: A person or legal person who transport animal and animal products into the Kingdom of Cambodia shall commit to the following implementations:

—Shall obtain the sanitary certificate issued by the exported country;

—Shall obey to the Article 9 (except the para 6), Article 10 and Article 11 of this Sub-decree.

Article 20: Animal and animal products which don not meet the criteria mentioned in trade agreement, MOU, convention, and other conditions of the Kingdom of Cambodia or have inappropriate certificate, the authority of sanitary inspection for animal and animal products shall apply the following measures:

—Shall send good to its original country;

—Shall redirect the use of good;

—Shall move of place good in the place assigned by the authority of sanitary inspection for animal and animal products;

—Shall keep animal in the quarantine place for investigation, confirming diagnosis, treatment, vaccination or disinfection;

—Shall destroy.

In case of destruction or sending good back to its original country, one shall request the principle measure from the Ministry of Agriculture, Forestry and Fisheries.

In case animals are kept for treatment, vaccination, disinfectant, holding, or destruction the owner or representative shall be responsible in all cost for animal care, other expenditure, and services.

Chapter Ⅴ: The export sanitary inspection of animal and animal products

Article 21: Good exported shall pass all veterinary technical sanitary inspection process as mention in the Article 15 of this Sub - decree.

Article 22: Exportation of good from the Kingdom of Cambodia shall process the sanitary inspection at the original place or at the animal Quarantine.

Good must appropriately meet the condition mentioning in trade agreement, MOU, convention and other conditions required by the imported countries.

Article 23: Any person or legal representative who transport animal or animal products abroad shall implement following the Article 9, Article 10, and Article 11 of this Sub - decree.

Article 24: Good subjected to the sanitary inspection for export, when it is found with the infectious disease sign, the authority of sanitary inspection for animal and animal products at that given check - point shall temporarily stop that good for a veterinary measure. For this temporary holding, the authority of sanitary inspection for animal and animal products shall immediately report to the Department of Animal Health and Production in order to request the measure from the Ministry of Agriculture, Forestry and fisheries.

Chapter Ⅵ: The transit sanitary inspection of animal and animal products

Article 25: Any person or legal representative who transport animal and animal products through the Kingdom of Cambodia shall respect to the following conditions:

—Shall obtain the sanitary certificate issued by the exported country;

—Shall obey to the Article 9 (except the para 6) of this Sub - decree;

—Shall not open the safety seal;

—All means of transport shall not contaminate with the infectious agents that can spread on the way the good is transported.

Article 26: The procedures of transit sanitary inspection of animal and animal products shall mention as the followings:

—The owner shall inform to authority of sanitary inspection at the checkpoint prior the good arriving at the entrance and exit border checkpoints.

—The authority of sanitary inspection for animal and animal products shall inspect the appearance means of transport for animal products, animal health and certificate of exported countries and shall facilitate timely transport of good.

Article 27: Good conditionally inappropriate as mentioning in trade agreement, MOU, convention, and other documents on sanitary of animal and animal products shall be applied the context in the Article 20 for this Sub - decree.

In case unpredicted accidence occurs during the transportation causing damage or disclose of packaging materials or harm to animal, the owner shall report immediately to the sanitary inspector authority, commune, district administration unit, or closest local authority. The sanitary inspection authority for animal and animal products shall inspect and apply the veterinary measures.

Chapter Ⅶ: The right and authority of the sanitary inspector for animal and animal products

Article 28: The sanitary inspection officers for animal and animal products has the following right and authority:

—Inspect animal and animal products sanitary and apply the veterinary measures on all transport means and good objected to the sanitary inspection for animal and animal products in the warehouse, factory, or station;

—Document, minute of case and submit the document, minute of case to the court house;

The owner or holder of the fixed asset mentioned above shall allow the sanitary inspection officer to inspect and shall cooperate in providing information to the sanitary inspection officers for animal and animal products.

Article 29: The Ministry of Agriculture, Forestry and Fisheries shall issue the Prakas defining the authority and the right for handling cases for the authority of animal health and production.

Article 30: The district, commune administration and local authority or army shall cooperate in execution of the animal and animal product sanitary inspection following the request from the sanitary inspection authority.

Chapter Ⅷ: Penalties

Article 31: Any person who fails to obey the Article 9, para 1, 3, 5, 6, 7 shall be entitled to the fine from one percent (1%) to two percent (2%) of the value of objective good; in case the false is repeated it shall be fined double.

Article 32: Any person who fails to obey the Article 9, para 4 and Article 11 shall be entitled to the fine from three percent (3%) to five percent (5%) of the value of the objective good; in case the false is repeated it shall be fined double.

Article 33: Any person who fails to obey the Article 9, para 2, Article 19, para 1, Article 25, para 1 shall be fined from ten percent (10%) to fifteen percent (15%) of the value of objective good; in case the false is repeated it shall be fined double.

Article 34: Any person who fails to obey the Article 14, para 2 shall be fined from fifteen percent (15%) to twenty percent (20%) of the value of objective good and shall be additionally applied with Article 20; in case the false is repeated it shall be fined double.

Article 35: If the fine is not paid, the document shall be filed to the court. The fee collecting from fine shall be allocated seventy percent (70%) for the National Treasury; and other thirty percent (30%) is allocated for incentive award to the outstanding person and other expenses for this mission.

Article 36: During the official operation, if the sanitary inspection officer for animal and animal product is careless, lack of responsibility in inspecting good, he/she shall be committed to the administration penalty.

If the carelessness causes damage to animal or results in disease spreading from region to another, the officer shall be subjected to the additional social law.

Article 37: Any person who cheats the duty, penalty fee, regulated misconduct, receives pride, offer pride or using the authority for own interest, a person shall be subjected to the criminal law.

Chapter Ⅸ: Final provisions

Article 38: The Sub – decree No. 14/ANK dated 29 July 1988 on the Sanitary Inspection of Animal and Animal Products and other regulations which have different context and meaning of this Sub – decree shall be abrogated.

Article 39: The Minister in charge of the Council Minister, Ministry of Agriculture, Forestry and Fisheries, Ministers, under Secretary of State of all Ministries, Institutions shall be responsible for implementation of this Sub – decree at their capacity from the date of signature.

马来西亚

植物检疫法

（马来西亚法律 167 号法）

1994 年 6 月

本法旨在修订和强化与农业害虫、恶性杂草和植物病害的控制、预防和根除有关的法律，旨在对控制有害生物随国际间的货物贸易而传播方面扩大合作。

本法由 Dewan Negara and Dewan Rakyat 在议会中提议和同意，经 the Duli Yang Maha Mulia Seri Paduka Baginda Yang di Pertuan Agong 通过并颁布，文本如下：

1. （1） 本法可被引述为《植物检疫法 1976》

（2） 本法适用于马来西亚全境。

2. 除非本法文本另有规定，否则本法所指—

有益生物　　指对农业生产有益，不会对植物造成危害的任何无脊椎动物（包括此类动物的卵）、真菌、细菌、病毒及其他生物体。

构成地区　　指本法实施地区包括西马来西亚地区，拉布安岛联邦，沙巴州，沙捞越州。

有害生物　　指为本法的实施，部长通过公报宣布其在马来西亚全境或部分地区为危险性有害生物的任何有害生物。

假如有害生物涉及沙巴州或涉及沙捞越州或同时涉及此两州时，部长在作出有害生物公告前，须根据不同的情况，事先与沙巴州或/和沙捞越州主管或负责农业的州部长磋商。

局长　　指西马来西亚农业总局局长，其职责扩及拉布安岛联邦，沙巴州农业局局长和沙捞越州农业局局长职责仅限于各自相应州。

染疫的　　指被任何有害生物侵染的。

进境　　由其语法变体和同源表达，指经陆、海、空由构成地区外的地方带进或造成带进构成地区的任何地区。

检查官员　　指经第 3 条（3）款任命的检查官员。

隔离　　指为第 10 条的目的并以该条规定的方法对任何土地的隔离。

土地　　包括：

（a） 陆地表面和构成地表的全部物质；

（b） 地表下的土壤和其内的全部物质；

（c） 全部的植物和其他自然产品，不管其生产是否需要周期性的劳动投入，也不管其是在地表或在地下；

（d） 附着于土壤的所有物体，或恒定地固着于前者的全部物体，不管其是在地表或地下；

（e） 被水淹没的土地。

部长　　指主管农业有害生物和有害植物的根除以及植物病害预防的部长。

有害植物　　指为本法的实施，部长通过公报宣布其为马来西亚全境或部分地区有害植物的任何植物，包括此类植物的种子和各部分器官当公报宣布的有害植物涉及沙巴州或涉及沙捞越州或同时涉及此两州时，部长在作出恶性杂草公报宣布前，须根据不同的情况，事先与沙巴州或沙捞越州负责农业的部长或这两个州部长磋商。

占用人　　包括承租人、租户、耕作者，以及对任何土地具有实际拥有、经营或控制的个人。

土地所有者　　指按相应的构成地区土地法，现时已登记为土地业主的任何个人，也包括沙捞越州按原住民的习俗拥有土地的任何土地拥有者。

有害生物 指任何对植物有害或能对植物造成危害的脊椎动物和无脊椎动物（包括此类动物的卵）、真菌、细菌、病毒、类病毒、类菌原体（MLO）、杂草、以及其他生物，也包括所有的危险性有害生物。

植物 指所有的植物种类，以及来自植物体的具有或不具有生命力的任何部分，包括茎、枝、块茎、球茎、鳞茎、砧木、接穗、插条、压条、分蘖、吸根、根、叶、花、果、种子，以及源自植株的与植株分离或不分离的其他部分和其他产品，而已经热处理和干燥处理的植物产品除外。

土壤 指植物生长的泥土或其他自然形成的有机物和无机物质。

3. （1）各局长仅对本法在其各自构成地区的贯彻或实施实行全面监督，本法授予局长的权力应被理解为与本条本款一致：各局长在执行第 19 条授予的相应职责时，其权力不受本条本款的约束，可超越局长所在的构成地区行使权力。

（2）各局长除了本法授予的权力外，还具有本法授予检查官员在其相应构成地区的所有权力。

（3）为使本法在相应构成地区得以贯彻或实施，局长任命各自相应地区的农业官员为该地区的检查官员，本法授予检查官员的权力应被理解为与本条本款一致：检查官员在执行第 19 条授予的相应职责时，其权力不受本条本款的约束，可超越检查官员所在的构成地区行使权力。

4. 每一个局长和检查官员在本法规定的权力和职责范围内行事时，应被视为相应构成地区刑法典意义上的公务人员。

5. （1）为下述目的，一个检查官员，不管有或无随行的助手、带或不带设备或者其他物件，在所有适当的时期，可进入任何土地并在其内停留必要的时间：

（a）为了检查相应的土地和其上的植物，以证实有害植物或有害生物是否存在，或者证实土地或其上的植物是否处于有利于有害植物或有害生物发生或传播的状态；以及

（b）为了检查或调查，检查官员认为必要时，可采用任何方式移动任何植物。

（2）相应土地的所有者或占用人，应该允许每一个检查官员为本条第（1）款所规定的目的而进行的检查，应向检查官员提供所有信息，同时为检查官员提供必要的邦助。

6. （1）检查官员鉴于对土地或植物的检查结果，如发现植物感染病害并且会对其他植物造成危害，检查官员必须对土地的所有者或占用人送达手签的书面通知，指示土地的所有者或占用人在书面通知所限定的时间内，采取检查官员认为必要的或适当的措施，以根除或防止有害生物的扩散。需采取的措施须在书面通知中加以具体限定，包括销毁、移除或以特定的方法处理有问题的植物、其他植物、有害生物、土地上的农具和设施。

（2）检查官员鉴于对土地或植物的检查结果，如发现土地或植物处于有利于有害生物发生或传播的状态，检查官员必须对土地的所有者或占用人送达手签的书面通知，指示土地的所有者或占用人在书面通知所限定的时间内，采取检查官员认为必要的或适当的措施，以根除或防止有害生物的扩散。需采取的措施须在书面通知中加以具体限定，包括销毁、移除或以特定的方法处理有问题的植物、其他植物、有害生物、土地上的农具和设施，以将土地或植物处于不利于有害生物发生或传播的状态。

（3）因本条第（1）款和第（2）款而采取的各项措施产生的费用由相应土地的所有者或占用人支付。

（4）本条第（1）和第（2）款中的所有书面通知，自其签发之日起，应当具体载明不少于 7 天的期限，在此期限内，土地的所有者或占用人可以用书面形式向下述机构申诉：

（a）当书面通知涉及的土地隶属西马来西亚时，可以书面形式向相应州的州务大臣或首席部长申诉；或

（b）当书面通知涉及的土地隶属沙巴州时，可以书面形式向沙巴州负责该州农业的州部长申诉；或

（c）当书面通知涉及的土地隶属沙捞越州时，可以书面形式向沙捞越州负责该州农业的州部长

申诉。

（5）对本条第（4）款的申诉，西马来西亚各州的州务大臣或首席部长以及沙巴州、沙捞越州负责相应州农业的州部长，就相应的书面通知，可以作出支持、中止、撤销相应通知的决定，也可作出其他合适的决定。

7.（1）对第6条或第12条第（1）款送达的书面通知，以第6条第（5）款的决定为条件，如果土地的所有者或占用人不能在书面通知规定的时间内履行书面通知的要求，检查官员可带必要的人员、设备和物件进入相应的土地，可以实施书面通知要求的事项，并通过法院从相应的土地所有者或占用人获得由此而产生的所有开支。

（2）本条不影响第8条或第13条规定的个人起诉权和处罚权。

8.（1）任何土地的所有者或占用人，对第6条送达的书面通知，如果不能在该通知规定的时间内履行其要求，即构成犯罪，可被判处不超过10,000令吉的罚款。当出现书面通知被西马来西亚各州的州务大臣或首席部长以及沙巴州、沙捞越州负责相应州农业的州部长按第6条第（5）款的规定，作出中止或撤销的情况时，则本条不追究书面通知的要求被中止或撤销时起的不履行罪。

（2）当西马来西亚各州的州务大臣或首席部长以及沙巴州、沙捞越州负责相应州农业的州部长按第6条第（5）款的规定，对书面通知作出变更，则变更了的书面通知适用于本条和第7条，亦适用于第6条。

9.（1）法院依照第8条、第11条或第13条款对罪犯定罪时，除了执行罚金外，可采取其认为必要的措施，如对罪犯判处一定时间的关押，以防止同罪行的重现。

（2）罪犯如不履行本条第（1）款的判处，则构成犯罪，并可能因其罪行的延续被判处每天不超过50令吉的罚款，另加按第8条、第11条或第13条规定的相应处罚。

10.（1）只要局长提出认为土地上有任何植物染疫的通知，西马来西亚各州的州务大臣或首席部长以及沙巴州、沙捞越州负责相应州农业的州部长，可对相应土地的全部或部分作出隔离令，此隔离令需述明隔离的期限；当对隔离令作修改或解除时，有关部长亦应倾听局长的意见和建议。

（2）无适当理由，任何人不得进入或离开本条第（1）款隔离的土地。除非得到检查官员的指示，否则不得将任何物品带离所隔离的土地。

（3）经本条第（1）款隔离的土地，其所有者或占用人为了获得对隔离令的修改或解除，可以向检查官员提出申请，要求其对被隔离的土地进行检查。检查官员应当在接到申请后的7天内，到相应土地进行检查，并将检查的结果和建议提交局长，局长再视情况相商有关州务大臣，首席部长。

（4）任何人蓄意地或无适当理由违反本条第（2）款的规定，则构成犯罪并被处以不超过2,000令吉的罚款。

11.（1）土地上一旦发现或出现危险性有害生物或植物被危险性有害生物危害的情况，相应土地的所有者或占用人应当：

（a）一经发现上述情况，需立即以书面或其他形式将其有关详细情况报告局长或检查官员；

（b）有效实施检查官员为消灭危险性有害生物或被有害生物侵染的植物而对其发出的所有指令；

（c）尽其所能对检查官员为消灭危险性有害生物的行动提供帮助。

（2）任何人违犯本条第（1）款即构成犯罪，并可被处不超过10,000令吉的罚款。

（3）收到本条（1）款（a）项有关通知的检查官员，须将相关通知转知局长。

12.（1）在其相应州的土地内，西马来西亚各州的州务大臣或其首席部长以及沙巴州、沙捞越州负责相应州农业的州部长，当认为需对被危险性有害生物侵染的植物或此类生物的易感植物采取实施根除、销毁或处理的措施时，或局长所在构成地区、其他构成地区或马来西亚境外植物上的有害生物，危及局长所在构成地区植物的生长安全，并认为其构成地区的土地全部或部分清空所有植物、部分植物或特定种类的植物，对防止有害生物的扩散是必要时，或需对相应土地上的植物实施根除、销毁或处理时，上述州务大臣或首席部长、负责相应州农业的州部长、或在某些情况下的局长，应该即刻对相关土地的所有者或占用人送达书面通知，要求他们中的一方或两方在通知所限定的时间内，对植物予以根除、销毁或处理，或对土地实施清空的措施。

（2）当西马来西亚各州的州务大臣或其首席部长以及沙巴州、沙捞越州负责相应州农业的州部长或各构成地区的局长认为本条第（1）款的指导性措施不能确保植物的安全时，上述官员应该即刻指派检查官员或其他人员进入相应土地，这些被指派的人员可带必要的随行助手、必要的设备或者其他物件，以采取或迫使采取特定的措施以根除、销毁或控制有害生物，或无论是否存在危险性有害生物，均对植物予以处理、或对土地上的特定植物实施清除。

（3）本条第（1）款和第（2）款之根除、销毁、控制、处理和清除的费用和所有支出均由相应土地的所有者或占用人支付，若是由土地所有者或占用人之外的他人垫支时，土地所有者或占用人应补偿其有关开支。

13.（1）除本条第（2）款的情况外，土地的所有者、占用人或其他人，无权取得因履行本法而产生的开支或引起的损失的赔偿权利，除非此损失系因为故意的玩忽职守行为造成。

（2）作为预防措施，当土地的所有者或占用人被要求对其土地上未染疫的植物进行销毁而造成的损失，局长可酌情对其给予适当的赔偿。

（3）赔偿的申请必须是书面形式，并须在要求销毁植物的相关通知发出之日起的三个月内送达局长办公室，否则赔偿的申请不予受理。同时，赔偿不得超过销毁植物的相关通知发出时植物的实际价值。

（4）植物价值方面的任何异议，应咨询负责土地收益的官员，并由该官员依照植物所在构成地区现时有效的有关土地法予以决定，此决定为最终结论性的决定。

（5）对正确履行本法规定的职责而导致植物、货物、土地或其他生物的损失，政府和本法授权的任何人，享有赔偿追诉豁免权。

14. 禁止任何人，除非局长允许：

（a）进口有害植物；

（b）拥有和持有有害植物，或在其所有或占用的土地上允许此类植物的生长；

（c）进口和持有任何有害生物，局长可通过书面许可的形式，豁免任何人对本条部分或全部条款的禁约。

15. 当土地上出现有害植物的生长而违反第 14 条的规定时，相应土地的所有者或占用人应当采取焚烧或检查官员、局长指导的其他方法尽快使此类植物完全彻底地被消灭。

16. 对第 15 条规定须被消灭的有害植物，当土地的所有者或占用人不履行其有关义务时，检查官员可带必要的人员、设备和物件进入此类植物生长的相应土地，对此类植物实施完全彻底的消灭，由此而发生的成本和所有费用由相应土地的所有者或占用人支付。

17.（1）当出现违反本法规定或第 14 条的的相关条件而进境、存放有害植物的情况，当地检查官员、海关关员应当：

（a）检查官员应直接扣留和彻底销毁相应的有害植物；

（b）海关关员应扣留直至将其转交检查官员，由检查官员对相应的有害植物实施彻底销毁；

（2）本条“海关官员”适用《海关法 1976》的相应定义。

18. 任何人违反本法第 14 条或第 15 条即构成犯罪——不管检查官员采取或可能会采取本法第 16 条和第 17 条的措施，并可被处不超过 10,000 令吉的罚款。

19. 任何人无法定的理由故意地在马来西亚境内移动或运输有害生物或有害植物，或造成此类生物或植物的移动或运输，即构成犯罪，并可被处不超过 10,000 令吉的罚款或不超过两年的监禁，或者两刑并处。

各构成地区的局长和检查官员为销毁此类有害生物或有害植物，或为研究如何销毁此类生物而引起的此类生物在马来西亚境内的移动或运输，不受本条的约束。

19A. 任何人从事或试图从事，造成或许可，或怂恿有违或不符本法及其相关法规的行为，即构成犯罪，当无明确的处罚可适用时，可对其处以不超过10,000令吉的罚款或不超过两年的监禁，或者两刑并处。

20. 本法书面通知的送达，可：

（a）直接投递其本人；或

（b）寄达

（ⅰ）其雇员或家庭的成年成员—通过其本人通常的或最新的住址或工作地址；或

（ⅱ）其雇员或代理人—通其本人的注册办公地址；或

（c）张帖送达：

（ⅰ）张帖于其本人通常的或最新的住址或工作地址；或

（ⅱ）张帖于其本人注册的办公地址；或

（d）采取第21条的替代方法送达。

21. 当检查官员确信书面通知的被送达人难以找到，同时本法第20条确立的送达方法不适用时，可采下列方式将书面通知予以送达和告知：

（a）在显要位置张贴书面通知的副本：

（ⅰ）在土地上；和

（ⅱ）在土地所属地区的法院、寺院、或村长的办公地址或警察局、市场或其他公共场所；和

（b）在报刊上公布书面通知的副本，如检查官员认为必要，还可在相应“构成地区”流通的一到多份报刊上刊登书面通知的副本。

22. 除非受到公诉人的书面指控，任何人违反本法及其相关法规，法院不对其实施司法程序。

23. （1）为使本法得到彻底有效的贯彻以及为强化本法的主旨，部长可不时地制定相关条例。在无损于前述一般原则的前提下，可制定如下条例：

（a）本法执法官员的权力和职责；

（b）进入土地的方式和书面通知，如有，先告知再进入；

（c）本法授权的植物检疫和其他程序的实施；

（d）土地所有者或占用人发现植物感染危险性有害生物的通知；

（e）局长或检查官员依据本法签发的通知、命令的格式；

（f）为控制和预防植物有害生物，对有害生物、有益生物、植物和土壤，对其进出境的管理状况和控制；

（g）为预防植物病害，对马来西亚现有的有害生物、植物的控制；

（h）在预防危险性有害生物和有害植物的侵入，或当此类生物已出现于马来西亚，在对其实施根除或控制时，有从马来西亚所有公民、军队、海军、空军、警察、其他组织或暂存或已成立的武装力量获得协助的权力；

（i）有关收费；

（j）不超过1000令吉的罚款或不超过6个的监禁，或者两罪并处。

（2）依据本条制定的法规，如涉及沙巴州或沙捞越州，在法规制定之前，应先与相应州主管农业的州部长磋商。

24.《农业有害生物和有害植物条例1953》，《沙巴州农业有害生物条例》和《沙捞越州农业有害生物条例》，除下述情况外，特此废止。

除非：

（a）上述被废止条例的任命与本法条文没有不一致，且被认为是本法的任命时；

（b）上述被废止条例的有关通知、指导说明、条令、法规与本法条文没有不一致，且被认为是本法的有关通知、指导说明、条令、法规的，可继续生效。

Plant Quarantine Act

(Laws of Malaysia Act. 167)

(June 1994)

An Act to amend and consolidate the laws relating to the control, prevention and eradication of agricultural pests, noxious plants and plant diseases and to extend co – operation in the control of the movement of pests in international trade for matters connected therewith.

BE IT ENACTED by the Duli Yang Maha Mulia Seri Paduka Baginda Yang di Pertuan Agong with the advice and consent of the Dewan Negara and Dewan Rakyat in Parliament assembled, and by the authority of the same, as follows:

1. (1) This Act may be cited as the Plant Quarantine Act, 1976

(2) This Act shall apply throughout Malaysia.

2. In this Act unless the context otherwise requires

"beneficial organism" means any invertebrate animal (including the eggs such animal), fungus, bacterium, virus, or any other organism which is beneficial to agriculture and which is not capable of being injurious to plants;

"component region" mean the region constituting West Malaysia, the Federal Territory of Labuan, the State of Sabah or the State of Sarawak, as the case may be, for the purpose of the implementation of this Act;

"dangerous pest" means any pest which the Minister may by notification in the Gazette declares to be a dangerous pest for the purposes of this Act for the whole or any part of Malaysia;

Provided that where the declaration of a dangerous pest affects the State of Sabah or Sarawak or both such States, the Minister shall consult the State Minister charged with or responsibility for agriculture of Sabah or Sarawak or both such State Ministers, as the case may be, prior to making such declaration;

"Director" means the Director – General of Agriculture for West Malaysia, whose responsibility extends to the Federal Territory of Labuan, the Director of Agriculture for the State of Sabah or the Director of Agriculture for the State of Sarawak, as the case may be;

"diseased" means bearing any pest;

"import", with its grammatical variation and cognate expression, means to bring or cause to bring into any component region from a place outside such region, by land, sea, or air;

"Inspecting Officer" means an Inspecting Officer appointed under section 3 (3);

"isolation" means the isolation of any land for the purpose and in the manner provided under section 10;

" land" includes:

(a) the surface of the earth and all substances forming the surface;

(b) the earth below the surface and all substances therein;

(c) all vegetation and other natural products whether or not requiring the periodical application of labor for their production and whether on or below the surface;

(d) all things attached to the earth, or permanently fastened to any thing attached to the earth, whether on or below the surface; and

(e) land covered by water;

"Minister" means the Minister charged with theresponsibility for the eradication of agricultural pests and noxious plants and prevention of plant diseases;

"noxious plant" means any plant which the Minister may by notification in the Gazette declare to be a noxious plant for purposes of this Act for the whole or any part of Malaysia and includes the seed and every part of such plant; Provided that where the declaration of a noxious plant affects the State of Sabah or Sarawak or both such States, the Minister shall consult the State Minister charged with the responsibility for agriculture of Sabah or Sarawak or both such State Ministers, as the casemay be, prior to making such declaration;

"occupier" includes a lessee or tenant or cultivator or person in actual possession, management or controlor any land;

"owner" in relation to any land means any person for the time being registered as the proprietor of any land under the law relating to land applicable in the respective component regions and shall include in the case of Sarawak the holder by customary rights of anyland;

"pest" means any vertebrate or invertebrate animal (including the eggs of such animal), fungus, bacterium, virus, viroid, *mycoplasm like organism*, *weed*, and or any other organism which is or is capable of being injurious to plants and includes any dangerous pest;

"plant" means any species of plant or any part thereof whether living or dead and includes the stem, branch, tuber, bulb, corn, stock, budwood, cutting, layer, slip, sucker, root, leaf, flower, fruit, seed or any other part or product whatsoever of a plant whether severed or attached but does not include any plant product that has undergone a process of heat and drying treatment;

"soil" means any earth, ground or other naturallyoccurring organic and mineral material in which plants may be grown.

3. (1) The Directors shall have general supervision of all matters for purposes of carrying out or putting into effect the provision of this Act in respect of their respective component regions and the powers of the Directors conferred under this Act, shall be construed in accordance with the provision of this subsection: Provided that the power conferred upon the Directors under section 19 shall not be construed as if the exercise of such power by any of the Directors is confined within the component region of such Director.

(2) The Directors shall in addition to the powers conferred upon them by this Act have all the powers conferred upon an Inspecting Officer under this Act in respect of their respective component regions.

(3) The Directors may appoint any officers of the Department of Agriculture of the respective component regions to be Inspecting Officers for purposes of carrying out or putting into effect the provisions of this Act in respect of the component region for which the appointments are made and the powers conferred upon an Inspecting Officer under this Act shall be construed in accordance with the provision of this subsection:

Provided that the powers conferred upon theInspecting Officers under section 19 shall not be construed as if the exercise of such power by any of the Inspecting officers is confined within the component region of such Inspecting Officer.

4. Every Director and Inspecting Officer when acting within the scope of the power and duties under this Act shall be deemed to be public servants within the meaning of the Penal Code applicable in the respective component regions.

5. (1) An Inspecting Officer may at all reasonable times, with or without assistants, instruments or thing, enter upon any land and may remain there for so long as may be reasonably necessary for the following purposes:

(a) to inspect and examine such land and any plant thereon to ascertain whether any noxious plant or pest is present on such land or whether such land or any plant thereon is in a condition favorable to the introduction or spread of any noxious plant or pest; and

(b) to remove in any way such portions of any such plant as he may deem necessary for purposes of examination or investigation.

(2) The owner or occupier of such land shall permit every Inspecting Officer to have access thereto for the purposes specified in subsection (1) and shall supply to the Inspecting Officer all such information as may be requested by him, and shall afford the Inspecting Officer such assistance as may be reasonably necessary for such purposes.

6. (1) If, on or as a result of any inspection or examination of land or plants by an Inspecting Officer, it appears to him that any plant is diseased in a manner and to an extent which might endanger other plants he may, by notice in writing under his hand, served on the owner or occupier of the land wherever such plant is found, direct such owner or occupier to take within the time specified in the notice such measures as seem to the Inspecting Officer necessary or expedient for the eradication or prevention of the spread of the either by destruction, removal or treatment in a manner to be specified in the said notice of any diseased plant or any other plant, or of any pest or tools or utensils or structure used for agricultural purposes on the land.

(2) If, on or as a result of any inspection or examination of land or plants by an Inspecting Officer, it appears to him that any land or plant is in a condition favorable to the introduction or spread of any pest he may, by notice in writing under his hand, served on the owner or occupier of the land whereon such condition exists, direct such owner or occupier to take within the time specified in the notice such measures as seem to the Inspecting Officer necessary or expedient for the eradication or prevention of the spread of the pest either by destruction, removal or treatment in a manner to be specified in the said notice of such plant or any other plant, or of any pest or tools or utensils or structure used for agricultural purposes on the land with a view to bringing the same into a condition not favorable to the introduction or spread of any pest.

(3) The cost of the measures and of the taking thereof mentioned in subsections (1) and (2) shall be defrayed by the owner or occupier of the land.

(4) Any notice under subsection (1) or (2) shall specify a time not being less than seven days from the date of the notice within which the owner or occupier of the land may make representation in writing:

(a) to the Menteri Besar or Chief Minister, as the case may be, of the State in West Malaysia in which the land specified in the notice is situated; or

(b) to the State Minister charged with the responsibility for griculture of Sabah in the case of the land specified in the notice being situated in Sabah; or

(c) to the State Minister charged with the responsibility for agriculture of Sarawak in the case of the land specified in the notice being situated in Sarawak, with respect to any or all of the directions specified in the notice.

(5) The Menteri Besar or Chief Minister of any State in West Malaysia or the State Minister charged with the responsibility for agriculture of Sabah or Sarawak to whom representation under subsection (4) is made may confirm, or suspend the operation of the notice or cancel the notice or make such other order as he may deem fit.

7. (1) If an owner or occupier of land on whom a notice under section 6 or subsection (1) of section 12 has been served fails to comply with the requirements of such notice within such time as is stated in the notice for the performance of the acts thereby required to be done, the Inspecting Officer may, subject to any order made under subsection (5) of section 6, enter upon the land to which the notice refers together with such persons, instruments and things as may be necessary and may proceed to perform and do thereon all acts and things required by the said notice to be performed or done, and may recover the cost of, and all expenses incurred in, so doing from the said owner or occupier in any Court.

(2) Nothing in this section shall affect any liability of any person to prosecution and punishment under sec-

tion 8 or 13.

8. (1) If any owner or occupier of land on whom a notice under section 6 has been served fails to comply therewith within the time therein stated, he shall be guilty of an offence and shall on onviction be liable to a finenot exceeding ten thousand ringgit; Provided that no person shall be punished under this section for failure to comply with any notice from the time that its requirements may have been suspended or cancelled by the Menteri Besar or Chief Minister of any State in West Malaysia or the State Minister charged with the responsibility for agriculture of Sabah or Sarawak, as the case may be, under the provisions of subsection (5) of section 6.

(2) Where the Menteri Besar or Chief Minister of any State in West Malaysia or the State Minister charged with the responsibility for agriculture of Sabah or Sarawak, as the case may be, has under the provisions of subsection (5) of section 6 made an order varying the terms of any such notice, the notice as varied shall for the purposes of this section and of section 7 be deemed to be the notice under section 6.

9. (1) Upon the conviction of any person under section 8, 11 or 13, the Court before which the person is convicted may in addition to any penalty imposed by such Court order the convicted person within a time to be fixed by the Court to take such measures as the Court may deem necessary to prevent any further commission of the offence for which the person has been convicted.

(2) If any person fails to comply with an order made under ubsection (1) he shall be guilty of an offence and shall on conviction be liable to a fine not exceeding fifty ringgit for every day during the continuance of such offence in addition to the respective penalty under section 8, 11 or 13.

10. (1) Whenever the Menteri Besar or Chief Minister of a State in West Malaysia or the State Minister charged with the responsibility for agriculture of Sabah or Sarawak, on the advice of the Director is of the opinion that any plants on any land are diseased he may make an order placing such land or any part thereof in isolation for such period as may be prescribed by the order and may at any time amend or revoke such order.

(2) No person shall, without reasonable excuse, enter or leave any land to which an order made under subsection (1) refers and nothing shall be removed there from except in accordance with any directions issued by an Inspecting Officer.

(3) Any owner or occupier of land which is placed in isolation by an order issued under subsection (1) may apply to an Inspecting Officer to examine the land so placed under isolation with a view to btaining amendment or revocation of the order and the Inspecting Officer shall within seven days after receipt of such application visit and examine the said land and submit has findings and recommendations to the Director who shall then advice the Menteri Besar, Chief Minister of the State Minister, as the case may be.

(4) Any person who knowingly or without reasonable excuse commits a breach of the provisions of subsection (2) shall be guilty of an offence and shall on conviction be liable to a fine not exceeding two thousand ringgit.

11. (1) Whenever a dangerous pest, or any plant diseased by a dangerous pest, is found or appears on any land, the owner or occupier of such land shall:

(a) as soon as he becomes aware that the same has been found or has appeared thereon forthwith give notice thereof in writing or otherwise to the Director or to any Inspecting Officer with such particulars as may be prescribed;

(b) carry into effect all instructions given to him by any Inspecting Officer for the destruction of the dangerous pest of plants diseased by a dangerous pest on such land; and

(c) render all assistance in his power the carrying out of any action taken by any Inspecting Officer for the purpose of destroying the dangerous pest on such land.

(2) Any person who commits a breach of the provisions of subsection (1) shall be guilty of an offence and

shall on conviction be liable to a fine not exceeding ten thousand ringgit.

(3) Any Inspecting Officer receiving any notice in accordance with the provisions of paragraph (a) of subsection (1) shall inform the Director of such notice.

12. (1) If in opinion of the Menteri Besar or Chief Minister of a State in West Malaysia of the State Minister charged with the responsibility for agriculture of Sabah or Sarawak that which respect to any land within his State the eradication, destruction, or treatment of any diseased plant which is affected by a dangerous pest or of any plant liable to become so affected is a matter of necessity or urgency or if in the opinion of the Director the safety of any plant growing in his component region is endangered by the existence of a dangerous pest on any plant growing in such region or in any other component regions or growing outside Malaysia and he considers it necessary for the prevention of the spread of such dangerous pest that any land within his component region be entirely or partly cleared of all plants or of any particular species of plants or that the eradication or destruction or any from of treatment of any plant present on any such land, is required, such Menteri Besar, Chief Minister, State Minister charged with the responsibility for agriculture, or Director, as the case may be, may forthwith serve a notice in writing on the owner or the occupier of the land connected therewith requiring any or both of them to take such measures for the eradication, estruction or treatment of any plants or clearing of the land within such time as may be specified in the notice.

(2) If it appears to the Menteri Besar or Chief Minister of a State in West Malaysia or the State Minister charged with the responsibility for agriculture of Sabah or Sarawak or any Director as the case may be that safety of plant cannot be properly ensured by the action directed to be taken under subsection (1), such Menteri Besar, Chief Minister, State Minister charged with the responsibility for agriculture or Director may forthwith direct an Inspecting Officer or any person to enter any specified land together with such other persons or with such instruments or things as may be necessary and to take or cause to be taken any specified action for the eradication, destruction or control of the dangerous pest, or the treatment of any plants or clearing of the land of any plants whether or not the dangerous pest is present on such land.

(3) The cost of, and all expenses incurred in such eradication, destruction, control, treatment or clearing as mentioned in subsections (1) and (2) shall be defrayed by the owner or occupier of the land whereon such eradication, destruction, control, treatment or clearing is carried out and where the cost and the expenses have been incurred by any person other than the owner or occupier such person may recover the cost and expenses from the owner or occupier.

13. (1) Except as provided by subsection (2), no owner or occupier of land or other person shall be entitled to compensation for any xpense incurred or damage occasioned by any order given or act done in pursuance of this Act unless such damage was occasioned by willful negligence.

(2) The Director may, in his discretion, order that such compensation as he thinks fit shall be paid to the owner or occupier of any land who is required to destroy as a measure of precaution plant thereon not being diseased.

(3) No application for compensation shall be entertained unless it is in writing and is received in the office of the Director within three months from the date of the notice requiring the destruction of the plant, and in no case shall compensation be paid in excess of the actual value of the plant destroyed at the date of notice.

(4) If any question arises as to the value of an plant, such question shall be referred to and decided by the officer charged with the collecting of land revenue pursuant to any written law concerning land for the time being in force in the component region in which such plant is located and the decision of such officer shall be final and conclusive.

(5) If in the proper exercise of their function of administering the provisions of this Act loss or damage to

plants, goods, soil or other organisms occurs, the government and every person authorized under this Act shall be exempted from all claims for compensation for such loss or damage.

14. No person, except the Director shall:

(a) import any noxious plant;

(b) possess or keep any noxious plant or allow the same to grow in or on any land of which he is the owner or occupier; or

(c) import or keep any pest. Provided that the Director may in writing exempt any person from any or all of the provisions of this section subject to such conditions as he may impose in the exemption.

15. Where any noxious plant is growing in or on any land in contravention of section 14 the owner and occupier thereof shall as soon as possible cause such noxious plant to be completely and effectually destroyed by fire or by such other means as the Inspecting Officer or Director may direct.

16. Where default is made by any person in the complete and effectual destruction of any noxious plant which, by the provisions of section 15 he is required so to destroy, an Inspecting Officer may enter upon the land in or on which such noxious plant is growing, together with such persons and with such instruments and things as may destroy the same and may recover the cost of, and all expenses incurred in, so doing from the owner or occupier of the said land

17. (1) Any Inspecting Officer; or any officer of customs at any place at which any noxious plants is imported or kept, in contravention of this Act or of any condition that may be imposed under section 14, shall:

(a) in the case of an Inspecting Officer, seize and effectively destroy such plant; and

(b) in the case of an officer of customs, seize and detain such plant until it is placed in the charge of an Inspecting Officer who shall effectively destroy it.

(2) In this section "officer of customs" shall have the meaning assigned to it in the Customs Act, 1976.

18. Any person who contravenes any of the provisions of section 14 or 15 shall be guilty of an offence and shall on conviction be liable to a fine not exceeding ten thousand ringgit, notwithstanding that an Inspecting Officer may take, or may have taken action under section 16 or 17.

19. Any person who shall knowingly and without any lawful excuse move or convey or cause to be moved or conveyed within Malaysia any dangerous pest or noxious plant shall be guilty of an offence and shall on conviction be liable to a fine not exceeding ten thousand ringgit or to imprisonment for a term not exceeding two years or to both: Provided that nothing in this section shall apply to any Director or Inspecting Officer of any component region who may move or convey within Malaysia any dangerous pest or noxious plants for purposes of the destruction of such pests or plants of for any other purposes relating to any research or study to eliminate such pests or plants.

19A. Any person who does or attempts to do, or causes or permits to be done, or abets, an act contrary to, or fails to comply with, the provisions of this Act or any regulation made there under shall be guilty of an offence and shall on conviction, if no penalty is expressly provided, be liable to a fine not exceeding ten thousand ringgit or to imprisonment for a term not exceeding two years or to both.

20. A notice may be served on a person for the purposes of this Act:

(a) by delivering the notice to the person; or

(b) by delivering the notice:

(i) to his servant or to an adult member of his family at the person's usual or last known place of abode or business; or (ii) to his servant or agent at the person's registered office; or (c) by sending the notice by post to the person;

(ii) at his usual or last known abode or place of business; or

(iii) at his registered office; or

(c) by substituted service in accordance with section 21.

21. Where the Inspecting Officer is satisfied that the person on whom the notice is to be served cannot by the exercise of due diligence be found and service cannot be effected as set out in section 20, the service may be effected:

(a) by affixing a copy of the notice in a conspicuous position –

(i) on the land; and

(ii) on a court – house, mosque or penghulu's office or balai, or in a market or other public place, in the area in which the land is ituated; and

(b) by publishing a copy of the notice in the Gazette and, if he thinks fit, in one or more of the newspapers circulating in the component region.

22. No proceeding shall be instituted in any Court against any person for any breach of any provision of this Act or of any regulations made there under except with the written section of the Public Prosecutor.

23. (1) The Minister may from time to time make regulations for fully and effectively carrying out and giving effect to the purpose of this Act, and without prejudice to the generality of the foregoing such regulations may provide for:

(a) the powers and duties of officers appointed under this Act;

(b) the manner of entry upon lands and the notice, if any, to be given prior to such entry;

(c) the conduct of the examination and inspection of plants and of other proceedings authorized by this Act;

(d) the notification by owners or occupier of land of any plant found to be diseased with a dangerous;

(e) the form of notices and orders to be made by the Director or any Inspecting Officer under this Act;

(f) the control of, and the conditions governing the import or export of pests, beneficial organisms, plants and soil for purposes of controlling and prevention of plant pests;

(g) the control of any pest or plant present in Malaysia for purposes of the prevention of plant diseases;

(h) the obtaining from all civil, military, naval, air, police or other organizations or forces present for the time being or established in Malaysia, of assistance directed to preventing the introduction of any dangerous pest or noxious plant or to the eradication or control of such dangerous pest or noxious plant if present inMalaysia;

(i) the imposition of fees;

(j) the imposition of penalties of a fine not exceeding one thousand ringgit or imprisonment of not exceeding six months or both.

(2) Where the regulations made under this section would affect Sabah or Sarawak the Ministers charged with responsibility for agriculture of Sabah or Sarawak as the case may be, shall be consulted prior to the making of such regulations.

24. The Agricultural Pests and Noxious Plants Ordinance, 1953, the Sabah Agricultural Pests Ordinance, and the Sarawak Agricultural Pests Ordinance are hereby repealed: Provided that –

(a) any appointment made under such repealed Ordinances shall, in so far as the same is not inconsistent with the provisions of this Act, be deemed to havebeen made under this Act; and

(b) any notice, direction, order, regulation or rule issued or made under such repealed Ordinances shall, in so far as the same is not inconsistent with the provisions of this Act, continue in force and have effect as if it had been issued or made under this Act.

植物检疫条例

（1981 年）

为履行《植物检疫法 1976》第 23 条赋予的权力，部长制定条例如下：

1.（1）本法规可被引述为《植物检疫条例 1981》，并于 1981 年 3 月 31 日生效。

（2）本条例不适用于有益生物、运输工具和装载容器、生长介质、非植物材料、有害生物、植物、堆肥和土壤在沙巴州和拉布安岛联邦之间的运输。

2. 除非本条例文本另有规定，否则本条例所指—

美洲热带地区　指美州及其毗连岛屿被南回归线（南纬 23.5）和北回归线（北纬 23.5）及西经 30 和西经 120 所包围的地区，也包括墨西哥北回归线以北的地区。

指定的入境检查点　指附录 5 所规定的海关检查点。

运输工具和装载容器　包括运输和装载有益生物、生长介质、非植物材料、有害生物、植物、堆肥和土壤的各种车辆、船只、飞机和装载容器。

直接过境　指来自或发自一国的货物进入到马来西亚的构成地区，不经清关而直接通过相同的运输工具或另一运输工具运往另一国家。

废料　指全部或部分源自水果、蔬菜或植物其他部位的所有废弃物质，以及与此类废弃物有关联的其他废弃物。

进境检查官员　指在指定的入境检查点和《海关法 1967》规定的其他法定陆地检查点的海关、农业或邮政值勤人员。

间接过境　指来自或发自一国的货物进入到马来西亚的构成地区，经在该构成地区清关后，再通过相同的运输工具或另一运输工具运往另一国家。

植物检疫证书　指附录 2 所列的证书，由检查官员签发，证明有关的植物或其代表样品在发运前已经过彻底的检查，未发现其含有任何有害生物和病害。

植物检疫官员　指农业部门的进境检查官员。

（禁止进境）植物清单　指附录 3 规定的植物。

土壤　指植物生长的泥土、母岩和其他自然形成的有机和无机物。

东南亚和太平洋地区　指东南亚的所有地区（巴基斯坦东部边界以东，喜马拉雅山南以东，中国南部边界以东，越南东海岸以东），以及全部或部分位于太平洋、南中国海、印度洋的所有地区（东经 100°，南纬 45°，西经 135°，北纬 38°所围与韩国西海岸交接点，从此交接点与台北的连线，以及北纬 15°与越南东部海岸交叉点的连线，包括香港地区。）

非洲可可（有害生物）疫区　指非洲境内危害可可的病害或盲蝽的已知发生区或可能发生区。

3. 禁止进口土壤，不论其是单独进口或附着于植物的根或其他部位而传带进境：获附录 6 所列进境许可为分析或研究的目的而进境的土壤除外。

4.（1）这些法规不适用于：

（a）用于食用、药用、加工或制造的进境植物；

（b）已加工了的植物；

（c）作为包装或包装材料的植物全株或其一部分；

（d）废料、衬板和托板。

但上述（a）（b）（c）款豁免的物品须经检查，如发现有害生物，可作销毁或处理；但上述（d）

款豁免的物品须经局长确定的方法处理。

（2）从美洲热带地区空运进境法规 4 第（1）条（a）和（b）款豁免的植物到构成地区，须遵照法规 7 第（i）和第（ii）款的要求。

（3）法规 4 第（1）条（a）、（b）款和（c）款的规定，不适用于已被危险性有害生物感染的椰子（不论全果或去壳）、油棕和法规 5 第（5）款和第（6）款列明的植物。

5.（1）除非获得许可，否则任何植物、堆肥或其他生长介质均被禁止输入构成地区。此类物品，应获得局长签发的进境植物许可证（附录 1）及堆肥或其他生长介质许可证（附录 6），在符合植物检疫法规及许可证载明的相关条件下方可进境。

（2）除了遵照条例 6 载明的禁止和限制条件外，输入到构成地区的每一批植物必须随附植物检疫证书（附录 2），适用时还要随附转口国出具的转口植物检疫证书（附录 7），或其他单证。这些证书或单证应由相关国家植物保护部门的授权官员对发货人签发，（当植物系由马来西亚的一构成地区输入到另一构成地区时）或应由植物生长地的构成地区局长对发货人签发。证书须在货物发运前的 14 天内签发，并随货同行。

（3）植物、有益生物、根肥、土壤和其他生长介质只能通过条例 3 和条例 5 第（1）条和第（4）条相关许可证指定的入境检查点进境。

（4）除非获得许可，否则任何有益生物均被禁止输入构成地区。有益生物应获得局长签发的进境有益生物许可证（附录 8），在符合植物检疫条例及许可证载明的相关条件下方可进境。

（5）自附录 9 谷斑皮蠹疫区国家输入条例 4 第（1）条（a）款、（b）款和（c）款豁免的植物，应由输出国依照局长确定的剂量进行处理，并须随附植物检疫证书。

（6）尽管有条例 4 第（1）条（a）款的规定，禁止产自菲律宾、印度尼西亚和马来西亚本国一构成地区的可可荚果、红毛丹、山荔枝、龙眼果和喃喃果向另一构成地区进境。

6.（1）禁止从任何国家或本国的其他构成地区输入橡胶树属的任何物种，除非：

（ⅰ）输入系研究的需要；

（ⅱ）输入由局长批准；且

（ⅲ）输入前，由局长咨询马来西亚橡胶研究院院长，院长对其入境作出建议。

（2）禁止从美洲热带地区和橡胶南美叶疫病疫区的其他国家输入具生长或繁殖能力的橡胶树属的任何种类植物，除非此类植物符合本法规第（1）款的要求，且满足下列条件：

（ⅰ）已在局长批准的橡胶属植物检疫站进行充分的隔离种植，该隔离点需位于东南亚和太平洋地区、美洲热带地区和橡胶南美叶疫病疫区的其他地区或国家之外的非疫区；

（ⅱ）不带有有害生物；且

（ⅲ）随附由相关植物检疫站主管检疫官员签发的证书，证明其符合上述（i）款和（ii）款的要求。

（3）禁止从美洲热带地区和橡胶南美叶疫病发生区或疑似发生区的其他国家输入橡胶树属的任何植物种子，除非此类种子符合本法规第（1）款的要求，且满足下列条件：

（ⅰ）在局长批准的地点进行了检查和消毒，检查和消毒的地点应位于东南亚和太平洋地区、美洲热带地区和橡胶南美叶疫病疫区的其他地区或国家之外的非疫区；

（ⅱ）置新的容器，用新的包装材料重新包装；

（ⅲ）随附由相关检查消毒地点主管检疫官员签发的证书，证明其符合上述（ⅰ）款和（ⅱ）款的要求。

（4）禁止输入不具生长或繁殖能力的橡胶树属的任何种类植物（如鲜的或干制的植物标本），除非此类植物符合本法规第（1）款的要求，为研究需要或为局长批准的其他目的需要，且用局长认可的方法在原产国进行了处理。

7. 禁止从美洲热带地区和橡胶南美叶疫病疫区的其他国家输入非橡胶树属的任何种类植物，除非此类植物符合下列条件：

（ⅰ）输入系研究的需要；

（ⅱ）输入由局长批准；且

（ⅲ）在局长批准的地点进行了检疫或处理，检疫或处理的地点应位于东南亚和太平洋地区、美洲热带地区和橡胶南美叶疫病疫区的其他地区或国家之外的非疫区，同时不含有害生物，且随附由相关检疫或处理地点主管检疫官员签发的证书，证明其符合上述的要求。

8. 禁止进境可可树、椰子树、油棕、或任何已知可被可可根肿病毒、致死黄化病、类病毒病或病毒、重要病害作为寄主的植物，除非：

（ⅰ）输入系研究的需要；

（ⅱ）输入委托给局长；且

（ⅲ）在局长批准的地点进行了检疫或处理，检疫或处理的地点应位于美洲热带地区、非洲可可有害生物疫区和可可、油棕、椰子其他病害之外的非疫区，同时不含有害生物，且随附由相关检疫地点主管检疫官员签发的证书。

9.（1）禁止附录4所列危险性有害生物的进境。

（2）被上述危险性有害生物感染的进境植物、或被局长认为具特定危险性质的其他有害生物或病害感染的进境植物，以及与此类被感染植物同置一包装容器的其他植物，应当被立即销毁。

（3）为预防危险性有害生物和有害植物的侵入，或当此类生物已出现于马来西亚的构成地区，为对其实施根除或控制时，局长有从马来西亚现时存在的民间、军队、海军、空军、警察或其他组织和力量获得协助的权力。

10.（1）在指定的入境检查点，进境检查官可扣留输入构成地区的植物，直至扣留的植物被交付局长，局长可对其实施放行处理，当发现或认为其感染有害生物时，可对其实施销毁或其他适宜的方法予以处置。

（2）输入构成地区的每一批植物须由进境检查官在入境地点或局长批准的其他地点实施检查。

（3）对已被有害生物感染的入境植物的整批或其部分，由局长确定其检疫处理或销毁的方法。

（4）对入境植物实施检查、检疫、处理和销毁而造成的损失或发生的开支，包括运输费用，均由进口商负担。除非局长酌处而免除进口商此类损失和开支的全部或部分。

10A. 有可能感染有害生物的非植物材料、运输工具及装载容器，须实施检查和处理。

11. 违反这些条例而入境的植物将被进境检查官予以扣留，并被按照局长指示的方法进行处置。

12.（1）没有获得局长的事先许可，直接过境或间接过境的植物和有害生物不得卸离入境时的运输工具。

（2）条例5的规定，适用于直接过境或间接过境的植物。

13.（1）对违反这些条例入境或持有的任何有害生物，进境检查官可进行扣留。

（2）只要植物检疫官员认为任何人非法携带或持有植物、土壤、有害生物、有益生物、堆肥、生长介质和非植物材料，或者任何个人物品、运输工具和包装容器非法含有或夹带此类物品，可依法叫停、检查、找寻相关的人，可依法扣留相关个人物品、运输工具和包装容器，并采取条例载明的适当措施。

（3）对来自外国或本国别的构成地区的轮船、车辆和飞机，植物检疫官员被授权登轮、登车、登机，以检查、处理和处置有益生物、运输工具和包装容器、生长介质、非植物材料（包括下脚料和废料）、有害生物和可能带病或感染有害生物的堆肥、土壤。

14.（1）任何人

（a）故意地对抗、抵制、妨碍或阻止进境官员履行这些条例所赋予的权力和职责；

（b）蓄意地将有害生物或植物从国外或本国的一构成地区传入另一构成地区；

（c）无恰当的理由，不能提供或拒绝提供进境官员要求其提供的信息，或故意提供虚假或不完全的信息；

（d）作出其本人明知为虚假的、或不真实的声明或陈述，或故意地利用此类虚假的、或不真实的声明或陈述，为自己或他人骗取进境许可证、植物检疫证书或其他证明文书；

（e）违反这些条例条款的规定；

（f）没有履行局长依照这些条例而签发的许可证所载明的限制措施和条件；

（g）没有填写或拒绝填写附录10所载植物检疫申报表，或进行了虚假申报；

将构成犯罪。

（2）违反法规14第（1）条（a）款、（c）款、（d）款、（e）款、（f）款和（g）款的规定，可被处不超过1000令吉的罚款，或不超过6个月的监禁，或者两罚并处。

（3）违反条例14第（1）条（b）款的规定，可被处以《植物检疫法1976》第19A所载明的处罚。

15.（1）货物的进境许可证的签发收费为每份15令吉，许可证从签发之日起有3个月的有效期限。

（1A）有效期限已到的货物进境许可证，只能延期一次，所延长的有效期限从该证原有效期满之日起不得超过1个月，延期需付5令吉。

（2）检查官员或植物检疫人员从事检验，处理植物、植物产品，杀灭有害生物时按下列价格收取费用。

（ⅰ）（a）最先半小时或其不足部分　$10

（b）第2个半小时或其不足部分　$10

（c）每增加1小时或其不足部分　$20

（ⅱ）检查官员在其办公场所以外的地点对货物或田间生长的植物实施检查或实施消毒监督，作相应检查和监督的时间包括来回的旅途时间。

（ⅲ）检查官员或植物检疫官员实施消毒和处理，由此发生的药品和其他物品的费用由货主或收货人依照局长在不同时期确定的相应价格承担。

（ⅳ）检查官员或植物检疫官员应货主或收货人的要求，在上班时间外对货物或房屋实施检查，加班补贴由收货人视情况来支付—

（a）普通日加班每小时4令吉；

（b）周末和公共假日加班每小时8令吉。

（3）对实施检查和监督的旅行，要收取旅途乘飞机、火车或/和汽车的交通费，对全部或部分为陆路的旅行，按每公里50仙的价格收取其陆路旅途交通费。

（4）应任何人的申请或进境许可证规定的进境条件的要求，检查官员到其职责以外的马来西亚境内外其他地方实施检查，相关人应按当时的政务价格向局长补偿食宿费用。

（5）检查官员除检查货物外，还可自由裁定去检查植物生产场地，本条例第2条规定而发生的检查费用由货主承担。

16. 需实施入境后续检疫的植物和进口商未能及时提走的植物，其保管费如下：

（ⅰ）保管或入境后续检疫第1周内，每株每天2令吉；

（ⅱ）保管或入境后续检疫第2周，每株每天3令吉；

（ⅲ）保管或入境后续检疫第3周，每株每天4令吉；

（ⅳ）保管或入境后续检疫第4周，每株每天5令吉；

（ⅴ）入境后续检疫隔离一个生长季节或一个生长季的一段时期，每株10林吉特元；

（ⅵ）尽管有条款（ⅰ）、条款（ⅱ）、条款（ⅲ）、条款（ⅳ）和条款（ⅴ）的规定，局长可自主决定按一次付清征收费用来代替上述条款的收费。

17. 进入构成地区的所有人，均需填写附录10所载明的植物检疫申报单，并递交到指定的进境检查点。

18.（1）从附录5所列指定海港进入构成地区的船只，船主或其代理需在船只到达后的24小时内，且未卸下任何货物之前，向植物检疫官员提交一份符合《海关法 1967》第52条（1）款要求的船舶入境情况明细复印件。

（2）从附录5所列指定空港进入构成地区的飞机，驾驶员或其代理需在飞机未卸下任何货物之前，向植物检疫官员提交一份符合《海关法 1967》第56条要求的飞机入境情况明细复印件。

19.（1）根据检查和处理的情况，应出口商的要求，对出境和在构成地区间运递的植物、植物产品和非植物产品，植物检疫官员可以签发附录2所载明的植物检疫证书，以满足入境构成地区或入境国家的植物检疫法规的要求。

（2）应出口商的要求，对产自第三国或另一构成地区的转口植物和植物产品，植物检疫官员可以签发附录7所载明的植物检疫证书，以满足入境构成地区或入境国家的植物检疫法规的要求。

（3）对植物、植物产品和非植物产品实施检查和处理而发生的一切费用，依照法规15第（2）至第（5）款设定的费率由出口商承担。

附录 1
植物进境许可证

Permit No ....

Name and address of consignee ....

(Name)

of ....

(Address)

Name and address of consignor ....

(Name)

of ....

(Address)

Permission is hereby granted to the consignee to import the plants contained in the Schedule here to through

....

(Appointed entry check – point)

This permit is issued subject to the following conditions –

(1) Import Licence is to be sought from the relevant Ministry.

(2) Plants must be accompanied with a Phytosanitary Certificate from the country of origin of the plants issued within 14 days prior to dispatch of the consignment.

(3) A copy of this Import Permit must be sent to the consignor and must accompany the consignment.

(4) Plants must be free from soil and pest.

(5) Plants are subject to inspection or examination prior to clearance from the Customs Office.

(6) This Import Permit is valid for one consignment only until ....

(Date)

Further conditions ....

....

....

Schedule:

Descriptions	Quantity	Country of origin

Date of issue ....

....

Director of Agriculture

附录2
植物检疫证书

No ....

Plant Protection Organization

of ....

To: Plant Protection Organization (s)

of ....

Description of consignment

Name and address of exporter ....

Declared name and address of consignee ....

Number and description of packages ....

Distinguishing marks ....

Place of origin ....

Declared means of conveyance ....

Declared point of entry ....

Name of produce and quantity declared ....

Botanical name of plants ....

This is certify that the plants or plant products described above have been inspected according to appropriate procedures and are considered to be free from quarantine pests, and practically free from other injurious pests; and that they are considered to conform with the current phytosanitaryregulations of the importing country.

Disinfestation and/or disinfection treatment

Date .... *Treatment* ....

Chemical (active ingredient) .... *Duration and temperature* ....

Concentration .... *Additional information* ....

....

Additional declaration ....

Place of issue ....

(Stamp of Organization) *Name of authorized*

Officer ....

Date: .... *Signature* ....

No financial liability with respect to this certificate shall attach to the Government of Malaysia or to any of its officers or representatives.

附录3 （条例8和11）
违反本条例的植物产品销毁名录

Ananas comosus（L.）Merr.（Pineapple）	凤梨（菠萝）
All species of *Artocarpus*（Keledang）	菠萝密属所有种
Camellia sinensis（L.）Kuntze.（Tea）	茶
Carica papaya L.（Papaya）	番木瓜
All species of *Citrus* and allied genera	柑桔属和其亲缘属的所有种
All species of *Coffea*（Coffee）	咖啡属所有种
All species of *Colocasia* and *Zanthosoma*（Taro）	芋属和 *Zanthosoma* 属的所有种
Durio zibethinus Murr.（Durian）	榴莲
All species of Forest trees	所有林木树种
Glycine max（L.）Merr.	大豆（黄豆）
All species of *Gossypium*（Cotton）	棉属所有种
All species of *Hevea*（Rubber）	橡胶树属所有种
Ipomoea batatas Poir.（Sweet potato）	甘薯（甘薯）
All species of Leguminosae	所有豆科植物
All species of *Mangifera*	所有芒果品种
All species of *Manihot*（Cassavae）	木薯属所有种
All species of *Musa* and allied genera（Banana, Plantains and Manila hemp）	芭蕉属及其类似属植物（香蕉、芭蕉、马尼拉蕉麻）所有种
All species of *Nephelium*	所有韶子属植物
All species of *Nicotiana*（Tobaccoes）	所有烟草属植物
All members of the Orchidaceae	所有兰科植物
Oryza sativa L.（Rice）	水稻属（水稻）
All members of the Palmaceae（coconut, oil palm and other palms）	所有棕榈科植物（椰子、油棕榈树、其他棕榈树）
All members of the *Piperaceae*（Peppers）	所有胡椒科植物（胡椒）
All species of *Saccharum*（Sugarcane）	所有甘蔗属植物（甘蔗）
Solanum tuberosum L.（Potato）	马铃薯（马铃薯）
Zea mays L.（Maize）	玉米（玉米）
All species of *Theobroma*（Cacao）and other plants known, or likely to be, hosts, of virus diseases of cacao（including all members of the families Bombacaceae and Sterculiaceae）	所有可可属植物和其他已知的可以携带可可病毒病的植物（包括木棉科和梧桐科）
Plants grown in the American Tropics	生长在美国热带地区的植物
Plants grown in the African Cacao Region	生长在非洲可可产区的植物
All species of Zingiberaceae	所有姜科植物

附录4
危险性有害生物

AVOCADO（*Persea* spp.）	**鳄梨 *Persea* spp.**
Sunblotch virus of avocado	鳄梨日斑病毒
BANANA（*Musa* spp.）	**香蕉 *Musa* spp.**
Bunchy top virus	香蕉束顶病毒
Mycosphaerella musicola var *difformis*	香蕉叶斑病菌
Pseudomonas solanacearum	青枯病菌
Mycosplasma – Like organism	香蕉支原体类病
BARLEY（*Sorghum* spp.）	**大麦 *Sorghum* spp.**
Barley stripe mosaic	大麦条纹花叶病
CASSAVA（*Manihot esculenta*）	**木薯 *Manihot esculenta***
Phaeolus manihotis	（暗孔菌属）
Cassava brown streak virus	木薯褐条斑病毒
Cassava mosaic virus	木薯花叶病毒
Cassava witch's broom	木薯丛枝病
Super elongation disease	木薯徒长病
Caliothrips masculinus	巢针蓟马属
Monomychelus tanajoa	木薯单爪螨
Oligonychus peruvianus	（小爪螨属）
Mycoplasma – like organism	木薯支原体类病
Sphaceloma manihotis	木薯痂圆孢徒长病
Frog's skin	木薯蛙皮病
Cassava latent virus disease	木薯潜伏性病毒病
African mosaic	非洲花叶病
CITRUS（*Citrus* spp.）	**柑橘 *Citrus* spp.**
Anastrepha fraterculus	南美按实蝇
Anastrepha ludens	墨西哥按实蝇
Anastrepha mombinpraeoptans	西印度按实蝇
Anastrepha spp.	按实蝇属
Ceratitis rasa	纳塔尔实蝇
Ceratitis capitata	地中海实蝇
Dacus tryoni	昆士兰实蝇
Deuterophoma tracheiphila	嗜管半知点霉菌
Citrus stubborn disease	柑橘顽固病
Citrus green	柑橘绿霉
Quadraspidiotus perniciosus	梨圆盾蚧
Impietratura virus	柑橘石果病毒
Exocortis virus	柑橘裂皮病毒
Satsuma dwarf virus	柑橘矮化病
Spiroplasma citri	柑橘顽固病

Yellow virus	柑橘干坚病毒
Xyloporosis virus	柑橘木孔病
COCOA（***Theobroma cacao***）	**可可 *Theobroma cacao***
Sahlbergella singularis	可可褐盲蝽
Distantiella theobroma	可可瘤盲蝽
Helopeltis bergrothis	角盲蝽属
Stenoma decora	油棕果蛾
Bathycoella thalassina	*Bathycoella thalassina*
Marasmius perniciosus	小皮伞属
Monilia roreri	可可念珠霉果腐病
Trachysphaera fructigena	粉荚病菌
Cacao swollen shoot virus complex	可可肿茎病毒
Cacao red mottle virus	可可红斑病毒
Cacao vein – clearing virus	可可脉明病毒
Acrocercops cramerella	可可细蛾
Cacao yellow mosaic virus	可可黄色花叶病毒
Monalonium sp.	盲椿象
Oncobasidium theobromae	可可缘斑梢枯病
Phytophthora palmivora	棕榈疫霉
Water mark	可可水印斑病
Yellow vein banf\ ding	可可黄脉斑病
COCONUT（***Cocos nucifera***）	**椰子 *Cocos nucifera***
Pachymerus nucleorum	（粗腿豆象属）
Pseudotheranthus wayi	椰缘蝽
Pseudotheranthus devastans	橡胶缘蝽
Rhynchophorus palmarum	棕榈象甲
Oryctes monocerus	单角犀甲
Oryctes boas	暴蛀犀金龟
Coelaenomenodera elaeidis	油棕潜叶甲
Melitomma insulara	*Melitomma insulara*
Tatipaka/Coconut wilt	椰子萎蔫病
Cadang – Cadang	棕榈类顶死病
Lethal yellowing	椰子致死黄化病
Kaincope（Togo）	棕榈类致死黄化病（多哥）
Cape St. Paul wilt（Ghana）	枯萎病（加纳）
Kribi（Cameroons）	克里比（喀麦隆）
Awka（Nigeria）	奥卡（尼日利亚）
Natuna wilt	纳吐纳枯萎病
Rhadinaphelenchus cocophilus	椰子红轮线虫
Eriophyes guerreronis	椰子穗瘿螨
Artona catoxantha	马来亚椰斑蛾
Oryctes rhinoceros	椰子犀角金龟
Setora nitens	铜斑褐刺蛾

Rickettsiae	立克次菌
Marasmiellus cocophilus	(微皮伞属)
Phytophthora palmivora	棕榈疫霉
Head droop	类菌原体
Leaf scorch	椰子叶焦病
Little leaf	椰子小叶病
Mycoplasma – Like organism	椰子支原体类病
Phytophthora heveae	橡胶条溃疡病
COFFEE (*Coffea* spp.)	**咖啡 *Coffea* spp.**
Antestiopsis spp.	拟丽蝽属
Leucoptera coffeella	咖啡潜叶蛾
Planococcus kenyae	肯尼亚咖啡粉蚧
Omphalia flavida	咖啡叶斑病
Trachysphaera fructigena	粉荚病菌
Gibberella xylarioides	咖啡导管萎焉病
Coffee blister spot virus	咖啡疱状斑病毒
Mancha mantecosa	*Mancha mantecosa*
Colletotrichum coffeanum var virulens	(炭疽菌属)
Colletotrichum sp.	炭疽菌属
Hemileia coffeicola	咖啡新叶锈病
Phytomonas garcae	(植生滴虫属)
Bacterial leaf spot	咖啡细菌性叶斑病
Ring spot	咖啡环斑病
COTTON (*Gossypium* spp.)	**棉花 *Gossypium* spp.**
Anthonomus grandis	棉铃象甲虫
Anthonomus vestitus	短梗花象
Anthonomus spp.	花象属
Phymatotrichum omnivorum	棉根腐病
Sacadedes pyralis	南美红铃虫
Cotton leaf curl virus	棉花卷叶病毒病
GRAPE (*Vitis Vinifera*)	**葡萄 *Vitis Vinifera***
Agrobacterium tumefaciens	根癌农杆菌
Pierce's disease	葡萄皮尔斯病
Fan leaf virus	葡萄扇叶病毒
Guignardia bidwellii	葡萄球座菌
Leaf – roll virus	葡萄卷叶病
Mycoplasma – like organism	葡萄支原体类病
Nepo viruses (Grapevine fanleaf virus and its strains, Arabis mosaic, Hungarian chrome mosaic virus, Rasberry ring spot virus)	(葡萄扇叶病毒及其株系、南芥菜花叶病毒、匈牙利铬花叶病毒、树莓环斑病毒)
Grapevine corky bark	葡萄栓皮病毒
Grape 'legno ricco' or stem pitting	葡萄茎纹病

Xanthomonas ampelina	冰核活性细菌
GROUNDNUT (***Arachis hypogaea***)	**落花生 *Arachis hypogaea***
Marginal chlorosis virus	花生叶边褪绿病毒
Peanut stunt virus	花生矮化病毒
Phymatotrichum omnivorum	花生根腐病
Rosette viruses	玫瑰花形病毒
Sphaceloma arachidis	花生疮痂病
Verticillium dahliae	花生大丽轮枝菌
HEVEA RUBBER (***Hevea brasilliensis***)	**橡胶树 *Hevea brasilliensis***
Leptopharsa heveae	(网蝽科)
Microyclus ulei	南美叶枯病
Aleurodicus cocois	(粉虱科)
Erinnyis ello	木薯天蛾
Premolis semirufa	巴西蛾
Phytophthora spp.	橡胶疫霉属
Thanatephorus cucumeris	橡胶瓜亡革菌
Syn. *Pellicularia filamentosa*	橡胶丝核薄膜革菌
Catacauma huberi	橡胶黑壳病
HONEY BEES (***Apis* spp.**)	**蜜蜂 *Apis* spp.**
Acarapis woodi	武氏蜂盾螨
Bacillus larvae	幼虫芽孢杆菌
Streptococcus pluton	蜂房链球菌
Nosema apis	微孢子虫
Sacbrood	幼蜂皱萎病
MAIZE (***Zea mays***)	**玉米 *Zea mays***
Diatraea spp. esp. *D*, *saccharalis*	杆草螟属尤其是小蔗螟
Sesamia cretica	高粱蛀茎夜蛾
Erwina stewartii	玉米青枯病
Maize chlorotic dwarf virus	玉米黄化病毒
Maize dwarf mosaic virus	玉米矮化花叶病毒
Maize stripe virus	玉米条斑病毒
Maize streak virus	玉米条纹病毒
Maize stunt virus	玉米矮化病毒
Claviceps gigantean	(麦角菌属)
Corn stunt spiroplasma	玉米矮小螺原体
Dreschlera maydis	玉米叶病
Peronosclerospora philippensis	菲律宾霜霉病菌
Prostephanus truncatus	大谷蠹
MANGO (***Mangifera indica***)	**芒果 *Mangifera indica***
Noorda albizonalis	芒果汝达野螟
Sternochetus magifera	芒果果核象甲
Mango malformation and bunchy top	芒果畸形及束顶病
Woody gall & scaly bark	木瘤及鳞皮病

Elsinoe mangifera	芒果疮痂病
OIL PALM (Elaeis guineensis)	**油椰子 *Elaeis guineensis***
Pachymerus lacerdae	巴西粗腿豆象
Pachymerus nucleorum	(粗腿豆象属)
Pimelephila ghesquierei	非洲油棕蛀心螟
Fusarium oxysporum	尖孢镰刀菌
Cercospora elaeidis	油棕雀斑病
Coelaenomennodera elaeidis	油棕潜叶甲
Darna trema	(刺蛾科)
Leptopharsa gibbicarina	(网蝽科)
Mahasena corbetii	(蓑蛾科)
Metisa plana	油棒钩角蓑蛾
Oryctes rhinoceros	二疣犀甲
Retracrus elaeis	油棕后弯瘿螨
Rhynchophorus phoenicis	紫棕象甲
Setora nitens	褐刺蛾
Sibine fusca	(矛刺蛾属)
Rhadinaphelenchus cocophilus	椰子红轮线虫
Ganoderma lucidum	(灵芝菌属)
Phytomonas staheli	史氏植生滴虫
Fatal yellowing	椰子死亡类病毒
Leaf mottle	椰子叶斑病
Viroid Cadang – cadang	椰子死亡类病毒
ORCHIDS	**兰花**
Cymbidium mosaic virus	兰花花叶病毒
Orchid mosaic virus	兰花叶病毒
PAPAYA (*Carica papaya*)	**番木瓜 *Carica papaya***
Papaya bunchy top virus	番木瓜束顶病毒
Papaya mosaic virus	番木瓜花叶病毒
Papaya ring spot virus	番木瓜环斑病毒
***PEPPER* (*Piper nigrum*)**	**胡椒 *Piper nigrum***
Phytophthora palmivora	胡椒疫霉菌
***PINE* (*Pinus* spp.)**	**松属 *Pinus* spp.**
Cronartium harkensii	(柱锈菌属)
Cronartium ribicola	松疱锈病
Dothistroma pini	松座囊菌
Fusarium moniliforme var *subglutinans*	串珠镰刀菌
Scirrhia acicola	松针褐斑病
Scleroderris abietina	松针枝枯病
POTATO (Solanum tuberosum)	**马铃薯 *Solanum tuberosum***
Leptinotarasa decemlineata	马铃薯甲虫
Corynebacterium sepedonicum	马铃薯环腐病
Synchytrium endobioticum	马铃薯癌肿病

Heterodera rostochiensis	马铃薯金线虫
Oospora pustulans	马铃薯斑点病
Ditylenchus destructor	马铃薯茎线虫
RICE（Oryza sativa）	**稻 *Oryza sativa***
Aphelenchoides besseyi	水稻干尖线虫
Diatraea spp.	杆草螟属
Orseolia oryzae	稻瘿蚊
Sogatodes oryzicola and Cubana	条斑病
Rice dwarf virus	水稻矮化病毒
Rice stripe virus	水稻条斑病毒
Rice Hoja blanca virus	水稻白叶病毒
Lissorhopterus oryzaephilus	稻水象虫
Fusarium moniliforme	串珠镰孢菌
Ephelia pallida	（柱香菌属）
Rice waika virus	水稻矮化病毒
Transitory yellowing	水稻黄化（短暂）病毒
SILKWORM（*Bombyx mori*）	**蚕 *Bombyx mori***
Nosema bombycis	家蚕微孢子虫
Infectious flacherie, grasserie	蚕软化症病毒
SOYA BEAN（*Glycine max*）	**大豆 *Glycine max***
Cercospora kikuchii	大豆紫斑病菌
Colletotrichum truncatum	大豆炭疽菌
Peronospora manshurica	大豆霜霉病
Pseudomonas glycinea	大豆细菌性斑点病
Pseudomonas tabaci	烟草野火病
Soyabean dwarf virus	大豆矮缩病毒
Soyabean mosic virus	大豆花叶病毒
SUGARCANE（*Saccharum officinarum*）	**甘蔗 *Saccharum officinarum***
Diatraea spp.	杆草螟属
D. saccharalis	小蔗螟
Diaprepes abbreviatus	甘蔗根螟虫
Xanthomonas albilinean	（黄单胞菌属）
Xanthomonas rubrisubalicans	（黄单胞菌属）
Xanthomonas rubilineaus	（黄单胞菌属）
Xanthomonas vasculorum	甘蔗流胶病菌
Clemonra smithi	（甘蔗蛴螬）
Grassy shoot	甘蔗绿茎病
Fiji disease	甘蔗斐济病
Streak virus	甘蔗条纹病毒
Ring mosaic	甘蔗环斑花叶病
Ustilago scitaminea	甘蔗黑穗病
Dwarf virus	甘蔗矮小病毒
Sugarcane mosaic	甘蔗花叶病毒

SUNFLOWER（*Helianthus* sp.）	**向日葵 *Helianthus* sp.**
Sunflower mosic virus	向日葵花叶病毒
STONE FRUIT	**核果**
Stone fruit virus	核果病毒
SWEET POTATO（*Ipomoea batatas*）	**甘薯 *Ipomoea batatas***
Euscepes postfasciatus	西印度甘薯象甲
Sweet potato internal cork virus	甘薯内木栓病毒
Sweet potato mosaic virus	甘薯花叶病毒
Sweet potato dwarf virus	甘薯矮化病毒
TEA（Camellia sinensis）	**茶（茶属）**
Exobasidium reticulatum	网状外担菌
TOBACCO（*Nicotiana* spp.）	烟草 ***Nicotiana* spp.**
Ephestia elutella	烟草螟
Pseudomonas tabaci	假单胞菌
Peronospora tabacina	烟草霜霉菌
TUNG（Aleurites fordii）	**桐树 *Aleurites fordii***
Septobasidium aleuritidis	（隔坦菌属）
Trogoderma granarium	谷斑皮蠹
Popillia japonica	日本金龟子
Quadraspidiotus perniciosus	梨圆蚧
WEEDS	**杂草**
Alternanthera philoxeroides	空心莲子草
Baccaris halimifolia	（菊科）
Chondrilla juncea	灯芯草粉苞苣
Momosa pigra	刺轴含羞木
Myriophyllum brasiliense	巴西艽
Parthenium hysterophorus	银胶菊
Rottboellia exaltata	筒轴茅
Christisonia wightii	假野菰
Aeginetia indica	野菰
Striga angustifolia	（独脚金属）
Striga densiflora	密花独脚金
Striga gesnerioides	独脚金
Striga hermonthica	弯叶独脚金
Oryza barthii	短舌野生稻
Oryza longistaminata	长花药野生稻
Oryza punctata	斑点野生稻
Pennisetum polystachyon	狼尾草

附录 5
指定入境植物检验检疫站

	AIR –	**空港**
1	Subang International Airport	吉隆坡苏耶国际机场
2	Bayan Lepas Airport	槟城峇六拜国际机场
3	Senai Airport	士乃机场
4	Kuching Airport	古晋机场
5	Miri Airport	米里机场
6	Bintulu Airport	民机场都鲁
7	Kota Kinabalu Airport	亚庇国际机场
8	Labuan Airport	纳闽机场
9	Sandakan Airport	山打根机场
10	Tawau Airport	斗湖机场
	LAND –	**陆路口岸**
1	Johor Bharu	柔佛巴鲁
2	Padang Besar	巴当勿刹
3	Kroh	高乌
4	Changloon	樟仑
5	Wang Kelian	旺吉辇
6	Rantau Panjang	兰都班让
7	Pengkalan Kubor	彭加兰古堡
8	Miri	米里
9	Lawas	老越
10	Lubok Antu	鲁勃安都
11	Lundu	隆杜
12	Long Pa Sia	龙巴夏
13	Pensiangan	冰厢岸
14	Sindumin	实必丹
	SEA –	**海港口岸**
1	Butterworth	巴特沃思
2	Georgetown	乔治城
3	Port Kelang	巴生港
4	Melaka Port	马拉卡
5	Pasir Gudang	巴西古单
6	Kuantan Port	昆坦港
7	Tanah Putih	丹那美拉
8	Sim Kheng Hong	沉肯香港
9	Rejang Port (Sibu, Sarikei)	拉让港口

10	Bintulu	民都鲁
11	Miri	米里
12	Limbang	林梦
13	Sandakan	山打根
14	Lahad Datu	拉哈达图
15	Tawau	斗湖
16	Labuan	纳闽岛
17	Kudat	古达
18	Kota Kinabalu	哥打基纳巴卢
	PARCEL OFFICE –	**邮政中心**
1	Kuala Lumpur	吉隆坡
2	Penang	槟榔屿
3	Johor Bharu	新山
4	Kuching	古晋
5	Kota Kinabalu	哥打基纳巴卢

附录6
进口许可证—土壤/生根堆肥/生长介质

Permit No: ....

Name and address of consignee: ....

(*Name*)

of ....

(*Address*)

Permission is hereby granted to the consignee to import * *soil/rooting compost/growing media contained in the Schedule here to through* ....

....

(*appointed entry checkpoint*)

This permit is issued subject to the following conditions:

1. *Import licence is to be sought from the relevant Ministry*
2. *A copy of this Import Permit must be sent to the consignor and must accompany the consignment.*
3. *The* * *soil/rooting compost/growing media are subject to inspection and examination prior to clearance by the customs.*
4. *This Import Permit is valid until the* ....

For one consignment only.

5. *The consignment must be accompanied by a phytosanitary certificate or a statement from the official Plant Protection Service of the country of origin bearing the following certification*:

(*a*) *Treatment*: ....

(*b*) *Other declaration*: ....

....

6. *Further conditions*: ....

Schedule:

Description	*Quantity*	*Country of origin*

Date of issue: ....

....

Director of Agriculture

Delete whichever inapplicable.

附录 7
植物检疫证书—出口

Plant Protection Organization | *No.* ....
of .... | *(country of re - export)*
TO: Plant Protection Organization (s)
of ....

Description of consignment

Name and address of exporter ....
Declared name and address of consignee ....
Number and description of packages ....
Distinguishing marks ....
Place of origin ....
Declared means of conveyance ....
Declared point of entry ....
Name of produce and quantity declared ....
Botanical name of plants ....

This is to certify that the plants or plant products described above were imported into .... *(country of re - export)* .... *from* .... *(country of * origin)* .... *Covered by Phytosanitary Certificate No.* .... *original * certified true copy of which is attached together with this * certificate. That they are packed repacked in original * new containers, and that based on the original Phytosanitary * Certificate and additional inspection, they are considered to conform with the current phytosanitary regulations of the importing country, and that during storage in* .... *(country of re - export)* .... *the consignment has not been subjected to the risk of infestation or infection.*

Please tick (/) appropriate box

Disinfestation/and/or disinfection treatment

Date .... | *Treatment* ....
Chemical (active ingredient) .... | *Duration and temperature* ....
concentration .... | *Additional information* ....

....

Additional declaration: ....

....

Place of issue ....
Name of Authorized Officer ....

....

Signature ....

(*Stamp of Organization*)

Date: ....

No financial liability with respect to this Certificate shall attach to the Government of Malaysia or to any of its officers or representatives.

附录8
有益生物进境许可证

Permit No: ____________

Name and address of consignee: ____________

of ____________

(*Address*)

Name and address of consignee: ____________

of ____________

(*Address*)

*Permission is hereby granted to the consignee to import * soil/rooting compost/growing media contained in the Schedule here to through* ____________

____

(*appointed entry checkpoint*)

This permit is issued subject to the following conditions:

1. *Import licence is to be sought from the relevant Ministry*
2. *A copy of this Import Permit must be sent to the consignor and must accompany the consignment.*
3. *The consignment is subject to inspection prior to clearance by the customs.*
4. *This Import Permit is valid until the* ____________

For one consignment only.

5. *The consignment must be accompanied by a phytosanitary certificate or a statement from the official Plant Protection Service of the country of origin bearing the following certification*:

(*c*) *Treatment*: ____________

(*d*) *Other declaration*: ____________

____

Schedule:

Description	*Quantity*	*Country of origin*

Date of issue: ____________

____

Director of Agriculture

附录9（法规5条第5）
来自发生谷斑皮蠹国家的植物产品

***Name of plant* * –**	**植物名称***
1. *Peas and beans – seeds and meal*	豌豆和豆类 – 种子和谷物粗粉
2. *Cashew nuts*	腰果
3. *Groundnut – seeds and cake*	花生 – 种子和块状物
4. *Maize – seeds, meal and dried cobs*	玉米 – 种子，谷物粗粉和干棒子
5. *Rice – milled and bran*	水稻 – 碾磨过的和麸
6. *Sesame – seeds and cake*	芝麻 – 种子和块状物
7. *Wheat – bran and seeds*	小麦 – 麸和种子
8. *Spices*	香料
9. *Tapioca – flour, chips and pearls*	木薯 – 淀粉，干片和粒
10. *Sorghum – grain*	高粱 – 粒
11. *Gunny sacks*	麻布袋
(* *This does not apply to plants that are chilled, preserved or hermetically sealed.*)	这些并不适用于冷藏，经防腐加工或密封的植物及其产品
***Countries of export* –**	**出口国家**
1. *Bangladesh*	孟加拉共和国
2. *India*	印度
3. *Pakistan*	巴基斯坦
4. *Sudan*	苏丹
5. *Turkey*	土耳其
6. *Thailand*	泰国
7. *Philippines*	菲律宾
8. *Burma*	缅甸
9. *Indonesia*	印度尼西亚
10. *Morocco*	墨西哥
11. *Sri Lanka*	斯里兰卡

附录 10
植物检疫申报表

All persons entering a component region (West Malaysia, Labuan, Sabah or Sarawak) are required to supply the information required in this form.

---

1. Full Name (Use block letters) Male ☐ Female ☐

....

2. Age .... 3. Passport No ....

4. Flight No/Vessel's Name ....

5. Last place of embarkation ....

1 * (a) Have you been to Africa, # South or Central America or the # Caribbean during the last 30 days?

Yes ☐ No ☐

(b) If yes, please state of departure from last country visited (from any of the above).

2 * Are you carrying any plant, parts of plant or any other living organisms?

Yes ☐ No ☐

....

Date Signature

Penalty for failure to complete this From or providing false information is a fine up to one thousand ringgit or to imprisonment for a term not exceeding six month or to both on conviction.

Please tick (/) appropriate box

#Countries in the South America and Caribbean as follows.

"Brazil, Paraguay, Bolivia, Peru, Ecuador, Colombia, Venezuela, Guyana, Surinam, French, Guiana, Trinidad & Tobago, Barbados, Puerto Rico, Jamaica, Dominican Republic, Haiti, Cuba, Panama Canal Zone, Costa Rica, Nicaragua, Honduras, Guatemala, Belize, Mexico, El Salvador".

Date the 21_{st} April 1992.

[KP/LA/529/4; PN. (PU^2) 303/II]

DATUK SERI SANUSI JUNID

Minister of Agriculture

Plant quarantine regulations 1981

(1981)

IN exercise of the powers conferred by section 23 of the Plant Quarantine

1976, the Minister makes the following regulations:

1. (1) These Regulations may be cited as the Plant Quarantine Regulations 1981 and shall come into force on the 31st March, 1981.

(2) Nothing in these Regulations shall apply to the movement of beneficial organisms, carrier, growing media, non – plant articles, pests, plants, rooting compost and soil between Sabah and Federal Territory of Labuan.

2. In these Regulations, unless the context otherwise requires:

"American tropics" means those parts of the Continent by America, including adjacent islands, which are bounded by the Tropics of Capricorn (latitude 23½°S) and the Tropic of Cancer (latitude 23½°N) and by Longitudes 30°W and 120°W and includes that part of Mexico which is North of the Tropic of Cancer;

"appointed entry check – points" means the customs check – points specified in the Fifth Schedule;

"carrier" means and includes any type of vehicle, vessel, aircraft, or container in which beneficial organisms, growing media, non – plant articles, pests, plants, rooting compost and soil may be moved from one place toanother;

"direct transit" means a consignment taken or sent from any country and brought into a component region for the sole purpose of being carried toanother country by the same or another conveyance without having obtained clearance from the customs;

"garbage" means all materials derived in whole or in part from vegetables, fruits or other parts of a plant and other refuse which are associated with any such material;

"import officer" means any officer of the customs, agricultural or postal services on duty at an appointed entry check – point and other legal landing places defined under the Customs Act 1967;

"indirect transit" means a consignment taken or sent from any country and brought into a component region for the sole purpose of being carried to another country by the same or another conveyance, after having obtained clearance from the customs into a omponent region;

"phytosanitary certificate" means the certificate set out in the Second Schedule issued by an inspecting officer certifying that he has, before dispatch, thoroughly examined the plants to which the statement relates, or a representative sample thereof, and found the plants or sample to be free, from any pests or disease;

"plant quarantine inspector" means an import officer of the Agricultural Services;

"schedule plant" means the plants specified in the Third Schedule;

"soil" means any earth, ground or other naturally occurring organic and mineral in which plants may be grown;

"South East Asia and Pacific Region" means the region comprisingall the territories in South East Asia east of the western border of Pakistan and south of the Himalayas, the southern border of China and of the eastern coast of Vietnam together with all those territories in the Pacific Ocean, the South China Sea and the Indian Ocean situated wholly or partly in the area bounded by longitude 100℃ East, latitude 45℃ South, longitude

130℃ West, latitude 38℃ North, to the point of its interception with the western coast of the Republic of Korea and from that point to a straight line to Taipei and thence a straight line to the point of interception of the eastern coast of Vietnam and latitude 15° North including Hong Kong;

"the African Cacao Region" means any African territory in which any disease of cacao or Mirid (Capsid) bug affecting cacao is known, or believed, to occur.

3. The importation into a component of soil whether by itself or attached to the roots or other parts of plants is prohibited:

Except where the soil is imported for analysis or for research purposes under a permit as set out in the Sixth Schedule.

4. (1) Nothing in these Regulations shall apply to:

(a) Any plant imported for consumption, medicinal, processing or manufacturing purposes;

(b) Any processed plants;

(c) Any plant or parts of a plant used as packaging or packing material; or

(d) Any garbage, dunnage and pallets.

But items exempted under paragraphs (a), (b) and (c) are subject to inspection, and if found to be diseased of infested may be treated or destroyed and items exempted under paragraph (d) are subject to disposal in a manner to be determined by the Director.

(2) Importation of plants exempted under paragraphs (a) and (b) of sub – regulations (1) by air from the American tropics into a component region is subject to the requirements as specified under regulation 7 (ii) and (iii).

(3) The provisions of paragraphs (a), (b) and (c) of subregulation (1) do not apply to items, including coconut (whole or dehusked), oil palm (fruit bunch) and plants listed under subregulation (5) and (6) of regulation 5, where they are reasonably suspected to be diseased or infested with dangerous pests. Non – application of these Regulations.

5. (1) The importation into a component region of any plant, or any rooting compost or other growing media is prohibited except under a permit in the First Schedule in respect of plants and the Sixth Schedule in respect of rooting compost or other growing media issued by the Director in a accordance with these Regulation and subject to such conditions as the Director may, by endorsement on the permit, impose.

(2) Subject to the prohibitions and restrictions contained in regulation 6, each consignment of plants imported into a component region shall be accompanied by a phytosanitary certificate as contained in the Second Schedule and where applicable a phytosanitary certificate for re – export as contained in the Seventh Schedule from the country of re – export or any other documents signed by or on behalf of an authorized official of the plant protection service in the country concerned or in the case of a component region, the Director of the component region in which the plants were grown, which is issued to the consignor not more than fourteen days prior to dispatch of the consignment and shall accompany the consignment.

(3) A plant, beneficial organisms, rooting composts, soil or other growing media may only be imported through an appointed entry check – point as specified in the respective permits in regulation 3 and sub – regulations (1) and (4) of regulation 5. Prohibition of import of plant etc. except under permit.

(4) The importation into a component region of any beneficial organism is prohibited except under a permit contained in the Eighth Schedule issued by the Director in accordance with the regulations and subject to such conditions as the Director may, by endorsement on the permit, impose.

(5) Plants, which are exempted under regulation 4 (1) (a), (b) and (c) and imported from countries where the khapra beetle is found, as contained in the Ninth Schedule, shall be treated by the exporting countries according to the dosage rates to be determined by the Director and such a consignment of plants shall be accom-

panied by a phytosanitary certificate.

(6) Notwithstanding regulation 4 (1) (a), the importation into a component region of cocoa pods, rambutan, pulasan, longan and nam – nam fruits produced in another component region, the Philippines and Indonesia is prohibited.

6. (1) The importation into a component region of any plant of any species of *Hevea* from any country or another component region is prohibited except where –

(i) the importation is made for research purposes;

(ii) the importation is consigned to the Director; and

(iii) prior to such importation, the importation has been referred by the Director to the Director of the Rubber Research Institute of Malaysia who may make such recommendations there on as he thinks fit, to which the Director shall not be found.

(2) The importation into a component region of any plant of any species of *Hevea* which is capable of further growth or propagation from the American Tropics or from any other country in which South American Leaf Blight (*Microcyclus ulei* (*P. Henn.*) Arx.) is present or believed to be present is prohibited unless, in addition to the requirements of paragraph (1), such plant –

(i) has been grown for an adequate period at a plant quarantine station for *Hevea* approved by the Director for this purpose which is situated outside the South East Asia and Pacific region, the American Tropics or any other region or country in which the South American Leaf Blight (*Microcyclus ulei* (P. Henn.) Arx.) is present;

(ii) has been found to be free from pests; and

(iii) is accompanied by a certificate to the effect that requirements of sub – paragraph (i) and (ii) have beenfulfilled and signed by the officer – in – charge of such quarantine station.

(3) The importation into a component region of any seed of any species of *Hevea* from the American Tropics or from any other country in which the South American Leaf Blight (*Microcyclus ulei* (*P. Henn.*) Arx.) is present or believed to present is prohibited unless, in addition to the requirements of paragraph (1) such seed –

(i) has been examined and disinfected at a place approved by the Director for this purpose which is situated outside the South East Asia and Pacific Region, the American Tropics or any other region or country where the South American Leaf Blight (*Microcyclus ulei* (P. Henn.) Arx.) is present;

(ii) has been repacked with new packing materials in new containers; and

(iii) is accompanied by a certificate to the effect that the requirements of sub – paragraphs (i) and (ii) have been fulfilled and signed by the officer – in – charge of the place of such examination and disinfection.

(4) The importation into a component region of any plant of any species of *Hevea* not capable of further growth or propagation (such as fresh or dried herbarium specimens) is prohibited unless it complies with provisions of paragraph (1) and such plant is required for research purposes or any other purposes approved by the Director and has been sterilised in the country of origin by a method which the Director considers to be satisfactory.

7. The importation of plant, other than those belonging to the species of *Hevea*, from the American Tropics or from any other country in which the South American Leaf Blight (*Microcyclus ulei* (P. Henn.) Arx.) is present is also prohibited except where –

(i) the importation is made for research purposes;

(ii) the importation is consigned to the Director; and

(iii) such plant has been subjected to quarantine or treatment at a place approved by the Director for this purpose situated outside the South East Asia and Pacific Region, and the American Tropics or any other region or country where the South American Leaf Blight ((Microcyclus ulei (P. Henn.) Arx.) is present or believed to be present, and has been found to be free from pests and is accompanied by a certificate to that effect and signed by the officer – incharge of the place of such quarantine or treatment.

8. The importation into a component region of any plant *Theobroma cacao* L. (cacao), *Cocos nucifera* (coconut), *Elaeis guineensis* (oil palm), or any scheduled plant which is known to be a host of the cacao swollen shoot virus complex, lethal yellowing, kaincope, cadang – cadang or any virus or serious disease is prohibited except where –

(i) the importation is made for research purposes;

(ii) the importation is consigned to the Director; and

(iii) such plant has been subjected to quarantine or treatment at a place approved by the Director for this purpose situated outside the American Tropics, the African Cacao Region or any other diseases of cacao, oil palm and coconut is present or believed to be present, and has been found to be free from pests and is accompanied by a certificate to that effect and signed by the officer – in – charge of the place of such.

9. (1) The importation of Dangerous Pests set out in the Fourth Schedule is prohibited.

(2) Any plant imported into a component region which appears to be infested with such dangerous pests or with any other pest or disease which, in the opinion of the Director, is of a particularly dangerous nature, and any other plant kept in the same container with such plants, shall be destroyed immediately.

(3) The Director may direct all civil, military, naval, air, police or other organizations or forces present for the time being or established in Malaysia to provide the necessary assistance for the purpose of preventing the introduction of any dangerous pests or noxious plants into a component region or for the purpose of the eradication or control of such dangerous pests or noxious plants if present in a component region.

10. (1) Any plant imported into a component region may be detained by the import officer at the appointed entry check – point until such plant is placed in the charge of the Director who may release it, or if it is found or suspected to be diseased, the Director may destroy or otherwise dispose of it as he thinks fit.

(2) Every consignment of plants imported into a component region shall be examined by the import officer either at the place of entry or at any other place approved by the Director.

(3) The Director may determine the method for quarantine treatment or destruction, of any consignment of plants or part thereof which has been imported into a component region which is found or is suspected to be diseased.

(4) Any loss or cost incurred, including the cost of transport, for the purpose of inspection, quarantine, treatment or destruction of any plant imported into a component region shall be borne by the importer: Provided that the Director may, in his discretion exempt the importer from the whole or any part thereof.

10A. Non – plant articles and carriers which are reasonably suspected to be diseased or infested with pests are subject to inspection and treatment.

11. Any plant which has been imported into a component region in contravention of these Regulations shall be detained by the import officer and may be disposed of in such manner as the Director shall direct.

12. (1) Plants or pests in direct transit or indirect transit shall not be removed from the conveyance in which they have been brought into a component region without the prior permission of the Director who may impose any condition as he deems fit.

(2) The provisions of regulation 5 shall apply to plants in direct or indirect transit.

13. (1) An import officer may seize any pests imported or kept contravention of these Regulations.

(2) Whenever it appears to any plant quarantine inspector that there is reasonable cause to believe that any person carries or possesses or any personal effects or carrier contains or carries any plants, soil, pests, beneficial organisms, rooting compost or growing media or any non – plant articles in contravention of the provisions of these Regulations, it shall be lawful for the plant quarantine inspector to stop, inspect and search such person,

and to seize such personal effects or carrier and to take any appropriate action asprovided by these Regulations.

(3) A plant quarantine inspector is authorized to board any vessel, vehicle or aircraft arriving from any foreign country or another component region to inspect, treat or dispose of beneficial organisms, containers, growing media, non-plant articles including garbage and dunnage, pests, rooting compost and soil, which are likely to be diseased or infested with pests.

14. (1) Any person who -

(a) willfully resists, obstructs, impedes or hinders an import officer in the exercise of his powers or the performance of his duties under these Regulations;

(b) maliciously introduces a pest or a plant into a component region from another component region or foreign country.

(c) fails or refuses without reasonable cause to give information to an import officer when required to do so or knowingly gives false or incomplete information.

(d) for the purpose of obtaining, whether for himself or any other person, a permit, phytosanitary certificate or other document, makes a declaration or statement which he knows to be false, or does not know or does not believe to be true or knowingly makes use such declaration or statement;

(e) contravenes any provision of these Regulations.

(f) fails to comply with any restrictions or conditions imposed by the Director on any permit issued under these Regulations or

(g) fails or refuses to complete the Plant Quarantine Declaration Form as set out in the Tenth Schedule or provides false information therein, shall be guilty of an offence.

(2) on conviction of any offence under paragraphs (a), (c), (d), (e), (f) or (g) of sub-regulation (1) of regulation 14, the offender shall be liable to fine not exceeding one thousand ringgit or to imprisonment for a term not exceeding six month or both.

(3) On convention of any offence under paragraph (b) of sub-regulation (1) of regulation 14, the offender shall be liable to the penalty as set out under section 19A of the Plant Quarantine Act 1976.

15. (1) A fee of 15 ringgit shall be charged for the issue of an import permit in respect of a consignment which shall be valid for a period of three months from the date is issued.

(1A) An import permit which has expired may be extended only once for a further period not exceeding one month from the date of its expiry upon payment of five ringgit.

(2) Fees at the following rates shall charged for the inspection of a consignment or premise, disinfection of pests, treatment of plant or plant produce by the Inspecting Officer or plant quarantine inspector:

(i) (a) for the first half manhour or part thereof $10

(b) for the second half manhour or part thereof $10

(c) for every additional manhour or part thereof $20

(ii) Where an Inspecting Officer inspects or supervises disinfection of a consignment at any place other than at his office premises or inspects or supervises disinfection of growing crops in the field, the time taken to carry out such inspection or supervision shall include the time taken for his journey to and from such place.

(iii) Where disinfection or treatment is carried out by the Inspecting Officer or the plant quarantine inspector as the case may be, the cost of chemicals or other materials incurred in carrying out the disinfection or treatment shall be borne by the consignor or consignee according to the rates to be determined by the Director from time to time.

(iv) Overtime allowance for an Inspecting Officer or plant quarantine inspector who conducts inspection on any consignment or premise as required by either the consignor or consignee shall be borne by the consignee as the case may be -

(a) at the rate of four ringgit per hour beyond the usual office hours; and

(b) at the rate of eight ringgit per hour during weekends or public holidays.

(3) Travelling expenses by air, rail or/and road, whichever is applicable, shall be charged in respect of any journey made for the purpose of carrying out any inspection or supervision provided that where the journey is wholly or partly by road, the charge will be at the rate of 50 sen for every kilometer or part thereof.

(4) Where an Inspecting Officer, on the application of any person or as a requirement under the condition of import specified in the Import Permit attends at place away from his place of duty within Malaysia or outside Malaysia to carry out any inspection, subsistence and accommodation expenses in accordance with current government rates shall be reimbursed by such person to the Director.

(5) An Inspecting Officer may, in his discretion, inspect the source of plant produce in addition to the inspection of a particular consignment, and the consignor shall pay the fees specified in paragraph (2) in respect of such inspection.

16. Fees at the following rates shall be charged for keeping plants under post entry quarantine or which are not removed promptly by an importer –

(i) for every plant, per day for the first week of keeping or post – entry quarantine. $2

(ii) for every plant, per day for the second week of keeping or post – entry quarantine. $3

(iii) for every plant, per day for the third week of keeping or post – entry quarantine. $4

(iv) for every plant, per day for the fourth week of keeping or post – entry quarantine. $5

(v) for every plant, which is grown in post – entry quarantine for the full growing season or part for observation. $10

(vi) not withstanding paragraphs (i), (ii), (iii), (iv) and (v) the Director may in his discretion levy a lump sum in lieu of the fees chargeable under the said paragraphs.

17. All persons entering a component region are required to complete the Plant Quarantine Declaration Form as set out under the Tenth Schedule and shall surrender the Form at an appointed entry checkpoint.

18. (1) The Master or agent of every vessel entering a component region at an appointed sea port listed under the Fifth Schedule shall, within twenty four hours of the arrival, and before any cargo is unshipped, present to a plant quarantine inspector a copy of the true inward manifest of the vessel with the particulars as required under section 52 (1) of the Customs Act 1967.

(2) The pilot or agent of every aircraft entering a component region at an appointed airport, as listed under the Fifth Schedule shall, before any cargo is delivered, present to a plant quarantine inspector a copy of the true inward manifest of the aircraft with the particulars as required under section 56 of the Customs Act 1967.

19. (1) An Inspecting Officer may issue a phytosanitary certificate as set out in the Second Schedule for plants, plant products and nonplant articles exported from or moving between the component region based on inspections and treatment performed at the request of exporters to meet the requirements of the phytosanitary regulations of the importing component region or country.

(2) set out in the Seventh Schedule for the re – export of plants or plant products grown or produced in the third country or a component region at the requested of exporters to meet the requirements of the phytosanitary regulations of the importing component region of country.

(3) All expenses incurred in carrying out the inspection and treatment of the plants, plant products or non – plant articles shall be borne by the exporter according to the rates set out under regulation.

First schedule
[Regulation 5 (1)]
Permit to import plants

Permit No ________________

Name and address of consignee ____

(Name)

of ____

(Address)

Name and address of consignor ____

(Name)

of ____

(Address)

Permission is hereby granted to the consignee to import the plants contained in the Schedule here to through ____

(Appointed entry check – point)

This permit is issued subject to the following conditions –

(1) Import Licence is to be sought from the relevant Ministry.

(2) Plants must be accompanied with a Phytosanitary Certificate from the country of origin of the plants issued within 14 days prior to dispatch of the consignment.

(3) A copy of this Import Permit must be sent to the consignor and must accompany the consignment.

(4) Plants must be free from soil and pest.

(5) Plants are subject to inspection or examination prior to clearance from the Customs Office.

(6) This Import Permit is valid for one consignment only until ________________

(Date)

Further conditions ____

____

____

Schedule:

Descriptions	Quantity	Country of origin

Date of issue ________________

____

Director of Agriculture

Second schedule
[Regulation 5 (2)]
Phytosanitary certificate

No ....

Plant Protection Organization

of ....

To: Plant Protection Organization (s)

of ....

Description of consignment

Name and address of exporter ....

Declared name and address of consignee ....

Number and description of packages ....

Distinguishing marks ....

Place of origin ....

Declared means of conveyance ....

Declared point of entry ....

Name of produce and quantity declared ....

Botanical name of plants ....

This is certify that the plants or plant products described above have been inspected according to appropriate procedures and are considered to be free from quarantine pests, and practically free from other injurious pests; and that they are considered to conform with the current phytosanitary regulations of the importing country.

Disinfestation and/or disinfection treatment

Date .... *Treatment* ....

Chemical (active ingredient) .... *Duration and temperature* ....

Concentration .... *Additional information* ....

....

Additional declaration ....

Place of issue ....

(Stamp of Organization) *Name of authorized*

Officer ....

Date: .... *Signature* ....

No financial liability with respect to this certificate shall attach to the Government of Malaysia or to any of its officers or representatives.

Third schedule
(Regulations 8 and 11)
Plants which shall be destroyed if imported in contravention of these regulations

Ananas comosus (L.) Merr. (Pineapple)
All species of *Artocarpus* (Keledang)
Camellia sinensis (L.) Kuntze. (Tea)
Carica papaya L. (Papaya)
All species of *Citrus* and allied genera
All species of *Coffea* (Coffee)
All species of *Colocasia* and *Zanthosoma* (Taro)
Durio zibethinus Murr. (Durian)
All species of Forest trees
Glycine max (L.) Merr.
All species of *Gossypium* (Cotton)
All species of *Hevea* (Rubber)
Ipomoea batatas Poir. (Sweet potato)
All species of Leguminosae
All species of *Mangifera*
All species of *Manihot* (Cassavae)
All species of *Musa* and allied genera (Banana, Plantains and Manila hemp)
All species of *Nephelium*
All species of *Nicotiana* (Tobaccoes)
All members of the Orchidaceae
Oryza sativa L. (Rice)
All members of the Palmaceae (coconut, oil palm and other palms)
All members of the Piperaceae (Peppers)
All species of *Saccharum* (Sugarcane)
Solanum tuberosum L. (Potato)
Zea mays L. (Maize)
All species of *Theobroma* (Cacao) and other plants known, or likely to be, hosts, of virus diseases of cacao (including all members of the families Bombacaceae and Sterculiaceae)
Plants grown in the American Tropics
Plants grown in the African Cacao Region
All species of Zingiberaceae

Fourth schedule
(Regulation 9)
Dangerous pests

AVOCADO (***Persea* spp.**)

Sunblotch virus of avocado

BANANA (***Musa* spp.**)

Bunchy top virus

Mycosphaerella musicola var *difformis*

Pseudomonas solanacearum

Mycosplasma – Like organism

BARLEY (***Sorghum* spp.**)

Barley stripe mosaic

CASSAVA (***Manihot esculenta***)

Phaeolus manihotis

Cassava brown streak virus

Cassava mosaic virus

Cassava witch's broom

Super elongation disease

Caliothrips masculinus

Monomychelus tanajoa

Oligonychus peruvianus

Mycoplasma – like organism

Sphaceloma manihotis

Frog's skin

Cassava latent virus disease

African mosaic

CITRUS (***Citrus* spp.**)

Anastrepha fraterculus

Anastrepha ludens

Anastrepha mombinpraeoptans

Anastrepha spp.

Ceratitis rasa

Ceratitis capitata

Dacus tryoni

Deuterophoma tracheiphila

Citrus stubborn disease

Citrus green

Quadraspidiotus perniciosus

Impietratura virus

Exocortis virus

Satsuma dwarf virus

Spiroplasma citri
Yellow virus
Xyloporosis virus
COCOA (***Theobroma cacao***)
Sahlbergella singularis
Distantiella theobroma
Helopeltis bergrothis
Stenoma decora
Bathycoella thalassina
Marasmius perniciosus
Monilia roreri
Trachysphaera fructigena
Cacao swollen shoot virus complex
Cacao red mottle virus
Cacao vein – clearing virus
Acrocercops cramerella
Cacao yellow mosaic virus
Monalonium sp.
Oncobasidium theobromae
Phytophthora palmivora
Water mark
Yellow vein banf\ ding
COCONUT (***Cocos nucifera***)
Pachymerus nucleorum
Pseudotheranthus wayi
Pseudotheranthus devastans
Rhynchophorus palmarum
Oryctes monocerus
Oryctes boas
Coelaenomenodera elaeidis
Melitomma insulara
Tatipaka/Coconut wilt
Cadang – Cadang
Lethal yellowing
Kaincope (Togo)
Cape St. Paul wilt (Ghana)
Kribi (Cameroons)
Awka (Nigeria)
Natuna wilt
Rhadinaphelenchus cocophilus
Eriophyes guerreronis
Artona catoxantha
Oryctes rhinoceros

Setora nitens

Rickettsiae

Marasmiellus cocophilus

Phytophthora palmivora

Head droop

Leaf scorch

Little leaf

Mycoplasma – Like organism

Phytophthora heveae

COFFEE (***Coffea* spp.**)

Antestiopsis spp.

Leucoptera coffeella

Planococcus kenyae

Omphalia flavida

Trachysphaera fructigena

Gibberella xylarioides

Coffee blister spot virus

Mancha mantecosa

Colletotrichum coffeanum var *virulens*

Colletotrichum sp.

Hemileia coffeicola

Phytomonas garcae

Bacterial leaf spot

Ring spot

COTTON (***Gossypium* spp.**)

Anthonomus grandis

Anthonomus vestitus

Anthonomus spp.

Phymatotrichum omnivorum

Sacadedes pyralis

Cotton leaf curl virus

GRAPE (***Vitis Vinifera***)

Agrobacterium tumefaciens

Pierce's disease

Fan leaf virus

Guignardia bidwellii

Leaf – roll virus

Mycoplasma – like organism

Nepo viruses (Grapevine fanleaf virus and its strains, Arabis mosaic, Hungarian chrome mosaic virus, Rasberry ring spot virus)

Grapevine corky bark

Grape 'legno ricco' or stem pitting

Xanthomonas ampelina

GROUNDNUT（***Arachis hypogaea***）

Marginal chlorosis virus

Peanut stunt virus

Phymatotrichum omnivorum

Rosette viruses

Sphaceloma arachidis

Verticillium dahliae

HEVEA RUBBER（***Hevea brasilliensis***）

Leptopharsa heveae

Microyclus ulei

Aleurodicus cocois

Erinnyis ello

Premolis semirufa

Phytophthora spp.

Thanatephorus cucumeris

Syn. *Pellicularia filamentosa*

Catacauma huberi

HONEY BEES（***Apis* spp.**）

Acarapis woodi

Bacillus larvae

Streptococcus pluton

Nosema apis

Sacbrood

MAIZE（***Zea mays***）

Diatraea spp. esp. *D*, *saccharalis*

Sesamia cretica

Erwina stewartii

Maize chlorotic dwarf virus

Maize dwarf mosaic virus

Maize stripe virus

Maize streak virus

Maize stunt virus

Claviceps gigantean

Corn stunt spiroplasma

Dreschlera maydis

Peronosclerospora philippensis

Prostephanus truncatus

MANGO（***Mangifera indica***）

Noorda albizonalis

Stenochetus magifera

Mango malformation and bunchy top

Woody gall & scaly bark

Elsinoe mangifera

OIL PALM（Elaeis guineensis）
Pachymerus lacerdae
Pachymerus nucleorum
Pimelephila ghesquierei
Fusarium oxysporum
Cercospora elaeidis
Coelaenomennodera elaeidis
Darna trema
Leptopharsa gibbicarina
Mahasena corbetii
Metisa plana
Oryctes rhinoceros
Retracrus elaeis
Rhynchophorus phoenicis
Setora nitens
Sibine fusca
Rhadinaphelenchus cocophilus
Ganoderma lucidum
Phytomonas staheli
Fatal yellowing
Leaf mottle
Viroid Cadang – cadang
ORCHIDS
Cymbidium mosaic virus
Orchid mosaic virus
PAPAYA（Carica papaya）
Papaya bunchy top virus
Papaya mosaic virus
Papaya ring spot virus
PEPPER（*Piper nigrum*）
Phytophthora palmivora
PINE（*Pinus* spp.）
Cronartium harkensii
Cronartium ribicola
Dothistroma pini
Fusarium moniliforme var *subglutinans*
Scirrhia acicola
Scleroderris abietina
POTATO（*Solanum tuberosum*）
Leptinotarasa decemlineata
Corynebacterium sepedonicum
Synchytrium endobioticum
Heterodera rostochiensis

Oospora pustulans

Ditylenchus destructor

RICE（*Oryza sativa*）

Aphelenchoides besseyi

Diatraea spp.

Orseolia oryzae

Sogatodes oryzicola and *Cubana*

Rice dwarf virus

Rice stripe virus

Rice Hoja blanca virus

Lissorhopterus oryzaephilus

Fusarium moniliforme

Ephelia pallida

Rice waika virus

Transitory yellowing

SILKWORM（*Bombyx mori*）

Nosema bombycis

Infectious flacherie, grasserie

SOYA BEAN（*Glycine max*）

Cercospora kikuchii

Colletotrichum truncatum

Peronospora manshurica

Pseudomonas glycinea

Pseudomonas tabaci

Soyabean dwarf virus

Soyabean mosic virus

SUGARCANE（*Saccharum officinarum*）

Diatraea spp.

D. saccharalis

Diaprepes abbreviatus

Xanthomonas albilinean

Xanthomonas rubrisubalicans

Xanthomonas rubilineaus

Xanthomonas vasculorum

Clemonra smithi

Grassy shoot

Fiji disease

Streak virus

Ring mosaic

Ustilago scitaminea

Dwarf virus

Sugarcane mosaic

SUNFLOWER (*Helianthus* sp.)

Sunflower mosic virus

STONE FRUIT

Stone fruit virus

SWEET POTATO (*Ipomoea batatas*)

Euscepes postfasciatus

Sweet potato internal cork virus

Sweet potato mosaic virus

Sweet potato dwarf virus

TEA (*Camellia sinensis*)

Exobasidium reticulatum

TOBACCO (*Nicotiana* spp.)

Ephestia elutella

Pseudomonas tabaci

Peronospora tabacina

TUNG (*Aleurites fordii*)

Septobasidium aleuritidis

Trogoderma granarium

Popillia japonica

Quadraspidiotus perniciosus

WEEDS

Alternanthera philoxeroides

Baccaris halimifolia

Chondrilla juncea

Momosa pigra

Myriophyllum brasiliense

Parthenium hysterophorus

Rottboellia exaltata

Christisonia wightii

Aeginetia indica

Striga angustifolia

Striga densiflora

Striga gesnerioides

Striga hermonthica

Oryza barthii

Oryza longistaminata

Oryza punctata

Pennisetum polystachyon

Appointed entry check – points

AIR –

1	Subang International Airport
2	Bayan Lepas Airport
3	Senai Airport
4	Kuching Airport
5	Miri Airport
6	Bintulu Airport
7	Kota Kinabalu Airport
8	Labuan Airport
9	Sandakan Airport
10	Tawau Airport

LAND –

1	Johor Bharu
2	Padang Besar
3	Kroh
4	Changloon
5	Wang Kelian
6	Rantau Panjang
7	Pengkalan Kubor
8	Miri
9	Lawas
10	Lubok Antu
11	Lundu
12	Long Pa Sia
13	Pensiangan
14	Sindumin

SEA –

1	Butterworth
2	Georgetown
3	Port Kelang
4	Melaka Port
5	Pasir Gudang
6	Kuantan Port
7	Tanah Putih
8	Sim Kheng Hong
9	Rejang Port (Sibu, Sarikei)
10	Bintulu

11	Miri
12	Limbang
13	Sandakan
14	Lahad Datu
15	Tawau
16	Labuan
17	Kudat
18	Kota Kinabalu

PARCEL OFFICE –

1	Kuala Lumpur
2	Penang
3	Johor Bharu
4	Kuching
5	Kota Kinabalu

Sixth schedule

[Regulations 3 and 5 (1)]

Permit to import ∗ soil/rooting compost/growing media

Permit No: ....

Name and address of consignee: ....

(*Name*)

of ....

(*Address*)

Permission is hereby granted to the consignee to import ∗ soil/rooting compost/growing media contained in the Schedule here to through ....

....

(*appointed entry checkpoint*)

This permit is issued subject to the following conditions:

1. *Import licence is to be sought from the relevant Ministry*
2. *A copy of this Import Permit must be sent to the consignor and must accompany the consignment.*
3. *The ∗ soil/rooting compost/growing media are subject to inspection and examination prior to clearance by the customs.*
4. *This Import Permit is valid until the* ....
For one consignment only.
5. *The consignment must be accompanied by a phytosanitary certificate or a statement from the official Plant Protection Service of the country of origin bearing the following certification*:
(*a*) *Treatment*: ....
(*b*) *Other declaration*: ....
....
6. *Further conditions*: ....

Schedule:

Description	*Quantity*	*Country of origin*

Date of issue: ....

....
Director of Agriculture

Delete whichever inapplicable.

Seventh schedule
[Regulation 5 (2)]
Phytosanitary certificate for re – export

Plant Protection Organization *No.* ....

of .... *(country of re – export)*

TO: Plant Protection Organization (s)

of ....

Description of consignment

Name and address of exporter ....

Declared name and address of consignee ....

Number and description of packages ....

Distinguishing marks ....

Place of origin ....

Declared means of conveyance ....

Declared point of entry ....

Name of produce and quantity declared ....

Botanical name of plants ....

This is to certify that the plants or plant products described above were imported into .... *(country of re – export)* ....*from* .... *(country of * origin)* ....*Covered by Phytosanitary Certificate No.* ....*original * certified true copy of which is attached together with this * certificate. That they are packed repacked in original * new containers, and that based on the original Phytosanitary * Certificate and additional inspection, they are considered to conform with the current phytosanitary regulations of the importing country, and that during storage in* .... *(country of re – export)* ....*the consignment has not been subjected to the risk of infestation or infection.*

Please tick (/) appropriate box.

Disinfestation/and/or disinfection treatment

Date .... *Treatment* ....

Chemical (active ingredient) .... *Duration and temperature* ....

concentration .... *Additional information* ....

....

Additional declaration: ....

....

Place of issue ....

Name of Authorized Officer ....

....

Signature ....

(Stamp of Organization)

Date: ....

No financial liability with respect to this Certificate shall attach to the Government of Malaysia or to any of its officers or representatives.

Eighth schedule
[Regulation 5 (4)]
Permit to import beneficial organism

Permit No: ....

Name and address of consignee: ....

of ....

(Address)

Name and address of consignee: ....

of ....

(Address)

Permission is hereby granted to the consignee to import * *soil/rooting compost/growing media contained in the Schedule here to through* ....

....

(appointed entry checkpoint)

This permit is issued subject to the following conditions:

1. *Import licence is to be sought from the relevant Ministry*
2. *A copy of this Import Permit must be sent to the consignor and must accompany the consignment.*
3. *The consignment is subject to inspection prior to clearance by the customs.*
4. *This Import Permit is valid until the* ....

For one consignment only.

5. *The consignment must be accompanied by a phytosanitary certificate or a statement from the official Plant Protection Service of the country of origin bearing the following certification*:

(c) *Treatment*: ....

(d) *Other declaration*: ....

....

Schedule:

Description	*Quantity*	*Country of origin*

Date of issue: ....

....

Director of Agriculture

Ninth schedule
[Regulation 5 (5)]
Plants from countries where khapra beetle is found

Name of plant * –

1. *Peas and beans – seeds and meal*
2. *Cashew nuts*
3. *Groundnut – seeds and cake*
4. *Maize – seeds, meal and dried cobs*
5. *Rice – milled and bran*
6. *Sesame – seeds and cake*
7. *Wheat – bran and seeds*
8. *Spices*
9. *Tapioca – flour, chips and pearls*
10. *Sorghum – grain*
11. *Gunny sacks*

(* *This does not apply to plants that are chilled, preserved or hermetically sealed.*)

Countries of export –

1. *Bangladesh*
2. *India*
3. *Pakistan*
4. *Sudan*
5. *Turkey*
6. *Thailand*
7. *Philippines*
8. *Burma*
9. *Indonesia*
10. *Morocco*
11. *Sri Lanka*

Tenth schedule
[Regulation 17]
Plant quarantine declaration

All persons entering a component region (West Malaysia, Labuan, Sabah or Sarawak) are required to supply the information required in this form.

---

1. Full Name (Use block letters) Male ☐ Female ☐

....

2. Age .... 3. Passport No ....

4. Flight No/Vessel's Name ....

5. Last place of embarkation ....

1 * (a) Have you been to Africa, # South or Central America or the # Caribbean during the last 30 days?

Yes ☐ No ☐

(b) If yes, please state of departure from last country visited (from any of the above) .

2 * Are you carrying any plant, parts of plant or any other living organisms?

Yes ☐ No ☐

....

Date Signature

Penalty for failure to complete this From or providing false information is a fine up to one thousand ringgit or to imprisonment for a term not exceeding six month or to both on conviction.

Please tick (/) appropriate box

#Countries in the South America and Caribbean as follows.

"Brazil, Paraguay, Bolivia, Peru, Ecuador, Colombia, Venezuela, Guyana, Surinam, French, Guiana, Trinidad & Tobago, Barbados, Puerto Rico, Jamaica, Dominican Republic, Haiti, Cuba, Panama Canal Zone, Costa Rica, Nicaragua, Honduras, Guatemala, Belize, Mexico, El Salvador" .

Date the 21st April 1992.

[KP/LA/529/4; PN. (PU^2) 303/II]

DATUK SERI SANUSI JUNID

Minister of Agriculture

植物检疫限制进境名录

（1976 年《植物检疫法》以及 1981 年《植物检疫法规》规定的限制进境名录进口要求以及植物检疫）

1. 栽培用种植原料（种子、植株、苗木、嫁接秧苗、树桩、花卉、植物组织培养以及其他植物可培育部分）

作 物 类 型	进 口 要 求
1. 橡胶属 *Hevea* 的所有种类* 仅限研究用途，并与马来西亚橡胶局保持联络： ⅰ. 来自高风险国家（南美叶疫病（SALB disease））－种子、发芽种子、幼苗 ⅱ. 来自以上国家之外的国家	进口许可（IP），植物检疫证书（PC） 对无地方性流行南美叶疫病的国家进行媒介植物检疫以及入境后检疫（PEQ） 入境后检疫（PEQ）
2. 棕榈油、椰子以及棕榈科植物* 仅限研究用途，并与马来西亚棕榈油局（MPOB）保持联络： ⅰ. 来自高风险国家（枯萎病 *Fusarium* Wilt disease）－种子、发芽种子、幼苗 ⅱ. 来自以上国家之外的国家	进口许可（IP）、植物检疫证书（PC） 对无地方性流行枯萎病的国家进行媒介植物检疫以及入境后检疫（PEQ） 入境后检疫（PEQ）
3. 可可属 *Theobroma* 以及其他可可病毒宿主，包括木棉科和梧桐科* ⅰ. 来自高风险国家（可可病毒病 cocoa virus disease）－种子、发芽种子、幼苗 ⅱ. 来自以上国家之外的国家	进口许可（IP）、植物检疫证书（PC） 对无地方性流行可可病毒病的国家进行媒介植物检疫以及入境后检疫（PEQ） 入境后检疫（PEQ）
4. 美洲热带地区的所有植物*	进口许可（IP）、植物检疫证书（PC） 对无地方性流行南美叶疫病的国家进行媒介植物检疫以及入境后检疫（PEQ）
5. 非洲可可地区的所有植物*	进口许可（IP）、植物检疫证书（PC）以及入境后检疫（PEQ）
6. 菠萝 *Ananas cosmosus**	进口许可（IP）、植物检疫证书（PC）以及入境后检疫（PEQ）
7. 菠萝蜜属 *Artocarpus* 所有植物	进口许可（IP）、植物检疫证书（PC）以及入境后检疫（PEQ）
8. 茶树 *Camellia sinensis**	进口许可（IP）、植物检疫证书（PC）以及入境后检疫（PEQ）
9. 番木瓜 *Carica papaya**	进口许可（IP）、植物检疫证书（PC）以及入境后检疫（PEQ） —商业用途的进口只允许以组织培养的形式进行，并需对出口国的组织培养实验室和组培母本进行检疫检查
10. 柑橘属 *Citrus* 及其相关属的所有植物*	进口许可（IP）、植物检疫证书（PC）以及入境后检疫（PEQ）

续表

作物类型	进口要求
11. 咖啡属 *Coffee* 的所有植物*	进口许可（IP）、植物检疫证书（PC）以及入境后检疫（PEQ）
12. 芋头以及千年芋 *Zanthosoma*（Taro）的所有种类*	进口许可（IP）、植物检疫证书（PC）以及入境后检疫（PEQ）
13. 榴莲 *Durio zibethinus**	进口许可（IP）、植物检疫证书（PC）以及入境后检疫（PEQ）
14. 所有种类的林木*，并与马来西亚林业部以及马来西亚森林研究院（FRIM）保持联络	进口许可（IP）、植物检疫证书（PC）、濒临物种野生动植物国际贸易公约许可证仅适用于计划种类的林木以及入境后检疫（PEQ）。
15. 甘薯 *Ipomoea batatas**	进口许可（IP）、植物检疫证书（PC）以及入境后检疫（PEQ）
16. 所有种类的豆科植物（坚果，如被护作物坚果或豆荚）*	进口许可（IP）、植物检疫证书（PC）
17. 芒果属 *Mangifera* 的所有种类*	进口许可（IP）、植物检疫证书（PC）以及入境后检疫（PEQ）
18. 木薯属 *Manihot* 的所有种类*	进口许可（IP）、植物检疫证书（PC）以及入境后检疫（PEQ）
19. 芭蕉属 *Musa* 以及其相关属（香蕉 Banana、大蕉 *Plantains* 以及马尼拉 *Manila*）的所有种类*	进口许可（IP）、植物检疫证书（PC）以及入境后检疫（PEQ） —商业用途的进口只允许以组织培养的形式进行，并需对出口国的组织培养实验室和组培母本进行检疫检查
20. 红毛丹属 *Rambutan* 的所有种类*	进口许可（IP）、植物检疫证书（PC）以及入境后检疫（PEQ）
21. 烟草属 *Tobaccoes* 的所有种类*	进口许可（IP）、植物检疫证书（PC）以及入境后检疫（PEQ）
22. 兰科 Orchidaccae 的所有种类*	进口许可（IP）、植物检疫证书（PC），濒临绝种野生动植物国际贸易公约许可证适用于计划种类的兰花以及入境后检疫（PEQ）。 —商业用途的进口只允许以组织培养的形式进行
23. 水稻 *Oryza sativa**	马来西亚农业以及农基工业部（稻谷和大米产业司）进口批准，进口许可（IP）、植物检疫证书（PC）以及入境后检疫（PEQ）。 ——允许仅用于政府机构和私人机构研究目的的进口，且该两者必须同马来西亚农业发展研究所（MARDI）进行合作研究
24. 胡椒科 Piperaceae 的所有植物*	进口许可（IP）、植物检疫证书（PC）以及入境后检疫（PEQ）
25. 甘蔗属 *Sugarcane* 的所有种类*	进口许可（IP）、植物检疫证书（PC）以及入境后检疫（PEQ）

续表

作　物　类　型	进　口　要　求
26. 玉米 *Zea mays* *	进口许可（IP）、植物检疫证书（PC）
27. 马铃薯 *Solanum tuberosum* *	进口许可（IP）、植物检疫证书（PC）以及入境后检疫（PEQ）
28. 姜属 *Zingiberaceae* 的所有种类 *	进口许可（IP）、植物检疫证书（PC）以及入境后检疫（PEQ）
29. 其他果实类植物，如草莓，苹果，葡萄	进口许可（IP）、植物检疫证书（PC）以及入境后检疫（PEQ）
30. 禾草	进口许可（IP）、植物检疫证书（PC）以及 PEQ（入境后检疫 - 仅适用于匍匐茎）
31. 观赏性植物	进口许可（IP）、植物检疫证书（PC）
32. 蔬菜种子	进口许可（IP）、植物检疫证书（PC）
33. 花种	进口许可（IP）、植物检疫证书（PC）
34. 其他目前尚未进口或尚未进入电子许可系统的植物、或来自新的出口国家的植物、或对某种已进口植物已存在经修改的进口要求、或高风险进口植物、或来自高风险国家的进口植物。	经过有害生物风险分析（PRA）确定作物是否允许进口、或在清关前需要检疫检查或入境后检疫、或仅限研究用途、或能够进口以作商用或他用

* 为已在 1981 年《植物检疫法规》表 3 中规定的植物。

2. 植物产品（加工或未加工）

植物产品种类	进　口　要　求
1. 新鲜芒果果实	进口许可（IP）、植物检疫证书（PC）
2. 来自泰国的蒲桃 *Syzygium samarangense*	进口许可（IP）、植物检疫证书（PC） 来自泰国的蒲桃暂停进口，以待与泰国相关的生产农场获得资格认定
3. （1）、（2）以外的新鲜水果	不要求有进口许可（IP）、植物检疫证书（PC），但一旦到达进口口岸需接受马来西亚检疫检查服务（MAQIS）的人员进行检疫检查
4. 黄麻麻袋（包装材料）	进口许可（IP）、植物检疫证书（PC）
5. 包装材料以及竹制品	进口许可（IP）、植物检疫证书（PC）
6. 椰子（新鲜果实、茎、杆、纤维以及椰子树其他的部分）	进口许可（IP）、植物检疫证书（PC） —进口成熟椰子后，仅限于将椰子产品出口到其他国家的椰子工厂。成熟椰子进口数量取决于工厂的生产能力。此生产能力受到控制，以防止引入椰子中所含的危险害虫，并控制本地市场成熟椰子过剩，否则将影响当地小型椰农的收入。椰子产业发展委员会将会首先对工厂的检查进行审议
7. 槟榔（新鲜果实、茎，杆、纤维以及槟榔其他的部分）	进口许可（IP）、植物检疫证书（PC）
8. 香料、木薯、玉米、大米、坚果/豆荚、腰果、花生、BIJAN、小麦、高粱、黄麻麻袋	发生谷斑皮蠹的国家，如印尼、印度、巴基斯坦、缅甸、苏丹、土耳其、孟加拉国、菲律宾、摩洛哥和斯里兰卡，需要植物检疫证书（PC）

续表

植物产品种类	进口要求
9. 来自高风险国家的烟草：美洲热带地区和非洲国家。	进口许可（IP）、植物检疫证书（PC）
10. 美洲热带地区和非洲国家（可可地区）的可可以及咖啡	进口许可（IP）、植物检疫证书（PC）
11. 橡胶原木（成型木材）	进口许可（IP）、植物检疫证书（PC）
12. 木材（成型木材）以及其他木制品	进口许可（IP）、植物检疫证书（PC）
13. 原木	禁止从美洲热带国家（南美叶疫病发生地区）、非洲以及中南美洲国家（枯萎病发生地区）以及印尼进口。 以上国家以外的需有进口许可（IP）、植物检疫证书（PC）
14. 木片	进口许可（IP）、植物检疫证书（PC）
15. 干花	进口许可（IP）、植物检疫证书（PC）
16. 鲜切花	进口许可（IP）、植物检疫证书（PC）
17. 草本植物（高风险国家）	进口许可（IP）、植物检疫证书（PC）
18. 巴西胡桃 *Bertholletia excels*	进口许可（IP）、植物检疫证书（PC）
19. 加工产品： 谷物； 果实； 香料； 球根； 根茎	不要求有进口许可（IP）、植物检疫证书（PC）
20. 美洲热带国家果实	禁止进口； （关于热带美洲国家农产品进口问题，亚太植物保护公约正在确立一个标准）
21. 来自泰国的 12 种物品： 甘薯 *Ipomea batatas*； 芋头 *Colocasia esculenta*； 花生 *Arachis hypogeae*； 土豆 *Solanum tuberosum*； 小花鞘蕊花 *Coleus parviplorus*； 柠檬草 *Cymbopogon citrates*； 朝天椒/辣椒 *Capsicum frustescens*； 姜黄 *Curcuma domestica*； 生姜 *Zingiber officinale*； 大高良姜 *Alpinia galangal*； 地瓜 *Panchyrhizus erosus*； 青柠檬叶 *Citrus hystrix*	进口许可（IP）、植物检疫证书（PC）
22. 从高风险国家来的玉米谷物以及其他谷物饲料	进口许可（IP），植物检疫证书（PC）

3. 植物媒介

植物媒介类型	进口要求
1. 泥煤苔	进口许可（IP）、植物检疫证书（PC）
2. 泥炭藓	进口许可（IP）、植物检疫证书（PC）
3. 珍珠岩	进口许可（IP）、植物检疫证书（PC）
4. 蛭石	进口许可（IP）、植物检疫证书（PC）
5. 椰纤土	进口许可（IP）、植物检疫证书（PC）

4. 土壤

土壤类型	进口要求
海砂	进口许可（IP）、植物检疫证书（PC） —进口后仅限用于铸造海堤； —进口商需要出示谅解备忘录，特许经营权合约并应在出口国接受检疫检查
土壤样品	进口许可（IP） —仅限研究与分析用途，并需接受实验室检疫检查
卵石（小于一英寸）	进口许可（IP）、植物检疫证书（PC）
加工过的矿石	进口许可（IP）

5. 有机肥/微生物

材料类型	进口要求
有机肥	进口许可（IP）以及出口国家说明无危险微生物的正式信函。 —要求进口样品，用于分析； —要求出示文件与研究文献证明有机肥无危险微生物； —要获取进口微生物和有机肥料技术委员会的进口许可
有益生物/人工培育生物	见上文 1.

6. 有益生物

材料类型	进口要求
蜜蜂（工蜂、蜂王）	进口许可（IP）、植物检疫证书（PC） —蜂房先需接受检疫检查，再进行入境后检疫（PEQ）
蜂巢	不允许进口
蠕虫	进口许可（IP）、植物检疫证书（PC） —先进行检疫检查再进行入境后检疫（PEQ）
生物制剂	进口许可（IP）、植物检疫证书（PC） —在国家入境后检疫站 Insektori 进行入境后检疫
植物害虫： 活的 死的	 需要农业局长允许进口的批准书，且仅限研究用途 需要农业局长允许进口的批准书

7. 进口许可（IP） 由农业部颁发的许可证，这些许可证规定了准许进口物品的种类和数量。这些许可证中也提到了所需检疫处理的类型、补充声明以及进口商必须遵守的其他规定。

8. 植物检疫证书（PC） 是由出口国家（国家植保机构）签发的植物卫生证书，作为已满足进口许可所列的检疫处理或全部要求的认证或认可。

9. 入境后检疫（PEQ） 为已获准少量进口的植物，且进口保留时间为 3 ~ 12 个月或一个季节，取决于植物种类，以及政府或进口商所有的入境后检疫站筛选或监控的疾病。批准进口货物的数量取决于所准备的地方或网室的承受能力。接受入境后检疫的进口货物一般用于研究、种植或者 janaplasm 项目。批准在进口商的场所进行入境后检疫的情况视所有需要遵守的入境后检疫规范要求而定。

10. 进口口岸检疫检查 所有进口植物材料需在进口口岸接受由马来西亚检疫检查服务（MAQIS）人员进行的检疫检查。如果发现植物感染疾病或带有害虫，被没收该植物，并采取退回、销毁、拒绝进口或送回原产国的检疫措施。产生的所有费用将由进口商承担。

需要在进口商或出口商处进行的入境后检疫或检疫检查，仅允许由该进口商进行，且只允许从批准的出口商处进口。

理由：

1976 年《植物检疫法》与 1981 年《植物检疫法规》的执行目的是控制、预防和消灭农业害虫、危险植物以及植物病害，并且在国际贸易以及相关的所有议题中控制害虫活动这一方面扩大合作。

为了这个目的，在上表中提到的所有进口植物材料均被要求持有进口许可，在 1981 年《植物检疫法规》的第 5 项中有所规定。

基于这一点，进口许可的目的为：

ⅰ. 防止危险性有害生物传入马来西亚。

ⅱ. 保护马来西亚的农业产业不受来自马来西亚境外的危险性有害生物的损害或威胁。

ⅲ. 如进口农业材料受到了污染或有害生物攻击，确保可以检测其可追溯性，并可以立即采取行动。

1981 年《植物检疫法规》并没有要求对来自热带美洲国家和中非国家的新鲜水果以及蔬菜之外的其他新鲜水果以及蔬菜持有进口许可。然而，对于芒果和蒲桃这两种类型的新鲜水果，仍需持有进口许可。这是因为这两种水果都可以携带检疫性有害生物 –

ⅰ. 芒果 – 芒果果核象 *Sternochetus mangiferae*；

ⅱ. 蒲桃 – 番石榴实蝇 *Bactrocera correcta*

为使进口的新鲜水果不带有规定的检疫性有害生物，需要有进口许可要求的出口国遵守马来西亚已经执行的植物检疫要求，以确保这些检疫性有害生物不会进入马来西亚。

从美洲热带地区、非洲、亚洲和中南美洲国家以外进口的原木、成型木材/木料/木块以及其他未加工的木制品也需要进口许可。以确保木制品不带有植物上的危险检疫性有害生物，如：

ⅰ. 金线虫 *Globodera rostochiensis*

ⅱ. 松材线虫 *Bursaphelenchus xylophilus*

ⅲ. 羽状疫病菌 *Phytophthora pinifolia*

ⅳ. 栎树脂溃疡病 *Phytophthora kernoviae*

ⅴ. 栎树猝死病菌 *Fusarium circinatum*

ⅵ. 松间溃疡病菌 *Fusarium circinatum*

ⅶ. 粉蠹科 Lyctidae、长蠹科 Bostrichidae、天牛科 Cerambycidae、蚁科 Formicidae、树蜂科 Siricidae、毒蛾科 Lymantriidae、窃蠹科 Anobiidae、小蠹科 Scolytidae、长小蠹科 Platypodidae、吉丁虫科 Buprestidae 有害生物。

• 请参阅农业部网站 www. doa. gov. my 的《原木、成型木材/木料/木块和其他未加工的木制品进口指南》，该指南将持续更新。

List of Import Control Item

(Under Plant Quarantine Act 1976 and Plant Quarantine Regulations 1981)

Importation requirement and plant phytosanitary

1. Planting material for cultivation (Seeds, plants, seedlings, cuttings, stumps, flowers, tissue cultures and other cultivated parts of plants).

TYPE OF CROPS	IMPORT REQUIREMENTS
1. All species of Rubber (*Hevea*) * For research purpose only, liaise with Malaysian Rubber Board: i. From high risk countries (SALB disease) - seed, germinated seed, seedling ii. From countries other than above	IP (Import Permit), PC (Phytosanitary certificate) Intermediate Quarantine at country not endemic SALB disease and PEQ (Post Entry Quarantine) PEQ (Post Entry Quarantine)
2. Palm oil, coconut and Palmae Family * For research purpose only, liaise with Malaysian Palm Oil Board (MPOB): i. From high risk countries (Fusarium Wilt disease) - seed, germinated seed, seedling ii. From countries other than above	IP (Import Permit), PC (Phytosanitary Certificate) Intermediate Quarantine at country not endemic Fusarium Wilt disease and PEQ (Post Entry Quarantine) PEQ (Post Entry Quarantine)
3. Cocoa (*Theobroma*) and other plants known as host of cocoa virus disease including Family Bombacacaeae dan Sterculiaceae * i. From high risk countries (cocoa virus disease) - seed, germinated seed, seedling ii. From countries other than above	IP (Import Permit), PC (Phytosanitary Certificate) Intermediate Quarantine at country not endemic to cocoa virus diseases and PEQ (Post Entry Quarantine) PEQ (Post Entry Quarantine)
4. All plant species from America Tropics *	IP (Import Permit), PC (Phytosanitary Certificate). Intermediate Quarantine at country not endemic to SALB disease and PEQ (Post Entry Quarantine)
5. All plant species from African Cacao Region *	IP (Import Permit), PC (Phytosanitary Certificate) and PEQ (Post Entry Quarantine)
6. Pineapple (*Ananas cosmosus*) *	IP (Import Permit), PC (Phytosanitary Certificate) and PEQ (Post Entry Quarantine)
7. All species of Keledang	IP (Import Permit), PC (Phytosanitary Certificate) and PEQ (Post Entry Quarantine)
8. Tea (*Camellia sinensis*) *	IP (Import Permit), PC (Phytosanitary Certificate) and PEQ (Post Entry Quarantine)

Continue Table

TYPE OF CROPS	IMPORT REQUIREMENTS
9. Papaya (*Carica papaya*)*	IP (Import Permit), PC (Phytosanitary Certificate) and PEQ (Post Entry Quarantine). —Importation for commercial used only allowed in the form of tissue culture subjected to quarantine inspection on tissue culture lab and plant mother host in exporting country.
10. All species of *Citrus* and allied genera*	IP (Import Permit), PC (Phytosanitary Certificate) and PEQ (Post Entry Quarantine)
11. All species of coffea (*Coffee*)*	IP (Import Permit), PC (Phytosanitary Certificate) and PEQ (Post Entry Quarantine)
12. All species of Colocasia and *Zanthosoma* (Taro)*	IP (Import Permit), PC (Phytosanitary Certificate) and PEQ (Post Entry Quarantine)
13. Durian (*Durio zibethinus*)*	IP (Import Permit), PC (Phytosanitary Certificate) and PEQ (Post Entry Quarantine)
14. All species of forest trees* Liaise with Malaysian Forestry Department and Forestry Research Institute Malaysia (FRIM)	IP (Import Permit), PC (Phytosanitary Certificate), permit CITES only for scheduled species of forest trees and PEQ (Post Entry Quarantine)
15. Sweet potato (*Ipomoea batatas*)*	IP (Import Permit), PC (Phytosanitary Certificate) and PEQ (Post Entry Quarantine)
16. All species of Leguminosae (Nut such as cover crop nut/legume)*	IP (Import Permit), PC (Phytosanitary Certificate)
17. All species of mango (*Mangifera*)*.	IP (Import Permit), PC (Phytosanitary Certificate) and PEQ (Post Entry Quarantine)
18. All species of Cassava (*Manihot*)*	IP (Import Permit), PC (Phytosanitary Certificate) and PEQ (Post Entry Quarantine)
19. All species of *Musa* and allied genera (Banana, Plantains and Manila)*	IP (Import Permit), PC (Phytosanitary Certificate) and PEQ (Post Entry Quarantine). —Importation for commercial used only allowed in the form of tissue culture subjected to quarantine inspection on tissue culture lab and plant mother host in exporting country.
20. All species of *Nephelium* (Rambutan)*	IP (Import Permit), PC (Phytosanitary Certificate) and PEQ (Post Entry Quarantine)
21. All species of *Nicotiana* (Tobaccoes)*	IP (Import Permit), PC (Phytosanitary Certificate) and PEQ (Post Entry Quarantine)
22. All species of Orchidaccae*	IP (Import Permit), PC (Phytosanitary Certificate), permit CITES for scheduled species of orchid and PEQ (Post Entry Quarantine). —Importation for commercial used only allowed in the form of tissue culture.

Continue Table

TYPE OF CROPS	IMPORT REQUIREMENTS
23. Paddy/Rice (*Oryza sativa*) *	Import approval from Ministry of Agriculture and Agro – Based Industry Malaysia (Paddy and Rice Industry Division), IP (Import Permit), PC (Phytosanitary Certificate) and PEQ (Post Entry Quarantine). —Importations allowed for research purpose only for government agencies and for private agencies must have collaboration research with Malaysian Agricultural Research and Development Institute (MARDI)
24. All members of *Piperaceae* (Peppers) *	IP (Import Permit), PC (Phytosanitary Certificate) and PEQ (Post Entry Quarantine)
25. All species of *Saccharum* (sugarcane) *	IP (Import Permit), PC (Phytosanitary Certificate) and PEQ (Post Entry Quarantine)
26. *Zea mays* (Maize/Corn) *	IP (Import Permit), PC (Phytosanitary Certificate)
27. *Solanum tuberosum* (Potato) *	IP (Import Permit), PC (Phytosanitary Certificate) and PEQ (Post Entry Quarantine)
28. All species of Zingiberaceae *	IP (Import Permit), PC (Phytosanitary Certificate) and PEQ (Post Entry Quarantine)
29. Other fruits plant such as strawberry, apple, grape	IP (Import Permit), PC (Phytosanitary Certificate) and PEQ (Post Entry Quarantine)
30. Grass	IP (Import Permit), PC (Phytosanitary Certificate) and PEQ (Post Entry Quarantine – only for stolon)
31. Ornamental plants	IP (Import Permit), PC (Phytosanitary Certificate)
32. Vegetables seeds	IP (Import Permit), PC (Phytosanitary Certificate)
33. Flowers seeds	IP (Import Permit), PC (Phytosanitary Certificate)
34. Other plant that has not yet been imported or not yet has in ePermit system or from new exporting country or revising import requirement already exist for plants that had already been imported or importation of high – risk plants or importation of plants from high – risk countries	Subjected to pest risk analysis (PRA) whether the crop can be allowed for import or not or require to do quarantine inspection visit pre – clearance or PEQ or allowed only for research or can be imported for commercial use and others

* Plants that had been stated in Table Three Plant Quarantine Regulations 1981.

2. Plant Products (process or not process).

Type of Plants Products	Import Requirements
Manggo fresh fruits	IP (Import Permit), PC (Phytosanitary Certificate)
Rose apple fruits (*Syzygium samarangense*) from Thailand	IP (Import Permit), PC (Phytosanitary Certificate). Importation of rose apple from Thailand is temporarily halted pending accreditation of the production farm involved in Thailand.
Fresh fruits other than (1) and (2)	Not require IP (Import Permit), PC (Phytosanitary Certificate) but are subjected to quarantine inspection upon arrival at the entry point by the Malaysian Quarantine and Inspection Services (MAQIS) officers

Continue Table

Type of Plants Products	Import Requirements
Jute gunny sack (Packing material)	IP (Import Permit), PC (Phytosanitary Certificate)
Packing material and products from bamboo	IP (Import Permit), PC (Phytosanitary Certificate)
Coconut (fresh fruits, stem, stick, fiber and other coconut parts)	IP (Import Permit), PC (Phytosanitary Certificate). —Importation of matured coconut only allowed to operational coconut mill where as their coconut products will be exported to other countries. The quantity importation of matured coconut will depends on the production capacity of the mill. This capacity is controlled because to prevent the introduction of dangerous pest of coconut and to control excess of matured coconut in local market, which can affect income of the small local coconut farmers. Inspection of the mill will be carried out first for Coconut Industrial Development Committee deliberation
Betelnut palm Areca catechu (fresh fruits, stem, stick, fiber and other betelnut palm parts)	IP (Import Permit), PC (Phytosanitary Certificate)
Spices, cassava, corn, rice, nuts/legume, cashew nut, ground nut, bijan, wheat grain, sekoi, jute gunny sack	PC (Phytosanitary Certificate) required from countries endemic to khapra bettle such as Indonesia, India, Pakistan, Myanmar, Sudan, Turkey, Bangladesh, Philippines, Morocco and Sri Lanka
Tobacco from high risk countries: American Tropics and African Countries	IP (Import Permit), PC (Phytosanitary Certificate)
Cocoa and coffee from American Tropics Countries and African Countries (Cocoa region)	IP (Import Permit), PC (Phytosanitary Certificate)
Rubber wood (sawn timber)	IP (Import Permit), PC (Phytosanitary Certificate)
Wood (sawn timber) and other wood articles	IP (Import Permit), PC (Phytosanitary Certificate)
Logs	Importation PROHIBITED from American Tropic Countries (endemic to SALB diseases), Africa and South & Middle of America countries (endemic to Fusarium wilt disease) and Indonesia. IP (Import Permit), PC (Phytosanitary Certificate) for country other than the above
Wood chips	IP (Import Permit), PC (Phytosanitary Certificate)
Dried flowers	IP (Import Permit), PC (Phytosanitary Certificate)
Fresh cutflowers	IP (Import Permit), PC (Phytosanitary Certificate)
Herbs (High risk country)	IP (Import Permit), PC (Phytosanitary Certificate)
Brazil Nut (Bertholletia excels)	IP (Import Permit), PC (Phytosanitary Certificate)
Processed products: Grain; Fruits; Spices; Umbisi; Rhizome	Not required IP (Import Permit), PC (Phytosanitary Certificate)
Fruits from American Tropic countries	Importation is PROHIBITED; (A standard is being legislated by The Asia - Pacific Plant Protection Convention regarding the importation of agricultural products from American Tropic countries

Continue Table

Type of Plants Products	Import Requirements
12 types of commodities from Thailand only: Sweet potato (*Ipomea batatas*); Taro/dasheen (*Colocasia esculenta*); Groundnuts (*Arachis hypogeae*); Ubi kentang (*Solanum tuberosum*); Ubi kemili/kembili (*Coleus parviplorus*); Lemon grass (*Cymbopogon citrates*); Bird/Hot pepper (*Capsicum frustescens*); Turmeric (*Curcuma domestica*); Ginger (*Zingiber officinale*); Greater galangal (*Alpinia galangal*); Yambean (*Panchyrhizus erosus*); Kaffir lime leaf (*Citrus hystrix*)	IP (Import Permit), PC (Phytosanitary Certificate)
Corn grain or other grains for animal feed from high risk countries	IP (Import Permit), PC (Phytosanitary Certificate)

3. Plant medium

Type of Plant Medium	Import Requirement
1. Peat moss	IP (Import Permit), PC (Phytosanitary Certificate)
2. Sphagnum moss	IP (Import Permit), PC (Phytosanitary Certificate)
3. Perlite	IP (Import Permit), PC (Phytosanitary Certificate)
4. Vermiculite	IP (Import Permit), PC (Phytosanitary Certificate)
5. Coco peat	IP (Import Permit), PC (Phytosanitary Certificate)

4. Soil

Type of Soil	Import Requirement
Sea sand	IP (Import Permit), PC (Phytosanitary Certificate) —Importation is for sea embankment only. —Importers require presenting the MOU, concession contract and subjected to quarantine inspection in the exporting country
Soil sample	IP (Import Permit) —For research or analysis only and subjected to quarantine inspection at the laboratory premise
Pebble stone (size less than 1 inch)	IP (Import Permit), PC (Phytosanitary Certificate)
Processed mineral stone.	IP (Import Permit)

5. Organic fertilizer/Microorganism

Type of Material	Import Requirement
Organic fertilizer	IP (Import Permit) and formal letter from exporting country stated that free from dangerous microbe. —Require to import sample for analysis purposes. —Require to present documents and research literature to prove that the organic fertilizer had no dangerous microbe. —Import approval from Importation of Microorganism & Organic Fertilizer Technical Committee
Beneficial microorganism/Cultured microorganism	As stated in (1) above

6. Beneficial organism

Type of Material	Import Requirement
Bee (workers, queen)	IP (Import Permit), PC (Phytosanitary Certificate) —PEQ at apiary subjected to quarantine inspection first
Hive and comb	Not allowed to import
Worm	IP (Import Permit), PC (Phytosanitary Certificate) —PEQ at the importer premise subjected to quarantine inspection first
Biological agent	IP (Import Permit), PC (Phytosanitary Certificate) —PEQ at the Insektori in National Post Entry Quarantine Station
Plant pests: Live	Approval letter to allow importation from Director General of Agriculture only for research purpose
Dead	Approval letter for allowing importation from Director General of Agriculture

7. IP (Import Permit) Permit issued by the Department of Agriculture. These permit stated approved type and quantity for importation. In these permit also mentioned type of quarantine treatment required, additional declaration and other requirements that importer must followed.

8. PC (Phytosanitary certificate) is a plant health certificate issued by the exporting country (NPPO) as an acknowledgement or accreditation that quarantine treatment or the entire requirement stated in import permit had followed.

9. PEQ (Post Entry Quarantine) are plants that had been allowed to be imported in the small quantity and will be kept for duration between 3 – 12 months or one season subjected to plant species and diseases that will be screen or monitored at the Post Entry Quarantine Station either own by the government or importer. The approved quantity of the consignment to be imported is subjected to capacity of the place or screen house prepared. Usually importations that are subjected to PEQ are for research or cultivation or janaplasm. Approval for the PEQ at the importer premise is depending on all PEQ specification requirements that need to follow.

10. Quarantine Inspection at the Entry Point all imported plant material are subjected to quarantine inspection at the entry point by the Malaysia Quarantine and Inspection Services (MAQIS) officers. If the plant is found to be infected with diseases or infested with pest, will be confiscate and subjected to quarantine action that is whether retreated or destroyed or refuse entry or sent back to origin country. All cost incurred will be borne by the importer.

For importation of plants required PEQ or quarantine inspection at the importer's premise or exporter's premise, approval only allowed for that importer and only allowed imported from the approved exporter.

Justification:

Enforcement of Plant Quarantine Act 1976 and Plant Quarantine Regulations 1981 is for the purpose to control, prevent and destroyed agriculture pests, dangerous plants and plant diseases and to expend cooperation in controlling the pests' movement in the international trade and all issues related to it.

For that purpose, import permit is required to all importation of plant materials as mention in the above table, since stated in item number 5 Plant Quarantine Regulations 1981.

Based on that, import permit is for the purpose to:

Prevent introduction of dangerous pests into Malaysia.

Protect agriculture industry in Malaysia from damage or threaten by the dangerous pests from outside Malaysia.

To make sure if imported agriculture materials have a contamination or attack on the consignment, it can detect traceability and immediately action can be take.

Plant Quarantine Regulations 1981 did not required import permit for importation of fresh fruits and fresh vegetables except from American Tropic countries and Central African countries. Nevertheless, import permit is still required for importation of this 2 type of fresh fruits that are mango and rose apple. This is because both of them can carry quarantine pest:

Mango—Mango seed weevil (*Sternochetus mangiferae*)

Rose apple—*Bactrocera correcta*

To oblige importation of this fresh fruits are free from the stated quarantine pests, permit import is required for exporting country follow phytosanitary requirement that had been enforce by Malaysia to make sure that introduction of these quarantine pests can be prevent from entering Malaysia.

Importation of logs, sawn timber/lumber/pieces of wood and other unmanufactured wood articles from countries other than American Tropic, Africa and South and Middle of America countries also require import permit. This to make sure the woods are free from dangerous quarantine pests to plants, such as: -

ⅰ—Golden nematode (*Globodera rostochiensis*)

ⅱ—Wood nematode (*Bursaphelenchus xylophilus*)

ⅲ—Phytophthora pinifolia

ⅳ—Phytophthora kernoviae

ⅴ—Phytophthora ramorum

ⅵ—Pine pitch canker (*Fusarium circinatum*)

ⅶ—Peot of family Lyctidae, Bostrichidae, Cerambycidae, Formicidae, Siricidae, Lymantriidae, Anobiidae, Scolytidae, Platypodidae, Buprestidae.

- Please refer to Guidelines Importation of Logs, Sawn Timber/Lumber/ Pieces of Wood/and Other Unmanufactured Wood Articles at the Department of Agriculture website www. doa. gov. my . This guideline will always be updated.

马来西亚动物法

(法令 647　动物法 1953)

为了防止动物疫病传入并在马来西亚国内传播，控制动物进出马来西亚，控制动物的宰杀，防止虐待动物，制定马来西亚国内相关的动物福利、动物保护的贮备和动物改良措施，以及处理相关事务，特根据法令制订本法。

(1953 年 4 月 30 日)

第 I 部分　总　　章

简称

1. 本法为《动物法 1953》。

注释

2. 在本法中，除非在文中另有所指

航空器　包括所有空运兽类或禽类动物的飞行器。

动物　包括各种年龄和性别，不论圈养或放牧的马、牛、绵羊、山羊、猪、狗、猫等四腿动物。

动物检疫站　指依照第 80 条建立的检疫场所。

禽类　包括各种日龄和性别的驯养的鸡、鸭、鹅、火鸡、珍珠鸡和鸽子及其产下的蛋。

建筑物　用作圈养或关禁兽类或禽类的无论是否有屋顶的房屋、小屋、棚屋、厩房、畜栏及其栏架、笼、墙、门、柱、桩、木栅、栏框、临时围墙、篱笆、装卸台、路面、小径、梯级、脚手架、船架、码头、船坞、堆场、防波堤、登陆梯或桥等与上述相关的建筑。

公牛　指各个品种的雄性牛。

动物尸体　指包括死亡的畜类和禽类动物及其无论是否肢解的肉、骨（无论是否完整、破损或磨碎）、废弃物、皮革、皮毛、毛、发、羽毛、蹄、角等部分。

猫类　指各个品种或性别经驯养的猫。

牛类　指各种年龄或性别的公牛、母牛、阉公牛、小母牛、犊牛和野牛。

涉疫动物　指所有因通过直接或间接方式接触染疫兽类或禽类而易受疫病感染的动物或禽类。

局长　指依照第 3 条任命的兽医局的正副局长。

疫病　指在兽类或禽类动物间传播或传染的疾病，包括炭疽、气肿性炭疽、牛瘟、肺疫、布氏杆菌病、结核病、流行性淋巴管炎、口蹄疫、鼻疽病、山羊痘、出血性败血症、狂犬病、绵羊痘、猪瘟、猪丹毒、锥虫病、禽肺脑炎、鸡白痢、禽霍乱、鸡瘟、禽痘、传染性喉气管炎，或农牧部依据本法，时常在政府公报中公布的其他疫病。

[注：农牧部公布的其他疫病，参见 P. U. （B） 86/1999，P. U. （B） 96/1999 & P. U. （B） 247/2000.]

犬类　指各个品种或性别的驯养狗。

检查　正如其文字所表述一样，包括进行各种实验和验尸检查（如果必要）。

饲料　用作兽类或禽类动物食物的任何物质。

马类　包括各种母马、阉马、小型马、马驹、小马、小雌马、驴或骡。

感染　指染上某种疾病。

垫料　指用于兽类或禽类的铺垫材料。

主管　指船长或机长，包括曾经管理船舶或航空器的人员（领航员除外）。

农牧部　指主管动物事务的部门。

违反本法　指违背或不符合本法或依照本法制订的指令、条例或命令的行为。

海关官员　同义于 海关法 1967［法令 235］。

物主　包括曾经管理兽类或禽类或使用某建筑物的人员。

隔离检疫　指在隔离场对兽类、禽类或其他动物进行强制性留检。

隔离检疫站　指包括检查站或废旧船舶在内的执行隔离检疫的建筑或场所。

船舶　包括各种大船或小艇，水上引航艇除外。

州兽医局局长　指依照第 3 条任命的州兽医局局长。

疫苗　包括病原培养物或致病介质的活性配制物。

兽医负责人　指兽医局的正副局长、州兽医局局长、以及由兽医局正副局长、州兽医局局长依照第 3 条书面任命为兽医负责人的兽医官员、兽医官副职、助理兽医官和其他人员。

兽医中心　释义参见第 82 条。

兽医警察官　指在兽医行政机构领导下行动的警察成员。

官员的任命

3.（1）由最高元首任命兽医局正副局长。

（2）由州长或元首依照本法认为需要时，可任命州兽医局局长，并确定执行本法所需兽医官、兽医官副职和助理兽医官的数量。

（3）兽医局正副局长和州兽医局局长依照本法书面任命兽医负责人或委派人员，依照本法被委派人员应视为官员。

（4）依照本法任命的官员应视为刑法［法令 574］所指的公务员。

出示的身份卡

4.（1）所有兽医负责人、海关官员、兽医警察官或警察官在依据本法法执行公务时，如果没有穿着制服，按要求应向被执行人出示身份卡。身份卡标示为依照本法任命的兽医局长、海关关长、警察总检疫长或海关官员和警察官员。

（2）不服从依据本法任命的，但未穿着制服、不表明自己的职务和拒绝出示符合要求的身份卡的官员、海关官员、警察官员所作的要求、查询或命令的，不能认定为违法。

第Ⅱ部分　兽类和禽类动物的进出口

进口

制定进口相关规则的权力

5.（1）农牧部可以规定：

（a）确定是否对出口动物和禽类或某些特定动物和禽类动物的国家或地区施加限制措施。

（b）完全或部分禁止从特定的国家或地区进口可能传播疫病的动物尸体、精液、饲料、垫料、粪料、动物或禽类产品以及任何可能携带或传播疾病物品或材料。

（2）对违反依照本条（1）（b）规定的任何人，应被单处或并处 5000 林吉特罚款或2 年有期徒刑。

未经许可任何人不得进口兽类和禽类动物

6.（1）除第 5 条（1）（a）规定外，任何人不得进口没有本法签发的许可证或不符合许可证规定的条件的动物或禽类动物。

（2）通过向各州的州兽医局局长书面申请并交纳规定的费用后，可以取得进口动物或禽类动物的许可证。

（3）任何人违反本条（1）的规定进口动物或禽类动物，应被单处或并处5000林吉特罚款或2年有期徒刑。

进口兽类和禽类动物的检疫和留检

7.（1）由兽医负责人在到达地或指定的场所对进口或即将进口的动物或禽类进行检疫。如果动物或禽类可能感染了疫病，兽医负责人认为必要时，可以进行血清学或其他检疫，并按规定收取费用。

（2）兽医负责人根据情况决定对进口动物或禽类进行留检的时间和场所，以进行观察、检查、检疫或处理。

动物到达报告

8.（1）运输动物或禽类的船长、机长和列车押运员，不管动物或禽类是否在马来西亚卸货，应在马来西亚境内第一到达地向港口官员、机场负责人或站长报告。港口官员、机场负责人或站长应立即通知附近的兽医负责人。

（2）兽医负责人可以登轮、登机或登车对动物进行检查。

（3）没有兽医负责人的允许，港口官员、机场负责人或站长不得同意将动物或禽类卸离运输工具。

（4）尽管取得了第6条规定的许可证或动物或禽类的来源国符合第5条（1）（a）的规定，本条第（3）的规定仍须执行。

（5）（a）不能按（1）要求提交报告的，将被罚款50林吉特。

（b）任何人违反本条（3）的规定装载或转移动物或禽类动物，应被罚款200林吉特。

染疫和涉疫的兽类和禽类动物的进口

9.（1）兽医负责人认为进口或即将进口的动物、禽类及其动物尸体可能染疫或涉疫，可以：

（a）拒绝此类染疫和涉疫的动物、禽类、动物尸体或涉疫动物的卸货或转移。

（b）立即销毁此类染疫和涉疫的动物、禽类、动物尸体或涉疫动物并监督动物尸体按其认可的方式进行处理。

（c）扣留染疫和涉疫的动物、禽类、动物尸体或涉疫动物进行一段时间的隔离检疫。

（2）根据本条（1）（b）规定销毁的动物和禽类动物，其处理畜禽尸体的费用由物主支付。

（3）根据本条规定销毁的动物和禽类动物，将不作任何补偿。

船上的犬类和猫类动物

10.（1）任何通过海运进境的犬类和猫类动物，无论船舶到达哪个港口，船上的犬类和猫类动物应该限制在笼子或窝里，除非兽医负责人同意其登岸。

（2）如果犬类和猫类动物死亡或逃离原船舶，船长应立即报告兽医负责人。

（3）船长违反本条（1）或没有合理的理由违反本条（2）中的规定，将被罚款100林吉特。

受伤动物或禽类的扑杀

11.（1）如果任何动物或禽类，经兽医负责人进行进境检疫时，发现其受伤且无法医救时，兽医负责人就可以立即销毁此类动物并监督畜禽尸体的处理。

（2）根据本条规定销毁的动物或禽类，其处理畜禽尸体的费用物主支付。

（3）根据本条规定销毁的动物或禽类，将不作任何补偿。

动物尸体上岸许可

12.（1）没有兽医负责人出具有处理意见的许可，任何人不得将动物尸体从船舶、航空器或火车上卸货或转移。

（2）违反本条（1）的规定转移动物尸体或没有按兽医负责人的意见处理动物尸体的，将被罚款100林吉特。

某些物品的销毁或消毒

13. 当兽医负责人发现从海、陆、空进境的垫料、草料、饲料、粪料、精液、私人物品或其他物品可以传播疫病时，他可以查封、扣留该物品，并按其意见进行销毁或消毒。

出口

任何人不得出口无证动物

14.（1）任何人不得出口动物或动物尸体，除非其符合本法签发的许可证及许可证规定的条件。

（2）通过向各州的州兽医局首长书面申请并交纳规定的费用后，可以取得出口动物或动物尸体的许可证。

（3）任何人违反本条（1）的规定出口动物或动物尸体，应被单处或并处500林吉特罚款或6个月有期徒刑。

出口到新加坡

15. 负责将动物出口到新加坡的物主应在依据第14条签发许可证前出示由新加坡农业食品兽医局局长签发同意向新加坡出口动物的书面许可证。

出口前检疫

16. 兽医负责人在指定的地点对将要出口的动物进行检疫。

染疫动物或禽类的出口

17. 兽医负责人认为将要出口的动物染疫时，他可以拒绝同意此类染疫动物出口。

第Ⅲ部分　疫病扩散的预防

概述

对动物和禽类可疑疫病的检疫

18.（1）如果兽医负责人有理由认为动物、禽类或动物尸体可能染疫，必要时，他可以通过采血样、奶样、尿样或其他物质样品对动物、禽类或动物尸体实施检疫。

（2）为实施（1）项下的检疫时，兽医负责人可以命令将动物、禽类或动物尸体在规定的时间送到指定的地点，未经许可，不得将这些动物、禽类或动物尸体移离以下地点：任何人不得将动物留检地3英里以内的动物、禽类或畜禽尸体进行转移。

（3）没有合法的理由违反（2）项下的命令的人，应被处50林吉特罚款。

染疫动物和禽类的销毁

19. 不管根据第18条进行检疫的结果如何，兽医负责人对发现或有理由认为动物、禽类或动物尸体染疫或疑似染疫时，可以命令立即进行隔离或销毁。

销毁动物和禽类的赔偿

20.（1）依据兽医负责人的命令，对确认已染疫的动物、禽类或动物尸体进行销毁的，不作赔偿。

（2）依据兽医负责人的命令，对有理由认为动物、禽类或动物尸体已染疫并已销毁的，应对物主进行赔偿。赔偿数额由州兽医局首长评估并由州主管部长确认。

验尸检查

21.（1）兽医负责人可以对动物、禽类的尸体实施检疫，实验需要时，他可以抽取动物尸体的部分样品或命令将动物尸体在指定的时间运到指定的地点。

（2）兽医负责人可以命令将已埋土的动物、禽类的尸体挖掘出来以实施验尸检查。

（3）没有合法的理由违反本项下的命令的人，应被处100林吉特罚款。

染疫和涉疫的动物和禽类

22.（1）如果兽医负责人认为动物或禽类已经染疫，他可以下命令对动物或禽类进行预防或治疗处理，这包括病毒、疫苗或免疫血清治疗，他认为必要时，可以进行多种方法复合治疗。

（2）没有合法的理由违反本项下的命令的人，应被处100林吉特罚款。

畜栏等物体的消毒

23.（1）兽医负责人可以签署命令并指挥对发现或饲养染疫动物或禽类的畜栏、畜棚、栏架、笼或其他地方进行消毒，也可以签署命令禁止在消毒完成前将饲养染疫动物或禽类的畜栏、畜棚、栏架、笼或其他地方挪作他用。

（2）没有合法的理由违反本项下的命令的人，应被处100林吉特罚款。

畜栏等物体的销毁

24.（1）如果兽医负责人认为被染疫动物占用的畜栏、畜棚、栏架、笼或其他地方不能进行有效的消毒，可以命令物主或拥有者在规定的时间内销毁畜栏、畜棚、栏架、笼或其他地方并将其原材料进行焚烧。

（2）如果在规定的时间内不执行（1）项中签署的命令，兽医负责人可以指挥销毁畜栏、畜棚、栏架、笼并将其原材料进行焚烧。

（3）兽医负责人应向州主管部长汇报依据本项签署的命令的执行情况，州主管部长可以决定对被销毁畜栏、畜棚、栏架、笼或其他地方给予或拒付补偿。

（4）没有合法的理由违反本项（1）下的命令的人，应被处100林吉特罚款。

物品的消毒或销毁

25.（1）兽医负责人可以命令对接触染疫的动物或禽类动物的草垫、织物、马具、用具、木桶、提桶或器具等进行消毒或销毁，被销毁的物品经兽医负责人评估后应得到补偿。

（2）没有合法的理由违反本项下的命令的人，应被处100林吉特罚款。

人员和衣服的消毒

26.（1）兽医负责人可以命令对接触、经营、照看染疫或有理由认为已染疫动物或禽类的人员及其衣物进行消毒。

（2）没有合法的理由违反本项下的命令的人，应被处100林吉特罚款。

运输工具的消毒

27.（1）兽医负责人可以命令对进出第36条规定的疫区、运输染疫或有理由认为染疫动物或禽类的运输工具进行消毒。

（2）没有合法的理由违反本项下的命令的人，应被处100林吉特罚款。

染疫动物、禽类或动物尸体的处理

28.（1）任何人不应故意丢弃、指使或允许别人丢弃或以其他方式暴露正在或曾经染疫的动物、禽类及其尸体或是其接触过的草料、垫料、粪便等物到排水沟、壕沟、水渠、街道或空地。

（2）违反本项规定的人，应被处100林吉特罚款。

29.（已依据法令147号进行删除）

持有培养物或疫苗的许可证

30.（1）局长可以签发许可证，允许持有者将其持有的活体培养物或疫苗接种到动物或禽类。

（2）除兽医负责人或注册医师因为职业的正当用途需要外，未经许可，任何人不得拥有培养物或疫苗并将其接种到动物或禽类。

（3）（a）违反本项规定拥有培养物或疫苗的个人，应被处100林吉特罚款。

（b）违反本项规定接种动物或禽类的个人，应被单处或并处250林吉特罚款或3个月有期徒刑。

物主报告染疫或死亡的动物或禽类

31.（1）任何物主或个人管理的兽类或禽类动物出现染疫或有理由怀疑正患上疫病时，应立即向兽医负责人或最近的警察局、彭古鲁、县长报告，并应立即指挥将这些染疫的动物或禽类及其他与其接触过的动物和禽类进行隔离直到兽医负责人抵达。

（2）任何物主或个人管理的动物或禽类有理由怀疑死于疫病时,应立即向兽医负责人或最近的警察局、彭古鲁、县长报告,即使只有一个动物,未经兽医负责人或警察局主管官员的许可,不得将其畜禽尸体转移。由于报告后24小时内没有接到指示或由于路程、路途或通信困难的原因,24小时内未能向有关部门报告,掩埋染疫动物的畜禽尸体不作为违法论处。

（3）警察局主管官员、彭古鲁或县长人员接到依据本项（1）或（2）下所作的汇报后，应立即通过电话或电报等可能的方式，向最近的兽医负责人汇报。兽医负责人通过书面通信方式向州兽医局局长汇报并确认此事。

（4）（a）没有合法的理由，未能依照本项的要求进行报告的人，应被处50林吉特罚款。

（b）没有合法的理由，未能依照本项（1）的要求隔离动物或禽类或违反本项（2）的要求允许移动动物尸体的人，应被处100林吉特罚款。

与动物（犬类和猫类动物除外）和禽类相关的特别规定

适用范围

32. 第33至37条不适用于犬类和猫类动物。

死亡动物或禽类的处理

33.（1）对于经兽医负责人签发命令销毁或死于疫病的兽类和禽类动物，经营者或物主应使用焚烧或兽医负责人指定的方法处理畜禽尸体。

（2）没有合法的理由，违反本条（1）中兽医负责人的指示的人，应被处100林吉特罚款。

染疫或疑似染疫动物的移动或处置

34.（1）没有州兽医局局长的书面许可，即使是通过购买方式得到的，任何人不得移动或处置染疫或有理由怀疑染疫或涉疫动物或禽类、或者是这些动物或禽类的尸体、奶类或粪便。

（2）任何人违反本项规定，每项罪名应被处100林吉特罚款。

受污染场所的物品的搬移

35.（1）兽医负责人可以通过发布命令，禁止奶类、肥料、草料、垫料或其他有可能传播疫情的物品从正在或最近饲养过染疫动物或禽类的场所进行搬移。

（2）任何人没有合法的理由违反本项发布的命令，应被处100林吉特罚款。

疫区、疫病控制区和疫病扑灭区

36.（1）当有理由地认为：

（a）全州或州内部分地区的动物或禽类群内存在疫病；

（b）全州或州内部分地区很可能已经传入疫病或

（c）希望遏制或清除全州或州内部分地区的疫病时，主管部长可以根据具体情况发布命令宣布该州或州内部分地区为某种疫病的疫区、疫病控制区和疫病扑灭区，并可以在同一命令中或后续命令中：

（ⅰ）完全或有条件地禁止从该地区转移动物及其畜禽尸体；

（ⅱ）完全或有条件地禁止在该地区屠宰动物；

（ⅲ）完全或有条件地禁止在该地区买卖动物动物尸体；

（ⅳ）禁止在该地区保存动物尸体或者保存及饲养动物或禽类；

（ⅴ）加强对经营或运输动物或禽类的市场、屠宰房、屠宰场、笼、箱、货车和集装箱的清洁和消毒；

（ⅵ）要求对畜禽产品进行检疫（包括畜禽动物的血、奶、尿等物质），对动物或禽类免疫并加以烙印或其他标记；

（ⅶ）全区或部分地区禁止保存或饲养动物或禽类；

（ⅷ）尽管本法或其他条例中的一些规定依据许可证来执行，但仍可撤消依据本法签发的动物、禽类及动物尸体的进口许可或对原许可增加条件；

（ⅸ）为了防止疫病的传入、扩散或有利于疫病的控制和消除，必要时，可以增加检疫条件或制订新的规定。

（2）在本项（1）所提的情况下，当一个地区被宣布为疫区、疫病控制区和疫病扑灭区时，州兽医局局长认为有必要去控制或制止疫情的扩散或消除疫病时，可以签发与本项（1）不相矛盾的命令，以利于在区内管制动物或禽类的紧急隔离、分离场、转移和屠宰，利于采取其他疫病预防措施或采取打烙印等方法标识动物。当动物货主或经营者违反上述命令时，州兽医局局长可以采取必要的步骤分开或隔离这些动物，而因此产生的费用应由货主或经营者单独或共同补偿。

（3）本项（1）或（2）下所制订的各项命令都应公布在政府公告上，但应立即实施。

（4）在疫区、疫病控制区和疫病扑灭区发现的流浪动物或禽类，违反了本项（1）或（2）下所发布的命令的，兽医负责人可以将其立即销毁或抓捕并扣押直到交齐罚款。

（5）屠宰、迁移或买卖的动物、禽类或动物尸体，违反了本项（1）或（2）下所发布的命令的，兽医负责人可以命令立即销毁或将其抓捕并扣押直到交齐罚款。

（6）为了执行本项（2）下检测、免疫和预防性治疗措施，兽医负责人可以命令在规定时间将动物或禽类送到规定的地点，没有他的允许，这些动物不得移离规定的地点。

（7）任何人没有合法的理由违反本项（1）和（2）发布的命令的，应被处不高于100林吉特罚款。

（8）依据本项命令销毁或抓捕动物、禽类或动物尸体，不作赔偿。

特别许可

37. 在条件允许的情况下，州兽医局局长可以准许物主将动物或禽类转移进出疫区。

与犬类动物和狂犬病相关的特别规定

许可

38.（1）未经许可，任何人不得拥有、经营、寄养或饲养3月龄以上的犬类动物。

（2）犬类动物在每年1月31日前依规定程序办理、达到3月龄、抵达马来西亚后14天内或依据第42条签发的接种防狂犬病疫苗令结束后14天内都可获得许可证，且许可证生效后可在当年12月31日前使用。

（3）在邮局或规定的地点，状况正常的犬类动物可以获得许可证。

（4）农牧部可以规定犬类动物取得许可证的费用。

（5）收取规定的费用后，许可机构应发给犬的主人一个标有一串数字的证章。

（6）每个取得许可证的狗的主人应为依据本条（5）发出的证章准备一条颈链。佩带时，颈链牢牢地系上，并使证章清晰可见。外出时，取得许可证的狗应一直佩带颈链和证章。没有佩带颈链和证章的狗将被扑杀。

（7）（a）相关的负责人将书面授权人员依据本条（6）规定扑杀狗类。为了实施本条（6）的规定，被授权人员可以进出任何地方，而并不限于其住所。同时应遵守规定：如果有人要求，被授权人应向现场的物主、住户或负责人出示书面授权状。

（b）本条中“相关的负责人”指州兽医局局长、市长、地区理事会或地方机构的首长、乡镇总长或州警察局主管。

（8）（a）任何人违反本条（1）的规定拥有、经营、寄养或饲养犬类动物，应被处100林吉特罚款。

（b）任何人没有合法的理由违反本条（6）的规定，应被处50林吉特罚款。

（9）州立法会的会长或元首可以通过颁布命令宣明本条（1）的规定不适用于州的某些特定地区或豁免某些人或某类人按本条规定要求的犬类动物许可证或取得许可证的部分或全部费用。

（10）本条规定在下列情况下对狗不适用：

（a）依据第42条在全州或部分地区实施接种防狂犬病疫苗令期间。

（b）依照其他成文的法律已经注册或获得许可证。

狂犬病疫区

39.（1）作为防狂犬病的预防措施，州主管部长可以在任何时间通过签发命令的方式宣布某州或部分地区为狂犬病疫区。

（2）本条（1）下所制订的各项命令都应公布在适当的政府公告上，并应立即实施。

（3）未经州兽医局局长签发的书面许可，任何人不应将狗带出狂犬病疫区或有部分地区为狂犬病疫区的州。

（4）狂犬病疫区的狗的主人或管理者应能有效的控制住他的狗：

（a）将狗关在一个不可能逃出的封闭的地方。

（b）安全地绑住。

（c）用链条或结实的绳索、皮革适当地、牢牢地固定在狗戴的颈链或狗服上：

规定：不管是否是由于预防疫病的处理措施或其他原因，如果州兽医局首长认为某种狗来自狂犬病疫区并已接种免疫，他认为合适时，可以让此种狗免于符合本条的要求。

（5）当在狂犬病疫区发现的狗类没有按本条（4）的规定进行有效的控制时，被州兽医局首长或州主管警察局书面授权的被授权人可以扑杀此类狗只。为了执行本条的规定，被授权人可以进出任何场地、高楼或建筑物：

规定；被授权人 -

（ⅰ）不应进入住宅，除非是在白天

（ⅱ）如果有人要求，被授权人应向当时负责管理场地、高楼或建筑物的物主、住户或负责人出示书面授权状。

（6）（a）任何人违反本条（3）的规定的，应被处500林吉特罚款或3个月有期徒刑。

（b）任何人没有合法的理由违反本条（4）的规定的，应被处250林吉特罚款。

疑似感染狂犬病动物的扑杀或留检

40.（1）当兽医负责人有理由地怀疑动物可能染上狂犬病或已经接触了狂犬病病例时，可以根据自己的判断指导立即扑杀这些动物或命令动物的主人或管理者立即将动物赶进动物检疫站进行留检和观察。

（2）当这些动物的主人或管理者违反上述命令，兽医负责人可以指导立即扑杀这些动物或控制这些动物并将其迁移到动物检疫站。

（3）兽医负责人可以在动物检疫站将这些动物销毁或留下来治疗直至其治愈。

（4）兽医负责人可以控制这些死亡或被扑杀动物的畜禽尸体，有理由认为这些畜禽尸体已感染狂犬病，可以采用他认为合适的方法处理这些畜禽尸体。

（5）依据本条规定销毁动物不作任何赔偿。

（6）任何人没有合法的理由违反本条（1）的规定的，应被处100林吉特罚款。

（7）本条规定中的“动物”指圈养或受控饲养的四腿兽类。

咬人后犬只的留检

41.（1）兽医负责人或警衔不低于检疫官的警察可以命令已经或有理由确信咬人的狗只的主人或管理者将狗带到他们那里进行检疫，并且他们认为合适时，可以在此时此地留检此狗。如果狗的主人或管理者违反这些命令，上述兽医负责人或警察可以立即控制该狗只并将其迁移到动物检疫站。

（2）任何人没有合法的理由违反本条签发的命令的，应被处100林吉特罚款。

犬类抗狂犬病疫苗

42.（1）当时间合适时，州主管部长可以签发命令（在本条中指“接种防狂犬病疫苗令”），要求全州或命令中规定的部分地区的狗只应接受防狂犬病疫苗接种，亦可以随时取消此项命令。

（2）“接种防狂犬病疫苗令”的签发和取消应公布在适当的政府公告上。

（3）每个接种防狂犬病疫苗令应维持实施到12月31日，在此期间会制订新的命令或取消该命令。如取消该命令，原实施周期就会缩短，应无偏差地制订新的接种防狂犬病疫苗令并在原命令废止时实施。

（4）当制订命令时，州兽医局首长可以规定狗或狗类接种的时间和地点。

（5）所有的狗类接种疫苗的安排应公布在适当的政府公告上或州兽医局首长认为其他必要的方式。

（6）（a）州兽医局首长可以政府公告上发布通知，要求每只按接种防狂犬病疫苗令规定接种的狗，在通知规定的时间之后，在接种防狂犬病疫苗令实施的地区和时期内，佩带有序列号的金属证章、标识或耳牌等接种标记（不管其大小）。没有佩带正确的标记的狗只将被捕杀。

（b）相关的负责人可以书面授权某些人按本条（a）的规定捕杀此类狗只。为了执行本条的规定，被授权人可以进出任何场地、高楼或建筑物：

规定；被授权人 -

（ⅰ）不应进入住宅，除非是在白天。

（ⅱ）如果有人要求，被授权人应向当时负责管理场地、高楼或建筑物的物主、住户或负责人出示书面授权状。

（c）本条中的“相关负责人”指州兽医首长、城市理事会或市政的首脑、市政理事会首长、特区首长、地方机构首长、乡镇总长和州警察局主管。

（7）如果狗的主人或管理者违反本条（1）或（4）中的命令或指令，兽医负责人可以立即捕杀这些狗类。

（8）如果狗的主人或管理者没有合理的理由违反本条（1）或（4）中的命令或指令，应被处 250 林吉特罚款。

（9）农牧部可以规定狗的接种费：

任何按照第 38 条在接种时获得许可证的，或按市政当局施行的成文法律进行注册或取得许可证的狗只在接种时，免收任何费用。

（10）州立法会的会长或元首可以通过颁布命令豁免某些人或某类人部分或全部的狗只接种费用。

（11）任何在某年按照接种防狂犬病疫苗令进行接种并持有正确的接种标识的狗只，应被认为在当年 12 月 31 日前按照本法取得了许可，并按成文法律进行注册或取得许可证。

第Ⅳ部分 防止虐待动物

注释

43. 在本部分，除非在文中另有所指，否则 -

动物：指除人类以外任何活的生物，包括兽类、禽类、鱼类、爬行类或昆虫类，不管是野生的或驯养的。

对虐待动物行为的处罚

44.（1）任何人：

（a）粗暴地抽打、脚踢、虐待、践踏、过度驱使、过度负载、折磨、激怒或惊吓动物；

（b）在行为上参与或经主人的允许，使动物受到上述对待的；

（c）作为动物在分娩期或从一地点到另一地点运输途中的管理者，忘记向动物提供足够的食物或饮水的；

（d）由于某些嬉闹、不合理的行为或疏忽某些工作，或者经主人的允许，造成动物不必要的疼痛或苦楚的；

（e）在行为上参与或经主人的允许，将动物关押、运输、抬起或携带时所在的地点或采用方式让动物遭受不必要的疼痛或苦楚的；

（f）雇用患病、体质虚弱、受伤或有伤痛的动物进行劳作的；

（g）参与或协助动物打架或诱捕，或拥有、使用、经营或协助管理用于动物打架或诱捕的设施或场所，或者允许别人使用这些设施或场所，或者收取或让别人收取某人使用这些设施或场所所支付的费用的，应被判犯有虐待罪，应被单处或并处 200 林吉特罚款或有期徒刑 6 个月。

（2）如果物主在防止动物受虐待方面没有做出合理的关心和实施监督，应被认为允许本部分所指的虐待行为：

如果物主仅仅因为没有做出合理的关心和实施监督而被证明允许本部分所指的虐待行为，他没有被处罚金时就不能被判有期徒刑。

（3）在本条中，作为人们食物的动物的宰杀或准备宰杀的行为不认为是犯罪或不负法律责任，除非这些宰杀或准备宰杀的行为对动物施加了不必要的痛苦。

（4）尽管本条（1）（g）中有所规定，但州主管部门可以通过书面许可批准在本州的斗牛活动，其应符合的条件可以在许可证中加以规定，即斗牛活动在公众关注的特殊场合开展，或者州主管部门认为斗牛活动利于品种的繁育，并在斗牛活动不出现虐待动物的情况。当活动符合许可证里相关的条件时，本条（1）（g）中的规定不应适用于这类斗牛活动。

兽医负责人和警察官员的权力

45.（1）当兽医负责人和警察官员看到有人违反第44条的规定时，可以不需要任何凭证地逮捕违法的人员、抓捕相关的动物、收缴相关的运输工具和物品。

（2）被逮捕的人员和被收缴的运输工具和物品应立即送往警察局。

（3）被抓捕的动物应送到警察局、畜栏或兽医中心，并根据地方签发的有关动物的命令，可以将动物扣押直到被告被审问。

（4）兽医负责人和警察官员有理由地认为动物违反或正在违反第44条的规定时，他可以在任何街道或公众场所拦截并检查这些动物。

地方官员或乡镇机构的权力

46. 在地方或乡镇机构的权限内，根据第45条赋予兽医负责人和警察官员的权力由城市理事会或市政的首脑、市政理事会首长、特区首长、地方机构首长、乡镇总长根据情况委派的官员来授予。

地方行政官员对违法行为签发的命令

47.（1）当地方行政官员认为某人违反第44条时，他可以签发命令：

（a）违法的相关动物被送往兽医中心，由兽医负责人进行扣留和处理直到命令中声明的期限的结束，或地方行政官员签发新的命令来释放，或由官衔不低于助理兽医官的兽医负责人书面证明其可以完全地释放。

（b）动物由兽医负责人处理且不得使用直到命令中声明的期限的结束，或地方行政官员、官衔不低于助理兽医官的兽医负责人签发使用许可证。

（c）如果认为动物患病或受伤已不可治愈时，可以命令警察官或兽医负责人根据指示立即销毁此动物，埋葬畜禽尸体等处理费用由违法人员支付。

（2）如果依照上述（1）中的命令，动物被送往兽医中心或由兽医负责人进行处理，违法的人员应支付规定的费用用于动物在释放或使用前的饲养和处理：

如果动物的主人书面要求主管兽医中心的官员销毁此类动物，他应向官员支付规定的动物销毁和埋葬费。主管兽医中心的官员立即安排销毁此类动物，并免收动物的饲养费和处理费。

（3）任何人违反本条规定下的命令，应被处200林吉特的罚款。

签发指令扑杀动物的权力

48.（1）地方官员、政府医学官员、官衔不低于助理兽医官的兽医负责人或官衔不低于检查官的警察经检疫后认为：

（a）动物患病或受伤已不可治愈或使其生存只是增加痛苦；

（b）动物患病或受伤十分严重，或根据其身体情况，考虑到转移动物的有效方法时，不可能无痛苦将其转移，其生存只是增加痛苦；可以通过书面命令指示扑杀此类动物且此类命令由上述官员、警察亲自或根据其指示立即执行：

如果患病或受伤严重的动物关在适当的房子、畜栏、畜棚或围栏里，并不在公共通道、市场或重要场所，在动物的主人或管理者（如果有）知道其动物状况前，不应签发此类命令。

（2）根据本条规定执行命令扑杀动物，其迁移动物和埋葬畜禽尸体的费用应由动物的主人或管理者来支付，其赔偿的数额由地方官员来考虑。

对患有不可救治的疾病、损伤的动物或根据公开承认是物主的要求，扑杀动物不作赔偿

49. 在任何情况下，根据第 47 条（1）（c）、第 48 条（1）的规定来执行命令，或根据第 47 条（2）的规定，公开承认是物主的人向主管兽医中心的官员书面要求，扑杀动物不作任何赔偿：

在上面最后一种情况里，主管兽医中心的官员应确认作书面要求的人就是物主。

给举报者报酬

50.（1）法院根据本法本部分的规定执行的罚款，可以将不超过一半的数额酬谢举报者。

（2）关于这种报酬，根据本法规定，违法行为限于地方的，其罚款应缴入议会，地方法令的实施可以使用这些资金。

未经许可，不得囚禁出售、出口或展览的兽类和禽类动物

50A.（1）根据本法的规定，任何人未经许可，不得在任何地方囚禁出售、出口或展览的兽类和禽类动物：

本条规定在实施细则中另有规定的地区不适用。

（2）任何人违反本条（1）的规定，应被单处或并处 200 林吉特的罚款或 6 个月有期徒刑。

第Ⅴ部分　牲畜的贮备

禁止屠杀或迁移牛只等

51.（1）州主管部门可以签发命令：

（a）在命令规定的时期内，未经许可，禁止牛、猪或其他特定的牛、猪品种在州与州之间、本州内地方之间或本州地方与其他州之间进行迁移。

（b）在命令规定的时期内，未经许可，禁止在州范围内屠宰牛、绵羊、山羊、猪、禽或其他特定的品种。

（c）完成规定的程序和交纳规定的费用后，才能取得上述许可证。

（2）根据本条（1）制订的命令签发的许可证应符合命令或依照本条（1）授权签发许可证的人规定的条件。

（3）任何人违反本条规定签发的命令，每个违法行为应被处 500 林吉特罚款。

在州公报上发布命令

52. 根据第 51 条制订的命令应在相关的州公报上发布。

第Ⅵ部分　牲畜的改良

适用的州

53. 本部分应在吉打州和吉兰丹州实施，除了上述的州外，除非州议会根据具体情况，通过相关的动议，认为这些规定对州或地区有利，否则不应在其他州或地区实施。

54.（已删除）

禁止拥有未去势的公牛

55.（1）根据第 56 条，除非经州兽医局局长确认公牛已去势，否则任何人不应拥有或管理大于 15 月龄的公牛。

（2）任何人违反本条规定，应被处 100 林吉特的罚款。

州兽医局局长可豁免的情况

56.（1）经物主书面申请且公牛是在州兽医局局长管辖的地区上繁育的，州兽医局局长认为公牛适于品种的繁育时，可以准予免于遵守第55条的规定。类似的申请中应包含有动物所有细节的描述，并且陈述其年龄、关养地点和其他规定的细节。

（2）公牛出现下列情况时，州兽医局局长不应根据本条（1）的规定进行豁免：

（a）很可能有缺陷或品种低劣。

（b）感染传染性疫病。

（3）本条中州兽医局局长的权力和义务可以由他正式授权的个人来行使和履行。

种公牛的注册

57. 州兽医局局长应对依照第56条豁免的公牛（下称“种公牛”）进行登记注册，应记录这些动物的概况，还有物主的姓名和住址，并免费发给物主一份登记注册情况的副本（下称“认可书”）。

种公牛的出售、死亡或迁移应上报

58.（1）在遵守其他成文法律的情况下，种公牛的物主应在公牛的出售、死亡或转移后一个月内向彭古鲁、县长或兽医负责人报告种公牛的出售、死亡或迁移的情况，并出示依据第57条签发的认可书。州兽医局局长应该对这些出售、死亡或转移的情况在注册表和认可书上加以记录。

（2）彭古鲁或县长依据本条（1）的规定收集信息并尽快向兽医负责人汇报是其应尽的义务。

（3）任何人没有合理的理由，没有根据本条的规定进行报告或没有出示认可书，将被处以50林吉特罚款。

种公牛的检疫

59.（1）州兽医局局长随时可以要求种公牛的物主牵出种公牛进行检疫，并可根据自己的判断，撤消种公牛根据第56条规定获得的豁免权。

（2）与此类种公牛有关的注册表和认可书应记录豁免权的撤消情况。

给种公牛的物主的通知

60.（1）当豁免申请被拒、认可书被取消或认为适用于本部分规定的公牛不适于繁育时，州兽医局局长可以在不少于14天内向物主或公牛管理者发送一份通知，指示他们在通知规定的时间内将公牛屠宰或去势。

（2）当有人违反本条（1）中的通知的规定时，州兽医局局长可以指导将公牛屠宰或去势，费用由物主支付。为了达到上述目的，被授权人可以进入公牛正在或将要出现在的建筑物里。与公牛屠宰或去势有关的费用由州兽医局局长考虑作为公民负债来列支，但由物主来支付。

（3）任何人没有合理的理由违反依据本条发出的通知的，将被处100林吉特的罚款。

必要时出示认可书

61.（1）当下列人员按要求扣留种公牛时，种公牛的物主出示或指示别人出示与种公牛相关的认可书：

（a）官衔不低于助理兽医师的兽医负责人。

（b）官衔不低检查官的警察。

（c）管理牛只的人员。

（2）任何人没有合理的违反本条（1）的规定的，将被处50林吉特罚款。

免费去势

62. 如果在州兽医局局长管辖的地区内的公牛在当时符合去势条件，经物主或公牛（非种公牛）管理者的请求，州兽医局局长或经州兽医局局长特别授权的人员应免费给这样的公牛去势。

官员的保护

63. 法庭对州兽医局局长或被授权的人员执行第62条的规定可能导致公牛的损失或损伤的赔偿行为不予支持。

批准起诉制

64. 未经州兽医局局长的事先批准不得对本部分的规定提起诉讼。

物证的责任

65. 在因为违反本部分的规定而提起的诉讼中，公牛依照第56条的规定得以免责的证据应取决于被起诉人，在反方被检定之前，公牛应被假定为15月龄以上。

免责的权利

66. 州主管部门可以在州政府公报上刊登公告，依照本部分的规定，对某个、某种或几种的公牛给予免责。

第Ⅶ部分　搜查、收缴和拘留

搜查染疫动物或禽类的权利

67. 为了确认动物或禽类是否染疫或是否有违反本法的行为：

（a）为了检查动物、畜禽尸体、场所、楼房或建筑物，兽医负责人或兽医警察官可以进入并检查他怀疑可能扣押动物或贮藏畜禽尸体的任何场所、楼房或建筑物，这些场所、楼房、建筑物、动物或畜禽尸体的物主应向兽医负责人或兽医警察官提供所有必要的帮助及其所需的信息。

（b）兽医负责人、兽医警察官或海关官员可以任何拦截、进入和检查运输动物或畜禽尸体的运输工具，这类运输工具的物主或管理者拒绝停车应被处200林吉特罚款。

动物、禽类、动物尸体或相关物品的收缴

68.（1）当兽医负责人、兽医警察官有理由认为违反本法的行为已经发生或正在发生，或者海关官员有理由认为违反本法有关的进出境规定的行为已经发生或正在发生，兽医负责人、兽医警察官或海关官员可以收缴与违法行为有关的动物、禽类、动物尸体、运输工具或相关物品并迁移到兽医负责人选定的兽栏、围栏进行扣押。

（2）当兽医负责人、兽医警察官或海关官员依据本条（1）的规定将要收缴并扣押动物、禽类、动物尸体、运输工具或相关物品时，他应向地方首长报告。地方首长认为合适时，可以为动物、禽类、动物尸体、运输工具或相关物品的扣押或释放签发命令。

（2A）虽然本法有所规定，但是由于地方首长未能及时行动且被扣押的动物尸体或物品会自然、快速地腐烂，兽医负责人、兽医警察官或海关官员认为合适时可以销毁、出售或用其他方法进行处理。

（3）动物、禽类、动物尸体、运输工具或相关物品的物主将支付这些费用，费用的数额由地方首长合理地考虑，其中包括将物品运送到扣押地的支出。除非在规定的时间内支付这些费用，否则这些动物、禽类、动物尸体、运输工具或相关物品将被罚没。

拘留的权利

69.（1）兽医负责人、海关官员或警察官发现正在、试图或其有理由怀疑正着手从事违反本法的人时，如果这些人拒绝提供他的姓名、地址、马来西亚境外的地址或有合理的依据认为其提供虚假的姓名或地址、或有意潜逃，可以不用许可证将其进行拘留。

（2）这种被拘留的人将被带到警察局并根据刑事处理法［法令 593］进行处理。

第Ⅷ部分 增　补

防碍官员执行公务

70. 任何人没有合理的理由防碍、阻止或协助防碍、阻止兽医负责人、警察官或海关官员执行本法或依据本法签发的条例和命令中的规定时，应被单处或并处 500 林吉特罚款或 6 个月有期徒刑。

更改许可证

71. 任何人没有合法的授权，擅自更改依据本法规定签发的许可或允许，或者有意地更改这些许可或允许的，应被单处或并处 500 林吉特罚款或 6 个月有期徒刑。

一般的处罚

72. 任何人违反本法且没有特定的处罚规定的，处 200 林吉特罚款。

累犯的处罚

73. 任何人因违反本法以相同或相似的罪名第二次被判有罪之日起 12 个月内再次违反本法，但此次违法没有判处死刑的惩罚时，应被处罚款之外增加 2 个月的刑期或用 2 个月的刑期代替罚款。

罚没

74.（1）当任何人已经违反本法时，法院在宣判当事人有罪同时，作为补充或代替的惩罚措施，可以签发命令将与此次违法有关的动物、禽类、动物尸体、运输工具或物品进行罚没。

（2）当根据第 68 条的规定收缴动物、禽类、动物尸体、运输工具或物品时，犯罪嫌疑人不明或失踪时，如果地方首长确信这些动物、禽类、动物尸体、运输工具或物品已经违法，他可以签发命令将与这些动物、禽类、动物尸体、运输工具或物品进行罚没：

相关规定：除非有具体姓名或住址的物主已经有机会出庭陈述不能签发罚没命令的理由时，不能签发命令罚没运输工具。

（3）根据本条或第 68（3）条的规定罚没的动物、禽类、动物尸体、运输工具或物品，应遵照地方首长的指示来处理。

推定原则

75.（1）当患病动物或禽类的主人或管理者被指控违反本法时，在他向法庭证明他在被指控前不知道且不留意获取相关信息以前，他将被法庭推定为知晓患病畜类或禽类的有关情况。

（2）当对动物或禽类的物主有疑问时，管理这些动物的人或常年使用这些设备的人将被推定为物主直到其非物主身份得以确认。

起诉

76. 对任何违反本法的行为应由民事诉讼副长、官衔不低于助理兽医官的兽医负责人或官衔不低于副检疫官的警察提起诉讼。

费用

77. 由兽医负责人或其他官员行使本法或依据本法规定签发的命令、条例、指示赋予的权力所产生的费用应根据具体情况向相关动物、禽类、动物尸体、物品、房屋或运输工具的物主、发货人、收货人或进口商收取，并考虑作为公民负债来列支。

行动的风险和费用由物主负责

78.（1）依据本法或依据本法规定签发的命令、条例、指示对动物、禽类、动物尸体、物品、房屋或运输工具采取的行动产生的风险应由其物主负责。

（2）政府部门或官员对行使本法赋予的权力产生的费用、损失、伤害或延误不负任何责任。

可以对动物施加铭牌或其他标识

79.（1）兽医负责人如果认为出于识别的目的，可以对动物施加临时或永久铭牌或其他标识。

（2）任何人伪造、复制、更改、损坏或擦掉兽医负责人施加的铭牌或标识的，应被处 200 林吉物罚款。

动物检疫站

80.（1）动物检疫站应由国家和州政府在马来西亚合适的地点修建并维护，这些动物检疫站的位置及名称应在相应的政府公报中通报。

（2）除了上述（1）中通报的动物检疫站外，州兽医局局长可以指定合适的地点或建筑作为临时或紧急的动物检疫站。

动物检疫站管理的议事程序

81.（1）兽医局长在联邦动物检疫站和州兽医局局长在州动物检疫站在问题上，经与兽医局长磋商，可以制订动物检疫站管理和维护的议事程序。

（2）农牧部可以规定动物在联邦动物检疫站的检疫费用，州议长或首长可以规定动物在州动物检疫站的检疫费用。

（3）动物进出动物检疫站所产生的费用应由物主或动物管理者来支付。

兽医中心的建立

82. 州主管部门可以指定州内某个合适的地方或数个地方作为兽医中心或动物中心，可以制订兽医中心或动物中心管理规定，可以规定在兽医中心或动物中心内饲养、治疗和扣押或处理后畜禽尸体的销毁或深埋等费用。

州无疫病证明

83. 州兽医局局长可以向动物或货物出口商签发证书证明本州无疫病，收费 2 林吉特。

有害生物和病原的进口

84.（1）未经兽医局长的书面允许，任何人不得故意向马来西亚进口或拥有天然对动物有害或危险的有害生物活体、毒虫活体、病原体活体、病毒和细菌培养物。

（2）任何人违反本条规定应被处 100 林吉特罚款。

检疫站的动物或禽类视为未进入马来西亚境内

85. 根据本法及依据本法规定制订的条例和细则的宗旨，通过海、陆、空运输带入马来西亚并进入兽医负责人指定检疫站的动物或禽类，视为未进入马来西亚境内，但应服从本法及依据本法规定制订的条例和细则。

制订条例的权利

86.（1）为了进一步执行本法的规定和目标，农牧部可以制订条例。

（2）不违背上述（1）赋予的权利的情况下，农牧部可以通过条例为以下情况制订规定：

（a）放置装运受检疫的动物、禽类或动物尸体的船舶。

（b）规范动物、禽类或动物尸体从船上的卸货。

（c）规范动物通过海、陆、空的进出口。

（d）规定进口动物或禽类的检疫实验及检疫方法。

（e）规范屠宰用进口动物的卸货及移动。

（ea）规范和管理屠宰场。

（eb）规范和许可孵卵所、繁殖场、人工授精中心和场所、禽类加工厂、肉类打包和罐装厂、肉类贮存厂和其他家畜和家禽繁殖和改良场所。

（f）清洁和消毒曾经饲养或装载染疫动物或禽类的建筑物、畜棚、场所或运输工具。

（g）清洁和消毒曾经装载或运送染疫动物或禽类的市场、销售场所、铁道路基、铁路车厢和货车。

（h）来自疫区的动物或禽类或涉疫动物的消毒。

（i）接触染疫或疑似染疫动物、禽类、动物尸体或涉疫动物的人员及其衣服的消毒。

（j）不管是否有赔偿，对接触染疫动物、禽类或动物尸体或者是有理由被怀疑为已在传播疫病的运输工具上的其他畜禽尸体、铺草、饲料或其他物品进行收缴、消毒和销毁（如果合适时）。

（k）犬类动物的饲养、销毁或其他处理方法的条件和规则，以及许可证的使用方法。

（ka）圈养动物用于销售、出口或展览的场所的许可、管理、监督和检疫。实施细则可以：

（ⅰ）规定动物或禽类的饲养条件。

（ⅱ）规定从何机构取得许可证。

（ⅲ）规定许可证撤销或暂停的条件。

（l）确定依据本法规定需付费的项目及其金额。

（m）违反实施细则将被罚款，但每个违法行为的罚款不超过100林吉特。在一个持续违法的行为的情况下，在违法过程中每天罚款20林吉特。

废止条文的方式

87.（1）废止表中列出的成文法律其废止的范围在第三列中规定。

（2）用“（已删除）”来表示。

（3）雌性动物屠宰通告和动物迁移和屠宰的基本规定从此撤销。

废止表（略）

附录

农业部公布的其他疫病
（参见文 P. U.（B）86/1999）

1. 非洲马瘟
2. 萎缩性鼻炎
3. （已删除，见文 P. U. （B） 247/2000）

4. 蓝舌病
5. 疯牛病
6. 马传染性子宫炎
7. 鸭病毒性肠炎
8. 鸭病毒性肝炎
9. 马流感
10. 马传染性贫血
11. 马病毒性动脉炎
12. 日本脑炎
13. 梅迪 - 维斯纳病
14. 黏液瘤病
15. 副结核
16. 猪蓝耳病
17. 肺腺瘤病
18. 鹦鹉热
19. 马腺疫
20. 传染性胃肠炎
21. 委内瑞拉马脑脊髓炎

病毒性脑炎（参见文 P. U.（B）96/1999）

禽伤寒（参见文 P. U.（B）247/2000）

Laws of Malaysia ACT 647

(Animals ACT 1953)

An Act to amend and consolidate the laws for preventing the introduction into, and the spreading within, the Malaysia of diseases of animals; for the control of the movement of animals into, within and from the Malaysia; for the control of the slaughter of animals; for the prevention of cruelty to animals; for measures pertaining to the general welfare, conservation and improvement of animals in the Malaysia; and for purposes connected therewith.

(30th April, 1953)

Part Ⅰ Preliminary

Short title

1. This Act may be cited as the Animals Act 1953.

Interpretation

2. In this Act, unless the context otherwise requires –

aircraft includes any kind of craft which may be used for the conveyance of animals or birds by air;

animal includes horses, cattle, sheep, goats, swine, dogs, cats and any fourfooted beast kept in captivity or under control, of any age or sex;

animal quarantine station means a quarantine station established under section 80;

bird includes domestic fowls, ducks, geese, turkeys, guinea fowls and pigeons of any age or sex and their eggs;

building includes any house, hut, shed, stable or enclosure, whether roofed or not, used for sheltering or confining any animal or bird and any pen, cage, wall, gate, pillar, post, paling, frame, hoarding, fence, platform, roadway, path, steps, staging, slip, wharf, dock, piles, jetty, landing stage or bridge, or any structure connected with the foregoing;

bull means a male of any species of cattle;

carcass means the dead body of an animal or bird and includes any part thereof and the meat, bones (whether whole, broken or ground), offal, ide, skin, wool, hair, feathers, hoof, horns or other part of an animal or bird, separately or otherwise, or any portion thereof;

cat means a domesticated cat of any breed or sex;

cattle means bulls, cows, oxen, heifers, and calves and includes buffaloes of any age or sex;

contact means any animal or bird which has by contact direct or indirect with a diseased animal or bird been exposed to the risk of contracting a disease;

Director General means the Director General of Veterinary Services appointed under section 3 and includes the Deputy Director General appointed under the same section;

disease means any disease infectious or contagious amongst animals or birds and includes anthrax, blackquarter, cattle plague (rinderpest), contagious pleuropneumonia, contagious abortion, tuberculosis, epizootic lymphangitis, foot and mouth disease, glanders and farcy, goat pox, haemorrhagic septicaemia, rabies, sheep pox, swine fever, swine erysipelas, trypanosomiasis, avian pneumoencephalitis (Ranikhet disease), bacillary white diarrhoea (pullorum disease), fowl cholera, fowl plague, fowl pox, infectious laryngotracheitis and any other disease which the Minister may from time to time, by notification in the Gazette, declare to be a disease * within the meaning of this Act;

[* Note—For other diseases declared by the Minister – see P. U. (B) 86/1999, P. U. (B) 96/1999 & P. U. (B) 247/2000.]

dog means domesticated dog of any breed or sex;

examine with its grammatical variations and cognate expressions, includes the carrying out of any tests and post – mortem examination, after exhumation of the carcass (if necessary);

fodder means any substance used for food of animals or birds;

horse includes any mare, gelding, pony, foal, colt, filly, ass or mule;

infected means infected with any disease;

litter means any substance used for bedding or otherwise for or about animals or birds;

master means the captain of any ship or aircraft and includes any person for the time being in charge on any ship (other than a pilot) or aircraft;

Minister means the Minister charged with the responsibility for animal husbandry;

offence against this Act means any contravention of or failure to comply with any of the provisions of this Act or of any order, rule or direction made or given under it;

officer of customs has the same meaning as in the Customs Act, 1967 [Act 235];

owner includes any person for the time being in charge of any animal or bird and any person for the time being in occupation of any building;

quarantine means the compulsory detention in isolation of any animal, bird or thing;

quarantine station means any building or place where quarantine is carried out and includes an examination station or hulk;

ship includes every description of vessel or craft, however propelled, which may be used in navigation by water;

State Director means the State Director of Veterinary Services appointed under section 3;

vaccine includes any culture or living preparation of the causative agent of any disease;

veterinary authority means the Director General of Veterinary Services, the Deputy Director General of Veterinary Services and any State Director of Veterinary Services, any Veterinary Officer, Deputy or Assistant Veterinary Officer and includes any person appointed in writing by the Director General of Veterinary Services, the Deputy Director General of Veterinary Services and any State Director of Veterinary Services, to be a Veterinary authority under section 3;

veterinary centre has the meaning assigned to it in section 82;

veterinary police officer means any member of the Police Force acting under the direction of a veterinary authority.

Appointment of officers

3. (1) The Yang di – Pertuan Agong may appoint an officer to be known as the Director General of Veterinary Services and an officer to be known as the Deputy Director General of Veterinary Services.

(2) The Ruler or Yang di – Pertua Negeri of a State may appoint a State Director of Veterinary Services and as many Veterinary Officers, Deputy and Assistant Veterinary Officers as he may consider necessary for the pur-

poses of this Act.

(3) The Director General of Veterinary Services, the Deputy Director General of Veterinary Services and any State Director of Veterinary Services may appoint any person in writing to be a veterinary authority for all the purposes of this Act or for such of the purposes of this Act as he shall specify in so appointing such person, and such person shall, for the purposes of this Act in respect of which he is so appointed, be deemed to be an officer appointed under this Act.

(4) All officers appointed under this Act shall be deemed to be public servants within the meaning of the Penal Code [Act 574].

Identification card to be produced

4. (1) Every veterinary authority, officer of customs, veterinary police officer or police officer when exercising any powers under this Act shall, if not in uniform, declare his office and shall, on demand, produce to any person affected by the exercise of such powers such identification card as the Director General, the Director General of Customs or the Inspector General of Police respectively may direct to be carried by officers appointed under this Act, officer of customs or police officers.

(2) It shall not be an offence for any person to refuse to comply with any request, demand or order made or given by any officer appointed under this Act, or by any officer of customs or police officer not in uniform, who fails to declare his office and refuses to produce his identification card on demand being made by such person.

Part Ⅱ Importation and exportation of animals and birds

Importation

Power to make orders with regard to importation

5. (1) The Minister may make orders –

(a) specifying the countries or the parts of any country from which animals and birds, or any specified kinds of animals or birds, may be imported, either with or without restriction; and

(b) prohibiting, either absolutely or conditionally, the import from any specified country or any specified part of a country of any carcass, semen, fodder, litter, dung or any product of animals or birds or any article or substance that is likely to convey or spread disease.

(2) Any person who contravenes any order made under paragraph (1) (b) shall be liable to a fine of five thousand ringgit or to imprisonment for a term of two years or to both.

No person to import any animal or bird without licence

6. (1) Except as specifically provided in any order made under paragraph 5 (1) (a), no person shall import any animal or bird except in accordance with a licence in that behalf issued under this Act and in accordance with the conditions of such licence and such conditions as may be prescribed.

(2) A licence to import any animal or bird under this Act may be obtained in any State by application made in writing to a State Director and upon payment of the prescribed fee.

(3) Any person who imports an animal or bird contrary to subsection (1) shall be liable to a fine of five thousand ringgit or to imprisonment for a term of two years or to both.

Examination and detention of imported animals and birds

7. (1) Every animal or bird imported or about to be imported may be required to undergo an examination by a veterinary authority either at the place of arrival or at such other place as the veterinary authority may ap-

point and if any such animal or bird is considered likely to have been exposed to infection with any disease the veterinary authority may subject it to such biological or other test or treatment as he may think necessary, and may charge such fees for such examination, test or treatment as may be prescribed.

(2) Any such animal or bird may on importation be detained by a veterinary authority for observation, examination, test or treatment for such period and at such place as in the circumstances of the case he thinks proper.

Arrival of animals to be reported

8. (1) The master of any ship or aircraft and the guard of any train on board of which there is any animal or bird, whether such animal or bird is intended to be landed in the Malaysia or not, shall immediately on the first arrival of the ship, aircraft or train at a port, airfield or station in the Malaysia report the fact to a Port Officer or the officer in charge of the airfield or the station master, as the case may be, who shall without delay inform the nearest veterinary authority.

(2) A veterinary authority may board any ship, aircraft or train for the purpose of examining such animal.

(3) A Port Officer or officer in charge of an airfield or station master shall not permit any animal or bird which has arrived in the Malaysia to be landed from the ship or removed from the aircraft or the train until he is satisfied that the veterinary authority has granted a permit for the landing or removal of such animal or bird.

(4) Subsection (3) shall apply, notwithstanding that a licence may have been granted under section 6 or that the animal or bird comes from a country or part of a country specified in an order made under paragraph 5 (1) (a).

(5) (a) Any person who fails to make a report as required by subsection (1) shall be liable to a fine of fifty ringgit.

(b) Any person who permits an animal or bird to be landed or removed contrary to subsection (3) shall be liable to a fine of two hundred ringgit.

Importation of diseased animal or bird and contact

9. (1) If any animal, bird or carcass which has been or is about to be imported is, in the opinion of a veterinary authority, infected with any disease or likely to have been in contact with any infected or diseased animal, bird or carcass or any other infected articles or materials, the veterinary authority may in his discretion either—

(a) refuse to permit such animal, bird or carcass or any contacts thereof to be landed or removed; or

(b) cause such animal, bird or carcass and any contacts thereof to be destroyed at once and the carcass to be disposed of in such manner as he may direct; or

(c) cause such animal, bird or carcass and any contacts thereof to be detained in quarantine for such period as he may consider necessary.

(2) If any animal or bird is destroyed under paragraph (1) (b) the expense of disposing of the carcass shall be payable by the owner or person in charge.

(3) No compensation shall be payable in respect of any animal or bird destroyed under this section.

Dogs and cats on board ship

10. (1) Any dog or cat imported by sea shall, unless a veterinary authority has authorized its landing, at all times while on board the ship in any port be confined in an enclosed part of the ship or in a cage or kennel.

(2) If any dog or cat dies or is lost from a ship in any port the master of the ship shall immediately notify

the veterinary authority of such death or loss.

(3) The master of any ship on board of which any contravention of subsection (1) occurs or who fails without reasonable excuse to comply with subsection (2) shall be liable to a fine of one hundred ringgit.

Destruction of injured animals or birds

11. (1) If any animal or bird examined by a veterinary authority for the purposes of importation is found to be suffering from injury which in the opinion of the veterinary authority cannot be relieved, the veterinary authority may cause such animal or bird to be destroyed at once and its carcass to be disposed of in such manner as he may direct.

(2) If any animal or bird is destroyed under this section the expense of disposing of the carcass of any animal or bird shall be payable by the owner or person in charge.

(3) No compensation shall be payable in respect of any animal or bird destroyed under this section.

Permission to land carcass

12. (1) No person shall land from any ship or remove from any aircraft, train or vehicle the carcass of any animal or bird without the written permission of a veterinary authority who shall give directions as to the manner of its disposal.

(2) Any person who lands or removes the carcass of an animal contrary to subsection (1) or fails to comply with any direction given by a veterinary authority as to the manner of disposal of carcass shall be liable to a fine of one hundred ringgit.

Destruction or disinfection of certain article

13. Whenever it appears to a veterinary authority that any bedding, litter, fodder, dung, semen, personal belongings or other substance or material imported by land, sea or air may convey or spread disease, he may seize and detain the same and at his discretion may order its or their destruction or disinfection.

Exportation

No person to export any animal without licence

14. (1) No person shall export any animal or the carcass of any animal except in accordance with a licence in that behalf issued under this Act and in accordance with the conditions of such licence and such conditions as may be prescribed.

(2) A licence to export any animal or the carcass of any animal may be obtained in any State by application made in writing to a State Director and upon payment of the prescribed fee.

(3) Any person who exports any animal or the carcass of any animal contrary to subsection (1) shall be liable to a fine of five hundred ringgit or to imprisonment for a term of six months or to both.

Exportation to Singapore

15. The owner or person in charge of any animal to be exported to the Singapore shall produce evidence in writing of the permission of the Director General of Agri – Food and Veterinary Services of Singapore to import the animal into Singapore before any licence under section 14 is issued.

Examination before exportation

16. Every animal which is about to be exported may be required to undergo an examination by a veterinary

authority at such place as the veterinary authority may appoint.

Exportation of diseased animal or bird

17. If any animal which is about to be exported is in the opinion of the veterinary authority infected with any disease the veterinary authority may refuse to permit such animal or any contacts of the animal to be exported.

Part Ⅲ Prevention of the spread of disease

General

Examination for animals or birds suspected of disease

18. (1) If a veterinary authority has reason to believe that any animal, bird or carcass may be infected with any disease, he may subject such animal, bird or carcass to such examination or test as he may consider necessary, and for the purposes of such examination or test may take blood, milk, urine, or any other substance from such animal, bird or carcass.

(2) For the purpose of carrying out any examination or test under subsection (1) the veterinary authority may order that the animal, bird or carcass be delivered to him at a specified place and time, and no such animal, bird or carcass shall be removed from such place without the permission of the veterinary authority: Provided that no person shall be required to deliver any animal, bird or carcass at any place more than three miles from the place at which such animal is kept.

(3) Any person who fails without lawful excuse to comply with any order made under subsection (2) shall be liable to a fine of fifty ringgit.

Destruction of diseased animal or bird

19. A Veterinary authority may order the immediate isolation or destruction of any animal, bird or carcass found or reasonably believed to be infected with disease or suspected to have been in contact with a diseased animal or bird, or infected carcass or material, whether as a result of examination or test made under section 18 or otherwise.

Compensation for any animal or bird destroyed

20. (1) No compensation shall be payable in respect of any animal, bird or carcass infected with disease and destroyed by order of any veterinary authority.

(2) There shall be payable as compensation to the owner in respect of any animal, bird or carcass reasonably believed to be infected with disease which has been destroyed by order of any veterinary authority such sum as may be assessed by the State Director and approved by the Chief Minister of the State.

Post – mortem examination

21. (1) A veterinary authority may conduct a post – mortem examination of the carcass of any animal or bird and may remove such portions of the carcass as he may deem necessary for laboratory examination, and for the purposes of such examination may order that the carcass be delivered to him at such place and time as he shall specify.

(2) A veterinary authority may order the carcass of an animal or bird which has been buried to be exhumed for the purpose of such post – mortem examination.

(3) Any person fails without lawful excuse to comply with any order given under this section shall be liable to a fine of one hundred ringgit.

Diseased and contact animals and bird

22. (1) If a veterinary authority considers that any animal or bird has been exposed to infection with any disease he may order that such animal or bird be subjected to such prophylactic or curative treatment, including virus, vaccine or serum therapy, or any such combination thereof as he may think necessary.

(2) Any person who fails without lawful excuse to comply with any order given under this section shall be liable to a fine of one hundred ringgit.

Disinfection of stables, etc.

23. (1) A veterinary authority may order any stable, shed, pen, cage or other place in which an infected animal or bird has been found or kept to be disinfected in such manner as he may direct; and may by order prohibit the further use of such stable, shed, pen, cage or place for the keeping of any animal or bird until such disinfection has been completed.

(2) Any person who fails without lawful excuse to comply with any order made under this section shall be liable to a fine of one hundred ringgit.

Destruction of stables, etc.

24. (1) If a veterinary authority is of opinion that any stable, shed, pen, cage or other place which has been occupied by an infected animal cannot be effectively disinfected, he may order the owner or occupier thereof, within a time specified in such order to destroy such stable, shed, pen, cage or place and to burn the materials thereof.

(2) If an order made under subsection (1) is not complied with within he specified time the veterinary authority may cause such stable, shed, pen, cage or place to be destroyed and the materials to be burned.

(3) The veterinary authority shall make a report to the Chief Minister of the State upon every order made under this section and the Chief Minister may in his discretion give or withhold compensation for any stable, shed, pen, cage or place so destroyed.

(4) Any person who fails without lawful excuse to comply with any order made under subsection (1) shall be liable to a fine of one hundred ringgit.

Disinfection or destruction of articles

25. (1) A veterinary authority may order the disinfection or destruction of any bedding, clothing, harness, fittings, buckets, pails, or utensils whatsoever used in connection with any infected animal or bird, and compensation to be assessed by the veterinary authority shall be payable for any articles so destroyed.

(2) Any person who fails without lawful excuse to comply with any order made under this section shall be liable to a fine of one hundred ringgit.

Disinfection of person and clothing

26. (1) A veterinary authority may order the disinfection of the body and clothing of any person who has been in contact with, in charge of, or attendant upon, any animal or bird infected with or reasonably believed to be infected with disease.

(2) Any person who fails without lawful excuse to comply with any order made under this section shall be liable to a fine of one hundred ringgit.

Disinfection of vehicles

27. (1) A veterinary authority may order the disinfection of any vehicle or conveyance entering or leaving

an area declared to be an infected area under section 36, or which has been used in the transport of any animal or bird infected with or reasonably believed to be infected with disease.

(2) Any person who fails without lawful excuse to comply with any order made under this section shall be liable to a fine of one hundred ringgit.

Disposal of infected animal, bird or carcass

28. (1) No person shall knowingly cast or cause or permit to be cast into any drain, ditch, water channel, street or open space, or otherwise expose any animal or bird or the carcass of any animal or bird which is or has been infected with disease or any fodder, litter, dung or thing which has been used in connection with any infected animal or bird.

(2) Any person who contravenes this section shall be liable to a fine of one hundred ringgit.

29. (Deleted by Act 147).

Licences to possess culture or vaccine

30. (1) The Director General may issue licences permitting the holder of such a licence to possess live cultures or vaccines and to inoculate animals or birds with such culture or vaccine.

(2) No person other than a veterinary authority or registered medical practitioner for the bona fide purpose of his profession shall have in his possession any such culture or vaccine or shall inoculate any animal or bird with such culture or vaccine unless licensed in that behalf.

(3) (a) Any person who has in his possession any culture or vaccine contrary to this section shall be liable to a fine of one hundred ringgit.

(b) Any person who inoculates any animal or bird contrary to this section shall be liable to a fine of two hundred and fifty ringgit or to imprisonment for a term of three months or both.

Owner of diseased or dead animal or bird to report

31. (1) Every owner or person in charge of any animal or bird infected with or reasonably suspected to be infected with disease shall immediately make a report to a veterinary authority or to the nearest Police Station, penghulu or penggawa and shall at once cause such animal or bird and all other animals and birds which have been in contact with it to be confined and isolated until the arrival of a veterinary authority.

(2) Every owner or person in charge of any animal or bird reasonably suspected to have died of disease shall immediately report such death to the veterinary authority or the nearest Police Station, penghulu or penggawa and, in the case of an animal, the carcass shall not be moved without permission from the veterinary authority or officer in charge of such Police Station Provided that it shall not be an offence to bury the carcass of such animal if no instructions have been received within twenty – four hours of making such report or where through distance, difficulty of terrain or of communications the report cannot be made within twenty – four hours.

(3) The officer in charge of a Police Station, a penghulu or penggawa who receives a report made under subsections (1) or (2) shall immediately forward, by telephone or telegram where possible, any such report to the nearest veterinary authority, confirming such report by a written communication to the State Director.

(4) (a) Any person who fails without reasonable excuse to make any report required under this section shall be liable to a fine of fifty ringgit.

(b) Any person who fails without reasonable excuse to cause any animal or bird to be confined and isolated as required by subsection (1) or permitting the carcass of an animal to be moved contrary to subsection (2) shall be liable to a fine of one hundred ringgit.

Special Provisions Relating To Animals (other than Dogs and Cats) and Birds

Application

32. Sections 33 to 37 shall not apply to dogs and cats.

Disposal of dead animal or bird

33. (1) The owner or person in charge of any animal or bird that has died from disease or has been destroyed by order of a veterinary authority shall burn or otherwise dispose of the carcass as the veterinary authority may direct.

(2) Any person who fails without reasonable excuse to comply with any direction given by a veterinary authority under subsection (1) shall be liable to a fine of one hundred ringgit.

Moving or disposal of diseased or suspected animals

34. (1) No person shall move or dispose, whether by sale or otherwise, of any animal or bird diseased or reasonably suspected of being diseased or of being a contact or of the carcass of such animal or bird, or of the milk or dung of such animal, except under and in accordance with the written permission of a State Director.

(2) Any person who contravenes this section shall be liable for each offence to a fine of one hundred ringgit.

Removal of articles from infected premises

35. (1) A veterinary authority may by order prohibit the removal of milk, manure, fodder, litter or other articles likely to carry or convey infection from premises on which there is or recently has been, any animal or bird infected with disease.

(2) Any person who fails without reasonable excuse to comply with any order made under this section shall be liable to a fine of one hundred ringgit.

Infected area, disease control area and disease eradication area

36. (1) Whenever there is reasonable cause to believe that –

(a) any disease exists amongst any animals or birds in any State or part of a State; or

(b) any disease is likely to be introduced into any State or part of a State; or

(c) it is desired to control or eradicate any disease from any State or part of a State, the Chief Minister may issue an order declaring such State or part of a State to be an infected area, a disease control area or a disease eradication area for the specified disease as the case may be, and may by the same or subsequent order—

(i) prohibit either absolutely or conditionally the removal into or out of such area any animal, bird or carcass of any animal or bird;

(ii) prohibit either absolutely or conditionally the slaughter of any animal or bird within such area;

(iii) prohibit either totally or conditionally the sale of any carcass within such area;

(iv) prohibit the keeping of carcass or the keeping or rearing of any animal or bird within such area;

(v) impose conditions as to the cleansing and disinfection of market places, slaughter houses, abattoirs or any other places, or of baskets, crates, lorries and any other container or vehicle in which animals or birds have been kept or carried;

(vi) require the production of animals or birds for examination (including the taking of blood, milk, urine or other substance from such animals or birds), vaccination and the tattooing or otherwise marking of such animals or birds;

(vii) prohibit the keeping or rearing of any animal or bird in the whole or part of the area;

(viii) notwithstanding any other provision of this Act or regulations made under it, withdraw any licence or permit for the importation of any animal, bird or carcass issued under this Act or impose any further conditions on such licences or permits;

(ix) impose any other conditions or make any provisions that may be necessary to prevent the introduction or spread of or to control or eradicate such disease.

(2) Subject to subsection (1) when an area has been declared to be an infected area, a disease control area or a disease eradication area the State Director may issue such order not inconsistent with any order made under subsection (1) to regulate the tying – up isolation, segregation, movement or slaughter of animals or birds or to carry out other prophylactic measures or the tattooing or otherwise marking of animals or birds within the area as he may deem necessary to control and check the spread of or to eradicate the disease and in the event of any owner or person in charge of any animal or bird failing to comply with such order the State Director may take such steps as are necessary to effectively isolate or segregate such animal or bird and all expenses incurred thereby shall be recoverable from the owner or person in charge or both.

(3) Every order made under subsection (1) or (2) shall be published in the State Gazette, but shall come into operation immediately upon the making of the order.

(4) Any animal or bird found straying within an infected area, a disease control area or a disease eradication area in contravention of an order given under subsection (1) or (2) may be destroyed immediately by a veterinary authority or may be seized and detained until its forfeiture has been ordered.

(5) Any animal, bird or carcass which is slaughtered, moved or offered for sale or sold in contravention of an order given under subsection (1) or (2) may be ordered by a veterinary authority to be destroyed immediately or may be seized and detained until its forfeiture has been ordered.

(6) For the purpose of carrying out any test, vaccination or prophylactic treatment under subsection (2) a veterinary authority may order that the animals or birds be delivered to him at a specified place or time and no such animal or bird shall be removed from such place without the permission of the veterinary authority.

(7) Any person who fails without reasonable excuse to comply with any order made under subsections (1) and (2) shall be liable to a fine not exceeding one thousand ringgit.

(8) No compensation shall be payable for any animal, bird or carcass destroyed or seized under this section.

Special permits

37. The State Director may grant, subject to such conditions as he may consider advisable, permission to the owner of any animal or bird to remove it into or out of any infected area.

Special Provisions relating to Dogs and in connection with Rabies

Licensing

38. (1) No person shall own, keep, harbour or maintain any dog that is over three months old unless such dog is licensed.

(2) Dogs shall be licensed only in the manner prescribed before the 31 January each year or on reaching the age of three months or within fourteen days after arrival in Malaysia or within fourteen days of the cancellation of an Anti – rabies Vaccination Order made under section 42, whichever is the later, and such licence shall remain in force until the 31 December of the year in respect of which such licensing was effected.

(3) Dogs may be licensed at any Post Office in the State in which they are normally kept or at such other places as may be prescribed.

(4) The Minister may prescribe the fee for the licensing of a dog.

(5) On receipt of the prescribed fee the licensing authority shall supply the owner of the dog with a serially numbered metal badge.

(6) The owner of every licensed dog shall provide a collar to which the badge issued in accordance with subsection (5) shall be securely fastened in such a manner as to be clearly visible when worn, and such collar and badge shall be continually worn by such licensed dog when out – of – doors; and any dog found out – of – doors and not wearing such collar and badge may be destroyed.

(7) (a) The proper authority may authorize in writing persons to destroy dogs in accordance with subsection (6) and such persons may enter upon and into any place, not being a dwelling house, for the purpose of enforcing that subsection:

Provided that such person shall, if so required, produce and show his written authority to the owner, occupier or person for the time being in charge of such place.

(b) In this subsection the 'proper authority' means a State Director, Mayor of a City Council or City Hall, President of a District Council or Local Authority, General Manager of a Town Board or the Chief Police Officer of a State.

(8) (a) Any person who owns, keeps, harbours or maintains any dog contrary to subsection (1) shall be liable to a fine of one hundred ringgit.

(b) Any person who fails without reasonable excuse to comply subsection (6) shall be liable to a fine of fifty ringgit.

(9) The Ruler in Council or the Yang di – Pertua Negeri in Council in a State may by order declare that subsection (1) shall not apply within any specified part of such State or may exempt any person or any class of persons either from licensing any dog which is required by this section to be licensed or from the payment of all or any part of the fee payable in respect of such licensing.

(10) This section shall not apply to any dog –

(a) within any State or any part of it for so long as the Anti – rabies Vaccination Order made under section 42 is in force therein; or

(b) which is liable to be or has been registered or licensed in accordance with any other written law.

Rabies – infected areas

39. (1) The Chief Minister in a State may at any time as a precaution against rabies by order declare such State or any part of it specified in such order to be a rabies – infected area.

(2) Every order made under subsection (1) shall be published in the appropriate State Gazette but shall come into operation immediately upon the making of the order.

(3) No person shall take any dog out of a rabies – infected area or out of any State of which any part is a rabies – infected area except in accordance with a written permit issued by the State Director.

(4) The owner or person in charge of any dog within a rabies – infected area shall cause such dog to be kept under effective control, either

(a) by confining it within an enclosed area from which it is impossible for the dog to escape; or

(b) by tying it up securely; or

(c) by leading it by a chain or lead of strong cord or leather properly secured to a collar or harness worn by the dog:

Provided that the State Director, if he is satisfied that any class of dogs, whether by reason of prophylactic treatment or otherwise, is immune from infection by rabies, may exempt such class of dogs from the requirements of this subsection subject to such conditions as he may think fit.

(5) Any dog found within a rabies – infected area which is not under effective control in accordance with subsection (4) may be destroyed by any person authorized in writing in that behalf by the State Director or the Chief Police Officer of a State and any person so authorized may enter any land, building or premises for the purpose of carrying out the provisions of this subsection:

Provided that such person –

(i) shall not enter into any dwelling house for such purpose except during the hours of daylight; and

(ii) shall, if so required, produce and show his written authority to the owner, occupier or person for the time being in charge of such land, building or premises.

(6) (a) Any person who contravenes subsection (3) shall be liable to a fine of five hundred ringgit or to imprisonment for a term of three months.

(b) Any person who fails without reasonable excuse to comply with subsection (4) shall be liable to a fine of two hundred and fifty ringgit.

Destruction or detention of animal suspected to be infected rabies

40. (1) Whenever a veterinary authority reasonably suspects that any animal may be infected with rabies or has been exposed to rabies infection he may in his discretion either cause the animal to be destroyed immediately or may order the owner or person in charge of such animal to take it immediately to an animal quarantine station for detention and observation.

(2) If the owner or person in charge of any such animal fails to comply with such order the veterinary authority may immediately either cause the animal to be destroyed or take possession of the animal and remove it to an animal quarantine station.

(3) The veterinary authority may either destroy any such animal in the animal quarantine station or may detain it until he is satisfied that it is free from disease.

(4) A veterinary authority may take possession of the body of any animal that has died or has been destroyed and which is reasonably suspected to have been infected with rabies and may dispose of it in such manner as he may think fit.

(5) No compensation shall be payable to any person in respect of the destruction of any animal under this section.

(6) Any person who fails without reasonable excuse to comply with subsection (1) shall be liable to a fine of one hundred ringgit.

(7) For the purposes of this section "animal" means any four – footed beast in captivity or under control.

Detention of any dog that has bitten a person

41. (1) A veterinary authority or a police officer not below the rank of Inspector may order the owner or person in charge of any person dog that has or is reasonably believed to have bitten any person to produce the dog to him for examination, and he may detain the dog at such place and for such time as he may deem advisable. If the owner or person in charge of such dog fails to comply with such order, the veterinary authority or police officer may immediately take possession of the dog and remove it to an animal quarantine station.

(2) Any person who fails without lawful excuse to comply with any order made under this section shall be liable to a fine of one hundred ringgit.

Anti rabies vaccination of dogs

42. (1) The Chief Minister in a State, whenever it appears to him to be expedient, may make an order (in this section referred to as an 'Anti – rabies Vaccination Order') that all dogs within such State, or any part of it specified in such order, shall be submitted to anti – rabies vaccination, and may at any time cancel any such order.

(2) Every Anti – rabies Vaccination Order and the cancellation thereof shall be published in the appropriate State Gazette.

(3) Every Anti – rabies Vaccination Order shall remain in force until the 31 December of the year in which the order was made or until its cancellation, whichever period shall be the shorter, but without prejudice to the making of a further Anti – rabies Vaccination Order to take effect upon the expiry of the period.

(4) Whenever an Anti – rabies Vaccination Order has been made the State Director may specify periods of time within which, and the places at which, dogs, or groups of dogs, shall be produced for the purposes of such vaccination.

(5) All such arrangements for vaccination of dogs shall be published in the appropriate State Gazette and also in such other manner as the State Director may consider necessary.

(6) (a) The State Director may by notification in the Gazette require that every dog which has been vaccinated in accordance with an Anti – rabies Vaccination Order shall, after such date as may be specified in such notification, at all times during the continuance in force of the Order and within the area to which the Order applies, carry upon it a serially numbered metal badge or mark, tag or other evidence of vaccination, and any dog found within such area after the date specified in the notification, whether at large or not, which does not carry the proper evidence of vaccination may be destroyed.

(b) The proper authority may authorize in writing persons to destroy dogs in accordance with paragraph (a) and any person so authorized may enter any land, building or premises for the purpose of carrying out this subsection:

Provided that such person –

(i) shall not enter into any dwelling for such purpose except during the hours of daylight; and

(ii) shall, if so required, produce and show his written authority to the owner, occupier or person for the time being in charge of such land, building or premises.

(c) In this subsection the 'proper authority' means the State Director, Mayor of a City Council or City Hall, President of a Municipal Council, District Council or Local Authority, General Manager of a Town Board or the Chief Police Officer of the State.

(7) If any owner or person in charge of a dog fails to comply with any order or direction made or given under subsection (1) or (4), the veterinary authority may immediately destroy such dog.

(8) Any owner or person in charge of a dog who fails without reasonable excuse to comply with any order or direction made or given under subsection (1) or (4) shall be liable to a fine of two hundred and fifty ringgit.

(9) The Minister may prescribe the fee for the vaccination of a dog:

Provided that no person shall be liable to pay any fee for the vaccination of any dog which at the date of such vaccination has already been licensed in accordance with section 38 or has been registered or licensed in accordance with any written law in force in a Municipality.

(10) The Ruler in Council or the Yang di – Pertua Negeri in Council in a State may by order exempt any person or class of persons from the payment of all or any part of the fee payable in respect of the vaccination of any dog.

(11) Any dog which has been vaccinated in any year in accordance with an Antirabies Vaccination Order

and is carrying the proper evidence of vaccination shall be deemed to be licensed under this Act, and to be registered or licensed under or in accordance with any other written law, until 31 December of such year.

Part Ⅳ Prevention of cruelty to animals

Interpretation

43. In this Part, unless the context otherwise requires –

"animal" means any living creature other than a human being and includes any beast, bird, fish, reptile or insect, whether wild or tame.

Penalty for cruelty to animals

44. (1) Any person who

(a) cruelly beats, kicks, ill – treats, overrides, overdrives, overloads, tortures, infuriates or terrifies any animal; or

(b) causes or procures or, being the owner, permits any animal to be so used; or

(c) being in charge of any animal in confinement or in course of transport from one place to another neglects to supply such animal with sufficient food or water; or

(d) by wantonly or unreasonably doing or omitting to do any act, causes any unnecessary pain or suffering, or, being the owner, permits any unnecessary pain or suffering to any animal; or

(e) causes, procures or, being the owner, permits to be confined, conveyed, lifted or carried any animal in such manner or position as to subject it to unnecessary pain or suffering; or

(f) employs or causes or procures or being the owner, permits to be employed in any work or labour, any animal which in consequence of any disease, infirmity, wound or sore, or otherwise is unfit to be so employed; or

(g) causes, procures or assists at the fighting or baiting of any animal, or keeps, uses, manages, or acts or assists in the management of any premises or place for the purpose, or partly for the purpose, of fighting or baiting any animal, or permits any premises or place to be so kept, managed or used, or receives or causes or procures any person to receive, money for the admission of any person to such premises or place, shall be guilty of an offence of cruelty and shall be liable to a fine of two hundred ringgit or to imprisonment for a term of six months or to both.

(2) For the purposes of this section an owner shall be deemed to have permitted cruelty within the meaning of this Part if he shall have failed to exercise reasonable care and supervision in respect of the protection of the animal from cruelty:

Provided that where an owner is convicted of permitting cruelty within the meaning of this Act by reason only of his having failed to exercise such care and supervision, he shall not be liable to imprisonment without the option of a fine.

(3) Nothing in this section shall apply to the commission or omission of any act in the course of the destruction, or the preparation for destruction, of any animal as food for mankind, unless such destruction or such preparation was accompanied by the infliction of unnecessary suffering.

(4) Notwithstanding paragraph (1) (g) the Chief Minister in a State may by written permit authorize the wrestling of bulls in such State, subject to such conditions as may be specified in the permit either on a special occasion of public interest or if he is satisfied that such wrestling is beneficial to the breed and, in either case, that no cruelty to any animal will arise from such wrestling, and where such wrestling is conducted in accordance with the conditions of such permit paragraph (1) (g) shall be deemed not to apply to such wrestling.

Power of veterinary authorities and police officers

45. (1) Any veterinary authority and any police officer may arrest without warrant any person whom he sees committing any offence under section 44, and may seize any animal in respect of which and any conveyance or article with or by means of which such offence has been committed.

(2) Any person so arrested and any conveyance or article so seized shall be immediately taken to a police station.

(3) Any animal so seized shall be taken to a police station or a pound or a veterinary centre and may, subject to any order made in respect of the animal by a Magistrate, be there detained until the accused has been tried.

(4) Any such officer may stop in any street or public place and examine any animal in respect of which he has reason to believe that an offence has been or is being committed under section 44.

Power of Town Board or Municipal Officers

46. Within any town or Municipal limits the powers given by section 45 to veterinary authorities and police officers may be exercised by any officer appointed in that behalf by the Mayor of a City Council or City Hall, President of a Municipal Council, District Council or Local Authority or General Manager of a Town Council or Town Board, as the case may be.

Orders by Magistrate when an offence has been committed

47. (1) When any person has been convicted by a Magistrate of an offence under section 44, the Magistrate may order—

(a) that the animal in respect of which the offence was committed be taken to a veterinary centre and there detained and treated by a veterinary authority for any period stated in such order, or until released by further order of a Magistrate or until a veterinary authority not below the rank of Assistant Veterinary Officer has certified in writing that it may properly be released; or

(b) that the animal be treated by a veterinary authority and not used during such period as may be stated in such order or until permission to use it has been given by a Magistrate or a veterinary authority not below the rank of Assistant Veterinary Officer; or

(c) may, if satisfied that the animal is incurably diseased or injured, order that such animal be destroyed immediately by or under the direction of a police officer or veterinary authority and that the cost of burying or otherwise disposing of the carcass be borne by the person convicted.

(2) If any animal is taken to a veterinary centre or treated by a veterinary authority in accordance with an order under subsection (1) any person who has been convicted of an offence in respect of such animal shall be liable to pay the prescribed fees for its maintenance and treatment until it shall be declared fit for release or use:

Provided that if the owner of such animal shall request in writing the officer in charge of the veterinary centre to destroy such animal and shall pay to such officer any fee that may be prescribed for the destruction or burial of such animal, such officer shall immediately cause the animal to be destroyed, and no fee shall be payable in respect of the maintenance or treatment of such animal for any time subsequent to such request and payment.

(3) Any person who contravenes any order made under this section shall be liable to a fine of two hundred ringgit.

Power to order destruction of animals

48. (1) A Magistrate, Government Medical Officer, or veterinary authority not below the rank of Assistant

Veterinary Officer or police officer not below the rank of Inspector who has satisfied himself by personal inspection –

(a) that an animal is diseased or injured and that the disease or injury from which the animal is suffering is incurable or that it is cruel to keep the animal alive; or

(b) that an animal is so diseased or so severely injured or in such a physical condition that, in his opinion, having regard to the means available for removing the animal, there is no possibility of removing it without cruelty and that it is cruel to keep it alive, may by order in writing direct that such animal be destroyed, and such order may immediately be carried out by or under the direction of such officer or of any police officer:

Provided that if the animal so diseased or injured is in any house, stable, shed, or enclosure proper for such animal and not in a public thoroughfare, market or place no order shall be made until the owner of the animal (if known) or person in charge (if any) has been duly notified of the state of the animal.

(2) If any animal is destroyed in pursuance of an order made under this section the expense of the removal and burial of the carcass of the animal shall be paid by the owner or person in charge and the amount may be recovered from such owner or person in charge in a summary manner before a Magistrate.

No compensation for destruction of an animal incurably diseased or injured or destroyed at request of professed owner

49. No compensation shall in any case be payable to any person in respect of the destruction of any animal in pursuance of an order made under paragraph (47) (1) (c) or subsection 48 (1) or in compliance with a request in writing to an officer in charge of a veterinary centre as provided in subsection 47 (2) by any person professing to be the owner of such animal:

Provided that in the last case the officer in charge of the veterinary centre in good faith believed that the person making the request was in fact the owner.

Award to informer

50. (1) The Court by which any fine is imposed under this Part of this Act may award any portion not being more than half thereof to the informer.

(2) Subject to such award, every fine imposed under this Act in respect of any offence committed within the limits of any Municipality shall be paid to the Councillors, to be applied by them for the purposes of any Municipal Ordinance for the time being in force.

Animals and birds not to be kept in captivity for sale, export or exhibition without licence

50A. (1) No person shall keep in captivity for sale, export or exhibition any animal or bird in any place which is not licensed in that behalf in accordance with rules made under this Act:

Provided that this section shall not apply except in such areas as shall be prescribed by such rules.

(2) Any person who contravenes subsection (1) shall be liable to a fine of two hundred ringgit or to imprisonment for a term of six months or to both.

Part V Conservation of livestock

Movement or slaughter of cattle, etc., may be prohibited

51. (1) The Chief Minister of a State may by order—

(a) prohibit for such period as may be specified in the order the movement of any cattle and swine or any specified class of cattle and swine from such State to any other State or from part of such State to any other part of such State or to any other State except under licence;

(b) prohibit during such period or periods as may be specified in the order the slaughter in such State of any cattle, sheep, goats, swine or poultry or any specified class of them except under licence;

(c) prescribed fees and procedures for obtaining such licences.

(2) A licence issued under any order made under subsection (1) shall be subject to such conditions as may be imposed by such order or by the person authorized to issue the licence by order made under subsection (1).

(3) Any person who contravenes any order made under this section shall be liable for each offence to a fine of five hundred ringgit.

Publication of order in Gazette

52. Any order made under section 51 shall be published in the appropriate State Gazette.

Part Ⅵ Improvement of livestock

Application in States

53. This Part shall be in force in the States of Kedah and Kelantan, but save as aforesaid this Part shall not extend to any State or any part of it unless a resolution has been passed by the Council of State that it is expedient that such provisions should apply in such State or such part of it, as the case may be.

54. (Omitted)

Prohibition of possession of unsterilized bull.

55. (1) Subject to section 56 no person shall have in his possession or under his control any bull over fifteen months of age unless such bull shall have been sterilized in a manner approved by a State Director.

(2) Any person who contravenes this section shall be liable to a fine of one hundred ringgit.

State Director may exempt

56. (1) The State Director on application being made to him in writing by the owner of any bull and on the bull being produced at such place as the State Director may direct, may grant an exemption from section 55 in respect of any bull which he considers suitable for breeding purposes. Such application shall contain a full description of the animal and shall state its age, the place where it is usually kept and any other particulars that may from time to time be prescribed.

(2) The State Director shall not grant an exemption under subsection (1) in respect of any bull which appears to him –

(a) to be likely to beget defective or inferior progeny; or

(b) to be infected with any contagious or infectious disease.

(3) The powers and duties of the State Director under this section may be exercised and performed by any person duly authorized by him in that behalf.

Register of stud bulls

57. The State Director shall keep a register of bulls in respect of which exemptions have been granted under section 56 (hereinafter called "stud bulls"), and shall enter therein a description of every such animal together with the name of the owner and his place of residence and shall issue to the owner, free of charge, a copy of the entry in such register (hereinafter referred to as "a licence").

Sale, death or transfer of a stud bull to be reported

58. (1) Without prejudice to any other written law, the owner of a stud bull shall report to a penghulu or penggawa or to a veterinary authority the sale, death or transfer of a stud bull within one month of such sale, death or transfer, and shall produce the licence issued under section 57. The State Director shall record such sale, death or transfer in the register and upon the licence.

(2) It shall be the duty of a penghulu or penggawa receiving information under subsection (1) to report it as soon as possible to a veterinary authority.

(3) Any person who fails without reasonable excuse to make any report required to be made under this section or fails to produce a licence as required by this section shall be liable to a fine of fifty ringgit.

Inspection of stud bulls

59. (1) The State Director may at any time require the owner of a stud bull to produce such bull for inspection, and may, at his discretion, withdraw the exemption granted in respect of such bull under section 56.

(2) The entry in the register of stud bulls relating to such bull together with the licence shall upon the withdrawal of the exemption be cancelled.

Notice to owner of stud bull

60. (1) Where an application for exemption has been refused or a licence cancelled or where the State Director is of opinion that a bull to which this Part applies is not suitable for breeding purposes he may serve on the owner or person in charge of the bull to which such application or licence or opinion refers a notice in the prescribed form requiring such person within the time specified in such notice, not being less than fourteen days, to have such bull slaughtered or sterilized.

(2) Where a notice under subsection (1) is not complied with, the State Director may cause the bull to be slaughtered or sterilized at the expense of the owner and for that purpose any person authorized in that behalf may enter upon any premises where the bull may be or may reasonably be expected to be and any expenses incurred in connection with such slaughter or sterilization may be recovered by the State Director from the owner as a civil debt.

(3) Any person who fails without reasonable excuse to comply with any notice given under this section shall be liable to a fine of one hundred ringgit.

Licence to be produced on demand

61. (1) The owner of a stud bull shall produce or cause to be produced the licence relating to such bull at the place where the bull is kept upon being required to do so by any of the following:

(a) a veterinary authority not below the rank of Assistant Veterinary Officer;

(b) a Police Officer not below the rank of Inspector;

(c) the person in charge of a cow about to be served by such bull.

(2) Any person who fails without reasonable excuse to comply with subsection (1) shall be liable to a fine of fifty ringgit.

Sterilization free of charge

62. At the request of the owner or person in charge of a bull (not being a stud bull) the State Director or other person specially authorized to sterilize bulls by the State Director shall, if the bull is produced for the purpose at such time and place as the State Director may direct, sterilize such bull free of charge.

Protection of officers

63. No action shall be maintainable in any Court for compensation for any loss or injury that may result from anything done by a State Director or other authorized person in accordance with section 62.

Sanction to prosecute

64. No prosecution under this Part shall be brought without the previous sanction of the State Director.

Burden of proof

65. In any prosecution for an offence under this Part the burden of proof that exemption has been granted in respect of a bull under section 56 shall lie on the person prosecuted and it shall be presumed until the contrary is proved that a bull is over fifteen months of age.

Power of exempt

66. The Chief Minister of a State may by notification in the State Gazette grant exemption from any of the provisions of this Part in respect of any bull or class or classes of bull.

Part Ⅶ Search, Seizure and Arrest

Power of search for diseased animals or birds

67. For the purpose of ascertaining whether any animal or bird is suffering from disease or for the purpose of ascertaining whether any offence against this Act has been or is being committed –

(a) any veterinary authority or veterinary police officer may enter and examine any land, building or premises on or in which he suspects any animal, bird or carcass is being kept for the purpose of examining such animal, bird, carcass, land, building or premises and the owner of such land, building, premises, animal, bird or carcass shall render such veterinary authority or veterinary police officer all necessary assistance and furnish such information as may be required of him;

(b) any veterinary authority, veterinary police officer or officer of customs may stop, enter and examine any conveyance used for carrying animals, birds or carcasses and any person owning or being in charge of any such conveyance refusing to stop when required shall be liable to a fine of two hundred ringgit.

Seizure of animal, bird, carcass or article

68. (1) When any veterinary authority or police officer has reason to believe that any offence against this Act has been or is being committed or when any officer of customs has reason to believe that an offence against this Act relating to importation or exportation has been or is being committed such veterinary authority, officer of customs or police officer may seize any animal, bird, carcass, conveyance or article the subject matter of such offence and may remove such animal, bird, carcass, conveyance or article to any pound, enclosure or other place selected by a veterinary authority and there detain it.

(2) Whenever any animal, bird, carcass, conveyance or article shall have been seized and detained under subsection (1) the veterinary authority, officer of customs or police officer shall report the same to a Magistrate and the Magistrate may make such order for the further detention or release of the animal, bird, carcass, conveyance or article as he may think fit.

(2A) Notwithstanding any other provisions of this Act where a Magistrate is not immediately available and the carcass or article seized is subject to speedy and natural decay the veterinary authority, officer of customs or police officer may destroy, sell or otherwise dispose of the property as he thinks fit.

(3) The owner of such animal, bird, carcass, conveyance or article shall pay such sum as the Magistrate may consider reasonable to cover the expenses connected with its removal to a place of detention and unless such sum is paid within a specified time such animal, bird, carcass, conveyance or article shall be forfeited.

Powers of arrest

69. (1) Any veterinary authority, officer of customs or police officer may arrest without warrant any person whom he sees or finds committing or attempting to commit or whom he reasonably suspects of being engaged in committing or attempting to commit any offence against this Act, if such person refuses to furnish his name and address or furnishes an address out of the Malaysia, or there are reasonable grounds for believing that he has furnished a false name or address or that he is likely to abscond.

(2) Every person so arrested shall be taken to a police station and shall be dealt with as if has been arrested under the Criminal Procedure Code [Act 593].

Part Ⅷ Supplemental

Obstructing officers in the execution of their duties

70. Any person who without lawful excuse obstructs or impedes or assists in obstructing or impeding any veterinary authority, police officer or officer of customs in the exercise of his duty under this Act or any rule or order made under it shall be liable to a fine of five hundred ringgit or to imprisonment for a term of six months or to both.

Altering licences

71. Any person who without lawful authority alters any licence or permit issued under this Act or knowingly makes use of any licence or permit so altered shall be liable to a fine of five hundred ringgit or to imprisonment for a term of six months or to both.

General penalty

72. Any person guilty of an offence against this Act shall, where no other penalty is specified, be liable to a fine of two thousand ringgit.

Penalty on second conviction

73. Any person convicted of any offence against this Act who is within a period of twelve months from the date of such conviction convicted of a second or subsequent like offence against this Act shall where no penalty of imprisonment is provided for such offence be liable to imprisonment for two months in addition to or in lieu of any fine.

Forfeiture

74. (1) Whenever any person shall have been convicted of an offence against this Act the Court convicting such person may, in addition to or in lieu of imposing any other punishment, order that any animal, bird, carcass, conveyance or article in respect of which such offence has been committed shall be forfeited.

(2) When any animal, bird, carcass, conveyance or article has been seized under the provisions of section 68 but the person who is alleged to have committed the offence is unknown or cannot be found, the Magistrate may, if it is proved to his satisfaction that an offence has been committed in respect of such animal, bird, carcass, conveyance or article, order that such animal, bird, carcass, conveyance or article be forfeited:

Provided that no order of forfeiture shall be made in respect of a conveyance unless the owner, if his name and place or residence is known, shall have had an opportunity of appearing to show cause why such order should not be made.

(3) Any animal, bird, carcass, conveyance or article forfeited under this section or under subsection 68 (3) shall be disposed of in accordance with the directions of the Magistrate.

Presumptions

75. (1) Where the owner or person in charge of a diseased animal or bird is charged with an offence against this Act relative to such disease, he shall be presumed to have known of the existence of such disease in such animal or bird until he shows to the satisfaction of the Court before which he is charged that he had not such knowledge and could not with reasonable diligence have obtained such knowledge.

(2) Where there is any doubt regarding the ownership of any animal or bird, the person found in possession of such animal or bird or the occupier of the premises frequented by it may be presumed to be the owner until the contrary is proved.

Conduct of prosecution

76. Any prosecution in respect of an offence against this Act shall be conducted by a Deputy Public Prosecutor, a veterinary authority not below the rank of Assistant Veterinary Officer or a police officer not below the rank of Sub – Inspector.

Expenses

77. Any expense incurred by a veterinary authority or other officer in the exercise of the powers conferred on him by this Act or any order, rule, or direction made or given under it shall be charged against the owner, consignor, consignee or importer, as the case may be, of the animal, bird, carcass, article, building or conveyance concerned and may be recovered as a civil debt.

Action to be at risk and expense owner

78. (1) Any action taken under this Act or of any order, rule, or direction made or given under it in respect of any animal, bird, carcass, article, building or conveyance shall be at the risk of it's owner.

(2) No liability shall attach to any Government or to any officer thereof in respect of any expense, loss, damage or delay arising in or from the lawful exercise of the powers conferred by this Act.

Brands or other identification marks may be applied to animals

79. (1) A veterinary authority may, if he deems it necessary for purposes of identification, brand, label or otherwise mark either permanently or temporarily any animal.

(2) Any person who counterfeits, copies, alters, defaces or erases, any brand or mark applied by a veterinary authority shall be liable to a fine of two hundred ringgit.

Quarantine Stations for animals

80. (1) Animal quarantine stations shall be established and maintained by the Government and by State Governments at suitable places in the Malaysia. The position and name, if any, of any such quarantine station shall be notified in the appropriate Gazette.

(2) In addition to the animal quarantine stations notified under subsection (1) the State Director may ap-

point suitable places or premises to be temporary or emergency quarantine stations for animals.

By – laws for management of animal quarantine stations

81. (1) The Director General in the case of Federal animal quarantine stations and the State Director in the case of State animal quarantine stations, after consultation with the Director General, may make by – laws for regulating the management and maintenance of animal quarantine stations.

(2) The Minister may prescribe fees for the quarantine of animals in Federal animal quarantine stations and the Ruler in Council or the Yang di – Pertua in Council may prescribe fees for the quarantine of animals in State animal quarantine stations respectively.

(3) Any charges incurred on account of transport of an animal to or from an animal quarantine station shall be paid by the owner or person in charge of the animal.

Establishment of Veterinary centres

82. The Chief Minister of a State may appoint a suitable place or places within the State, to be a veterinary centre or centres for animals and birds or for any kind of animal or bird and may make rules for the management of the veterinary centre or centres, and may prescribe the fees to be paid for the maintenance and treatment in the veterinary centre or centres of any kind of animal or bird and the fees to be paid for the destruction or burial of the carcass of any animal or bird treated or detained in the veterinary centre or centres.

Certificates of freedom of State from disease

83. A State Director may on payment of a fee of two ringgit issue to the exporter of any animal or goods a certificate certifying that a State is free from disease.

Importation of noxious insects or pests

84. (1) No person shall knowingly import into the Malaysia or shall have in his possession any living noxious insect, or any living pest, or any living disease germ or virus or any bacterial culture, of a nature harmful or dangerous to animals or birds without the previous written permission of the Director General.

(2) Any person who contravenes this section shall be liable on conviction to a fine of one hundred ringgit.

Animal or bird in a quarantine not deemed to be entering Malaysia

85. For the purposes of this Act and any rules and regulations made under it any animal or bird brought to the Malaysia by land, sea or air, and entering a quarantine station under instructions of a veterinary authority shall not be deemed to have entered the Malaysia, but shall be subject to all appropriate provisions of this Act and any rules and regulations made under it.

Power to make rules

86. (1) The Minister may make rules for the further carrying out of the objects and provisions of this Act.

(2) Without prejudice to the generality of the powers conferred by subsection (1) the Minister may by rules make provision for –

(a) placing vessels carrying animals, birds or carcasses in quarantine;

(b) regulating the landing of animals, birds or carcasses from vessels;

(c) regulating the importation or exportation of animals or birds by land, sea or air;

(d) prescribing the examination of animals or birds on importation, the tests to be applied, and the measures to be taken;

(e) regulating the landing and movement of animals imported for slaughter;

(ea) regulating or controlling any abattoirs and slaughter – houses;

(eb) regulating and licensing of hatcheries, breeding farms, artificial insemination centres and service, poultry processing plants, meat packing and canning plants, meat storage plants and other facilities for livestock and poultry breeding and improvement;

(f) the cleansing or disinfection of buildings, sheds, places or conveyances in which diseased animals or birds have been kept or carried;

(g) the cleansing or disinfection of markets, sale yards, railway premises and railway vans or trucks wherein any animals or birds have been kept or carried;

(h) the disinfection of contacts or animals or birds which have been in an infected area;

(i) the disinfection of persons and the clothing of persons who have been in contact with or employed about diseased or suspected animals, birds or carcasses or contacts;

(j) the seizure, disinfection and, if expedient, the destruction, with or without compensation, of carcass, litter, fodder or other articles which have been in contact with any diseased animal, bird or carcass or which are reasonably suspected of being a vehicle for spreading disease;

(k) the conditions and regulations under and in accordance with which dogs may be kept and the circumstances in which they may be destroyed or otherwise disposed of, and the manner in which licensing may be effected; (ka) the licensing, control, supervision and inspection of places in which animals or birds are or may be kept in captivity for sale, export or exhibition, and such rules may –

(i) prescribe the conditions which animals or birds may be so kept;

(ii) specify the authorities by which such licences may be granted; and

(iii) prescribe the circumstances in which such licences may be revoked or suspended;

(l) the payment of fees for anything to be done under this Act and fixing the amount of such fees;

(m) the fine with which the contravention of any rule may be punished, but so that such fine shall not exceed one hundred ringgit for any one offence, or, in the case of a continuing offence, the sum of twenty ringgit for every day during which the offence continues.

Repeal

87. (1) The written laws set out in the Schedule are hereby repealed to the extent specified in the third column.

(2) (Omitted)

(3) The Slaughter of Female Animals Proclamation and the Essential (Control of Movement and Slaughter of Animals) Regulations are hereby revoked.

Schedule

(Appendix)

List of diseases declared by the minister P. U. (B)86/1999

1. African horse sickness
2. Atropic rhinitis
3. (Deleted by P. U. (B) 247/2000)
4. Bluetongue
5. Bovine spongiform encephalophathy

6. Contagious equine metritis
7. Duck virus enteritis
8. Duck virus hepatitis
9. Equine influenza
10. Equine infectious anemia
11. Equine viral arteritis
12. Japenese encephalitis
13. Maedi – visna
14. Myxomatisos
15. Paratuberculosis
16. Porcine reproductive and respiratory syndrome (PRSS)
17. Pulmonary adenomatosis
18. Psittacosis – Ornithosis
19. Strangles
20. Transmissible gastroenteritis
21. Venezuelan equine encephalomyelitis

P. U. (B)96/1999 viral encephalitis

P. U. (B)247/2000 Avian salmonellosis

缅　甸

植物有害生物检疫法

（国家法律和规则修正委员会法令 8/93 号）

1993 年 6 月 16 日

国家法律和规则修正委员会由此制定以下法律：

第一章 名称和定义

1. 本法名称为《植物有害生物检疫法》。

2. 本法下列术语的定义是：

a. **植物** 指可种植的植物和繁殖部分。其中包括种子、块茎、穗、鳞茎、根和茎等。

b. **植物产品** 指任何未加工的植物原材料或即使经过自然方法加工仍然可能造成有害生物传播风险的植物材料。也包括可食用的块茎、穗、鳞茎、果以及叶。

c. **非植物产品** 指本身不是植物产品，但存在被有害生物侵染而造成传播风险的任何材料。也包括其他与植物有害生物有关的进口物。

d. **有害生物** 指毁坏作物、食物或商品，或者那些妨碍人类或动物的昆虫、节肢动物、鼠、鼹鼠、蜗牛、杂草。也包括其他导致植物病害的有害生物和缅甸农业局规定的生物有机体。

e. **检疫性有害生物** 指对植物构成危害，但在缅甸尚未存在的有害生物和那些已经存在但尚未广泛分布需要控制的有害生物。

f. **有益生物** 指一种生物，通过直接感染有害生物，或寄生它的卵，或掠食有害生物，使得农业受益。也包括以一种或另外一种方式使农业受益的昆虫、节肢动物、真菌类、细菌、病毒、线虫和不同种类的可食用菌类，以及缅甸农业局规定的其他生物。

g. **临时隔离场** 指在出口前，用于临时贮存植物、植物产品、有害生物、有益生物或土壤的场所。

h. **进口许可证** 指由缅甸农业局签发的，允许从国外输入植物、植物产品、有害生物、有益生物或土壤的证书。

i. **植物检疫证书** 指由缅甸农业局签发的，依照 1951 年的国际植物保护公约规定格式的国际通行证书。

j. **部门** 指农业部。

k. **部长** 指农业部部长。

l. **行政领导** 指缅甸农业局局长。

第二章 立 法 目 的

3. 本法的立法目的是：

a. 防止检疫性有害生物通过任何途径进入缅甸。

b. 有效地控制检疫性有害生物的传播蔓延。

c. 检疫官员对输入的植物或植物产品进行必要的除害处理并签发植物检疫证书。

第三章 进口检疫和出口检疫

4. 植物、植物产品、有害生物、有益生物或土壤

a. 进口商在有关部门或机构办理营业执照前，须先在缅甸农业局申请办理进口许可证。

b. 进口检疫物或旅客携带检疫物在抵达时要接受缅甸农业局的检查。

c. 证书费和检查费由进口商或携带者承担。

5. 有出口植物或植物产品资质的出口商，如果需要植物检疫证书、消毒证书、除害处理证书的，可在支付规定费用之后通过缅甸农业局办理。

6. 转口贸易的植物、植物产品、有害生物、有益生物或土壤，经临时隔离场出口时：

a. 缅甸农业局有权实施检疫。

b. 如果检查时发现检疫性有害生物的，缅甸农业局有权进行消毒或除害处理，货主须承担相关费用。

c. 如需要出具植物检疫证书的，可在支付规定费用后，向缅甸农业局申请办理。

第四章　检　疫　站

7. 根据本法，为了开展工作，缅甸农业局可在以下地区设立检疫站：

a. 仰光国际机场；

b. 仰光港；

c. 缅甸邮政、电讯、外国邮件部；

d. 临时隔离场。

8. 农业部可根据需要在其他合适的地区设立检疫站。

第五章　行政领导的义务和权力

9. 行政领导的义务和权力如下：

a. 指定检测的技术和方法，对进口的植物、植物产品、有害生物、有益生物、非植物产品或土壤实施检疫。

b. 制定临时隔离场卫生管理规范，对转口贸易的植物、植物产品、有害生物、有益生物或土壤实施监管。

c. 按照目的地国家的卫生要求，对转口贸易的植物、植物产品、有害生物、有益生物或土壤实施检疫和管理。

d. 为防止境内植物疫情的发生，制订必要的检疫卫生措施。

e. 进口贸易的植物、植物产品、有害生物、有益生物或土壤植物卫生证书申请的审核。

f. 指导并组织实施消毒或除害处理工作。

g. 根据申请，决定是否允许进口。

h. 发布命令，防止被污染或被检疫性有害生物侵染的植物、植物产品、有害生物、有益生物或土壤在国内调运。

i. 制定行政处罚制度。

j. 完成部长分配的其他工作。

10. 行政领导：

a. 有权从缅甸农业局挑选检疫官和检疫员。

b. 规定检疫官和检疫员的工作职责。

c. 可以下放职权给检疫官或缅甸农业局的官员。

d. 可以赋予缅甸农业局官员执行行政处罚的权力。

第六章　禁止和处罚

11. 无进口许可证的，不得输入植物、植物产品、有害生物、有益生物或土壤。

12. 从国外进口或随身携带允许进口的植物、植物产品、有害生物、有益生物或土壤的，须接受缅甸农业局的检查和监督。

13. 按照缅甸农业局规定需实施检疫的非植物产品，进口商必须配合。

14. 经缅甸农业局确认被污染或被检疫性有害生物侵染的植物、植物产品、有害生物、有益生物或土壤，未经允许，任何人不得在境内调运。

15. 不得违反本法规定的其他有关要求。

16. 违反本法第 11 条或 12 条规定的，应受到以下处罚：

a. 首次违反的，处以 1000 至 5000 缅元罚款。

b. 再次违反的，处以 5000 至 10000 缅元罚款。

17. 违反本法第 13 条、14 条或 15 条规定的，应受到以下处罚：

a. 首次违反的，处以 500 至 3000 缅元罚款。

b. 再次违反的，处以 3000 至 5000 缅元罚款。

18. 除了第 16 条、17 条规定的行政处罚外，还可以对相关货物作销毁处理，或者在货主支付规定费用后作消毒或除害处理。

第七章　申　　述

19. 对行政领导根据本法所作的裁决和命令不满的，可在 60 天内向部长申述。

20. 部长的决定为最终裁决。

第八章　其　　他

21. 参与进口管理的其他政府部门或职能机构在进口的植物、植物产品、有害生物、有益生物、土壤或非植物产品入境时应该：

a. 及时通知缅甸农业局实施检疫。

b. 经缅甸农业局检疫合格后，才能入境和流通。

22. 依照本法实施检疫时：

a. 不得阻碍正常的贸易；

b. 及时实施检疫。

23. 依照卫生除害法规定组建，并经卫生除害注册委员会批准注册的机构，可依照本法开展消毒和卫生除害处理。

24. 除植物、植物产品、有害生物和土壤外，经农业部批准，政府部门和政府机构进口其他物品的，可免于履行本法其他的相关要求。

25. 只有事先获得缅甸农业局的进口许可，其他参与管理进口植物、植物产品、有害生物、有益生物或土壤的政府部门和机构政府才可以办理相关入境许可。

26. 缅甸农业局可以依法追回罚款。

27. 为了确保贯彻落实本法的规定：

a. 经中央政府批准，农业部可以颁布必要的实施条例和操作规程。

b. 农业部和农业局可以发布必要的命令和指导意见。

28. 1914 年颁布实施的《昆虫和有害生物法案》自本法实施之日起废止。

Sd/Than Shwe

首席主任委员

国家法律和规则修正委员会

The plant pest quarantine law

(The State Law and Order Restoration Council Law No. 8/93)
The 12th Waning Day of Nayon, 1355 ME.
(16th June, 1993)

The State Law and Order Restoration Council hereby enacts the following Law: –

Chapter Ⅰ Title and Definition

1. This Law shall be called the Plant Pest Quarantine Law.

2. The following expressions contained in this Law shall have the meanings given hereunder: –

(a) Plant means the cultivable plant and propagative parts thereof Such expression also includes seed, tuber, corn, bulb, root or stem part of the plant;

(b) Plant Product means any unprocessed material of plant origin or even though processed which by the nature and that of the processing method may create a risk for the spread of pests. Such expression also includes tuber, corn, bulb, grain, fruit or vegetable for consumption;

(c) Non – plant Product means any material which is not a product of plant and which is contaminated with pest constituting risk of spread. This expression also includes imported materials which have been prescribed for the purpose of this Law by the Ministry for inspection;

(d) Pest means insects, arachnids, rats, moles, snails, weeds that destroy crops, food or commodities or those interfering with human being or animal. Such expression also includes other pests that cause plant disease and living organisms prescribed by the Myanmar Agriculture Service;

(e) Quarantine Pest means pest dangerous to plant but not yet in existence in Myanmar and even those in existence but not widely spread yet needs to be controlled;

(f) Beneficial Organism means an organism which benefits the agriculture by causing disease to or parasitize its eggs or by predating the pest. Such expression also includes insects, arachnids, fungi, bacteria, viruses, nematodes and various kinds of edible mushrooms which in one way or another benefits agriculture and other organisms prescribed by the Myanmar Agriculture Service;

(g) Transit Camp means a camp being stationed for the purpose of temporary storage of plant, plant product, pest, beneficial organism or soil from the arriving carrier to Myanmar before being transferred to the outgoing carrier destined to any foreign country;

(h) Import Certificate means the certificate issued by the Myanmar Agriculture Service for the purpose of importing from abroad, plant, plant product, pest, beneficial organism or soil;

(i) Phytosanitary Certificate means an internationally recognized certificate issued by the Myanmar Agriculture Service after phytosanitary inspection in accordance with the model prescribed in the 1951 International Plant Protection Convention;

(j) Ministry means the Ministry of Agriculture;

(k) Minister means the Minister for the Ministry of Agriculture:

(l) Managing Director means the Managing Director of the Myanmar Agriculture Service.

Chapter Ⅱ　Objectives

3. This Law shall be implementted in accordance with the objective given hereunder: –

(a) to prevent quarantine pests from entering into Myanmar by any mean;

(b) to suppress effectively the spread of quarantine pests;

(c) to carry out, if necessary, disinfestation, disinfection treatment of plant or plant product to be exported and the issuance of phytosanitary certificate.

Chapter Ⅲ　Import and Export

4. Plant, product, pest, beneficial organism or soil: –

(a) shall be imported by a person on application for import certificate from the Myanmar Agriculture Service before obtaining licence or permit from the department or organization concerned;

(b) When on arrival by importing or when brought personally shall be subject to inspection by the Myanmar Agriculture Service;

(c) shall be subject to payment of fees as prescribed for import certificate and to payment of inspection fees by the person who imports or brings along with him.

5. A person, who has been permitted to export plant or plant product, if desirous of obtaining phytosanitary certificate or disinfestation or disinfection treatment may apply to the Myanmar Agriculture Service after payment of the prescribed fee.

6. In re – exporting plant, plant product, pest, beneficial organism or soil through transit camp to abroad: –

(a) the Myanmar Agriculture Service has the right to inspect;

(b) if quarantine pests are found while inspecting under sub – section (a), the Myanmar Agriculture Service has the right to carry out disinfestation or disinfection treatment. The person so concerned shall incur the costs;

(c) if desirous of obtaining phytosanitary certificate, application may be made to the Myanmar Agriculture Service after payment of the prescribed fee.

Chapter Ⅳ　Inspection camps

7. In order to carry out inspection works under this Law, the Myanmar Agriculture Service shall establish inspection camps at the following places: –

(a) Yangon International Airport;

(b) Yangon Port;

(c) Myanmar Posts and Telecommunications, Foreign Mail Service;

(d) Transit Camp.

8. The Ministry may extend the establishment of pest inspection camps.

Chapter Ⅴ　The duties and powers of the managing director

9. The duties and powers of the Managing Director are as follows: –

(a) prescribing methods of inspection in respect of plant, plant product, pest, beneficial organism, non – plant product or soil imported from abroad as to whether they are infested or infected with quarantine pest;

(b) prescribing conditions relating to the temporary custody in the transit camp, transferring from one vehicle to another of plant, plant product, beneficial organism or soil for reexport;

(c) prescribing necessary measures for inspection in accordance with the requirements of the receiving country in respect of plant, plant product, pest, beneficial organism or soil for reexport;

(d) prescribing necessary measures for the effective suppression of quarantine pest in case of outbreak of such pest in the country.

(e) permitting or refusing after scrutinizing the applications for import certificate made in respect of plant, plant product, pest, beneficial organism or soil;

(f) making arrangements for carrying out disinfestation or disinfection treatment;

(g) permitting or refusing after scrutinizing the applications for phytosanitary certificate:

(h) issuing order preventing the transportation from one place to another within the country of plant, plant product, beneficial organism or soil that is infested or infected with quarantine pest;

(i) imposing administrative penalty;

(j) carrying out duties as are assigned by the Minister.

10. The Managing Director: -

(a) shall assign the duty of Inspector General and Inspectors to the suitable personnel from the Myanmar Agriculture Service;

(b) shall prescribe the duties and powers of the inspector General and the Inspectors;

(c) may assign his powers to the Inspector General or any officer of the Myanmar Agriculture Service;

(d) may assign on suitable officers of the Myanmar Agriculture Service the power to impose administrative penalty.

Chapter Ⅵ Prohibition and Penalty

11. No person shall, without obtaining the import certificate, import plant, plant product, pest, beneficial organism or soil.

12. No person, who imports plant, plant product, pest, beneficial organism or soil with import certificate or who brings along with him from abroad, shall fail to submit to inspection and control of the Myanmar Agriculture Service.

13. An importer of non - plant product which has been prescribed by the Myanmar Agriculture Service for inspection shall not fail to submit to inspection.

14. No person shall, knowingly transport from one place to another within the country, plant, plant product, beneficial organism or soil which has been declared to be infested or infected with quarantine pest by the Myanmar Agriculture Service.

15. No person shall violate any provision of the rules, procedures, made under this Law.

16. A person shall violates any of the provisions contained in section 11 or section 12 shall be liable to the following administrative penalty: -

(a) in the case of a first offence imposition of a fine which may extend from a minimum of Kyats 1,000 to a maximum of kyats 5,000;

(b) in the case of a subsequent offence, imposition of a fine which may extend from a minimum of Kyats 5.000 to a maximum of Kyats 10,000.

17. A person who violates the provisions contained in section 13, section 14 or section 15 shall be liable to the following administrative penalty: -

(a) in the case of a first offence, imposition of a fine which may extend from a minimum of Kyats 500 to a maximum of Kyats 3,000;

(b) in the case of a subsequent offence. imposition of a fine may extend from a minimum of Kyats 3,000 to a maximum of Kyats 5,000.

18. In respect of the administrative penalty imposed under section 16 or section 17 may require the exhibits involved in the offence to be destroyed or after payment of the prescribed fee may require them to be disinfested or disinfected.

Chapter Ⅶ Appeal

19. A person dissatisfied with the order or decision made by the Managing Director under this Law may appeal to the Minister within 60 days from the date such order or decision was made.

20. The decision of the Minister shall be final.

Chapter Ⅷ Miscellaneous

21. The respective government department or government organization shall, in respect of plant, plant product, pest, beneficial organism, soil or non-plant product on arrival from abroad: -

(a) promptly inform the Myanmar Agriculture Service for inspection;

(b) permit an importer to take delivery only when it has been found to be free from pests on inspection by the Myanmar Agriculture Service.

22. The inspection work under this Law shall be done: -

(a) without affecting the smooth and steady flow of trade

(b) without delay in inspection.

23. Any organization recognized by the Pesticide Registration Board formed under the Pesticide Law may carry out the disinfestation or disinfection treatment under this Law.

24. The Ministry may exempt any government department or government organization from complying with any of the provisions of this Law apart from the inspection of plant, plant product, pest or soil.

25. The government department or the government organization that is authorized to issue import licence or permit in respect of plant, plant product, pest, beneficial organism or soil imported from abroad may issue the licence or permit only on submission of the import certificate granted by the Myanmar Agriculture Service.

26. The Myanmar Agriculture Service may recover the fine payable under this Law as if it were arrears of land revenue.

27. For the purpose of carrying out the provisions of this Law: -

(a) the Ministry may, issue rules and procedures as may be necessary, with the approval of government:

(b) the Ministry and the Myanmar Agriculture Service may issue orders and directives as may be necessary.

28. The Insects and Pests Act, 1914 is hereby repealed.

Sd./Than Shwe
General
Chairman
The State Law and Order Restoration Council

动物健康和发展法

（国家法律法规修正委员会法令文件号 17/93）

[Tazaungmon 月 12 蜡日，缅甸历 1355 年（1993 年 11 月 25 日）]

国家法令法规修正委员会颁布下列法规：

第一章　标题和定义

1. 本法名称为《动物健康和发展法》。

2. 本法下列用语的含义是：

（a）动物　指人工养殖的家畜和为满足特定需求捕获的野生动物，也包括上述动物的精子、卵子和胚胎。

（b）动物产品　为奶制品、蛋类和其他构成动物机体的组织成分。

（c）动物饲料　通过商业途径出售，并用于动物饲养的，经过科学配制或依照常规标准混合，或是未经配制或混合的饲料。

（d）传染性疾病　指所有政府公布为具有传染性的动物疾病。

（e）推荐证书　指依据本法第 8 条（b）款规定签发的证书。

（f）部门　指畜牧水产部。

（g）部长　指畜牧水部部长。

（h）局　指畜牧兽医局。

（i）局长　指畜牧业兽医局负责人。

第二章　目　　的

3. 本法立法目的：

（a）促进动物健康事业发展。

（b）促进畜牧业发展。

（c）防止动物传染性疾病的爆发，确保一旦疾病爆发，能够采取系统的控制措施。

（d）检查进口的动物，动物产品和动物饲料。

（e）签发出口动物、动物产品和动物饲料的检疫证书。

（f）保障动物福利。

第三章　动物健康和发展

4. 畜牧兽医局应该为动物健康和发展采取下列措施：

（a）向动物饲养的从业人员传授技术知识。

（b）为缅甸引进优良品种的动物。

（c）监管进口种用动物。

（d）为预防传染病进行疫苗研发和生产。

（e）开发本土自然植物和农作物用于动物饲料的生产。

（f）检查进口动物产品和动物饲料的是否达到标准的质量以及是否存在有害病原体或毒素。

第四章　国内销售的动物饲料的检查

5. 局长应该：

（a）依照规程检查国内销售的动物饲料。

（b）一旦发现销售的动物饲料对动物有害，可以下令禁止该产品的销售。

（c）建立动物饲料销售商清单。

6. 动物饲料销售商应该：

（a）服从畜牧水产部的监督检查。

（b）遵守畜牧水产部依据本法颁布的禁令。

第五章　出口动物、动物产品和动物饲料的检查

7. 出口动物、动物产品或动物饲料的人，可以按照规定格式向相关部门提交申请，以便获取推荐证书。

8. 受理推荐证书申请后局长应：

（a）依照规定程序检查该动物是否携带传染性疾病；该动物产品或动物饲料是否符合质量标准，或是否携带有害病原体或毒素。

（b）如果符合上述条件，则发放推荐证书。

9. （a）申请人应支付规定的费用。

（b）检验费、证书费和其他相关费用的数额由局长确定。

第六章　进口动物、动物产品和动物饲料的检查

10. 进口动物、动物产品和动物饲料的进口商，应向畜牧兽医局提出检查申请。

11. 经过政府部门的批准后，相关部门应在所需地区建立检查站，以进行进口的动物、动物产品和动物饲料的检查。

12. 在进口动物、动物产品或动物饲料的时候，局长应该：

（a）依照规定流程检查动物是否携带传染性疾病，或动物产品、动物饲料是否符合质量标准，是否携带有害病原体或毒素。

（b）可以禁止特定动物的进口；或可以临时扣留特定动物，经过传染病检查后，再决定是否可以进口或进行销毁处理。

（c）可以禁止特定动物产品或动物饲料的进口；或可以将其临时扣留，在完成有害病原体或毒素的检验后，再决定是否可以进口或进行销毁处理。

（d）如果依照条款（a）进行检查后，证明该动物不携带传染性疾病，或该动物产品或动物饲料符合质量标准或不携带有害病原体或毒素，应签发推荐证书。

13. （a）动物、动物产品或动物饲料的进口商应该支付规定的费用。

（b）检查费用，证书费和其他费用可由局长确定。

第七章　传染性疾病的预防和控制

14. 水产畜牧部应定期公布动物传染病疫情。

15. 畜牧兽医局：

（a）应采取必要的预防措施，控制动物传染病的发生。

（b）及时根除疫区内的动物传染病，并防止向外传播。

（c）应依法定程序公布非疫区名单。

（d）可以采取必要的措施，以防止或控制传染病。

16. 畜主或者动物共有人，一旦发现动物传染病迹象，或发现疑似动物传染病迹象的，应尽快向相关部门报告，或向政府部门指定的人员报告。

17. 如果兽医发现动物患传染病的，应迅速向距离最近的畜牧兽医局主管人员报告。

第八章　动物福利的保护

18. 畜牧兽医局局长应该：

（a）采取行政措施防止虐待动物。

（b）可以规定特定种类动物允许拉载或承载货物的最大重量。

（c）指导公众正确运输、捆绑以及饲养动物的方法。

（d）对在政府部门设立的机构收容的受虐待的动物进行护理。

（e）收容中心治疗、饲养和照顾动物的相关费用由畜主或者动物共有人承担。

第九章　上　　诉

19. 对畜牧兽医局官员的决定或命令不服的，可以在接到决定或命令的 60 天内向局长上诉。

20. 对畜牧兽医局局长的决定或命令不服的，可以在收到决定或命令的 30 天内向畜牧水产部上诉。

21. 部长的决定将作为最后决定。

第十章　处　　罚

22. 如果动物饲料经销商有以下违法行为的，将被判有罪，处以不超过 5000 缅元罚款，单处或并处不超过 6 个月的监禁：

（a）拒不服从畜牧兽医局对经营动物饲料进行检查的。

（b）经销畜牧兽医局禁止交易的动物饲料。

23. 如果进口动物、动物产品或动物饲料经销商有以下违法行为的，将被判有罪，处以不超过 5000 缅元罚款，单处或并处不超过 6 个月的监禁：

（a）拒不服从畜牧兽医局对进口的动物、动物产品或动物饲料进行检查的。

（b）在没有获得畜牧兽医局颁布的许可证的情况下，向国内输入、分发或销售进口的动物、动物产品或动物饲料。

24. 如果畜主或者动物共有人有以下违法行为的，将被判有罪，处以不超过 5 000（缅甸）元罚款，单处或并处不超过 6 个月的监禁：

（a）违反畜牧兽医局颁布的关于控制传染病的指导或命令。

（b）对传染病疫情隐瞒不报的。

（c）对发现疑似传染病死亡动物隐瞒不报的。

25. 任何人有以下违法行为的，处以不超过 1000 缅元的罚款：

（a）粗暴对待动物或让动物搬运或拉载超过规定重量货物的。

（b）任意虐待动物的。

（c）不必要的致残。

（d）对圈养的动物不供应水和食物的。

（e）不及时治疗和照顾受伤或生病的动物。

（f）遗弃患有感染性疾病或受伤的动物。

26. 法院应依照第 22 条或第 23 条的规定对相关违法行为的进行处罚，另外可以发布命令，没收或销毁有关违法物品。

第十一章　其他规定

27. 畜牧水产部可以授权机构对进出口动物产品或者动物饲料进行检查并签发推荐性的证书，基于本法规定，被授权机构可以是适当的任何政府部门或组织机构。

28. 畜牧水产部可以免除政府部门或者任何机构的检验费、推荐证书费和本法规定的其他费用。

29. 任何获畜牧水产部签发动物、动物产品或者动物饲料进口执照或者许可证的政府部门，（签发前）应当当获得优先签发此类证书的（农牧渔业部）司局的建议。

30. 畜牧兽医局局长可以委托本局任何官员代其行使本法授予的权力。

31. 依本法对动物、动物产品或者动物饲料的检查工作，应当：-

a. 不影响贸易的流通和稳定；

b. 不因检查而造成延误。

32. 当畜牧兽医人员依本法对违犯行为采取行动时，公共安全部队应当提供必要的协助。

33. 为了执行本法所规定的内容；

（a）畜牧水产部可在获经政府批准后签发必要的规定和流程。

（b）畜牧水产部或畜牧兽医局可颁布必要的命令和指导。

34. 废除下列法案：

（a）1898 年《牲畜进口法》

（b）1899 年《鼻疽病法》

（c）1910 年《媾疫法》

（d）1930 年《防止虐待动物法》

（e）1939 年《动物寄生虫病法》

（Sd）Than Shwe

大将主席

国家法律法规修改委员会

Animal Health and Development Law

(The State Law and Order Restoration Council Law No. 17/93)
The 12th Waxing Day of Tazaungmon, 1355 ME
(25 th November, 1993)

The State Law and Order Restoration Council hereby enacts the following Law: —

Chapter Ⅰ Title and Definition

1. This Law shall be called the Animal Health and development Law.

2. The following expressions contained in this Law shall have the meanings given hereunder: -

(a) Animal means domestic animal bred by man or captured for a certain purpose. This expression also includes the semen, ovum or embryo of the animal;

(b) Animal Product means milk, egg or any part of an animal;

(c) Animal Feed means feed sold on a commercial scale for the purpose of feeding animals and which is scientifically prepared or conventionally mixed or without preparation or mixing;

(d) Infectious Disease means any animal disease notified as a contagious disease by the Ministry;

(e) Recommendation Certificate means a certificate issued under section 8 sub - section (b) of this Law;

(f) Ministry means the Ministry of Livestock Breeding and Fisheries;

(g) Minister means the Minister for Livestock Breeding and Fisheries;

(h) Department means the Livestock Breeding and Veterinary Department;

(i) Director General means the Director General of Livestock Breeding and Veterinary Department.

Chapter Ⅱ Objectives

3. The objectives of this Law are as follows: -

(a) to carry out animal health and development work;

(b) to promote livestock development;

(c) to prevent outbreak of contagious disease in animals and to control the outbreak systematically when it occurs;

(d) to inspect imported animal , animal product and animal feed;

(e) to issue recommendation certificate concerning animal, animal product and animal feed for export;

(f) to protect animals by law from being ill - treated.

Chapter Ⅲ Animal health and development

4. The Department shall for the purpose of animal health and development carry out the following functions: -

(a) disseminating technical know how to those desiring to raise animal under modern technology;

(b) carrying out works for obtaining improved breed animals suitable for Myanmar;

(c) supervising importation of improved breed animals;

(d) carrying out research on vaccines that protect animals from contagious diseases and producing the vaccines;

(e) carrying out research on utilizing natural vegetation, crops in the country for animal feed;

(f) inspecting of imported animal product and animal feed for standard quality, the presence of harmful pathogens or toxins.

Chapter Ⅳ Inspection of animal feed for domestic sale

5. The Director General may: -

(a) inspect animal feed for domestic sale in the prescribed manner;

(b) prohibit further sale of animal feed if it is found that the animal feed for sale is harmful to animals;

(c) make a list of animal feed sellers.

6. A person who sells animal feed shall, in respect of the animal feed he sells: -

(a) submit for inspection by the Department;

(b) abide by the prohibition made by the Department in accordance with the Law.

Chapter Ⅴ Inspection of Animal, Animal Product and Animal Feed for Exportation

7. A person exporting animal, animal product or animal feed may, on desiring a recommendation certificate, apply to the Department in the prescribed manner.

8. The Director General shall, in respect of the application for recommendation certificate: -

(a) inspect in the prescribed manners, an animal if it is free from contagious disease, animal product or animal feed if it is of standard quality and free from harmful pathogens or toxins;

(b) issue recommendation certificate if it is found to be in conformity with the prescribed stipulations.

9. (a) The applicant for the recommendation certificate shall pay the prescribed fees;

(b) Examination fee, recommendation certificate fee and other expenses shall be as determined by the Director General.

Chapter Ⅵ Inspection of Imported Animal, Animal Product and Animal Feed

10. A person importing animal, animal product or animal feed shall submit to inspection by the Department.

11. The Department shall, with the approval of the Ministry, establish Inspection Stations in required regions for inspection of imported animal, animal product or animal feed.

12. The Director General, in respect of the imported animal, animal product or animal feed: -

(a) shall inspect in the prescribed manner an animal if it is free from the contagious disease, animal product or animal feed if it is of standard quality and free from harmful pathogens or toxins;

(b) may prohibit the animal from being transported into the country, may temporarily detain the animal, may allow retransportation or destruction if found to be infected with contagious disease;

(c) may prohibit the animal product or animal feed being transported into the country, may temporarily detain it, may allow retransportation or destruction, if, on inspection, it is found that it is not of the standard quality and if it contains harmful pathogens or toxins;

(d) shall issue recommendation certificate if, on inspection in accordance with clause (a), the animal is found to be free from contagious disease, the animal product or animal feed is found to be of standard quality and free from harmful pathogens or toxins.

13. (a) A person importing animal, animal product or animal feed shall pay the prescribed fees;

(b) Examination fee, recommendation certificate fee and other expenses shall be as determined by the Director General.

Chapter Ⅶ Prevention and Control of Contagious disease

14. The Ministry shall notify the contagious diseases of animals from time to time.

15. The Department: -

(a) shall lay down necessary preventive measures to the effect that no contagious disease occur in animals;

(b) shall make arrangement to eradicate the disease in the contagious disease affected areas and to prevent spreading of disease to other regions;

(c) shall notify the Disease Free Zone in accordance with the prescribed manners;

(d) may issue necessary order or directive for prevention or control of contagious disease.

16. The owner of an animal or a person who has in his possession an animal shall report promptly to the employee in charge of the Department of either a village tract or a township or a person designated for this purpose by the Ministry, if he knows the occurrence of contagious disease in the animal or finds symptoms of contagious disease in the dead animal.

17. A veterinarian shall report promptly to the nearest employee of the Department if he finds that the animal he treats is suffering from contagious disease.

Chapter Ⅷ Prevention of cruelty to Animal

18. The Director General: -

(a) shall carry out educative measures to prevent man from wilfully ill - treating the animal;

(b) may prescribe the maximum weight of load to be carried by or load to be drawn by a certain species of animal;

(c) shall carry out educative measures regarding the methods to be observed by the public in respect of transporting, binding or keeping of animals;

(d) shall take measures for treatment of ill - treated animals at the Veterinary Centre established by the Department;

(e) shall prescribe the expenses payable by the owner of an animal or a person who has an animal in his possession for treatment, feeding and taking care of the animals at the Veterinary Centre.

Chapter Ⅸ Appeals

19. A person dissatisfied with the decision or order made under this Law by any officer of the Department may appeal to the Director General within 60 days of the receipt of such decision or order.

20. A person dissatisfied with the decision or order made by the Director General may appeal to the Minister within 30 days of the receipt of such decision or order.

21. The decision of the Minister shall be final.

Chapter Ⅹ Offences and Penalties

22. If a person who sells animal feed commits any of the following act, he shall on conviction be punishable with fine which may extend to kyats 5,000 or with imprisonment for a term which may extend to 6 months or with both: -

(a) refusing to submit for inspection by the Department of the animal feed for sale;

(b) selling animal feed prohibited by the Department from furture sale.

23. If a person who imports animal, animal product or animal feed commits any of the following acts, he shall on conviction be punishable with fine which may extend to kyats 5,000 or with imprisonment for a term which may extend to 6 months or with both: -

(a) refusing to submit for inspection by the department of imported animal, animal product or animal feed;

(b) transporting into the country, distributing, selling of imported animal, animal product or animal feed without obtaining a recommendation certificate issued by the Department.

24. If the owner of an animal, or a person who has an animal in his possession fails to comply with any of the following acts, in respect of the animal, he shall, on conviction, be punishable with fine which may extend to kyats 5,000 or with imprisonment for a term up to 6 months or with both: -

(a) failing to comply with the order or directive issued by the Department regarding control of contagious disease;

(b) failing to report to the concerned knowingly of the outbreak of contagious disease;

(c) failing to report to the concerned knowingly of the contagious disease symptom in the dead animal.

25. Whoever commits any of the following acts in respect of the animal shall on conviction be punishable with fine which may extend to kyats 1,000: -

(a) causing to work cruelly or causing to carry or draw more than the prescribed weight;

(b) wilfully ill - treating;

(c) unnecessarily maiming;

(d) wilfully keeping it without food and water;

(e) neglecting to give proper treatment and care though being sick or wounded;

(f) letting to stray in public place though being suffering from contagious disease or wounded.

26. The Court shall on conviction under section 22 or section 23, impose punishment as prescribed for the relevant offence and in addition pass orders for confiscation or destruction of exhibits in respect of which the offence has been committed.

Chapter XI Miscellaneous

27. The Ministry may delegate the authority to inspect animal product or animal feed for exportation or importation and to issue recommendation certificate, which is to be performed under this Law, to any appropriate Government department or organization.

28. The Ministry may exempt Government department or any organization from payment of inspection fee, recommendation certificate fee and other expenses payable under this Law.

29. A Government department which has the authority to issue import licence or permit for importation of animal, animal product or animal feed shall obtain the opinion of the Department prior to the issuance of such licence or permit.

30. The Director General may delegate the powers conferred on him under this Law to any officer of the Department.

31. Inspection work on animal, animal product or animal feed under this Law shall be done: -

(a) without affecting the smooth and steady flow of trade;

(b) without delay in inspection.

32. The People's Police Force shall render necessary assistance when the personnel of the Department are

taking action against offences under this Law.

33. For the purpose of carrying out the provisions of this Law: -

(a) the Ministry may, with the approval of the Government, issue such rules and procedures as may be necessary;

(b) the Ministry or Department may issue such orders and directives as may be necessary.

34. The following Acts are hereby repealed: -

(a) The Live - stock Importation Act, 1898;

(b) The Glanders and Farcy Act, 1899;

(c) The Dourine Act, 1910;

(d) The Prevention of Cruelty to Animals Act, 1930;

(e) The Animal Pests Act, 1939.

(Sd) **Than Shwe**

Senior General

Chairman

The State Law and Order Restoration Council

泰　国

图 表

植物检疫法

（B. E. 2507）

经国民大会宪法修订会议审议通过，由国王颁布如下法令：

第 1 条 本法为“植物检疫法，B. E. 2507”。

第 2 条 本法在政府公报上公布 90 天期满后开始生效。

第 3 条 植物病害及植物有害生物防治法 B. E. 2495 将废止。

第 4 条 本法中“植物”是指所有植物种类，包括陆生的、水生的和其他植物种类，包括植物的任何一部分，例如茎、芽、树干、蘖、分蘖、枝条、叶、根、根茎、鳞茎、花、果实、种子、及菌类营养体和孢子，无论是否存活；包括捕食性生物、寄生物、蚕、蚕卵、蚕茧、蜜蜂、蜂巢和微生物；

受控植物 指由部长在政府公报上公布的受控植物；

特定性受控植物 指由部长在政府公报上公布的植物。要求在出口前，按照进口国要求，采取保护措施并检查微生物或对人类健康有害的项目。

植物种质 指具有各种遗传基因的一组细胞，其构成活的可繁殖的植物片断，这些植物片断可以是种子、组织或植物的其他任何部分，也包括用于繁殖目的可遗传其控制特征的遗传物质；

土壤 指具有有机物质或者具有适合植物有害生物栖息的土壤；

植物有害生物 是指危害植物的生物，如：植物病原体、昆虫、动物、或对植物有害的植物；

载体 指栽培材料、土壤、沙、包装植物的容器或其他材料、有机肥或其他植物有害生物媒介物；

禁止物 指部长在政府公报上宣布的被禁止的植物、植物有害生物及其载体；

限制物 指部长在政府公报上宣布的被限制的植物、植物有害生物及其载体；

未禁物 指未被禁止或限制的其他植物；

货主 包括货主代理商、货物所有者及承运者；

有害生物风险分析 从生物的或系统及经济方面的评估过程，以确定一种有害生物是否应被管制及采取何种植物检疫措施的依据。

进口 指通过一切方式引进泰国；

过境 指经过泰王国转运或不转运；

出口 指通过一切方式输出泰王国；

植物检疫站 指部长在政府公报上宣布的作为检查进口或过境的植物、禁止物和限制物及植物种质的场所；

入境后隔离场 指部长在政府公报宣布的用于对扣留的植物、禁止物和限制材料以及植物种质进行观察研究的场所；

植物有害生物控制区 指局长在政府公报上宣布的作为防止或根除植物有害生物的地区；

植物检疫证书 指由出口国主管部门签发的官方文件，旨在确认植物、植物种质或载体未携带有害生物，并符合进口国的要求；

转口植物检疫证书 指由出口国主管部门签发的官方文件，旨在确认输入并从泰王国输出到其他国家的植物、植物种质或载体，未携带转口国家的有害生物，并符合进口国的要求；

健康证书 指由出口国主管部门签发的官方文件，旨在确认特定性受控植物未携带微生物或其他对人类健康有害的物质，并符合进口国的要求；

委员会　指植物检疫委员会；

局长　指农业局局长；

植物检疫官　指执行本法的局长及部长任命的执法人员；

部长　指负责执行本法的部长。

第5条　植物检疫官员应佩带内阁条例中所规定形式的证件，且在执法过程中，应要求，须向相关人出示证件。

第5.1条　将成立植物检疫委员会，该委员会由渔业局局长、牲畜发展局局长、皇家林业局局长、农业局局长、海关关长、农业推广局局长、麻醉品管委会秘书长、泰国港务局局长、泰国航空公司常务董事、泰国电信局董事长、国家遗传工程和生物工艺中心主任、商业部和内务部代表（每部选派一名代表和部长指派不超过4名专家）组成，由农业合作部常任秘书担任主席，农业局法规处处长为委员会秘书。

在委员会的领导下，农业局将负责委员会技术的、管理的以及程序上的事务。

第5.2条　专家委员会任职期限为两年，可以再重新委任。

如果专家委员会在任职期满之前以任何理由辞职，或者如果部长在专家委员会任职期间任命其他专家委员会，继任的专家委员会将续任前任专家委员会的任职，直到任职期满。

第5.3条　根据第5.3条规定，部长任命的专家委员会任职期满前，只有在以下情况下才能离职：

（1）死亡；

（2）辞职；

（3）被部长调离的；

（4）不称职及类似之人；

（5）终审被判监禁在服刑期，疏忽或轻微犯罪除外。

第5.4条　委员会召开的会议中，需要超过半数的成员出席才能达到法定人数。如果大会主席不能出席或者不能履行职责，出席会议的委员会成员将从他们自己当中选举一位，作为主席来主持会议。

会议的每个决议将由大多数选票通过。委员会的每一位成员只能投一票。如果票数相等，主持会议的主席可再投一票，作最终决定。

第5.5条　委员会将有以下权力：

（1）向部长提供建议以决定禁止或限制的植物、植物有害生物或禁止或限制的载体、植物种质的名录，以及受控植物种质、受控植物的名录；

（2）向部长提供建议以决定植物检疫站和入境后检疫站；

（3）向局长提供建议以决定依据第8（2）条规定的进口或引进禁止携带物的企业注册登记类型，以及通过依据第8（2）条的商业渠道或其他企业进口或引进禁止携带物的标准、程序和条件。

（4）向局长提供建议以决定通过依据第10条的商业渠道或其他企业进口或引进禁止携带物的标准、程序和条件，并决定依据第15条的植物有害生物的检查和处理费用，植物检疫证书或转口植物检疫证书的要求及签发。

（5）向局长提供建议以决定出境特定性受控植物的检查费用，包括依据第15.6条的卫生证书的要求和签发的标准、程序和条件。

（6）向部长提供建议以颁布依据本法的部长条例。

（7）若不利于履行植物检疫，可向部长或局长建议对本法，部长条例，规章，依据本法或其他法律与植物检疫相关的告示或指引制订修正案。

（8）执行本法或其他法律赋予委员会的其他职能。

第5.6条　委员会将有权任命一个或多个下附委员会来执行由委员会负责的任何职责。

法令的相应规定将适用于下附委员会召开的会议。

第6条　为防止植物有害生物传入泰国后传播或暴发，或有利于保护环境或人类健康，根据植物检疫委员会的建议，依本法规定，视情况而定，部长有权在政府公报上宣布被禁止进境植物、植物有害生物、载体以及被限制物的名单。被禁止进境植物、植物有害生物或者载体的来源地，其免除情况或条件亦应在上述政府公报中予以限定。

为保证防止各种植物有害生物传入王国，部长可要求途经发生特殊植物有害生物国家的人按局长指定的形式向植物检疫官员报告。

当不再必要时，将在政府公报上宣布废除第一段中提及的被禁止和被限制物。

第6.1条　为了控制和防止植物有害生物的传入，部长根据委员会的建议将有权在政府公报上宣布将被控植物种质名称。

非经局长许可，且附有植物检疫证书，任何人不得进出口由部长在第一段中宣布的植物种质。

要求许可和第二段规定的许可应在局长指定的标准、程序和条件下执行。

第6.2条　在白天或工作时间，植物检疫官将有权进入第6.1条第一段中由部长宣布的植物种质的种植区、集散地或存放地对植物种质的使用进行检查和研究。执行此公务时，植物检疫官有权向种植区或上述场所的业主及所有者了解情况，要求许可或相关证明。

第7条　根据委员会的建议，部长将有权在政府公报上宣布任何港口、机场或者某一特定限制的地方为植物检疫站或入境后隔离场，视具体情况而定。

第8条　任何人进口或中转禁止物，需经局长批准并符合以下规定：

（1）进口或转运禁止物作科研用途，应附有植物检疫证书，或如果进口或中转禁止进境植物有害生物或非植物的载体，要求随货附上输出国授权机构出具的证书。

（2）进口或转运作为商业或由局长在委员会建议下公告的其他用途，应随附植物检疫证书，经过有害生物风险分析并遵守局长在委员会建议下规定并在政府公报上公布的的标准、程序和条件。

第9条　任何人不得进口或中转任何限制物，除非上述的限制物附有植物检疫证书。

第10条　进口或过境禁止物或限制物经植物检疫站的植物检疫官检查，并遵守局长在委员会建议下规定并在政府公报上公布的的标准、程序和条件。

第11条　任何人进口或中转非禁止物应附上植物检疫证书并用局长规定的格式向植物检疫官员申报。

第12条　执行本法时，植物检疫官员有以下权力：

（1）当有合理理由怀疑违反本法进口或过境植物、禁止物、限制物或非禁止物时，有权调查植物检疫站或植物有害生物控制区管辖的任何仓库、交通工具、包装和任何人员。

（2）假如有合理理由怀疑违反本法进口或过境植物、禁止物、限制物或非禁止物，带有会引起严重危害的植物有害生物，且假如搜查令需要较长时间签发，上述非法物或或任何 会被迁移、隐藏、破坏或改变原貌，且假如该调查不能及时执行，可允许持续在白天或在上述房屋的营业时间，调查在植物检疫站或植物有害生物控制区范围外的任何房屋、人员或交通工具，直到调查结束。

（3）收集或抽取足够数量的植物、禁止物、限制物或非禁止物或其他相关物的样本进行检查或分析，假如有足够理由怀疑上述物为植物有害生物或带有引起严重危害的植物有害生物。

（4）必要时，没收或扣留植物或禁止物、限制物或非禁止物或其他相关物，假如有足够理由怀疑上述物为植物有害生物或带有引起严重危害的植物有害生物。

第13条　为防止植物有害生物传入王国，植物检疫官有权对进口或过境的植物、禁止物、限制物、非禁止物或植物种质作如下处理：

（1）诊断植物有害生物，进行熏蒸或喷雾方式的化学处理，或其他处理手段，费用由货主负担；

（2）必要时，没收或扣留上述物到入境植物检疫站或其他地方。

（3）责令进口商将感染或会传染植物有害生物的植物、禁止物、限制物、非禁止物或植物种质运出泰王国；

（4）有合理理由怀疑上述植物有害生物会引发严重的危害且依据第（1）条规定无可供选择的补救

措施，必要时进行销毁处理。

第13.1条 假如货主未提出要求，或公诉人撤诉，或最后判决为非没收物品，且货主未在没收或截留、或公诉人撤诉或最终判决为非没收物品之日起90天内提出要求，所有依据第12（3）、（4）条及第13（2）条规定收集、没收或扣留的物品，为农业部门所有。

如果依据上述第一段中规定收集、没收或扣留的物品为易腐坏物，或容易在存储时受损或保存费超出其价值，局长有权下令销毁或用其他方式处理。

第14条 没有下述植物检疫官的书面批准，任何人不得从植物检疫站、入境后隔离场、过境的运输工具或植物检疫官下令查扣的货物处调离植物、禁止物或限制物及植物种质。

第15条 任何人要申请一份植物检疫证书或转口植物检疫证书，应支付检查及处理费用，该费用由局长在委员会建议下规定并在政府公报上公布。

植物检疫官员有权依据第1条规定签发植物检疫证书和转口植物检疫证书，并收取签发证书的费用，费用由部长条例规定。

申请和签发植物检疫证书或转口植物检疫证书，应符合由局长在委员会建议下规定并在政府公报上公布的标准、程序和条件。

第15.1条 为防止植物有害生物从泰王国传出，部长根据委员会的建议将有权在政府公报上宣布受控植物的名单。

任何人出口第一段中规定的受控植物，必须随附上述受控植物的植物检疫证书。

第15.2条 如果植物检疫证书或转口植物检疫证书正本丢失或损坏，证书的持有者如需补发应向植物检疫官申请补发的植物检疫证书。补发的植物检疫证书的申请和签发须符合局长规定的标准、程序和条件。

第15.3条 为便利植物生长物的出口，任何要求植物检疫官对提供出口的苗圃或大田实施检疫或推荐控制植物有害生物的方法者，应到农业局对上述供出口的苗圃或大田进行注册登记。

申请注册和登记须符合局长规定的标准、程序和条件。

第15.4条 为调控出口植物，部长根据委员会建议可有权在政府公报上公布特定性受控植物，并标明名称、品种、种类或按进口国要求为对人类健康有害的植物，微生物或其他物品的特性。

第15.5条 任何人想要进口特定性受控植物，需随附植物检疫证书并支付检查费用，该费用的收取由局长根据委员会的建议而规定并在政府公报上发布。

植物检疫官员有权向第一段中规定的申请人签发健康证书，并且收取证书的签发费用，该费用由部长条例规定。

第16条 任何人要求植物检疫官在法定假日和工作时间以外的时间履行本法赋予的职责，或者出差（不管是否在规定的工作时间内），按照部长条例的规定必须支付加班费，同时还要支付植物检疫官必要的及实际产生的差旅费。

根据第一段要求应支付附加费和差旅费，须符合农业合作部规定的标准、程序和条件。

第17条 如果爆发植物有害生物可能造成严重损失的，或者有根据确定某地需要控制植物有害生物的，局长有权以公告的形式宣布该地为植物有害生物控制区。公告上须详细列出受控植物、植物有害生物和载体的名称和种类，必要时在当地设立检查站。公告应张贴在省政府办公场所，镇办公室，Kumnan和Phuyai Ban办公室的这些位置。

第18条 第17条法令规定的植物有害生物控制区公告后，非经植物检疫官检验和书面许可，任何人不得将公告上规定的植物、植物有害生物或载体带出或带入植物有害生物控制区。

第19条 相应的，第12条和13条的有关规定，将适用于第17条涉及的植物有害生物控制区内及带出、带入该控制区的植物、植物有害生物和载体。

如果发生某种植物有害生物，可能会造成重大损失，且不及时销毁将导致更严重的损失，植物检疫官可责令货主销毁植物、植物有害生物和载体，必要时，植物检疫官可以亲自销毁。在此情况，局长可根据需要和实际支出要求货主支付一切销毁费用。

第 20 条　当局长发现第 17 条中发布声明的植物有害生物已经全部被销毁或者不再必要时，这个声明将被废除。

第 20.1 条　根据第 15 条规定所收取的检验费和第 16 条规定的附加费不列入财政预算法规定的收入，只能用于本法规定的活动范围，而不能用于其他任何目的。

第 20.2 条　任何不遵守第 6 条第二段或违背第 6.1 条第二段、第 9 条或第 18 条规定者，处以 20000 铢以下罚款。

第 20.3 条　任何防碍植物检疫官履行第 6.2 条职责者，处以 10000 铢以下罚款。

第 21 条　任何违反第 8 条、第 14 条或者不遵守第 10 条法令者，处以一年以下监禁或者 20000 铢以下罚款，或者两项并处。

第 22 条　任何不遵守第 11 条或者第 15.1 条第二段规定者，将被罚款 2000 铢以下。

第 23 条　任何防碍植物检疫官履行第 12、13 条第一、二、四段规定的职责者，或不遵守第 13 条第三段规定的植物检疫官指令者，处以 6 个月以下监禁，或者 10000 铢以下罚款，或者两项并处。

第 24 条　任何不服从或阻碍植物检疫官员履行第 19 条第二段规定的职责者，处以 6 个月以下监禁，或 10000 铢以下罚款，或者两项并处。

第 25 条　在本法内，所有只被处以罚款的违法，局长或者局长任命的任何人都有权执行罚款。

第 26 条　本法规定的所有植物、植物有害生物或载体如没有经过植物检疫场检查，或者违反本法规定进口或过境引进，或者违反第 8、9、14、18 条关于植物有害生物控制区相关规定的，不管相关人被法院判罪与否，都将予以没收。法庭判定没收的所有物品都归农业部自行处理。

第 27 条　农业合作部部长负责本法的执行，有权任命植物检疫官员，签发部级规章规定不超过下面附录中所限定费率的收费，准予减免行政管理费以及规定执行本法的其他行为。

这些部级规章在政府公报上公布之后开始有效。

行政性收费率

禁止物的进口和转口许可证	200 铢/份
植物种质的进出口许可证	200 铢/份
（1）植物检疫证书	200 铢/份
（2）转口植物检疫证书	200 铢/份
（3）健康证书	200 铢/份
（4）植物检疫证书补发证	100 铢/份
（5）转口植物检疫证书补发证	100 铢/份
（6）健康证书补发证	100 铢/份

联署：

陆军元帅 **Thanom Kittikachorn**

总理

- 植物检疫法 B. E. 2507（1964）：政府公报，第 81 卷，27 章，3 月 21 日 B. E. 2507（1964）.
- 植物检疫法（第二版）B. E. 2542（1999）：政府公报，第 116 卷，39a 章，3 月 18 日 B. E. 2542（1999）.
- 植物检疫法（第三版）B. E. 2551（2008）：政府公报，第 125 卷，40a 章，B. E. 2551（2008）.
- 非官方翻译
- 如果泰语原文与英语译文之间存在任何差异，以泰语原文为准.

Plant quarantine

(ACT B. E. 2507)

Enacted by the King, by and with the advice and consent of the Constituent Assembly acting as the National Assembly, as follows:

Section 1 This Act shall be called the "Plant Quarantine Act, B. E. 2507".

Section 2 This Act shall come into force after the expiration of ninety days from the date of its publication in the Government Gazette.

Section 3 The Plant Diseases and Plant Pests Prevention Act, B. E. 2495 shall be repealed.

Section 4 In this Act, "plant" means all species of plants including terrestrial, aquatic, and other kinds of plants, including any parts thereof such as the stems, buds, stocks, shoots, offshoots, branches, leaves, roots, rhizomes, bulbs, flowers, fruits, seeds, and cultures and spores of mushrooms, be they propagable or dead; including predators, parasites, silkworms, silkworm - eggs, silk - cocoons, bees, bee - hives, and microorganisms;

controlled plant means plants declared by the Minister in the Government Gazette as controlled plant;

specific controlled plant means plants declared by the Minister in the Government Gazette. It shall require protective measures and inspection on microorganisms or other articles that are harmful to human health, in compliance with the importing country requirements prior to exportation.

plant germplasms means a group of cells with diverse inheritable genes that form pieces of plants which are alive and propagable, be they in a form of seeds, tissues, or any part of plants, including genetic materials that may inherit any characteristics controlled by them, herein specific only to those useful for breeding purposes;

soil means soil with organic matters or with livable conditions for plant pests.

plant pests means those which are harmful to plants, such as plant pathogens, insects, animals or plants which may do harm to plants.

carriers means planting materials, soil, sand, containers or other materials in which plants are packed, organic fertilizers or others which may serve as media for the plant pests;

prohibited materials means plants, plant pests and carriers declared by the Minister in the Government Gazette;

restricted materials means plants, plant pests and carriers declared by the Minister in the Government Gazette;

unprohibited materials means other plants which are not prohibited or restricted materials;

owner includes agent of the owner, person in possession of the materials and person in charge of the conveyance transporting the materials;

pest risk analysis means the process of evaluating biological or other scientific and economic evidence to determine whether a pest should be regulated and the strength of any phytosanitary measures to be taken against it;

importation means bringing or ordering into the Kingdom by any means whatsoever;

bringing in transit means bringing or sending through the Kingdom with or without transshipment;

exportation means bringing or sending out of the Kingdom by any means whatsoever;

plant quarantine station means a station declared by the Minister in Government Gazette for inspecting plants, prohibited and restricted materials, and plant germplasms imported or brought in transit;

post – entry quarantine station means a place declared by the Minister in the Government Gazette as a place for holding plants, prohibited and restricted materials, and plant germplasms for observation and research;

plant pest control area means a locality declared by the Director – General in the Government Gazette as area for prevention or eradication of plant pests;

phytosanitary certificate means an official document issued by the competent authority of exporting country to verify that plant, plant germplasm or carrier is free from pests, in compliance with the importing country requirements;

phytosanitary certificate for re – export means an official document issued by the competent authority of exporting country to verify that plant, plant germplasm or carrier brought or sent into and transshipped out of the Kingdom to other countries is free from pests of re – exporting country, in compliance with the importing country requirements;

health certificate means an official document issued by the competent authority of exporting country to verify that a specific controlled plant is free from microorganisms or other articles which are harmful to human health, in compliance with the importing country requirements;

Committee means the Plant Quarantine Committee;

Director – General means the Director – General of the Department of Agriculture;

plant quarantine official means the Director – General and a person appointed by the Minister for the execution of this Act;

Minister means the Minister in charge of the execution of this Act.

Section 5 The plant quarantine official shall bear an identification card in the form prescribed in the Ministerial Regulation, and in the execution of this Act, upon request, shall provide the said identification card to the person concerned.

Section 5bis There shall be a Committee called "The Plant Quarantine Committee," comprising the Permanent Secretary of Ministry of Agriculture and Cooperatives as the chairman, Director – General of the Department of Fisheries, Director – General of the Department of Livestock Development, Director – General of the Royal Forestry Department, Director – General of the Department of Agriculture, Director – General of the Custom Department, Director – General of the Department of Secretary – General Office of the Narcotics Control Board, Director – General Port Authority of Thailand, Managing Director Airport Authority of Thailand, President the Communications Authority of Thailand, Director of the National Center for Genetic Engineering and Biotechnology, Representatives of the Ministry of Commerce and the Ministry of Interior, one for each Ministry, and no more than 4 Experts appointed by the Minister as the Committee and the Director of Agricultural Regulatory Division of the Department of Agriculture as the Committee and Secretary.

The Department of Agriculture, for the Committee, shall be charged with the duties on technical, administrative, and procedural under the decision of the Committee.

Section 5ter The Expert Committee shall be in office for a two – year – term, nevertheless may be reappointed.

In case there is any reason for the Expert Committee to leave the office before the end of the term or in case the Minister appoints additional Expert Committee during the office term of the Committee, the substituted Expert Committee shall be in the office for as long as the term left for the earlier appointed Expert Committee.

Section 5tetra Notwithstanding the end of office term under Section 5ter, the Expert Committee appointed by the Minister shall leave the office in case of:

(1) death;

(2) resignation;

(3) removed by the Minister;

(4) become incompetent or quasi – incompetent person;

(5) imprisoned by the final judgement to a term of imprisonment, except for an offence committed through negligence or a petty offence.

Section 5penta In a meeting of the Committee, the presence of not less than one – half of the total number of members of the Committee shall be required to constitute the quorum. In case where the chairman is not present or is unable to perform the duty, the members of the Committee present shall elect a member among themselves to preside over the meeting as a chairman.

A decision of the meeting shall be met by a majority vote. Each member of the Committee shall have one vote. In case of equality of the votes, the presiding chairman shall have an additional vote as the final vote.

Section 5hexa The Committee shall have the authorityas following:

(1) provide recommendations to the Minister for the determination on name of plants, plant pests, or carriers to be prohibited or restricted articles, and of plant germplasms that shall be controlled, and of controlled plants and specific controlled plants;

(2) provide recommendations to the Minister for the determination on plant quarantine station and post – entry quarantine station;

(3) provide recommendations to the Director – General for the determination on type of business enterprises that are eligible to import or bring in transit of prohibited articles under Section 8 (2) as well as the determination on criteria, procedures and conditions for the importation or bringing in transit of prohibited articles through commercial channel or other business enterprises under Section 8 (2);

(4) provide recommendations to the Director – General for the determination on criteria, procedures and conditions for importation or bringing in transit of prohibited or restricted articles under Section 10, and for the determination on plant pest inspection and treatment fees, the request for a phytosanitary certificate or phytosanitary certificate for re – export and the issuance of certificates under Section 15;

(5) provide recommendations to the Director – General for the determination on inspection fees for exportation of specific controlled plants, including criteria, procedures and conditions on the request and issuance of health certificate under Section 15hexa;

(6) provide recommendations to the Minister for the promulgation of the Ministerial Regulations under this Act;

(7) make recommendations to the Minister or Director – General for the amendment of this Act, Ministerial Regulations, rules, notifications or guidelines related to plant quarantine under this Act or other laws elsewhere, that cause adverse effect to the plant quarantine implementation;

(8) perform other actions stipulated by this Act or other laws to be the duties of the Committee.

Section 5hepta The Committee shall have the authority to appoint one or more Sub – Committee (s) to perform any duties charged by the Committee.

The provisions of Section 5penta shall be applied to the meeting of the Sub – Committee *mutatis mutandis*.

Section 6 In case, where it is necessary to prevent the spread or outbreak from introduction of any kind of plant pests into the Kingdom or where it is advantageous to protect possibly adverse effect on environment or human health, the Minister by the recommendation of the Committee shall have the authority to declare, where propriate, in the Government Gazette the names of plants, plant pests or carriers to be prohibited or restricted articles under this Act, as the case may be. Under the said declaration, the names of any plants, plant pests or carriers from any sources may be stated or any exceptions or conditions may be specified.

In stipulating the conditions for prevention of the introduction of any kind of plant pests into the Kingdom, the Minister may require that any person travelling from the place where there is the occurrence of that particular plant pest, report to the plant quarantine official with the form specified by the Director – General.

When it is no longer necessary, the prohibited and restricted materials mentioned in paragraph one shall be revoked by declaration in the Government Gazette.

Section 6bis For the purpose of controlling and prevention of the introduction of plant pests, the Minister by the recommendation of the Committee shall have the authority to declare the name of plant germplasms that shall be controlled in the Government Gazette.

No one shall import or export any plant germplasms declared in paragraph 1 by the Minister, unless otherwise permitted by the Director – General, and the importation of which shall be accompanied with a phytosanitary certificate.

The request for permission and the permission under paragraph 2 shall be performed under the criteria, processes, and conditions specified by the Director – General.

Section 6ter The plant quarantine official shall have the authority to enter the planting area, places of collection, or preservation of plant germplasms declared by the Minister under Section 6bis paragraph 1, during sunrise and sunset of the day or the official hours to inspect and study the use of plant germplasms. In such action, the plant quarantine official shall have the authority to inquire the fact or request for the permit, or related evidence from the owner or the possessor of the planting area or the said place.

Section 7 The Minister under the recommendation of the Committee shall have the authority to declare in the Government Gazette, any port, airport, or place with certain limit as plant quarantine station or post – entry quarantine station, as the case may be, in the Government Gazette.

Section 8 Any person importing or bringing in transit prohibited
articles shall receive permission from the Director – General and comply with the following rules.

(1) The importation or bringing in transit of prohibited articles for research purpose shall be accompanied with a phytosanitary certificate, or in case where the importation or bringing in transit of prohibited plant pest or carrier which is not plant, a certification letter from the authorized agency of the exporting country shall be required to accompany with such prohibited articles.

(2) The importation or bringing in transit for commerce or other purposes which shall be declared by the Director – General under the recommendation of the Committee, shall be accompanied by a phytosanitary certificate, subjected to pest risk analysis and complied with the criteria, procedures and conditions stipulated by the Director – General under the recommendation of the Committee and published in the Government Gazette.

Section 9 No one shall import or bring in transit any restricted articles unless the said restricted articles are accompanied with a phytosanitary certificate .

Section 10 The importation or bringing in transit of prohibited or restricted articles shall be made through the plant quarantine station for inspection by the plant quarantine official, and shall be complied with criteria, procedures and conditions stipulated by the Director – General under the recommendation of the Committee and published in the Government Gazette.

Section 11 Any person importing or bringing in transit unprohibited articles shall attach with a phytosanitary certificate and shall declare to the plant quarantine official in a format form specified by the Director – General.

Section 12 In the execution of this Act, the plant quarantine official shall have the authority as follows;

(1) search any warehouse, conveyance, package as well as any person within the jurisdiction of plant quarantine station or plant pest controlled area when there is reasonable ground to suspect that plants, prohibited articles, restricted articles or unprohibited articles have been imported or brought in transit in violation or non – compliance of this Act;

(2) search any premise, person or conveyance outside the jurisdiction of plant quarantine station or plant pest controlled area, during sunrise to sunset of the day, or during the business hours of that premise in case where there is reasonable ground to suspect that plants, prohibited articles, restricted articles or unprohibited articles under possession are plant pests or harbor plant pests that may cause very serious damage and in case where there is reasonable ground to suspect that if the search warrant shall take longer time to be issued, such unlawful articles or any wrongdoings shall be removed, hidden, destroyed or changed from the original appearances, and in case where the search can not be carried out in time, it is allowable to continue until the search is completed;

(3) collect or draw sample in an adequate amount of plants, prohibited articles, restricted articles or unprohibited articles or other related articles for inspection or analysis, in case where there is reasonable ground to suspect that such articles are plant pests or harbor plant pests that may cause very serious damage;

(4) confiscate or hold plants or prohibited articles, restricted articles or unprohibited articles or other related articles in due time, where necessary, in case where there is reasonable ground to suspect that such articles are plant pests or harbor plant pests that may cause very serious damage.

Section 13 To prevention of the introduction of plant pests into the Kingdom, the plant quarantine official shall have the authority to deal with the plants or prohibited articles, restricted articles, unprohibited articles or plant germplasms imported or brought in transit as follows;

(1) diagnose plant pests, fumigated or treated with chemical by means of spraying or by any other means as deemed necessary at the owner's expenses;

(2) confiscate or hold them at the post – entry quarantine station or at any other places in due time, where necessary;

(3) order the importer to send the plants, prohibited articles, restricted articles, unprohibited articles or plant germplasms infected or infested with plant pests out of the Kingdom;

(4) destroy them, where necessary, when there is reasonable ground to suspect that such plant pests may cause very serious damage and there is no alternative remedial measures under subparagraph (1).

Section 13bis All articles that are collected, confiscated or held under Section 12 (3) and (4) and Section 13 (2), shall fall into the possessions of the Department of Agriculture, in case if there is no claim from the owners, or in case where the case is withdrew by the public prosecutor, or the final judgement is not to confiscate the articles, and the owner does not claim within ninety days counting from the date of confiscation or hold, or the date of public prosecutor withdrawal or the date of the final judgement not to confiscate the articles, wherever the cases shall be.

If the articles collected, confiscated or held under paragraph 1 are perishable, or if the articles shall be at risk to be damaged from storage or the expenses to keep the articles exceed their values, the Director – General shall have the authority to order destroying or any other means of disposal, where appropriate.

Section 14 No one shall remove any plants, prohibited or restricted articles, or plant germplasms from any plant quarantine station, post – entry quarantine station, or conveyance in case of transit, or from any places where such articles are confiscated or held by the order of the plant quarantine official unless permission in writing has been obtained from the said plant quarantine official.

Section 15　Any person who would like to apply for a phytosanitary certificate or phytosanitary certificate for re – export shall pay inspection and treatment fees at the rates specified by the Director – General under the recommendation by the Committee and shall be published in the Government Gazette.

The plant quarantine official has the authority to issue a phytosanitary certificate and phytosanitary certificate for re – export to the applicant under paragraph 1 and the plant quarantine official shall collect fees for the issuance of a phytosanitary certificate or phytosanitary certificate for re – export, where applicable to the rates prescribed in the Ministerial Regulation.

The request for and issuance of a phytosanitary certificate or phytosanitary certificate for re – export shall be complied with the criteria, procedures, and conditions stipulated by the Director – General under the recommendation by the Committee and shall be published in the Government Gazette.

Section 15bis　To prevent the spread of the plant pests out of the Kingdom, the Minister under the recommendation of the Committee shall have the authority to declare the name of plants to be considered as controlled plant in the Government Gazette.

Any person who would like to export controlled plants under paragraph 1 shall have a phytosanitary certificate accompanied with the said controlled plant.

Section 15ter　In case of loss or damage in the essential matters of the phytosanitary certificate or phytosanitary certificate for re – export, the holder of the said phytosanitary certificate requiring a substitution shall request for such substituted phytosanitary certificate from the plant quarantine official.

The request for and issuance of the substitution of the phytosanitary certificate shall be in complied with the criteria, processes, and conditions as stipulated by the Director – General.

Section 15tetra　To facilitate plant growers for purpose of exportation, any person who would like to request that the plant quarantine official inspect or recommend the means to control plant pests in nursery or field for exportation, shall request for registration of the said nursery or field for exportation to the Department of Agriculture.

The request for registration and the registration shall be in line with the criteria, processes, and conditions stipulated by the Director – General.

Section 15penta　To regulate plants for exportation, the Minister under the recommendation of the Committee shall have the authority to declare a plant to be specific controlled plant by indicating name, type, species or characteristic aspects of the plant, microorganism or other articles that may be harmful to human health in compliance with the importing country requirements, as well in the Government Gazette.

Section 15hexa　Any person who would like to export specific controlled plant shall have a phytosanitary certificate accompanying with the consignment and pay inspection fee at the rates specified by the Director – General under the recommendation by the Committee and shall be published in the Government Gazette.

The plant quarantine official shall have the authority to issue a health certificate to the applicant under paragraph 1 and the plant quarantine official shall collect fee for the issuance of a health certificate at the rates prescribed in the Ministerial Regulation.

Section 16　Any person would like to request that the plant quarantine official to perform his duties under this Act on official holidays, after official working hours, or outside Government offices whether during or after official working hours, shall pay additional fees for performing his duties at the rates prescribed in the Ministerial Regulation and pay all travel expenses as necessary and actually paid to the plant quarantine official.

The criteria, processes, and conditions of the payment of additional fees and travel expenses under paragraph 1 shall be in line with the Ministerial Rule.

Section 17　In the event of an outbreak of plant pests which might bring about serious damages, or where there is proper reason to place control in respect of plant pests in any locality, the Director – General shall have the power to determine by notification such locality as plant pests control area. The notification shall specify the names and species of plants, plant pests, and carriers under the control and determined the local checking stations as are necessary. Such notification shall be posted up at the Provincial Government Office, Amphur Office, Office of Kumnan and Phuyai Ban of such locality.

Section 18 After a declaration of the plant pests control area under Section 17 has been made, no one shall take out of or bring into the plant pests control area any plants, plant pests or carriers specified in the declaration unless inspected and permitted in writing by the plant quarantine official.

Section 19 The provisions of Sections 12 and 13 shall apply mutatis mutandis to the plants, plant pests and carriers stated in Section 17 which are within the plant pests control area, or to be taken out of or brought into the said area.

In case there is any plant pests which may cause serious damages and, if it is not destroyed in time, it will cause more severe damages, the plant quarantine official may order the owner to destroy the plants, plant pests and carriers, or if necessary the plant quarantine official may destroy them by himself. In such case, the Director – General may order the owner to pay all expenses for such destruction as necessary and actually paid.

Section 20 When the Director – General finds that the plant pests according to the declaration under Section 17 have all been destroyed or that necessity no longer exists, such declaration shall be revoked.

Section 20bis The money obtained from the inspection fees under Section 15 and the additional fees under Section 16 shall not be considered as income under the law of fiscal budget, and shall be used only in those activities specified by this Act, not for any other purposes whatsoever.

Section 20ter Any person who does not comply with Section 6 paragraph 2 or is in violation of Section 6bis paragraph 2, Section 9, or Section 18 shall be fined not exceeding 20,000 Baht.

Section 20tetra Any person resists or obstructs the plant quarantine official from performing his duties under Section 6ter shall be fined not exceeding 10,000 Baht.

Section 21 Any person violates Section 8 or 14 or does not comply with Section 10 shall be imprisoned not exceeding one year or fined not exceeding 20,000 Baht, or both.

Section 22 Any person who does not comply with Section 11 or 15bis paragraph 2, shall be fined not exceeding 2,000 Baht.

Section 23 Any person resists or obstructs the plant quarantine official from performing his duties under Section 12 or 13 (1) (2) or (4) or does not comply with the order of the plant quarantine official under Section 13 (3) shall be imprisoned not exceeding six months, or fined not exceeding 10,000 Baht, or both.

Section 24 Any person disobeys or obstructs the plant quarantine official from performing his duties under Section 19 paragraph 2, shall be imprisoned not exceeding six months, or fined not exceeding 10,000 Baht, or both.

Section 25 For all the offences under this Act that are only punishment by fine, the Director – General or any person appointed by him shall have the authority to perform administrative fine.

Section 26 For all plants, plant pests or carriers under this Act which are not imported through plant quarantine station or imported or brought in transit in violation of this Act in any respect, or those which are objects of offences in connection with the plant pests control area as provided in Section 8 Section 9 Section 14 Section or Section 18 shall be confiscated regardless of whether any person is convicted by the order of the court. All articles confiscated by the order of the court shall belong to the Department of Agriculture to be managed under its discretion.

Section 27 The Minister of Agriculture and Cooperatives shall be in charge of the execution of this Act, and shall have the authority to appoint the plant quarantine official, to issue Ministerial Regulations fixing fees not exceeding the rates annexed hereto, to grant exemption of administrative fees, and to prescribe other activities for carrying out this Act.

Such Ministerial Regulations shall become effective upon their publication in the Government Gazette.

Rate of Administrative Fees

(1) An Import and transit permits of prohibited articles	200 Baht per each
(2) An Import and export permits of plant germplasms	200 Baht per each
(3) A Phytosanitary certificate	200 Baht per each
(4) A phytosanitary certificate for re – export	200 Baht per each
(5) A health certificate	200 Baht per each
(6) Substitute certificate of phytosanitary certificate	100 Baht per each
(7) Substitute certificate of phytosanitary certificate for re – export	100 Bath per each
(8) Substitute certificate of health certificate	100 Baht per each

Countersigned by:
Field Marshal **Thanom Kittikachorn**
Prime Minister

• Plant Quarantine Act B. E. 2507 (1964): The Government Gazette, VoL. 81, Part 27, dated 21 March B. E. 2507 (1964).

• Plant Quarantine Act (NO. 2) B. E. 2542 (1999): The Government Gazette, VoL. 116, Part 39a, dated 18 May B. E. 2542 (1999).

• Plant Quarantine Act (No. 3) B. E. 2551 (2008): The Government Gazette, VoL. 125, Part 40a, dated 1 March B. E. 2551 (2008).

• UNOFFICIAL TRANSLATION

• This is an English translation. In case of any difference in meaning between the Thai text and the English translation, the Thai text shall be applied.

植物检疫进口条例

植物检疫法

目前正在执行的植物检疫法 B. E. 2507（1952）是经植物检疫法（第二版）B. E. 2542（1999）修订而来。该法共包含 27 条。为防止国外植物有害生物的入侵，法令中规定了针对进口植物及植物产品的一系列条例、公告和指令。

行政执法机构

植物检疫法 B. E. 2507（1952）经植物检疫法（第二版）B. E. 2542（1999）修订后，由农业合作部下属的农业局负责执行，农业局指派植物检疫分支局、农业法规处来具体实施该法规定的各项职责。

植物检疫进口要求

本法规定，进口的植物及植物产品根据其在原产地的经济价值，以及携带的病虫害在原产地的流行性而划分为 3 类，即禁止物、限制物和非禁物。以下是禁止物、限制物和非禁物的进口要求。

- **禁止物：**

表 1 中所列的是禁止进境物名单，预先经农业局批准，仅用于实验研究目的的除外。

（1）农业合作部公告中列出的植物、植物产品以及从列入疫区名单的地区运来的植物、植物产品。

（2）植物、植物有害生物及载体。

（3）土壤和有机肥。

禁止物进口要求规定如下：

（1）必须经由曼谷国际机场、曼谷港口和曼谷邮政植物检疫站 3 个植检站的检疫；

（2）必须出具出口国官方政府机构签发的植物检疫证书；

（3）植物检疫证书必须申明货物不带有植物检疫性病虫害，符合农业局局长所规定的条件。

- **限制物**

表 2 所列的物品是允许进口的。限制物进口要求规定如下：

（1）必须出具出口国官方政府机构签发的植物检疫证书；

（2）必须依照植物检疫官员的要求对货物进行处理；

（3）此外，进口限制物，特别是植物繁殖材料，必须进行彻底检查。

- **非禁物**

禁止物和限制物以外的植物材料，都属于非禁物。进口时不需要植物检疫证书和许可证。但是，进口非禁物须在入境口岸申报检查。所有非禁物都须进行检查，如发现检疫性病虫害要进行检疫处理或销毁。

表 1　禁止进境物

编号	植物、有害生物及其携带者	来　源	例　外　情　况
	植物		
1	柑桔属 *Citrus*、金桔属 *Fortunella*、枳属 *Poncirus* 植物	非洲 澳大利亚 中美洲 斯里兰卡 欧洲 印度 印度尼西亚 日本 中东 地中海地区 南美洲 美国	1. 罐装食品。 2. 来自澳大利亚且必须依照农业局2004年1月15日签发的公告：澳大利亚输往泰国新鲜柑橘类水果要求，进行处理的橘子（包括 navels，valencias，mandarins 及其杂交种如 tangor）、柠檬、葡萄柚（包括 pummelo）。 3. 来自美国加利福尼亚州且必须依照特定的商品规定1（SCU 1）：美国加利福尼亚输往泰国新鲜柑橘类水果要求，进行处理的桔子（包括 avels，tangerines，tangelos，valencias）柠檬和葡萄柚（包括 pummelo）。 4. 来自美国佛罗里达州且必须依照特定的商品规定2：美国佛罗里达输往泰国新鲜柑橘类水果要求，进行处理的橘子（包括 avels，tangerines，tangelos，valencias）、葡萄柚（包括 pummelo）和柠檬（sour lemon，Citrus limon 除外）。 5. 来自美国亚利桑那州且必须依照特定的商品规定4：美国亚利桑那州输往泰国新鲜柑橘类水果要求，进行处理的橘子（avels，tangerines，tangelos，valencias）、柠檬、酸橙和葡萄柚（包括 pummelo）。 6. 来自美国加利福尼亚、法国、西班牙、以色列、南非和澳大利亚且必须依照农业局局长规定的要求进行处理的柑橘属种子，并出具植物检疫证书
2	椰子 *Cocos nucifera*	东非 西非 中美洲 南美洲 西印度群岛 菲律宾 印度 关岛	1. 罐装食品 2. 椰子植物制成品，在进口前货主向农业局局长申报了其加工的方法，且局长确定经此方法加工的椰子植物制成品不带有植物有害生物。 3. 去壳的椰子，必须依照农业局局长规定的要求进行处理
3	棉花属 *Gossypium* 植物	非洲 墨西哥 美国 委内瑞拉 西印度群岛 中美洲	进口工业用棉花，须附有原产国植物检疫证书
4	橡胶树 *Hevea* 属植物（如橡胶）及其粘合物质（如鲜胶乳、杯凝胶）	中美洲 南美洲 西印度群岛	
5	木薯 *Manihot esculenta*	非洲 巴西 印度尼西亚	罐装食品、面粉、西米

续表

编号	植物、有害生物及其携带者	来　源	例 外 情 况
6	稻属 *Oryza* 植物	中美洲 斯里兰卡 印度 日本 菲律宾 中国 南美洲 美国 西非 西印度	1. 罐装食品 2. 稻属植物加工品，必须依照农业局局长规定的要求进行处理 3. 大米、糙米碎磨米和蒸煮米，必须附有植物检疫证书
	转基因植物		
1	剪股颖属 *Agrostis* 植物	所有国家	
2	奇异果 *Actinidia chinensis* Planch	所有国家	
3	洋葱 *Allium cepa* L.	所有国家	
4	康棣属 *Amelanchier* 植物	所有国家	
5	菠萝 *Ananus comosus*（L.）Merr.	所有国家	
6	芹菜 *Apium graveolens* var. *dulce*（MilL.）D. C.	所有国家	
7	拟南芥 *Arabidopsis thaliana* L.	所有国家	
8	落花生属 *Arachis*	所有国家	
9	马萝卜 *Armoracia rusticana* P. Gaertner，Meyer & Scherb.	所有国家	
10	芦笋 *Asparagus officinalis* Linn.	所有国家	
11	颠茄 *Atropa belladonna* L.	所有国家	
12	燕麦 *Avena sativa* L.	所有国家	
13	甜菜属 *Beta vulgaris* L. sub sp. vulgaris	所有国家	
14	油菜属 *Brassica* 植物	所有国家	
15	茶属 *Camellia* 植物	所有国家	
16	番椒属 *Capsicum* 植物	所有国家	
17	木瓜 *Carica papaya* L.	所有国家	

续表

编号	植物、有害生物及其携带者	来　源	例　外　情　况
18	菊花属 *Chrysanthemum* 植物	所有国家	
19	菊苣 *Cichorium intybus* L.	所有国家	
20	西瓜 *Citrullus lanatus* (Thumb) Matsun & Nakai	所有国家	
21	柑桔属 *Citrus* 植物	所有国家	
22	可可椰子 *Cocos nucifera* L.	所有国家	
23	咖啡属 *Coffea* 植物	所有国家	
24	黄瓜属 *Cucumis* 植物	所有国家	
25	瓜属 *Cucurbita* 植物	所有国家	
26	胡萝卜 *Daucus carota* L.	所有国家	
27	菊属 *Dendranthema* 植物	所有国家	
28	康乃馨 *Dianthus caryophyllus* L.	所有国家	
29	油棕 *Elaeis guineensis* Jacq.	所有国家	
30	桉树属 *Eucalyptus* 植物	所有国家	
31	金桔属 *Fortunella* 属植物	所有国家	
32	草莓属 *Fragaria* 植物	所有国家	
33	唐菖蒲属 *Gladiolus* 植物	所有国家	
34	黄豆 *Glycine max* L.	所有国家	1. 罐装食品 2. 大豆，用于生产动物饲料或人类消费品的原料，或者用于工业目
35	棉属 *Gossypium* 植物	所有国家	
36	向日葵属 *Helianthus* 植物	所有国家	
37	橡胶属 *Hevea* 植物	所有国家	
38	大麦属 *Hordeum* 植物	所有国家	
39	甘薯属 *Ipomoea* 植物	所有国家	

续表

编号	植物、有害生物及其携带者	来 源	例 外 情 况
40	核桃属 *Juglans* 植物	所有国家	
41	莴苣 *Lactuca sativa* L.	所有国家	
42	兵豆 *Lens culinaris* Medik.	所有国家	
43	麻属 *Linum* 植物	所有国家	
44	北美枫香树 *Liquidambar styraciflua* L.	所有国家	
45	羽扇豆属 *Lupinus* 植物	所有国家	
46	番茄 *Lycopersicon esculentum* Miller	所有国家	
47	苹果属 *Malus* 植物	所有国家	
48	树薯 *Manihot esculenta* Crantz.	所有国家	
49	芭蕉属 *Musa* 植物	所有国家	
50	苜蓿 *Medicago sativa* L.	所有国家	
51	烟草 *Nicotiana tabacum* L.	所有国家	
52	兰科 Orchidaceae 植物	所有国家	
53	稻属 *Oryza* 植物	所有国家	
54	罂粟属 *Papaver* 植物	所有国家	
55	天竺葵属 *Pelargonium* 植物	所有国家	
56	矮牵牛花属 *Petunia* 植物	所有国家	
57	菜豆属 *Phaseolus* 植物	所有国家	
58	云杉属 *Picea* 植物	所有国家	
59	豌豆 *Pisum sativum*	所有国家	
60	枸橘属 *Poncirus* 植物	所有国家	
61	杨树属 *Populus* 植物	所有国家	
62	李属 *Prunus* 植物	所有国家	
63	梨属 *Pyrus* 植物	所有国家	
64	穗醋栗 *Ribes nigrum*	所有国家	
65	蓖麻属 *Ricinus* 植物	所有国家	
66	蔷薇属 *Rosa* 植物	所有国家	
67	树莓属 *Rubu* 植物	所有国家	

续表

编号	植物、有害生物及其携带者	来　源	例 外 情 况
68	*Saccharum* 属植物	所有国家	
69	茄属 *Solanum* 植物	所有国家	
70	高粱属 *Sorghum* 植物	所有国家	
71	笔花豆属 *Stylosanthes* 植物	所有国家	
72	可可 *Theobroma cacao* L.	所有国家	
73	夏堇 *Torenia fournieri* Lind.	所有国家	
74	车轴草属 *Trifolium* 植物	所有国家	
75	小麦属 *Triticum* 植物	所有国家	
76	越橘属 *Vaccinium* 植物	所有国家	
77	豇豆属 *Vigna* 植物	所有国家	
78	葡萄属 *Vitis* 植物	所有国家	
79	玉米 *Zea mays* L.	所有国家	1. 罐装食品 2. 玉米，用于生产动物饲料或人类消费品的原料或者用于工业目的
80	结缕草属 *Zoysia* 植物	所有国家	
	载体		
1	土壤	所有国家	
2	有机肥	所有国家	1. 动物有机肥（动物粪便除外） 2. 植物有机肥，在进口前货主向农业局局长申报了其加工的方法，且局长确定经此方法加工的植物有机肥不带有植物有害生物
	植物有害生物		
	真菌		
1	棉壳二孢菌 *Ascochyta gossypii*	所有国家	
2	番木瓜座糙孢菌 *Asperisporium caricae*	所有国家	
3	可可花瘿病菌 *Calonectria rigidiuscula*	所有国家	
4	甘薯长喙壳菌 *Ceratocystis fimbriata*	所有国家	
5	可可丛枝病菌 *Crinipellis perniciosa*	所有国家	

续表

编号	植物、有害生物及其携带者	来 源	例 外 情 况
6	柠檬干枯菌 *Deuterophoma tracheiphila*	所有国家	
7	柑橘澳洲痂囊腔菌 *Elsinoe australis*	所有国家	
8	稻柱香菌 *Ephelis oryzae*	所有国家	
9	肉座菌目 *Haplobasidion musae*	所有国家	
10	橡胶南美叶疫病菌 *Microcyclus ulei*	所有国家	
11	念珠菌 *Moniliophthora roreri*	所有国家	
12	香蕉黑条叶斑病菌 *Mycosphaerella fijiensis*	所有国家	
13	柑橘斑点病菌 *Phaeoramularia angolensis*	所有国家	
14	褐根病菌 *Phellinus noxius*	所有国家	
15	棉根腐病 *Phymatotrichum omnivorum*	所有国家	
16	柑橘生疫霉 *Phytophthora citricola*	所有国家	
17	冬生疫霉 *Phytophthora hibernalis*	所有国家	
18	桂氏疫霉 *Phytophthora katsurae*	所有国家	
19	锥孢座坚壳菌 *Rosellinia bunodes*	所有国家	
20	黑根病 *Rosellinia pepo*	所有国家	
21	柑橘斑枯病 *Septoria limonum*	所有国家	
22	木薯痂圆孢徒长病 *Sphaceloma manihoticola*	所有国家	
23	单胞锈菌属 *Uromyces musae*	所有国家	

续表

编号	植物、有害生物及其携带者	来　源	例　外　情　况
	细菌		
1	番茄溃疡病菌 *Clavibacter michiganensis* subsp. *michiganensis*	所有国家	
2	玉米内州萎蔫病菌 *Clavibacter michiganensis* subsp. *nebraskensis*	所有国家	
3	马铃薯环腐病菌 *Clavibacter michiganensis* subsp. *sepedonicus*	所有国家	
4	柑橘黄龙病非洲株系 *Liberobacter africanum*	所有国家	
5	草螺菌 *Pseudomonas rubrisubalbicans*	所有国家	
6	番茄溃疡假单胞菌 *Pseudomonas corrugat*	所有国家	
7	柑桔溃疡病 *Xanthomonas axonopodis* pv. *citrumelo*	所有国家	
8	木薯细菌性黑斑病 *Xanthomonas campestris* pv. *cassavae*	所有国家	
9	香蕉细菌性萎焉病菌 *Xanthomonas campestris* pv. *celebensis*	所有国家	
10	苟养木杆菌 *Xylella fastidiosa*	所有国家	
	原生动物		
1	家蚕微孢子 *Nosema bombycis*	所有国家	
2	史氏植生滴虫 *Phytomonas staheli*	所有国家	
	病毒		
1	非洲木薯花叶病毒 African cassava mosaic virus	所有国家	
2	香蕉线条病毒 Banana streak virus	所有国家	

续表

编号	植物、有害生物及其携带者	来　源	例 外 情 况
3	木薯褐条病毒 Cassava brown streak virus	所有国家	
4	木薯花叶病毒 Cassava common mosaic virus	所有国家	
5	木薯蛙皮病毒 Cassava frog skin virus	所有国家	
6	科特迪瓦木薯病毒 Cassava ivorian virus	所有国家	
7	木薯脉花叶病毒 Cassava vein mosaic virus	所有国家	
8	柑橘皱叶病毒 Citrus leaf rugose virus	所有国家	
9	柑桔疯病毒 Citrus leprosies virus	所有国家	
10	柑橘鳞片病毒 Citrus psorosis virus	所有国家	
11	柑橘环斑病毒 Citrus ringspot virus	所有国家	
12	柑橘胶木病毒 Citrus rubbery wood virus	所有国家	
13	柑橘碎叶病毒 Citrus tatter leaf virus	所有国家	
14	柑橘杂斑病毒 Citrus variegation virus	所有国家	
15	柑橘脉突病毒 Citrus vein enation virus	所有国家	
16	可可炭疽病毒 Cocao necrosis virus	所有国家	
17	可可红斑病毒 Cocao red mottle virus	所有国家	
18	可可肿枝病毒 Cocao swollen shoot virus	所有国家	
19	可可黄化花叶病毒 Cocao yellow mosaic virus	所有国家	

续表

编号	植物、有害生物及其携带者	来　源	例外情况
20	可可黄化脉带病毒 Cocao yellow vein banding virus	所有国家	
21	可可果叶片腐烂病毒 Coconut foliar decay virus	所有国家	
22	棉花黄萎病毒 Cotton anthocyanosis virus	所有国家	
23	棉花皱叶病毒 Cotton leaf crumple virus	所有国家	
24	棉花花叶病毒 Cotton leaf mosaic virus	所有国家	
25	棉花斑驳病毒 Cotton leaf mottle virus	所有国家	
26	棉花狭窄病毒 Cotton stenosis virus	所有国家	
27	棉花晚矮病毒 Cotton terminal stunt virus	所有国家	
28	东非木薯花叶病毒 East African cassava mosaic virus	所有国家	
29	印度木薯花叶病毒 Indian cassava mosaic virus	所有国家	
30	玉米褪绿矮缩病毒 Maize rayado fino virus	所有国家	
31	番木瓜束顶病毒 Papaya bunchy top virus	所有国家	
32	番木瓜卷叶病毒 Papaya leaf curl virus	所有国家	
33	番木瓜花叶病毒 Papaya mosaic virus	所有国家	
34	怀厄卢阿番木瓜病毒 Papaya waialua virus	所有国家	
35	水稻矮缩病 Rice dwarf virus	所有国家	
36	水稻白叶病毒 Rice hoja blanca virus	所有国家	

续表

编号	植物、有害生物及其携带者	来 源	例 外 情 况
37	水稻黄斑驳病毒 Rice yellow mottle viru	所有国家	
38	温州蜜柑萎缩病 Satsuma dwarf virus	所有国家	
39	甘蔗拉姆线条病毒 Sugarcane ramu stunt virus	所有国家	
40	番茄黑环病毒 Tomato black ring viru	所有国家	
41	番茄丛矮病毒 Tomato bushy stunt virus	所有国家	
42	番茄环斑病毒 Tomato ring spot virus	所有国家	
43	番茄斑萎病毒 Tomato spotted wilt virus	所有国家	
	类病毒		
1	柑橘木孔病类病毒 Citrus cachexia viroid	所有国家	
2	柑桔裂皮病类病毒 Citrus exocortis viroid	所有国家	
3	椰子死亡类病毒 Coconut cadang - cadang viroid	所有国家	
4	马铃薯纺锤形块茎类病毒 Potato spindle tuber viroid	所有国家	
5	败生类病毒 Tinangaja viroid	所有国家	
	植原体		
1	香蕉大理石状肉病原体 Banana marbling disease MLO	所有国家	
2	柑橘丛枝病植原体 Citrus witches broom MLO	所有国家	
3	椰子致死黄化类菌原体 Coconut lethal yellowing MLO	所有国家	
4	甘蔗丛蘖病菌原体 Sugarcane grassy shoot MLO	所有国家	

续表

编号	植物、有害生物及其携带者	来 源	例 外 情 况
	昆虫		
1	南美按实蝇 *Anastepha fraterculus*	所有国家	
2	墨西哥按实蝇 *Anastepha ludens*	所有国家	
3	西印度按实蝇 *Anastepha oblique*	所有国家	
4	加勒比按实蝇 *Anastepha suspensa*	所有国家	
5	墨西哥棉铃象 *Anthonomus grandis*	所有国家	
6	短梗花象 *Anthonomus vestitus*	所有国家	
7	马来亚椰斑蛾 *Artona catoxantha*	所有国家	
8	香蕉果实蝇 *Bactrocera musae*	所有国家	
9	昆士兰实蝇 *Bactrocera tryoni*	所有国家	
10	（巢针蓟马属）*Caliothrips masculinus*	所有国家	
11	地中海实蝇 *Ceratitis capitata*	所有国家	
12	果小条实蝇 *Ceratitis cosyra*	所有国家	
13	五点实蝇 *Ceratitis quinaria*	所有国家	
14	非洲蜡实蝇 *Ceratitis rosa*	所有国家	
15	小蔗螟 *Diatraea saccharalis*	所有国家	
16	木薯天蛾 *Erinnyis ello*	所有国家	
17	（网蝽科）*Leptopharsa heveae*	所有国家	

续表

编号	植物、有害生物及其携带者	来 源	例 外 情 况
18	稻水象甲 *Lissorhoptrus oryzophilus*	所有国家	
19	蔗扁蛾 *Opogona sacchari*	所有国家	
20	（蛀犀金龟属）*Oryctes boas*	所有国家	
21	单角犀甲 *Oryctes monoceros*	所有国家	
22	（豆象属）*Pachymerus nucleorum*	所有国家	
23	玫瑰短喙象 *Panthomorus cervinus*	所有国家	
24	木薯粉蚧 *Phenacoccus manihoti*	所有国家	
25	大谷蠹 *Prostephanus truncatus*	所有国家	
26	橡胶缘蝽 *Pseudotheraptus devastans*	所有国家	
27	椰缘蝽 *Pseudotheraptus wayi*	所有国家	
28	棕榈象甲 *Rhynchophorus palmarum*	所有国家	
29	棉芽三纹夜蛾 *Sacadodes pyralis*	所有国家	
30	非洲桔硬蓟马 *Scirtothrips aurantii*	所有国家	
31	蛀茎夜蛾 *Sesamia calamistis*	所有国家	
32	高粱蛀茎夜蛾 *Sesamia cretica*	所有国家	
33	非洲木虱 *Trioza erytreae*	所有国家	
34	谷斑皮蠹 *Trogoderma granarium*	所有国家	

续表

编号	植物、有害生物及其携带者	来　源	例　外　情　况
	螨类	所有国家	
1	（瘿螨科）*Aceria guerreronis*	所有国家	
2	桔芽瘿螨 *Aceria sheldoni*	所有国家	
3	木薯单爪螨 *Mononychellus tanajoa*	所有国家	
4	（小爪螨属）*Oligonychus peruvianus*	所有国家	
	线虫		
1	剪股颖粒线虫 *Anguina agrostis*	所有国家	
2	禾谷类粒线虫 *Anguina graminis*	所有国家	
3	小麦粒线虫 *Anguina tritici*	所有国家	
4	叶芽线虫 *Aphelenchoides arachidis*	所有国家	
5	刺线虫 *Belonolaimus longicaudatus*	所有国家	
6	松材线虫 *Bursaphelenchus xylophilus*	所有国家	
7	仙人掌波线虫 *Cactodera cacti*	所有国家	
8	马铃薯腐烂茎线虫 *Ditylenchus destructor*	所有国家	
9	起绒草茎线虫 *Dytylenchus dipsaci*	所有国家	
10	异尾锥线虫 *Dolichodorus heterocephalus*	所有国家	
11	马铃薯白线虫 *Globodera pallida*	所有国家	
12	马铃薯金线虫 *Globadera rostochiensis*	所有国家	

续表

编号	植物、有害生物及其携带者	来源	例外情况
13	燕麦胞囊线虫 *Heterodera avenae*	所有国家	
14	大豆胞囊线虫 *Heterodera glycines*	所有国家	
15	杂草异皮线虫 *Heterodera graminis*	所有国家	
16	水稻异皮线虫 *Heterodera oryzae*	所有国家	
17	稻居异皮线虫 *Heterodera oryzicola*	所有国家	
18	点异皮线虫 *Heterodera punctata*	所有国家	
19	甘蔗异皮线虫 *Heterodera sacchari*	所有国家	
20	甜菜胞囊线虫 *Heterodera schachtii*	所有国家	
21	蜀黍异皮线虫 *Heterodera sorghi*	所有国家	
22	三叶草胞囊线虫 *Heterodera trifolii*	所有国家	
23	线蚀潜根线虫 *Hirschmaniella miticausa*	所有国家	
24	矛状线虫 *Hoplolaimus columbus*	所有国家	
25	印度纽带线虫 *Hoplolaimus indicus*	所有国家	
26	森林长针线虫 *Longidorus sylphus*	所有国家	
27	山茶根结线虫 *Meloidogyne camelliae*	所有国家	
28	奇特拉德根结线虫 *Meloidogyne chitwooki*	所有国家	
29	咖啡根结线虫 *Meloidogyne coffeicola*	所有国家	

续表

编号	植物、有害生物及其携带者	来　源	例 外 情 况
30	禾本科根结线虫 *Meloidogyne graminis*	所有国家	
31	假根结线虫 *Nacobbus aberrans*	所有国家	
32	咖啡根腐线虫 *Pratylenchus coffeae*	所有国家	
33	椰子红环腐线虫 *Rhadinaphelenchus cocophilus*	所有国家	
34	大囊小盘旋线虫 *Rotylenchulus macrodoratus*	所有国家	
35	山药螺旋线虫 *Scutellonema bradys*	所有国家	
36	具毒毛刺线虫 *Trichodorus viruliferus*	所有国家	
37	美洲剑线虫 *Xiphinema americanum*	所有国家	
38	裂尾剑线虫 *Xiphinema diversicaudatum*	所有国家	
	杂草		
1	野燕麦 *Avena fatua*	所有国家	
2	藜 *Chenopodium album*	所有国家	
3	丝路蓟 *Cirsium arvense*	所有国家	
4	欧洲蓟（翼蓟）*Cirsium vulgare*	所有国家	
5	猪殃殃 *Galium aparine*	所有国家	
6	卷茎蓼 *Polygonum convolvulus*	所有国家	
7	小酸模 *Rumex acetosella*	所有国家	
8	土大黄 *Rumex obtusifolius*	所有国家	
9	人厌槐叶苹 *Salvinua molesta*	所有国家	
10	菥蓂 *Thlaspi arvense*	所有国家	

续表

编号	植物、有害生物及其携带者	来 源	例 外 情 况
	未知病因		
1	苞片花叶病 Bract mosaic diseases	所有国家	
2	苞片花叶病 Bristle top	所有国家	
3	柑橘枯萎病菌 Citrus blight	所有国家	
4	棉花蓝病害 Cotton blue disease	所有国家	
5	干腐病 Dryout rot	所有国家	
6	Head drop	所有国家	
7	小叶病 Little leaf	所有国家	
8	小斑病 Little mottle	所有国家	
9	枯萎病 Natuna wilt	所有国家	
10	枯萎病 Sacorro wilt	所有国家	
11	枯萎病 Tatipaka wilt	所有国家	

表 2 限 制 物

编号	植物和携带者	来 源	例外情况
1	菠萝 *Ananus comosus*	所有国家	罐装食品
2	落花生 *Arachis hypogaea*	所有国家	罐装食品
3	茶属 *Camellia* 植物	所有国家	罐装食品
4	辣椒属 *Capsicum* 植物	所有国家	罐装食品
5	番木瓜 *Carica papaya*	所有国家	罐装食品
6	西瓜 *Citrullus lanatus*	所有国家	罐装食品
7	柑橘属 *Citrus* 植物	所有国家（注明的禁止物除外）	罐装食品
8	椰子 *Cocos nucifera* 及其干椰肉、干椰粉、椰壳纤维	所有国家（注明的禁止物除外） 所有国家	罐装食品
9	咖啡属 *Coffea* 植物	所有国家	罐装食品
10	野芋 *Colocasia antiquorum* var. *esculent* 及其粉状物	所有国家	罐装食品
11	甜瓜 *Cucumis melo*	所有国家	罐装食品
12	油棕 *Elaeis guineensis*	所有国家	—

续表

编号	植物和携带者	来　源	例外情况
13	大豆 *Glycine max* 及其大豆粉、全脂大豆粉	所有国家	罐装食品
14	棉属 *Gossypium* 植物及其棉籽粉	所有国家（注明的禁止物除外） 所有国家	—
15	橡胶属 *Hevea* 及其新鲜乳胶、块胶、废料	所有国家（注明的禁止物除外）	—
16	大麦 *Hordeum vulgare*	所有国家	罐装食品
17	甘薯 *Ipomoea batatas* 及甘薯粉	所有国家	罐装食品
18	羽扇豆属 *Lupinus* 植物	所有国家	—
19	番茄 *Lycopersicon esculentum*	所有国家	罐装食品
20	木薯 *Manihot esculenta* 以及木薯粉	所有国家（注明的禁止物除外） 所有国家	罐装食品
21	芭蕉属 *Musa* 及其粉状物	所有国家	罐装食品、绳索
22	烟草 *Nicotiana tabacum*	所有国家	香烟、丝烟、雪茄、和小雪茄
23	兰科 Orchidaceae 植物	所有国家	—
24	稻属 *Oryza* 植物及其米粉、米糠、脱脂米糠、去胚芽、米糠	所有国家（注明的禁止物除外） 所有国家	罐装食品
25	甘蔗属 *Saccharum* 植物	所有国家	—
26	马铃薯 *Solanum tuberosum* 及其面粉	所有国家	罐装食品
27	高粱 *Sorghum bicolor* 及其粉状物	所有国家	罐装食品
28	可可 *Theobroma cacao*	所有国家	罐装食品
29	小麦属 *Triticum* 植物及其粉状物	所有国家	罐装食品
30	绿豆 *Vigna radiata* 及其粉状物	所有国家	罐装食品
31	玉米 *Zea mays*、玉米碎块、玉米粗粉、玉米面	所有国家	罐装食品

Plant Quarantine Import Regulations

Plant Quarantine Act

Presently, the Plant Quarantine Act B. E. 2507 (1952) amended by the Plant Quarantine Act(No. 2) B. E. 2542(1999) is being enforced. The Act contains 27 Sections. In order to prevent the invasion of plant pests and diseases from outside the country, a number of regulations, notifications and orders are applied to imported plants and plant products under the Plant Quarantine Act.

Administrative Body of the Act

The Plant Quarantine Act B. E. 2507 (1952) amended by the Plant Quarantine Act (No. 2) B. E. 2542 (1999) is administered by the Department of Agriculture, Ministry of Agriculture and Cooperatives. The Department of Agriculture has assigned the Plant Quarantine Sub – Division, Agricultural Regulatory Division to carry out various functions authorized by the Act.

Plant Quarantine Import Requirements

Under the Act, the import of plants and plant products is categorized into 3 groups namely prohibited, restricted and unprohibited materials according to their economic importance and prevalence to plant pests and diseases at their place of origin. Following are import requirements of prohibited, restricted and unprohibited materials.

- **Prohibited materials:**

The import of the following items listed in Table 1 is not allowed. Exceptions are permitted only for cases approved in advance by the Department of Agriculture for the purpose of experimentation or research only.

(1) Plants and plant products designated by the Ministerial Notification, shipped from the areas specify by the Ministerial Notification.

(2) Plants, plants pests and diseases and carriers

(3) Soil and organic fertilizer

The requirement for importation of prohibited materials is set as follows:

(1) They must be imported via 3 plant quarantine stations namely; Bangkok International Airport, Bangkok Maritime Port and Bangkok General Post Office Plant Quarantine Station.

(2) They must bear phytosanitary certificate issued by the proper government agency of the exporting country.

(3) Phytosanitary certificate should be declared that the consignment is free from plant quarantine pests and diseases according to conditions prescribed the Director – General of the Department of Agriculture.

- **Restricted materials**

The import of the following items listed in Table 2 is allowed. The requirement for importation of restricted materials is set as follows:

(1) They must bear phytosanitary certificate issued by the proper government agency of the exporting country.

(2) The must be handled according to conditions prescribed by plant quarantine officer.

(3) Furthermore, importation of restricted materials, particularly, plants intended for propagation must be subjected to thoroughly examination.

- **Unprohibited materials**

Plant materials other than those classified as prohibited and restricted materials areunprohibited materials. Permission and a Phytosanitary Certificate are not required for importation. However, the imported unprohibited materials have to be notified for inspection at ports of entry. All materials are subjected to inspection and also put under quarantine treatment or destruction if plant quarantine pests and diseases are found.

Table 1　Prohibited Materials

No.	Plant, Plant pest or Carrier	Source	Exception
	Plant		
1	Plant in the genus *Citrus*, *Fortunella* and *Poncirus*	Africa Australia Central America Ceylon Europe India Indonesia Japan Near East Mediterranean Region South America United States of America	1. Preserved food. 2. Oranges (including navels, valencias, mandarins and its hybrids such as tangor), lemons, grapefruit (including pummelo) from Australia which must be handled according to the Department of Agriculture Notification: Conditions for Import of Fresh Citrus Fruit from Australia to Thailand dated 15 June 2004. 3. Oranges (including navels, tangerines, tangelos, valencias), lemons and grapefruit (including pummelo) from California, USA which must be handled according to specific commodity understanding 1 (SCU1): conditions for export of fresh citrus from California, USA to Thailand. 4. Oranges (including navels, tangerines, tangelos, valencias), grapefruit (including pummelo) and lemon (excluding sour lemon, Citrus limon) from Florida, USA which must be handled according to specific commodity understanding 2: Conditions for export of fresh citrus fruit from Florida, USA to Thailand. 5. Oranges (navels, tangerines, tangelos, valencias), lemons, limes, and grapefruit (including pommelo) from Arizona, USA which must be handled according to specific commodity understanding 4: Conditions for export of fresh citrus fruit from Arizona, USA to Thailand. 6. Citrus seeds from California, USA, French, Spain, Israel, South Africa and Australia which must be handled according to conditions stipulated by the Director – General of the Department of Agriculture and accompanied by Phytosanitary Certificate.
2	Coconut (*Cocos nucifera*)	Central America East Africa Guam India Philippines South America West Indies West Africa	1. Preserved food. 2. Finished products of coconut plants which have been processed by the method declared by the owner to the Director – General of the Department of Agriculture before the importation and the Director – General of the Department of Agriculture has decided the same are free of plant pests. 3. Dehusked coconut which must be handled according to conditions stipulated by the Director – General of the Department of Agriculture.
3	Plants in the genus *Gossypium*	Africa Central America Mexico United States of America Venezuela West Indies	Cotton lint imported for industrial use which must be accompanied by a Phytosanitary Certificate of the country of origin.

Continue Table

No.	Plant, Plant pest or Carrier	Source	Exception
4	Plants in the genus *Hevea* such as rubber etc. and carrier such as Fresh latex, Cup lump, Scrap.	Central America South America West Indies	
5	Cassava (*Manihot esculenta*)	Africa Brazil Indonesia	Preserved food Flour Sago
6	Plants in the genus *Oryza*	Central America Ceylon India Japan Philippines Republic of China South America United States of America West Africa West Indies	1. Preserved food 2. Finished products of plants in the genus Oryza spp. Which much be handled according to conditions stipulated by the Director – General of the Department of Agriculture 3. Rice, broken – milled rice and steamed rice which much be accompanied by Phytosanitary Certificate
	Genetically modified plant		
1	Plants in the genus *Agrostis*	All countries	
2	*Actinidia chinensis* Planch	All countries	
3	*Allium cepa* L.	All countries	
4	Plants in the genus *Amelanchier*	All countries	
5	*Ananus comosus* (L.) Merr.	All countries	
6	*Apium graveolens* var. *dulce* (MilL.) D. C.	All countries	
7	*Arabidopsis thaliana* L.	All countries	
8	Plants in the genus *Arachis*	All countries	
9	*Armoracia rusticana* P. Gaertner, Meyer & Scherb.	All countries	

Continue Table

No.	Plant，Plant pest or Carrier	Source	Exception
10	*Asparagus officinalis* Linn.	All countries	
11	*Atropa belladonna* L.	All countries	
12	*Avena sativa* L.	All countries	
13	*Beta vulgaris* L. sub sp. *vulgaris*	All countries	
14	Plants in the genus *Brassica*	All countries	
15	Plants in the genus *Camellia*	All countries	
16	Plants in the genus *Capsicum*	All countries	
17	Papaya （*Carica papaya* L.）	All countries	
18	Plants in the genus *Chrysanthemum*	All countries	
19	*Cichorium intybus* L.	All countries	
20	*Citrullus lanatus* (Thumb) Matsun & Nakai	All countries	
21	Plants in the genus *Citrus*	All countries	
22	*Cocos nucifera* L.	All countries	
23	Plants in the genus *Coffea*	All countries	
24	Plants in the genus *Cucumis*	All countries	
25	Plants in the genus *Cucurbita*	All countries	
26	*Daucus carota* L.	All countries	
27	Plants in the genus *Dendranthema*	All countries	
28	*Dianthus caryophyllus* L.	All countries	
29	*Elaeis guineensis* Jacq.	All countries	
30	Plants in the genus *Eucalyptus*	All countries	

Continue Table

No.	Plant, Plant pest or Carrier	Source	Exception
31	Plants in the genus *Fortunella*	All countries	
32	Plants in the genus *Fragaria*	All countries	
33	Plants in the genus *Gladiolus*	All countries	
34	*Glycine max* L.	All countries	1. Preserved food 2. Soybean use as raw material to produce animal feed or food for human consumption or use for industrial purpose
35	Plants in the genus *Gossypium*	All countries	
36	Plants in the genus *Helianthus*	All countries	
37	Plants in the genus *Hevea*	All countries	
38	Plants in the genus *Hordeum*	All countries	
39	Plants in the genus *Ipomoea*	All countries	
40	Plants in the genus *Juglans*	All countries	
41	*Lactuca sativa* L.	All countries	
42	*Lens culinaris* Medik.	All countries	
43	Plants in the genus *Linum*	All countries	
44	*Liquidambar styraciflua* L.	All countries	
45	Plant in the genus *Lupinus*	All countries	
46	*Lycopersicon esculentum* Miller	All countries	
47	Plant in the genus *Malus*	All countries	
48	*Manihot esculenta* Crantz.	All countries	

Continue Table

No.	Plant, Plant pest or Carrier	Source	Exception
49	Plant in the genus *Musa*	All countries	
50	*Medicago sativa* L.	All countries	
51	Tobacco (*Nicotiana tabacum* L.)	All countries	
52	Plant in the family Orchidaceae	All countries	
53	Plant in the genus *Oryza*	All countries	
54	Plant in the genus *Papaver*	All countries	
55	Plant in the genus *Pelargonium*	All countries	
56	Plants in the genus *Petunia*	All countries	
57	Plant in the genus *Phaseolus*	All countries	
58	Plant in the genus *Picea*	All countries	
59	*Pisum sativum*	All countries	
60	Plant in the genus *Poncirus*	All countries	
61	Plants in the genus *Populus*	All countries	
62	Plant in the genus *Prunus*	All countries	
63	Plant in the genus *Pyrus*	All countries	
64	*Ribes nigrum*	All countries	
65	Plant in the genus *Ricinus*	All countries	
66	Plant in the genus *Rosa*	All countries	
67	Plants in the genus *Rubus*	All countries	
68	Plants in the genus *Saccharum*	All countries	

Continue Table

No.	Plant, Plant pest or Carrier	Source	Exception
69	Plants in the genus *Solanum*	All countries	
70	Plants in the genus *Sorghum*	All countries	
71	Plants in the genus *Stylosanthes*	All countries	
72	*Theobroma cacao* L.	All countries	
73	*Torenia fournieri* Lind.	All countries	
74	Plants in the genus *Trifolium*	All countries	
75	Plants in the genus *Triticum*	All countries	
76	Plants in the genus *Vaccinium*	All countries	
77	Plants in the genus *Vigna*	All countries	
78	Plants in the genus *Vitis*	All countries	
79	Corn (*Zea mays* L.)	All countries	1. Preserved food 2. Maize use as raw material to produce animal feed or food for human consumption or use for industrial purpose
80	Plants in the genus *Zoysia*	All countries	
	Carrier		
1	Soil	All countries	—
2	Organic fertilizer	All countries	1. Organic fertilizer from animals except excrement of animal. 2. Organic fertilizer from plants which have been processed by the method declared by the owner to the Director – General of the Department of Agriculture before the importation and the Director – General of the Department of Agriculture has decided the same are free of plant pests.
	Plant pest		
	Fungi		
1	*Ascochyta gossypii*	All countries	
2	*Asperisporium caricae*	All countries	

Continue Table

No.	Plant, Plant pest or Carrier	Source	Exception
3	*Calonectria rigidiuscula*	All countries	
4	*Ceratocystis fimbriata*	All countries	
5	*Crinipellis perniciosa*	All countries	
6	*Deuterophoma tracheiphila*	All countries	
7	*Elsinoe australis*	All countries	
8	*Ephelis oryzae*	All countries	
9	*Haplobasidion musae*	All countries	
10	*Microcyclus ulei*	All countries	
11	*Moniliophthora roreri*	All countries	
12	*Mycosphaerella fijiensis*	All countries	
13	*Phaeoramularia angolensis*	All countries	
14	*Phellinus noxius*	All countries	
15	*Phymatotrichum omnivorum*	All countries	
16	*Phytophthora citricola*	All countries	
17	*Phytophthora hibernalis*	All countries	
18	*Phytophthora katsurae*	All countries	
19	*Rosellinia bunodes*	All countries	
20	*Rosellinia pepo*	All countries	
21	*Septoria limonum*	All countries	
22	*Sphaceloma manihoticola*	All countries	
23	*Uromyces musae*	All countries	
	Bacteria		
1	*Clavibacter michiganensis* subsp. *michiganensis*	All countries	
2	*Clavibacter michiganensis* subsp. *nebraskensis*	All countries	
3	*Clavibacter michiganensis* subsp. *sepedonicus*	All countries	
4	*Liberobacter africanum*	All countries	
5	*Pseudomonas rubrisubalbicans*	All countries	

Continue Table

No.	Plant, Plant pest or Carrier	Source	Exception
6	*Pseudomonas corrugate*	All countries	
7	*Xanthomonas axonopodis* pv. *citrumelo*	All countries	
8	*Xanthomonas campestris* pv. *cassavae*	All countries	
9	*Xanthomonas campestris* pv. *celebensis*	All countries	
10	*Xylella fastidiosa*	All countries	
	Protozoa		
1	*Nosema bombycis*	All countries	
2	*Phytomonas staheli*	All countries	
	Virus		
1	African cassava mosaic virus	All countries	
2	Banana streak virus	All countries	
3	Cassava brown streak virus	All countries	
4	Cassava common mosaic virus	All countries	
5	Cassava frog skin virus	All countries	
6	Cassava ivorian virus	All countries	
7	Cassava vein mosaic virus	All countries	
8	Citrus leaf rugose virus	All countries	
9	Citrus leprosies virus	All countries	
10	Citrus psorosis virus	All countries	
11	Citrus ringspot virus	All countries	
12	Citrus rubbery wood virus	All countries	
13	Citrus tatter leaf virus	All countries	
14	Citrus variegation virus	All countries	
15	Citrus vein enation virus	All countries	
16	Cocao necrosis virus	All countries	
17	Cocao red mottle virus	All countries	
18	Cocao swollen shoot virus	All countries	

Continue Table

No.	Plant, Plant pest or Carrier	Source	Exception
19	Cocao yellow mosaic virus	All countries	
20	Cocao yellow vein banding virus	All countries	
21	Coconut foliar decay virus	All countries	
22	Cotton anthocyanosis virus	All countries	
23	Cotton leaf crumple virus	All countries	
24	Cotton leaf mosaic virus	All countries	
25	Cotton leaf mottle virus	All countries	
26	Cotton stenosis virus	All countries	
27	Cotton terminal stunt virus	All countries	
28	East African cassava mosaic virus	All countries	
29	Indian cassava mosaic virus	All countries	
30	Maize Rayado fino virus	All countries	
31	Papaya bunchy top virus	All countries	
32	Papaya leaf curl virus	All countries	
33	Papaya mosaic virus	All countries	
34	Papaya waialua virus	All countries	
35	Rice dwarf virus	All countries	
36	Rice hoja blanca virus	All countries	
37	Rice yellow mottle virus	All countries	
38	Satsuma dwarf virus	All countries	
39	Sugarcane ramu stunt virus	All countries	
40	Tomato black ring virus	All countries	
41	Tomato bushy stunt virus	All countries	
42	Tomato ring spot virus	All countries	
43	Tomato spotted wilt virus	All countries	
	Viroid		
1	Citrus cachexia viroid	All countries	

Continue Table

No.	Plant, Plant pest or Carrier	Source	Exception
2	Citrus exocortis viroid	All countries	
3	Coconut cadang – cadang viroid	All countries	
4	Potato spindle tuber viroid	All countries	
5	Tinangaja viroid	All countries	
	Mycoplasma		
1	Banana marbling disease MLO	All countries	
2	Citrus witches broom MLO	All countries	
3	Coconut lethal yellowing MLO	All countries	
4	Sugarcane grassy shoot MLO	All countries	
	Insect		
1	*Anastepha fraterculus*	All countries	
2	*Anastepha ludens*	All countries	
3	*Anastepha oblique*	All countries	
4	*Anastepha suspensa*	All countries	
5	*Anthonomus grandis*	All countries	
6	*Anthonomus vestitus*	All countries	
7	*Artona catoxantha*	All countries	
8	*Bactrocera musae*	All countries	
9	*Bactrocera tryoni*	All countries	
10	*Caliothrips masculinus*	All countries	
11	*Ceratitis capitata*	All countries	
12	*Ceratitis cosyra*	All countries	
13	*Ceratitis quinaria*	All countries	
14	*Ceratitis rosa*	All countries	
15	*Diatraea saccharalis*	All countries	
16	*Erinnyis ello*	All countries	
17	*Leptopharsa heveae*	All countries	
18	*Lissorhoptrus oryzophilus*	All countries	
19	*Opogona sacchari*	All countries	

Continue Table

No.	Plant, Plant pest or Carrier	Source	Exception
20	*Oryctes boas*	All countries	
21	*Oryctes monoceros*	All countries	
22	*Pachymerus nucleorum*	All countries	
23	*Panthomorus cervinus*	All countries	
24	*Phenacoccus manihoti*	All countries	
25	*Prostephanus truncatus*	All countries	
26	*Pseudotheraptus devastans*	All countries	
27	*Pseuotheraptus wayi*	All countries	
28	*Rhynchophorus palmarum*	All countries	
29	*Sacadodes pyralis*	All countries	
30	*Scirtothrips aurantii*	All countries	
31	*Sesamia calamistis*	All countries	
32	*Sesamia cretica*	All countries	
33	*Trioza erytreae*	All countries	
34	*Trogoderma granarium*	All countries	
	Mite		
1	*Aceria guerreronis*	All countries	
2	*Aceria sheldoni*	All countries	
3	*Mononychellus tanajoa*	All countries	
4	*Oligonychus peruvianus*	All countries	
	Nematode		
1	*Anguina agrostis*	All countries	
2	*Anguinagraminis*	All countries	
3	*Anguina tritici*	All countries	
4	*Aphelenchoides arachidis*	All countries	
5	*Belonolaimus longicaudatus*	All countries	
6	*Bursaphelenchus xylophilus*	All countries	
7	*Cactodera cacti*	All countries	
8	*Ditylenchus destructor*	All countries	
9	*Dytylenchus dipsaci*	All countries	

Continue Table

No.	Plant, Plant pest or Carrier	Source	Exception
10	*Dolichodorus heterocephalus*	All countries	
11	*Globodera pallida*	All countries	
12	*Globadera rostochiensis*	All countries	
13	*Heterodera avenae*	All countries	
14	*Heterodera glycines*	All countries	
15	*Heterodera graminis*	All countries	
16	*Heterodera oryzae*	All countries	
17	*Heterodera oryzicola*	All countries	
18	*Heterodera punctata*	All countries	
19	*Heterodera sacchari*	All countries	
20	*Heterodera schachtii*	All countries	
21	*Heterodera sorghi*	All countries	
22	*Heterodera trifolii*	All countries	
23	*Hirschmaniella miticausa*	All countries	
24	*Hoplolaimus columbus*	All countries	
25	*Hoplolaimus indicus*	All countries	
26	*Longidorus sylphus*	All countries	
27	*Meloidogyne camelliae*	All countries	
28	*Meloidogyne chitwooki*	All countries	
29	*Meloidogyne coffeicola*	All countries	
30	*Meloidogyne graminis*	All countries	
31	*Nacobbus aberrans*	All countries	
32	*Pratylenchus coffeae*	All countries	
33	*Rhadinaphelenchus cocophilus*	All countries	
34	*Rotylenchulus macrodoratus*	All countries	
35	*Scutellonema bradys*	All countries	
36	*Trichodorus viruliferus*	All countries	
37	*Xiphinema americanum*	All countries	
38	*Xiphinema diversicaudatum*	All countries	

Continue Table

No.	Plant, Plant pest or Carrier	Source	Exception
	Weed		
1	*Avena fatua*	All countries	
2	*Chenopodium album*	All countries	
3	*Cirsium arvense*	All countries	
4	*Cirsium vulgare*	All countries	
5	*Galium aparine*	All countries	
6	*Polygonum convolvulus*	All countries	
7	*Rumex acetosella*	All countries	
8	*Rumex obtusifolius*	All countries	
9	*Salvinua molesta*	All countries	
10	*Thlaspi arvense*	All countries	
	Unknown Ethiology		
1	Bract mosaic diseases	All countries	
2	Bristle top	All countries	
3	Citrus blight	All countries	
4	Cotton blue disease	All countries	
5	Dryout rot	All countries	
6	Head drop	All countries	
7	Little leaf	All countries	
8	Little mottle	All countries	
9	Natuna wilt	All countries	
10	Sacorro wilt	All countries	
11	Tatipaka wilt	All countries	

Table 2 Restricted Materials

No.	Plant and Carrier	Origin	Exception
1	*Ananus comosus*	All countries	Preserved food
2	*Arachis hypogaea*	All countries	Preserved food
3	Plants in the genus *Camellia*	All countries	Preserved food
4	Plants in the genus *Capsicum*	All countries	Preserved food
5	*Carica papaya*	All countries	Preserved food
6	*Citrullus lanatus*	All countries	Preserved food
7	Plants in the genus *Citrus*	All countries other than those indicated in prohibited materials	Preserved food

Continue Table

No.	Plant and Carrier	Origin	Exception
8	*Cocos nucifera* and the following carries: dried copra, dried copra meal and coir	All countries other than those indicated in prohibited materials All countries	Preserved food
9	Plants in the genus *Coffea*	All countries	Preserved food
10	*Colocasia antiquorum* var. *esculenta* and the following carrier: flour	All countries	Preserved food
11	*Cucumis melo*	All countries	Preserved food
12	*Elaeis guineensis*	All countries	—
13	*Glycine max* and the following carriers: flour, soy meal and full fatted soy flour	All countries	Preserved food
14	Plants in the genus *Gossypium* and the following carriers: cotton seed meal	All countries other than those indicated in prohibited materials All countries	—
15	Plants in genus *Hevea* and the following carriers: fresh latex, cuplump, scrap	All countries other than those indicated in prohibited materials	—
16	*Hordeum vulgare*	All countries	Preserved food
17	*Ipomoea batatas* and the following carriers: flour	All countries	Preserved food
18	Plants in the genus *Lupinus*	All countries	—
19	*Lycopersicon esculentum*	All countries	Preserved food
20	*Manihot esculenta* and the following carriers flour	All countries other than those indicated in prohibited materials All countries	Preserved food
21	Plants in the genus *Musa* and the following carriers: flour	All countries	Preserved food, rope
22	*Nicotiana tabacum*	All countries	Cigarettes, smoking tobacco, cigars and cigarillos
23	Plants in family Orchidaceae	All countries	—
24	Plants in the genus *Oryza* and the following carriers: flour, rice bran, defatted rice bran and rice malt extract.	All countries other than those indicated in prohibited materials All countries	Preserved food
25	Plants in the genus *Saccharum*	All countries	—

Continue Table

No.	Plant and Carrier	Origin	Exception
26	*Solanum tuberosum* and the following carriers: flour	All countries	Preserved food
27	*Sorghum bicolor* and the following carriers: flour	All countries	Preserved food
28	*Theobroma cacao*	All countries	Preserved food
29	Plants in the genus *Triticum* and the following carriers: flour	All countries	Preserved food
30	*Vigna radiata* and the following carriers: flour	All countries	Preserved food
31	*Zea mays* and the following carriers: flour, cob, corn meal and corn flour	All countries	Preserved food

禁止进境的植物有害生物

（《植物检疫法案》B. E. 2507、(No. 7) B. E. 2550 规定）

基于《植物检疫法案》B. E. 2507 第 6 款及《植物检疫法案》（第 2 号）B. E. 2542 修正案，农业合作部部长根据植物检疫委员会的建议发布以下通知。

本通知中列出的任何来源的植物有害生物都被视为违禁物，因为这些有害生物属于检疫性有害生物。

本通知在政府公报上发布 60 日后开始生效，并持续有效。

发布于 7 月 27 日，B. E. 2550
Thira Sutabutra
（Thira Sutabutra 教授）
农业合作部部长

植物有害生物名录

真菌类

1. 禾谷角担菌 *Ceratobasidium cereale* Murray & Burpee
2. 黄色镰刀菌 *Fusarium culmorum*（W. G. Sm.）Sacc.
3. 尖孢镰刀菌瓜类致病变种 *Fusarium oxysporum* f. sp. *melonis*（Leach & Currence）Snyder &Hansen
4. 尖孢镰刀菌百合致病变种 *Fusarium oxysporum* f. sp. *lilii* Imle
5. 尖孢镰刀菌水仙致病变种 *Fusarium oxysporum* f. sp. narcissi Snyder & Hansen
6. 玉蜀黍球梗孢菌 *Kabatiella zeae* Narita & Y. Hirats.
7. 雪腐明梭孢 *Monographella nivalis*（Schaffnit）E. MulL.
8. 麝香石竹霜霉 *Peronospora dianthicola* Barthelet
9. 安第斯茎点霉 *Phoma andigena* Turkenst.
10. 天冬柄锈菌 *Puccinia asparagi* DC.
11. 瓜角斑壳针孢 *Septoria cucurbitacearum* Sacc.
12. 向日葵壳针孢 *Septoria helianthi* ElL. & Kellerman
13. 小麦矮腥黑穗病菌 *Tilletia controversa* J. G. Kuhn
14. 唐菖蒲生条黑粉菌 *Urocystis gladiolicola* Ainsworth
15. 唐菖蒲单胞锈菌 *Uromyces gladioli* Henn.

细菌类

16. 香石竹凋萎病菌 *Burkholderia caryophylli*（Burkholder）Yabuuchi et al.
17. 萎蔫短杆菌萎蔫致病变种 *Curtobacterium flaccumfaciens* pv. *flaccumfaciens*（Hedges）Collins & Jones
18. 郁金香黄色疱斑病菌 Curtobacterium flaccumfaciens pv. oortii（Saaltink & Maas Geest.）Collins & Jones
19. 边缘假单胞菌边缘致病变种 *Pseudomonas marginalis* pv. *marginalis*（Brown）Stevens
20. 恶臭假单胞菌 *Pseudomonas putida*（Trevisan）Migula

21. 丁香假单胞菌致黑致病变种 *Pseudomonas syringae* pv. *atrofaciens* （McCulloch） Young et al.
22. 丁香假单胞菌 *Pseudomonas syringae* pv. *coronafaciem* （Elliott） Young et al.
23. 葡萄根瘤菌 *Rhizobium vitis* （Ophel & Kerr） Young et al.
24. 葡萄溃疡病菌 *Xanthomonas axonopodis* pv. *vitians* （Brown） Vauterin et al.
25. 野油菜黄单胞菌 *Xanthomonas campestris* pv. *zantedeschiae* （Joubert & Truter） Dye
26. （黄单胞菌属） *Xanthomonas hortorum* pv. *carotae* （Kendrick） Vauterin et al.
27. 葡萄细菌性疫病菌 *Xylophilus ampelinus* （Panagopoulos） Willems et al.

病毒类

28. 南芥菜花叶病毒 Arabis mosaic nepovirus
29. 芦笋病毒 1 Asparagus virus－1
30. 芦笋病毒 2 Asparagus virus－2
31. 芹菜花叶病毒 Celery mosaic virus
32. 葡萄藤病毒 A Grapevine virus A
33. 葡萄藤病毒 B Grapevine virus B
34. 木槿黄萎环斑病毒 Hibiscus chlorotic ring spot virus
35. 凤仙花坏死斑点病毒 Impatiens necrotic spot virus
36. 凤仙花坏死病毒 Impatiens necrotic virus
37. 玉米褪绿斑驳病毒 Maize chlorotic mottle virus
38. 天竺葵属黄萎环状病毒 Pelargonium chlorotic ring pattern virus
39. 天竺葵属带状斑驳病毒 Pelargonium line pattern carmo virus
40. 天竺葵属环斑病毒 Pelargonium ring spot virus
41. 天竺葵属脉明病毒 Pelargonium vein clearing virus
42. 天竺葵属环斑病毒 Pelargonium zonate spot virus
43. 黄瓜花叶病毒 Pepino mosaic virus
44. 土豆病毒 S Potato virus S
45. 郁金香花色变异病毒 Tulip breaking virus
46. 马蹄莲属花叶病毒 Zantedeschia mosaic virus
47. 西葫芦黄叶病毒 Zucchini yellow mosaic virus

植原体类

48. 葡萄藤枯黄植原体 *Grapevine yellows phytoplasmas* Seemuller et al.

昆虫类

49. 茶长本圆蚧 *Abgrallaspis cyanophylli* （Signoret）
50. 茶小卷叶蛾 *Adoxophyes honmai* （Yasuda）
51. 茶角纹小卷蛾 *Adoxophyes privatana* （Walker）
52. （黄卷蛾属） *Archips machlopis* Meyrick
53. （黄卷蛾属） *Archips podana* （Scopoli）
54. 角纹卷叶虫 *Archips xylosteanus* （Linnaeus）
55. 春藤圆蚧 *Aspidiotus nerii* （Bouche）
56. （柏盾蚧属） Carulaspis minima Borchsenius
57. 相思子异型小卷蛾 *Cryptophlebia illepida* （Butler）
58. 小卷蛾 *Cydia fabivora* （Meyrick）
59. 黑姬卷叶蛾 *Cydia leucostoma* （Meyrick）
60. 波氏白背盾蚧 *Diaspis boisduvalii* Signoret

61. 围盾介壳虫 *Fiorinia fioriniae*（Targioni）
62. 茶尖角盾蚧 *Fiorinia theae* Green
63. 东花蓟马 *Frankliniella tritici*（Fitch）
64. 麻小食心虫 *Grapholita delineana* Walker
65. 李小食心虫 *Grapholita funebrana* Treitschke
66. 苹小食心虫 *Grapholita inopinata* Heinrich
67. （白片盾蚧属）*Lopholeucaspis cockerelli*（Grandpre & Charmoy）
68. 茶片盾蚧 *Parlatoria theae* Cocekrell
69. 智利果卷蛾 *Proeulia auraria*（Clarke）
70. 卷蛾 *Proeulia chrysopteris*（Butler）
71. 桑蓟马 *Pseudodendrothrips mori*（Niwa）
72. 葡萄黑蓟马 *Retithrips syriacus*（Mayet）
73. 刺盾蚧 *Selenaspidus articulatus*（Morgan）
74. 甘蔗小卷蛾 *Tetramoera schistaceana*（Snellen）
75. 褐翅蓟马 *Thrips fuscipennis* Haliday
76. 唐菖蒲简蓟马 *Thrips simplex*（Morison）

螨类

77. *Amphitetetranychus viennensis*（Zacher）
78. （苔螨属）*Bryobia graminum*（Schrank）
79. （苔螨属）*Bryobia lagodechiana* Reck
80. 长腿红蜘蛛 *Bryobia praetiosa* Koch
81. 果苔螨 *Bryobia rubrioculus*（Scheuten）
82. 食菌嗜木螨 *Caloglyphus mycophagus*（Megnin）
83. 斑真叶螨 *Eutetranychus banksi*（McGregor）
84. 枥始叶螨北方亚种 *Eotetranychus carpini*（Oudemans）
85. 路易氏始叶螨 *Eotetranychus lewisi*（McGregor）
86. 弯钩始叶螨 *Eotetranychus uncatus* Garman
87. （单爪螨属）*Mononychellus planki*（McGregor）
88. （小爪螨属）*Oligonychus gossypii*（Zacher）
89. （小爪螨属）*Oligonychus grypus* Baker & Pritchard
90. （小爪螨属）*Oligonychus ilicis*（McGregor）
91. 印度小爪螨 *Oligonychus indicus*（Hirst）
92. 樟小爪螨 *Oligonychus yothersi*（McGregor）
93. 长毛根螨 *Rhizoglyphus setosus* Manson
94. 野生叶螨 *Tetranychus desertorum* Banks
95. 伊氏叶螨 *Tetranychus evansi* Baker & Pritchard
96. 草莓叶螨 *Tetranychus lambi* Pritchard & Baker
97. （叶螨属）*Tetranychus lombardinii* Baker & Pritchard
98. （叶螨属）*Tetranychus mexicanus*（McGregor）
99. 长毛粉螨 *Tyrophagus dimidiatus*（Hermann）
100. （食酪螨属）*Tyrophagus similis* Volgin

线虫类

101. 菊花滑刃线虫 *Aphelenchoides ritzemabosi*（Schwartz）Steiner and Buhrer

102. 马铃薯腐败线虫 *Ditylenchus destructor*（Thorne）

103. 盔形纽带线虫 *Hoplolaimus galeatus*（Cobb）Thorne

- 皇家公报，第124卷，109 D 专区，第6页，日期：9月5日 B E. 2550（2007）
- 本文为非官方英文翻译件。如泰文与英文的含义有任何不一致之处，以泰语版本为准。

Specification of plant pests as prohibited articles

(under the Plant Quarantine Act B. E. 2507 (No. 7) B. E. 2550)

By virtue of Article 6 of the Plant Quarantine Act B. E. 2507, revised by the Plant Quarantine Act (No. 2) B. E. 2542, the Minister of Agriculture and Cooperatives, through the recommendation of the Plant Quarantine Committee, hereby issue the following notification.

Plant pests from any source listed with this notification are considered as prohibited articles because they are quarantine pests.

This notification shall enter into force 60 days after the date of its proclamation in the Royal Gazette, and shall remain valid henceforth.

Given on 27 July B. E. 2550
Thira Sutabutra
(Professor Thira Sutabutra)
Minister
Ministry of Agriculture and Cooperatives

List of plant pests

Fungi

1. *Ceratobasidium cereale* Murray & Burpee
2. *Fusarium culmorum* (W. G. Sm.) Sacc.
3. *Fusarium oxysporum* f. sp. *melonis* (Leach & Currence) Snyder & Hansen
4. *Fusarium oxysporum* f. sp. *lilii Imle*
5. *Fusarium oxysporum* f. sp. *narcissi* Snyder & Hansen
6. *Kabatiella zeae* Narita & Y. Hirats.
7. *Monographella nivalis* (Schaffnit) E. Mull.
8. *Peronospora dianthicola* Barthelet
9. *Phoma andigena* Turkenst.
10. *Puccinia asparagi* DC.
11. *Septoria cucurbitacearum* Sacc.
12. *Septoria helianthi* Ell. & Kellerman
13. *Tilletia controversa* J. G. Kuhn
14. *Urocystis gladiolicola* Ainsworth
15. *Uromyces gladioli* Henn.

Bacteria

16. *Burkholderia caryophylli* (Burkholder) Yabuuchi et al.
17. *Curtobacterium flaccumfaciens* pv. *flaccumfaciens* (Hedges) Collins & Jones
18. *Curtobacterium flaccumfaciens* pv. *oortii* (Saaltink & Maas Geest.) Collins & Jones

19. *Pseudomonas marginalis* pv. *marginalis* (Brown) Stevens
20. *Pseudomonas putida* (Trevisan) Migula
21. *Pseudomonas syringae* pv. *atrofaciens* (McCulloch) Young et al.
22. *Pseudomonas syringae* pv. *coronafaciens* (Elliott) Young et al.
23. *Rhizobium vitis* (Ophel & Kerr) Young et al.
24. *Xanthomonas axonopodis* pv. *vitians* (Brown) Vauterin et al.
25. *Xanthomonas campestris* pv. *zantedeschiae* (Joubert & Truter) Dye
26. *Xanthomonas hortorum* pv. *carotae* (Kendrick) Vauterin et al.
27. *Xylophilus ampelinus* (Panagopoulos) Willems et al.

Virus

28. Arabis mosaic nepovirus
29. Asparagus virus - 1
30. Asparagus virus - 2
31. Celery mosaic virus
32. Grapevine virus A
33. Grapevine virus B
34. Hibiscus chlorotic ring spot virus
35. Impatiens necrotic spot virus
36. Impatiens necrotic virus
37. Maize chlorotic mottle virus
38. Pelargonium chlorotic ring pattern virus
39. Pelargonium line pattern carmovirus
40. Pelargonium ring spot virus
41. Pelargonium vein clearing virus
42. Pelargonium zonate spot virus
43. Pepino mosaic virus
44. Potato virus S
45. Tulip breaking virus
46. Zantedeschia mosaic virus
47. Zucchini yellow mosaic virus

Phytoplasma

48. Grapevine yellows phytoplasmas Seemuller et al.

Insect

49. *Abgrallaspis cyanophylli* (Signoret)
50. *Adoxophyes honmai* (Yasuda)
51. *Adoxophyes privatana* (Walker)
52. *Archips machlopis* Meyrick
53. *Archips podana* (Scopoli)
54. *Archips xylosteanus* (Linnaeus)
55. *Aspidiotus nerii* (Bouche)
56. *Carulaspis minima* Borchsenius
57. *Cryptophlebia illepida* (Butler)
58. *Cydia fabivora* (Meyrick)

59. *Cydia leucostoma* (Meyrick)
60. *Diaspis boisduvalii* Signoret
61. *Fiorinia fioriniae* (Targioni)
62. *Fiorinia theae* Green
63. *Frankliniella tritici* (Fitch)
64. *Grapholita delineana* Walker
65. *Grapholita funebrana* Treitschke
66. *Grapholita inopinata* Heinrich
67. *Lopholeucaspis cockerelli* (Grandprè & Charmoy)
68. *Parlatoria theae* Cocekrell
69. *Proeulia auraria* (Clarke)
70. *Proeulia chrysopteris* (Butler)
71. *Pseudodendrothrips mori* (Niwa)
72. *Retithrips syriacus* (Mayet)
73. *Selenaspidus articulatus* (Morgan)
74. *Tetramoera schistaceana* (Snellen)
75. *Thrips fuscipennis* Haliday
76. *Thrips simplex* (Morison)

Mite

77. *Amphitetetranychus viennensis* (Zacher)
78. *Bryobia graminum* (Schrank)
79. *Bryobia lagodechiana* Reck
80. *Bryobia praetiosa* Koch
81. *Bryobia rubrioculus* (Scheuten)
82. *Caloglyphus mycophagus* (Megnin)
83. *Eutetranychus banksi* (McGregor)
84. *Eotetranychus carpini* (Oudemans)
85. *Eotetranychus lewisi* (McGregor)
86. *Eotetranychus uncatus* Garman
87. *Mononychellus planki* (McGregor)
88. *Oligonychus gossypii* (Zacher)
89. *Oligonychus grypus* Baker & Pritchard
90. *Oligonychus ilicis* (McGregor)
91. *Oligonychus indicus* (Hirst)
92. *Oligonychus yothersi* (McGregor)
93. *Rhizoglyphus setosus* Manson
94. *Tetranychus desertorum* Banks
95. *Tetranychus evansi* Baker & Pritchard
96. *Tetranychus lambi* Pritchard & Baker
97. *Tetranychus lombardinii* Baker & Pritchard
98. *Tetranychus mexicanus* (McGregor)
99. *Tyrophagus dimidiatus* (Hermann)
100. *Tyrophagus similis* Volgin

Nematode

101. *Aphelenchoides ritzemabosi* (Schwartz) Steiner and Buhrer
102. *Ditylenchus destructor* (Thorne)
103. *Hoplolaimus galeatus* (Cobb) Thorne

• The Royal Gazette, Vol. 124, Special Part 109 D, Page 6, Dated 5 September B. E. 2550 (2007)

• This is an unofficial English translation. In case of any different in meaning between the Thai text and the English translation, the Thai text shall be applied.

动物疫病法

（B. E. 2499（1956））

普密蓬．阿度德国王陛下

在泰历 2499 年 9 月 28 日

即在位 11 年颁布

根据普密蓬．阿度德国王陛下颁布王室命令，在此宣布从现在开始执行一个关于动物疫病的法律；根据人民代表通过的提议，国王陛下很荣幸地颁布下列法规：

第 1 条 本法应称为“动物疫病法 B. E. 2499（1956）”。

第 2 条 本法在其在政府公报中公布后 90 天后实施。

第 3 条 废止下列法规：

（1）家畜和野生动物疫病法 B. E. 2474

（2）家畜和野生动物疫病法（修订）B. E. 2478

（3）家畜和野生动物疫病法（第 3 版）B. E. 2497

所有以此法相抵触的法律、条例或实施细则，均以此法为准。

第 4 条 在本法中：

动物指

*（1）大象、马、奶牛、水牛、驴、骡、山羊、绵羊、猪、狗、猫、兔、长臂猿及其用于繁殖的精液和胚胎（未发育出完整内脏组织的幼小动物）。

（2）禽类：鸟、鸡、鸭、鹅及其受精卵。

（3）由部颁条例规定的其他动物。

畜体 指未成为食品或最终成品的动物的整个或部分胴体，还包括未加工成最终成品的动物生前的牙齿、角和鬃毛。

疫病 指牛瘟、出血性败血症、炭疽、伊（凡斯）氏锥虫病、鼻疽病、流行性淋巴管炎（腺疫）、口蹄疫、猪霍乱（猪瘟）和其他由部颁条例规定的疾病。

物主 指物权的拥有者。它还应包括在涉及动物时物主不出现的情况下，动物的管理者或监护者。

进境口岸 指动物和畜体进口的地点。

出境口岸 指动物和畜体出口的地点。

动物检疫站 指扣押动物或畜体进行疫病检疫的地点。

交易 指中间人式的买卖。

主管官员 指部长指派的人员。

检疫官 指家畜发展部检疫人员或总长委任的人员。

注册主任 指由部长委任负责登记的人员。

兽医师 指家畜发展部的兽医人员或由部长委任的人员。

司长 指家畜发展部的首长。

主管部门 指本法规定的负责实施的部门。

第 5 条 从属于国防部的动物不在本法管理之内。

（译者注：公元年 = 泰历年（B. E.）－543）

第6条　本法应只对进口、出口或过境的狗、猫、兔、猴、长臂猿及其精液、禽类、鸟、鸡、鸭、鹅及其受精卵实施检疫，其他情况由皇家政令规定。

第7条　实施本法的主管部门是农业部，其有权委任主管官员、注册主任和兽医师，有权签发部颁条例规定应执行的实施细则，有权签发许可证和确定不高于附表中规定的收费，有权在特殊情况下减免收费和有权规定执行本法时其他事情。

签发的部颁条例应在政府公报中公布后实施。

*依据动物疫病法（第2版）B. E. 2542 第3条废止原第4条中“动物”的释义并从此用现印刷的内容替代。

第1章　疫病的预防

第8条　在未依据第2章的规定宣布为非疫区的地方，或未依据第3章的规定宣布为疫区、疑似疫区、暂时疫区的地方，如果动物染上或死于已知疫病，或不明原因地患病或死亡，或在同一村庄或相邻的地方在7天的时间内有2只以上的动物患病或死于相同的症状，物主应在动物患病或死亡后24小时内通知当地主管官员、检疫官或兽医师。

在上述的情况中，如果动物患病，物主应在病畜附近看守，禁止物主和其他人将病畜迁移；如果动物病死，物主应在畜体附近看守，禁止物主和其他人将畜体迁移、分割等操作。在遇到大畜体的情况下，如果主管官员、检疫官或兽医师在动物死亡后48小时内未处理畜体，物主应将畜体深埋至少50厘米深，并盖土高于地面50厘米。

第9条　接到第8条中的通知或有理由怀疑动物染上或死于某种疫病时，主管官员或检疫官应有权签发书面命令让物主做如下处理：

（1）在当地按照规定的方法将病畜或疑似患病的动物进行关押、隔离和迁移。

（2）在无法烧毁的情况下，可以命令用其他被认为合适的方法进行销毁。

（3）在当地按照规定的方法将与病畜、疑似患病的动物或死亡动物同群的其他动物进行关押、隔离和迁移。

第10条　接到第8条中的通知或发现疑似病畜发病或死于某种疫病时，兽医师有权进入相关地方并对动物或畜体进行检疫，并有权签发书面命令让物主做如下处理：

（1）在当地按照规定的方法或提出合适的处理方法将病畜或疑似患病的动物进行关押、隔离和迁移。

（2）在规定的地方深埋或烧毁整具畜体或其部分。在无法深埋或烧毁的情况下，可以要求用其他被认为合适的方法进行销毁。

（3）在当地按照规定的或认为适于动物受到保护、抵御疫病的方法，将与病畜、疑似患病的动物或死亡动物同群的其他动物进行关押、隔离和迁移。

（4）由部委任的总长按照条例的规定，销毁染疫的或接触携带疫病的动物或畜体的动物。在这种情况下，除非物主故意违反本法的规定，否则物主应取得部颁条例规定的、金额不低于动物在疫病出现前的当地市场价的一半的补偿。

（5）用规定的方法消除动物饲料或畜体中的疫病原。

（6）用规定的方法清洁并消毒场地、建筑物和运输工具等物体。

第2章　非　疫　区

第11条　为了防止动物疫病的传播，部长有权在他认为合适的时候在政府公报中公告某个地方或其部分区域为非疫区。这种公告应指出针对何种动物和何种疫病。

第12条　当依据第11条的规定公告为非疫区的，未经总长或总长授权的兽医师的书面许可，任何不得将动物或畜体移入或通过这些区域。

第13条　在非疫区内，动物的物主有义务遵守第8条的规定，主管官员和检疫官具有第9条赋予的权力，兽医师具有第 10 条和第 18 条赋予的权力。

第 14 条 在非疫区内，如果有疫病出现或有理由认为有疫病存在，市级政府首长或兽医师根据第 3 章的规定将该地区宣布为疫区、疑似疫区或暂时疫区。

第 3 章 疫 区

第 15 条 在市级地区，如果出现疫病或疑似疫病时，政府首长根据具体情况有权公告该地区或其部分区域为疫区或疑似疫区。这种公告应指出是何种疫病，并在该地区的政府办公室、市府办公室、村镇办公室、村长办公室及集会的地方张贴。

第 16 条 如果兽医师认为在他那里或附近出现的疫病会扩散时，他应有权书面公告发现疫点的半径不大于 5 公里的区域为暂时疫区。公告中应指出是何种动物和何种疫病，并在该地区的村镇办公室、村长办公室及集会的地方张贴。公告发布后 30 天内有效。

第 17 条 当依据第 16 条的规定公告为疫区或疑似疫区或依据第 16 条的规定公告为暂时疫区的，未经兽医师的书面许可，任何人不得将上述区域内的动物、畜体迁移或进出该区域。

第 18 条 在依据第 16 条的规定公告为疫区或疑似疫区或依据第 16 条的规定公告为暂时疫区内，兽医师具有第 10 条赋予的权力和以下权力：

（1）向所有物主的签发通知或指示，要求物主上报某一种动物的数量，并在他认为合适时，将动物带来进行检疫、保护或疫病预防。

（2）命令动物的物主给经检疫或经防疫处理的动物施加标识。

（3）命令对运送动物或畜体来检疫的运输工具进行检疫，并在必要时，对相关的动物和畜体进行检疫观察。

第 19 条 在依据第 16 条的规定公告为疫区或疑似疫区或依据第 16 条的规定公告为暂时疫区内，如果动物患病或死亡，其物主应在动物出现症状或死亡后 12 小时内通知主管官员、检疫官或兽医师。第 8 条第 2 段应根据实际情况来执行。

第 20 条 在宣布为疫区或疑似疫区的政府行政区，如果疫情出现消除或未发现任何疫点，政府首长应撤消该通告。

第 4 章 动物和畜体的交易管理

第 21 条 未取得注册主任的许可，任何人不得买卖部颁条例中规定的大象、马、水牛、绵羊、山羊、猪等动物及其畜体。

* **第 21 条** （b）未取得注册主任的许可，任何人不得出售、配送、处理、交换或用于买卖目的地拥有部颁条例规定的大象、马、奶牛、水牛、山羊、绵羊、猪等动物用于繁殖的精液和胚胎。应依据由总长制订并在政府公报中公告的实施细则、步骤和条件来申请并取得许可。

** **第 22 条** 依据第 21 条或第 21 条（b）取得的许可应在签发当年内有效。

第 23 条 从事动物或畜体交易的人应遵守许可证规定的条件。

*** **第 24 条** 依据第 21 条或第 21 条（b）取得的许可条证的人违反本法的规定或许可证规定的条件，兽医师应有权将许可证收缴回注册主任。注册主任认为合适时，可以命令中止或撤消该许可证。

* 依据动物疫病法（第 2 版）B. E. 2542 第 4 条修订第 21 条（b）。

** 依据动物疫病法（第 2 版）B. E. 2542 第 5 条废止原文并从此用现印刷的内容替代。

*** 依据动物疫病法（第 2 版）B. E. 2542 第 6 条废止原文并从此用现印刷的内容替代。

第 5 章 其 他

第 25 条 如果动物在其他场所上患病或死亡时其物主并未出现，该场所的主人应有义务作为动物的主人依据本法的规定来处理。当动物的真正主人明确后，场所的主人应有权从动物的主人那里得到实际费用的补偿。

第 26 条　如果动物在公共场所上患病或死亡时其物主并未出现或场所的主人未明确，主管官员、检疫官或兽医师有权在他认为该场所合适的地方对动物或畜体实施检疫。当认为这些相关的畜体需要深埋时，在必需防止疫病扩散的情况下，兽医师可以在上述场所销毁动物或畜体或深埋这些畜体。

当动物的真正主人明确后，主管官员、检疫官或兽医师应有权得到在上述场所实际花费的补偿。

* **第 27 条**　有物主跟从或由运输运输工具运送的动物，如果其明显接触过疫病或已成为疫病携带者，兽医师应有权在必要的情况下命令在合适的地点实施检疫。

第 28 条　未经兽医师的书面许可，任何人不得解剖按本法规定深埋的畜体。

第 29 条　当在运输工具、建筑物或其他场所很明显或有理由地认为已出现疫情或疫病携带动物时，兽医师应有权召集上述运输工具来实施检疫或进入上述建筑物或场所，物主应给予合理的便利。

进入上述建筑物或场所应在白天进行。

第 30 条　主管部门应有权在政府公报上刊登通告：

（1）规定进出境口岸。

（2）在国外出现疫情或疑似疫情的情况下，禁止该国的动物或畜体进境或过境。

（3）在下列情况下，制定无偿扣押、销毁或退运动物、畜体的实施细则：

a. 动物或畜体违反本法的规定进境或过境。

b. 在动物或畜体按照本法的规定进境或过境过程中，动物、畜体染疫或携带病原。

第 31 条　未取得总长的许可证，任何人不得将动物或畜体进口、出口或过境。总长或总长授权的人认为合适时，可以将这些相关条件在许可证上加以规定。

依据本条规定，动物或畜体应根据具体情况，在原定的进出境口岸进口、出口或过境，除非总长或总长授权的人命令在其他口岸进行。

第 32 条　从事动物或畜体进口、出口或过境的任何人应遵守部颁条例。

* **第 33 条**　总长应有权在政府公报中通告：

（1）任命检查员检查本法的实施情况。

（2）建立动物检疫站和动物中转仓库。

（3）制订销毁染疫动物或携带疫病的动物、畜体的条例。

（4）制订对进口、出口、过境或在国内迁移的动物及其畜体的检疫和消毒条例。

第 34 条　任何人将大象、马、奶牛、水牛、山羊、绵羊、猪、用于繁殖的精液和胚胎、部颁条例规定的其他动物或部颁条例规定的动物畜体转移到其他省区，应首先取得当地相关兽医师的许可。

关于上述的许可证的签发，兽医师可以在许可证上增加符合由总长制订的条例规定的运输动物的工具的类型、运输途径、途经的动物中转站和动物检疫站等必要的条件。偶尔引领动物进行觅食或劳作不在此范围内。

第 35 条　带动物穿越动物检疫站区域的人应遵守相关的部颁条例。

第 36 条　出口动物或畜体进行海外销售的人应遵守相关的部颁条例。

第 37 条　收取诸如出口动物或畜体的租房费等费用的 50% 应截留并作为基金用于管理支出或海外销售动物、畜体的出口支出等。其余的应限定为国家税收。

第 38 条　检疫员应有权拘留违反本法规定的人，扣押与违法行为相关的动物、畜体或其他物品，并根据犯罪程序法的规定交付质询官，以执行第 51 条的规定。

* 依据动物疫病法（第 2 版）B. E. 2542 第 7 条废止原文并从此用现印刷的内容替代。

* 依据动物疫病法（第 2 版）B. E. 2542 第 7 条废止原文并从此用现印刷的内容替代。

* 依据动物疫病法（第 2 版）B. E. 2542 第 8 条废止原文并从此用现印刷的内容替代。

* 依据动物疫病法（第 2 版）B. E. 2542 第 9 条废止原文并从此用现印刷的内容替代。

第 6 章　处　　罚

* **第 39 条**　违反第 8 条第 1 节的，应被处不高于 2000 铢的罚款。

*第40条 违反第8条第2节、第9条中有主管官员和检疫官的命令、第19条或第29条第1节中运输工具、建筑物或相关场所的物主阻碍或未能向兽医师提供相关的便利，应被单处或并处不超过2个月的有期徒刑或不高于4000铢的罚款。

*第41条 违反第10条、第18条或第23条规定中兽医师的命令的，应被单处或并处不超过6个月的有期徒刑或不高于10000铢的罚款。

*第42条 违反第12条、第17条、第21条、第21（b）条或第28条的规定的，应被单处或并处不超过1年的有期徒刑或不高于20000铢的罚款。

第43条 违反第13条的规定或在违反第8条第1节的情况下，应按第39条进行处罚。

在违反第8条第2节的情况下或违反第9条中有主管官员和检疫官的命令的，应按第40条进行处罚。

在违反第10条或第18条兽医师的命令的情况下，应按第41条进行处罚。

**第44条 场地的主人不能履行第25条规定的义务的，应被处不高于2000铢的罚款。

***第45条 （此条已废止）。

****第46条 违反第30条（2）中部长公告的，应被单处或并处不超过2年的有期徒刑或不高于40000铢的罚款。

*第47条 违反第31条第1节或第3节、第31条第2节许可证中规定的条件的，应被单处或并处不超过2年的有期徒刑或不高于40000铢的罚款。

*第48条 违反第32条、第35条或第36条的，应被单处或并处不超过2个月的有期徒刑或不高于4000铢的罚款。

*第49条 违反第34条第1节或第34条第2节许可证中规定的条件的，应被单处或并处不超过2个月的有期徒刑或不高于10000铢的罚款。

*第50条 使用假标识、更改动物标识伪造主管官员手迹、销毁或更改有资格官员放置在动物、集装箱或动物畜体包装上的标识的，应被单处或并处不超过2个月的有期徒刑或不高于10000铢的罚款。

**第51条 当根据本法的规定，违法行为只是给予罚款处罚，总长或由其委派的官员应有权处理这种案件。当被指控的违法者在规定的时间内支付规定的数量的罚款后，案件应被视为结案。

***第52条 总长被授权根据由其起草并经财政部核准的条例的规定支付奖金或酬金。

*依据动物疫病法（第2版）B. E. 2542第10条废止原文并从此用现印刷的内容替代。

**依据动物疫病法（第2版）B. E. 2542第11条废止原第45条。

***依据动物疫病法（第2版）B. E. 2542第12条废止原第45条。

****依据动物疫病法（第2版）B. E. 2542第13条废止原文并从此用现印刷的内容替代。

*依据动物疫病法（第2版）B. E. 2542第13条废止原文并从此用现印刷的内容替代。

**依据动物疫病法（第2版）B. E. 2542第14条修订第51条和第52条。

由部委理事会首长、P. Pibulsonggram军区将军签署。

Animal Epidemics Act

(B. E. 2499 (1956))

BHUMIBOL ADULYADEJ P. R.

Given on the 28th of September B. E. 2499

Being the 11th year of the Present Reign.

Authorized UnOfficial Translation

By Royal Command of His Majesty King Bhumibol Adulyadej it is hereby proclaimed that

Whereas it is proper that there be a law on animal epidemics;

His Majesty the King. by and with the advice and consent of the Assembly of the People's Representatives, is graciously pleased to en an Act as follows:

Section 1 This Act shall be called the "Animal Epidemics Act B. E. 2499"

Section 2 This Act shall come into force after the expiration of ninety days form its publication in the Government Gazette.

Section 3 The following are repealed:

(1) the Epidemics of Livestock and Beasts of Burden Act B. E. 2474;

(2) the Epidemics of Livestock and Beasts of Burden Amendment Act B. E. 2478; and

(3) the Epidemics of Livestock and Beasts of Burden Act (No. 3) B. E. 2497

Provisions of all laws, regulations or rules insofar as the conflict with or are contrary to the provisions of this Act shall be governed hereby

Section 4 In this Act

Animal means

*(1) Elephants, horses, cattle, buffaloes, donkeys, mules, goats, sheep, pigs, dogs, cats, rabbits, gibbons and shall mean to include the semen for breeding purposes and embryo (youngs of animals not yet develop completed visceral organs) of these animals."

(2) Poultry of the classifications: birds, chicken, duck, geese, and shall include the eggs for fertilisation, and,

(3) Other kinds of animals as may by determined by Ministerial Regulations;

Carcass means the body or part of the body of a dead animal which has not yet been changed into cooked food or a finally processed product and shall include tusks, horns, and hair cut from animal while alive but which have not yet been changed into things in final processed forms.

Epidemic disease means rinderpest, hemorrhagic septicaemia, anthrax, surra, glanders, epizootic lymphangitis (strangles), foot and mouth disease, hog cholera (swine fever) and other diseases as may by determined by Ministerial Regulation;

Owner shall include the person in possession. In cases involving animals whose owner is not apparent, it shall also include the person tending the animals or in whose custody the animals are;

Port of entry means a place for the importation of animals and carcasses;

Port of exit means a place for the exportation of animals and carcasses;

Animal quarantine station means the place for the confinement of animals or carcasses for examination for epidemics;

Trade means middleman – type trade;

Competent official means persons appointed by the Minister;

Inspector means inspectors of the Department of Livestock Development or persons appointed by the Director General;

Registrar means the persons appointed by the Minister as registrar;

Veterinarian means veterinarians of the Department of Livestock Development or persons appointed by the Minister;

Director General means the Director General of the Department of Livestock Development,

Minister means the Minister in Charge under this Act.

Section 5 Animals which belong to the Ministry of Defence are not under this Act.

Section 6 With respect to dog, cats, rabbits, monkeys, gibbons, including the semen of such animals, and poultry of the classifications; birds, chicken, ducks, geese including eggs for fertilisation, this Act shall apply only to importation, exportation, transit through the kingdom, or other act as may be prescribed by Royal Decree.

Section 7 The Minister of Agriculture shall be in charge under this Act and shall have the power to appoint competent officials, registrars, and veterinarians, and to issue Ministerial Regulations prescribing rules for applying for and issuing licenses, fixing fees at no higher than the rates prescribed in the annexed schedule, or giving exemptions from fees in specific cases, and prescribing other matters to carry out the provisions of this Act.

Such Ministerial Regulations shall come into force upon publication in the Government Gazette.

* the previous clause in Section 4, the word "animals" is repealed nas the printed clause hereby is used instead by virtue of Section 3 of the Animal Epidemics Act (No. 2) B. E. 2542.

Chapter 1 Prevention of Epidemics

Section 8 In localities not yet proclaimed free zone of epidemic under Chapter 2 or in localities not yet proclaimed epidemic areas, suspected epidemic areas, or temporary epidemic areas under Chapter 3, if an animal is sick or dies of an epidemic disease where it is known, or if an animal becomes sick or dies suddenly from an unknown cause, or if in the same village or adjacent area there are two or more animals which have become sick of die having the same symptoms within seven days or each other, the owner shall notify the competent official, inspector, or veterinarian of the locality within twenty – four hours from the time the animal becomes sick or dies.

In the event animals become sick under the preceding paragraph, the owner shall see that all sick carcsses in the vicinity where they are. The owner and all other persons are forbidden to move any sick animal from that vicinity. In the event animals dies under the preceding paragraph, the owner shall see that the carcasses of such animals in the place where the animals dies. The owner and all other persons are forbidden to move, cut up, or do anything else to such carcasses. If the competent official, inspector, or veterinarian is unable to insect the carcasses within forty – eight hours from the time the animal dies the owner shall bury such carcasses at least fifty centimetres below the surface, also be covered over with earth extending fifty centimetres above the surface of the land, in case of large carcasses.

Section 9 When notification is given under section 8 or there are reasonable grounds to suspect an animal is sick or has dies because of epidemic disease, the competent official or inspector shall have have the power to issue orders in writing to have the owner do as follows;

(1) confine, separate, or move the sick animal or animal suspected of being sick within the area and according to the method prescribed.

(2) Burning are not possible, orders may by given for destruction by other means as may be deemed appropriate, or

(3) confine, separate, or remove animal which are or were in the same group with a sick animal or animal suspected of being sick or dead animal within the area and according to the method prescribed.

Section 10 Upon notification under section 8, or upon finding of reasonably suspecting an animal to be sick or be sick or to have died of an epidemic disease, veterinarians shall have the power to enter and examine the animal or carcasses and shall have the power to issue orders in writing to have the owner do as follows;

(1) confine, separate, or move the sick animal or animal suspected of being sick within the area and according to the method prescribed, or give treatment as may be thought proper.

(2) bury or burn all or part of the carcasses at the place prescribed. If burial or burning is not possible, destruction by other means as may be thought appropriate may be required.

(3) confine, separate, or remove animal which are or were in the same group with a sick or suspected sick or dead animal within the area and by the method prescribed or have the animals receive protection against epidemic as may be thought proper.

(4) destroy animals affected with epidemic disease or animals or carcasses which are carriers of epidemic disease in accordance with the regulations prescribed by the Director Genral with the approval of the Minister. In such case, the owner shall receive compensation provided in Ministerial Regulations with the amount not less than one half of the local market value of the animal before the epidemic occurs unless the owner has intetionally contravened the provisions of this Act.

(5) destroy epidemic carrying germs in animal feed or carcasses by the methods precribed, or

(6) cleanse and disinfect land, building, vehicles, or things by the methods precribed.

Chapter 2　Epidemic Free Zone

Section 11 The Minister shall have the power he thinks fit in order to prevent the occurrence of epidemic for any kind of animal in any locality to proclaim in the Government Gazette all or part of such locality an epidemic - free zone. Such proclamation shall give the kind of animal and epidemic.

Section 12 When an epidemic - free zone has been proclaimed under Section 11, no one may move animals or carcasses into or through such area unless by permission in writing with from the Director General or veterinarian authorized by the Director General.

Section 13 Within epidemic - free zone, animal owner shall have the duty to comply with section 8, competent officials and inspectors shall have the power granted in section 9, and veterinarians shall have the power granted in section 10 and 18.

Section 14 Within epidemic - free zone, if it appears that there is epidemic disease, or there is reason to believe there is epidemic disease, the Changwat Governor or veterinarian may proclaim it an epidemic area, suspected epidemic area, or temporary epidemic area as the case may be under chapter 3.

Chapter 3　Epidemic Areas

Section 15 In any Changwat locality if there is epidemic disease or suspected epidemic, the Governor of Changwat shall have the power to proclaim all or part of the locality an epidemic area or suspected epidemic area as the case may be. This proclamation shall give the kinds of epidemic and shall be posted at the Changwat office, Amphur Offices, kamnans'houses, village chiefs' houses, at the meeting place within the area.

Section 16 If a veterinarian is of the opinion that epidemic disease discovered in his or an adjacent locality will spread, he shall have the power to proclaim in writing a temporary epidemic area with a radius not more than five kilometres from the place the epidemic disease was discovered. This proclamation shall give the kinds of animals and kind of epidemic disease and shall be posted at Kamnans' houses, village chiefs' houses and at meeting place within the area and shall remain effective for thirty days from its issuance.

Section 17 When there has been a proclamation of an epidemic area or suspected epidemic area under section 15 or proclamation of temporary epidemic area under section 16, no one may move animals and carcasses within such are or move animals or carcasses into or out of such area except by permission in writing from the veterinarian.

Section 18 Within an epidemic area or suspected epidemic area under section 15 or temporary epidemic area under section 16, veterinarians shall have the power granted under section 10 and the following power:

(1) to issue notices or instructions in writing to all owners to report the number of animals of certain kinds and if deemed proper to bring the animals for examination or protection or protection epidemic disease.

(2) to order owners of animals which have been examined or protected against epidemic disease to take the animals to be marked, or

(3) to order the quarantine of vehicles which carry animals or carcasses for inspection for epidemic disease and if deemed proper animals or carcasses may be ordered quarantined for observation as may be necessary.

Section 19 Within epidemic area or suspected epidemic area under section 15 or temporary epidemic area under section 16, if any animal is sick or dies its owner shall inform the competent officials, inspectors, or veterinarians within twelve hours from the time the animal becomes sick or dies and the provisions of section 8, paragraph 2 shall apply mutatis mutandis.

Section 20 In any Changwat locality proclaimed an epidemic area or suspected epidemic area, if it appears that the epidemic disease has subsided or that there is absolutely no epidemic disease, the Changwat Governor shall withdraw the proclamation.

Chapter 4 Control of Trade in Animals and Carcasses

Section 21 No one may trade in elephants, horses, buffaloes, sheep, goats, pigs or other animals as prescribed in Ministerial Regulations or trade in carcasses as prescribed in Ministerial Regulations except upon obtaining a license from the registrar.

* **Section 21** (b) No one is permitted to sell, distributed, dispose of, exchange or to possess for purposes of trade, semen for breeding purposes, or embryo of elephants, horses, cattle, buffaloes, goats, sheep, pigs or other kinds of animals specified in the Ministerial Regulations, except upon obtaining a licence from the registrar. Application for and granting of the permit shall follow the rules, procedures and conditions set by the Director General to be announced in the Government Gazette.

** **Section 22** The licences under section 21 or section 21 (b) shall remain vailid till the last day of the calendar year they are issued.

Section 23 Persons engaged in animal or carcass trade shall comply with the conditions prescribed in the license.

*** **Section 24** In the event a person, who received his licence issued from section 21 or section 21 (b), violates provisions of this Act or the conditions specified in his licence, veterinarians shall have the power to seize his licence for submission to the registrar. The registrar may, if he thinks fit, order the suspension or revocation of the licence.

A person whose licence has been sezied, suspended, or revoked under paragraph 1 has the right to appeal to the Minister or officail designated by him within thirty days from the date of seizure, or revocation as the case may be. The decision of the Minister or officail entrusted by him shall be considered final.

* Section 21 (b) is amended by virtue of section 4 of the Animal Epidemics Act (No. 2) B. E. 2542

** the previous clause is repealed and the printed clause hereby is used instead by virtue of Section 5 of the Animal Epidemics Act (No. 2) B. E. 2542

*** the previous clause is repealed and the printed clause hereby is used instead by virtue of Section 6 of the Animal Epidemics Act (No. 2) B. E. 2542

Chapter 5 Miscellaneous

Section 25 If an animal whose owner is not apparent is sick or dies on the land of any person, the owner of that land shall have the duty to comply with the provisions of this Act just as the owner of the animal and when the owner of the animal becomes known later, the owner of the land shall have the right to recover actual expeness from the owner of the animal.

Section 26 If an animal whose owner is not apparent is sick or dies of an epidemic disease on public or on land whose owner is unknown. Competent officials, inspectors, or veterinaians shall have the power to quarantine the animal or carcasses at a place deemed appropriate upon such land. When deemed appropriate such carcasses may be buried. In case of necessity to keep the epidemic disease from spreading, veterinaian may destroy the animals or carcasses or bury such carcasses, upon such land.

When the owner of the animal becomes known later, competent officials, inspectors, or veterinaians shall have the right to recover actual expenses, upon such land.

* **Section 27** For animals accompanying their owners or transported by vehicles, if it appears that they contact epidemic diseases or become carriers of epidemic disease, the veterinarian shall have the power to order their quarantine at appropriate places as need be.

All expenses arising therefrom shall be for the account of the animal owners.

Section 28 No one may dissect carcass buried in accordance with the provisions of this Act except by permission in writing of the veterinarian.

Section 29 When it appears that there is epidemic disease or carriers of epidemic disease or there is reason to believe there is epidemic disease or carriers of epidemic disease in any vehicle, building, or other place, veterinarians shall have the power to summon such vehicle for inspection or enter into such building or other place, and the owner shall give reasonable convenience to the veterinarian.

Entering into a building or other place under the preceding paragraph may done between sunrise and sunset.

Section 30 The Minister shall have the power to give notice in Government Gazette:

(1) prescribing ports of entry and ports of exit,

(2) forbidding the importation or transit through the kingdom of animals or carcasses from areas outside the kingdom in the event such areas have or are suspected of having epidemic disease, and

(3) laying down rules for the seizure, destruction, or return of animals or carcasses without compensation in case of;

a. importation or transit through the kingdom in violation of the provisions of this Act. or

b. importation or transit through the kingdom in compliance with the provision of this Act of animals having epidemic disease or of animals or carcasses is carrying epidemic disease upon or after importation or entry for transit.

Section 31 No one may import, export, or transit though the kingdom animals or carcasses without having obtained a license from the Director General.

The Director General or person authorized by the Director General may prescribe such conditions as may deemed appropriate in the license.

Importation, exportation, or transit through the kingdom of animal or carcasses under this section shall be done at ports of entry or ports or exits as the case may be unless the Director General or person authorized by the Director General shall order otherwise.

Section 32 Whoever imports, exports or transit through the kingdom animals or carcasses shall comply with the Ministerial Regulations.

* **Section 33** The Director general shall have the power by notification in the Government Gazettle:

(1) to appoint inspectors to oversee implementation of this Act;

(2) to set up animal quarantine station and animals transportation depots;

(3) to set up the regulations for destroying animals tainted by the epidemic disease or animals or carcasses of animals becoming carriers of epidemic disease;

(4) to set up the regulations for inspections and disaffection of animals and carcasses of animals in case of importation, exportation, exportation or transit through or on domestic movement in the Kingdom.

Section 34 Any person moving elephants, horses, cattle, buffaloes, goats, sheep, pigs, embryo, semen for breeding purposes or other kinds of animals specified in the Ministerial Regulations, or animal carcasses specified in the Ministerial regulations, to the provincial area, shall first obtain a permit from the local Veterinarian concerned.

Upon issuing a permit under the preceding paragragh, the veterinarian may impose necessary conditions in the permit regarding the routes and types of vehicles to be used for transporting the animals, as well as animal transportation stations and animal quarantine station to be passed in accordance with the regulations set up by the Director General. The leading to animals for feeding or working from time to time is exempted.

Section 35 Whoever takes animals through animal quarantine station shall comply with Ministerial Regulations.

Section 36 Whoever exports animals or carcasses for sale abroad shall comply with Ministerial Regulations.

Section 37 Fifty percent of all fees collected as lodging house charges for animals or carcasses to be exported shall be retained as a fund for expenses in the control or exportation of animals and carcasses for sale abroad. Whatever remains shall be limited as state revenue.

Section 38 Inspectors shall have the power to arrest those who violate the provision of this Act, and to seize animals, carcasses of animals or other objects connected with the violation of this act for delivery to the inquiry officers for him to proceed under the criminal procedures Act, so to take action under section 51.

* the previous clause is repealed and the printed clause hereby is used instead by virtue of Section 7 of the Animal Epidemics Act (No. 2) B. E. 2542

* The previous clause is repealed and the printed clause hereby is used instead by virtue of Section 7 of the Animal Epidemics Act (No. 2) B. E. 2542

* the previous clause is repealed and the printed clause hereby is used instead by virtue of Section 8 of the Animal Epidemics Act (No. 2) B. E. 2542

* the previous clause is repealed and the printed clause hereby is used instead by virtue of Section 9 of the Animal Epidemics Act (No. 2) B. E. 2542

Chapter 6　Penalties

* **Section 39**　The violator of the Provisions of Section 8, paragraph 1, shall be liable to a fine not exceeding Bath 2,000.

* **Section 40**　The violator of the Provisions of section 8, paragraph 2 or of the orders of competent officials and inspectors under section 9, or of provisions of section 19, or owner of vehicles, premises or locations, who obstructs or fails to provide apropriate facilities to the veterinarian under section 29, paragraph 1, shall be liable to imprisonment not exceeding 2 months or a fine not exceeding Bath 4,000, or both.

* **Section 41**　The violator of orders of the veterinarians under section 10 or section 18 or section 23 shall be liable to imprisonment not exceeding 6 months or a fine not exceeding Bath 10,000, or both.

* **Section 42**　The violator of section 12, section 17, section 21, section 21 (b), or section 28 shall be liable to imprisonment not exceeding 1 year or a fine not exceeding Bath 20,000, or both.

Section 43　Whoever contravenes section 13. In the event of non – compliance with section 8, paragraph 1 shall be subject to the penalty provided in Section 39,

In the event of non – compliance with section 8, paragraph 2 or contravened orders of Competent officials or inspectors under section 9 shall be subject to the penalty provided in section 40.

In the event of non – compliance with an order of a veterinarian under section 10 or 18 shall be subject to the penalty provided in section 41.

** **Section 44**　The land owner who fails to fulfill his duties specified under section 25 shall be liable to fine not exceeding Bath 2,000.

*** **Section 45**　(this section is repealed)

**** **Section 46**　The violator of proclamation of the Minister under section 30 (2) shall be liable to imprisonment not exceeding 2 years, or to a fine not exceeding Bath 40,000, or both.

* **Section 47**　The violator of section 31, paragraph 1 or paragraph 3 or of the conditions specified in the license under section 31, paragraph 2 shall be liable to imprisonment not exceeding 2 years, or a fine not exceeding Bath 40,000, or both.

* **Section 48**　The violator of section 32, section 35 or section 36 shall be liable to imprisonment not exceeding 2 months, or to a fine not exceeding Bath 4,000, or both.

* **Section 49**　The violator of section 34, paragraph1 or of the conditions specified in the license under section 34, paragraph 2 shall be liable to imprisonment not exceeding 2 months, or a fine not exceeding Bath 10,000, or both.

* **Section 50**　Any person using a false mark or changing the marking on an animal to give the impression of marking of the competent official, or destroying or changing any marking placed by competent official of animals, or container, or wrapper of carcass of animals, shall be liable to imprisonment not exceeding 2 months, or a fine exceeding Bath 10,000, or both.

** **Section 51**　For offenses under this Act that are to punishment by fine only, the Director General or official designated by him shall have the authority to settle the case. When the alleged offender has paid the fine the amount settled within the specified period, the case shall be considered terminated.

*** **Section 52**　The Director General is authorized to disburse the prize money or reward under the regulations set up by him and approved by the Ministry of Finance."

* the previous clause is repealed and the printed clause hereby is used instead by virtue of Section 10 of the Animal Epidemics Act (No. 2) B. E. 2542

** Section 45 is repealed by virtute of Section 11 of the Animal Epidemics Act (No. 2) B. E. 2542

[***] Section 45 is repealed by virtute of Section 12 of the Animal Epidemics Act（No. 2）B. E. 2542

[****] the previous is repealed and the printed clause hereby is used instead by virtue of Section 13 of the Animal Epidemics Act（No. 2）B. E. 2542

[*] the previous clause is repealed and the printed clause hereby is used instead by virtue of Section 13 of the Animal Epidemics Act（No. 2）B. E. 2542

[**] Section 51 and Section 52 is amended by Section 14 of the Animal Epidemics Act（No. 2）B. E. 2542

Countersigned by：

Field Marshal P. PIBULSONGGRAM,
President of the Council of Ministers.

文　　莱

农业有害生物及有害植物

（文莱法律1997年修订版43章）

本法旨在保护植物及其产品不受病害侵染以及有害生物、有害植物的侵害。

引言

1. 本法为农业有害生物及有害植物法。

释义

2. 本法令下列用语的含义是：

危险性有害生物　指苏丹王陛下及 Yang Di – Pertuan 议会在宪报上公布的所有危险性有害生物；

病害　指被任何有害生物侵袭或侵染或传染；

检查官员　指依据第3条任命的所有检查官员并包括农业主管；

国土　包括附属于土地的或永久性依附于土地和房屋的所有东西；

有害植物　指苏丹王陛下及 Yang Di – Pertuan 议会在宪报上公布的所有有害植物并包括种子及植物的各个部分；

占用者　包括承租者或租客和耕作者或土地的实际占有、经营或支配者；

海关官员　见《海关法案》；

所有者　指土地的注册所有人；

有害生物　包括直接或间接对植物有害的所有昆虫、无脊椎动物、啮齿动物、蠕虫、真菌、寄生植物、细菌、病毒包括所有有害生物的卵；

植物　指所有种类的植物及其任何存活的或死的部分（包括茎、根、叶、花、果）或从植物上切除、嫁接到植物上的部分或产品；

检疫　指依据本法令或衍生条例，隔离任何土地和房屋，以阻断其与不符合上述法令或衍生条例的土地及房屋间的交流或运输；

检验官员的任命

3. 议会最高君主可以书面形式任命农业部门的任何官员为检查官员。

授权

4. 检查官员可以书面形式授权任何下级官员行使和履行本法令赋予的所有权力或义务。

检查官员为公务员

5. 授权的所有官员，在行使本法案或衍生条例赋予的权力和义务时，被视为刑典法承认的公务员。

检查官员进入并检查土地等的权力

6.（1）检查官员有权在带有或未带有助理的情况下，在合理时间进入所有正在栽培或曾经栽培并残留有任何植物的土地，只要以下列为目的—

（a）检验和调查该土地及其所有植物以确认是否有任何植物染病，或是否该地或其上任何植物有利于有害生物的传入或传播；并且

（b）有权以割取、挖走或以其他方式，取走有利于检验和调查的植物的任何部分。

（2）土地所有者或占用者应准许检查官员因上述目的进入该土地，并应提供所有被问及和因上述目的所需要的信息。

直接销毁或处理植物及有害生物或土地的权力

7.（1）检查官员在检验或调查土地、植物或动物产品后，认为某植物或动物产品染病并有可能危

及其他植物，则可以书面形式通知生产该植物或动物产品的土地所有者或占用者，令其在通知规定的时间内执行检查官员认为必需的或有利于扑灭或防止有害生物传播的措施，通过销毁、转移或按上述通知规定的处理方法，对染病的或其他植物、动物产品、任何有害生物或农业生产器具进行处理，执行上述措施的产生的费用由土地所有者或占用者支付。

（2）检查官员在检验或调查土地、植物或动物产品后，认为某土地、植物或动物产品有利于有害生物的传入或传播，则可以书面形式通知土地所有者或占用者，令其在通知规定的时间内执行通知所列针对上述土地、植物或农业生产器具的措施，以杜绝有害生物的传入及传播；通过销毁、转移或按上述通知规定的处理方法，对染病的或其他植物、动物产品、任何有害生物或农业生产器具进行处理，以阻止有害生物的传入或传播的措施产生的费用由土地所有者或占用者支付。

上诉权

8.（1）如果土地所有者或占用者收到依据第7条规定发出的通知后，认为该通知的要求是不合理的或不必要的，可以在收到上述通知14天内以挂号信或其他投递方式直接向部长提交书面申请，并赴上述申请所在地，申请取消或更改上述通知要求，并立即通知签署上述通知的检验官员。

（2）部长在收到申请后7天内，批准或延缓或取消通知的实施，也可制定其认为合适的其他命令。

强制执行第7条或13（1）条的要求

9.(1)如果依照第7条规定通知的土地所有者或占用者或第13(1)条规定涉及的个人,未能在规定时间内履行通知或规定(视具体情况而定)的要求,检查官员可依据由部长根据第8条规定下发的命令,携带必要的设备和工具与上述人员一同进入通知和规定所指的地区,执行上述通知及规定的要求,新产生的费用及已产生的费用应由上述法定的所有者支付。

（2）本条款与个人检举权以及依据第10条或第14条刑罚不冲突。

罚金

10. 如果土地所有者或占用者未能在第7条规定的时间内履行通知的犯罪行为，即构成犯罪，处以1000美元罚款：

依据第8条，如部长暂停或取消上述通知，从暂停或取消日起，不予处罚：

如部长依据第8条更改上述通知的条款，则更改后的通知应依据第7条的要求，并符合本条及第9条要求。

法院下达执行命令的权力

11.（1）依据第10条或第14条定罪的个人，法院在对其定罪前会责令其在法院允许的时间内证明其无罪。

（2）如果个人未能执行上述第（1）条的规定，即构成犯罪：在不履行责任期间处以每天50美元罚款。

存在危险性有害生物的责任

12.（1）只要在任何土地上发现危险性有害生物或由危险性有害生物引起的植物病害，该地的所有者或占用者应—

（a）一旦发现上述情况，应立即将详细情况以书面形式或其他形式通知农业主管或授权的检查官员；

（b）执行检验官员对其下达的所有指令以销毁该地的危险性有害生物或染病植物；

（c）检查官员应尽量提供援助以销毁该地的危险性有害生物或染病植物。

（2）任何人违反上述第（1）条规定应处以罚金，即构成犯罪：处罚2000美元罚款。

（3）检查官员收到依据本条款的第1（a）条规定的任何通知，应立即报告农业主管。

处理危险性有害生物的权力

13.（1）如果部长认为有必要或急需扑灭、销毁或处理在所有感染危险性有害生物的植物及其他容易被感染的植物，或必需防止任何危险性有害生物的传播，则可要求完全清除土地上的所有植物或任何异常的植物种类，或根除或销毁、处理地上现存的所有植物，并以书面形式下令直接根除或销毁或处理该类植物，指定人员使用规定的设备清理该地，上述措施产生的所有费用由土地所有者或占用者支付，如这些费用是由其他人引起的，则上述人员应向法定土地所有者或占用者补偿所有费用。

（2）如果部长认为本国的植物安全性受到危险性有害生物的威胁，且土地所有者或占用者执行第（1）条规定亦不能确保上述植物安全时，不论该危险性有害生物是否存在于该地区，将立即派检查官员与上述人员一起进入该地区，使用必需的设备和器具，扑灭、销毁或控制该危险性有害生物。

违约罚金

14. 土地所有者或占用者未能执行第13（1）条款的要求的，即构成犯罪：处以6个月监禁并罚款2000美元。

赔偿规定

15.（1）按规定销毁植物、或是按第13条规定执行后，议会最高领导可酌情支付合理的赔偿给上述人员。

（2）农业主管对于所有非书面的、及从下达销毁植物的通知之日起超过3个月的赔偿申请均不受理。

（3）任何因履行本法令或衍生条例所造成的花费和损失，土地所有者或占用者或其他人员均不享有赔偿资格，除非该损失是由于疏忽或故意、不合理原因造成的。

禁止进口或拥有有害植物

16. 任何个人、农业主管或其书面授权的人除外，均禁止：

（a）进口任何有害植物；

（b）在其为物主或居住者的土地上，拥有或保存任何有害植物或允许种植上述植物。

销毁有害植物的责任

17. 任何有害植物被非法种植在所有者或占用者的土地之内或之上，应尽快用焚烧或其他手段将其完全、有效地销毁。

不及时销毁有害植物的行为

18. 若有人不按第17条的规定，完全、有效地销毁有害植物时，检查官员可与上述人员一起在有害植物生长的区域，使用必需的设备及物品销毁该有害植物，新产生的费用及已产生的费用应由上述法定的所有者支付。

海关官员销毁有害植物的权力

19. 海关官员及检查官员有权查封并销毁非法入境有害植物，并不需对所查封及销毁的有害植物进行赔偿。

罚金

20. 任何人违反第16条或17条款规定，尽管检查官员将执行或已经执行第18条规定的，即构成犯罪，处以1000美元罚款。

非法转移危险性有害生物或有害植物

21. 任何个人在文莱境内对所有危险性有害生物或有害植物，进行有意转移或运输或引起转移或将要转移或运输的，即构成犯罪：处以6个月监禁并罚款2000美元。

通告和命令的传达

22.（1）依据本法令发布或制定的任何通告或命令会用以下形式送达，即——。

（a）如果联系人的地址是在文莱境内，通告或命令会直接送达给他或交由其成年的家庭成员（仆人除外）送达；或

（b）如果通告或命令未能以上述（a）的形式送达，则将以挂号信形式邮寄到该人员最新的地址；或

（c）如果通告或命令在上述（a）或（b）的形式不能送达，或土地物主或居住者不明，则将其粘

贴在该地显著的地方。

（2）通告或命令不得注明土地物主或居住者的姓名，除非涉及的土地是以姓名来形容或区别的。

（3）每个此类通告或命令应使用马来语或其他的签署通告或命令的官员认为所受送达人可以理解的语言，通告或命令不因语言问题而影响实施。

检察官执行的制裁

23. 检察官提出书面批准，方可对违反违反本法令任何条款或衍生条例的人员提出诉讼。

条例

24.（1）国王陛下在不损害前述的原则下，制定确保本法令得以全面有效的贯彻及实施条例，这些条例规定—

（a）依据本法令授予官员的权力和职责；

（b）进入土地的方式，如有通知，需提前送达；

（c）实施检查，检验植物和其他由本法令授权的诉讼；

（d）物主或土地居住者对受危险性有害生物侵染的植物的通报；

（e）依据本法令的通知、命令和申请的形式；

（f）进出口植物或有害生物的控制、调整情况；

（g）土地的隔离；

（h）控制任何文莱境内所有植物或有害生物；

（i）收费；

（j）违反或不履行本条规定下的任何条例，或限制、制约依据上述条例的许可，处以不超过1000美元的罚款。

（2）依本法令制订的所有条例应提交立法委员会，并且，如果决议在提交后的4个月内获得通过，要废除该条例或其中的一部分，则从指定日期起要废除部分将无法律效力，但不影响已执行条例的有效性或新制订的条例。

Agricultural pests and noxious plants

(Laws of Brunei revised edition 1997 chapter 43)

An Act to provide for the protection of plants and cultivated products from diseases and to provide for the destruction of pests and noxious plants.

Short title

1. This Act may be cited as the Agricultural Pests and Noxious Plants Act.

Interpretation

2. In this Act unless the context otherwise requires—

dangerous pest means any pest which His Majesty the Sultan and Yang Di – Pertuan in Council by notification in the Gazette declares to be a dangerous pest for the purposes of this Act;

disease means attacked by or infected or affected with any pest;

inspecting officer means any inspecting officer appointed under section 3 and includes the Director of Agriculture;

land includes things attached to the earth or permanently fastened to anything attached to the earth and premises;

noxious plant means any plant which His Majesty in Council by notification in the *Gazette* declares to be a noxious plant for the purposes of this Act and includes the seed and every part of such plant;

occupier includes alessee or tenant and a cultivator or person in actual possession, management or control of any land;

Cap. 36

officer of Customs shall have the same meaning as in the Customs Act;

owner means the registered proprietor of any land;

pest includes any insect, invertebrate animal, rodent, vermin, fungus, parasite, bacteria, virus or disease, destructive or injurious, directly or indirectly, to any plant and includes the eggs of any pest;

plant means any species of vegetable and any part of a plant whether living or dead and includes the stem, root, leaf, flower, fruit or any part or product whatsoever of any plant whether severed or attached;

quarantining means isolating any land and premises for the purposes of this Act or of any rules made thereunder so that there shall be no communication or traffic with any other land and premises except in accordance with this Act or any rules made thereunder ;

Appointment of inspecting officers

3. His Majesty in Council may appoint in writing any officer of the Department of Agriculture to be an inspecting officer for the purposes of this Act.

Delegating powers

4. Any inspecting officer may by writing under his hand delegate to any officer subordinate to him the exercise and performance of any powers or duties assigned to an inspecting officer by this Act, and such subordinate officer may thereupon exercise and perform the powers and duties so performed.

Inspecting officers to be public servants

Cap. 22

5. All officers to whom powers and duties shall have been delegated when acting within the scope of the powers and duties so delegated under this Act or any rules made thereunder, shall be deemed to be public servants within the meaning of the Penal Code.

Powers of an Inspecting officer to enter and inspect land, etc.

6. (1) Every inspecting officer has power to enter a tall reasonable times with or without assistants, upon any land whereon any plants are or have been cultivated and to remain there so long as may be reasonably necessary for the following purposes—

(a) to inspect and examine such land and all plants thereon for the purposes of ascertaining whether any of such plants are diseased or whether such land or any plant thereonis in a condition favourable to the introduction or spread of any pest; and

(b) to remove by cutting, digging or otherwise, such portion of any plant as he may think expedient for the purposes of examination or investigation.

(2) The owner or occupier of such land shall permit every inspecting officer to have access thereto for the said purposes and shall supply to such officer all such information as may be requested by him and may be reasonably necessary for the said purposes.

Power to direct destruction or treatment of plants and pests or treatment of land

7. (1) If, on or as a result of any inspection or examination of land or plants or animal product by an inspecting officer, it shall appear to such inspecting officer that any plant or animal product is diseased in a manner and to an extent which might endanger other plants, such inspecting officer may by notice in writing under his hand, addressed to the owner or occupier of the land whereon such plant or animal product is, direct him to take within a time to be stated in the notice such measures as seem to the inspecting officer necessary or expedient for the eradication or prevention of the spread of the pest either by destruction, by removal or by treatment in a manner to be specified in the said notice of such diseased or any other plant, or such animal product, or of any pest or of any tools or utensils used for agricultural purposes on such land and the cost of such measures and of the taking thereof shall be defrayed by such owner or occupier of the land.

(2) If, on or as a result of any inspection or examination of land or plants or animal product by an inspecting officer, is shall appear to such officer that any land or plant or animal product is in a condition favourable to the introduction or spread of any pest, such inspecting officer may by notice in writing under his hand, addressed to the owner or occupier of the land whereon such condition exists, direct him to take within a time to be stated in the notice such measures as shall in the said notice be specified for the treatment of such land or plant or of any tools or utensils used for agricultural purposes on such land with a view to the bringing of the same into a condition not favourable to the introduction or spread of any pest and the cost of such measures as seem to the inspecting officer necessary or expedient for the eradication or prevention of the spread of the pest either by destruction, by removal or by treatment in a manner to be specified in the said notice of such diseased or any other plant, or such animal product, or of any pest or of any tools or utensils used for agricultural purposes onsuch land with a view to the bringing of the same into a condition not favourable to the introduction or spread of any pest, and the cost of such measures and of the taking thereof shall be defrayed by such owner or occupier.

Right of appeal

8. (1) If any owner or occupier of land on whom a notice under the provisions of section 7 has been served is of the opinion that any act or thing required by such notice to be performed or done is unreasonable or unnecessary, he may, by an application in writing addressed to the Minister and despatched by registered post, or otherwise delivered, to the said the Minister, within 14 days from the service of the said notice, and setting forth the grounds on which such application is based, apply for an order cancelling or varying the requirements of the said notice and shall forthwith notify the inspecting officer by whom the said notice was signed that the said application has been made.

(2) The the Minister shall within 7 days of receipt of such application, confirm or suspend the operation of the notice or cancel the notice or make such other order as he may deem fit.

Enforcement of any action required under any notice under section 7 or orderunder section 13 (1)

9. (1) If any owner or occupier of land on whom a notice under the provisions of section 7 or the person specified in any order made under section 13 (1) has been served shall fail to comply with the requirements of such notice or order (as the case may be) within such time as is stated in the notice or order for the performance of the acts thereby required to be done, the inspecting officer may, subject to any order made under section 8 by the Minister in respect of a notice given under section 7, enter upon the land to which the notice or order refers together with such persons with such instruments and things as may be necessary and may proceed to perform and do thereon all such acts and things required by the said notice or order to be performed or done, and may recover the cost of, and all expenses incurred in so doing from the said owner in any Court of competent jurisdiction.

(2) Nothing in this section shall affect any liability of any person to prosecution and punishment under section 10 or section 14.

Penalty for default

10. If any owner or occupier of land on whom a notice under the provisions of section 7 has been served fails to comply therewith within the time therein stated, he shall be guilty of an offence: Penalty, a fine of $1,000:

Provided that no person shall be punished under this section for failure to comply with any notice from the time that its requirements may have been suspended or cancelled by the Minister under the provisions of section 8:

Provided further that where the Minister has under the provisions of section 8 made an order varying the terms of any such notice, the notice as so varied shall for the purposes of this section and of section 9 be deemed to be the notice under section 7.

Power of convicting Court to order action to be taken

11. (1) Upon the conviction of any person under section10 or section 14 the Court before which the conviction is had may order the convicted person to take, within a time to be fixed by the Court, the measures for failure to take which such conviction was had.

(2) If any person fails to comply with an order made under subsection (1), he shall be guilty of an offence: Penalty, a fine of $50 for every day during which such default continues.

Duty on appearance of a dangerous pest

12. (1) Whenever a dangerous pest, or any plant diseased by a dangerous pest, is found or appears on any land, the owner or occupier of such land shall—

(a) as soon as he becomes aware that the same has been found or has appeared thereon, forthwith give notice thereof in writing or otherwise to the Director of Agriculture or to any inspecting officer with such particulars as may be prescribed; and

(b) carry into effect all instructions given to him by any inspecting officer for the destruction of the dangerous pest or diseased plants on such land; and

(c) render all assistance in his power towards the carrying out of any action taken by any inspecting officer for the purpose of destroying such dangerous pest or diseased plants on such land.

(2) Any person who commits a breach of the provisions of subsection (1) shall be guilty of an offence: Penalty, a fine of $2,000.

(3) Any inspecting officer receiving any notice in accordance with the provisions of paragraph (a) of subsection (1) shall forthwith inform the Director of Agriculture of the receipt of such notice.

Power to take action against a dangerous pest

13. (1) If in the opinion of the Minister the eradication, destruction or treatment on any land of any diseased plant which is affected by a dangerous pest, or of any plant liable to become so affected, is a matter of necessity or urgency, or if the Minister considers it necessary for the prevention of the spread of any dangerous pest that any land be entirely cleared of all plants or of any particular species of plant, or that the eradication or destruction or any form of treatment of any plant present on any land is required, the 42 may forthwith make anorder in writing directing the eradication or destruction or prescribing the treatment of such plant, or the clearing of such land by any person specified in such order and in accordance with any instructions contained in such order, and the cost of, andall expenses incurred in such eradication, destruction, clearing or treatment shall be defrayed by the owner or occupier of theland whereon the action required by the order is taken and where such cost or expenses have been incurred by any person other than the owner or occupier such person may recover such cost and expenses from the owner or occupier in any Court of competent jurisdiction.

(2) If in the opinion of the Minister the safety of any plant growing in Brunei is endangered by the existence of a dangerous pest on the said plant or on any other plant, and it appears to him that the safety of such plant cannot properly be ensured by the action ordered to be taken under subsection (1) by any individual owner or occupier of any land the Minister may forthwith direct an inspecting officer to enter upon any specified land together with such persons with such instruments or things as may be necessary and to take or cause to be taken any action authorised by the Minister for the eradication, destruction or control of such dangerous pest, whether or not such dangerous pest is present on such land.

Penalty for default

14. If any owner or occupier of land on whom an order under the provisions of section 13 (1) has been served fails to comply with the requirements thereof, he shall be guilty of an offence: Penalty, imprisonment for 6 months and to a fine of $2,000.

Provisions as to compensation

15. (1) Where any plants have been destroyed in pursuance of an order, or as a result of any action taken under section 13, His Majesty in Council may, in his discretion, direct the payment to such persons as he may specify of such sum as he considers reasonable as compensation.

(2) No application for compensation shall be entertained unless it is in writing and is received in the office of the Director of Agriculture within 3 months from the date of the order requiring the destruction of such plant.

(3) Subject to this section no owner or occupier of land nor any other person be entitled to compensation for any expense incurred or damage occasioned by any notice or order given or act done in pursuance of this Act or any rules made thereunder unless such damage was occasioned by negligence or maliciously, and without reasonable cause.

Prohibition of importation or possession of noxious plants

16. No person except the Director of Agriculture, or a person authorised by him in writing in that behalf and subject to such conditions as the Director of Agriculture shall see fit to impose, shall—

(a) import any noxious plant; or

(b) possess or keep any noxious plant or allow the same to grow in or on any land of which he is the owner or occupier.

Duty to destroy noxious plants

17. Where any noxious plant is unlawfully growing in or on any land the owner and occupier thereof shall as soon as possible cause such noxious plant to be completely and effectually destroyed by fire or any other means.

Action where noxious plants not duly destroyed

18. Where default is made by any person in the complete and effectual destruction of any noxious plant which, by the provisions of section 17 he is required so to destroy, an inspecting officer may enter upon the land in or on which such noxious plant is growing, together with such persons with such instruments and things as may be necessary for the purpose of destroying, and may destroy, the same and may recover the cost of and all expenses incurred in so doing from the owner or occupier of the said land in any Court of competent jurisdiction.

Power of customs officers to destroy noxious plants

19. Any officer of customs and any inspecting officer at any place at which any noxious plant is unlawfully imported may seize and destroy the same and no person shall be entitled to any compensation for any noxious plant so seized and destroyed.

Penalty

20. Any person who contravenes any provision of section 16 or 17 shall be guilty of an offence: Penalty, a fine of $1,000, notwithstanding that an inspecting officer may take, or may have taken, action under section 18.

Criminal transfer of dangerous pests or noxious plant

21. Any person who shall knowingly move or convey or cause to move or to be moved or conveyed within Brunei any dangerous pest or noxious plant shall be guilty of an offence: Penalty, imprisonment for 6 months and a fine of $2,000.

Serving of notices and orders

22. (1) Any notice or order issued or made under this Act may be served in the manner following, namely—

(a) if the person to whom it is addressed is within Brunei, the notice or order may be delivered to him or left with some adult member of his family (other than a servant) residing with him; or

(b) if the notice or order cannot be servedas described in paragraph (a), it may be sent by registered post addressed to him at his last known address; or

(c) if the notice or order cannot be servedas described in paragraphs (a) or (b), or if there is no known owner or occupier of the land, it may be posted up in some conspicuous place on the land.

(2) It shall not be necessary in any such notice or order to name the owner or occupier of the land if the land to which the notice or order relates is therein described or identified by name or otherwise.

(3) Every such notice or order shall be in the Malay language or in such other language as may, in the opinion of the officer signing the notice or order be likely to render it intelligible to the person on whom it is to be served: Provided that no notice or order shall be deemed to be bad or insufficient by reason merely of the language wherein the same is rendered.

Prosecutions to be sanctioned by Public Prosecutor

23. No proceedings shall be instituted in any Court against any person for any breach of any provision of this Act or of any rules made thereunder except with the written sanction of the Public Prosecutor.

Rules

24. (1) His Majesty in Council may from time to time make rules for fully and effectively carrying out and giving effect to the purpose of this Act, and, without prejudice to the generality of the forgoing, such rules may provide for—

(a) the powers and duties of officers appointed under this Act;

(b) the manner of entry upon lands and the notice, if any, to be given prior to such entry;

(c) the conduct of the examination and inspection of plants and of other proceedings authorised by this Act;

(d) the notification by owners or occupiers of land of any plant found to be diseased with a dangerous pest;

(e) the form of notices, orders and applications under this Act;

(f) the control of, and the conditions governing, the import or export of plants or pests;

(g) the quarantining of land;

(h) the control of any plant or pest present in Brunei;

(i) the fees to be charged;

(j) penalties, not exceeding a fine of $1,000 for any contravention or failure to comply with any of the provisions of any rules made under this section or with the restrictions or conditions of any licence granted under any such rules.

(2) All rules made under this Act shall be laid before the Legislative Council as soon as may be after they are made, and, if a resolution is passed within the next subsequent 4 months after any such rules are so laid annulling the rules or any part thereof as from a specified date, such rules or such part thereof, as the case may be, shall thereupon be void as from such date, but without prejudice to the validity of anything previously done thereunder or to the making of new rules.

疾病预防和检疫法规[①]

（文莱1997年修订法）

为了防止传染病传入传出文莱和在文莱境内传播，制定本法。

第1部分　前言

简称

1. 该修订法案称为疾病预防和检疫法规。

定义

2. 除非文中另有规定，在本法中：

动物　包括马、驴、骡、牛、狗、绵羊、山羊、猪和所有的四足动物。

动物尸体　指动物的尸体，包括畜体的组成部分，肉、骨骼、皮、毛、蹄、角、内脏以及动物的其他所有部分。

牛　包括公牛，母牛，黄牛，水牛，小牝牛和牛犊。

工作人员　指受雇于船运服务或货物运送的有关人员，而不是指出入境旅游的人员。

疾病　指所有危害人类或动物的感染性或传染性疾病。

患病　指染上疾病。

消毒　指消灭或清除传染病病因，包括采取合理、适当的措施来防止病菌携带媒介的传播。

行政区　指本法案中的所有地方行政区域。

卫生官员　指在市政卫生机构或主管检疫站中履行卫生或助理卫生官员职责的官员，包括书面授权的代理或助理人员。

染疫　指受到某种传染病侵染。

传染病流行区　指政府颁布公告宣布为疫区的所有地区，从公告之日开始到公告解除之日或被宣布为疑似疫区之日为止。

主管　指雇主、船长或其他船舶临时负责人。

口岸　指修建在海边或有水路通到海边的所有城镇，包括城镇周围的所有区域。

检疫　是根据本法或以下规章规定，强制将任何船、人、动物或物品与其他船、人、动物、物品、建筑物或地方隔离并检疫，本法或以下条例另有规定的除外。

检疫站　所有实施隔离检疫的岛屿、建筑物或其他地方，包括检查站、废船和传染病医院。

鼠类　指所有啮齿类动物，包括所有已知可以传播瘟疫的动物和昆虫。

船　指所有能用作水上航行的船只。

疑似疫区　指被政府颁布公告从公告之日起一直到公告解除为止都是疑似疫区的局部地区。

兽医官　指政府兽医，或政府机关根据本法任命的官员，称为兽医官或代理兽医官。

第6部分　进出口家养牲畜的检疫

家畜进出口

1. 苏丹通过立法会可制定基于本法的相关条例，用于禁止或调控家畜的进出口。

---

① 只摘录了与动物有关部分内容。

第7部分 条 例

制定条例的权力

2. 为了更好地防止疫病传入或传出文莱国境或在境内传播,苏丹通过立法会制定本条例。

相关事项的规定

3. (1) 本法案制定的条例可以规定

(a) 指定船只抵达任何文莱的港口进行检疫;

(b) 禁止或有条件地控制船上的人员上岸;

(c) 除了在规定的地点外,禁止或控制通过水、陆、空运从文莱境内或境外进来的动物入境或上岸。

(d) 隔离所有患病的人或动物。

(e) 建立、维持人和动物的检疫站,并制定管理规定。

(g) 禁止或控制患病动物或疑似患病动物的转运和动物尸体的销毁;

(h) 在应急处置中,不管是否有补偿,扑杀染疫动物以及带有补偿性的扑杀可疑染疫动物或者曾暴露于疫区的易感动物。

(i) 清洁和消毒被患者或动物占用的房屋、建筑物、房间和其他地方,或其他不符合卫生条件的地方。

(j) 在应急处置中,对与患病的人或动物有密切接触史的家具、衣物、垫草、饲料和其他物品在都可能成为传播介质的物品,不管是否有补偿,实施消毒或销毁处理;

(p) 绝对地或有条件禁止或控制家畜从文莱的任何口岸或港口出口,不管这个口岸或港口是一般的还是特殊的;

(q) 指定、建立和维持家畜出口前观察和检查的场所,制定管理规定,并对出口家畜进行强制检查;

(r) 清洁和消毒所有装载出口家畜的船只;

(s) 禁止和控制饲料、垫草、粪便和其他物品的搬运;

(t) 规定和控制对违反本法制定条例的任何动物实施没收、扣留和处理,同时规定和控制动物进口商应缴纳的没收、扣留和处理费用;

(u) 规定由诊治患者的医师向政府报告疫情;

(v) 任命执行本法和以下所有规定的检查员和其他的官员,规定他们的职责和行为,授予他们履行职责所必须的权力。

(w) 本法或以下所有规章赋予的所有权力和职责由当地政府实施和执行。

(x) 规定本法制定的所有条例的发行,并规定服务或公告分送或其他文件的形式和方式;

(y) 规定违反本法制定的任何条例的罚款,最高不超过1000美元;

(z) 根据本法确定所收取费用的数量;

(za) 建立和维持航空卫生监督的地点、工作和服务,和涉及国际航空所采取的卫生措施(普通或者特殊疾病),与当时生效的国际卫生条例的条款一致。

(2) 在第(1)分段中没有提到的事项,本法案授予苏丹经立法会采取任何形式的限定,但该权力延伸至所有事项,无论是否与第(1)分段中提到的事项相似,以至于很有必要制定条例使本法案的目的得到更好实行。

(3) 依据本法案制定的所有条例必须在公报上发布。

第8部分 其他规定

违法

4. 任何人没有合法权限或理由,证据

(a) 违反本法案或根据本法案制定的条例要求;

（b）阻碍或协助阻碍本法案授权的官员、其他执法者或警察的执法行为。

以上行为将被认为违反了本法案。

处罚

5.（1）任何违反本法案的人，没有罚款规定的，将处以500美元的罚款。

（2）任何违反本法被判罪的人，在12个月内第2次或连续犯同样的罪将被地方法院判处两个月监禁和处以1000美元的罚款。

（3）本部分所涉及的处罚不会影响本违法行为在普通法律或除本法之外其他法令中规定应当受到的处罚，但不能一罪两罚。

没收

6.（1）任何人携带违反根据本法案制定的条例规定的动物或物品入境的，将被没收。

（2）根据本法，没收由地方法院裁决，被没收的动物和物品由部长直接处置。

逮捕

7.（1）当任何人被看见或被发现或被怀疑违反了本法案时，任何本法案授权的检疫官或其他官员或警察在没有许可证的情况下，可以阻止或扣留他，如果不知道此人的姓名和住址，也可以逮捕他。

（2）根据本法案，检疫官或其他官员可以在没有许可证的情况下逮捕任何妨碍和协助妨碍其执法行为的人。

（3）根据本部分被逮捕的人应尽快带到法院进行审判。

（4）不管本部分是否颁布，将不会削除或削弱警察的任何权力。

推定

8. 当患者的监护人或动物的所有者，被指控违反了本法案中与疫病有关的条款，应当认为他已经知道患者或动物患有该疫病，除非他能让法院确信被控告前他不了解该疫病，也没有合理的途径获得这些知识。

公务员

9. 本法案授权的检疫员和其他官员视为刑法典中的公务员。

违法判决

10. 根据本法案，除非另有规定，每个犯罪必须经过地方法院的审判，不管刑事诉讼法有任何规定，法院可以对此违法行为进行充分裁决。

补充法案（2）动物检疫和疫病预防条例

引证

1. 这些条例称为动物检疫和疫病预防条例。

释义

2. 在这些条例中

动物　　包括鸟类；

卫生官员　　指这个地区的卫生官员，包括他书面委托作为他的代理或助手的人；

进口　　指通过陆运、海运、空运进入文莱；

海关官员　　与海关法中的意思相同。

进口动物限制

3. 没有兽医官的书面许可，禁止进口动物或在文莱境内将动物转船。

进口动物要向兽医官申报

4. 货主在进口动物的应该抵达入境点、入境或着陆前向兽医官书面申报。

进口狗和猫要出示动物无狂犬病证书

5. 进口狗或猫的人应该向兽医官出示由合格的兽医师签发的证书，证明：狗或猫在出口时，没有患狂犬病或类似的疾病，并且在这此前六个月或从出生到现在，一直饲养在没有狂犬病或类似疾病发生的地区。

过境动物入境或着陆时可以拒绝入境

6. 如果任何动物在由出口地过境的过程中，在任何港口入境或着陆时，兽医官可以拒绝动物进入文莱。

兽医官签发兽医官许可证

7. 如果兽医官

（a）在确信狗或猫符合条例5中提到的证书要求的情况下，狗或猫是健康的；或

（b）在确信任何其他动物健康的情况下，他将签发证书证明动物—

（i）没有任何形式的传染病；并

（ii）符合进口条件。

扑杀感染或患病的动物

8.（1）如果兽医官认为动物染疫或是处于须紧急处置的状况下，可以命令作扑杀处理。

（2）兽医官依据（1）款规定下达命令后，应该尽快通知卫生官员并提供所有与这个案例相关的信息。

隔离检疫染病的动物

9.（1）如果兽医官认为染疫或患病动物不必要采取扑杀处理，可以下令由进口商承担风险和费用，将动物进行隔离监管，直到认为：

（a）动物是健康的，可以交付给货主；或

（b）动物应该被扑杀，那么他将采取相应的措施。

（2）兽医官作出决定后，应该尽快通知卫生官员并提供所有与这个案例相关的信息。

部长有禁止动物进口或在文莱境内调运的权力

10.（1）根据兽医官的建议，卫生官员可以向部长提议，以便部长行使第（2）的权力。

（2）如果部长认为由于狂犬病或其他类似疾病的流行，他可以通过公告宣布在这段时间内的规定：

（a）禁止进口动物；

（b）没有兽医官的书面许可，禁止在文莱境内调运动物。

处罚

11. 某人：

（a）在任何动物到达文莱境内时应该申报，却不申报；

（b）没有得到兽医官的许可就进口任何动物；或

（c）违反第10条的规定，在文莱境内调运动物，将处以200美元的罚款，并没收或扑杀动物。

如果未获得许可，海关官员可以拒绝动物入境或着陆

12. 根据海关法，海关官员可以拒绝任何动物入境直到获得兽医官的书面许可。

根据第10条例发布的公告

宣布禁止所有的马、驴和骡从文莱任何港口进口或转运：

本禁令不适用于从澳大利亚、新西兰、美国和沙巴州（马来西亚）直接进口或转运马、驴和骡。

S. 114/70

宣布禁止从马来西亚（沙巴州和沙捞越除外）进口狗和猫及其相关种类。

S. 87/73

宣布除非有兽医官书面批准的运输工具，否则禁止从任何法定的码头运输动物到斯里巴加湾市。

S. 93/75

宣布从除澳大利亚、爱尔兰、新西兰、沙巴州、沙捞越、新加坡和英国之外的国家进口的狗、猫和相关种类，从它们到达之日算起在文莱、沙巴或沙捞越批准的检疫站内进行为期6个月的隔离检疫。

S. 77/74

宣布没有兽医官的书面许可，禁止在文莱境内调运牛或水牛。

补充法案（3）动物出口检疫和疾病预防条例

从1962年1月20日开始实行

引证

1. 这些条例为《动物出口检疫和疾病预防条例》。

释义

2. 在这些条例中：

动物　　包括鸟类；

出口　　指通过陆运、海运、空运运出文莱；

卫生官员　　与检疫和疾病预防法中的意思相同；

兽医官　　与检疫和疾病预防法中的意思相同；

动物出口限制

3. 没有兽医官的书面许可，禁止动物出口、转船运输或以出口为目的在文莱境内调运。

动物健康证书的申请

4.（1）根据这些条例的规定，如果想要将动物出口到文莱境外的任何地方，不管是为了销售还是其他原因，都应该向动物所在地区的兽医官递交申请。

（2）假如是同一种类，申请检疫动物的数量不受限制。

动物检查和动物健康证书的签发

5. 收到申请后，兽医官应该安排对动物进行检查，如果没有发现疫病和动物的健康良好，将按规定的形式签发动物健康证书。

费用

6.（1）签发动物健康证书的费用：

（a）家养牲畜包括水牛，每头20美元；

（b）山羊、狗和猫，每只10美元；和

（c）鸟类包括小鸡，每只2美元 。

（2）如果由于动物或鸟类的归类不清引发第（1）段的收费问题，以兽医官出具的证书中所界定的种类为准。

扑杀感染或患病的动物

7.（1）根据兽医官在检查后的意见，如果动物已感染或处在扑杀是更有利的状况下，兽医官可以下令将它扑杀。

（2）兽医官在下令后，应该尽快通知卫生官员并提供所有与这个案例相关的信息。

隔离检疫染病动物

8.（1）如果兽医官认为动物已染病或健康状况不好、或处在扑杀是更有利的状况下，他可以下令由出口商承担风险和费用，将动物进行隔离监管，直到他认为：

（a）动物是健康的，可以交给出口商；或

（b）动物应该扑杀，他将采取相应的措施。

（2）兽医官发布命令后，应该尽快通知卫生官员并提供所有与案例相关的信息。

部长有禁止动物出口或在出口前在文莱境内调运的权力

9.（1）根据兽医官的意见，卫生官员可以向部长提议，以便部长行使第（2）段的权力。

（2）如果部长认为由于狂犬病或其他类似疾病的流行，他可以通过公告宣布在这段时间内的规定：

（a）禁止动物出口；

（b）没有兽医官的书面许可，禁止在出口前在文莱境内调运动物。

处罚

10. 某人

（a）没有兽医官的许可，出口任何动物；或

（b）违反第 9 条条例的规定，在出口前在文莱境内调运动物。

根据具体情况，处以 200 美元的罚款，并没收或扑杀动物。

当局关于出口的现有权力和权限

11. 应用关于出口动物到文莱境外任何地方的条例时，应当不损害当局、政府或其他部门的现有权力和权限。

Quarantine and Prevention of Disease

(Laws of Brunei Revised Edition 1997)

Chapter 47

Act to prevent the introduction and spread in Brunei, and the transmission from Brunei, of infectious diseases.

Part I Preliminary

Short title

1. This Act may be cited as the Quarantine and Prevention of Disease Act.

Interpretation

2. In this Act, unless there is something repugnant in the subject or context

animals includes horses, asses, mules, cattle, dogs, sheep, goats and swine and any kind of four – footed beast;

carcase means the carcass of an animal, and includes part of a carcass and the meat, bones, hide, skin, hoofs, horns, offal or other part of an animal separately or otherwise or any portion thereof;

cattle means bulls, cows, oxen, buffaloes, heifers and calves;

crew includes any person who is not on board for the sole purpose of travelling from one country to another but who is employed in some way in the ship's service or in connection with the cargo;

disease means any disease of an infectious or contagious nature dangerous to mankind or animals;

diseased means affected with disease;

disinfection means the destruction or removal of the cause of an infectious disease and includes the taking of any reasonable and appropriate measures to render a germ carrier free from infection;

district means the district of any local authority under this Act;

health officer means the officer for the time being performing the duties of health officer or assistant health officer to a Municipal Board or of health officer in charge of a quarantine station, and includes any person authorised in writing by such officer to act as his deputy or assistant;

infected means affected with an infectious disease;

infected local area means any local area which has been declared by public notification to be an infected local area from the date of such declaration until the date of the withdrawal of such public declaration or until the date it is declared to be a suspected local area;

master means the master, officer or other person for the time being in charge of any ship;

port means any town built by the sea or having water access to the sea, and includes any district surrounding such town;

quarantine means the compulsory detention in isolation for the purpose and under the provisions of this Act or of the regulations made thereunder of any ship, person, animal or thing, so that there shall be no communication or traffic with any other ship, person, animal or thing, or with any building or place except in accordance with this Act or the regulations made thereunder;

quarantine station means any island, building or place where quarantine is carried out, and includes an examination station, a hulk and an infectious diseases hospital;

rat means any rodent and includes any animal or insect known to be a means of spreading plague;

ship includes any vessel or craft which may be used in navigation by water;

suspected local area means any local area which has been by notification published in the Gazette to be a suspected local area from the date of such declaration until the date of the withdrawal of such declaration;

veterinary officer means a Government veterinary surgeon, or an officer appointed by office or name to be a veterinary officer or deputy veterinary officer for the purpose of this Act.

Part Ⅵ Prevention of the importation and exportation of cattle

Importation and exportation of cattle

1. The importation and exportation of cattle may be prohibited or regulated by regulations to be made by His Majesty in Council under this Act.

Part Ⅶ Regulations

Power to make regulations

2. His Majesty in Council may make such regulations as seem to him necessary or expedient for the purpose of preventing the introduction into and the spread in Brunei of any disease and the transmission of any disease from Brunei

Matters in respect of which regulations may be made

3. (1) The regulations made under this Act may provide for

(a) placing vessels arriving at any port of Brunei in quarantine;

(b) prohibiting or regulating the landing of persons from vessels either absolutely or conditionally;

(c) prohibiting or regulating the entry or landing of animals brought by land, sea or air from any place without or within Brunei, and for prohibiting such entry or landing except at specified places;

(d) isolating all cases of disease, whether in persons or animals;

(e) establishing and maintaining quarantine stations for persons and animals, and for regulating the management of the same;

(g) prohibiting or regulating the movement of diseased animals or animals suspected of being diseased and the removal of carcases;

(h) slaughtering with or without compensation, as is deemed expedient, diseased animals or with compensation animals suspected of being diseased or of having been in circumstances in which they were likely to have become infected with disease;

(i) cleansing and disinfecting houses, buildings, rooms and other places which have been occupied by any diseased person or animal or which are otherwise in an insanitary condition;

(j) disinfecting and, if expedient, destroying with or without compensation, as is deemed expedient, furniture, clothing, litter, fodder and other articles which have been in contact with any diseased person or animal or which are reasonably suspected of being a vehicle for spreading disease;

(p) prohibiting or regulating the export of cattle from any port or ports of Brunei either absolutely or conditionally and either generally or to any particular port or ports;

(q) appointing, establishing and maintaining places for the observation and examination of cattle previous to export, and for regulating the management of the same, and for compelling the examination of cattle intended to be exported;

(r) cleansing and disinfecting any vessels in which cattle are to be exported;

(s) prohibiting and regulating the removal of fodder, litter, dung and other things;

(t) prescribing and regulating the seizure, detention and disposal of any animal dealt with in contravention of any regulation made under this Act, and for prescribing and regulating the importer of the animal to the expenses connected with the seizure, detention and disposal thereof;

(u) prescribing the notification to Government by medical practitioners of cases of disease treated by them;

(v) the appointment of inspectors and other officers to carry out this Act or any regulations made thereunder, and for regulating their duties and conduct, and for investing them with all powers necessary for the due execution of their duties;

(w) the performance and execution by local authorities of any powers and duties conferred and imposed by this Act or any regulations made thereunder;

(x) prescribing the publication of any regulations made under this Act, and for prescribing and regulating the form and mode of service or delivery of notices and other documents;

(y) prescribing the fine with which the contravention of any regulation made under this Act shall be punishable, but so that such fine shall not exceed $1,000;

(z) fixing the amount of fees to be paid under this Act;

(za) establishing and maintaining places, works and services for the sanitary control of aerial navigation and for prescribing sanitary measures to be taken in respect of international aerial navigation (either generally or in relation to specific diseases) in accordance with the provisions of the International Sanitary Regulations for time being in force.

(2) Nothing in subsection (1) shall in any way restrict or be construed to restrict the generality of the powers conferred on His Majesty in Council by this Act, but such powers shall extend to all matters, whether similar or not, to those in subsection (1) mentioned, as to which it is expedient to make regulations for the better carrying into effect the objects of this Act.

(3) All regulations made under this Act shall be published in the Gazette.

Part Ⅷ Miscellaneous provisions

Offences

4. Any person who, without lawful authority or excuse, proof whereof shall lie on him—

(a) does or omits to do anything which under this Act or any regulations made thereunder he ought not to do or omit to do; or

(b) obstructs, or impedes, or assists in obstructing or impeding, any inspector or other officer appointed under this Act or any police officer in the execution of this Act or of any regulation made thereunder;

shall be guilty of an offence against this Act.

Penalties

5. (1) Any person who is guilty of an offence against this Act for which no penalty is prescribed by this Act or by any regulation made thereunder shall be guilty of an offence: Penalty, a fine of $500.

(2) Any person convicted of any offence against this Act who is within a period of 12 calendar months convicted for a second or subsequent like offence against this Act shall be liable in the Court of a Magistrate to imprisonment for 2 months and to a fine of $1,000.

(3) Nothing in this section shall affect the liability of any person to any punishment or penalty to which he is liable at common law or under any enactment other than this Act, but so that a person shall not be punished twice for the same offence.

. **Forfeitures**

6. (1) If any person lands or brings or attempts to land or bring in or into Brunei any animal or thing in contravention of any regulation made under this Act, such animal or thing shall be forfeited.

(2) Forfeitures under this Act may be declared by a Court of a Magistrate and all animals and things forfeited shall be dealt with as the Minister directs.

Power to arrest

7. (1) When a person is seen or found committing or is reasonably suspected of being engaged in committing an offence against this Act, any inspector or other officer appointed under this Act or any police officer may without warrant stop and detain him and, if his name and address are not known, may arrest him without warrant.

(2) Any person who obstructs or impedes an inspector or other officer appointed under this Act or any police officer in the execution of this Act or of any regulation made thereunder, or assists in any such obstructing or impeding, may be apprehended by such inspector or other officer without warrant.

(3) A person arrested under this section shall be taken with all practicable speed before the Court of a Magistrate.

(4) Nothing in this section shall take away or abridge any power or authority that a police officer would have had if this section had not been enacted.

Presumption

8. When the person in charge of a diseased person, or the owner or person in charge of a diseased animal, is charged with an offence against this Act relative to such disease, he shall be presumed to have known of the existence of such disease in such person or animal, unless and until he show to the satisfaction of the Court of a Magistrate before which he is charged that he had no such knowledge and could not with reasonable diligence have obtained such knowledge.

Officers to be public servants.

Cap. 22

9. Inspectors and other officers appointed under this Act shall be deemed to be public servants within the meaning of the Penal Code.

Offences how triable

Cap. 7

10. Unless otherwise provided every offence under this Act may be tried by the Court of a Magistrate and such Court may, notwithstanding anything in the Criminal Procedure Code, award the full punishment with which such offence is punishable.

Subsidiary legislation

(2) Quarantine and prevention of disease (animals)

REGULATIONS

Citation

1. These Regulations may be cited as the Quarantine and Prevention of Disease (Animals) Regulations.

Interpretation

2. In these regulations—

animal includes a bird;

health officer means the health officer of the district and includes a person authorised in writing by him to act as his deputy or assistant;

import means to bring or cause to be brought into Brunei by land, sea or air;

Cap. 36

officer of customs has the same meaning as in the Customs Act.

Restriction on importation of animals

3. No animal shall be imported, or transhipped from one ship to another within Brunei, without the express permission in writing of the veterinary officer.

Importers of animals to report to veterinary officer

4. A person importing any animal shall, immediately upon arrival and before entering or landing it, report in writing the fact to the veterinary officer.

Importers of dogs and cats to produce certificate that animal is free from rabies

5. A person importing a dog or cat shall produce to the veterinary officer a certificate from a duly qualified veterinary surgeon that, at the time of despatch from the place of export, the dog or cat was free from rabies or similar disease and that, for 6 months prior thereto or from birth, it had been kept in a district in which no case of rabies or similar disease had occurred.

Animals entered or landed in transit may be refused entry

6. If, in the course of transit from the place of export, any animal has been entered or landed at any port, the veterinary officer may refuse permission to enter or land it in Brunei.

Veterinary officer to issue permit on production of veterinary officer's certificate

7. If the veterinary officer—

(a) in the case of a dog or cat, is satisfied that the certificate referred to in regulation 5 is in order and that the dog or cat is in good health; or

(b) in the case of any other animal, is satisfied that the animal is in good health, he shall issue a certificate stating that the animal—

(i) is free from any form of infectious disease; and

(ii) is fit to be imported.

Animals infected or diseased may be destroyed

8. (1) If, in the opinion of the veterinary officer, any animal is infected or is in such a condition that it is expedient that it should be destroyed, he may order it to be destroyed.

(2) Where the veterinary officer has, under paragraph (1), made an order, he shall as soon as possible inform the health officer thereof and give him all relevant information as to the case.

Animals subject to infection may be put in quarantine

9. (1) If, in the opinion of the veterinary officer, any animal has been subject to infection or not being in good health is not in such a condition that it is expedient that it should be destroyed, he may direct that it shall be kept under supervision at the risk and expense of the importer until he is satisfied either—

(a) that it is healthy and may be delivered to the owner, or

(b) that it should be destroyed and he shall take action accordingly.

(2) Where the veterinary officer has, under paragraph (1), given a direction, he shall as soon as possible inform the health officer thereof and give him all relevant information as to the case.

Minister's power to prohibit importation of animals or their conveyance from one place to another in Brunei

10. (1) The health officer, on the advice of the veterinary officer, may recommend to the Minister that it is expedient for the Minister to exercise either or both of his powers under paragraph (2).

(2) If the Minister is satisfied that, owing to the prevalence of rabies or other similar disease, it is expedient, he may declare by public notification that for such time as he may prescribe—

(a) no animal shall be imported;

(b) no animal shall be conveyed from one place in Brunei to another place in Brunei without the express permission in writing of the veterinary officer.

Penalties

11. A person who—

(a) being bound to report, fails to report the arrival in Brunei of any animal;

(b) without the permission of the veterinary officer imports any animal; or

(c) contrary to the provisions of a notification made in that behalf under rule 10, conveys any animal from one place in Brunei to another place in Brunei, shall be guilty of an offence: Penalty, a fine of $200 and the animal may be confiscated or destroyed.

Customs officials may refuse entry or landing of animal if permit is not produced Cap. 36

S. 89/61

12. Subject to the Customs Act, an officer of customs may refuse to permit the importation of any animal until permission in writing of the veterinary officer is produced in respect of that animal.

Declarations under regulation 10

It is declared that the importation or transhipment of all horses, asses and mules into or at any port in Brunei shall be prohibited:

Provided that this prohibition shall not apply to horses, asses and mules imported or transhipped directly from Australia, New Zealand, the United States of America and Sabah.

S. 165/63

S. 114/70

Declaration that the importation of dogs and cats on related species from Malaysia (excluding Sabah and Sarawak) is prohibited.

S. 87/73

Declaration that no animals shall be conveyed from any legal landing place to abbation facilities in Bandar Seri Begawan except in such vehicle as has been approved for that purpose in writing by a veterinary officer.

S. 70/74

S. 93/75

Declaration that the entry of dogs, cats and related species from all countries except Australia, Ireland, New Zealand, Sabah, Sarawak, Singapore and teh United Kingdom shall be subject to their having been kept in quarantine in an approval station in Brunei, Sabah or Sarawak for a period of six months from the time of their arrival.

S. 77/74

Declaration that no cattles or buffalo may be conveyed from one place in Brunei to another place in Brunei without the express permission in writing of a veterimary officer.

(3) Quarantine and prevention of disease (exportation of animals) regulations

Commencement: 20th January 1962

Citation

1. These regulations may be cited as the Quarantine and Prevention of Disease (Exportation of Animals)

Regulations.

Interpretation

2. In these regulations— "animal" includes a bird;

export means to take or cause to be taken out of Brunei by land, sea or air;

health officer has the same meaning as in the Quarantine and Prevention of Disease Act;

veterinary officer has the same meaning as in the Quarantine and Prevention of Disease Act.

Restriction on the exportation of animals

3. No animal shall be exported or transhipped from one ship or conveyance to another ship or conveyance within Brunei for the purpose of export, without the express permission of the veterinary officer.

Application for an Animal Health Certificate

4. (1) Subject to the provisions of these regulations, a person wishing to export an animal, either for sale or otherwise, to any place outside Brunei shall, in the first instance, make an application in the ordinary way to a veterinary officer of the district wherein the animal is situated.

(2) An application may be made for any number of animals, provided they are of the same species.

Inspection of animals and issue of Animal Health Certificate

5. On receipt of such application, the veterinary officer shall arrange for an inspection of the animal and if he is satisfied after such inspection that the animal is free from disease and is in good health, he shall issue an Animal Health Certificate in the form prescribed in the Schedule.

Fee

6. (1) The fee for an Animal Health Certificate shall be:

(a) Cattle including buffalo— $20 per animal;

(b) Goats, dogs and cats— $10 per animal; and

(c) Birds including chicken— $2 per bird.

(2) If any question arises as to which category any animal or bird belongs for the purposes of determining the fees under paragraph (1), a certificate by the veterinary officer for this purpose shall be conclusive;

Animals infected or diseased may be destroyed

7. (1) If, in the opinion of the veterinary officer after such inspection, any animal is infected or is in such a condition that it is expedient that it should be destroyed, he may order it to be destroyed.

(2) Where the veterinary officer has, under paragraph (1) made an order, he shall as soon as possible inform the health officer and give him all relevant information as to the case.

Animals subject to infection may be put in quarantine

8. (1) If the veterinary officer is of the opinion that any animal, which has been subject to infection or not been in good health, is not in such a condition that it is expedient that it should be destroyed, he may direct that it shall be kept under supervision at the risk and expense of the exporter until he is satisfied—

(a) that it is healthy and may be delivered to the exporter; or

(b) that it should be destroyed and he shall take action accordingly.

(2) Where the veterinary officer has, under paragraph (1), given a direction, he shall as soon as possible inform the health officer and give him all relevant information as to the case;

Minister's power to prohibit exportation of animals or their conveyance from one place in Brunei to another prior to exportation

9. (1) The health officer, on the advice of the veterinary officer, may recommend to the Minister that it is expedient for the Minister to exercise either or both of his powers under the following paragraph.

(2) If, owing to the prevalence of an infectious animal disease, the Minister is satisfied that it is expedi-

ent so to do, he may declare by public notification that for such time as he may prescribe—

(a) that no animal shall be exported;

(b) that no animal shall be conveyed from one place to another in Brunei prior to exportation without the express permission in writing of the veterinary officer.

Penalties

10. A person who—

(a) without the permission of the veterinary officer, exports any animal; or

(b) contrary to the provisions of a notification made in that behalf under regulation 9, conveys an animal from one place in Brunei to another prior to exportation,

shall be guilty an offence: Penalty, a fine of $200 and may also suffer the confiscation or destruction, as the case may be, of the animal.

Existing powers and jurisdiction of authorities in respect of exportation

11. The application of these regulations shall not prejudice the existing powers and jurisdiction of authorities, Government or otherwise, in respect of exportation of animals to any place outside Brunei.

新 加 坡

植物控制法案

第一部分　序　　言

简称

1. 此法为《植物控制法案》。

释义

2. 在本法案中，除非上下文有特别释义—

授权分析师　指依据第 3 节条款（3）项，由局长任命的分析员；

授权官员　指依据第 3 节条款（2）项，由局长任命的官员；

主管当局　指根据 2000 年通过的《农业食品和兽医管理法案》（2000 年第 16 号法案）中第 3 节而建立的农业食品和兽医管理局；

具有农药使用资质证书的人员　指根据第 12 节规定被授权作为使用农药的人员；

运输工具　包括所有由机械或他方式驱动的、或者能够被使用的作为陆上、水面、空中运输手段的航空器、船舶、列车、汽车或者其他人造物品；

局长　指根据《动物和禽鸟法》第 7 章第三节第（1）款任命的农业食品和兽医管理局最高行政长官；

染疫　指被某种有害生物侵袭或者感染；

新鲜的水果和蔬菜　指供人类食用的、未经加工的天然水果和蔬菜；

进口　从其语法和词源上讲，系指从新加坡之外的某处经陆运、水运或者空运进入或者由于某种原因被带入新加坡，但是不包括经陆运、水运或者空运进入新加坡（无论在新加坡内装卸或者转运）仅仅是为通过同一或者另一运输工具运往另一个国家；

标签　指手写、打印、图示或者其他类型描述性的材料；

陆地　包括：

（a）地表和地表上的所有物质；

（b）地表下的所有物质；

（c）所有植物及其自然产物，无论这些产物是否需要定期劳作来生产或者产于地上或地下；

（d）与土地有关的或者永久性地附着于与土地有关的某种物体有关的任何物体，无论是地上或地下；

（e）被水覆盖的陆地。

认证种植人　指根据第 10 节规定获得认证的人；

占有人　指包括实际拥有、管理或者控制陆地的人；

物主　指包括租用或借用该土地的人；

包装　指为从某地运往他处，用于植物、植物产品、有害生物的装箱、覆盖、封装、盛放或者捆扎的方式；

有害生物　指对植物或者植物产品产生危害的或者能够产生危害的，任何种、属、目的植物、动物或者病原物；

农药　指任何配置或者使用的用于防止、杀灭、驱除、减轻有害生物的物质或者混合物，以及任何配置或者使用的作为植物调节剂、落叶剂、干燥剂的物质或者混合物；

农药残留 指使用任何一种农药导致的残留，依据本法案中规定的残留水平；

植物检疫证书 指第30节第（1）款中所指的植物检疫证书；

植物 指任何用于繁殖或者可能用于繁殖的植物或者植物的一部分，无论是死的还是活的，无论是蔬菜、水果、花卉、叶、茎、枝、孢子、种子、根、插条、接枝、幼芽还是植物的任何部分；

植物产品 指源于植物的任何产品，无论是天然的、制造的还是加工处理过的；

房屋 应包括其土地；

禁用农药 指在《食品法》附录十中（Cap. 283，Rg 1）未列明的农药；

禁用农药残留 指因使用禁用农药导致的残留；

违禁植物 指第17节禁止的植物；

出售 包括提供或试图出售、收购出售、拥有出售、展示出售、邮寄或发送出售，允许出售、为出售而提供或展示，以及存在和“出售”相同的意义；

土壤 指能够维持植物生存或者能传播有害生物的泥土、水、泥炭、肥料、堆肥、沙、粘土等，无论其是否被用作栽培媒介、或者处于任何加工阶段、或者作为压舱物，或者其他任何目的；

提供 包括供给、试图提供、正在为提供而加工、引起或允许要被提供；

有毒化学残留 指非农药的任何化学物质导致的残留，本法案中规定了残留水平；

转运 从其语法和词源上讲，系指任何植物从新加坡外的某处经陆运、水运或者空运进入或者带入新加坡后—

（a）从进入新加坡的交通工具中转移或者因故被转移；

（b）重新装回或者因故重新装回同一交通工具，或者该植物被转移或者因故被转移到另一交通工具以便出口，无论该植物是在交通工具间直接被转移的，还是在它被带进新加坡后卸载在新加坡并储藏待出口的。

处理 指为确保安全进行的消毒和灭虫，即通过适当的方法杀灭有害生物。[*32/98*；*16/2000*]

法案的执行和授权官员的任命等

3.（1）局长对本法案的执行负责，由部长任命。[*16/2000*]

（2）为实现本法案及其衍生法规的目标，局长可以书面任命各类官员无论本机构或者其他法定机构的官员为授权官员。[*16/2000*]

（3）为实现本法案及其衍生法规，局长可以任命一位或者多位具有合适资质和实际经验的人作为授权分析师。[*16/2000*]

（4）局长可委派授权官员来代其行使本法所赋予他的权力或义务。[*16/2000*]

公务员

4. 根据刑法典（第224章）的宗旨，所有授权官员均为公务员。

出示身份证明

5. 当行使本法案的权力时，任何授权官员都应当申明其职责，如果有关人员提出要求时，还应当出示由局长签发的身份卡。[*16/2000*]

局长可以授权公务员等，行使权力和履行职责

6. 本法案及其衍生法规授予的权力或者赋予的职责，由以局长的名义授权或者特别授权的官员或者其他法定机构的官员执行和贯彻。[*32/98*；*16/2000*]

第二部分　进口和转运新鲜水果和蔬菜

禁止无证新鲜水果和蔬菜进口或者转运

7.（1）任何人不得进口或转运销售、供应、批发新鲜水果和蔬菜，经局长签发许可证按许可要求的除外。[*32/98*；*16/2000*]

（2）违反上述第（1）款的，将视为犯罪并处以不超过＄10,000的罚金或不超过3年的监禁，或

两项并罚。[*32/98*]

禁止进口或转运未经许可的新鲜水果或者蔬菜

8. （1）获许可证的人可从事进口销售、供应、批发新鲜水果和蔬菜，应满足下列条件：

（a）获许可证的人已经从局长处获得允许进口某批新鲜水果或者蔬菜的许可证，且该批货物是按照许可证的规定进口的；

（b）整批货物符合许可证中的内容；

（c）整批货物不含有任何禁用农药残留，或者农药残留和有毒化学残留的水平未超标。

（d）整批货物符合（国家发展部）部长规定的卫生标准；

（e）获许可证的人向农业食品和兽医管理局提交符合要求的证明材料，证明货物与上述（c）、（d）两款的要求相符合；

（f）装运该批新鲜水果或者蔬菜的包装物应显示生产商的名称和地址以及规定的其他要求。[*32/98*；*16/2000*]

（2）获许可证的人获得某批新鲜水果或者蔬菜运输的许可证后，方可从事新鲜水果和蔬菜的运输，该批货物按照许可证的规定运输；[*32/98*；*16/2000*]

（3）违反或者不遵循上述第（1）款或者第（2）款的要求，视为犯罪，将处以不超过＄10,000的罚金，或不超过3年的监禁，或两项并罚。[*32/98*]

（4）除第（5）款的规定情形外，按第（3）款审理的案件，被告人可以依据下列情形发起辩护—

（a）此违法行为应归于他人的行为或者过错，或者超出本人控制的其他原因；

（b）被告人通过本人或其代理人，采取了合理的预防措施、实施了所有必要的手段防止该违法行为的发生。[*32/98*]

（5）在任何一个案件中，如果援引上述第（4）款提出的违法行为归于他人的行为或过错的，未经法庭允许，被告人将无权以此作辩，除非在听证会之前的7个完整工作日内，他已经作为检举人收到书面通知，告知上述信息属实，并且尽其所能确认或者协助查明该人。[*32/98*]

（6）本节所述—

包装物　指用于盛装新鲜水果、蔬菜的篮筐、纸箱、袋子、盒子、包裹或者其他容器，有时某容器装在另一同类容器中，也应包括所有容器；

持证人　指按如第7节要求获得新鲜水果或者蔬菜进口或转运许可的人员。[*32/98*]

第三部分　植物种植的控制

本部分的应用范围

9. 本部分不应用于—

（a）以园艺为目的种植植物；

（b）不以销售为目的种植植物。

禁止种植无证植物

10. 任何人不得以任何理由种植任何植物，除非取得并遵循局长签发的许可证。[*16/2000*]

农药的使用

11. （1）任何人不得在植物种植过程中使用农药，除非—

（a）该农药经局长注册登记；

（b）具有农药使用资质证书的人员或者在其指导下使用。[*16/2000*]

（2）在植物种植过程中使用农药的，应当确保—

（a）农药按规定的方式妥善储藏；

（b）农药的包装按规定的方式处置；

（c）农药残留未超过规定的标准。

具有农药使用资质证书的人员

12. （1）希望获得农药使用资质证书的人员，可以向局长递交申请。[*16/2000*]

（2）局长依据以下条例签发农药使用资质证书—

（a）具有规定的资质和经验；

（b）具有适宜的、能够胜任安全使用农药的能力。[*16/2000*]

（3）具有农药使用资质的人员，局长将为其签发证书。[*16/2000*]

农药使用资质证书的暂停或者取消

13. 局长可以依据下列情形暂停或者取消农药使用资质证书—

（a）使用或者指导使用了未经局长注册登记的农药；

（b）使用或者指导使用了农药时，未按照该农药规定的用法施用；

（c）未能按规定的方法存储农药；

（d）包装的处置未按规定方法办理的；

（e）未能按照局长的要求填写农药使用记录的。[*16/2000*]

农药注册登记的申请

14. （1）用于植物种植的每一种农药都应当由局长注册登记。[*16/2000*]

（2）上述第（1）款项下申请注册登记的农药，应当根据局长的要求，按照规定的方法制作并随附相关的文件和详细资料。[*16/2000*]

（3）局长可以自主建立由他所任命的委员会，在农药注册登记申请及其相关事务方面为他提出建议。[*16/2000*]

新型农药保密条例

15. （1）1999 年 1 月 8 日之前局长已经受理的不超过 5 年的及之后受理的新型农药申请和保密申请材料，在保护期内，局长—

（a）应当采取合理措施保护农药的保密信息；

（b）不能使用该保密信息来决定是否准予其他同类的申请。[*32/98*；*16/2000*]

（2）本节和第 16 节所述内容当中，除非上下文有其他规定—

申请　　指第 14 节项下农药的注册申请；

保密信息　　包括：

（a）商业秘密；

（b）泄露会或可能会导致损害该农药的商业价值的信息；

“保密申请材料”是申请者提供的保密信息，包括—

（a）某项新型农药的申请或者与申请相关的材料；

（b）可能要求的其他申请材料。

局长　　包括负责第 14 节项和第 6 节项下任何被授权的官员、无论本机构或者其他法定机构的官员。

成分　　是化学或生物成分。

“新型农药申请”是—

（a）1999 年 1 月 8 日后提交的、农药有效成分相关的申请—

（i）申请涉及该农药的有效成分；

（ii）在局长受理该申请前，从未有关于该农药有效成分的其他申请；

（b）1999 年 1 月 8 日前提交的，申请所涉及有效成分—

（i）申请涉及该农药的某种有效成分；

（ii）在检疫官受理该申请前，从未有关于该农药有效成分的任何其他申请；

“保护期”，是从该新型农药申请提交之日或局长受理申请之日起 5 年。　　[*32/98*；*16/2000*]

第 15 节项下的保护不实施的情形

16.（1）在保密申请材料有关的保护期内，除第 15 节的规定，局长可以—

（a）公布该保密申请材料或者使用该保密申请材料来决定是否准予与该申请相关的其他同类申请—

（i）经该保密申请材料的申请人同意；

（ii）在局长看来，公布或者使用（该保密申请材料）对于保护大众的健康或者安全是必要的；

（b）在局长看来，即便对某政府部门或者法定机构公布该保密申请材料，该政府部门或者法定机构能够采取合理措施保密该申请材料；

（c）对以下人员或者机构公布该保密申请材料：

（i）世界卫生组织；

（ii）世界粮农组织；

（iii）世界贸易组织成员国的相关机构；

（iv）第 14 节第（3）款项下建立的委员会；

（v）如果该公布符合本法案规定的条件，经本法案规定授权的个人或者组织。[*32/98*；*16/2000*]

（2）上述第（1）款第（a）条第（i）点项下的准予同意的权力，可以由申请人实施—

（a）该申请人—

（i）已经书面通知局长可由其他人准予同意的授权；

（ii）未书面通知局长该人准予同意的授权已经被取消的；

（b）该申请人相关保密申请材料的权力已经被移交给其他人，而且该申请人和该人已经书面通知局长该项权利移交的。[*32/98*；*16/2000*]

（3）“世界贸易组织成员国”指 1994 年 4 月 15 日在马拉卡什签署的《关于建立世界贸易组织的协定》的所有成员国。[*32/98*]

第四部分　禁止植物

部长可以禁止植物的种植

17.（1）部长可以签署命令，禁止或者有条件地禁止某种植物在新加坡境内种植。

（2）上述第（1）条规定的任何人不得种植禁止植物，经局长签发许可并根据许可种植的除外。[*16/2000*]

经许可种植禁止植物的物主和占有人

18. 如果在任何地方被发现违反第 17 节的规定种植禁止植物，该土地的物主和占有人没有获得种植该植物的许可的，除非该物主和占有人证实—

（a）该植物系未经其知道和同意种植的；

（b）一经获悉存在该植物，立即采取有效措施对其进行根除和杀灭。

局长证书应有确凿证据

19. 局长签发说明某种植物是禁止植物的证书，应当指出确凿的事实证据。[*16/2000*]

禁止植物的根除和销毁

20.（1）任何违反第 17 节的规定种植的禁止植物，应当由局长或者授权官员实施根除和销毁。[*16/2000*]

（2）此类根除和销毁的费用，应当由禁止植物种植或者许可种植的土地的物主或者占有人、或者种植该植物的人偿还。[*16/2000*]

第五部分　有害生物的控制

销毁或者处理植物的权力

21.（1）为证实土地上或建筑物内存在某种有害生物，授权官员对土地或者建筑的物主或占有人宣读由局长签发的书面通知（如果被要求）并出示身份卡后，可以—

（a）在任何适当的时间内，进入该土地或者建筑，检查任何植物、植物产品、包装、土壤或者相关物品；

（b）无偿扦取部分植物、植物产品或者土壤作为样品。[*32/98*；*16/2000*]

（2）上述第（1）条的通知，应当在计划进入该土地或者建筑的时间前至少6小时，向该土地或者建筑的物主或者占有人宣读。[*32/98*]

（3）作为上述第（1）条授权官员检查的结果，如果该授权官员发现该土地或者建筑存在有害生物进入或者传播的可能，或者植物染疫，局长可以签发书面通知，告知该土地或者建筑的物主或者占有人，指导其在通知要求的时限内采取局长认可必要的措施，以便—

（a）按照通知规定的某种方式，对该土上地或者建筑内的植物、有害生物，用于农业或者工业的器具，通过进行销毁或者处理，包括停止从该土地或者建筑获得植物或者提炼产品，根除或阻止有害生物的传播；

（b）该土地上或者建筑内的植物、有害生物，用于农业或者工业的器具的处理，应考虑到防止有害生物引进或者传播。[*32/98*；*16/2000*]

（4）该土地或者建筑的物主或者占有人不能遵循上述第（3）条通知要求，或在通知规定的时限内完成措施，授权官员可以—

（a）控制该通知所指的土地或者建筑；

（b）由其授权的处理人员，携带必要的工具和材料进入；

（c）开始实施通知要求的全部措施，由此产生的开销和费用，由该土地或者建筑的物主或者占有人支付。[*32/98*；*16/2000*]

（5）上述第（3）条，均不影响第（7）条的惩罚。[*32/98*]

（6）任何人，阻拦或者妨碍局长或者授权官员行使上述第（1）条的权力的，将视为犯罪，将被处以不超过10000美元的罚金，或者不超过3年的监禁，或者两项并罚。[*32/98*；*16/2000*]

（7）土地或者建筑的物主或者占有人，在规定的时限内故意不遵循上述第（3）条的通知，视为犯罪，将被处以不超过10000美元的罚金，或者不超过3年的监禁，或者两项并罚。如果继续违反的，其定罪后的违法延续期间内，按每一天不超过100美元追加罚金。[*32/98*]

对土地实施检疫监管

22.（1）当检疫官认为某地的植物染疫，可以发布命令对该地或者相关之地实施检疫监管，并在命令中规定监管期限。[*16/2000*]

（2）实施了检疫监管命令，任何人不得转移该地的植物，除非由和遵循授权官员的指导。

（3）上述第（1）条款下实施检疫监管的土地将一直处于检疫监管之下，直到检疫官发证确认其中植物不再染疫。[*16/2000*]

申请进行疫区检查

23.（1）第22节第（1）条款中受检疫监管土地的物主或者占有人可以向授权官员申请检查疫区，以根据第22节第（3）条款获得授权官员签发的证书。

（2）在收到申请后，授权官员应当尽快检查疫区，并按此类检查的规定收费。

命令对植物销毁的权力

24.（1）当局长认为有必要销毁染疫植物，应立即签发书面命令，命令相关人对该植物进行销毁。[*16/2000*]

（2）染疫植物依法销毁的费用（包括处理感病植物相关人产生的费用）将由该染疫植物所在土地的物主或者占有人支付。

清理染疫土地

25.（1）当授权官员确认植物染疫，需清除染疫植物或者某些特定物种时，局长经部长同意，可以通过书面通知向该染疫植物所在地的物主或者占有人说明，指示其在通知规定的期限内、按授权官员的要求砍伐、焚烧或者用其他方式销毁通知所指明的植物或者特定物种。[*16/2000*]

（2）上述第（1）条款通知指示的措施应当依照第21节第（4）条款提供的方式执行，以便第21节第（3）条款通知所指示的措施得到强化。[*32/98*]

（3）土地的业主或者占有人不能遵循第（1）条款通知的要求，将视为犯罪，将被处以不超过10000美元的罚金，或者不超过3年的监禁，或者两项并罚。如果继续违反的，其定罪后的违法延续期间内，按每一天不超过500美元追加罚金。

赔偿

26. 执行第25节第（1）条款签发的通知销毁植物，部长可以在其权力范围内，可从“统一基金”支付赔偿：

（a）染疫植物将不被赔偿；

（b）植物的价值将参照其被销毁时此类植物的市场价值，如果对其市场价值有任何争议，局长的决定为最终的判定；

（c）如果该土地的物主或者占有人实施了违反或者不遵循销毁通知的要求，或者因其疏忽造成该有害生物的传入，部长可以完全取消或者削减对植物销毁的赔偿金额。[*16/2000*]

有害生物检疫员认证

27. 局长可以将具有规定资质和实际经验的合格人员注册为认证的有害生物检疫员：

（a）可对本法案及其条例规定的植物、植物产品、有害生物、土壤、与植物或者植物产品相关其他材料实施检查、鉴定、分析、处理、扣留、销毁和处置；

（b）签发植物检疫证书。[*32/98*；*16/2000*]

第六部分 植 物 出 口

部长可以禁止植物出口

28. （1）部长可以发布命令，完全禁止或根据命令中规定的要求禁止植物从新加坡出口到任何国家、地区或区域。

（2）上述第（1）条款命令中规定的不得出口的植物，经局长签发许可且符合该许可要求方可出口。[*16/2000*]

咨询委员会

29. 部长可以建立一个或者多个由他任命的成员组成的咨询委员会，对部长行使第28条权力及其相关事项提供建议。

植物检疫证书

30. （1）经局长规定的申请和相关程序，授权官员或者授权有害生物检疫员可以签发植物检疫证书，证明植物或者植物产品不存在有害生物。[*32/98*；*16/2000*]

（2）任何人，故意—

（a）为获得植物检疫证书而提供虚假信息的；

（b）伪造任何植物检疫证书的；

（c）使用为其他植物或者植物产品签发的植物检疫证书，明知该证书不是为该批植物或者植物产品所签发的，却意图证明该证书是批植物或植物产品的证书，将视为犯罪，将被处以不超过10000美元的罚金，或者不超过3年的监禁，或者两项并罚。

第七部分 认证和许可

申请认证或许可

31. （1）申请

（a）第7条或者第10条下的认证；

（b）第 8 条下的许可；

（c）根据第 17 条第（1）款或者第 28 条第（1）款项下由局长签发的有关许可，应当按照局长规定的方式和格式制作并提交，并按照局长的要求随附相关费用及样本、资料和文件。［*32/98*；*16/2000*］

（2）受理上述第（1）款的申请后，局长可以—

（a）有条件或者无条件地签发所申请的认证或者许可；

（b）拒绝签发所申请的认证或者许可。［*32/98*；*16/2000*］

（3）不影响上述第（2）款的情况下，关于第 7 条认证的申请或者第 8 条下许可的申请，局长可以—

（a）拒绝签发所申请的认证或者许可；

（b）如果认为这对于保护大众的健康或安全是必要的设定限制或者禁止来自其他国家和地区的新鲜水果、蔬菜的进口或者转运的条件。［*32/98*；*16/2000*］

（4）局长如果拒绝签发认证或者许可，应向申请人提供书面通知，说明拒绝的原因。［*32/98*；*16/2000*］

（5）局长可以变更或者废止上述第（2）（a）条下设定的条件，或者设定新条件。［*32/98*；*16/2000*］

（6）本节项下签发的认证或者许可—

（a）应当按照局长规定的格式；

（b）规定的期限内有效，在第 32 条下被取消的除外；

（c）可以延长有效期，第 8 条的许可除外。［*32/98*；*16/2000*］

（7）上述第（1）款至第（6）款，经必要的修改，可以用于第 7 条或者第 10 条认证、第 17 条第（1）款或者第 28 条第（1）款的许可的延期申请。［*32/98*］

认证或者许可的撤回或者中止

32.（1）局长都以撤回或中止某项认证或许可。［*16/2000*］

（2）在实施上述第（1）款前，局长应当通知当事人，给当事人提交不实施撤回或中止理由的机会。［*16/2000*］

（3）检疫官撤回或中止认证或许可，应当向当事人出具书面的中止或撤回通知。［*16/2000*］

（4）根据第 17 条由检疫官签发的认证被撤回或到期，该持证人应当根除和销毁凭证种植、培育和保有的全部或部分禁止植物。［*16/2000*］

（5）上述第（4）款的禁止植物没有被根除或者销毁的，将被视为违反第 17 条。

上诉

33.（1）被侵害的任何人—

（a）因局长拒绝签发或延期第 31 条的认证或者许可的；

（b）因局长决定中止或撤回第 32 条的认证或者许可的，在收到拒签、中止或撤回通知起 7 天内，可以书面向部长提请上诉。部长做最终判定。［*32/98*；*16/2000*］

（2）上述第（1）款中关于某个认证或许可的中止或撤回的申请处理过程中，除非经部长特别命令，该中止或撤回仍然自局长规定的日期起生效。［*32/98*；*16/2000*］

第八部分　综 合 事 项

罚则

34. 任何人—

（a）违反或者不遵循第 10 条、第 11 条第（1）款和第（2）款、第 22 条第（2）款、第 41 条；

（b）违反或者不遵循部长在第 17 条第（1）款和第 28 条第（1）款项下的命令的，视为犯罪，将

被处以不超过 10000 美元的罚金，或者不超过 3 年的监禁，或者两项并罚。[*32/98*]

法人团体犯罪

35. 法人或者该法人团体中的任何主管、经理、秘书、其他类似官员或者有能力实施此类违法的人，被证实因故意、默许、疏忽违反本法案及其条例，该人和该法人团体视为犯罪，将依法受到起诉和惩罚。

代理人或者雇员犯罪

36. 代理人或其雇员，或在违法实施期间受雇于另一人并负对其有监督或者指导职责的人，违反本法案及其条例，该人负首要责任，如果他本人违法或者被证实该违法行为的实施是经他同意、默许或者因其疏忽而导致的，同样负法律责任。

授权官员的一般权力

37. （1）违反或者正在违反本法案及其条例的，在调查期间（如果被要求，出示身份证），授权官员可以—

（a）进入土地或建筑，检查植物、植物产品、包装、土壤或相关物品；

（b）截获、检查、进入、扣留用于运输植物、植物产品或者包装物的运输工具；

（c）无偿扦取植物、植物产品或土壤作为样品；

（d）没收、移动、扣留植物、植物产品、包装、有害生物或者土壤；

（e）打开货舱、车厢、集装箱、容器，包括任何可以用于装载的地方。

（2）如果授权官员要求，土地、建筑或者运输工具的物主或者占有人应当为其提供协助以便其履行职责，并提供被检查的土地或者建筑的相关资料。

（3）无需授权，警务人员可以拘捕违反或者有充分嫌疑违反了本法案及其条例规定的人—

（a）该人拒绝提供姓名和住址；

（b）有依据怀疑其所提供的姓名和地址不符。

（4）被拘捕的人将被羁留直到他的姓名和地址被证实，但是其羁留期不得超过送交法庭审理必需的时间。

（5）妨碍或者阻拦授权官员履行本法案及其条例所赋予的权力，将视为犯罪，将被处以不超过 10000 美元的罚金，或者不超过 3 年的监禁，或者两项并罚。

加贴标志以鉴别的权力

38. （1）当认为有必要，授权官员可以对有关植物、植物产品的任何货物加贴永久或临时标志。

（2）故意伪造、变更、玷污、涂改、移动此类标志的，将视为犯罪，将被处以不超过 10000 美元的罚金，或者不超过 3 年的监禁，或者两项并罚。

抽样分析的权力

39. （1）为确定新鲜水果或者蔬菜中是否存在禁用农药残留、农药残留或者有毒化学残留的水平，授权官员可以进入建筑无偿抽取新鲜水果或者蔬菜的适当样品送交授权分析师化验，扣留经抽样的整批货物，按正常条件储存，直到获得该分析师的化验报告。[*32/98*]

（2）由授权分析师签署的化验报告可作为本法案及其条例诉讼的证据，并且，如果没有其他证据反对，该化验报告即是陈述的事实证明。[*32/98*]

处置新鲜水果和蔬菜等的权力

40. （1）新鲜水果或者蔬菜的样品被授权分析师确定含有禁用农药残留、农药残留或者有毒化学残留超标，局长在其权力范围内指示将整批新鲜水果或者蔬菜—

（a）再出口或者退运回原产地；

（b）按规定的方式处理，以便清除或者降低残留以达到规定的标准；

（c）按其他规定方式处置。[*32/98；16/2000*]

（2）上述第（1）款中产生的相关费用，如再出口、退运、处理、处置，应当由该批新鲜水果或者蔬菜的物主、种植人或者进口商支付。

有关准许的文件、手册、报告

41. 销售或者供应，进口的或种植新鲜水果和蔬菜，被检查时，应当提供由授权官员签发的许可，并出示该批新鲜水果、蔬菜相关的文件、手册或者报告。[*16/2000*]

罚没

42.（1）触犯本法案及其条例，法庭可以依照本法案及其条例规定收缴与该案有关的任何物品，罚没归政府。[*16/2000*]

（2）依据本法案及其条例起诉的被告被宣判无罪时，法庭可以命令依照本法案及其条例规定收缴的物品归还该人。

（3）上述物品的物主不能定罪的，政府可以罚没收缴来的物品。[*16/2000*]

（4）因罚没归属政府的物品将依照政府认为合适的方式处置。[*16/2000*]

所有权的设定

43. 依据本法案及其条例提起的诉讼，对植物、植物产品、有害生物或者物品的所有权有争议的，占有该植物、植物产品、有害生物或者物品的人将被定为物主，直到反对的申请被证实。

通知的送达

44.（1）依据本法案及其条例出具的通知、命令、文件送达将通过—

（a）亲自送达，或者委托某个至少知晓被送达人的居住地或者工作地点的成年人送达；

（b）在封面上注明收件人的姓名地址，送至通常的或最近的居住地或工作地，或张贴于建筑的显眼位置；

（c）使用注明该人的姓名地址挂号邮件邮递到收件人通常的或最近的居住地或工作地点。

（2）如果“物主”或者“占有人”声明的姓名地址没有更多的名称或者描述，送达任何建筑的物主或者占有人的通知、命令、文件，将被认为是已经注明姓名地址的。

保护责任

45. 诉讼或其他法律程序均不应当回避或欺瞒依据本法案及其条例履行职责的局长或授权官员，除非该事项是在欺诈的情况下被做出或者因疏忽做出。[*16/2000*]

向政府支付的费用

46. 本法案及其条例中收取的费用、开销、罚金、款项都应当向政府缴纳。[*45A* [*16/2000*]

罪罚的合并

47.（1）在其职权范围内，局长可以合并在本法案及其条例中规定可以合并的罪刑，向有充分理由怀疑犯有该罪刑的人收取不超过1000美元的罚金，[*16/2000*]

（2）部长可以规定能够合并的罪刑。

（3）本法案及其条例的罪刑并处的，任何收缴的物品都应当罚没归属政府。[*46* [*16/2000*]

豁免条款

48. 无论在一般案件还是特殊案件中，符合部长规定条件的，可以豁免本法案及其条例规定的违法情况。[*47*]

法规

49.（1）部长可以就本法具体条款制定相关条例，该条例有利于执行本法案的规定。

（2）不违背上述第（1）款而制定—

（a）规定授权官员的权力和职责；

（b）规定与注册登记、认证、出证和许可的签发相关的事项；

（c）为新鲜水果和蔬菜的进口或者转运规定程序、条件或者场所；

（d）规定与第39条分析而对新鲜水果和蔬菜进行抽样的相关事项，以及规定与此类分析相关的事项；

（e）规定授权分析师的资质和实际经验；

（f）规定第8条第（1）（d）点中相关的卫生标准；

（g）对植物、植物产品的检查、观察、羁留、鉴别、处理、销毁、转运或者处置做出规定；

（h）规定植物、植物产品之上或者其中的任何杀虫剂残留或者有毒化学残留的标准；

（i）对控制和根除有害生物以及阻止其在新加坡的传播做出规定；

（j）对进入土地的方式，对植物、植物产品、有害生物、土壤或者其他相关物品的检查、检验、羁留、检疫、处理或者销毁做出规定；

（k）禁止或者限制可能携带有害生物的植物、植物产品、有害生物、土壤、包装材料以及其他媒介进入新加坡；

（l）禁止或者限制任何禁止植物进入新加坡；

（m）规定对来自海外的航空器或者其他运输工具的处理方法以及它们到达时采取的程序，以防止任何有害生物传入新加坡；

（n）要求自海外抵达新加坡的人出示证书，按照规定的格式申明其是否携带其他植物、植物产品、菌类、细菌、病毒、微生物、昆虫、螨类、无脊椎动物或者土壤；

（o）对引进新加坡的任何植物极其后代、土壤、包装材料或者其他媒介的检查、观察、羁留、辩识、处理、销毁、转运或者处置做出规定；

（p）规定在隔离环境中或者检疫监管条件下所储存或者种植的植物的控制措施；

（q）规定在新加坡境内可以装卸植物、植物产品、有害生物或者包装材料的区域；

（r）规定对可能携带有害生物的植物、植物产品或者包装材料的羁留或者检疫措施，规定相关的处理或者销毁措施；

（s）控制农药在植物种植过程中的使用；

（t）规定具有农药使用资质证书的人员的具体资质和实际经验要求；

（u）规定与植物种植过程中所使用的农药相关的登记注册、加贴标志、包装、使用、储存、处置、档案保管等事项；

（v）规定对植物或者植物产品种植、生产、加工、销售、储存、使用的土地或者建筑的认证、控制、监督和检查等事项；

（w）规定对认可的有害生物检疫员的注册登记、控制和监督；

（x）规定某些用于本法案的格式、费率、注册登记事项；[*32/98*]

（3）在本法案及其条例中，部长可以规定对其中条款的违反或者不遵循将视为犯罪，可以对此类犯罪规定处罚：金额不超过 10000 美元的罚金，或者为期不超过 3 年的监禁，或者两项并罚。[*48*]

立 法 史

1. 1993 年 18 号法案——1993 植物控制法案

初审日期：1993 年 2 月 26 日（议案第 9/93 号，1993 年 2 月 27 日出版）

二审和三审日期：1993 年 4 月 12 日

施行日期：1994 年 2 月 18 日

2. 1998 年 32 号法案——1998 植物控制（修订）法案

初审日期：1998 年 6 月 29 日（议案第 31/98 号，1998 年 6 月 30 日出版）

二审和三审日期：1998 年 7 月 31 日

施行日期：1999 年 1 月 8 日

3. 2000 年 16 号法案——2000 农粮兽医局法案

（已经做重大修改）

初审日期：2000 年 2 月 21 日（议案第 11/2000 号，2000 年 2 月 22 日出版）

二审和三审日期：2000 年 3 月 17 日

施行日期：2000 年 4 月 1 日

Control of Plants Act

Part I Preliminary

Short title

1. This Act may be cited as the Control of Plants Act.

Interpretation

2. In this Act, unless the context otherwise requires—

authorised analyst means any person appointed by the Director – General as an authorised analyst under section 3 (3);

authorised officer means any person appointed by the Director – General as an authorised officer under section 3 (2);

Authority means the Agri – food and Veterinary Authority established under section 3 of the Agri – food and Veterinary Authority Act 2000 (Act 16 of 2000);

certified pesticide operator means a person who is certified as a pesticide operator under section 12;

conveyance includes any aircraft, vessel, train, vehicle or any other artificial contrivance, whether mechanically propelled or otherwise used or capable of being used as a means of transport on land, water or air;

Director – General means the Director – General, Agri – food and Veterinary Services appointed under section 3 (1) of the Animals and Birds Act (Cap. 7);

diseased means attacked by or infected with any pest;

fresh fruits and vegetables means unprocessed and raw fruits and vegetables which are intended for human consumption;

import with its grammatical variations and cognate expressions, means to bring or cause to be brought into Singapore by land, sea or air from any place which is outside Singapore but does not include the bringing into Singapore by land, sea or air (whether landed or transhipped in Singapore) for the sole purpose of being carried to any other country either by the same or another conveyance;

label includes any written, printed, pictorial or other descriptive matter;

land includes—

(a) the surface of the earth and all substances forming the surface;

(b) the earth below the surface and all substances therein;

(c) all vegetation and other natural products whether or not requiring the periodical application of labour for their production and whether on or below the surface;

(d) all things attached to the earth, or permanently fastened to any thing attached to the earth, whether on or below the surface; and

(e) land covered by water;

licensed grower means a person who is issued with a licence under section 10;

occupier in relation to any land, includes every person in actual possession, management or control thereof;

owner in relation to any land, includes every lessee or tenant of the land;

package includes every means by which plants, plant products and pests are encased, covered, enclosed, contained or packed for conveyance from one place to another;

pest means any species, strain or biotype of plant, animal or pathogenic agent which is or is capable of being injurious to plants or plant products;

pesticide means any substance or mixture of substances prepared or used for preventing, destroying, repelling or mitigating any pest and any substance or mixture of substances prepared or used as a plant regulator, defoliant or desiccant;

pesticide residue means the remains of any substance resulting from the use of any pesticide, the level of which is prescribed by rules made under this Act;

phytosanitary certificate means a phytosanitary certificate referred to in section 30 (1);

plant means any species of plant or any part thereof whether living or dead and includes any vegetable, fruit, flower, leaf, stem, branch, spore, seed, root, cutting, graft, scion and any other part whatsoever, whether severed or attached, intended for propagation or from which further plants may be propagated;

plant product means any product derived from plants, either in their natural, manufactured or processed form;

premises includes land;

prohibited pesticide means a pesticide not specified in the Tenth Schedule to the Food Regulations (Cap. 283, Rg 1);

prohibited pesticide residue means the remains of any substance resulting from the use of any prohibited pesticide;

prohibited plant means any plant prohibited under section 17;

sell includes offering or attempting to sell, or receiving for sale, or having in possession for sale, or exposing for sale, or sending or delivering for sale, or causing or allowing to be sold, offered or exposed for sale, and "sale" has a corresponding meaning;

soil includes earth, water, peat, manure, compost, sand, clay and any other substance capable of supporting plant life, or transmitting any pest, whether or not used or intended to be used as a growing medium, or in any process of manufacture, or as ballast or for any other purpose whatsoever;

supply includes offering or attempting to supply or having in possession for supply or causing or allowing to be supplied;

toxic chemical residue means the remains of any chemical substance, other than pesticides, the level of which is prescribed by rules made under this Act;

tranship with its grammatical variations and cognate expressions, means to bring or cause to be brought into Singapore by land, sea or air from any place which is outside Singapore any plant and thereafter to—

(a) remove or cause to be removed that plant from the conveyance in which it was brought into Singapore; and

(b) return or cause to be returned that plant to the same conveyance or transfer it or cause it to be transferred to another conveyance, for the purpose of export, whether such plant is to be transferred directly between conveyances or whether it is to be landed in Singapore after it was brought into Singapore and stored, pending export;

treatment means disinfection and disinfestation to ensure the removal, sterilisation or killing of any pest by appropriate means. [*32/98*; *16/2000*]

Administration of Act and appointment of authorised officer, etc.

3. (1) The Director - General shall be responsible for the administration of this Act, subject to the general or special directions of the Minister. [*16/2000*]

(2) The Director – General may in writing appoint any public officer or any officer of the Authority or of any other statutory authority to be an authorised officer for the purposes of this Act and any rules made thereunder. [*16/2000*]

(3) The Director – General may appoint one or more persons with the prescribed qualifications and practical experience to be authorised analysts for the purposes of this Act and any rules made thereunder. [*16/2000*]

(4) The Director – General may delegate the exercise of all or any of the powers conferred or duties imposed upon him by this Act to any authorised officer. [*16/2000*]

Officers deemed to be public servants

4. All authorised officers shall be deemed to be public servants for the purposes of the Penal Code (Cap. 224).

Officer to produce identification on request

5. Every authorised officer, when exercising any power under this Act, shall declare his office and shall, if requested by any person in relation to whom the power is sought to be exercised, produce such identification-card as the Director – General may provide. [*16/2000*]

Director – General may authorise public officer, etc., to exercise powers and perform duties

6. The powers conferred and the duties imposed on the Director – General under this Act or any rules made thereunder may be exercised and carried out by any public officer or officer of the Authority or of any other statutory authority generally or specially authorised by name or office by the Director – General and subject to his directions. [*32/98*; *16/2000*]

Part Ⅱ Import and Transhipment of Fresh Fruits and Vegetables

Prohibition of import or transhipment of fresh fruits or vegetables without licence

7. (1) No person shall import for sale, supply or distribution or tranship any fresh fruit or vegetable except under and in accordance with the conditions of a licence issued by the Director – General. [*32/98*; *16/2000*]

(2) Any person who contravenes subsection (1) shall be guilty of an offence and shall be liable on conviction to a fine not exceeding $10,000 or to imprisonment for a term not exceeding 3 years or to both. [*32/98*]

Prohibition of import or transhipment of fresh fruits or vegetables without permit

8. (1) No licensee shall import any fresh fruit or vegetable for sale, supply or distribution unless—

(a) the licensee has obtained a permit from the Director – General in respect of each consignment of fresh fruits or vegetables to be imported by him and the import of such consignment is carried out in accordance with the conditions of the permit;

(b) the whole consignment conforms to the description contained in the permit;

(c) the whole consignment does not contain any prohibited pesticide residue, or levels of pesticide residue or toxic chemical residue exceeding the prescribed levels;

(d) the whole consignment complies with such sanitary standards as may be prescribed by the Minister;

(e) the licensee provides the Director – General with satisfactory evidence that the whole consignment complies with paragraphs (c) and (d); and

(f) the container of the fruits or vegetables constituting the consignment bears the name and address of the producer and such other particulars as may be prescribed. [*32/98*; *16/2000*]

(2) No licensee shall tranship any fresh fruit or vegetable unless the licensee has obtained a permit from the Director - General in respect of each consignment of fresh fruits or vegetables to be transhipped by him and the transhipment is carried out by him in accordance with the conditions of the permit. [*32/98*; *16/2000*]

(3) Any licensee who contravenes or fails to comply with subsection (1) or (2) shall be guilty of an offence and shall be liable on conviction to a fine not exceeding $10,000 or to imprisonment for a term not exceeding 3 years or to both. [*32/98*]

(4) Subject to subsection (5), in any proceedings for an offence under subsection (3), it shall be a defence for the person charged to prove—

(a) that the commission of the offence was due to the act or default of another person or some other cause beyond his control; and

(b) that he took all reasonable precautions and exercised all due diligence to avoid the commission of such an offence by himself or by any person under his control. [*32/98*]

(5) If in any case the defence provided by subsection (4) involves the allegation that the commission of the offence was due to the act or default of another person, the person charged shall not, without leave of the court, be entitled to rely on that defence unless, within a period ending 7 clear days before the hearing, he has served on the prosecutor a notice in writing giving such information as was then in his possession identifying or assisting in the identification of that other person. [*32/98*]

(6) For the purposes of this section—

container means the basket, carton, bag, box, packet or other receptacle which contains the fresh fruits or vegetables and, where any such receptacle is contained in another such receptacle, includes the latter receptacle;

licensee means a person who has obtained a licence as required under section 7 for the import or transhipment, as the case may be, of any fresh fruit or vegetable. [*32/98*]

Part Ⅲ Control of cultivation of plants

Application of this Part

9. This Part shall not apply to—

(a) the cultivation of any plant for domestic and home gardening purposes; and

(b) the cultivation of any plant which is not for sale.

No cultivation of plants without licence

10. No person shall cultivate any plant on any premises except under and in accordance with a licence issued by the Director - General. [*16/2000*]

Use of pesticide

11. (1) No person shall use any pesticide in the cultivation of any plant unless—

(a) the pesticide is registered with the Director - General; and

(b) he is a certified pesticide operator or the use is supervised by a certified pesticide operator. [*16/2000*]

(2) Any person who uses any pesticide in the cultivation of any plant shall ensure that—

(a) the pesticide is properly stored in the prescribed manner;

(b) the pesticide container is disposed of in the prescribed manner; and

(c) the pesticide residue on any plant cultivated does not exceed the prescribed level.

Certified pesticide operator

12. (1) A person who desires to be certified as a pesticide operator may make an application to the Director – General. [16/2000]

(2) The Director – General may certify a person as a pesticide operator if the Director – General is satisfied that—

(a) he possesses the prescribed qualifications and practical experience; and

(b) he is in all other respects a fit and proper person to be entrusted to apply or otherwise use pesticides safely. [*16/2000*]

(3) Where a person is certified as a pesticide operator, the Director – General shall issue him a certificate to that effect. [*16/2000*]

Suspension or cancellation of certification of pesticide operator

13. The Director – General may suspend or cancel the certification of a person as a pesticide operator if the pesticide operator—

(a) uses or supervises the use of any pesticide which is not registered with the Director – General;

(b) uses or supervises the use of any pesticide otherwise than in accordance with the instructions specified by the manufacturer of the pesticide;

(c) is responsible for any failure to store any pesticide in the prescribed manner;

(d) disposes or causes or allows the disposal of any pesticide container otherwise than in the prescribed manner; or

(e) fails to keep such records of the use of any pesticide as the Director – General may require. [*16/2000*]

Application for registration of pesticide

14. (1) Every pesticide for use in the cultivation of any plant shall be registered with the Director – General. [*16/2000*]

(2) An application for registration under subsection (1) shall be made in such manner and form andaccompanied by such documents and particulars as may be required by the Director – General. [*16/2000*]

(3) The Director – General may establish one or more committees consisting of such persons as he may appoint for the purpose of advising him on such matters arising out of any application for registration under this section as are referred to any such committee by the Director – General [*16/2000*]

Protection of confidential supporting information about innovative pesticides

15. (1) Where the Director – General receives, or has received not more than 5 years before 8th January 1999, an innovative pesticide application and confidential supporting information, the Director – General, during the protected period in relation to that confidential supporting information—

(a) shall take reasonable steps to ensure that the confidential supporting information is kept confidential to the Director – General; and

(b) shall not use the confidential supporting information for the purposes of determining whether to grant any other application. [*32/98*; *16/2000*]

(2) For the purposes of this section and section 16, unless the context otherwise requires—

application means an application for registration of a pesticide under section 14;

confidential information includes—

(a) trade secrets; and

(b) information that has commercial value that would be, or would be likely to be, diminished by disclosure;

confidential supporting information means confidential information given—

(a) in, or in relation to, an innovative pesticide application; and

(b) about the pesticide that is or was, as the case may be, the subject of that application;

Director – General includes any public officer or officer of the Authority or of any other statutory authority authorised under section 6 to carry out registration of pesticides under section 14;

ingredient includes a chemical or biological entity;

innovative pesticide application means—

(a) in relation to an application made after 8th January 1999, an application that refers to an active ingredient—

(i) that is an active ingredient of the pesticide to which the application relates; and

(ii) that has not, before that application is received by the Director – General, been referred to in any other application as an active ingredient of the pesticide; and

(b) in relation to an application made before 8th January 1999, an application that referred to an active ingredient—

(i) that was an active ingredient of the pesticide to which the application related; and

(ii) that had not, before the application was received by the Director – General, been referred to in any other application as an active ingredient of the pesticide;

protected period in relation to confidential supporting information relating to an innovative pesticide application received by the Director – General, means a period of 5 years from the date the innovative pesticide application is or was, as the case may be, received by the Director – General. [*32/98*; *16/2000*]

Circumstances where protection under section 15 does not apply

16. (1) Notwithstanding section 15, the Director – General may, during the protected period in relation to confidential supporting information—

(a) disclose that confidential supporting information, or use that confidential supporting information for the purposes of determining whether to grant any application other than the application to which it relates or related, as the case may be—

(i) with the consent of the applicant who made the application to which the confidential supporting information relates or related; or

(ii) if that disclosure or use is, in the opinion of the Director – General, necessary to protect the health or safety of members of the public;

(b) disclose that confidential supporting information to a Government department or statutory body for the purposes of the Government department or statutory body if, in the opinion of the Director General, the Government department or statutory body will take reasonable steps to ensure the confidential supporting information is kept confidential; or

(c) disclose that confidential supporting information to any one or more of the following:

(i) the World Health Organisation;

(ii) the Food and Agriculture Organisation;

(iii) any regulatory agency of a WTO Country;

(iv) any committee established under section 14 (3);

(v) any person or organisation, or a person or an organisation within a class or classes of persons or organisations, approved by any rules made under this Act, if the disclosure is in accordance with such conditions as may be specified in the rules. [*32/98*; *16/2000*]

(2) The power to grant consent under subsection (1) (a) (i) may be exercised by a person other than the applicant referred to in that subsection if—

(a) that applicant—

(i) has notified the Director – General in writing that that other person may grant that consent;

(ii) has not notified the Director – General in writing that that person's authority to grant that consent has been withdrawn; or

(b) that applicant's rights in respect of the relevant confidential supporting information have been transferred to that person and the applicant or that other person has notified the Director – General in writing of the transfer. [*32/98*; *16/2000*]

(3) For the purposes of this section, "WTO Country" means a country that is a party to the Agreement establishing the World Trade Organisation adopted at Marrakesh on 15th April 1994. [*32/98*]

Part Ⅳ Prohibited plants

Minister may prohibit cultivation of plants

17. (1) The Minister may by order prohibit, either absolutely or conditionally, the cultivation of any plant in Singapore.

(2) An order made under subsection (1) may provide that no person shall cultivate any prohibited plant except under and in accordance with a permit issued by the Director – General. [*16/2000*]

Presumption that owner and occupier permitted growing of prohibited plants

18. If any prohibited plant is found growing on any land in contravention of any order made under section 17, the owner and the occupier of the land shall be deemed to have permitted the plant to grow unless the owner or the occupier, as the case may be, proves—

(a) that the plant was planted without his knowledge and consent; and

(b) that on becoming aware of the existence of the plant he forthwith effectually eradicated and destroyed it.

Certificate of Director – General to be conclusive evidence

19. A certificate under the hand of the Director – General stating that any plant is a prohibited plant shall be conclusive evidence of the facts stated therein. [*16/2000*]

Eradication and destruction of prohibited plants

20. (1) Any prohibited plant cultivated in contravention of any order made under section 17 may be eradicated and destroyed by the Director – General or any person acting under his authority. [*16/2000*]

(2) The cost of such eradication and destruction shall be recoverable from the owner or occupier of the land on which the prohibited plant was planted or permitted to grow or from the person who planted it, as a debt due to the Authority. [*16/2000*]

Part Ⅴ Control of pests

Power to direct destruction or treatment of plants, etc.

21. (1) For the purpose of ascertaining whether any pest is present on or in any land or premises, an authorised officer may, upon serving notice in writing under the hand of the Director – General on the owner or occupier of the land or premises and upon producing, if so requested, an identification card—

(a) enter the land or premises and examine any plant, plant product, package, soil or article thereon at all reasonable times; and

(b) take, without payment, any sample of any plant, plant product or soil. [*32/98*; *16/2000*]

(2) The notice referred to in subsection (1) shall be served on the owner or occupier of the land or premises at least 6 hours before the time of intended entry of the land or premises. [*32/98*]

(3) If, as a result of any examination by an authorised officer under subsection (1), it appears to the

authorized officer that any land or premises or plant is in a condition favourable to the introduction or spread of any pest or that any plant is diseased, the Director – General may, by notice in writing under his hand addressed to the owner or occupier of the land or premises where that condition exists or where the plant is, direct him to take within a time to be stated in the notice such measures as may appear to the Director – General necessary or expedient for—

(a) the eradication or the prevention of the spread of any pest, either by destruction or by treatment in a manner to be specified in the notice of that plant or any plant or of any pest or of any tool or utensil used for agricultural or industrial purposes on the land or premises including the cessation of obtaining or abstracting any product from any plant on the land or premises; and

(b) the treatment of the land or premises or plant or of any tool or utensil used for agricultural or industrial purposes on the land or premises with a view to bringing them into a condition not favourable to the introduction or spread of any pest. [*32/98*; *16/2000*]

(4) If the owner or occupier of any land or premises fails to comply with a notice under subsection (3) within the time stated for the performance of the acts required to be done, any authorised officer may—

(a) enter upon the land or premises to which the notice refers;

(b) cause any person authorised by him to enter with such instruments and things as are necessary; and

(c) proceed to perform all acts required by the notice, and the costs and expenses thereof shall be recoverable as a debt due from the owner or occupier to the Authority. [*32/98*; *16/2000*]

(5) Nothing in subsection (4) shall affect the liability of any person to prosecution and punishment under subsection (7). [*32/98*]

(6) Any person who obstructs or hinders the Director – General or an authorised officer in the exercise of any of his powers under subsection (1) shall be guilty of an offence and shall be liable on conviction to a fine not exceeding $10,000 or to imprisonment for a term not exceeding 3 years or to both. [*32/98*; *16/2000*]

(7) Any owner or occupier of any land or premises who wilfully fails to comply with the notice under.

subsection (3) within the time stated shall be guilty of an offence and shall be liable on conviction to a fine not exceeding $10,000 or to imprisonment for a term not exceeding 3 years or to both and, in the case of a continuing offence, to a further fine not exceeding $100 for every day during which the offence continues after conviction. [*32/98*]

Placing land under quarantine

22. (1) Where the Director – General is of the opinion that any plant on any land is diseased, he may make an order placing the land or any part thereof in quarantine for such period as may be prescribed by the order. [*16/2000*]

(2) So long as an order of quarantine applies to any land, no person shall remove any plant therefrom except under and in accordance with the direction of an authorised officer.

(3) Any land placed in quarantine under subsection (1) shall continue in quarantine until the Director – General certifies that no plant thereon is diseased. [*16/2000*]

Application for examination of quarantined area

23. (1) Any owner or occupier of any land quarantined under section 22 (1) may apply to an authorized officer to examine the quarantined area with a view to obtaining from the authorised officer the certificate referred to in section 22 (3).

(2) The authorised officer shall, as soon as possible after receipt of such an application, visit and examine the quarantined area and may charge such fees as may be prescribed for such visit and examination.

Power to order immediate destruction of plants

24. (1) If in the opinion of the Director – General the destruction of any diseased plant is a matter of necessity and extreme urgency, he may forthwith make an order in writing directing the immediate destruction of the plant by any person referred to in the order. [*16/2000*]

(2) Such plant shall be destroyed accordingly and the cost of the destruction, if incurred by any person other than the owner or occupier of the land where the diseased plant was, shall be defrayed by the owner or occupier.

Clearing diseased land

25. (1) Where it appears to an authorised officer that any plant on any land is diseased and he is of the opinion that it is necessary for the prevention of the spread of any pest that the land be entirely cleared of cultivation or cleared of all cultivation of any particular species, the Director – General may, with the approval of the Minister, by notice in writing addressed to the owner or occupier of the land where the plant is, direct him to fell and burn or otherwise destroy within a time to be stated in the notice and to the satisfaction of the authorised officer all cultivation or all cultivation of the species named in the notice. [*16/2000*]

(2) The action directed by a notice under subsection (1) may be enforced in the manner provided by section 21 (4) for the enforcement of the action directed by a notice under section 21 (3). [*32/98*]

(3) If the owner or occupier of any land on whom a notice under subsection (1) has been served fails to comply with the notice, he shall be guilty of an offence and shall be liable on conviction to a fine not exceeding $10,000 or to imprisonment for a term not exceeding 3 years or to both and, in the case of a continuing offence, to a further fine not exceeding $500 for every day during which the offence continues after conviction.

Compensation

26. Where any cultivation has been destroyed in pursuance of a notice issued under section 25 (1), the Minister may, in his discretion, direct the payment out of the Consolidated Fund of compensation for that cultivation subject to the following provisions:

(a) no compensation shall be paid for any diseased plant;

(b) the value of any cultivation shall be taken to be the market value of that cultivation at the time of its destruction and if any question arises as to the market value, the decision of the Director – General shall be final and conclusive; and

(c) the Minister may entirely withhold or may reduce the amount of compensation for the destruction of any cultivation if the owner or occupier of the land has done anything in contravention of, or has failed to comply with, any notice issued under this Part or has by his neglect contributed to the introduction of the pest. [*16/2000*]

Accredited pest control agency

27. The Director – General may register any fit and proper person possessing the prescribed qualifications and practical experience as an accredited pest control agency—

(a) to carry out, at any place, any inspection, identification, analysis, treatment, detention, destruction or disposal of any plant, plant product, pest, or any soil or other material attached to any plant or plant product under this Act and any rules made thereunder; and

(b) to issue phytosanitary certificates. [*32/98*; *16/2000*]

Part Ⅵ Export of plants

Minister may prohibit export of plants

28. (1) The Minister may by order prohibit, either absolutely or subject to such conditions as may be specified in the order, the export of any plant from Singapore to any country, territory or place.

(2) An order under subsection (1) may specify that no person shall export any plant except under and in accordance with a permit issued by the Director – General. [*16/2000*]

Advisory committee

29. The Minister may establish one or more advisory committees consisting of such members as he may appoint, for the purpose of advising the Minister on the exercise of his power to make any order under section 28, and on other subjects connected therewith.

Phytosanitary certificate

30. (1) Any authorised officer or accredited pest control agency may, on application and on such terms as the Director – General may require, issue a phytosanitary certificate stating that any plant or plant product is free from pests for the purpose of export. [*32/98*; *16/2000*]

(2) Any person who wilfully—

(a) gives false information for the purpose of obtaining a phytosanitary certificate;

(b) falsifies any phytosanitary certificate; or

(c) uses a phytosanitary certificate with intention of causing it to be believed that a plant or plant product which is not a plant or plant product in respect of which the phytosanitary certificate was issued, is a plant or plant product in respect of which the certificate was issued, shall be guilty of an offence and shall be liable on conviction to a fine not exceeding $10,000 or to imprisonment for a term not exceeding 3 years or to both.

Part Ⅶ Licence and permit

Application for licence or permit

31. (1) An application—

(a) for a licence under section 7 or 10;

(b) for a permit under section 8; or

(c) where provision is made by an order under section 17 (1) or 28 (1) for the issue by the Director – General of a permit, for a permit under that section, shall be made to the Director – General in such manner and form as the Director – General may require and shall be accompanied by the prescribed fee and such particulars, information and documents as the Director – General may require. [*32/98*; *16/2000*]

(2) On the receipt of an application under subsection (1), the Director – General may—

(a) issue the licence or permit applied for, with or without conditions; or

(b) refuse to issue the licence or permit applied for. [*32/98*; *16/2000*]

(3) Without prejudice to the generality of subsection (2), the Director – General may, in respect of an application for a licence under section 7 or a permit under section 8—

(a) refuse to issue the licence or permit; or

(b) impose a condition restricting or prohibiting the import or transhipment of any fresh fruit or vegetable from any country, territory, place or farm, if he considers that this is necessary to protect the health or safety of members of the public. [*32/98*; *16/2000*]

(4) Where the Director – General has refused to issue the licence or permit applied for, he shall give the applicant notice in writing of the reasons for his refusal. [*32/98*; *16/2000*]

(5) The Director – General may at any time vary or revoke any of the conditions imposed under subsection (2) (a) or impose new conditions. [*32/98*; *16/2000*]

(6) Every licence or permit issued under this section—

(a) shall be in such form as the Director – General may determine;

(b) shall be valid for the period stated therein unless it is sooner revoked under section 32;

(c) may, unless it is a permit under section 8, be renewed upon its expiry. [32/98; 16/2000]

(7) Subsections (1) to (6) shall apply, with the necessary modifications, to an application for the renewal of a licence under section 7 or 10 or a permit under section 17 (1) or 28 (1). [32/98]

Revocation or suspension of licence or permit

32. (1) The Director - General may at any time revoke or suspend a licence or permit. [16/2000]

(2) The Director - General shall, before taking any action referred to in subsection (1), notify the person concerned of his intention to take such action and shall give the person concerned an opportunity to submit reasons why such action should not be taken against him. [16/2000]

(3) Where the Director - General has revoked or suspended a licence or permit under this Act, he shall give notice in writing of the suspension or revocation to the person concerned. [16/2000]

(4) Where a licence issued by the Director - General pursuant to an order made under section 17 is revoked or has expired, the licensee shall eradicate and destroy all or any of the prohibited plants planted or cultivated or maintained in pursuance thereof. [16/2000]

(5) Any prohibited plant not eradicated and destroyed under subsection (4) shall be deemed to have been grown in contravention of section 17.

Appeal

33. (1) Any person who is aggrieved by—

(a) the refusal of the Director - General to issue or renew a licence or permit under section 31;

(b) the decision of the Director - General to suspend or revoke a licence or permit under section 32, may, within 7 days of the receipt of the notice informing him of the refusal, suspension or revocation, as the case may be, appeal in writing to the Minister whose decision shall be final. [32/98; 16/2000]

(2) Notwithstanding the pendency of any appeal under subsection (1) in respect of the suspension or revocation of a licence or permit, such suspension or revocation shall, unless the Minister otherwise orders, take effect from the date specified by the Director - General therefor. [32/98; 16/2000]

Part Ⅷ Miscellaneous

Penalty

34. Any person who—

(a) contravenes or fails to comply with section 10, 11 (1) and (2), 22 (2) or 41; or

(b) contravenes or fails to comply with any order made by the Minister under section 17 (1) or 28 (1), shall be guilty of an offence and shall be liable on conviction to a fine not exceeding $10,000 or to imprisonment for a term not exceeding 3 years or to both. [32/98]

Offences committed by body corporate

35. Where an offence under this Act or any rules made thereunder has been committed by a body corporate is proved to have been committed with the consent or connivance of, or to be attributable to any neglect on the part of, any director, manager, secretary or other similar officer of the body corporate, or any person who was purporting to act in any such capacity, he, as well as the body corporate, shall be guilty of that offence and shall be liable to be proceeded against and punished accordingly.

Offences committed by agent or servant

36. Where an offence under this Act or any rules made thereunder is committed by any person acting as the agent or servant of another person, or being otherwise subject to the supervision or instructions of another person for the purposes of any employment in the course of which the offence was committed, that other person shall, without prejudice to the liability of the first – mentioned person, be liable under this Act or any rules made thereunder in the same manner and to the same extent as if he had personally committed the offence if it is proved that the act which constituted the offence was committed with his consent or connivance or that it was attributable to any neglect on his part.

General powers of authorised officers

37. (1) For the purpose of ascertaining whether any offence under this Act or any rules made thereunder has been or is being committed, any authorised officer may, on producing, if so requested, an identification card—

(a) enter and inspect any land or premises and examine any plant, plant product, package, soil or article thereon at all reasonable times;

(b) stop, examine, board, enter or detain any conveyance used for carrying any plant, plant product or package;

(c) take, without payment, any sample of any plant, plant product or soil;

(d) seize, remove or detain any plant, plant product, package, pest or soil; or

(e) break open any hold, compartment or container or other receptacle including any place that could be used as a receptacle.

(2) The owner or occupier of any land, premises or conveyance shall, if requested by an authorised officer, provide reasonable assistance to the authorised officer for the purpose of the exercise of his powers under this section and furnish any information relating to the land or premises which is reasonably required by the authorised officer for the purposes of the discharge of his duties under this Act.

(3) A police officer may arrest without warrant any person who has committed or whom he reasonably suspects to have committed an offence under this Act or any rules made thereunder—

(a) if the person refuses to give his name and address; or

(b) if there is reason to doubt the accuracy of the name and address, if given.

(4) A person arrested under this section may be detained until his name and address are correctly ascertained except that no person shall be detained longer than is necessary for bringing him before a court.

(5) Any person who obstructs or hinders any authorised officer in the exercise of any of his powers under this Act or any rules made thereunder shall be guilty of an offence and shall be liable on conviction to a fine not exceeding $10,000 or to imprisonment for a term not exceeding 3 years or to both.

Power to label for identification

38. (1) Any authorised officer may, where he considers it necessary for the purposes of identification, label permanently or temporarily, any consignment of plants or plant products.

(2) Any person who wilfully counterfeits, alters, defaces, erases or removes any such label shall be guilty of an offence and shall be liable on conviction to a fine not exceeding $10,000 or to imprisonment for a term not exceeding 3 years or to both.

Power to take samples for analysis

39. (1) An authorised officer may, for the purposes of ascertaining the presence of prohibited pesticide residue, and the levels of pesticide residue or toxic chemical residue, contained in any fresh fruit or vegetable, enter any premises at all reasonable times to take, without payment, any reasonable sample of fresh fruits or vegetables for analysis by an authorised analyst and detain the whole lot from which the sample is taken under normal storage conditions until a report of the result of the analysis is obtained. [*32/98*]

(2) A report of the result of an analysis which is signed by an authorised analyst shall be admissible in evidence in any proceedings under this Act or any rules made thereunder and, in the absence of evidence to the

contrary, is proof of the matters stated in the report. [*32/98*]

Power to dispose of, etc., fresh fruits and vegetables

40. (1) Where any sample of fresh fruits or vegetables is determined by an authorised analyst to contain any prohibited pesticide residue, or any pesticide residue or toxic chemical residue exceeding the prescribed levels, the Director – General may, in his discretion, cause the whole lot of fresh fruits or vegetables from which the sample is taken, to be—

(a) re – exported or returned to its place of origin;

(b) treated in such manner as he may direct so as to remove or aid the dissipation of the residue to the prescribed levels; or

(c) disposed of in such manner as he may direct. [*32/98*; *16/2000*]

(2) The cost of, and all expenses incurred in, the re – exporting, returning, treatment or disposal under subsection (1) shall be defrayed by the owner, grower or importer of the fresh fruits or vegetables.

Access to documents, books and records

41. Every person who imports for sale or supply or who grows fresh fruits or vegetables shall, on demand, afford the Director – General access to, and produce, such documents, books or records relating to or reasonably believed to relate to the fresh fruits or vegetables as may be required by the Director – General. [*16/2000*]

Forfeiture

42. (1) Where any person is convicted of any offence under this Act or any rules made thereunder, the court may order that any article seized under this Act or any rules made thereunder or in respect of which the offence was committed, be forfeited to the Authority. [*16/2000*]

(2) Where a person who is charged for an offence under this Act or any rules made thereunder is acquitted, the court may order any article seized under this Act or any rules made thereunder to be released to the person from whom the article was seized.

(3) Where the owner of the article cannot be ascertained, the Authority may confiscate the article seized. [*16/2000*]

(4) Every article so forfeited to the Authority shall be disposed of in such manner as the Authority thinks fit. [*16/2000*]

Presumption of ownership

43. Where in any proceedings under this Act or any rules made thereunder a question arises as to the ownership of any plant, plant product, pest or article, the person found in possession of the plant, plant product, pest or article shall be presumed to be the owner thereof until the contrary is proved.

Service of notices

44. (1) Where under this Act or any rules made thereunder any notice, order or document is required or authorised to be served on any person, it may be served by—

(a) delivering it personally or by leaving it with some adult person at the last known place of residence or business of the person to be served;

(b) leaving it at the usual or last known place of residence or business of the person to be served in a cover addressed to that person, or posting it upon a conspicuous part of those premises;

(c) sending it by registered post addressed to the person to be served at his usual or last known place of residence or business.

(2) Any notice, order or document required or authorised by this Act to be served on the owner or the occupier of any premises shall be deemed to be properly addressed if addressed by the description of the "owner" or "occupier" of the premises without further name or description.

Protection from liability

45. No suit or other legal proceedings shall lie against the Director – General or any authorised officer in respect of anything done or omitted to be done in the discharge of their duties under this Act or any rules made thereunder unless the thing was done or omitted to be done in bad faith. [*16/2000*]

Fees, etc. , payable to Authority

46. All fees, charges, composition fines and moneys collected under this Act or any rules made thereunder shall be paid to the Authority. [*45A* [*16/2000*]

Composition of offences

47. (1) The Director – General may, in his discretion, compound any offence under this Act or any rules made thereunder which is prescribed as an offence which may be compounded by collecting from a person reasonably suspected of having committed the offence a sum not exceeding $1,000. [*16/2000*]

(2) The Minister may prescribe the offences which may be compounded.

(3) Where an offence is compounded under this Act or any rules made thereunder, any article seized shall be forfeited to the Authority. [*46* [*16/2000*]

Exemption

48. The Minister may, either generally or in any particular case, and subject to such conditions as he may impose, exempt any person from all or any of the provisions of this Act or any rules made thereunder. [*47*]

Rules

49. (1) The Minister may make rules for or with respect to any matter which may be necessary or expedient for carrying out the provisions of this Act.

(2) Without prejudice to the generality of subsection (1), rules may be made—

(a) providing for the powers and duties of the authorised officers;

(b) providing for matters relating to registration, licensing, certification and the issue of permits;

(c) prescribing the procedure, condition or location for the import or transhipment of any fresh fruit and vegetable;

(d) providing for matters relating to the taking of samples of fresh fruits and vegetables under section 39 for analysis, and for matters relating to such analysis;

(e) prescribing the qualifications and practical experience of an authorised analyst;

(f) prescribing the sanitary standards referred to in section 8 (1) (d);

(g) providing for the inspection, observation, detention, identification, treatment, destruction, reshipment or disposal of any plant or plant product;

(h) prescribing the levels of any pesticide residue or toxic chemical residue in or on any plant or plant product;

(i) providing for the control and eradication of pests and preventing their spread within Singapore;

(j) prescribing the manner of entry upon any land and the conduct of any examination, inspection, detention, quarantine, treatment or destruction of any plant, plant product, pest, soil or any other article thereon;

(k) prohibiting or restricting the introduction into Singapore of any plant, plant product, pest, soil or package or other thing which is likely to introduce pests into Singapore;

(l) prohibiting or restricting the introduction into Singapore of any prohibited plant;

(m) prescribing treatment for aircraft or any other conveyance arriving from overseas and the procedure to be adopted on their arrival so as to prevent the introduction of any pest into Singapore;

(n) requiring every person arriving in Singapore from overseas to give a certificate declaring in such form as may be prescribed whether he has any plant, plant product, fungus, bacterium, virus or micro – organism or any insect, mite or other invertebrate animal or any soil in his possession;

(o) providing for the inspection, observation, disinfection, treatment, destruction, reshipment or disposal of any plant introduced into Singapore and the progeny of any such plant or any soil, package or other thing;

(p) providing for the control of plants kept or grown in isolation or under quarantine conditions;

(q) prescribing the areas within Singapore where any plant, plant product, pest or package may be landed;

(r) providing for the detention or the quarantine of any plant, plant product or package suspected of harbouring any pest and prescribing the treatment or the destruction thereof;

(s) regulating the use of any pesticide in the cultivation of plants;

(t) prescribing the qualifications and practical experience of a certified pesticide operator;

(u) providing for matters relating to the registration, labelling, packing, use, storage, disposal and record keeping of any pesticide used in the cultivation of plants;

(v) providing for the licensing, control, supervision and inspection of any land or premises on which any plant or plant product is grown, produced, processed, sold, stored or used;

(w) providing for the registration, control and supervision of any accredited pest control agency;

(x) prescribing the forms, fees or registers for the purposes of this Act. [*32/98*]

(3) The Minister may, in any rules made under this Act, provide that any contravention of or failure to comply with any provision thereof shall be an offence and may prescribe a penalty for any such offence of a fine not exceeding $10,000 or imprisonment for a term not exceeding 3 years or both. [*48*]

Legislation history

1. Act 18 of 1993—Control of Plants Act 1993

Date of First Reading: 26. 2. 93 (Bill No. 9/93 published on 27. 2. 93)

Date of Second and Third Readings: 12. 4. 93

Date of commencement: 18. 2. 94

2. Act 32 of 1998—Control of Plants (Amendment) Act 1998

Date of First Reading: 29. 6. 98 (Bill No. 31/98 published on 30. 6. 98)

Date of Second and Third Readings: 31. 7. 98

Date of commencement: 8. 1. 99

3. Act 16 of 2000—Agri-Food and Veterinary Authority Act 2000

(Consequential amendments made by)

Date of First Reading: 21. 2. 2000 (Bill No. 11/2000 published on 22. 2. 2000)

Date of Second and Third Readings: 17. 3. 2000

Date of commencement: 1. 4. 2000

植物控制（植物进口）条例

历史：G. N. NO. S29/94 →1995 修正案 →R4 2000 修正案

［**1994 年 2 月 18 日**］

引言

1. 以下条文称为《植物控制（植物进口）条例》。

定义

2.（1）在以下条文中，除非上下文有例外要求：

美洲热带地区　指美洲大陆的一部分以及邻近的岛屿，位于南回归线（南纬 23 度）和北回归线（北纬 23 度）、西经 30 度和西经 120 度之间，包括墨西哥在北回归线以北的部分地区；

生物防治　指利用有害生物的天敌、对抗生物或者竞争生物；或者其他管制有害生物的生物体；

进口卫生要求　指局长根据本条例第 7 条所指定或者变更的进口卫生要求；

改性活生物体　指通过现代生物技术获得的遗传材料新异组合的活生物体。

（a）打破了自然界生物学上生物繁殖或者重新组合的壁垒；

（b）不属于传统育种和选种的技术；

非检疫性有害生物　指附件 1 第 2 部分所列的有害生物；

检疫性有害生物　指附件 1 第 1 部分所列的有害生物；

受管制的有害生物　指附件 1 第 1 部分或第 2 部分所列的有害生物；

过境　指（物品）从某国被携带或者邮寄带入新加坡，仅仅是为了通过在自由贸易区内的同一或者另一运输工具带入另一个国家。

（2）在以下条文中：

（a）提及的植物、植物产品或者材料的装运，应包括所涉及的集装箱、容器、包装材料或者构成该次装运的其他物品；

（b）提及的受管制植物、受管制植物产品或者受管制材料，应作为涉及植物、植物产品或者材料（的物品），在附件 2 中列明；

（c）提及的有害生物、植物、植物产品、植物材料的进口或者转运的，解释为贸易的有害生物、植物、植物产品、植物材料的进口或者移运；

（d）提及的证书或者文档，应包括涉及的证书或者电子文档格式。

本条例不适用情况

3. 依据条例第 12、13、14 条，这些规定不适用于

（a）局长根据特定条件许可进口的以实验或者研究为目的的植物、植物产品或者受管制材料，并带有局长书面许可的；

（b）携带管制植物、管制植物产品或者管制材料进入新加坡过境，必须遵循该植物、植物产品或者材料不能从入境新加坡的口岸移运新加坡其他地区的要求，除非

（i）获得局长或者授权官员的书面许可；

（ii）符合局长或者授权官员许可的期限和条件。

进口的植物、植物产品或原料不得携带检疫性有害生物

4. 植物、植物产品或者材料应当确保该货物及其装运的集装箱或相关的其他包装物不携带检疫性有害生物。

管制植物、管制植物产品或管制植物原料的进口

5. (1) 没有局长签发的许可，任何人不得进口管制植物、管制植物产品或管制植物原料。

(2) 根据上述第 (1) 条款是否签发许可时，局长应当判断许可的申请是否和相关进口卫生要求和下列第 (4) 条款的要求一致。

(3) 在此条款下签发的每份许可：

(a) 应当在指定的时限内，仅对其相关的货物有效；

(b) 应当遵循局长随附在许可证书后的时限和要求。

(4) 任何进口管制植物、管制植物产品或管制植物原料应当随附与货物相关的—

(a) 植物检疫证书；

(b) 发运地国家经局长认可的相关政府机构签发或者授权签发的此类其他证书、文件或者标志，并且根据检验满足进口卫生要求。

(5) 上述第 (4) 款中的植物检疫证书应当在不早于货物装运前 14 天，由发运国相关政府机构或者农业部门签发。他们应当经局长认可。

(6) 植物检疫证书、上述第 (4) 条款中的其他证书、文件或者标志应当证明相关的进口卫生要求得以满足。

局长决定是否禁止植物、植物产品或原料进入新加坡

6. (1)

(a) 受管制的植物、受管制的植物产品或者受管制的材料进口时：

(i) 未依照第 5 条第 (4) 款随附植物检疫证书、其他证书、文件或者标志的；

(ii) 已经依照第 5 条第 (4) 条款随附植物检疫证书、其他证书、文件或者标志但是与第 5 条第 (5) 条款或者第 (6) 条款不符的；

(b) 已经进口的植物、植物产品或者植物材料被发现非检疫有害生物寄生的；

(c) 已经进口的植物、植物产品或者植物材料被发现某种非新加坡原生的有害生物（检疫性有害生物除外）寄生，该有害生物被局长判定对新加坡某种植物或者某类植物生态系统存在潜在危害的，局长有权决定：

(i) 禁止该批植物、植物产品或者植物材料进入新加坡；

(ii) 在满足合适时限和条件要求后，允许该批植物、植物产品或者植物材料进入新加坡。

(2) 在此条款中，所提及的进口货物包括旅客携带进入新加坡自用的物品。

进口卫生要求

7. (1) 为实现本条例的目标，局长可以对管制植物、管制植物产品或者管制材料设定进口卫生要求。

(2) 局长可以变更进口卫生要求：

(a) 根据管制植物、管制植物产品或者管制材料的状况；

(b) 国际条约或者国家间谅解备忘录的条款设定的与检疫性有害生物、管制植物、管制植物产品或者管制材料的进口卫生要求。

(3) 局长应当对上述第 (1) 条款下所有进口卫生要求和上述第 (2) 条款下的变更进行注册登记。

(4) 上述第 (1) 条款下的注册登记，应当向社会公布。

(5) 在判定上述第 (1) 条款下的进口卫生要求是否必要，局长应当注意以下：

(a) 该批植物、植物产品或者植物材料的进入后，携带检疫性有害生物传入新加坡的可能性；

(b) 该种有害生物传入后对新加坡本地植物或者植物产品、生态环境、经济造成的影响；

(c) 新加坡签署的有关植物进口的相关条约、协定、协议、谅解备忘录、交换函件或者其他类似法律文件中，新加坡应负的义务；

（d）局长认为的有关其他事项。

申请许可的费用

8. 依据第 5 条签发的申请，应当按局长要求的格式制作并递交，依照附录 3 的规定缴费。

许可的取消

9. 如果许可的申请人违反了许可随附的时限和要求或者本条例当中的任何一项，据第5 条签发的申请许可可以被取消。

10. 已经由文件 S *258/2005*，*wef 25/04/2005* 废止。

11. 已经由文件 S *258/2005*，*wef 25/04/2005* 废止。

授权官员的权力

12.（1）授权官员有权：

（a）进入检查建筑物，或者检查运输工具，是否有进口的管制植物、管制植物产品或者管制材料；

（b）检查已经进口到新加坡的植物、植物产品类货物，包括包装，并扦取样品以便进行合理、必要地分析和评估；

（c）打开集装箱、包装或者容器检查：

（i）装有或者授权官员有充分理由认为其装有；或者

（ii）授权官员有充分理由认为其已经用于或将用于装载植物、植物产品或者受管制的材料或携带有有害生物；

（d）完全禁止或授权官员认为在适当的范围内禁止装载有受管制的有害生物或者第 6（1）（c）条规定的有害生物、管制植物、管制植物产品或者管制材料的运输工具或者同类货物进入新加坡；

（e）负责对已经进口到新加坡的装载有受管制的有害生物或者第 6（1）（c）条规定的有害生物、管制植物、管制植物产品或管制材料的运输工具或者同类货物，在规定的地点和按规定的方式扣留或者检疫；

（f）负责对装载进口到新加坡的植物或者植物产品的运输工具或者容器，按照局长在规定的地点和按规定的方式进行的处理，灭活受危害的植物或者植物产品中受管制的有害生物或者第 6（1）（c）条项下的有害生物；

（g）指导植物、植物产品或者材料的进口商或所有人，按照局长规定的方式对该批货物进行销毁（费用由其自理），或者对该批货物实行退运，如该批货物被发现：（i）受管制的有害生物或者第 6（1）（c）条的有害生物危害，并且该种有害生物不能通过除害措施有效控制；（ii）违反本条例进口的。

（h）在任何一批植物、植物产品或者材料的进口商或所有人无法按照以第（g）条的要求做到销毁或者退运时，按照局长规定的方式对该批货物进行销毁，销毁该批货物产生的费用由进口商或者所有人支付；

（i）没收与本条例或者进口卫生要求的不符已经进口的或正在进口的有害生物、植物、植物产品和管制材料；

（j）授权官员以依据本条例履行权利，符合本法案规定。

（2）任何人，故意妨碍或者阻止授权官员依照本条例行使职权的，或者故意违背授权官员规定的时限或者要求的，将视为犯罪。

植物、植物产品或材料的检验、检疫、销毁或处理产生的损耗或费用

13.（1）依据本条例进口或者进入新加坡的装载植物、植物产品或材料的运输工具和货物，因检验、检疫、销毁或处理产生的损耗或费用，包括运输费用本身，将由该运输工具或货物的进口商或所有人承担。

（2）局长可以在其权利范围内，取消进口或者进入新加坡的转载植物、植物产品或材料的运输工具和货物因检验、检疫、处理或者销毁产生的费用。

未用于与植物进口有关的货物和运输工具的检验、处理或销毁

14. 即使某物品或者运输工具未与植物、植物产品或材料的进口有关，但是局长有充分理由怀疑其染疫或者染虫，在授权官员检查核实后，局长可以令其在规定的地点和按规定的方式进行处理或者销毁。

检验费用

15. 在附件 3 中列明了本条例中因检验或者实验室检验产生的费用和附带费用。

虚假申报

16. 因本条例的要求或者与本条例相关，申请人作出的申报、声明、陈述或者出具书面文书，或为获得某项许可：

（a）无论何种原因，所作出的或者提供的申报、声明、陈述是不真实的；

（b）无论何种原因，出具的书面文书是不真实的，或者该文书尚未生效，或者该文书已经被修饰或者篡改，将视为犯罪。

违法情况

17.（1）任何人违背或者不遵循：

（a）第 4 条或者第 5 条第（1）款的；

（b）依据本条例的许可中时限和要求；

（c）依据本条例由局长或者授权官员给他的指令的；

将视为违法。

（2）进口与管制植物、管制植物产品或者管制材料相关的货物：

（a）未提供第 5 条第（4）款要求的植物检疫证书、其他证书、文件或者标志；

（b）提供了第 5 条第（4）款要求的植物检疫证书、其他证书、文件或者标志但是不符合第 5 条第（5）款和第（6）款的规定的；

将视为违法。

处罚

18. 本条例项下犯罪的任何人，将被处以不超过 10000 美元的罚金，或者不超过 3 年的监禁，或者两项并处。

定罪后，货物的处置

19. 依据在本条例定罪的，局长提交由法庭法院对于其有关违法的植物、植物产品、集装箱、包装材料、容器、其他物品或材料、运输工具和货物被政府没收和处置。

附件一

第2条第（1）款
管制性有害生物

第1部分 检疫性有害生物

BACTERIA	**细菌**
Curtobacterium flaccumfaciens	菜豆细菌性萎蔫病菌
Clavibacter michiganensis sub. sp. *nebraskense*	玉米高氏细菌性萎蔫病菌
Clavibacter michiganensis sub. sp. *sepedonicum*	马铃薯环腐病菌
Pseudomonas syringae pv. *garcae*	咖啡细菌性叶斑病菌
Pseudomonas syringae	细菌性叶斑病菌
Xanthomonas ampelina	冰核活性细菌
Xanthomonas campestris pv. *cassavae*	木薯细菌性条斑病菌
Xanthomonas campestris pv. *phaseoli*	菜豆细菌性条斑病菌
FUNGI	**真菌**
Aecidium cantensis	半知锈类
Angiosorus solani（*Thecophora solani*）	马铃薯楔孢黑粉菌
Ascochyta gossypii（*A. phaseolorum*）	棉花茎枯病
Cercospora elaeidis	油棕灰斑病菌
Claviceps gigantean	麦角菌属
Cochliobolus carbonum（*Drechslera zeicola*）	玉米圆斑病菌
Charred ear mould	Charred ear mould
Colletotrichum coffeanum	咖啡果实炭疽病菌
Crinipellis perniciosa（*Marasmius perniciosus*）	可可丛枝病菌
Witches broom	枣疯病
Cryptosporella eugeniae	桉树溃疡病菌
Deuterophoma tracheiphila（*Phoma tracheiphila*）	柑橘类干枯病菌
Diaporthe phaseolorum var. *caulivora*	大豆茎溃疡病菌
Erysiphe polygoni	豌豆枯萎病菌
Fusarium oxysporum f. sp. *elaeidis*	咖啡果苦腐病菌
Fusarium xylarioides（*Gibberella xylarioides*）	咖啡导管萎蔫病
Tracheomycosis	维管束真菌病
Hemileia coffeicola	咖啡叶锈病菌
Marasmiellus cocophilus	椰子树干腐烂病
Microcyclus ulei	南美叶疫病菌
Moniliophthora roreri（*Monilia roreri*）	可可灰色果腐病
Mycena citricolor（*Omphalia flavida*）	美洲叶斑病菌
Mycosphaerella fijiensis var. *difformis*	斐济球腔菌
Peronospora tabacina	烟草霜霉病
Phaeolus manihotis	从枝根腐病菌
Phoma exigua var *fourata*（*P. exigua* var. *exigua*）	甜菜坏疽病菌
Phomopsis theae	拟茎点霉病菌

Phymatotrichopsis omnivorum	德克萨斯根腐病菌
Polyscytalium pustulans （*Oospora pustulans*）	卵孢菌属
Puccinia pittieriana	马铃薯锈病菌
Puccinia psidii	番石榴锈病菌
Sphaceloma arachidis	花生疮痂病
Sphaceloma manihoticola	木薯结痂病
Synchytrium endobioticum	马铃薯癌肿病
Trachysphaera fructigena	粉荚病菌
Verticillium albo – atrum	茄黄萎病菌
Verticillium dahliae	棉花黄萎病菌
INSECTS	**昆虫**
Acanthosellides obtectus	菜豆象
Anastrepha oblique	西印度按实蝇
Anastrepha fraterculus	南美按实蝇
Anastrepha ludens	墨西哥按实蝇
Anastrepha spp.	按实蝇属
Antestiopsis spp.	丽蝽属
Anthomomus vestitus	秘鲁棉铃象甲
Anthomomus grandis	墨西哥棉铃象甲
Aonidomytilus albus	白蛎盾蚧
Bactrocera tryoni	昆士兰实蝇
Bathycoelia thalassina	非洲可可盾蝽（拟）
Bruchus pisorum	豌豆象
Caliothrips masculinus	蓟马科
Ceratitis rosa	纳塔尔实蝇
Ceratitis capitata	地中海实蝇
Chaetanaphotrips orchidii	香蕉锈蓟马
Chrysomphalus aonidium	黑褐圆盾蚧
Coelaenomenodera elaedis	潜叶虫类
Diatrea abbreviatus	螟蛾科
Distantiella theobroma	可可盲蝽
Epilachna varivestis	墨西哥豆瓢虫
Euscepes postfaciatus	西印度甘薯象
Helopeltis bergrothi	黑须腰果角盲蝽
Hercinothrip bicinctus	香蕉蓟马
Hypsipyla robusta	麻楝梢斑螟
Rynchophorus phoenicis	非洲浆叶象甲
Leguminivora glycinivorella	大豆食心虫
Leptinotarsa decemilineata	马铃薯甲虫
Leptopharsa heveae	网蝽科
Leptopharsa gibbicarina	网蝽科
Leucoptera coffeella	咖啡潜叶蛾
Lissorhoptrus oryzephilus	稻水象甲

Melittomma insulare	筒蠹属
Menalonium sp.	盲蝽科
Noorda albizonalis	芒果钻孔虫
Oryctes boas (= *O. monoceros*)	椰子犀甲
Pachymerus lacerdae	豆象属
Pachymerus nucleorum	豆象属
Pimelephila ghesquieri	非洲油棕蛀心螟
Planococcus kenyae	肯尼亚粉蚧
Prostephanus truncatus	大谷长蠹
Pseudotheraptus wayi	卫氏缘蝽
Quadraspidiotus perniciosus	梨圆盾蚧
Rhynchophorus palmarum	棕榈象
Sacadodes pyralis	南美红铃虫（棉芽三纹夜蛾）
Sahlbergella singularis	可可盲蝽象
Sesamia cretica	螟蛾科
Sophronica ventrallis	天牛科
Stenoma decora	织蛾科
Trogoderma granarium	谷斑皮蠹
Xyleborus ferrugineus	赤材小蠹
MITES	**螨类**
Aceria guerreronis	椰子螨
Mononychellus tanajoa	木薯绿螨
Oligonychus peruvianus	木薯螨
PHYTOPLASMAS	**植原体**
Phytoplasmas of apple	苹果软枝病
Phytoplasmas of banana	香蕉植原体病
Phytoplasmas of cassava	木薯丛枝病
Phytoplasmas of coconut	椰子致死黄化植原体
Phytoplasmas of grape Grapevine	葡萄植原体
Phytoplasmas of grape	细菌性叶焦病
Phytoplasmas of oil palm	油棕叶斑驳病
Phytoplasmas of papaya	番木瓜束顶病
Phytomonas staheli	玉米白条病/叶灼病
Phytomonas sp	柑橘螺原体
Spiroplasma citri	玉米顽固病
Spiroplasma kunkelii	玉米矮化病
NEMATODES	**线虫**
Anguina agrostis	剪股颖粒线虫
Anguina graminis	禾谷粒线虫
Anguina tritici	小麦粒线虫
Aphasmatylenchus straturatus	具层无侧尾腺垫刃线虫
Aphelenchoides arachidis	花生滑刃线虫
Aphelenchoides blastophorus	鳞茎滑刃线虫

Aphelenchoides fragariae	草莓滑刃线虫
Aphelenchoides lilium	百合滑刃线虫
Bursaphelenchus lignicolus	松材线虫
Ditylenchus destructor	马铃薯茎线虫
Ditylenchus myceliophagus	食菌茎线虫
Globodera pallida	马铃薯白线虫
Globodera rostochiensis	马铃薯金线虫
Hemicycliophora arenaria	花生鞘线虫
Heterodera avenae	小麦禾谷胞囊线虫
Heterodera cacti	仙人掌胞囊线虫
Heterodera cajani	木豆胞囊线虫
Heterodera carrotae	胡萝卜胞囊线虫
Heterodera cruciferae	芸苔根线虫
Heterodera cyperi	莎草胞囊线虫
Heterodera fici	无花果胞囊线虫
Heterodera geottingiana	豌豆胞囊线虫
Heterodera longicaudata	长针小麦胞囊线虫
Heterodera oryzicola	水稻胞囊线虫
Heterodera sacchari	甘蔗胞囊线虫
Heterodera schactii	甜菜胞囊线虫
Heterodera sorghi	高粱胞囊线虫
Heterodera vignae	长豇豆胞囊线虫
Heterodera zeae	玉米胞囊线虫
Hirschmanniella miticausa	野芋潜根线虫
Hirschmanniella spinicaudata	水稻潜根线虫
Hoplolaimus columbus	哥伦比亚纽带线虫
Hoplolaimus indicus	印度纽带线虫
Hoplolaimus pararobustus	纽带线虫属
Longidorus attenuatus	纤细长针线虫
Macroposthonia xenoplex	异盘大刺环线虫
Meloidogyne africana	非洲根结线虫
Meloidogyne baurensis	根结线虫属
Meloidogyne brevicauda	短尾根结线虫
Meloidogyne chitwoodi	奇氏根结线虫
Meloidogyne coffeicola	咖啡根结线虫
Meloidogyne decalineata	光纹根结线虫
Meloidogyne exigua	咖啡根结线虫
Meloidogyne graminis	禾本科根结线虫
Meloidogyne indica	甜菜根结线虫
Meloidogyne inornata	巴西叉鞭根结线虫
Meloidogyne mali	苹果根结线虫
Meloidogyne megadora	巨大根结线虫
Meloidogyne naasi	小麦禾谷根结线虫

Meloidogyne oteifae	欧氏根结线虫
Merlinius brevidens	短齿默林线虫
Nacobbus aberrans	异常珍珠线虫
Pratylenchus fallax	伪尖根腐线虫
Pratylenchus neglectus	加利福尼亚根腐线虫
Pratylenchus thornei	索雷根腐线虫
Pratylenchus zeae	玉米根腐线虫
Punctodera punctata	刻点斑皮线虫
Rhadinaphelenchus cocophilus (= *Bursaphelenchus cocophilus*)	椰子红环腐线虫
Scutellonema bradys	缓慢盾线虫
Trichodorus viruliferus	具毒毛刺线虫
Xiphinema index	剑线虫
VIRUSES	**病毒**
African cassava mosaic virus	非洲木薯花叶病毒
Anthocyanosis of cotton	棉花色素病
Arabis mosaic virus	南芥菜花叶病毒
Artichoke Italian latent virus	意大利洋蓟潜隐病毒
Blister spot virus of coffee	咖啡病毒病毒
Brown streak virus of papaya	番木瓜棕条斑病毒
Grapevine corky bark associated virus	葡萄栓皮伴随病毒
Rice dwarf virus	水稻矮化病毒
Dwarf virus of sugarcane	甘蔗矮化病毒
Sweet potato yellow dwarf virus	甜马铃薯黄矮化病毒
Grapevine fanleaf virus	葡萄扇叶病毒
Rice hoja blanca virus	水稻叶枯萎病毒
Grapevine chrome mosaic virus	葡萄铬黄病毒
Sweet potato feathery mottle virus	甜马铃薯羽状斑驳病毒
Cotton leaf crumple virus	棉枯叶病毒
Cotton leaf curl virus	棉卷叶病毒
Leaf mosaic virus of cotton	棉花叶病毒
Leaf mottle virus of cotton	棉花叶斑驳病毒
Grapevine leafroll – associated virus	葡萄卷叶伴随病毒
Leaf virus of grape	葡萄叶病毒
Marginal chlorosis virus of groundnut	大豆叶缘黄化病毒
Mosaic virus of maize	玉米花叶病毒
Papaya mosaic virus	番木瓜花叶病毒
Mosaic virus of rubber	橡胶花叶病毒
Mosaic virus of sweet potato	甜马铃薯花叶病毒
Peanut stunt virus of maize	玉米花生矮化病毒
Phloem necrosis virus of tea	茶叶韧皮部枯斑病毒
Peach rosette mosaic virus of grape	葡萄桃丛簇花叶病毒
Rayado fino virus of tea	(茶雷亚朵非纳病毒)
Cacao swollen shoot virus	可可树肿枝病毒

Rice transitory yellowing virus	水稻黄叶（暂黄）病毒
Rice yellow mottle virus	稻黄斑驳病毒
Ringspot virus of soybean	大豆环斑病毒
Rupestris stem pitting – associated virus	昆士兰瓶子树茎锈斑联合病毒
Stenosis, small leaf of cotton	棉花小叶病毒
Stunt virus of maize	玉米矮化病毒
Maize streak virus	玉米条斑病毒
Waialua disease of papaya	Waialua disease of papaya
Wrinkled stunt and witches broom virus of rice	水稻皱矮丛枝病毒
Tomato spotted wilt virus	番茄斑萎蔫病毒
Yellow vein banding virus of cocoa	可可黄脉带状病毒
DISEASE OF UNKNOWN ETIOLOGY	**未知病原性疾病**
Coconut awka	Coconut awka
Coconut bristle tip	椰子束顶病
Coconut wilt	椰子萎蔫病
Cassava frog's skin	木薯蛙皮病
Coconut head droop	椰子枯萎病
Coconut kerala wilt	椰子凋萎病
Coconut leaf mottle	椰子叶斑驳病
Coconut leaf scorch	椰子叶焦病
Coconut little leaf	椰子小叶病
Coconut thatipaka wilt	Coconut thatipaka wilt
Mango malformation	芒果畸形病
Cotton Terminal Stunt Graft Transmissible Pathogen	棉花枝端矮化传播性病
WEEDS	**杂草**
Rottboellia spp.	筒轴茅属
Striga spp.	独脚金属

第2部分　非检疫性有害生物

FUNGI	**真菌**
Cochliobolus eragrotidis.	叶斑病
Coleosporium plumeri	普卢梅里鞘锈病
Cylindrocladium spathiphylli.	绿巨人褐腐病菌
Fusarium oxysporum	尖孢镰刀菌
Ganoderma boninense	狭长孢灵芝
Marasmius inoderma	小皮伞属
Rhizoctonia solani	水稻纹枯病
Sclerotium rolfsii	白绢薄膜革菌
Ustulina zonata	炭根病
INSECTS	**昆虫**
Bemisia tabaci	烟粉虱
Brontispa longissima	椰心叶甲
Contarinia maculipennis	芽瘿蚊
Maconellicoccus hirsutus	木槿曼粉蚧

Neolithocolletis pentadesma	潜叶蝇
Oryctes rhinoceros	椰树犀牛甲
Plesispa reichei	椰心叶甲
Quadrastichus spp.	胯姬小蜂
Rhesala spp.	雨树结网毛虫属
Thrips palmi	米象
NEMATODES	**线虫**
Discocriconemella spp.	环线虫属
Hemicycliophora spp.	鞘线虫属
Meloidogyne arenaria	花生根结线虫
Meloidogyne graminicola	水稻根结线虫
Meloidogyne hapla	北方根结线虫
Pratylenchus brachyurus	短根腐线虫
Pratylenchus penetrans	穿刺短体线虫
Pratylenchus pratensis	草地根腐线虫
WEEDS	**杂草**
Cuscuta spp.	菟丝子属

第2条第（2）款和第5条

允许进口的生物

植物、植物产品及其他材料

1. 橡胶树属
2. 可可属
3. 椰子属
4. 油棕
5. 木薯
6. 柑橘属
7. 咖啡属
8. 棉属
9. 玉米
10. 香蕉属
11. 菠萝
12. 水稻
13. 甘蔗
14. 茶叶
15. 兰科
16. 盆装或不带盆的活的繁殖材料，诸如枝条、鳞茎、球茎、叶、地下茎、种子、块茎等
17. 利用现代技术研制的具有新型基因材料的所有活的植物
18. 新鲜或烘干的植物标本
19. 蘑菇菌柱
20. 产于热带美洲的新鲜花、水果、蔬菜
21. 所有活的环节动物、节肢动物、软体动物、线虫和微生物
22. 活的转基因生物
23. 生物防治作用物
24. 土壤和有机肥料

附录3　第8条、第15条

第一栏	第二栏
（1）植物、植物产品或者鲜切花的检验和出证	（a）下列非商品货物每批次收取12美元：
	（i）数量不超过10或10烧瓶的植物；
	（ii）重量不超过5千克的植物产品；
	（iii）数量不超过24支的鲜切花。
	（b）商品货物每批次收取50美元：
	（i）数量超过10或10烧瓶的植物；
	（ii）重量超过5千克的植物产品；
	（iii）数量超过24支的鲜切花。
（2）对植物、植物产品、鲜切花或者其他管制物品的虫害或病原体做实验室检验	每批次收取50美元
（3）进口植物、昆虫或者微生物的许可	每批次11美元。
（4）专业服务费用	（a）每小时（不满1小时），63美元。
	（b）每小时（不满1小时），133美元（加班时间或者加急情况）。
（5）技术服务费	（a）每小时（不满1小时）38美元。
	（b）每小时（不满1小时）80美元（加班时间或者加急情况）。

附录4

已经由S *258/2005*，*25/04/2005* 废止。

[*G. N. Nos. S 29/94*；*S 369/94*；*S368/96*；*S148/97*；*S 137/98*]

Control of plants (Plant importation) rules

History: G. N. NO. S29/94 →1995 revisd edition →R4 2000 revisd edition

[18th February 1994]

Citation

1. These Rules may be cited as the Control of Plants (Plant Importation) Rules.

Definitions

2. (1) In these Rules, unless the context otherwise requires—

American tropics means those parts of the continent of America, including the islands adjacent thereto, which are bounded by the Tropic of Capricorn (latitude 23°S) and the Tropic of Cancer (latitude 23°N) and by Longitudes 30°W and 120°W and includes that part of Mexico which is north of the Tropic of Cancer;

biological control agent means a natural enemy, an antagonist or a competitor of a pest, or any other self - replicating biotic entity, used for pest control;

import health requirement means any import health requirement specified or varied by the Director - General under rule 7;

living modified organism means any living organism that possesses a novel combination of genetic material obtained through the use of any modern biotechnology technique—

(a) that overcomes natural physiological reproductive or recombination barriers; and

(b) that is not a technique used in traditional breeding and selection;

non - quarantine pest means a pest specified in Part II of the First Schedule;

quarantine pest means a pest specified in Part I of the First Schedule;

regulated pest means a pest specified in Part I or II of the First Schedule;

transit means to be taken or sent from any country and brought into Singapore for the sole purpose of being carried to another country by the same or another conveyance within any free trade zone.

(2) In these Rules—

(a) any reference to a consignment of plants, plant products or materials shall include a reference to any container, receptacle, packaging material or other article forming part of such a consignment;

(b) any reference to a regulated plant, regulated plant product or regulated material shall be construed as a reference to a plant, plant product or material, respectively, specified in the Second Schedule;

(c) any reference to the importation or movement of any pest, plant, plant product or material shall be read as including a reference to the importation or movement, respectively, of the pest, plant, plant product or material by post; and

(d) any reference to a certificate or document shall include a reference to a certificate or documenting electronic form.

Persons to whom Rules do not apply

3. Subject to rules 12, 13 and 14, these Rules shall not apply to any person who—

(a) with the written permission of the Director - General and subject to such conditions as the Director - General thinks fit to impose, imports any plant, plant product or regulated material for experimental or research purposes; or

(b) brings any regulated plant, regulated plant product or regulated material into Singapore in transit, subject to the condition that the plant, plant product or material is not moved from the point of entry into Singapore to any other place within Singapore except—

(i) with the permission in writing of the Director – General or an authorised officer; and

(ii) in accordance with such terms and conditions as the Director – General or the authorized officer thinks fit to impose.

Imported plant, plant product or material to be free of quarantine pests

4. Any person who imports any plant, plant product or material shall ensure that the plant, plant product or material and the container or any other package thereof is free of any quarantine pest.

Importation of regulated plant, regulated plant product or regulated material

5. (1) No person shall import any regulated plant, regulated plant product or regulated material except under a permit issued by the Director – General.

(2) The Director – General shall, in determining whether to issue a permit under paragraph (1), consider whether the applicant for the permit has complied with every relevant import health requirement and the requirements under paragraph (4).

(3) Every permit issued under this rule—

(a) shall be valid only for the period specified therein and for the consignment in respect of which it has been issued; and

(b) may be subject to such terms and conditions as the Director – General thinks fit to impose, which terms and conditions shall be endorsed on the permit.

(4) Any person who imports any consignment of regulated plants, regulated plant products or regulated materials shall ensure that there is, in respect of that consignment—

(a) a phytosanitary certificate; or

(b) such other certificate or document or mark issued by or authorised to be issued by a competent government agency in the country of despatch, being an agency which is recognised by the Director – General, in such form and issued in such manner as may be required under any import health requirement.

(5) The phytosanitary certificate referred to in paragraph (4) (a) shall be issued not more than 14 days prior to the date of shipment of the consignment by a competent government agency or some other agricultural authority, of the country of despatch, being an agency or authority which is recognised by the Director – General.

(6) The phytosanitary certificate or other certificate or document or mark required under paragraph (4) shall certify that every relevant import health requirement has been complied with.

Discretion of Director – General to prohibit plant, plant product or material from entering Singapore

6. (1) Where— (a) a consignment of regulated plants, regulated plant products or regulated materials is imported—

(i) without a phytosanitary certificate or other certificate or document or mark referred to in rule 5 (4); or

(ii) with a phytosanitary certificate or other certificate or document or mark referred to in rule 5 (4) that does not comply with rule 5 (5) or (6);

(b) an imported consignment of plants, plant products or materials is found to be infested with a non – quarantine pest; or

(c) an imported consignment of plants, plant products or materials is found to be infested with a pest (other than a regulated pest) which is not native to Singapore and which the Director – General determines to be potentially damaging to any plant in Singapore or the ecosystem of any plant in Singapore, the Director – General may, in his discretion—

(i) prohibit the consignment of plants, plant products or materials from entering Singapore; or

(ii) permit the consignment of plants, plant products or materials to enter Singapore, subject to such terms and conditions as the Director – General thinks fit.

(2) In this rule, a reference to an imported consignment includes a reference to any consignment brought into Singapore by an incoming traveller for his own use.

Import health requirements

7. (1) For the purposes of these Rules, the Director – General may specify such import health requirements as are necessary in respect of any regulated plant, regulated plant product or regulated material.

(2) The Director – General may, from time to time, vary any of the import health requirements

(a) having regard to the status of any regulated pest, regulated plant, regulated plant product or regulated material; and

(b) in accordance with the provisions of any international agreement or memorandum of understanding pertaining to the international movement of quarantine pests, regulated plants, regulated plant products or regulated materials.

(3) The Director – General shall maintain a register of all the import health requirements for the time being specified under paragraph (1) and any variation to any such requirement under paragraph (2).

(4) The register referred to in paragraph (3) shall be made available for public information.

(5) In determining whether it is necessary to specify any import health requirement under paragraph (1), the Director – General shall have regard to the following matters:

(a) the likelihood that the importation of any plant, plant product or other material may bring any regulated pest into Singapore;

(b) the nature and possibility of the effect of any pest on any local plant or plant product, or the environment in or economy of Singapore;

(c) any obligation imposed under any treaty, convention, arrangement, memorandum of understanding, exchange of letters or other similar instrument relating to the import of plants to which Singapore is a party; and

(d) such other matter as the Director – General thinks relevant.

Application and fee for permits

8. Every application for the issue of a permit under rule 5 shall be made to the Director in such form as the Director – General may require and shall be accompanied by the appropriate fee specified in the Third Schedule.

Cancellation of permits

9. Any permit issued under rule 5 may be cancelled if the person to whom it was issued is in breach of any of the terms and conditions endorsed on the permit or of these Rules.

10. *Deleted by S 258/2005, wef 25/04/2005.*

11. *Deleted by S 258/2005, wef 25/04/2005.*

Powers of authorised officers

12. (1) An authorised officer may at any time—

(a) enter and inspect any premises or stop, detain, board or inspect any conveyance where he has reason to believe that such premises or conveyance has been used or is being used in connection with the importation of pests, plants, plant products or any regulated material;

(b) inspect any consignment of plants and plant products which has been imported into Singapore including their packaging and take such samples thereof as may reasonably be necessary for analysis and evaluation;

(c) open and examine any container, package or receptacle which—

(i) contains or which the authorised officer reasonably believes to contain; or

(ii) has been used or is being used or which the authorised officer reasonably believes to have been used or to be being used in connection with the importation into Singapore of, any pests, plants, plant products or any regulated material;

(d) prohibit entirely or to such extent as he thinks fit, the movement of any conveyance containing or consignment of, regulated pests or pests referred to in rule 6 (1)(c), regulated plants, regulated plant products or regulated materials which has arrived but which has not yet entered Singapore;

(e) direct that any conveyance containing or consignment of, plants or plant products imported into Singapore be detained or quarantined for such a period as he thinks fit at such place and in such manner as may be determined by the Director – General;

(f) direct that any conveyance containing or consignment of, plants or plant products imported into Singapore be subject to treatment at such place and in such manner as may be determined by the Director – General for the purpose of destroying any regulated pest or pest referred to in rule 6 (1) (c) infesting the plants or plant products;

(g) direct the importer or owner of any consignment of plants, plant products or materials to destroy the consignment, at his own expense, in such manner as may be determined by the Director – General or immediately export the consignment, where the consignment is found— (i) to be infested with any regulated pest or pest referred to in rule 6 (1) (c), and such pest cannot be effectively controlled through disinfection or disinfestation measures; or (ii) to have been imported in contravention of these Rules;

(h) where the importer or owner of any consignment of plants, plant products or materials has failed to destroy or immediately export the consignment as directed under paragraph (g), destroy the consignment in such manner as may be determined by the Director – General and recover the expenses incurred for the destruction from the importer or owner of the consignment; (i) seize any pest, plant, plant product or regulated material which has been imported or which is being kept in contravention of these Rules or any import health requirement; and

(j) do such other act or thing as may be reasonable or necessary for the purpose of carrying out his duties under these Rules.

(2) Any person who wilfully obstructs or impedes an authorised officer in the exercise of his power sunder these Rules, or acts in contravention of the terms and conditions imposed by an authorised officer shall be guilty of an offence.

Loss or expenses incurred for inspection, quarantine, destruction or treatment of plants, plant products or materials

13. (1) Any loss or expenses incurred for the inspection, quarantine, treatment or destruction under these Rules of any conveyance containing or any consignment of, plants, plant products or materials imported or brought into Singapore, including the cost of transporting the same, shall be borne by the importer or owner of the conveyance or consignment, as the case may be.

(2) The Director – General may, in his discretion, waive any expenses incurred by him for the inspection, quarantine, treatment or destruction under these Rules of any conveyance containing or any consignment of, plants, plant products or materials imported or brought into Singapore.

Inspection, treatment or destruction of articles and conveyances not used in connection with importation of plants

14. The Director – General may, if in his opinion the circumstances of the case so warrant, direct that any article or conveyance which has not been used in connection with the importation of plants, plant products or materials but which he reasonably suspects to be diseased or infested with any quarantine pest, be inspected by an authorised officer and, if necessary, be treated or destroyed at such place and in such manner as the Director - General may determine.

Fees for inspection

15. The fees for and incidental to any inspection or laboratory examination under these Rules shall be as specified in the Third Schedule.

Making of false declarations, etc.

16. Any person who, being required by or by virtue of these Rules to make any declaration, statement or representation or to produce any document or who, for the purpose of obtaining any permit—

(a) makes or presents any declaration, statement or representation which, to his knowledge, is false in any material particular; or

(b) produces any document which, to his knowledge, is false in any material particular or has not been made by the person by whom it purports to have been made, or has been in any way altered or tampered with, shall be guilty of an offence.

Offences

17. (1) Any person who contravenes or fails to comply with—

(a) rule 4 or 5 (1);

(b) any of the terms and conditions of any permit issued to him under these Rules; or

(c) any direction given to him under these Rules by the Director - General or an authorised officer, shall be guilty of an offence.

(2) Any person who imports any consignment of regulated plants, regulated plant products or regulated materials—

(a) without a phytosanitary certificate or other certificate or document or mark referred to in rule 5 (4); or

(b) with a phytosanitary certificate or other certificate or document or mark referred to in rule 5 (4) that does not comply with rule 5 (5) and (6), shall be guilty of an offence.

Penalty

18. Any person who is guilty of an offence under these Rules shall be liable on conviction to a fine not exceeding $10,000 or to imprisonment for a term not exceeding 3 years or to both.

Forfeiture of consignment, etc., upon conviction

19. Where any person is convicted of an offence under these Rules, the court may order that any conveyance containing or any consignment of, plants or plant products and any container, packaging material, receptacle or other article or material to which the offence relates shall be forfeited to the Government and disposed of in such manner as the Director - General thinks fit.

First schedule

Rule 2 （1）
Regulated pests

Part Ⅰ
Quarantine pests

Name of Pest	*Common Name*
BACTERIA	
Curtobacterium flaccumfaciens	Bean wilt
Clavibacter michiganensis sub. sp. *Nebraskense*	Leaf freckles and wilt
Clavibacter michiganensis sub. sp. *sepedonicum*	Bacteria ring rot
Pseudomonas syringae pv. *Garcae*	Coffee halo blight，Twig blight
Pseudomonas syringae	Leaf spot/blight
Xanthomonas ampelina（grapes）	Bacterial blight
Xanthomonas campestris pv. *cassavae*	Cassava bacterial necrosis
Xanthomonas campestris pv. *phaseoli*	Common bacterial blight
FUNGI	
Aecidium cantensis	Deforming rust
Angiosorus solani（*Thecophora solani*）	Potato smut
Ascochyta gossypii（*A. phaseolorum*）	Ascochyta blight
Cercospora elaeidis	Freckle
Claviceps gigantean	Ergot，Horse's tooth
Cochliobolus carbonum（*Drechslera zeicola*）	Charred ear mould
Colletotrichum coffeanum	Coffee berry disease
Crinipellis perniciosa（*Marasmius perniciosus*）	Witches broom
Cryptosporella eugeniae	Dieback
Deuterophoma tracheiphila（*Phoma tracheiphila*）	Mal secco
Diaporthe phaseolorum var. *caulivora*	Stem canker
Erysiphe polygoni	Powdery mildew
Fusarium oxysporum f. sp. *elaeidis*	Fusarium wilt
Fusarium xylarioides（*Gibberella xylarioides*）	Tracheomycosis
Hemileia coffeicola	Rust（Powdery，grey rust）
Marasmiellus cocophilus	Lethal bole rot
Microcyclus ulei	South American Leaf Blight
Moniliophthora roreri（*Monilia roreri*）	Pod rot，watery pod rot
Mycena citricolor（*Omphalia flavida*）	American leaf spot
Mycosphaerella fijiensis var. *difformis*	Black sigatoka
Peronospora tabacina	Blue mould
Phaeolus manihotis	Root rot
Phoma exigua var fourata（*P. exigua* var. *exigua*）	Gangrene
Phomopsis theae	Stem canker
Phymatotrichopsis omnivorum	Texas root rot

Continue Table

Name of Pest	*Common Name*
Polyscytalium pustulans (*Oospora pustulans*)	Skin spot
Puccinia pittieriana	Common rust
Puccinia psidii	Guava rust
Sphaceloma arachidis	Scab
Sphaceloma manihoticola	Super elongation
Synchytrium endobioticum	Black wart, black scab
Trachysphaera fructigena	Trachysphaera pod rot
Verticillium albo – atrum	Verticillium wilt
Verticillium dahliae	Verticillium wilt
INSECTS	
Acanthosellides obtectus	Bean bruchid
Anastrepha oblique	West Indian fruit fly
Anastrepha fraterculus	South American fruit fly
Anastrepha ludens	Mexican fruit fly
Anastrepha spp.	Fruit fly
Antestiopsis spp.	Antestia bug
Anthomomus vestitus	Peruvian cotton boll weevil
Anthomomus grandis	Mexican cotton boll weevil
Aonidomytilus albus	Cassava scale
Bactrocera tryoni	Queensland fruit fly
Bathycoella thalassina	Cocoa bug
Bruchus pisorum	Pea pod weevil
Caliothrips masculinus	Thrips
Ceratitis rosa	Natal fruit fly
Ceratitis capitata	Mediterranean fruit fly
Chaetanaphotrips orchidii	Banana rust thrip
Chrysomphalus aonidium	Florida red scale
Coelaenomenodera elaedis	Leaf miner
Diatrea abbreviatus	Sugarcane root stalk borer
Distantiella theobroma	Cocoa capsid
Epilachna varivestis	Mexican bean beetle
Euscepes postfaciatus	West Indian sweet potato weevil
Helopeltis bergrothi	Helopeltis bug
Hercinothrip bicinctus	Banana thrip
Hypsipyla robusta	Stem borer
Rynchophorus phoenicis	African palm weevil
Leguminivora glycinivorella	Soybean pod borer
Leptinotarsa decemilineata	Colorado potato beetle
Leptopharsa heveae	Lace bug
Leptopharsa gibbicarina	Lace bug
Leucoptera coffeella	Coffee leaf miner

Continue Table

Name of Pest	*Common Name*
Lissorhoptrus oryzephilus	Rice water weevil
Melittomma insulare	Wood borer
Menalonium sp	Mirid bug
Noorda albizonalis	Red banded caterpillar
Oryctes boas (= *O. monoceros*)	Rhinoceros beetle
Pachymerus lacerdae	Kernel borer
Pachymerus nucleorum	Kernel borer
Pimelephila ghesquierii	Palm moth
Planococcus kenyae	Kenya mealy bug
Prostephanus truncatus	Large grain borer
Pseudotheraptus wayi	Coreid bug
Quadraspidiotus perniciosus	San Jose scale
Rhynchophorus palmarum South	American palm weevil
Sacadodes pyralis	False pink boll worm
Sahlbergella singularis	Cocoa capsid
Sesamia cretica	Durra/sorghum stalk borer
Sophronica ventrallis	Berry borer
Stenoma decora	Cocoa shoot
Trogoderma granarium	Khapra beetle
Xyleborus ferrugineus	Black twig borer
MITES	
Aceria guerreronis (= *Eryophyes guerreronis*)	Coconut mite
Mononychellus tanajoa (= *Ononychelie tanajoe*)	Cassava green mite
Oligonychus peruvianus (= *Homonychus peruvianus*)	Cassava mite
PHYTOPLASMAS	
Phytoplasmas of apple	Flat limb
Phytoplasmas of banana	Cameroon marbling disease
Phytoplasmas of cassava	Witches broom
Phytoplasmas of coconut	Lethal yellowing Coconut Awka diseases
Phytoplasmas of grape Grapevine	Flavescence doree
Phytoplasmas of grape	Pierce's disease = Xylella fastidiosa
Phytoplasmas of oil palm	Leaf mottle
Phytoplasmas of papaya	Papaya bunchy top
Phytomonas staheli	Sudden wither
Phytomonas sp	Maize leaf blight/Leaf scald
Spiroplasma citri	Stubborn disease
Spiroplasma kunkelii	Corn stunt, Grassy root
NEMATODES	
Anguina agrostis	Bentgrass nematode
Anguina graminis	Leaf gall nematode
Anguina tritici	Wheat or seed gall nematode

Continue Table

Name of Pest	*Common Name*
Aphasmatylenchus straturatus	Lance nematode of pea
Aphelenchoides arachidis	Testa nematode
Aphelenchoides blastophorus	Stem and bulb nematode
Aphelenchoides fragariae	Strawberry, bud or foliar nematode
Aphelenchoides lilium	Bud nematode
Bursaphelenchus lignicolus	Pinewood nematode
Ditylenchus destructor	Potato rot nematode
Ditylenchus myceliophagus	Mushroom spawn nematode
Globodera pallida	Potato cyst nematode
Globodera rostochiensis	Golden nematode, potato cyst
NEMATODE	
Hemicycliophora arenaria	Sheath nematode
Heterodera avenae	Cereal cyst nematode
Heterodera cacti	Cactus cyst nematode
Heterodera cajani	Pigeon pea cyst nematode
Heterodera carrotae	Carrot cyst nematode
Heterodera cruciferae	Brassica root nematode
Heterodera cyperi	Nutgrass/Sedge cyst nematode
Heterodera fici	Fig cyst nematode
Heterodera geottingiana	Pea cyst nematode
Heterodera longicaudata	Wheat cyst nematode
Heterodera oryzicola	Rice cyst nematode
Heterodera sacchari	Sugarcane cyst nematode
Heterodera schactii	Sugar beet cyst
Heterodera sorghi	Sorghum cyst nematode
Heterodera vignae	Pea cyst nematode
Heterodera zeae	Corn cyst nematode
Hirschmanniella miticausa	Taro nematode
Hirschmanniella spinicaudata	Rice root tip nematode
Hoplolaimus columbus	Columbia nematode
Hoplolaimus indicus	Lance nematode
Hoplolaimus pararobustus	Lance nematode
Longidorus attenuatus	Needle nematode
Macroposthonia xenoplex	Ring nematode
Meloidogyne africana	Root knot nematode
Meloidogyne baurensis	Root knot nematode
Meloidogyne brevicauda	Tea root knot nematode
Meloidogyne chitwoodi	Columbia root knot nematode
Meloidogyne coffeicola	Root knot nematode
Meloidogyne decalineata	Root knot nematode
Meloidogyne exigua	Coffee root knot nematode

Continue Table

Name of Pest	*Common Name*
Meloidogyne graminis	Root knot nematode
Meloidogyne indica	Root knot nematode
Meloidogyne inornata	Brazilian root knot nematode
Meloidogyne mali	Apple root knot nematode
Meloidogyne megadora	Root knot nematode
Meloidogyne naasi	Cereal root knot nematode
Meloidogyne oteifae	Root knot nematode
Merlinius brevidens	Stunt nematode
Nacobbus aberrans	False root knot
Pratylenchus fallax	Lesion nematode
Pratylenchus neglectus	California root – Lesion nematode
Pratylenchus thornei	Thorne's root – Lesion nematode
Pratylenchus zeae	Corn root – Lesion nematode
Punctodera punctata	Grass cyst nematode
Rhadinaphelenchus cocophilus (= *Bursaphelenchus cocophilus*)	Red ring nematode
Scutellonema bradys	Yam nematode
Trichodorus viruliferus	Stubby root nematode
Xiphinema index	Dagger nematode
VIRUSES	
African cassava mosaic virus	
Anthocyanosis of cotton	
Arabis mosaic virus	
Artichoke Italian latent virus	
Blister spot virus of coffee	
Brown streak virus of papaya	
Grapevine corky bark associated virus	
Rice dwarf virus	
Dwarf virus of sugarcane	
Sweet potato yellow dwarf virus	
Grapevine fanleaf virus	
Rice hoja blanca virus	
Grapevine chrome mosaic virus	
Sweet potato feathery mottle virus	
Cotton leaf crumple virus	
Cotton leaf curl virus	
Leaf mosaic virus of cotton	
Leaf mottle virus of cotton	
Grapevine leafroll – associated virus	
Leaf virus of grape	
Marginal chlorosis virus of groundnut	
Mosaic virus of maize	

Continue Table

Name of Pest	*Common Name*
Papaya mosaic virus	
Mosaic virus of rubber	
Mosaic virus of sweet potato	
Peanut stunt virus of maize	
Phloem necrosis virus of tea	
Peach rosette mosaic virus of grape	
Rayado fino virus of tea	
Cacao swollen shoot virus	
Rice transitory yellowing virus	
Rice yellow mottle virus	
Ringspot virus of soybean	
Rupestris stem pitting – associated virus	
Stenosis, small leaf of cotton	
Stunt virus of maize	
Maize streak virus	
Waialua disease of papaya	
Wrinkled stunt and witches broom virus of rice	
Tomato spotted wilt virus	
Yellow vein banding virus of cocoa	
DISEASE OF UNKNOWN ETIOLOGY	
Coconut awka	
Coconut bristle tip	
Coconut wilt	
Cassava frog's skin	
Coconut head droop	
Coconut kerala wilt	
Coconut leaf mottle	
Coconut leaf scorch	
Coconut little leaf	
Coconut thatipaka wilt	
Mango malformation	
Cotton Terminal Stunt Graft Transmissible Pathogen	
WEEDS	
Rottboellia spp.	Inchgrass
Striga spp.	Witchweed

Part Ⅱ

Non – Quarantine pests

Name of Pest	*Common Name*
FUNGI	
Cochliobolus eragrotidis.	Leaf spot
Coleosporium plumeri	Rust
Cylindrocladium spathiphylli.	Root rot
Fusarium oxysporum	Fusarium wilt
Ganoderma boninense	Basal stem rot
Marasmius inoderma	Root rot
Rhizoctonia solani （ = *Thanatephorus cucumeris*）	Stem & Collar rot，seedling root rot，damping off
Sclerotium rolfsii	Southern blight/wilt，crown and root rot，stem cankers
Ustulina zonata	Charcoal stump rot
INSECTS	
Bemisia tabaci	White fly
Brontispa longissima	Hispid beetle
Contarinia maculipennis	Blossom midge
Maconellicoccus hirsutus	Hibiscus mealy bug
Neolithocolletis pentadesma	Leaf miner
Oryctes rhinoceros	Rhinoceros beetle
Plesispa reichei	Coconut leaf beetle
Quadrastichus spp.	Gall wasps
Rhesala spp.	Raintree webworm
Thrips palmi	Melon thrip
NEMATODES	
Discocriconemella spp.	Ring nematode
Hemicycliophora spp.	Sheath nematode
Meloidogyne arenaria	Peanut root knot nematode
Meloidogyne graminicola	Rice root knot nematode
Meloidogyne hapla	Northern root knot nematode
Pratylenchus brachyurus	Lesion nematode
Pratylenchus penetrans	Lesion nematode
Pratylenchus pratensis	Lesion nematode
WEEDS	
Cuscuta spp.	Dodders

Second schedule Rules 2（2） and 5

Importation under permit nematodes

1. Plants of rubber（*Hevea* spp.）
2. Plants of cocoa（*Theobroma cacao*）
3. Plants of coconut（*Cocos nucifera*）
4. Plants of oil palm（*Elaeis guineensis*）
5. Plants of cassava（*Manihot esculenta*）
6. Plants of citrus（*Citrus* spp.）

7. Plants of coffee (*Coffea* spp.)

8. Plants of cotton (*Gossypium* spp.)

9. Plants of maize (*Zea mays*)

10. Plants of banana (*Musa* spp.)

11. Plants of pineapple (*Ananas comosus*)

12. Plants of rice (*Oryza sativa*)

13. Plants of sugarcane (*Saccharum officinarum*)

14. Plants of tea (*Camellia sinensis*)

15. Plants of orchid (*Orchidaceae*)

16. All other living plants or propagating materials such as branches, bulbs, corms, foliages, rhizomes, seeds or tubers, with or without potting media

17. All living plants that have acquired novel genetic materials by techniques of modern technology

18. Fresh or dried herbarium specimens

19. Mushroom spawn

20. All fresh flowers, fruits and vegetables originated from American Tropics

21. All living Annelida, Arthropoda, Mollusca, Nematoda and micro – organisms

22. All living modified organisms

23. All biological control agents

24. Soil and organic fertilizers.

Third schedule

Rules 8 and 15

<table>
<tr><th>First column</th><th>Second column</th></tr>
<tr><td rowspan="8">(1) Inspection and certification of plants, plant products or fresh cut flowers</td><td>(a) Non – commercial $12 per consignment for the following:</td></tr>
<tr><td>(i) Plants not exceeding 10 numbers or flasks;</td></tr>
<tr><td>(ii) Plant products not exceeding 5kg;</td></tr>
<tr><td>(iii) Fresh cut flowers not exceeding 24 stalks or numbers;</td></tr>
<tr><td>(b) Commercial $50 per consignment for the following:</td></tr>
<tr><td>(i) Plants exceeding 10 numbers or flasks;</td></tr>
<tr><td>(ii) Plant products exceeding 5 kg;</td></tr>
<tr><td>(iii) Fresh cut flowers exceeding 24 stalks or numbers;</td></tr>
<tr><td>(2) Laboratory examination of flowers, plants, plant products or other regulated articles for any pest or pathogen</td><td>$50 per pest examination.</td></tr>
<tr><td>(3) Permit to import plants, insects or micro – organisms</td><td>$11 per consignment.</td></tr>
<tr><td rowspan="2">(4) Professional service fee</td><td>(a) $63 per hour or part thereof;</td></tr>
<tr><td>(b) $133 per hour or part thereof (outside office hours or on an urgent basis).</td></tr>
<tr><td rowspan="2">(5) Technical service fee</td><td>(a) $38 per hour or part thereof;</td></tr>
<tr><td>(b) $80 per hour or part thereof (outside office hours or on an urgent basis).</td></tr>
</table>

Fourth schedule

Deleted by S 258/2005, wef 25/04/2005.

[*G. N. Nos. S 29/94*; *S 369/94*; *S368/96*; *S148/97*; *S 137/98*]

植物控制（新鲜水果及蔬菜进口与转运）条例

（植物控制法案（第57A章，第49条））

［1999年1月8日］

引用

1. 本《条例》是《植物控制（新鲜水果及蔬菜进口与转运）条例》

定义

2. 在《条例》目的范围内

容器　在其与新鲜水果或蔬菜相关的方面，意指装放有水果或蔬菜的筐篮、纸箱、包裹、箱盒、包装或其他的容器，并且，在任何前述的容器被放置在另一个此种容器当中的情况下时，亦包括后一种容器；

执照　意指在《法案》第31条项下就任何新鲜水果或蔬菜的进口或转运所颁发的执照；

持证人　指的是任一执照的持有人；

许可证　指的是在《法案》第31条项下就任何新鲜水果或蔬菜的托运货物的进口或转运而向任一持证人所颁发的许可。

可予发放执照或许可证的人员

3. 除非其正在新加坡境内开展业务，并具有下列情况，否则局长不得向其他人员颁发执照或许可证：

（a）其已根据《商业登记法案》（第32章）进行了登记的；

（b）如其为公司，则其已根据《公司法案》（第50章）设立或注册。

执照与许可证不可转让

4.（1）任何持证人均不得将向其颁发的执照或许可证向其他人员进行转让或让渡。

（2）违反第（1）款规定的持证人均应承担违法的责任。

执照、许可证或任何标签或文件的更改

5. 无相关合法手续，而将涉及到任何新鲜水果或蔬菜的进口或转运的任何持照或许可证，抑或任何的申报单、文件或标签予以更改，或者蓄意地对上述经更改的任何持照、许可证及申报或文件进行使用的人员，均应承担违法的责任。

所进口或转运的货物违反《法案》的情况

6.（1）经合法授权的官员有合理理由认为进口或转运的新鲜水果或蔬菜已经或者将会违反《法案》第7条或第8条的方式，则其可

（a）货物已随船进入新加坡境内但未卸货，根据相关法令，禁止将该货物从其运输工具上卸下；

（b）如货物运入新加坡境内，责令货主将该货物予以退运、销毁或以其他方式进行处置；

（c）将该货物予以没收。

（2）未能遵从授权官员在第（1）（a）点所做出的命令，抑或授权官员在第（1）（b）点所做出的指令的任何人员，均应承担违法的责任。

货物的检查

7.（1）进口或转运新鲜水果或蔬菜的持证人均应—

（a）在将货物从将进入新加坡境内的运输工具上卸下之前，或在授权官员允许的时间范围内，向授权官员提交关于该托运货物的进口申报或货物清关许可的复印件，以及局长或授权官员要求的涉及到该货物的其他相关文件；

（b）在经授权官员做出指示的情况下，将该货物送至大沙坡批发中心或者授权官员指定的其他相关地点，以便在其进行销售、供应或批发之前对其进行检疫。

（2）未能遵从第（1）款规定的人员应承担违法的责任。

采样分析程序

8.（1）如新鲜水果或蔬菜已予进口，且经授权官员根据《法案》第39条规定对该货物进行了采样以供检验，授权官员则应：

（a）以合适的方式，对该样本进行封存；

（b）将该货主的相关详情，以及采样的日期予以贴标标明；

（c）在标签上签署采样者姓名；

（d）指示货主，如货主并未到场则指示该货物代理人签署确认函，表明该样本来源于其所进口、或者由其所负责的运货物，具体根据实际情况而定；

（e）立即将该样本交送至授权的分析员处进行分析。

（2）如授权官员决定在得出相关分析结果报告前对该托运货物予以扣留，则其应：

（a）标记该货物，以便识别；

（b）指示货主，如货主并未到场则指示该货物代理人将货物存放于授权官员指定的相关地点处，直至得出检验报告。

（3）如在该货物被扣留时货主并未到场的，授权官员则应在实际可行的情况下，尽快将扣留事项通知货主。

（4）具有下列情况的人员：

（a）如未能遵从授权官员在第（1）款及第（2）款项下所做出的指示；

（b）未获得授权官员授权，即将已被扣留的货物全部或部分卸下、出售或以其他方式予以处置的，均应承担相关违法责任。

（5）如样本检验结果确认该样本不存在以下任一种情况的：

（a）禁用农药残留；

（b）农药残留超过第9（1）（a）条中所述标准的；或者

（c）超过关于任何有毒化学品的第9（1）（b）条规则中所述规定标准的有毒化学品残留的。

如该货物已予扣留的，授权官员则应立即将其放还给货人。

农药残留的标准

9.（1）《法案》第8（1）（c）：

（a）农药残留标准为：

（i）《食品法规》（1号法规第283章）的《附表九》中制定的农药残留标准；

（ii）在《食品法规》的《附表九》并未对该农药制定标准的情况下，建议采用联合国粮农组织/世界卫生组织联合食品规范委员会制定的相关标准；

（b）有毒化学品残留的标准为：

（i）《食品法规》中制定的有毒化学品详细标准；

（ii）在《食品法规》并未针对该农药制定标准的情况下，建议采用联合国粮农组织/世界卫生组织联合食品规范委员制定的相关标准。

（2）《法案》第8（1）（d）条的，相关卫生标准如下：

（a）进口的新鲜水果或蔬菜不得含有或者其含量水平可能会危害人体健康的微生物或其他物质（不包括农药或有毒化学品）；

（b）货物中用以盛装新鲜水果或蔬菜的容器干净且符合卫生条件，适宜于存放水果或蔬菜。

容器标识

10. （1）《法案》第 8（1）（f）条，货主应保证盛装新鲜水果或蔬菜的容器均标有以下内容：

（a）该新鲜水果或蔬菜生产商的名称；

（b）该生产商的详细地址，而不是其电报或者邮寄地址；

（c）该容器中所盛装的新鲜水果或蔬菜的名称；

（d）局长合理要求的其他相关详情。

（2）如货物并未包含有第（1）款中所述的任何一项的，授权官员可：

（a）责令货主将货物予以退运、销毁或以其他方式进行处置；

（b）将该货物予以没收。

（3）未遵从授权官员在第（2）（a）款项下处罚的人员，应承担相关违法责任。

授权官员的职权

11. （1）授权官员在不违反《法案》第 7 条或第 8 条项下或者本《条例》，有权（除《法案》第 37（1）条中相关职权外）要求进口或转运任何新鲜水果或蔬菜的人员：

（a）向授权官员报告其名称、居住地、营业地址以及授权官员合理要求的其他相关详情；

（b）供应、销售或批发该进口、转运的新鲜水果或蔬菜相关文件，或者授权官员合理要求的与前述内容相关的文件。

（2）拒绝或未遵从第（1）款中授权官员提出的要求的人员，均应承担相关违法责任。

虚假和其他不实信息

12. 根据本《条例》的规定而要求提供的信息、文件或者为获取到执照或许可证而做出了下列行为的人员：

（a）在材料中提供了虚假的或做出了不实陈述或声明的；

（b）在材料中提供或伪造了虚假的信息、或者并未由相关人员提交，或者篡改过的任何文件的，均应承担相关违法责任。

罚金

13. 根据本《条例》的规定应承担相关违法责任的人员，一旦定罪，则均应承担不超过 10000 美元的罚款，或者最长不超过 3 年的监禁，或者两者一并适用。

相关费用

14. 《一览表》第二栏中所详细规定的相关费用，应就第一栏中所详述的相关事项而向局长进行支付。

一 览 表

规则 14

第一栏	第二栏
1. 执照颁发或续期	378 美元/年
2. 许可的颁发	3 美元
3. 执照或许可的验证真实副本	9.45 美元

［*G. N. Nos. S 9/99*；*S 89/2000*；*S 449/2006*］

Control of plants (import and transhipment of fresh fruits and vegetables) rules

Control of plants ACT
(Chapter 57A, Section 49)

History G. N. No. S9/99 - >R1 2006 REVISED EDITION

[**8th January 1999**]

Citation

1. These Rules may be cited as the Control of Plants (Import and Transhipment of Fresh Fruits and Vegetables) Rules.

Definitions

2. For the purposes of these Rules—

container, in relation to fresh fruits or vegetables, means the basket, carton, bag, box, packet or other receptacle which contains the fruits or vegetables and, where any such receptacle is contained in another such receptacle, includes the latter receptacle;

licence means a licence issued under section 31 of the Act for the import or transhipment of any fresh fruit or vegetable;

licensee means the holder of a licence;

permit means a permit issued under section 31 of the Act to a licensee for the import or transhipment of any consignment of fresh fruits or vegetables.

Person to whom licence or permit may be issued

3. The Director - General shall not issue a licence or permit to any person unless the person is carrying on business in Singapore and is—

(a) registered under the Business Registration Act (Cap. 32); or

(b) in the case of a company, incorporated or registered under the Companies Act (Cap. 50).

Licence and permit not transferable

4. (1) No licensee shall transfer or assign the benefit of his licence or any permit issued to him to any person.

(2) A licensee who contravenes paragraph (1) shall be guilty of an offence.

Alteration of licence, permit or any label or document

5. Any person who without lawful authority alters any licence or permit or any declaration form, document or label relating to the import or transhipment of any fresh fruit or vegetable or knowingly makes use of any licence, permit, declaration or document so altered shall be guilty of an offence.

Where consignment imported or transhipped in contravention of Act

6. (1) Where an authorised officer has reasonable grounds to believe that a consignment of fresh fruits or vegetables has been or is to be imported or transhipped in contravention of section 7 or 8 of the Act, he may—

(a) where the consignment has yet to be removed from the conveyance in which it was brought into Singapore, by order prohibit the removal of the consignment from the conveyance;

(b) direct the person who brought the consignment into Singapore to export, destroy or otherwise dispose of the consignment; or

(c) seize the consignment.

(2) Any person who fails to comply with an order of an authorised officer given under paragraph (1)(a) or a direction of an authorised officer given under paragraph (1)(b) shall be guilty of an offence.

Inspection of consignment

7. (1) Any licensee who imports or tranships a consignment of fresh fruits or vegetables shall—

(a) before removal of the consignment from the conveyance in which it was brought into Singapore or within such time as an authorised officer may allow, submit to an authorised officer a copy of the import declaration or cargo clearance permit in respect of the consignment, whichever is applicable, and such other document in respect of the consignment as the Director - General or authorised officer may reasonably require; and

(b) when directed by an authorised officer to do so, take the consignment to the Pasir Panjang Wholesale Centre, or such other place as may be specified by the authorised officer, for inspection prior to its sale, supply or distribution.

(2) Any person who fails to comply with paragraph (1) shall be guilty of an offence.

Procedure for taking samples for analysis

8. (1) Where a consignment of fresh fruits or vegetables has been imported and an authorised officer takes a sample of the consignment for analysis under section 39 of the Act, the authorised officer shall—

(a) seal the sample in such manner as its nature permits;

(b) label the sample with the particulars of the licensee of the consignment and the date the sample was taken;

(c) sign his name on the label;

(d) direct the licensee or, where the licensee is not present, the person having charge of the consignment to sign an acknowledgment that the sample comes from the consignment imported by him or of which he is in charge, as the case may be; and

(e) immediately deliver the sample to an authorised analyst for analysis.

(2) Where the authorised officer determines that the consignment is to be detained until a report of the result of the analysis is obtained, he shall—

(a) cause the consignment to be marked or labelled for identification; and

(b) direct the licensee or, where the licensee is not present, the person having charge of the consignment to store the consignment at such place as the authorised officer may specify until the report is obtained.

(3) Where the licensee is not present at the time the consignment is detained, the authorised officer shall, as soon as practicable, inform the licensee of the detention.

(4) Any person who—

(a) fails to comply with a direction of an authorised officer given under paragraph (1) or (2); or

(b) without the authority of the authorised officer, removes, sells or otherwise disposes of any part of a consignment which has been detained, shall be guilty of an offence.

(5) Where the result of the analysis of the sample confirms that the sample does not contain any—

(a) prohibited pesticide residue;

(b) residue of any pesticide which exceeds the prescribed level referred to in rule 9 (1)(a) in respect of the pesticide; or

(c) residue of any toxic chemical which exceeds the prescribed level referred to in rule 9 (1)(b) in respect of that toxic chemical, an authorised officer shall immediately release the consignment to the licensee if the consignment is detained.

Level of pesticide residue, etc.

9. (1) For the purposes of section 8 (1) (c) of the Act—

(a) the prescribed level of pesticide residue is—

(i) the level specified in the Ninth Schedule to the Food Regulations (Cap. 283, Rg 1) in respect of the pesticide in question; or

(ii) where the Ninth Schedule to the Food Regulations does not specify any level in respect of that pesticide, the level recommended by the Joint FAO/WHO Codex Alimentarius Commission in respect of that pesticide; and

(b) the prescribed level of toxic chemical residue is—

(i) the level specified in the Food Regulations in respect of the toxic chemical in question; or

(ii) where the Food Regulations does not specify any level in respect of that toxic chemical, the level recommended by the Joint FAO/WHO Codex Alimentarius Commission in respect of that toxic chemical.

(2) For the purposes of section 8 (1) (d) of the Act, the sanitary standards are as follows:

(a) a consignment of fresh fruits or vegetables which is to be imported must not contain any organism or substance (other than a pesticide or toxic chemical) that is likely to be, or of a level that is likely to be, injurious to human health;

(b) the container for the fresh fruits or vegetables constituting the consignment is clean and in a sanitary condition, and is appropriate for the keeping of such fruits or vegetables.

Container to bear certain particulars

10. (1) For the purposes of section 8 (1) (f) of the Act, a licensee shall ensure that each container of fresh fruits or vegetables constituting a consignment to be imported by him bears the following particulars:

(a) the name of the producer of the fresh fruits or vegetables;

(b) the address of the producer, not being a telegraphic or code address or an address at a post office;

(c) the names of the fresh fruits or vegetables contained in the container; and

(d) such other particulars as the Director – General may reasonably require.

(2) Where a consignment does not bear any of the particulars referred to in paragraph (1), an authorized officer may—

(a) direct the licensee to export, destroy or otherwise dispose of the consignment; or

(b) seize the consignment.

(3) Any person who fails to comply with a direction of an authorised officer given under paragraph (2)

(a) shall be guilty of an offence.

Powers of authorised officers

11. (1) For the purpose of ascertaining whether an offence under section 7 or 8 of the Act or under these Rules has been or is being committed, an authorised officer has (in addition to the powers referred to in section 37 (1) of the Act) the power to require a person who imports or tranships any fresh fruits or vegetables—

(a) to disclose to the authorised officer his name, place of residence, place of business and such other particulars as the authorised officer may reasonably require;

(b) to produce any document, which relates to, or which the authorised officer reasonably believes relates to, the import for sale, supply or distribution, or the transhipment of, fresh fruits or vegetables.

(2) Any person who refuses or fails to comply with a requirement of an authorised officer referred to in paragraph (1) shall be guilty of an offence.

Giving of false information, etc.

12. Any person who, being required under these Rules to provide any information or produce any document or who, for the purpose of obtaining a licence or permit—

(a) provides any information or makes any statement or declaration which, to his knowledge, is false in any material particular; or

(b) submits or produces any document which, to his knowledge, is false in any material particular or has not been made by the person by whom it purports to have been made, or has been in any way altered or tampered with, shall be guilty of an offence.

Penalty

13. Any person who is guilty of an offence under these Rules shall be liable on conviction to a fine not exceeding $10,000 or to imprisonment for a term not exceeding 3 years or to both.

Fees

14. The fees specified in the second column of the Schedule shall be payable to the Director – General in respect of the matters specified in the first column thereof.

THE SCHEDULE

Rule 14

First column	*Second column*
1. For the issue or renewal of a licence	$378 per year
2. For the issue of a permit	$3
3. For a certified true copy of a licence or permit	$9.45

[*G. N. Nos. S 9/99*; *S 89/2000*; *S 449/2006*]

植物控制(植物检疫证书)条例

(植物控制法案(57A章,48款))

历史:G. N. NO. S29/94 →1995修正案 →R4 2000修正案

[1994年12月30日]

引言

1. 此条例称为《植物控制(植物检疫证书)条例》。

定义

2. 在以下条文中—

授权有害生物检疫员　指根据本法案第27款经局长批准并注册的官员。

装运　指植物、植物产品及其他管制物品装运出口。

管制物品　指植物、植物产品、仓储地、包装材料、运输工具、集装箱、土壤或其他有机物,以及可能携带或传播有害生物的或在国际运输过程中要求实施植物检疫的物品或原料;

处理证书　指由授权有害生物检疫官员签发的证书,证明已经根据局长或进口国要求对管制物品进行了处理。

出口植物、植物产品及其他管制物品植物检疫证书的申请

3. (1) 根据本法案第30款向授权官员提交植物检疫证书的申请,应以按局长要求以固定的格式填写并提交,需详细说明以下内容:

(a) 是否需要除害或消毒证明;

(b) 证书上是否需要加注特殊的声明。

(2) 根据第3(1)条所做的申请,申请人应在征得检疫官员同意,在不影响植物、植物产品及其他管制物品的装运的情况下,确定检疫时间。

签证前的检验和检疫

4. (1) 申请提交后,为签发关于植物、植物产品及其他管制物品装运的植物检疫证书,授权官员或授权有害生物检疫员应当

(a) 对植物、植物产品及其他管制物品(包括包装材料)的装运进行检疫,并合理扦样以备必要的分析或实验室检验;

(b) 对装载植物、植物产品及其他管制物品的集装箱、容器及其类似物、运输工具进行检疫;

(c) 完成以上必要的工作后签发证书。

(2) 如果植物检疫证书中要求注明该批装运的植物、植物产品及其他管制物品已经除害或消毒处理,其除虫或消毒处理应当在授权官员或有害生物检疫员的监督下进行。

植物检疫证书的签发

5. (1) 植物检疫证书签发的条件—

(a) 该批装运的植物、植物产品及其他管制物品经授权官员检查后符合要求—

(i) 符合申请书中的描述;

(ii) 不存在进口国规定的检疫性有害生物;

(iii) 符合进口国现行植物检疫要求,包括对非管制类检疫性有害生物的要求;

(b) 根据本法案第7条,申请人已经缴清相关检验和签证费用。

(2) 对原产新加坡的管制物品签发的植物检疫证书,由局长决定其证书形式。

（3）对非原产新加坡的管制物品再出口签发的植物检疫证书，由局长决定其证书形式。

随附其他证书

6. 根据附录二的规定，申请人缴清费用后，检疫官员可以在该批装运的植物、植物产品及其他管制物品的植物检疫证书后随附其他处理证书或植物检疫证书的复本。

植物检疫证书的费用

7. 附录二中规定了签发植物检疫证书应缴纳的费用。

签证的条件和限制

8.（1）根据本法案签发的植物检疫证书，授权官员为确保植物检疫证书的有效性，可以实施下列条件和限制。

（2）在出口商签收植物检疫证书后，授权官员如有合理依据认为该批货物与根据上述第（1）条款的条件和限制不符合，该官员可以重新检查该批装运的植物、植物产品、其他管制物品、货物的包装、集装箱、容器或其类似物和运输工具。

（3）在重新检查之后，该检疫官员认为该批货物的不符合项影响了植物检疫证书的适用，他可以要求取消该证书或者进行修改。

（4）如被取消证书，已经缴纳的费用不再退还。

植物检疫证书的重发

9.（1）当一份植物检疫证书因受损、玷污或其他特殊情况导致字迹模糊，或者植物、植物产品、其他管制物品的出口商要求修改该证书，可以向主管部门申请重发。

（2）请求重发植物检疫证书的每一份申请，应按局长的要求以固定的格式填写并提交，并按附录二的规定缴纳费用。

（3）除非已经向主管部门退回原发的植物检疫证书，否则不能重发。

（4）上述第（3）条款下退回的失效证书，已经缴纳的费用不再退还。

费用的减免

10. 政府部门或科研机构根据本法案要求而申请植物检疫证书产生的所有费用，可以完全或部分免除—

（a）由局长决定；

（b）授权官员是新加坡国家公园局雇员，为新加坡国家公园局局长雇佣。

使用或伪造（证书）应负的法律责任

11. 任何人—

（a）伪造植物检疫证书并声称该证书为授权官员签发的；或者

（b）明知或者有理由相信一份证书系伪造或者仿造，但是仍以欺骗或不实手段按真正的植物检疫证书来使用的，视为犯罪，将被处以不超过10000美元的罚金，或者不超过3年的监禁，或者两项并罚。

附录一

以由 S 380/2009、01/09/2009. 废止

附录二

第 6 条、第 7 条、第 9 条

检疫服务的应缴费用

(1) 检查和证明植物、植物产品、鲜切花或者其他管制物品:

(a) 下列非商品货物每批次收取 12 美元:

(i) 数量不超过 10 或 10 烧瓶的植物;

(ii) 重量不超过 5 千克的植物产品;

(iii) 数量不超过 24 支的鲜切花。

(iv) 重量不超过 5 千克的其他管制物品。

(b) 商品货物每批次收取 50 美元:

(i) 数量超过 10 或 10 烧瓶的植物;

(ii) 重量超过 5 千克的植物产品;

(iii) 数量超过 24 支的鲜切花。

(iv) 重量超过 5 千克的其他管制物品。

(2) 担保证明计划下的植物、植物产品、鲜切花或者其他管制物品,每批次收取32 美元。

(3) 对植物、植物产品、鲜切花或者其他管制物品的虫害或病原体做实验室检验,每批次收取 50 美元。

(4) 植物检疫证书的重发,每套 12 美元。

(5) 处理证书和植物检疫证书附本的工本费,每套 15 美元。

(6) 专业服务费用

(a) 每小时(不满 1 小时),63 美元。

(b) 每小时(不满 1 小时),133 美元(加班时间或者加急情况)。

(7) 技术服务费

(a) 每小时(不满 1 小时),38 美元。

(b) 每小时(不满 1 小时),80 美元(加班时间或者加急情况)。

[G. N. Nos. S 490/94; S369/96; S149/97; S 138/98; S 39/99]

Control of plants (phytosanitary certification) rules

Control of plants ACT
(Chapter 57A, Section 48)

History: G. N. NO. S29/94 →1995 REVISD EDITION →R4 2000 REVISD EDITION
[30th December 1994]

Citation

1. These Rules may be cited as the Control of Plants (Phytosanitary Certification) Rules.

Definitions

2. In these Rules— "accredited pest control agency" means a person registered by the Director – General under section 27 of the Act; "consignment" means a consignment of plants, plant products or other regulated articles to be loaded onto a vessel at any one time on behalf of one exporter; "regulated article" means any plant, plant product, storage place, packaging, conveyance, container, soil or any other organism, object or material capable of harbouring or spreading pests and deemed to require phytosanitary measures where international transportation is involved; "treatment certificate" means any certificate issued by an accredited pest control agency for a treatment applied to regulated articles and completed in accordance with the requirements of the Director – General or the importing country.

Application for phytosanitary certificate to export plants, plant products or other regulated

3. (1) Every application for a phytosanitary certificate under section 30 of the Act shall be made to an authorised officer in such form and through such mode as the Director – General may determine and the application shall specify—

(a) whether any certification of disinfestation or disinfection treatment is required; and

(b) whether any specific declaration is required on the certificate.

(2) An application made under paragraph (1) shall be subject to the applicant making available a date for inspection, acceptable to the authorised officer, of the consignment of plants, plant products or other regulated articles in respect of which the application has been made.

Inspection and examination before certification

4. (1) For the purposes of phytosanitary certification of a consignment of plants, plant products or other regulated articles in respect of which the application has been made, the authorised officer or an accredited pest control agency may—

(a) inspect the consignment of plants, plant products or other regulated articles, including their packaging, and take such samples thereof as may reasonably be necessary for analysis or laboratory examination;

(b) inspect the containers, receptacles or premises containing or holding the plants, plant products or other regulated articles and the conveyance transporting the plants, plant products or other regulated articles; and

(c) do all such other things that are reasonably necessary for him to carry out the certification.

(2) Where a certification that disinfestation or disinfection treatment of the consignment of plants, plant products or other regulated articles has been carried out is required in a phytosanitary certificate, the disinfestation or disinfection treatment shall be carried out in the presence of an authorised officer or accredited pest con-

trol agency.

Issue of phytosanitary certificates

5. (1) No phytosanitary certificate shall be issued unless—

(a) the authorised officer is satisfied that the consignment of plants, plant products or other regulated articles inspected—

(i) fits the description stated in the application form;

(ii) is considered free from quarantine pests as specified by the importing country; and

(iii) conforms to the current phytosanitary requirements of the importing country, including those for regulated non-quarantine pests; and

(b) the applicant has paid, in accordance with rule 7, all the fees for the services rendered and expenses incurred for the phytosanitary certification.

(2) A phytosanitary certificate issued in respect of regulated articles that originate from Singapore shall be in such form as the Director-General may determine.

(3) A phytosanitary certificate for re-export issued in respect of regulated articles that do not originate from Singapore shall be in such form as the Director-General may determine.

Endorsement of other certificates

6. In the phytosanitary certification of a consignment of plants, plant products or other regulated articles, the authorised officer may, upon payment by the applicant of the fee specified in the Second Schedule, endorse any treatment certificate or any duplicate copy of a phytosanitary certificate issued.

Fees payable for phytosanitary certification

7. The fees payable for the services rendered for the phytosanitary certification are specified in the Second Schedule.

Conditions and restrictions imposed upon certification

8. (1) In issuing a phytosanitary certificate under this rule, the authorised officer may impose such conditions and restrictions as he thinks fit to ensure continued validity of the phytosanitary certification.

(2) Where, after the receipt by the exporter of the phytosanitary certificate, any authorised officer has reasonable cause to think that any condition or restriction imposed under paragraph (1) has not been complied with, the authorised officer may re-examine the consignment of plants, plant products or other regulated articles, its packaging, container and receptacle or the premises in which the consignment is kept or the conveyance in which the consignment is to be transported.

(3) Where upon re-examination the authorised officer is satisfied that the non-compliance with the condition or restriction imposed has affected the applicability of the phytosanitary certificate to the consignment, he may require the phytosanitary certificate issued to be produced for cancellation or amendment.

(4) No refund shall be made for the fees paid for any certificate which has been cancelled.

Replacement of phytosanitary certificate

9. (1) Where a phytosanitary certificate is torn, defaced or if any of the particulars therein has become illegible or requires an amendment, the exporter of the plants, plant products or other regulated articles in respect of which the certificate was issued may apply to the Director-General for the issue of a replacement.

(2) Every application for the issue of a replacement of a phytosanitary certificate shall be made in such form as the Director-General may determine, and shall be accompanied by the fee specified in the Second Schedule.

(3) No replacement shall be issued for a phytosanitary certificate unless all the copies of the original phytosanitary certificates are surrendered to the Director-General for cancellation.

(4) No refund shall be made for the fees paid for the certificate surrendered to the Director – General under paragraph (3).

Remission of fees

10. Any fee payable by any Government department or scientific institution under these Rules for the services rendered for phytosanitary certification may be remitted either wholly or in part—

(a) by the Director – General; or

(b) where the authorised officer is an employee of the National Parks Board, by the Chief Executive Officer of the National Parks Board.

Offences relating to use and forgery

11. Any person who—

(a) forges a phytosanitary certificate, purporting to be a phytosanitary certificate issued by an authorised officer; or

(b) fraudulently or dishonestly uses as genuine a phytosanitary certificate which he knows or has

reason to believe to be a certificate which is forged or falsified, shall be guilty of an offence and shall be liable on conviction to a fine not exceeding $10,000 or to imprisonment for a term not exceeding 3 years or to both.

First schedule

Deleted by S 380/2009、wef 01/09/2009.

Second schedule

Rules 6, 7 and 9

Service rendered Fee payable

(1) Inspection and certification of plants, plant products, fresh cut flowers or other regulated articles:

(a) Non – commercial $12 per consignment for the following:

(i) Plants not exceeding 10 numbers or flasks;

(ii) Plant products not exceeding 5 kg;

(iii) Fresh cut flowers not exceeding 24 stalks or numbers;

(iv) Other regulated articles not exceeding 5 kg.

(b) Commercial $50 per consignment for the following:

(i) Plants exceeding 10 numbers or flasks;

(ii) Plant products exceeding 5 kg;

(iii) Fresh cut flowers exceeding 24 stalks or numbers;

(iv) Other regulated articles exceeding 5 kg.

(2) Certification of plants, plant products, fresh cut flowers or other regulated articles under the Assurance Certification Scheme, $32 per consignment.

(3) Laboratory examination of flowers, plants, plant products or other regulated articles for any pest or pathogen, $50 per pest examination.

(4) Issuance of replacement set of phytosanitary certificate, $12 per set.

(5) Endorsement of treatment certificate or duplicate phytosanitary certificate, $15 per set.

(6) Professional service fee

(a) $63 per hour or part thereof;

(b) $133 per hour or part thereof (outside office hours or on an urgent basis).

(7) Technical service fee

(a) $38 per hour or part thereof;

(a) $80 per hour or part thereof (outside office hours or on an urgent basis).

[G. N. Nos. S 490/94; S369/96; S149/97; S 138/98; S 39/99]

动物与禽鸟法

（第 7 章）

本法令旨在： 防止动物、禽鸟或鱼类疫病传入并散播于新加坡境内；管理动物、禽鸟或鱼类进出口以及境内转运；防范残害动物、禽鸟或鱼类；规范和改善新加坡动物、禽鸟或鱼类的正常福利；应对以上事项相关的偶发事件。

［修订编号为：10/2002］

［1965 年 10 月 22 日发布］

第一部分　序　　言

简称

1. 本法称为动物与禽鸟法。

释义

2. 除非文中另有规定，在本法中：

飞机　　包括用作动物或禽鸟空中运输的各类型飞行器；

动物　　指各种哺乳动物（人类除外）或者鱼类，包括本法中指示为动物或者归为某个动物类别的其他生物；

动物检疫站　　指依据本法第 57 条建立的检疫站点；

授权检查员　　指获任命的官员，并包括依据本法第 4 条由局长委任的检查人员；

授权官员　　指局长按本法第 3 条（2）款委任的官员；

主管当局　　指按农粮与兽医局法（第 5 章）第 3 条组建的农粮与兽医局；

禽鸟　　指包括不同年龄或性别的驯养鸟、鸭、鹅、火鸡、珍珠鸡和鸽子以及它们所产的卵；

房舍　　包括盖有或无屋顶的用于庇护或圈养动物或禽鸟的房子、小屋、棚屋、马厩或圈养地，以及围栏、笼、墙壁、门、栋梁、柱子、木栅、框架、木板、栅栏、平台、路面、通道、台阶、运输带、滑道、入船坞、堆积物、防波堤、栈桥或架桥以及与前述建筑物相连接的任何结构；

公牛　　指各品种雄性牛；

动物尸体　　指动物或者禽鸟死尸，包括其肢体，如肉、骨头（整块、碎屑或粉状的）、碎屑、兽皮、皮毛、毛绒、毛发、羽毛、蹄、角，以及与动物或者禽鸟分离的或连接的任何肢体部分；

猫　　指任何品种或性别的驯养猫；

牛　　指公牛、母牛、牛类和小牛，以及各年龄或性别的水牛；

接触　　指动物或禽鸟直接地或间接地与染疫动物或禽鸟相接触，存在接触感染疫病风险；

局长　　指依据本法第 3 条（1）款任命的农粮与兽医局最高行政长官；

疫病　　指动物或禽鸟之间能间接或直接传染的疫病，包括本部门在某阶段公告宣称适用本法管理的相关疫病；

犬　　指任何品种或性别的驯养犬；

检查　　指对任何动物、禽鸟及其尸体的检查、检测和测试，以判定其是否染疫；

鱼类　　包括各种海生、咸水或淡水产出的鱼、甲壳纲动物、水生软体类动物、海龟、海绵体、海参以及其他形式的水生生物，并包括其幼苗和卵；

饲料　　指用于饲喂动物或禽鸟的任何物质；

转基因生物　指活体或死亡生物（人类或植物除外），或是其机体的某个部分，其中包含有来源于或改良自遗传学实验或操作的遗传物质或蛋白质，而不是自然进化的结果；

转运货物　指经过新加坡中转出境的入境货物，且在中转过程中货物始终保存在入境时的同一运载工具上；

马　包括各种母马、阉马、小型马、马驹、小母马、驴或骡；

进口　包括向新加坡输入转运货物或转口货物；

染疫　指被任何一种疾病所感染；

许可证　指局长签发的各种许可执照；

废弃物　指动物或禽鸟铺垫过或使用过的其他相关物品；

运输主管　指船长或者飞机机长，包括船只或飞机的时任主管人（飞行员除外）；

海关官员　与海关法（第70章）中的释义相同；

物主　包括任何动物或禽鸟以及建筑物的现任掌管者；

通行证　指局长签发的放行许可证；

港口　与新加坡海事与港口管理局法案（第170A章）中释义相同；

公共场所　指明令规定或默许的，公众或部分民众在特定时间可以负费或免费进入的地方或经营场所；

检疫　指强制扣留以隔离动物，鸟或相关物品；

检疫站　指实施检疫的场所，包括供检查用的场所或船体；

船舶　包括各种能浮于水面的容器或工具，且无论其驱动方式；

转口　指转运用于出口的进口货物，无论货物出口时是否将其重新装载到进口使用的同一的车辆、飞机或船舶上，无论货物是否在上述运载工具之间直接转移还是进口后曾卸货在新加坡某地；

兽用生物制品　包括各种病毒、血清、毒素以及天然的或人工合成的类似产品，包括转基因生物、诊断试剂、抗毒素、疫苗、活的或死的微生物、以及微生物抗原或者免疫成分，这些制剂可用于动物和禽鸟疫病的诊断、治疗及预防，或用于动物和禽鸟的研究；

兽医中心　指向民众提供以下服务的经营场所：

（a）动物和禽鸟疫病和伤病诊断和诊断性测试；

（b）对动物或禽鸟进行治疗、免疫或药物注射。

［修订编号：16/2000；10/2000］

局长等的委任

3.（1）农粮与兽医局局长由部长任命，并公报告示，负责执行本法及其附属法规；

［修订编号：16/2000］

（2）局长可以书面形式委任本局或其他法定政府机构的公务员或其他官员为授权官员，行使本法相应权利；

［修订编号：16/2000］

（3）局长可委派授权官员来代其行使本法所赋予他的权力或义务。

［修订编号：16/2000］

授权检查员的委派

4. 局长可在遵从部长常规或特别指令下，可书面任命称职人员为授权检查员，授权检查员可在本法授权范围内从事检测、处置、签证以及其他相关事务。

［修订编号：3A；16/2000］

公务员

5. 所有的授权官员均为公务员，适用刑法（第224章）相关规定。

［修订编号：4；10/2002］

出示身份证明

6. （1）授权官员、海关官员或警官在践行本法职权时，应该做到：

（a）如果不穿制服，声明其所属政府机构；并且

（b）一经要求，向相关人员出示分别由局长、海关关长或公安局长签发的个人职务证明。

［修订编号：16/2000］

（2）如果授权官员、海关官员或警察不穿制服，且不能证明其身份，任何人均可拒绝服其要求和指令。

［修订编号：5］

第二部分　动物与禽鸟的进出口、转口，以及携带外来有害生物

制定进口相关规定的权力

7. （1）部长可发布以下命令：

（a）划定可进口或转口动物与禽鸟的国家或地区，以及相应的动物或禽鸟种类，可附加限制条款或自由输入；

（b）完全地或限制性禁止从划定的国家或地区进口或转口任何动物或禽鸟的尸体、精液、草料、垫料、粪便以及其他任何可能传播疫病的动物或禽鸟产品、商品或物质。

（2）任何人违反依据本条（1）款规定所发布的命令，将被定罪并处以不超过 $10,000 的罚款或不超过 12 个月的监禁或两罚并施。

［修订编号：5；10/2002］

未经许可不能进口或转口动物、禽鸟或兽医生物制品

8. （1）个人必须依据第 7 条（1）款规定输入或者转口各种动物、禽鸟或者兽医生物制品，并获得局长签发的许可证，以及满足许可证中可能提出的任何要求。

［修订编号：16/2000］

（2）想要获取依据本法令发放的进口或转运任何动物、禽鸟或兽医生物制品许可证书，必须预先向局长递交申请并交纳相关费用。

［修订编号：16/2000］

（3）任何人违反本条（1）款规定进口或转口任何动物、禽鸟或兽医生物制品，将被定罪并处以不超过 $10,000 的罚款或不超过 12 个月的监禁或两罚并施。

［修订编号：7；20/2002］

输入或保留有毒有害生物或转基因生物等

9. （1）没有局长的书面同意，任何人均不能向新加坡输入或保留对动物或禽鸟存在天然毒性或危险性的活体有害昆虫、有害生物、病菌、病毒、细菌培养物或转基因生物。

［修订编号：16/2000；10/2002］

（2）任何人违反本条（1）款规定，将被定罪并处以不超过 $10,000 的罚款或不超过 12 个月的监禁或两罚并施。

［修订编号：67；10/2002］

进口动物与禽鸟的检查

10. （1）任何人在局长或授权官员的指导下进口任何动物或禽鸟时，在动物或禽鸟抵达新加坡境内时须立即接受授权检查员的检查，并自行承担所需费用。

［修订编号：10/2002］

（2）鉴于本条（1）款规定，授权官员可以将进境动物或禽鸟滞留在局长或授权官员认可的检疫站直至检查完毕。

［修订编号：10/2002］

（3）任何动物或禽鸟在接受本条（1）款规定的检查时，被证实患有：

（a）授权检查员认为无法治疗或不应释放的动物或禽鸟疫病或伤病；

（b）如果不销毁动物将可能致使疫病散布；

进口动物或禽鸟的人员必须立即自费并依照局长或授权官员指定方式销毁处理动物或禽鸟尸体。

[修订编号：10/2002]

（4）任何人违反本条（1）款或（3）款规定，将被定罪并处以不超过 $5,000 的罚款或不超过 6 个月的监禁或两罚并施。

[修订编号：8；10/2002]

动物或禽鸟的入境申报

11.（1）载运动物或禽鸟的船舶、飞机或火车的运输主管，在抵达新加坡境内时，必须马上向抵境港口、机场或站点主管报告，并立即通知授权官员。

[修订编号：16/2000]

（2）授权官员可以：

（a）登上任何船、飞机或火车对动物或禽鸟实施检查；

（b）指令船舶、飞机或火车的运输主管，自费安排使动物或禽鸟便于授权检查员实施检查。

[修订编号：10/2002]

（3）尽管满足：

（a）按第 8 条持有动物或禽鸟的进口或转口许可证；或者

（b）动物或禽鸟来自第 7 条（1）（a）款划定的国家或区域；

进境港口、机场或站点主管仍不能允许动物或禽鸟卸离运载工具，直至授权官员认为满足要求，并发放通行证。

[修订编号：16/2000]

（4）任何人：

（a）没有按（1）款 要求申报；

（b）没有按（2）款遵从授权官员所作指令；

（c）违反（3）款允许动物或者禽鸟从船舶、飞机或火车上卸下的，被定罪并处以不超过 $5,000 的罚款或不超过 6 个月的监禁或两罚并施。

[修订编号：9；10/2002]

处置染疫进口动物与禽鸟的权力

12.（1）在进入或计划进入新加坡的船舶、飞机或火车上，如果局长或授权官员有理由相信动物或禽鸟可疑染疫，可指令运输主管自费地采取以下措施：

（a）确保船舶、飞机或火车上装载的动物或禽鸟没有被转移下该交通工具至新加坡境内；

（b）安排入境动物或禽鸟接受授权检查员的检查；

（c）船舶、飞机或火车上感染或被怀疑染疫的动物或禽鸟以及这些动物或者禽鸟接触过的动物或禽鸟将被：

（i）依照局长或授权官员指定的方式销毁和处置；

（ii）退运出新加坡境内；

（iii）依照检查该批次动物或禽鸟的授权检查员所作指令进行处理；

（iv）按照局长或授权官员指定的方式、地点和时间进行隔离检疫；

（d）为了防止疾病传入或散布于新加坡，如果局长认为必要，可采取措施阻止车辆、飞机或者船舶不进入新加坡或者把已入境的车辆、飞机或者船舶退运出新加坡境外。

[修订编号：10/2002]

（2）按照本条（1）（c）（i）款规定处理任何动物或禽鸟时，无任何补偿。

［修订编号：10/2002］

（3）任何人违反局长或授权官员依据本条（1）款规定作出的指令，将被定罪并处以不超过＄10,000 的罚款或不超过 12 个月的监禁或两罚并施。

［修订编号：10；10/2002］

船上动物和禽鸟的管理

13.（1）在获得授权官员许可之前，所有经海港进口或转口的动物或禽鸟，必须滞留在船上并限制于封闭区域或笼窝内。

［修订编号：16/2000；10/2002］

（2）如果任何动物或禽鸟在港口死亡或丢失，船长须立即通知授权官员。

［修订编号：16/2000；10/2002］

（3）船长在任何情况下：

（a）经船舶向新加坡输入或转运动物或禽鸟时，违反本条（1）款规定没有将动物或禽鸟限制于海港停泊船只上；

（b）当任何动物或禽鸟在港口死亡或丢失，无合理缘由不通知授权官员；

将被定罪，并处以不超过＄5,000 的罚款或不超过 6 个月的监禁或两罚并施。

［修订编号：1；10/2002］

动物尸体的卸离许可

14.（1）没有获取附带有处置指导意见的授权官员书面许可之前，任何人不能从船舶、飞机、火车或车辆上卸下或移走任何动物或禽鸟。

［修订编号：16/2000］

（2）任何人：

（a）违反本条（1）款规定，从船舶、飞机、火车或车辆上卸下或移走任何动物或禽鸟；

（b）没有遵从授权官员根据本条（1）款规定作出的书面指令；

将被定罪，并处以不超过＄10,000 的罚款或不超过 12 个月的监禁或两罚并施。

［修订编号：13；16/2000；10/2002］

特定物品的销毁或消毒

15.（1）授权官员在认为通过陆地、海上或空中随动物或禽鸟一同输入的垫料、废弃物、草料或者其他物品有可能携带或散布疫病时，可以：

（a）查封或扣留；并且

（b）自行决定销毁或消毒处置这些物品

（2）无须对依据本条（1）款规定处理的任何物品进行赔偿。

［修订编号：14；10/2002］

出　口

出口动物或禽鸟的许可

16.（1）个人不能出口任何动物或禽鸟及其尸体，除非：

（a）获得局长签发的许可证；

（b）满足许可证（如果持有）要求的所有条件；

（c）满足其他法定条件。

［修订编号：16/2000］

（2）为获得动物或禽鸟及其尸体的出口许可证，必须提交法定表格向局长申请，并交纳相关法定费用。

［修订编号：16/2000］

（3）任何人违反本条（1）款规定出口任何动物或禽鸟及其尸体，将被定罪，并处以不超过 $ 10,000 的罚款或不超过 12 个月的监禁或两罚并施。

［修订编号：15；10/2002］

动物和禽鸟出口前的检查及处理

17.（1）从新加坡出口任何动物或禽鸟须遵从局长或授权官员的指导，自行承担必要的检查及处理费用。

［修订编号：10/2002］

（2）按照本条（1）款规定对动物或禽鸟进行检查或处理时，检查员可以将动物或禽鸟滞留在局长或授权官员认可的检疫站直至检查或处理完毕。

［修订编号：10/2002］

（3）在执行按照本条（1）款规定的检查时，如果动物或禽鸟被证实感染了任何一种疫病：

（a）如果没有局长或授权官员的许可，货主不能出口该批次的动物或禽鸟；

（b）局长或授权官员可命令指示货主按照其指定的方式处理或销毁该批次的动物或禽鸟。

（4）任何人违反本条（1）款或（3）（a）款规定以及局长或授权官员依据本条（3）（b）款规定作出的指令时，将被定罪并处以不超过 $ 10,000 的罚款或不超过 12 个月的监禁或两罚并施。

［修订编号：10/2002］

无疫病证书

18.（1）任何人，拟出口动物、禽鸟及其尸体或产品的，可以向授权检查员申请获取相关证书：

（a）证明该批产品不携带有新加坡为非疫区的疫病；或者

（b）经检测，确认该批产品无相关疫病以及其他健康疾患。

［修订编号：10/2002］

（2）进行本条（1）款规定的申请须交纳法定费用。

［修订编号：66；10/2002］

第三部分　防止疫病扩散

一 般 规 定

疑似染疫动物或禽鸟的检查

19.（1）对于可疑染疫任何动物或禽鸟，局长或授权官员有权要求对动物或禽鸟以及任何与其相触过的物品或物质进行检查。

（2）基于本款规定：

（a）局长或授权官员可以：

（i）查封动物或者禽鸟以及相关物品的全部或采取样品，并送去检测；

（ii）以书面方式指令物主或者掌管者将动物或禽鸟以及全部相关物品或采取样品递送至指定地点，交由授权检查员进行检测；

（b）授权检查员在进行检查时，可以按照其认为恰当的方法从动物或禽鸟取样检测或杀死后解剖检查，并依据公认的兽医实践知识来断定动物或禽鸟是否感染了某种特定的疾病。

［修订编号：10/2002］

（3）对按照本条（2）（b）款规定处理任何动物或禽鸟时，将不予任何补偿。

［修订编号：10/2002］

（4）任何人：

（a）无法律许可的藉口而不遵从依据本条（2）（a）（ii）款规定签发的书面指令；或

（b）没有局长或授权官员的许可，擅自把任何动物或禽鸟转移本条（2）（a）（ii）款所陈述的地方；

将被定罪并处以不超过＄5,000的罚款或不超过6个月的监禁或两罚并施。

［修订编号：10/2002］

染疫动物或禽鸟的隔离或销毁

20. （1）局长或授权官员可根据需要即时隔离或销毁任何动物或禽鸟，如果：

（a）依据第19条规定由授权检查员对动物或禽鸟的检测证实其染疫；

（b）局长或授权官员有充分的理由相信动物或禽鸟染疫；

（c）局长或授权官员有充分的理由相信动物或禽鸟：

（i）与染疫动物或禽鸟接触过；

（ii）已经暴露于疾病之下；

（iii）可能续存疾病。

［修订编号：10/2002］

（2）任何人在没有法律依据的情况下，拒绝或者没有执行如本条（1）款规定的由局长或授权官员要求隔离或销毁动物或禽鸟的命令，将被定罪并处以不超过＄5,000的罚款或不超过6个月的监禁或两罚并施。

［修订编号：10/2002］

销毁动物或禽鸟的补偿

21. （1）按照第20条规定销毁的任何动物或禽鸟，将不予以任何补偿。

（2）尽管可遵从本条（1）款的规定，但部长仍可自行决断并授权对被销毁的任何动物或禽鸟主人以适当补偿。

动物尸体检查

22. （1）局长或授权官员可以对任何死亡动物或禽鸟的尸体进行验尸检查。

［修订编号：10/2002］

（2）为了执行本条（1）款规定，局长或授权官员书面指令：

（a）对于已经埋葬了的尸体，可掘出以备验尸检查；

（b）在规定时间内将尸体递送至指定地点交给授权检查员。

［修订编号：10/2002］

（3）任何人：

（a）没有法律许可的藉口地不遵从依据本条（2）款规定签发的书面指令；或

（b）没有局长或授权官员的许可，擅自把任何动物或禽鸟转移本条（2）（b）款所陈述的地方；

将被定罪并处以不超过＄5,000的罚款或不超过6个月的监禁或两罚并施。

［修订编号：10/2002］

染疫动物或禽鸟的处理

23. （1）如果授权官员认为任何动物或禽鸟已暴露于传染病的感染，他可书面指令对动物或禽鸟采取认为必须的措施，包括注射疫苗或治疗血清或两法并用。

［修订编号：16/2000］

（2）任何人没有法律许可的藉口而不遵从依据本条（1）款规定签发的书面指令，将被定罪并处以不超过＄5,000的罚款或不超过6个月的监禁或两罚并施。

［修订编号：10/2002］

房舍消毒

24. （1）授权官员可书面发出指令：

（a）对被发现保留或饲养有动物或禽鸟的建筑物按照其指定的方法进行消毒；

（b）禁止使用建筑物直至达到本条款（a）规定所发出相关指令的要求。

［修订编号：16/2000］

（2）任何人没有法律许可的藉口而不遵从依据本条（1）款规定签发的书面指令，将被定罪并处以不超过 $5,000 的罚款或不超过 6 个月的监禁或两罚并施。

［修订编号：10/2002］

房舍销毁

25.（1）如果授权官员认为对圈养有染疫动物的任何建筑物无法实施彻底消毒，他可在征得部长的同意后书面指令在指定时间拆除此建筑物并烧毁拆除物。

［修订编号：16/2000］

（2）如果依据本条（1）款规定发出的指令在规定的时间内没有被执行，授权官员可强制拆除和销毁建筑物和材料。

［修订编号：16/2000］

（3）按照本条（1）和（2）款规定拆除的建筑物时，对其物主或占有者不予任何补偿金。

［修订编号：16/2000］

（4）尽管有本条（3）款的规定，但部长仍可自行决断并授权对被拆除建筑物的主人以适当补偿。

［修订编号：16/2000］

（5）任何人没有法律许可的藉口而不遵从依据本条（1）款规定签发的书面指令，将被定罪并处以不超过 $5,000 的罚款或不超过 6 个月的监禁或两罚并施。

［修订编号：10/2002］

物品的消毒或销毁

26.（1）授权官员可书面指令对任何与染疫动物或禽鸟接触过的被褥、衣服、马具、配件、铲、桶或者其他器具进行消毒或销毁处理。

［修订编号：16/2000］

（2）依据本条（1）款规定销毁的被褥、衣服、马具、配件、铲、桶或者器具，将不予以补偿。

（3）任何人没有法律许可的藉口而不遵从依据本条（1）款规定签发的书面指令，将被定罪并处以不超过 $5,000 的罚款或不超过 6 个月的监禁或两罚并施。

［修订编号：10/2002］

人员及衣物的消毒

27.（1）授权官员可要求对任何接触、掌管或管理过任何染疫的或授权官员认为染疫的动物或禽鸟的人员及其衣服进行消毒处理。

［修订编号：16/2000］

（2）任何人没有法律许可的藉口而不遵从依据本条（1）款规定签发的书面指令，将被定罪并处以不超过 $5,000 的罚款或不超过 6 个月的监禁或两罚并施。

［修订编号：10/2002］

运载工具消毒

28.（1）授权官员可根据需要消毒任何车辆或运输工具：

（a）依据第 35 条规定，进入或离开疫区的；

（b）被用来运输过染疫或授权官员认为染疫的动物或禽鸟的。

［修订编号：16/2000］

（2）任何人没有法律许可的藉口而不遵从依据本条（1）款规定签发的书面指令，将被定罪并处以不超过 $5,000 的罚款或不超过 6 个月的监禁或两罚并施。

［修订编号：10/2002］

染疫动物、禽鸟及其尸体的处理

29.（1）对于染疫动物或禽鸟或其尸体以及与染疫动物接触的任何草料、垫料、粪便或其他物品的处理，没有人可以故意抛弃或任由或允许抛弃到任何排水沟、沟渠、水道、街道或公共地方，也不能任由其暴露于自然界。

（2）任何人有不遵从依据本条（1）款规定，将被定罪并处以不超过＄10,000 的罚款或不超过 12 个月的监禁或两罚并施。

［修订编号：10/2002］

染疫或死亡动物及禽鸟的物主申报

30. （1）每个动物或禽鸟的拥有者或管理员在动物或禽鸟感染或合理怀疑染疫时，必须：

（a）立刻报告给授权官员或附近的警察局；

（b）立刻对该动物或者禽鸟以及其接触过的动物或禽鸟加以限制和隔离，直至授权官员抵达。

（2）每个动物或禽鸟的拥有者或管理员在合理怀疑动物或禽鸟因染疫死亡时，必须立即报告给授权官员或附近的警察局，没有授权官员的书面许可不能移走动物。

［修订编号：16/2000］

（3）如果在依照本条（2）款规定报告后 24 小时内没有受到任何指示，可自行埋葬动物。

［修订编号：16/2000］

（4）收到报告的警察局官员在电话告知授权官员须报告内容后，须尽可能地将报告送至授权官员。

［修订编号：16/2000］

（5）任何人没有法律许可的藉口而不遵从依据本条（1）或（2）款规定报告的，将被定罪并处以不超过＄10,000 的罚款或不超过 12 个月的监禁或两罚并施。

［修订编号：10/2002］

（6）任何的人，没有合理的藉口：

（a）不按照本条（1）款规定限制和隔离动物或禽鸟的；

（b）或违反本条（2）款规定，允许移动动物或禽鸟尸体的；

将被定罪并处以不超过＄10,000 的罚款或不超过 12 个月的监禁或两罚并施。

［修订编号：10/2002］

动物与禽鸟（除犬猫外）的特别规定

适用范围

31. 第 32 条到第 36 条规定的申请不适用于狗和猫。

死亡动物或禽鸟的处理

32. （1）动物或禽鸟的拥有者或管理员在动物或禽鸟染疫死亡或被授权官员命令扑杀后，须遵从授权官员的书面指令埋葬或以其他方法处理其尸体。

［修订编号：16/2000］

（2）任何人没有法律许可的藉口而不遵从授权官员依据本条（1）款规定签发的书面指令，将被定罪并处以不超过＄10,000 的罚款或不超过 12 个月的监禁或两罚并施。

［修订编号：16/2000；10/2002］

染疫或可疑染疫动物或禽鸟的清理或处置

33. （1）对于任何患病的或合理怀疑患病的或于患病动物或禽鸟以及尸体接触过的动物或禽鸟，以及其乳汁、粪便或血液，除非有授权官员的书面同意，否则任何人不可以出售或以其他的方式转移或者处理，

［修订编号：16/2000］

（2）任何人不遵从依据本条（1）款规定的，将被定罪并处以不超过＄10,000 的罚款或不超过 12 个月的监禁或两罚并施。

［修订编号：10/2002］

染疫场所物品的清理

34. （1）授权官员可签发书面指令来禁止转移保留有或近期圈养过染疫动物或禽鸟的场所内可能携带或传播疾病的乳汁、粪肥、草料、垫料或者其他物品。

［修订编号：16/2000］

（2）任何人没有法律许可的藉口而不遵从依据本条（1）款规定签发的书面指令，将被定罪并处以不超过 $10,000 的罚款或不超过 12 个月的监禁或两罚并施。

［修订编号：10/2002］

疫区

35. （1）当有足够理由相信新加坡某地区的动物或禽鸟染疫时，部长可命令宣布该地区为疫区，并命令：

（a）完全地或有条件地禁止任何动物或禽鸟或者任何指定类型的动物或禽鸟进入或离开该区域；

（b）限制人和车辆、飞机和船的进入或离开该区域。

［修订编号：10/2002］

（2）当一个区域被依据本条（1）款规定宣布为疫区时，局长或授权官员可要求动物或禽鸟的拥有者或者管理人员执行局长或授权官员所发出的指令，以控制和阻止疫病散播。

［修订编号：10/2002］

（3）依据本条（2）款规定签发的指令可以：

（a）对疫区动物或禽鸟进行绑缚、隔离、分离、转移或扑杀；

（b）要求执行局长或授权官员指定的任何措施。

［修订编号：10/2002］

（4）获准保留在疫区的动物或禽鸟，有违依据本条（2）款规定发出的书面指令的，可能：

（a）被授权官员或其指定的任何人员当即销毁；

（b）被捕捉和扣留，直至根据本法令规定宣布没收处置。

［修订编号：16/2000；10/2002］

（5）对按照本条（4）款规定销毁或扣留的动物或禽鸟，不予以补偿；

（6）任何人没有法律许可的藉口而不遵从依据本条（1）款规定发出的指令或者是依据本条（2）款规定发出的书面指令，将被定罪并处以不超过 $10,000 的罚款或不超过 12 个月的监禁或两罚并施。

［修订编号：10/2002］

特别许可

36. 授权官员可允许并签发书面通行证，许可动物或禽鸟主人在满足官员强加的条件后将动物或禽鸟转移出疫区。

［修订编号：16/2000］

犬猫狂犬病特别规定

狂犬病疫区

37. （1）部长可随时命令宣布新加坡或者任何地区为狂犬病疫区以达到预防狂犬病的目的。

（2）除非有授权官员签发的通行许可证，否则任何人不能将犬移进或移出疫区。

［修订编号：16/2000］

（3）疫区内犬的主人或监护人须对犬采取有效的控制措施：

（a）将其限制在界定区域，防止逃逸；

（b）安全地绑好；

（c）用链条、绳索、皮革系牢犬。

（4）对于犬或犬科动物，无论是否采取了预防性治疗措施，只要授权官员认为该犬对狂犬病有足够的免疫力，可豁免该犬在遵从其强加指令的前提下免于遵从本条（3）款的规定。

［修订编号：16/2000］

（5）对于在疫区内不按照本条（3）款规定加以控制的任何犬只，授权官员可以书面指令任何人将其销毁。

［修订编号：16/2000］

（6）基于本条（5）款规定，获得授权的人员：

（a）可进入任何地方、建筑物或场所以执行本条（2）款规定；

（b）不能进入任何住宅执行本条（2）款规定，除非在特定期限内；

（c）在任何地方、建筑物或场所执行公务时，如有要求，向物主、占有者或相关人员出示书面授权书。

［修订编号：16/2000］

（7）任何人不遵从本条（2）款规定，将被定罪并处以不超过＄10,000的罚款或不超过12个月的监禁或两罚并施。

［修订编号：10/2002］

（8）任何人没有合理藉口而不遵从依据本条（3）款规定所签发的书面指令，将被定罪并处以不超过＄10,000的罚款或不超过12个月的监禁或两罪并施。

［修订编号：38；10/2002］

狂犬病可疑染疫动物的销毁或拘留

38. （1）当授权官员有理由怀疑某动物患有狂犬病或曾接触狂犬病病例时，可酌情决定：

（a）立即扑杀动物；或者

（b）书面指令其主人或监护人将动物立即送至动物检疫站接受隔离和检查。

［修订编号：16/2000］

（2）如果动物的拥有者或监护人没有遵从本条（1）款规定，授权官员可立即扑杀动物或将其带至检疫站。

［修订编号：16/2000］

（3）授权官员可将检疫站内的动物扑杀，或扣留至确认无疫时。

［修订编号：16/2000］

（4）授权官员可占有死亡或被扑杀的狂犬病疑似动物的幼仔，并按其认为恰当的方法进行处理。

［修订编号：16/2000］

（5）依据本条（1）（2）或（3）款规定销毁动物时，不予以补偿。

（6）任何人没有法律许可的藉口而不遵从依据本条（1）款规定签发的书面指令，将被定罪并处以不超过＄10,000的罚款或不超过12个月的监禁或两罚并施。

［修订编号：10/2002］

（7）在本条中，“动物”定义为扣留或控制下的四足兽。

［修订编号：39］

伤人犬只的扣留

39. （1）授权官员或警察可命令被证实咬人的犬主人或监护人将犬在指定时间送至指定地点。

［修订编号：16/2000］

（2）如果犬主人或监护人没有遵从本条（1）款规定，授权官员可立即扣留该犬并送至检疫站。

［修订编号：16/2000］

（3）任何人没有法律许可的藉口而不遵从依据本条（1）款规定签发的书面指令，将被定罪并处以不超过＄2,000的罚款。

［修订编号：40；10/2002］

犬只狂犬病疫苗免疫接种

40. （1）部长可要求新加坡或指定地区的所有犬只接种抗狂犬病疫苗。

（2）根据本条（1）款的命令，授权官员可要求将犬或整群犬送至指定地点在指定时间段内接种抗狂犬病疫苗。

［修订编号：16/2000］

（3）所有的犬疫苗接种安排将以授权官员决定的方式进行公布。

［修订编号：16/2000］

（4）部长刊登公报告示，要求每只根据命令进行过接种的犬，按通知指示日期之后，在命令施行期限内和指定区域内，给犬系上的徽章、标志、标签或其他免疫接种标记。

（5）在本条（4）款规定的通知时间之后，在指定区域内的任何犬只，无论是否是流浪犬，如果没有系带免疫接种标志的，都将被扑杀。

（6）授权官员可书面授权任何人扑杀本条（5）款中提及的犬只。

［修订编号：16/2000］

（7）任何获得授权的人可进入任何土地、建筑物或场所以执行本条（6）款的规定。

（8）获得授权的工作人员不能在白天工作时间以外的时间段内进入民宅执行公务。在其检查任何土地、建筑物或场所时，如有要求，须向物主、占有者或相关人员出示书面授权书。

（9）任何人没有遵从依据本条（1）或（4）款规定的指令，授权官员可根据情况立即扑杀该犬。

［修订编号：16/2000］

（10）任何犬主人或监护人没有法律许可的藉口而不遵从依据本条（1）款规定签发的书面指令，将被定罪并处以不超过＄10,000的罚款或不超过12个月的监禁或两罚并施。

［修订编号：10/2002］

（11）任何人没有法律许可的藉口而不遵从依据本条（4）款规定的要求，将被定罪并处以不超过＄10,000的罚款或不超过12个月的监禁或两罚并施。

［修订编号：10/2002］

（12）对依据本节规定扑杀的犬只，将不予以任何补偿。

［修订编号：4；10/2002］

第四部分 保 护 动 物

本部分释义

41. 除非文中另有规定，在本部分中："动物"包括任何畜牲、鸟、鱼、爬虫动物或昆虫，无论是野生的或是驯服的。

［修订编号：42］

残害动物

42. （1）任何人：

（a）残忍地打、踢、虐待、蹂躏、过度驱使、超负荷、折磨、激怒或者恐吓任何动物；

（b）任何动物主人，允许动物被如此对待；

（c）在对动物加以禁锢或异地转运的过程中，没有给动物提供充足的食物和饮水；

（d）放纵地或不合理地或疏忽地行为致使动物遭受不必要的痛苦，或者作为动物主人而允许动物遭受不必要的痛苦；

（e）身为拥有者，允许动物被限制、转运、空运或者运载时，采用的方法或动物所处位置使动物遭受不必要的痛苦；

（f）身为任何动物的拥有者，无合理解释地永久或暂时抛弃动物至可能引起动物遭受不必要痛苦的环境，或允许如此对待动物；

（g）身为任何动物的拥有者，使动物被雇佣于进行能致病、减弱劳动力、使其遭受痛苦或伤害、或者使其他不适合雇用动物的地方；

（h）推行或协助进行动物争斗，或保留、使用、管理或促成或协助管理用于或部分功能用于动物争斗的经营场所，或允许任何场所或地方被如此保留、管理或使用，或使得任何人负费进入这些场所的，将被定罪并处以不超过的＄10,000罚款或不超过12个月的监禁或两罚并施；除此之外，如果动物主人按本条（2）款被宣告有罪的，将处以不超过＄10,000罚款。

［修订编号：10/2002］

（2）补充本条（1）款规定，如果拥有者不能合理的照顾和监护动物的，将被认为是残忍对待动物。

（3）本节规定将不适用于屠宰或准备屠宰动物作为食物的行为，除非在这些行动过程中使动物遭受了不必要的痛苦。

［修订编号：43］

授权官员和警察的权力

43. （1）任何授权官员或任何警官可以，无须授权：

（a）拘捕任何违反第42条规定的人以及在场人员；

（b）对其认为违反第42条规定的或被指控的任何场所进行搜查；

（c）扣留被指控违反规定的相关动物、运输工具和物品。

［修订编号：10/2002］

（2）授权官员或警官依照本条（1）（b）款规定可以在获得授权的情况下，在必要的协助下，移除所有阻碍其进入场所的物品或破坏门、窗、锁、扣件、支持物、隔间、箱子、容器或者其他任何物品。

［修订编号：10/2002］

（3）依照本条（1）款规定逮捕的任何人和扣留的任何运输工具和物品须立即送至警察局。

［修订编号：10/2002］

（4）任何依照本条（1）款规定被扣留的动物须被送至警察站、拘留所、兽医中心或任何其他授权官员或警官认为适合的地方，并服从滞留地点地方官员的任何命令直至当事人被法庭审判。

［修订编号：10/2002］

（5）对按照本条（2）款规定破坏或意外损害的财产，不予以补偿；

［修订编号：10/2002］

（6）任何授权官员或任何警官对于认为或被控告违反第42条规定的动物，可在任何街道或公共场所使其停止和进行检查。

［修订编号：44；10/2002］

对违法行为的治安处罚

44. （1）当任何人在被宣告违反第42条规定时，法院可命令：

（a）与犯罪事实相关的动物带至兽医中心或其他法院指定的地方，并且拘留和处理至指定期限，或者直至获得地方官员的释放命令或授权官员书面证实可以释放为止；

（b）授权官员或依据第53款规定授权的人员在处理动物的时期内，该动物不能使用直至地方官员或授权官员作出可以使用的命令为止；

（c）如果认为动物患有不可治愈的疾病或伤害时，动物将被即刻扑杀或遵照警官或授权官员的指令处理，尸体的埋葬或其他处置的费用将由违规者承担。

（2）当法院依据本条（1）（a）款规定执行命令时，犯罪人须承担动物维护和处理的费用直到宣告释放动物为止。

［修订编号：16/2000；10/2002］

（3）遵从本条（1）款规定的同时，法院可以对任何违反第 42 条规定的动物拥有者附加法院认为适合的其他惩罚，剥夺其动物所有权，并作出命令按法院认为合适的方式处理动物。

（4）除非动物主人以前的罪行或其性格或其他方面使法院认为，如果任动物保留在其主人身边，将可能使动物被残忍地对待，否则法院无须执行本条（3）款的规定。

（5）任何人没有遵从依据本条（1）款规定的指令，将被定罪并处以不超过 $5,000 的罚款或不超过 6 个月的监禁或两罚并施。

［修订编号：45；10/2002］

销毁动物的权力

45.（1）授权官员或警官通过亲自检查或其他方法认为：

（a）动物所患疾病或所受伤害无法治愈，任其存活将过于残忍；或者

（b）动物病情或伤情极为严重，或者在当时的物质条件下他认为不可能通过非残忍手段移动动物，任其存活将过于残忍，

可书面指令要求将动物销毁并立即执行，并在授权官员或警官或其他获得授权人员的监督下执行。

［修订编号：21/93；16/2000；10/2002］

（2）如果严重患病或受伤的动物在任何房子、马房、棚子或围栏内，而不是在公共街道或集市，在动物主人（如果知道）或监护人（任何人）被适时通知到之前，不作出书面指令。

［修订编号：21/73］

（3）对于依据本条（1）款规定书面指令销毁的动物，其移动和埋葬动物尸体的费用由其主人或监护人承担，如果之前垫付的，将由地方官员向其主人或监护人一并收取。

［修订编号：46］

应物主要求销毁无望治愈的患病或伤残动物，不予补偿

46. 在以下情形下销毁的动物，不予以补偿：

（a）遵照第 44 条（1）（c）款规定所发指令执行的；

（b）遵照第 45 条（1）款规定所作的书面指令执行的；

（c）遵从授权官员或兽医中心主管或第 44 条（1）款规定的地方的主管给动物拥有者作出的书面要求执行的。

［修订编号：47］

对举报者的奖赏

47. 法院在依据本部分法律规定对任何人宣判有罪前，可悬赏依据本法令征得的所有罚金或其中的一部分给举报者。

［修订编号：48］

未经许可，不能将圈养动物和禽鸟用于销售、出口或展览

48.（1）除非获得依据本法令签发的许可证书，否则任何人不能将动物和禽鸟用于售卖、出口或展览。

（2）任何人不遵从依据本条（1）款规定，将被定罪并处以不超过 $5,000 的罚款或不超过 6 个月的监禁或两罚并施。

［修订编号：49；10/2002］

第五部分 家 畜 管 理

对移动或屠宰动物与禽鸟的禁令

49.（1）部长可命令：

（a）在指定时期内，除非获得许可证，禁止在新加坡境内转运动物和禽鸟；

（b）在指定时期内，除非获得许可证，禁止屠宰动物和禽鸟。

（2）按本条（1）款签发的许可证时，须服从于命令或许可执照的要求。

（3）任何人违反遵从本条规定，将被定罪并处以不超过 $ 10,000 的罚款或不超过 12 个月的监禁或两罚并施。

[修订编号：50；10/2002]

第六部分 搜查、查封和拘留

对染疫动物或禽鸟的搜查权

50.（1）为了确认动物或禽鸟是否染疫，或者确认或调查本法界定的违规行为：

（a）授权官员或警官可进入并调查任何他怀疑的地方、建筑物或者场所以及其中的动物、禽鸟、土地、建筑物或者场所，其拥有者须协助检查并提供官员要求的信息；

（b）任何授权官员、警官或海关官员可停止、进入和检查运送动物的任何交通工具。

[修订编号：16/2000]

（2）任何执行本条（1）款规定的授权官员、警官或海关官员在获得授权的情况下和必要的协助下，可移除所有阻碍其进入场所的物品或破坏门、窗、锁、扣件、支持物、隔间、箱子、容器或者其他任何物品。

[修订编号：10/2002]

（3）对于执行依照本条（2）款规定所造成的或意外造成的财产损失，不予赔偿。

[修订编号：10/2002]

（4）任何交通运输工具的掌管者违背授权官员、警官或海关官员依据本条（1）（b）款规定所作要求拒绝停驶接受检查的，将被定罪并处以不超过 $ 5,000 的罚款或不超过 6 个月的监禁或两罚并施。

[修订编号：5；10/2002]

动物、禽鸟、动物尸体或物品的查封

51.（1）基于本法，授权官员或警官确认既定或现认的违法行为时，或者海关官员在进出口业务中确认既定或现认的违法行为时，他们可以：

（a）扣留任何动物、禽鸟、尸体或者物品、犯罪主体；

（b）将动物、禽鸟、尸体或者物品转移至授权官员指定的围栏或其他地方，并扣留好。

[修订编号：16/2000]

（2）当依照本条（1）款规定查封和扣留动物、禽鸟、尸体或者物品时，授权官员、警官或者海关官员均须报告给地方官员，由地方官员作出继续扣留或释放动物、禽鸟、尸体或者物品等他认为恰当的决定。

[修订编号：16/2000]

（3）被扣留的动物、禽鸟、尸体或者物品的主人须承担其转移去拘留地的费用，并由地方官员收取，如果没有交纳指定的费用，被扣留的动物、禽鸟、尸体或者物品将被没收。

[修订编号：52]

拘留权

52.（1）基于本法，对被发现正在或试图实施或可疑实施违法的人员，授权官员、警官或者海关官员在无授权许可的情况下，可依据以下情况实施拘留：

（a）此人拒绝提供其的姓名和住址；

（b）此人提供新加坡以外的一个住址；

（c）有合理理由确认此人提供错误的姓名和住址；或

（d）此人可能潜逃。

[修订编号：16/2000]

（2）任何授权官员、警官或者海关官员无授权而逮捕某人时，须遵从本条（3）款的规定，在提交地方法院之前，对此人的拘捕不要有不必要的耽搁。

［修订编号：16/2000］

（3）任何被授权官员、警官或者海关官员拘捕的人员，如没有获得保释或地方官员或局长的书面特别命令，不能释放。

［修订编号：53；16/2000］

第七部分　动物与禽鸟相关兽医中心、兽医生物制品和保留、繁殖等许可规定

动物或禽鸟治疗及免疫接种的许可规定

53.（1）除了授权官员外，其他人员不能对动物或禽鸟实施治疗或免疫接种，除非获得局长签发的许可。

［修订编号：10/2002］

（2）任何人违反本条（1）款规定，将被定罪并处以不超过＄10,000 的罚款或不超过 12 个月的监禁或两罚并施。

［修订编号：68］

兽医中心的许可

54.（1）须获得局长签发的许可证，才能使用或者允许任何场所作为兽医中心。

［修订编号：10/2002］

（2）任何人违反本条（1）款规定，将被定罪并处以不超过＄10,000 的罚款或不超过 12 个月的监禁或两罚并施。

［修订编号：65；10/2002］

持有或使用兽医生物制品的许可

55.（1）除了授权官员之外，没有人能：

（a）私自持有任何兽医生物制剂；

（b）给任何动物或禽鸟使用任何兽医生物制品，

除非获得局长签发的许可证允许如此。

［修订编号：10/2002］

（2）任何人违反本条（1）款规定，将被定罪并处以不超过＄10,000 的罚款或不超过 12 个月的监禁或两罚并施。

［修订编号：69；10/2002］

动物或禽鸟商标或身份标志

56.（1）局长或授权官员可指令动物或禽鸟主人或监护人给动物系带永久的或临时的商标、标签或其他标志，以备身份鉴定。

［修订编号：10/2002］

（2）本条（1）款提及的动物或禽鸟的商标、标签或其他标志须由局长依照本条（3）款规定委派的人员发放，其费用由动物或禽鸟的主人或监护人承担。

［修订编号：10/2002］

（3）局长可委派任何人发放本款规定的动物或禽鸟的商标、标签或其他标志。

［修订编号：10/2002］

（4）任何人：

（a）不遵从依据本条（1）款规定发出的指令；或

（b）伪造、摹仿、改造、伤毁外表或者除去本节规定使用的动物或禽鸟的任何商标、标签或其他标志；

将被定罪并处以不超过 $10,000 的罚款或不超过 12 个月的监禁或两罚并施。

［修订编号：62；10/2002］

第八部分　检　　疫

检疫站

57.（1）基于本法，局长可根据需要建立或者指定他认为必需数量的检疫站点。

［修订编号：10/2002］

（2）根据本条（1）款要求，局长可指定任何符合资格的人员来筹建检疫站，或是管理任何由他依据本条（1）款规定指定或建立的检疫站。

［修订编号：63；10/2002］

禁止使用未经授权的场所作为检疫站

58.（1）除非由局长依据第 57 条规定指定的场所，任何人不能擅自允许任何场所用作检疫站。

［修订编号：10/2002］

（2）任何人不遵从本条（1）款规定的，将被定罪并处以不超过 $10,000 的罚款或不超过 12 个月的监禁或两罚并施。

［修订编号：64；10/2002］

保留、繁育或饲养动物和禽鸟的管制

59.（1）部长可制定规则以达到以下目的：

（a）完全禁止，或在符合相关规定地在任何私人或公共场所保管、繁育或饲养任何动物或禽鸟或规定种类的动物；

（b）对在任何私人或公共场所保管、繁育或饲养任何动物或禽鸟或规定种类的动物加以管制；并且

（c）依法没收在公共场所的流浪猫狗。

［修订编号：10/2002］

（2）遵从本条（1）款规定的同时，还须遵守以下规则：

（a）准备在任何私人或公共场所保管、繁育或饲养任何动物或禽鸟或规定种类的动物的任何人须获得局长签发的许可证，并执行许可执照的相关规定；

（b）可签发以下方面的许可：

（i）保持或繁育动物或禽鸟的许可；

（ii）许可某地方用于保持或繁育动物或禽鸟；

（c）授权局长或者授权官员可以清除或扑杀或转移违反本节规定的任何动物或禽鸟。

［修订编号：10/2002］

（3）依据本条（2）（c）款规定扑杀的动物或禽鸟，不予以补偿。

［修订编号：10/2002］

（4）第 80 条（3）款规定须在服从本款规定范围内应用。

［修订编号：10/2002］

第九部分　违法与处罚

妨碍官员行使职权

60. 在没有法定原因下，任何人妨碍、阻止、协助妨碍或者阻止授权官员、海关官员或警官实施本法及其规章或条例赋予职责行驶的，将被定罪并处以不超过 $10,000 的罚款或不超过 12 个月的监禁或两罚并施。

［修订编号：54；16/2000；10/2002］

变更许可

61. 任何人，如果没有法律授权，不能转让或有意转让使用任何依据本法令签发的许可证书或通行许可，否则将被定罪并处以不超过 $10,000 的罚款或不超过 12 个月的监禁或两罚并施。

［修订编号：55；10/2002］

许可证和通行证的中止或废止

62. （1）局长可中止或废止许可证或通行证，如果他确认：

（a）许可执照或通行许可证的申领过程存在有欺诈或误导；

（b）获得许可执照或通行许可证的人违背了：

（i）本法令的任何规定；

（ii）许可执照或通行证的相关要求；

（iii）局长或授权官员藉着本法令作出的任何指令；

（c）基于照顾公共利益中止或废止许可证或通行证。

［修订编号：10/2002］

（2）局长依据本条（1）款规定中止或废止许可证或通行许可证时：

（a）给许可执照或通行许可证的持有者书面通知；

（b）通知书上应该明确施行时间，并对许可证或通行许可证的中止或废止作出解释。

［修订编号：10/2002］

（3）如果许可证或通行许可证的持有者：

（a）不能在规定的或局长允许延长的时间内按要求行事；

（b）无合理解释，

局长可书面通知持有者告知许可执照或通行许可证中止或废止决定的生效日期。

［修订编号：10/2002］

（4）任何人对中止或废止许可执照或通行许可证的决定不满，可在接到中止或废止通知后的 7 天内书面向部长申诉并由部长作出最终决定。

［修订编号：10/2002］

（5）在依照本条（4）款规定递交的申诉后未获决定之前，依照本条（3）款规定作出的许可执照或通行许可证的中止或废止决定的生效日期仍为照局长指定的日期，除非部长另作命令。

［修订编号：69A；10/2002］

未明确惩罚尺度的违法处罚

63. 任何人违背本法令或任何规则或基于此作出的命令，如没有明确惩罚尺度的，将被宣告有罪并处以不超过 $5,000 的罚款或不超过 6 个月的监禁或两罚并施。

［修订编号：56；10/2002］

没收

64. （1）法院在依据本法令审判任何人有罪之前，可命令没收依据本法令相关规定已作封存的所有物品，如果：

（a）法院认为：

（i）违法行为已被定罪；并且

（ii）封存物品为违法主体物质，或被用于犯罪；

（b）考虑到具体的情形，法院认为应当没收此物。

［修订编号：10/2002］

（2）如果没有社会团体对本条（1）款的没收决定提出疑问，法院将自行处置。

［修订编号：10/2002］

（3）法院可依据本法令规定命令没收本条（1）款被封存的任何物品，即使没有人被定罪。

［修订编号：10/2002］

（4）如果法院，考虑到具体的情形，认为不应该命令没收依据本法令规定封存的任何物品，法院须将其归还给主人或代收人。

［修订编号：10/2002］

（5）在没有任何关于依据本法令规定封存物品的起诉时，局长须书面通知被封存物品者或物品主人，告知物品在其通知指定时间后7天内物品将被没收，除非在执行本条（6）款规定前被认领。

［修订编号：10/2002］

（6）如果有人声称：

（a）他是依据本法令规定封存物品的拥有者或受益人；

（b）物品不能被没收，可亲自地或藉着其代理人以书面方式向局长认领。

［修订编号：10/2002］

（7）在收到本条（6）款的通知后，局长可指令将物品归还给通知人或法院决定的个人。

［修订编号：10/2002］

（8）在如本条（5）款通知指定时间后7天内没有任何人认领，这些物品将被没收。

［修订编号：10/2002］

（9）任何依据本法令规定处置的封存物品项目，这些物品将被认为没收。

［修订编号：10/2002］

（10）任何依照本款规定被没收或被认为没收的物品须被送至授权官员，并按局长认为适当的方式处理。

［修订编号：10/2002］

（11）本条中，“物品”是指任何动物、禽鸟、尸体或任何其他物品。

［修订编号：57；10/2002］

推定

65.（1）当染疫动物或禽鸟的拥有者或监护人被指控违反本法时，将事先假定他知晓动物或禽鸟所患疫病，除非他能使法院确信其无相关知识或无能力获取相关知识。

（2）在怀疑任何患病动物或禽鸟的所有权时，被发现动物或者禽鸟携带者或动物或者禽鸟经常出没场所的所有者将被认为是其主人，直到证明事实并非如此。

［修订编号：58］

企业、代理和雇员犯罪的规定

66.（1）如果社团、企业或个体户被指控违反本法规定，在犯罪实施期间在这些机构中任职的主管、经理、股东、秘书或其他类似职务人员或声称对该行为负责的人员，将被定罪，除非他证实：

（a）被指控的违法行为没有获得他的同意或默许；并且

（b）在其职责范围内以及所有的情况下，他已经竭力去预防该违法行为。

［修订编号：10/2002］

（2）当违反本法规定的人员，为他人代理或雇员或者在罪行实施进程中服从于他人监督或指示的，雇佣者、监督人或指示人应当与违法实施者一并负担法律责任，无论其是否具体实施、同意、默许或是处于本人职责疏忽。

［修订编号：69D；10/2002］

法院的司法权

67.（1）即使有悖刑法（第68章）规定的情况，行政区法院和地方法院有权审理违反本法的罪行，并依据本法处以惩戒或处罚。

［修订编号：10/2002］

（2）即使有悖刑法第133条（1）和（2）款的规定，地方法院可根据收到的局长或授权官员签字确认的书面投诉，裁定违反本法的相关犯罪。

［修订编号：69；10/2002］

证据

68. （1）服从于本条（3）款的规定：

（a）局长或授权官员递交的基于本法的调查性或管理性文件或证明材料，均可接受为基于本法的诉讼证据，其中所述可作为初步证据；并且

（b）授权检查员依据对动物或禽鸟或任何其他物质的检测结果出具的证书，并声明其检测结果可作为基于本法诉讼的证据，其中所述并确保正确，可作为初步证据。

［修订编号：10/2002］

（2）依据本条规定，起诉过程中出示的本条（1）款提及的证书等公文将作为初步证据，除非事实证明并非如此。

［修订编号：10/2002］

（3）本条（1）款提及的证书有可能不能被采纳为证据，除非被起诉人得到：

（a）证书的副本；

（b）在控诉开始至少10个完整工作日之前，获知将此证书用于诉讼证据。

［修订编号：10/2002］

（4）本条（1）款中出示被接受为证据的证明材料的局长、授权官员或授权检查员，被起诉人可要求他们作为原告证人，并交叉检查其所陈述的证据事实。

［修订编号：69；10/2002］

违法的和解

69. （1）局长或授权官员在代表当局行使权力时，当发现罚金不超过$1,000的可赦免违反本法的行为时，可根据自己判断，通过向嫌疑人收取罚金来赦免该违法行为。

［修订编号：10/2002］

（2）在交付这些款项后，将不再追究违法人的责任。

［修订编号：69K；10/2002］

第十部分 其 他 规 定

官方税费等

70. 所有依据本法收取的酬金、收费、各种罚款和财产都必须交付给当局。

［修订编号：59A；10/2002］

费用

71. 所有由授权官员或其他官员，在行使本法及相关条例、规则或指令赋予的职权时，所导致的费用由物主、发货人、收货人或进口商承担，例如处置动物、禽鸟、动物尸体、物品、建筑物或运输工具相关的费用或民事债务。

［修订编号：60；16/2000］

行动风险和物主花费

72. （1）任何基于本法令以及相关条例、规则或指令做出的行动，引起关于动物、禽鸟、动物尸体、物品、建筑物或运输工具可能导致的风险，将由其物主承担。

（2）当局或其官员在合法行使本法令权力时，不对其行动引起的相关花费、损失、损坏或延误承担任何责任。

［修订编号：6；16/2000］

局长和授权官员对不配合执法行为的权力

73. （1）对不配合执行本法及相关规定、指令或命令的人员，该行为可被起诉，局长或授权官员可根据相关规定、指令或命令的要求采取任何行动或措施，导致的费用将由不配合者承担。

［修订编号：10/2002］

（2）按本条（1）款行使权力时，局长或授权官员可无须授权地进入任何的场所、车辆、船舶或者飞机，对于需要授权进入的场所，可依据必要的授权进入。

［修订编号：69B；10/2002］

要求出示文件等的权力

74. （1）为了履行本法令赋予的职责，局长或授权官员可随时要求任何人：

（a）当局长或授权官员有理由相信在任何帐簿、运输单证、提单或其他公文或记录中包含有与本法管控相关信息时，向局长或授权官员提供该文件的原件、副本或摘录，

（b）向局长或授权官员提供其所要求的合理信息。

［修订编号：10/2002］

（2）局长或授权官员可记录由任何人依据本条（1）（b）款规定提供的任何信息，并可作为指控违反本法令行为的证据。

［修订编号：10/2002］

（3）任何人没有遵从局长或授权官员依据本条（1）（a）或（b）款规定提出的要求，将被定罪并处以不超过＄5,000的罚金或被不超过6个月的监禁或两罚并施。

［修订编号：69C；10/2002］

通知、命令和其他公文的发布形式和证明

75. （1）局长依据本法令授权发布的所有无论什么性质的通知、命令和其他公文，可采用局长或授权官员可能决定的发布方式。

［修订编号：10/2002］

（2）任何发布的通知、命令和其他公文需要有以下证明：

（a）局长或授权官员的签字；或

（b）含有如上签署的官方传真，以及另外能提供足够证明的附件。

［修订编号：69E；10/2002］

公文中错误的处理

76. （1）在依据本法令作出的、签发的或发布的任何通知、命令和其他公文中发生关于任何人、动物、禽鸟、场所、建筑物、街道、地方、车辆、飞机、船舶、或其他交通工具的用词不当或错误的描述时，如果通知、命令和其他公文中指定的人、动物、禽鸟、场所、建筑物、街道、地方、车辆、飞机、船舶、或其他交通工具是可以确认的话，将不能影响本法令关于相关人、动物、禽鸟、场所、建筑物、街道、地方、车辆、飞机、船舶、或其他交通工具的措施的施行。

［修订编号：10/2002］

（2）基于本法令发布的规定不能因为形式上的错误而失效。

［修订编号：69F；10/2002］

公文送达

77. （1）本法令要求或授权的任何通知、命令和其他公文被送至与违反本法令规定相关的任何人和法院签发的任何传唤对象，其递送方式可能是：

（a）递送至常用或最后获知的居住地，交给本人或其家庭或家族的成年成员或雇员；

（b）装在签有该人姓名的信封内留在其常用或最后获知的居住地或商行；

（c）邮寄至该人常用或最后获知的居住地或商行；

（d）就公司、合伙企业或法人团体而言：

（i）递送至其公司、合伙企业或法人团体的注册登记办公地点或主要营业地点，交给其秘书或相似职位人员；

（ii）邮寄至公司、合伙企业或法人团体的注册登记办公地点或主要营业地点。

［修订编号：10/2002］

（2）邮寄至本款（1）提及人员的任何通知、命令、公文或传唤，将被认为已经适时地被送至目的地。到达时间将按通常的邮寄过程和速度来确定，并以登记邮局在信封上签有的适当的地址、邮戳和邮寄时间来证实。

［修订编号：10/2002］

（3）本法令要求或授权的任何通知、命令或公文或者是其真实副本须被递送至与违反本法令相关的任何营业场所的主人或占用者或法院传唤对象，并交给场所中的成年人，如果场所中无有合理的智力接纳文件的的人员，可将通知、命令或公文粘附在场所醒目的位置。

［修订编号：10/2002］

（4）如果没有更多的姓名或说明，何须被递送至与违反本法令相关的任何营业场所的主人或占用者或法院传唤对象的本法令要求或授权的通知、命令或公文，将被认为已经适当地被送至因营业场所主人或占用者记述的地方。

［修订编号：69G；10/2002］

职权保护

78. 在当局、局长或任何一个授权官员、警官、海关官员或任何其他当局或局长指令的人员依据本法令行事时，不应设置其他法律程序或法规来阻止其执行事务。

［修订编号：69H；10/2002］

豁免

79. 遵从由部长作出的常规或特别指令，局长可能豁免任何人、场所、动物或禽鸟或各级别人员免于遵从本法令的任何规定。

［修订编号：69L；10/2002］

实施细则

80.（1）部长可制定实施细则，以执行本法规定及其要求规定的事项。

［修订编号：10/2002］

（2）遵从本条（1）款规定，部长可能制定以下方面的实施细则：

（a）委派授权检查员，授权检查员委派条件，以及中止或撤消这些任命；

（b）执行动物或禽鸟的隔离检疫、检测、处置和证明等；

（c）管理动物、禽鸟或动物尸体的进出口和转口；

（d）防止动物和禽鸟疫病的传入和散布，以及疫病的控制和根除；

（e）对曾保留或运输过染疫动物、禽鸟或其尸体的建筑物、车辆、飞机或船舶的清洗或消毒；

（f）与动物、禽鸟或其尸体接触过人员的消毒，以及相关动物、禽鸟或物品的消毒和处理；

（g）管理和控制动物、禽鸟及其产品的售卖、买卖和配送；

（h）对以售卖、出口、展览、生产或其他用途为目的保留动物或禽鸟的许可、控制、监督与检查；

（i）遵从本法，对运输动物和禽鸟的任何车辆、飞机或船舶实施检查；

（j）动物污染控制，以及相关费用的订立和收取，包括收费的时间、地点和方式；

（k）动物或禽鸟生产的控制和改进，包括相关的繁育、营养、健康、经营、管理和生产方式；

（l）动物和禽鸟及其产品信息和统计数据的提供、收集和整理；

（m）检疫站的建立和指定；

（n）检疫站和兽医中心的管理和维护；

（o）规范本法规定收取的费用；

（p）依据第 69 条规定确定可减缓违法的指定方式和程序。

[修订编号：10/2002]

（3）部长可制定实施细则，规定任何抵触、或没有或者疏于遵从局长依据本法作出的管理规定或指令的行为，将被定罪并处以不超过 $10,000 的罚款或不超过 12 个月的监禁或两罚并施。

[修订编号：10/2002]

（4）任何依据本法令制定的实施细则，如经公告可行之后，须递交议会审议。

[修订编号：70；10/2002]

立法历史

1. 1965 年第 3 项法令——动物与禽鸟法 1965
一读时间：1964 年 11 月 19 日（1964 年 12 月 12 日公布，修订编号为：39/64）
二读和三读时间：1965 年 6 月 16 日
发布时间：1965 年 10 月 22 日（第 71 条除外）
1966 年 5 月 20 日（第 71 条）

2. 1973 年修订法案第 21 项——新加坡共和国修订法案（各类法规修订）1973
一读时间：1973 年 3 月 7 日（1973 年 3 月 9 日公布，修订编号为：16/73）
二读和三读时间：1973 年 3 月 20 日
发布时间：1973 年 4 月 6 日

3. 1996 年修订法案第 7 项——新加坡海运与港口局法 1996
（相应的修订）
一读时间：1995 年 12 月 5 日（1995 年 12 月 6 日公布，修订编号为：46/95）
二读和三读时间：1996 年 1 月 18 日
发布时间：1996 年 2 月 2 日

4. 1997 年修订法案第 7 项——修订法案（各类法规修订）1997
一读时间：1997 年 7 月 11 日（1997 年 7 月 12 日公布，修订编号为：6/97）
二读和三读时间：1997 年 8 月 25 日
发布时间：1997 年 10 月 1 日（第 3 条除外）
1998 年 9 月 1 日（第 3 条）

5. 2000 年法案第 16 项——农粮与兽医局法 2000
（相应的修订）
一读时间：2000 年 2 月 21 日（2000 年 2 月 22 日公布，修订编号为：11/2000）
二读和三读时间：2000 年 3 月 17 日
发布时间：2000 年 4 月 1 日

6. 2002 年修订法案第 10 项——动物与禽鸟（修订）法 2002
一读时间：2002 年 4 月 3 日（2002 年 4 月 4 日公布，修订编号为：2/2002）
二读和三读时间：2002 年 7 月 8 日
发布时间：2002 年 9 月 15 日

对照表

动物与禽鸟 1985 年修订版已经被法律修订委员会于 2002 年修订版重编过。
本对照表仅用于为使用者提供方便，不属于动物与禽鸟法定组成部分。
（略）

Animals and birds ACT
(Chapter 7)

An Act for preventing the introduction into, and the spreading within, Singapore of diseases of animals, birds or fish; for the control of the movement of animals, birds or fish into, within and from Singapore; for the prevention of cruelty to animals, birds or fish; for measures pertaining to the general welfare and improvement of animals, birds or fish in Singapore and for purposes incidental thereto.

[10/2002]

[22nd October 1965]

Part I Preliminary

Short title

1. This Act may be cited as the Animals and Birds Act.

Interpretation

2. In this Act, unless the context otherwise requires—

aircraft includes any kind of craft which may be used for the conveyance of animals or birds by air;

animal means any mammal (other than man) or fish and includes any other living creature that is prescribed as an animal for the purposes of this Act or that falls within a class of animals that is prescribed for those purposes;

animal quarantine station means a quarantine station established under section 57;

authorised examiner means any authorised officer and includes any person who has been designated as an authorised examiner by the Director – General under section 4;

authorised officer means any person appointed by the Director – General to be an authorised officer under section 3 (2);

Authority means the Agri – Food and Veterinary Authority established under section 3 of the Agri – Food and Veterinary Authority Act (Cap. 5);

bird includes domestic fowls, ducks, geese, turkeys, guinea fowls and pigeons of any age or sex and the eggs thereof;

building includes any house, hut, shed, stable or enclosure, whether roofed or not, used for sheltering or confining any animal or bird and any pen, cage, wall, gate, pillar, post, paling, frame, boarding, fence, platform, roadway, path, steps, staging, slip, wharf, dock, piles, jetty, landing stage or bridge, or any structure connected with the foregoing;

bull means a male of any species of cattle;

carcase means the dead body of an animal or bird and includes any part thereof and the meat, bones (whether whole, broken or ground), offal, hide, skin, wool, hair, feathers, hoof, horns or other part of an animal or bird, separately or otherwise, or any portion thereof;

cat means a domesticated cat of any breed or sex;

cattle means bulls, cows, oxen, heifers, and calves and includes buffaloes of any age or sex;

contact means any animal or bird which has by contact direct or indirect with a diseased animal or bird been exposed to the risk of contracting a disease;

Director – General means the Director – General, Agri – Food and Veterinary Services appointed under section 3 (1);

disease means any disease that is infectious or contagious amongst animals or birds and includes any other disease which the Minister may, from time to time, by notification in the Gazette, declare to be a disease for the purposes of this Act;

dog means a domesticated dog of any breed or sex;

examine in relation to any animal or bird or the carcase thereof, means to carry out in respect of such animal, bird or carcase, such manner of inspection, examination and test as may be necessary for the purposes of determining whether the animal, bird or carcase thereof is infected with any disease;

fish includes any of the varieties of marine, brackish water or fresh water fishes, crustacea, aquatic mollusca, turtles, marine sponges, trepang and any other form of aquatic life and the young and eggs thereof;

fodder means any substance used for food of animals or birds;

genetically modified organism means any organism (other than a human being or a plant), whether living or dead, or parts of any such organism, containing genetic material or protein or both which have been derived or modified as a result of manipulation or experimentation of genetic material, or any means other than by natural process;

goods in transit means goods that are brought into Singapore solely for the purpose of taking them out of Singapore and that remain at all times on the vehicle, aircraft or ship that brought them into Singapore;

horse includes any mare, gelding, pony, foal, colt, filly, ass or mule;

import includes the importation into Singapore of goods in transit and goods which are to be transhipped;

infected means infected with any disease;

licence means any licence issued by the Director – General;

litter means any substance used for bedding or otherwise for or about animals or birds;

master means the captain of any ship or aircraft and includes any person for the time being in charge of any ship (other than a pilot) or aircraft;

officer of customs has the same meaning as is assigned to it in the Customs Act (Cap. 70);

owner includes any person for the time being in charge of any animal or bird and any person for the time being in occupation of any building;

permit means a permit issued by the Director – General;

port has the same meaning as is assigned to it in the Maritime and Port Authority of Singapore Act (Cap. 170A);

public place means any place or premises to which at the material time the public or any section of the public has access, on payment or otherwise, as of right or by virtue of express or implied permission;

quarantine means the compulsory detention in isolation of any animal, bird or thing;

quarantine station means any building or place where quarantine is carried out, and includes an examination station or hulk;

ship includes every description of vessel or craft, however propelled, which may be used in the water;

tranship means to remove any goods imported into Singapore from the vehicle, aircraft or ship in which they were imported and either return them to the same vehicle, aircraft or ship or transfer them to another vehicle, aircraft or ship before being exported, whether such goods are to be transferred directly between such vehicles, aircraft or ships or whether they are to be landed in Singapore after their importation and kept at any place pending exportation;

veterinary biologics means any viruses, serums, toxins, and analogous products of natural or synthetic origin, including genetically modified organisms, diagnostics, antitoxins, vaccines, live micro – organisms, killed micro – organisms, and the antigenic or immunizing component of micro – organisms intended for use in the diagnosis, treatment, or prevention of diseases of animals and birds, or for purposes of research in animals or birds;

veterinary centre means any premises used for the purpose of providing any of the following services to members of the public:

(a) the diagnosis of disease in, and injuries to, animals or birds, including tests performed for diagnostic purposes;

(b) the treatment, vaccination or innoculation of animals or birds.

[*16/2000*; *10/2002*]

Appointment of Director – General, etc.

3. (1) The Minister may, by notification in the Gazette, appoint any person to be the Director – General, Agri – Food and Veterinary Services who shall be responsible for the administration of this Act and any other written law.

[*16/2000*]

(2) The Director – General may in writing appoint any public officer or any officer of the Authority or of any other statutory authority to be an authorised officer for the purposes of this Act.

[*16/2000*]

(3) The Director – General may delegate all or any of the powers conferred or duties imposed upon him by this Act to any authorised officer.

[*16/2000*]

Designation of authorised examiners

4. The Director – General may, subject to any general or special directions of the Minister, in writing designate any suitably qualified person as an authorised examiner to carry out, at any appointed place, any examination, treatment or certification and any other similar, related or ancillary functions which are required by this Act to be carried out.

[*3A*

[*10/2002*]

Public servants

5. All authorised officers shall be deemed to be public servants for the purposes of the Penal Code (Cap. 224).

[*4*

[*10/2002*]

Identification card to be produced

6. (1) Every authorised officer, officer of customs or police officer when exercising any powers under this Act shall—

(a) if not in uniform, declare his office; and

(b) on demand, produce to any person affected by the exercise of those powers such identification card as the Director – General, the Director – General of Customs or the Commissioner of Police respectively may direct to be carried by the authorised officers, officers of customs or police officers.

[*16/2000*]

(2) It shall not be an offence for any person to refuse to comply with any request, demand or order made

or given by any authorised officer, officer of customs or police officer not in uniform, who fails to declare his office and refuses to produce his identification card on demand being made by that person.

[5

Part Ⅱ Importation, Transhipment, Exportation of animals and birds and possession of noxious Insects, ETC. Importation

Power to make orders with regard to importation, etc.

7. (1) The Minister may make orders—

(a) specifying the countries or the parts of any country from which animals and birds, or any specified kinds of animals or birds, may be imported or transhipped either with or without restriction; or

(b) prohibiting, either absolutely or conditionally, the import and transhipment from any specified country or any specified part of a country of any carcase, semen, fodder, litter, dung or any product of animals or birds or any article or substance that is likely to convey or spread any disease.

(2) Any person who contravenes the provisions of any order made under subsection (1) shall be guilty of an offence and shall be liable on conviction to a fine not exceeding $10,000 or to imprisonment for a term not exceeding 12 months or to both.

[*6*

[*10/2002*]

No person to import or tranship any animal, bird or veterinary biologics without licence

8. (1) Except as provided in any order made under section 7 (1), no person shall import or tranship any animal, bird or veterinary biologics, except in accordance with a licence issued in that behalf by the Director – General and in accordance with the conditions (if any) of that licence and such other conditions as may be prescribed.

[*16/2000*]

(2) A licence to import or tranship any animal, bird or veterinary biologics under this Act may be obtained on an application made in the prescribed form to the Director – General and upon the payment of such fees as may be prescribed.

[*16/2000*]

(3) Any person importing or transhipping an animal, bird or veterinary biologics in contravention of subsection (1) shall be guilty of an offence and shall be liable on conviction to a fine not exceeding $10,000 or to imprisonment for a term not exceeding 12 months or to both.

[*7*

[*10/2002*]

Importation or possession of noxious insects, pests or genetically modified organisms, etc.

9. (1) No person shall knowingly import into Singapore or shall have in his possession any living noxious insect, or any living pest, or any living disease germ or virus or any bacterial culture, of a nature harmful or dangerous to animals or birds, or any genetically modified organism without the prior written consent of the Director – General.

[*16/2000*; *10/2002*]

(2) Any person who contravenes subsection (1) shall be guilty of an offence and shall be liable on conviction to a fine not exceeding $10,000 or to imprisonment for a term not exceeding 12 months or to both.

[*67*

[*10/2002*]

Examination of imported animals and birds

10. (1) Any person who has imported any animal or bird shall, if so directed by the Director – General or an authorised officer, immediately upon the arrival of the animal or bird in Singapore, at his own expense arrange for the animal or bird to be examined by an authorised examiner.

[*10/2002*]

(2) For the purpose of carrying out the examination of any animal or bird under subsection (1), an authorized examiner may detain the animal or bird at a quarantine station or such other place as may be approved by the Director – General or an authorised officer until the completion of the examination.

[*10/2002*]

(3) If any animal or bird, upon being examined by an authorised examiner under subsection (1), is certified by the authorised examiner to be suffering from—

(a) any disease or injury which, in the opinion of the authorised examiner, cannot be treated or relieved; or

(b) any disease which is likely to spread unless the animal or bird is destroyed,

the person who imported the animal or bird shall, at his own expense, cause that animal or bird to be destroyed at once and the carcase thereof to be disposed of in such manner as may be specified by the Director – General or an authorised officer.

[*10/2002*]

(4) Any person who fails to comply with subsection (1) or (3) shall be guilty of an offence and shall be liable on conviction to a fine not exceeding $5,000 or to imprisonment for a term not exceeding 6 months or to both.

[*8*

[*10/2002*]

Arrival of animal or bird to be reported

11. (1) The master of any ship or aircraft and the guard of any train on which there is any animal or bird, whether that animal or bird is intended to be landed in Singapore or not, shall immediately on the first arrival of the ship, aircraft or train at a port, airfield or station in Singapore report the fact to a port officer or the officer in charge of the airfield or the station master, as the case may be, who shall without delay inform the authorized officer.

[*16/2000*]

(2) An authorised officer may—

(a) board any ship, aircraft or train for the purpose of examining any animal or bird therein; or

(b) direct the master of the ship or aircraft or the guard of the train to arrange, at his own expense, for the animal or bird to be examined by an authorised examiner.

[*10/2002*]

(3) Notwithstanding the fact that—

(a) a licence has been issued for the importation or transhipment of an animal or bird under section 8; or

(b) any animal or bird comes from a country or part of a country which has been specified in an order made under section 7 (1) (a),

the port officer or officer in charge of an airfield or station master shall not permit that animal or bird to be landed from the ship or removed from the aircraft or the train, as the case may be, until he has personally satisfied himself that the authorised officer has granted a permit for the landing or removal of that animal or bird from the ship, aircraft or train.

[*16/2000*]

(4) Any person who—

(a) fails to make a report as is required under subsection (1);

(b) fails to comply with any direction given to him by an authorised officer under subsection (2); or

(c) permits an animal or bird to be landed or removed from any ship, aircraft or train in contravention of subsection (3),

shall be guilty of an offence and shall be liable on conviction to a fine not exceeding $5,000 or to imprisonment for a term not exceeding 6 months or to both.

[*9*

[*10/2002*]

Power to deal with diseased animals and birds being imported into Singapore

12. (1) Where the Director – General or an authorised officer has reasonable grounds for suspecting that there is on board any vehicle, aircraft or ship that has entered or that is about to enter Singapore any animal or bird that is infected with any disease, the Director – General or authorised officer may direct the person who is or who appears to be in command or charge of the vehicle, aircraft or ship to take all or any of the following measures at his own expense:

(a) ensure that any animal or bird on board the vehicle, aircraft or ship is not (as the case requires) removed from the vehicle, aircraft or ship or brought into Singapore;

(b) arrange for any animal or bird on board the vehicle, aircraft or ship to be examined by an authorized examiner;

(c) cause any animal or bird on board the vehicle, aircraft or ship which is infected or reasonably suspected to be infected with any disease and any other animal or bird on board the vehicle, aircraft or ship which has or may have come into contact with such animal or bird to be—

(i) destroyed and disposed of in such manner as the Director – General or authorised officer may specify;

(ii) removed from Singapore;

(iii) treated in such manner as may be specified in the direction or by the authorised examiner who examined the animal or bird; or

(iv) quarantined in such manner, at such place and for such period as the Director – General or authorised officer may specify;

(d) ensure that the vehicle, aircraft or ship does not enter Singapore or remove the vehicle, aircraft or ship from Singapore (as the case requires), if the Director – General is satisfied that such measure is necessary for the prevention of the introduction or spread of any disease in Singapore.

[*10/2002*]

(2) No compensation shall be payable in respect of any animal or bird which is required to be destroyed under subsection (1) (c) (i).

[*10/2002*]

(3) Any person who fails to comply with any direction given to him by the Director – General or an authorized officer under subsection (1) shall be guilty of an offence and shall be liable on conviction to a fine not exceeding $10,000 or to imprisonment for a term not exceeding 12 months or to both.

[*10*

[*10/2002*]

Animals and birds on board ship

13. (1) Any animal or bird imported or transhipped by sea shall, unless an authorised officer has authorized its landing, at all times while on board the ship in any port be confined in an enclosed part of the ship or in a cage or kennel.

[*16/2000*; *10/2002*]

(2) If any animal or bird dies or is lost from a ship while in the port, the master of the ship shall immediately notify the authorised officer of the death or loss.

[*16/2000*; *10/2002*]

(3) The master of any ship, in any case—

(a) in which any animal or bird imported or transhipped by sea in that ship has, in contravention of subsection (1), not been confined while on board the ship in the port; or

(b) where he fails without reasonable cause to notify the death or loss of any animal or bird while the ship is in the port,

shall be guilty of an offence and shall be liable on conviction to a fine not exceeding $5,000 or to imprisonment for a term not exceeding 6 months or to both.

[*11*

[*10/2002*]

Permission to land carcases

14. (1) No person shall land from any ship or remove from any aircraft, train or vehicle the carcase of any animal or bird without the written permission of an authorised officer who may give directions in writing as to the manner of its disposal.

[*16/2000*]

(2) Any person—

(a) landing or removing the carcase of an animal or bird in contravention of subsection (1); or

(b) who fails to comply with the directions in writing of an authorised officer given under subsection (1),

shall be guilty of an offence and shall be liable on conviction to a fine not exceeding $10,000 or to imprisonment for a term not exceeding 12 months or to both.

[*13*

[*16/2000*; *10/2002*]

Destruction or disinfection of certain articles

15. (1) Where an authorised officer is of the opinion that any bedding, litter, fodder or other material imported by land, sea or air may convey or spread any animal disease, he may—

(a) seize and detain; and

(b) in his discretion order the destruction or disinfection of,

that bedding, litter, fodder or other material.

[*16/2000*]

(2) No compensation shall be payable in respect of any bedding, litter, fodder or other material that is destroyed under subsection (1).

[*14*

[*10/2002*]

Exportation

No person to export any animal or bird without licence

16. (1) No person shall export any animal or bird or the carcase of any animal or bird except in accordance with—

(a) a licence in that behalf issued by the Director-General;

(b) the conditions of that licence (if any); and

(c) such other conditions as may be prescribed.

[*16/2000*]

(2) A licence to export any animal or bird or the carcase of any animal or bird may be issued upon an application made in the prescribed form to the Director – General and upon the payment of such fees as may be prescribed.

[*16/2000*]

(3) Any person exporting any animal or bird or the carcase of any animal or bird in contravention of subsection (1) shall be guilty of an offence and shall be liable on conviction to a fine not exceeding $10,000 or to imprisonment for a term not exceeding 12 months or to both.

[*15*

[*10/2002*]

Examination and treatment of animals and birds before exportation

17. (1) Any person who intends to export any animal or bird from Singapore shall, if so directed by the Director – General or an authorised officer, arrange, at his own expense, for the animal or bird to be examined and, if necessary, treated by an authorised examiner before exporting the animal or bird.

[*10/2002*]

(2) For the purpose of carrying out the examination or treatment of any animal or bird under subsection (1), an authorised examiner may detain the animal or bird at a quarantine station or such other place as may be approved by the Director – General or an authorised officer until the completion of the examination or treatment.

[*10/2002*]

(3) If any animal or bird, upon being examined by an authorised examiner under subsection (1), is certified by the authorised examiner to be infected with any disease—

(a) the person intending to export the animal or bird shall not export the animal or bird without the prior approval of the Director – General or an authorised officer; and

(b) the Director – General or an authorised officer may direct the person intending to export the animal or bird to treat or destroy the animal or bird at his own expense in such manner as may be specified by the Director – General or authorised officer.

[*10/2002*]

(4) Any person who fails to comply with subsection (1) or (3) (a) or with any direction given to him by the Director – General or an authorised officer under subsection (3) (b) shall be guilty of an offence and shall be liable on conviction to a fine not exceeding $10,000 or to imprisonment for a term not exceeding 12 months or to both.

[*10/2002*]

Certificate of freedom from disease

18. (1) Any person intending to export any animal or bird or the carcase thereof or any product derived from such animal, bird or carcase may apply to an authorised examiner—

(a) for a certificate certifying that Singapore is free from such disease as may be specified in the certificate; or

(b) for the animal, bird, carcase or product, as the case may be, to be examined and thereafter certified as to whether it is free from any disease or other condition.

[*10/2002*]

(2) An application under subsection (1) shall be accompanied by the prescribed fee.

[*66*

[*10/2002*]

Part Ⅲ Prevention of spread of disease

General

Examination of animal or bird suspected of disease

19. (1) If the Director – General or an authorised officer has reason to believe that any animal or bird may be infected with any disease, he may subject that animal or bird and any article or substance which has been in contact therewith to an examination.

[*10/2002*]

(2) For the purpose of this section—

(a) the Director – General or authorised officer may—

(i) seize the animal or bird as well as the whole or any sample of any article or substance which has been in contact therewith and take them to the place of examination; or

(ii) in writing direct the owner or person in charge of the animal or bird to deliver the animal or bird as well as the whole or any sample of any article or substance which has been in contact therewith to an authorised examiner at a specified place and time; and

(b) the authorised examiner carrying out the examination may take any substance from the animal or bird or destroy the animal or bird and conduct a post – mortem examination on its carcase, if that is the appropriate method by which he may, in accordance with accepted veterinary practice, determine whether the animal or bird has been infected with any particular disease.

[*10/2002*]

(3) No compensation shall be payable in respect of any animal or bird which has been destroyed under subsection (2) (b).

[*10/2002*]

(4) Any person who—

(a) fails without lawful excuse to comply with any written direction given to him under subsection (2) (a) (ii); or

(b) without the permission of the Director – General or an authorised officer removes any animal or bird from the place to which it has been delivered under subsection (2) (a) (ii),

shall be guilty of an offence and shall be liable on conviction to a fine not exceeding $5,000 or to imprisonment for a term not exceeding 6 months or to both.

[*10/2002*]

Isolation or destruction of diseased animal or bird

20. (1) The Director – General or an authorised officer may require the immediate isolation or destruction of any animal or bird if—

(a) the animal or bird is certified by an authorised examiner, upon any examination carried out under section 19, to be infected with disease;

(b) the Director – General or authorised officer has other reasonable cause for believing that the animal or bird is infected with disease; or

(c) the Director – General or authorised officer has reasonable cause for believing that the animal or bird—

(i) may have been in contact with another animal or bird which is infected with disease;

(ii) may have been exposed to disease; or

(iii) may perpetuate any disease.

[*10/2002*]

（2） Any person who refuses or fails without lawful excuse to isolate or destroy any animal or bird when required to do so by the Director – General or an authorised officer under subsection （1） shall be guilty of an offence and shall be liable on conviction to a fine not exceeding $5,000 or to imprisonment for a term not exceeding 6 months or to both.

[*10/2002*]

Compensation for any animal or bird destroyed

21. （1） No compensation shall be payable in respect of any animal or bird which has been destroyed under section 20.

（2） Notwithstanding subsection （1）, the Minister may in his discretion authorise the payment of such sum as he may determine as compensation in respect of any animal or bird which has been destroyed.

Post – mortem examination

22. （1） The Director – General or an authorised officer may cause the carcase of any animal or bird to be subject to a post – mortem examination.

[*10/2002*]

（2） For the purposes of subsection （1）, the Director – General or authorised officer may give written directions—

（a） for the carcase, if already buried, to be exhumed for the purpose of a post – mortem examination; and

（b） for the carcase to be delivered to an authorised examiner at a specified place and time.

[*10/2002*]

（3） Any person who—

（a） fails without lawful excuse to comply with any written direction given to him under subsection （2）; or

（b） without the permission of the Director – General or an authorised officer removes the carcase from the place to which it has been delivered under subsection （2）（b），

shall be guilty of an offence and shall be liable on conviction to a fine not exceeding $5,000 or to imprisonment for a term not exceeding 6 months or to both.

[*10/2002*]

Animal or bird exposed to infection

23. （1） If an authorised officer considers that any animal or bird has been exposed to infection to any disease, he may give written directions for that animal or bird to be subjected to such treatment as he may consider necessary, including vaccine or serum therapy or a combination of such therapy.

[*16/2000*]

（2） Any person who fails, without lawful excuse, to comply with any written direction given to him under subsection （1） shall be guilty of an offence and shall be liable on conviction to a fine not exceeding $5,000 or to imprisonment for a term not exceeding 6 months or to both.

[*10/2002*]

Disinfection of building

24. （1） An authorised officer may give written directions for—

（a） the disinfection in such manner as he may determine of any building in which an infected animal or bird has been found or kept;

（b） prohibiting the use of any such building until the building has been disinfected in accordance with such directions as may have been given under paragraph （a）.

[*16/2000*]

(2) Any person who fails, without lawful excuse, to comply with any written direction given to him under subsection (1) shall be guilty of an offence and shall be liable on conviction to a fine not exceeding $5,000 or to imprisonment for a term not exceeding 6 months or to both.

[*10/2002*]

Destruction of building

25. (1) If an authorised officer is of the opinion that any building which has been occupied by an infected animal cannot be effectively disinfected, he may give written directions, with the approval of the Minister, to the owner or occupier thereof to destroy the building and to burn the materials thereof within such time as may be specified in the order.

[*16/2000*]

(2) If an order made under subsection (1) is not complied with within the time specified in the order, the authorised officer may cause the building and the materials thereof to be destroyed.

[*16/2000*]

(3) No compensation shall be payable in respect of any building which has been destroyed by the owner or occupier thereof in compliance with written directions or by an authorised officer under subsection (1) or (2), as the case may be.

[*16/2000*]

(4) Notwithstanding subsection (3), the Minister may in his discretion authorise the payment of such sum as he may determine as compensation in respect of any building referred to in subsection (3).

[*16/2000*]

(5) Any person who fails, without lawful excuse, to comply with any written direction given to him under subsection (1) shall be guilty of an offence and shall be liable on conviction to a fine not exceeding $5,000 or to imprisonment for a term not exceeding 6 months or to both.

[*10/2002*]

Disinfection or destruction of articles

26. (1) An authorised officer may give written directions for the disinfection or destruction of any bedding, clothing, harness, fitting, buckets, pails or utensils whatsoever used in connection with any infected animal or bird.

[*16/2000*]

(2) No compensation is payable in respect of any bedding, clothing, harness, fitting, buckets, pails or utensilsdestroyed under subsection (1).

(3) Any person who fails, without lawful excuse, to comply with any written direction given to him under subsection (1) shall be guilty of an offence and shall be liable on conviction to a fine not exceeding $5,000 or to imprisonment for a term not exceeding 6 months or to both.

[*10/2002*]

Disinfection of person and clothing

27. (1) An authorised officer may require the disinfection of the body and clothing of any person who has been in contact with or in charge of or attended upon any animal or bird infected with or in the opinion of the authorised officer infected with disease.

[*16/2000*]

(2) Any person who fails, without lawful excuse, to comply with any requirement under subsection (1) shall be guilty of an offence and shall be liable on conviction to a fine not exceeding $5,000 or to imprisonment for a term not exceeding 6 months or to both.

[*10/2002*]

Disinfection of vehicles

28. (1) An authorised officer may require the disinfection of any vehicle or conveyance—

(a) entering or leaving an area declared to be an infected area, under section 35; or

(b) which has been used in the transport of any animal or bird infected with or in the opinion of the authorised officer infected with disease.

[*16/2000*]

(2) Any person who fails, without lawful excuse, to comply with any requirement under subsection (1) shall be guilty of an offence and shall be liable on conviction to a fine not exceeding $5,000 or to imprisonment for a term not exceeding 6 months or to both.

[*10/2002*]

Disposal of infected animal, bird or carcase

29. (1) No person shall knowingly cast or cause or permit to be cast into any drain, ditch, water channel, street or open space, or otherwise expose any animal or bird or the carcase of any animal or bird which is or has been infected with disease or any fodder, litter, dung or thing which has been used in connection with any infected animal or bird.

(2) Any person who acts in contravention of subsection (1) shall be guilty of an offence and shall be liable on conviction to a fine not exceeding $10,000 or to imprisonment for a term not exceeding 12 months or to both.

[*10/2002*]

Owner of diseased or dead animal or bird to report

30. (1) Every owner or person in charge of any animal or bird infected with or reasonably suspected to be infected with disease shall—

(a) immediately make a report to an authorised officer or to the nearest police station; and

(b) at once cause that animal or bird and all other animals or birds which have been in contact with it to be confined and isolated until the arrival of an authorised officer.

[*16/2000*]

(2) Every owner or person in charge of any animal or bird reasonably suspected to have died of disease shall immediately report its death to the authorised officer or the nearest police station and, in the case of an animal, the carcase shall not be moved without written permission from the authorised officer.

[*16/2000*]

(3) It shall not be an offence to bury the carcase of the animal, if no instructions have been received within 24 hours of making the report referred to in subsection (2).

[*16/2000*]

(4) Where the officer in charge of a police station has communicated the contents of a report by telephone to an authorised officer, he shall as soon as possible transmit the report to the authorised officer.

[*16/2000*]

(5) Any person who fails, without reasonable excuse, to make a report as required under subsection (1) or (2) shall be guilty of an offence and shall be liable on conviction to a fine not exceeding $10,000 or to imprisonment for a term not exceeding 12 months or to both.

[*10/2002*]

(6) Any person who without reasonable excuse—

(a) fails to cause any animal or bird to be confined and isolated as is required by subsection (1); or

(b) permits the carcase of an animal or bird to be moved in contravention of subsection (2), shall be guilty of an offence and shall be liable on conviction to a fine not exceeding $10,000 or to imprisonment for a term not exceeding 12 months or to both.

[*10/2002*]

Special provisions relating to animals (other than dogs and cats) and birds

Application

31. Sections 32 to 36 shall not apply to dogs and cats.

Disposal of dead animal or bird

32. (1) The owner or person in charge of any animal or bird that has died from disease or has been destroyed by order of an authorised officer shall burn or otherwise dispose of the carcase thereof in accordance with the written directions of the authorised officer.

[*16/2000*]

(2) Any person who fails, without reasonable excuse, to comply with any written directions given to him by an authorised officer under subsection (1) shall be guilty of an offence and shall be liable on conviction to a fine not exceeding $10,000 or to imprisonment for a term not exceeding 12 months or to both.

[*16/2000*; *10/2002*]

Moving or disposal of diseased or suspected animal or bird

33. (1) No person shall move or dispose, whether by sale or otherwise, of any animal or bird diseased or reasonably suspected of being diseased or of being a contact of any diseased animal or bird or of the carcase of such an animal or bird, or of the milk, dung or blood of such an animal, except with the written consent of an authorised officer.

[*16/2000*]

(2) Any person who contravenes subsection (1) shall be guilty of an offence and shall be liable on conviction to a fine not exceeding $10,000 or to imprisonment for a term not exceeding 12 months or to both.

[*10/2002*]

Removal of articles from infected premises

34. (1) An authorised officer may give written directions prohibiting the removal of milk, manure, fodder, litter or other articles likely to carry or convey infection, from premises on which there is or recently has been, any animal or bird infected with disease.

[*16/2000*]

(2) Any person who fails, without reasonable excuse, to comply with any written directions given to him under subsection (1) shall be guilty of an offence and shall be liable on conviction to a fine not exceeding $10,000 or to imprisonment for a term not exceeding 12 months or to both.

[*10/2002*]

Infected areas

35. (1) Whenever there is reasonable cause to believe that any disease exists amongst any animals or birds in any part of Singapore, the Minister may by order declare that part to be an infected area and may in the order—

(a) prohibit, either absolutely or conditionally, the removal of any animal or bird or any specified kind of animal or bird into or out of that area; and

(b) restrict the movement of persons and vehicles, aircraft and ships into, within or out of that area.

[*10/2002*]

(2) When an area has been declared to be an infected area under subsection (1), the Director-General

or an authorised officer may give the owner or person in charge of any animal or bird in that area such written directions as the Director – General or authorised officer may consider necessary to control and check the spread of the disease.

[*10/2002*]

(3) Directions issued under subsection (2) may—

(a) regulate the tying – up, isolation, segregation, movement or slaughter of animals or birds in the infected area; and

(b) require the taking of any measure as may be specified by the Director – General or authorised officer.

[*10/2002*]

(4) Any animal or bird allowed to stray within an infected area, in contravention of any written direction given under subsection (2), may—

(a) be destroyed immediately by an authorised officer or any person acting under his direction; or

(b) be seized and detained until its forfeiture has been declared under the provisions of this Act.

[*16/2000*; *10/2002*]

(5) No compensation shall be payable in respect of any animal or bird so destroyed or seized under subsection (4).

(6) Any person who fails, without reasonable excuse, to comply with any order given to him under subsection (1) or with any written directions given to him under subsection (2) shall be guilty of an offence and shall be liable on conviction to a fine not exceeding $10,000 or to imprisonment for a term not exceeding 12 months or to both.

[*10/2002*]

Special permission

36. The authorised officer may grant, subject to such conditions as he may impose, written permission to the owner of any animal or bird to remove it into or out of any infected area.

[*16/2000*]

Special provisions relating to dogs and cats in connection with rabies

Rabies infected areas

37. (1) The Minister may at any time as a precaution against rabies by order declare Singapore or any part thereof to be a rabies – infected area.

(2) No person shall take any dog out of a rabies – infected area or out of Singapore when any part thereof is a rabies – infected area, except in accordance with a written permit issued by an authorised officer.

[*16/2000*]

(3) The owner or person in charge of any dog within a rabies – infected area shall cause the dog to be kept under effective control—

(a) by confining it within an enclosed area from which it would be impossible for the dog to escape;

(b) by tying it up securely; or

(c) by leading it with a chain or lead of strong cord or leather properly secured to a collar or harness worn by the dog.

(4) If the authorised officer is satisfied that any dog or class of dogs, whether by reason of prophylactic treatment or otherwise, is immune from infection by rabies, he may exempt that dog or class of dogs from the requirements of subsection (3), subject to such conditions as may be imposed by him.

[*16/2000*]

(5) Any dog found within a rabies – infected area which is not under effective control under subsection (3) may be destroyed by any person authorised in writing in that behalf by the authorised officer.

[*16/2000*]

(6) Any person authorised under subsection (5) —

(a) may enter any land, building or premises for the purpose of carrying out the provisions of thatsubsection;

(b) shall not enter into any dwelling – house for that purpose specified under that subsection, except duringthe day; and

(c) shall, if required, produce and show his written authority to the owner, occupier or person for the time being in charge of the land, building or premises.

[*16/2000*]

(7) Any person who acts in contravention of subsection (2) shall be guilty of an offence and shall be liable on conviction to a fine not exceeding $10,000 or to imprisonment for a term not exceeding 12 months or to both.

[*10/2002*]

(8) Any person who fails, without reasonable excuse, to comply with subsection (3) shall be guilty of an offence and shall be liable on conviction to a fine not exceeding $10,000 or to imprisonment for a term not exceeding 12 months or to both.

[*38*

[*10/2002*]

Destruction or detention of animal suspected to be infected with rabies

38. (1) Where an authorised officer reasonably suspects that any animal may be infected with rabies or has been exposed to rabies infection he may, in his discretion, either—

(a) cause the animal to be destroyed immediately; or

(b) give written directions to the owner or person in charge of the animal requiring that owner or person to take it immediately to any animal quarantine station for detention and observation.

[*16/2000*]

(2) If the owner or person in charge of the animal fails to comply with the written directions given under subsection (1), the authorised officer may either cause the animal to be destroyed immediately or take possession of the animal and remove it to an animal quarantine station.

[*16/2000*]

(3) The authorised officer may either destroy the animal in the animal quarantine station or may detain it until he is satisfied that it is free from disease.

[*16/2000*]

(4) The authorised officer may take possession of the body of any animal that has died or has been destroyed and which is reasonably suspected to have been infected with rabies and may dispose of it in such manner as he may think fit.

[*16/2000*]

(5) No compensation shall be payable to any person in respect of the destruction of any animal under subsection (1), (2) or (3).

(6) Any person who fails, without reasonable excuse, to comply with any written directions given to him under subsection (1) shall be guilty of an offence and shall be liable on conviction to a fine not exceeding $10,000 or to imprisonment for a term not exceeding 12 months or to both.

[*10/2002*]

(7) In this section, "animal" means any four – footed beast in captivity or under control.

[39

Detention of any dog that has bitten a person

39. (1) An authorised officer or police officer may give directions requiring the owner or person in charge of any dog that has or is reasonably believed to have bitten any person to produce the dog at such place and time as he may determine.

[16/2000]

(2) If the owner or person in charge of the dog fails to comply with the directions given to him under subsection (1), the authorised officer or police officer may immediately take possession of the dog and remove it to an animal quarantine station.

[16/2000]

(3) Any person who fails, without lawful excuse, to comply with the directions given to him under subsection (1) shall be guilty of an offence and shall be liable on conviction to a fine not exceeding $2,000.

[40

[10/2002]

Anti – rabies vaccination of dogs

40. (1) The Minister may make an order requiring that all dogs within Singapore or any part thereof specified in the order shall be submitted to anti – rabies vaccination.

(2) Where an order has been made under subsection (1) the authorised officer may specify periods of time within which, and the place at which, dogs or groups of dogs, shall be produced for the purpose of such vaccination.

[16/2000]

(3) All such arrangements for vaccination of dogs shall be published in such manner as the authorised officer may determine.

[16/2000]

(4) The Minister may, by notification in the *Gazette*, require that every dog which has been vaccinated in accordance with the order shall, after such date as may be specified in the notification, at all times during the continuance in force of the order and within the area to which the order applies, carry upon it a serially numbered badge, mark, tag or other evidence of vaccination.

(5) Any dog within the area after the date specified in the notification made under subsection (4), whether the dog is at large or not, which does not carry the proper evidence of vaccination may be destroyed.

(6) The authorised officer may authorise in writing any person to destroy dogs to give effect to subsection (5).

[16/2000]

(7) Any person so authorised may enter any land, building or premises for the purpose of carrying out the provisions of subsection (6).

(8) The person so authorised shall not enter into any dwelling for that purpose, except during the hours of daylight and shall, if required, produce and show his written authority to the owner, occupier or person for the time being in charge of the land, building or premises.

(9) If any person in charge of a dog fails to comply with any order or requirement under subsection (1) or (4), as the case may be, the authorised officer may immediately destroy that dog.

[16/2000]

(10) Any owner of or person in charge of a dog who fails, without reasonable excuse, to comply with an

order made under subsection (1) shall be guilty of an offence and shall be liable on conviction to a fine not exceeding $10,000 or to imprisonment for a term not exceeding 12 months or to both.

[*10/2002*]

(11) Any person who fails, without reasonable excuse, to comply with a requirement contained in a notification made under subsection (4) shall be guilty of an offence and shall be liable on conviction to a fine not exceeding $10,000 or to imprisonment for a term not exceeding 12 months or to both.

[*10/2002*]

(12) No compensation shall be payable in respect of any dog that is destroyed under this section.

[*41*

[*10/2002*]

Part Ⅳ Prevention of cruelty to animals

Interpretation of this Part

41. In this Part, unless the context otherwise requires, "animal" includes any beast, bird, fish, reptile or insect, whether wild or tame.

[*42*

Cruelty to animals

42. (1) Any person who—

(a) cruelly beats, kicks, ill - treats, over - rides, over - drives, over - loads, tortures, infuriates or terrifies any animal;

(b) causes or procures or, being the owner, permits any animal to be so used;

(c) being in charge of any animal in confinement or in the course of transport from one place to another neglects to supply the animal with sufficient food and water;

(d) by wantonly or unreasonably doing or omitting to do any act, causes any unnecessary pain or suffering or, being the owner, permits any unnecessary pain or suffering to any animal;

(e) causes, procures or, being the owner, permits to be confined, conveyed, lifted or carried any animal in such a manner or position as to subject it to unnecessary pain or suffering;

(f) being the owner of any animal, abandons the animal without reasonable cause or excuse, whether permanently or not, in circumstances likely to cause the animal any unnecessary suffering or distress, or causes or permits the animal to be so abandoned;

(g) employs or causes or procures or, being the owner, permits to be employed in any work of labour, any animal which in consequence of any disease, infirmity, wound or sore, or otherwise is unfit to be so employed; or

(h) causes, procures or assists at the fighting or baiting of any animal, or keeps, uses, manages, or acts or assists in the management of any premises or place for the purpose, or partly for the purpose, of fighting or baiting any animal, or permits any premises or place to be so kept, managed or used, or receives or causes or procures any person to receive money for the admission of any person to the premises or place,

shall be guilty of an offence and shall be liable on conviction to a fine not exceeding $10,000 or to imprisonment for a term not exceeding 12 months or to both; except where an owner is convicted of having permitted cruelty to an animal under subsection (2), he shall be liable to a fine not exceeding $10,000.

[*10/2002*]

(2) For the purposes of subsection (1), an owner shall be deemed to have permitted cruelty to an animal, if hehas failed to exercise reasonable care and supervision in respect of the animal.

(3) Nothing in this section applies to the commission or omission of any act in the course of the destruction, or the preparation for destruction of any animal as food, unless that destruction or preparation was accompanied by the infliction of unnecessary suffering.

[*43*

Powers of authorised officers and police officers

43. (1) Any authorised officer or any police officer may, without warrant—

(a) arrest any person who, in his presence, commits an offence under section 42;

(b) enter and search any premises in which he has reasonable cause for suspecting that an offence under section 42 has been or is being committed; and

(c) seize any animal in respect of which, and any conveyance or article with or by means of which, that offence is reasonably suspected to have been committed.

[*10/2002*]

(2) An authorised officer or a police officer acting under subsection (1)(b) may, if the circumstances so warrant, with such assistance as he thinks necessary, remove anything obstructing his entry to the premises or break open any door, window, lock, fastener, hold, compartment, box, container or any other thing.

[*10/2002*]

(3) Any person arrested and any conveyance or article seized under subsection (1) shall immediately be taken to a police station.

[*10/2002*]

(4) Any animal seized under subsection (1) shall be taken to a police station, pound, veterinary centre or any other place which the authorised officer or police officer thinks fit and may, subject to any order made in respect thereof by a Magistrate, be detained there until the accused has been tried by a court.

[*10/2002*]

(5) No compensation shall be payable to any person in respect of any damage to his property caused or occasioned by any act authorised by subsection (2).

[*10/2002*]

(6) Any authorised officer or any police officer may stop and examine in any street or public place any animal in respect of which he has reason to believe that an offence under section 42 has been or is being committed.

[*44*

[*10/2002*]

Orders by Magistrate when an offence has been committed

44. (1) When any person has been convicted of an offence under section 42, the court may order—

(a) that the animal in respect of which the offence was committed be taken to a veterinary centre or such other place as the court may specify and there detained and treated for any period stated in the order, or until released by further order of a Magistrate or until an authorised officer has certified in writing that it may properly be released;

(b) that the animal be treated by an authorised officer or by a person licensed under section 53 to treat animals and not used during such period as may be stated in the order or until permission to use it has been given by a Magistrate or an authorised officer; or

(c) if satisfied that the animal is incurably diseased or injured, that it be destroyed immediately by or under the direction of a police officer or an authorised officer and that the cost of burying or otherwise disposing of the carcase be borne by the person convicted.

[*16/2000*; *10/2002*]

(2) Where the court makes an order under subsection (1)(a), the person who has been convicted of an offence in respect of the animal shall be liable to pay the costs and expenses for its maintenance and treatment until it is declared fit for release or use.

[*10/2002*]

(3) Without prejudice to subsection (1), where the owner of any animal is convicted of an offence under section 42, the court may, upon convicting him, if it thinks fit, in addition to any other punishment, deprive him of the ownership of the animal and make such order as to the disposal of the animal as the court thinks fit.

[*10/2002*]

(4) The court shall not make an order under subsection (3) unless it is satisfied by evidence as to a previous conviction, or as to the character of the owner or otherwise, that the animal, if left with the owner, is likely to be exposed to cruelty.

[*10/2002*]

(5) Any person who acts in contravention of the provisions of an order made under subsection (1) shall be guilty of an offence and shall be liable on conviction to a fine not exceeding $5,000 or to imprisonment for a term not exceeding 6 months or to both.

[*45*

[*10/2002*]

Power to order destruction of animals

45. (1) An authorised officer or a police officer who has satisfied himself by personal inspection or otherwise—

(a) that an animal is diseased or injured and that the disease or injury from which the animal is suffering is incurable or that it is cruel to keep the animal alive; or

(b) that an animal is so diseased or so severely injured or in such a physical condition that, in his opinion, having regard to the means available for removing the animal there is no possibility of removing it without cruelty and that it is cruel to keep it alive,

may give written directions requiring the animal to be destroyed and those directions may immediately be carried out by or under the supervision of that authorised officer or police officer or any other person authorized in that behalf by the authorised officer or police officer.

[*21/93*; *16/2000*; *10/2002*]

(2) If the animal so diseased or injured is in any house, stable, shed, or enclosure proper for that animal and not in a public thoroughfare, market or place, no written directions shall be given until the owner of the animal (if known) or person in charge (if any) has been duly notified of the state of the animal.

[*21/73*]

(3) If any animal is destroyed under written directions given under subsection (1), the expenses of the removal and burial of the carcase of the animal shall be paid by the owner or person in charge thereof and the amount thereof may be recovered from that owner or person in charge in a summary manner before a Magistrate.

[*46*

No compensation for destruction of an animal incurably diseased or injured or destroyed at request of professed owner

46. No compensation shall in any case be payable to any person in respect of the destruction of any animal—

(a) under an order made under section 44 (1)(c);

(b) under written directions given under section 45 (1); or

(c) in compliance with a request in writing to an authorised officer or a person in charge of a veterinary centre or such other place as provided for in section 44 (1) by any person professing to be the owner of the animal.

[47

Award to informer

47. The court before which any person is convicted of an offence under this Part may direct any fine or portion of any fine imposed and levied under this Act to be paid to the informer.

[48

Animals and birds not to be kept in captivity for sale, export or exhibition without licence

48. (1) No person shall keep in captivity for sale, export or exhibition any animal or bird in any place which has not been licensed in that behalf under this Act.

(2) Any person who contravenes subsection (1) shall be guilty of an offence and shall be liable on conviction to a fine not exceeding $5,000 or to imprisonment for a term not exceeding 6 months or to both.

[49

[10/2002]

Part V Control of livestock

Movement or slaughter of animals and birds may be prohibited

49. (1) The Minister may by order—

(a) prohibit for such period as may be specified in the order the movement of any animals and birds from one part of Singapore to another except under a licence;

(b) prohibit during such period or periods as may be specified in the order the slaughter of any animal or bird except under a licence.

(2) A licence issued in accordance with an order made under subsection (1) shall be subject to such conditions as may be contained in the order or the licence.

(3) Any person who contravenes the provisions of an order made under this section shall be guilty of an offence and shall be liable on conviction to a fine not exceeding $10,000 or to imprisonment for a term not exceeding 12 months or to both.

[50

[10/2002]

Part Ⅵ Search, seizure and arrest

Power of search for diseased animals or birds

50. (1) For the purpose of ascertaining whether any animal or bird is suffering from disease or for the purpose of ascertaining whether any offence under this Act has been or is being committed—

(a) any authorised officer or police officer may enter and examine any land, building or premises on or in which he suspects any animal or bird is being kept for the purpose of examining the animal, bird, land, building or premises and the owner of the land, building, premises, animal or bird shall render the authorised officer or police officer all necessary assistance and furnish such information as may be required of him; and

(b) any authorised officer, police officer or officer of customs may stop, enter and examine any conveyance used for carrying animals.

[16/2000]

(2) Any authorised officer, police officer or officer of customs acting under subsection (1) may, if the circumstances so warrant, with such assistance as he thinks necessary, remove anything obstructing his entry to

the premises or conveyance or break open any door, window, lock, fastener, hold, compartment, box, container or any other thing.

[*10/2002*]

(3) No compensation shall be payable to any person in respect of any damage to his property caused or occasioned by any act authorised by subsection (2).

[*10/2002*]

(4) Any person in charge of a conveyance who does not stop when he is required to do so by any authorized officer, police officer or officer of customs under subsection (1)(b) shall be guilty of an offence and shall be liable on conviction to a fine not exceeding $5,000 or to imprisonment for a term not exceeding 6 months or to both.

[*51*

[*10/2002*]

Seizure of animal, bird, carcases or articles

51. (1) Where any authorised officer or police officer has reason to believe that any offence under this Act has been or is being committed or where any officer of customs has reason to believe that an offence under this Act relating to importation or exportation has been or is being committed, the authorised officer, officer of customs or police officer may—

(a) seize any animal, bird, carcase or article, the subject – matter of such an offence; and

(b) remove that animal, bird, carcase or article to any compound, enclosure or other place selected by the authorised officer and there detain it.

[*16/2000*]

(2) Where any animal, bird, carcase or article has been seized and detained under subsection (1), the authorized officer, officer of customs or police officer shall report the same to a Magistrate and the Magistrate may make such order for the further detention or release of the animal, bird, carcase or article as he may think fit.

[*16/2000*]

(3) The owner of the animal, bird, carcase or article shall pay such sum as the Magistrate may consider reasonable to cover the expenses connected with its removal to a place of detention and unless that sum is paid within a specified time the animal, bird, carcase or article shall be forfeited.

[*52*

Powers of arrest

52. (1) Any authorised officer, officer of customs or police officer may arrest without warrant any person whom he sees or finds committing or attempting to commit or whom he reasonably suspects of being engaged in committing or attempting to commit any offence under this Act, if—

(a) the person refuses to furnish his name and address;

(b) the person furnishes an address out of Singapore;

(c) there are reasonable grounds for believing that the person has furnished a false name or address; or

(d) the person is likely to abscond.

[*16/2000*]

(2) Any authorised officer, officer of customs or police officer making an arrest without warrant shall, subject to subsection (3), without unnecessary delay bring the person arrested before a Magistrate's Court.

[*16/2000*]

(3) No person who has been arrested by any authorised officer, officer of customs or police officer shall be

released, except on his own bond or on bail or on the special order in writing of the Magistrate or the Director – General.

[*53*

[*16/2000*]

Part Ⅶ Licensing of veterinary centre, veterinary biologics and keeping, breeding, ETC., of animal or bird

Licence to treat, vaccinate and innoculate animal or bird

53. (1) No person other than an authorised officer shall treat, vaccinate or innoculate any animal or bird except under and in accordance with the conditions of a licence issued by the Director – General.

[*10/2002*]

(2) Any person who contravenes subsection (1) shall be guilty of an offence and shall be liable on conviction to a fine not exceeding $10,000 or to imprisonment for a term not exceeding 12 months or to both.

[*68*

[*10/2002*]

Veterinary centres to be licensed

54. (1) No person shall use or permit any premises to be used as a veterinary centre except under and in accordance with the conditions of a licence issued by the Director – General.

[*10/2002*]

(2) Any person who contravenes subsection (1) shall be guilty of an offence and shall be liable on conviction to a fine not exceeding $10,000 or to imprisonment for a term not exceeding 12 months or to both.

[*65*

[*10/2002*]

Licence to possess or innoculate veterinary biologics

55. (1) No person other than an authorised officer shall—

(a) have in his possession any veterinary biologics; or

(b) innoculate any animal or bird with any veterinary biologics, except under and in accordance with the conditions of a licence issued by the Director – General.

[*10/2002*]

(2) Any person who contravenes subsection (1) shall be guilty of an offence and shall be liable on conviction to a fine not exceeding $10,000 or to imprisonment for a term not exceeding 12 months or to both.

[*69*

[*10/2002*]

Brands or other identification marks may be applied to animals and birds

56. (1) The Director – General or an authorised officer may give directions to the owner or person in charge of any animal or bird to have that animal or bird branded, labelled or otherwise marked, either permanently or temporarily, for the purpose of identification.

[*10/2002*]

(2) The branding, labelling or marking of any animal or bird under subsection (1) shall be carried out by a person designated by the Director – General under subsection (3) and the costs thereof shall be borne by the owner or person in charge of the animal or bird.

[*10/2002*]

(3) The Director – General may designate any person to carry out the branding, labelling or marking of

animals and birds for the purpose of this section.

[*10/2002*]

(4) Any person who—

(a) fails to comply with any direction given to him under subsection (1); or

(b) counterfeits, copies, alters, defaces or erases, any brand, label or mark applied on any animal or bird under this section, shall be guilty of an offence and shall be liable on conviction to a fine not exceeding $10,000 or to imprisonment for a term not exceeding 12 months or to both.

[*62*

[*10/2002*]

Part Ⅷ Quarantine

Quarantine stations

57. (1) The Director - General may establish or designate such number of quarantine stations as he thinks necessary for the purposes of this Act.

[*10/2002*]

(2) For the purposes of subsection (1), the Director - General may engage the service of any suitably qualified person to provide such number of quarantine stations as he thinks necessary and to manage any quarantine station established by him under subsection (1).

[*63*

[*10/2002*]

Prohibition against use of premises as unauthorised quarantine stations

58. (1) No person shall use or permit any premises to be used as a quarantine station for animals or birds unless such premises have been designated by the Director - General as a quarantine station under section 57.

[*10/2002*]

(2) Any person who contravenes subsection (1) shall be guilty of an offence and shall be liable on conviction to a fine not exceeding $10,000 or to imprisonment for a term not exceeding 12 months.

[*64*

[*10/2002*]

Regulation and control of keeping, breeding or feeding of animals and birds

59. (1) The Minister may make rules for the following purposes:

(a) to prohibit, either absolutely or subject to such conditions as may be prescribed, the keeping, breeding or feeding in any private or public place of any animal or bird or type thereof;

(b) to regulate the keeping, breeding or feeding in any private or public place of any animal or bird or type thereof; and

(c) to provide for the impounding of stray cats or dogs found in any public place.

[*10/2002*]

(2) Without prejudice to the generality of subsection (1), rules made under that subsection may—

(a) require any person intending to keep or breed any animal or bird or type thereof in any private or public place to obtain a licence from the Director - General and to comply with the conditions of such licence;

(b) provide for the licence to be issued in respect of either or both—

(i) the animal or bird to be kept or bred; and

(ii) the place at which the animal or bird is to be kept or bred; and

(c) empower the Director - General or an authorised officer to remove or destroy or cause the removal or destruction of any animal or bird in connection with which any contravention of any rule made under this section has been committed.

[*10/2002*]

(3) No compensation shall be payable in respect of any animal or bird which is required by any rules made under subsection (2)(c) to be destroyed.

[*10/2002*]

(4) Section 80 (3) shall apply in respect of rules made under this section.

[*53A*

[*10/2002*]

Part IX Offences and penalties

Obstructing officers in execution of their duties

60. Any person who without lawful excuse obstructs or impedes or assists in obstructing or impeding any authorised officer, officer of customs or police officer in the exercise of his duties under this Act or any rule or order made thereunder shall be guilty of an offence and shall be liable on conviction to a fine not exceeding $10,000 or to imprisonment for a term not exceeding 12 months or to both.

[*54*

[*16/2000*; *10/2002*]

Altering licences

61. Any person who without lawful authority alters any licence or permit issued under this Act or knowingly makes use of any licence or permit so altered shall be guilty of an offence and shall be liable on conviction to a fine not exceeding $10,000 or to imprisonment for a term not exceeding 12 months or to both.

[*55*

[*10/2002*]

Suspension and revocation of licences and permits

62. (1) The Director – General may suspend or revoke a licence or permit if he is satisfied that—

(a) the issue of the licence or permit has been obtained by fraud or misrepresentation;

(b) the person to whom the licence or permit has been issued is contravening or has contravened or has failed to comply with—

(i) any of the provisions of this Act;

(ii) any condition of his licence or permit; or

(iii) any direction given to him by the Director – General or an authorised officer under this Act; or

(c) it is in the public interest to suspend or revoke the licence or permit.

[*10/2002*]

(2) The Director – General shall, before suspending or revoking the licence or permit under subsection (1) —

(a) give the holder of the licence or permit notice in writing of his intention to do so; and

(b) in such notice call upon the holder of the licence or permit to show cause within such time as may be specified in the notice as to why his licence or permit should not be suspended or revoked.

[*10/2002*]

(3) If the holder of the licence or permit—

(a) fails to show cause within the period of time given to him to do so or such extended period of time as the Director – General may allow; or

(b) fails to show sufficient cause,

the Director – General shall give notice in writing to the holder of the licence or permit of the date from which the suspension or revocation of his licence or permit is to take effect.

[*10/2002*]

(4) Any person who is aggrieved by the suspension or revocation of his licence or permit may, within 7 days from the date of receipt of the notice informing him of the suspension or revocation, appeal in writing to the Minister whose decision shall be final.

[*10/2002*]

(5) Notwithstanding that any appeal under subsection (4) is pending, the suspension or revocation of a licence or permit under subsection (3) shall take effect from the date specified by the Director – General therefor, unless the Minister otherwise orders.

[*69A*

[*10/2002*]

Penalties for offences for which no expressed penalty is provided

63. Any person guilty of an offence under this Act, or any rule or order made thereunder for which no expressed penalty is provided shall be liable on conviction to a fine not exceeding $5,000 or to imprisonment for a term not exceeding 6 months or to both.

[*56*

[*10/2002*]

Forfeiture

64. (1) The court before which any person is tried for an offence under this Act may make an order for the forfeiture of any item which has been seized under the provisions of this Act if—

(a) the court is satisfied that—

(i) an offence under this Act has been committed; and

(ii) the item seized was the subject – matter, or was used in the commission, of the offence; and

(b) having regard to the circumstances of the case, the court thinks it fit to order the forfeiture of the item.

[*10/2002*]

(2) Where no party raises the question of forfeiture under subsection (1), the court shall consider the question on its own motion.

[*10/2002*]

(3) The court may make an order under subsection (1) for the forfeiture of any item which has been seized under the provisions of this Act notwithstanding that no person may have been convicted of an offence.

[*10/2002*]

(4) If the court, having regard to the circumstances of the case, does not think it fit to order the forfeiture of any item which has been seized under the provisions of this Act, the court shall order that the item be released to the owner thereof or to the person entitled thereto.

[*10/2002*]

(5) In the absence of any prosecution with regard to any item which has been seized under the provisions of this Act, the Director – General shall give the person from whom the item was seized or the owner of the item notice in writing that the item shall, on the expiration of 7 days from the date specified in the notice, be deemed to be forfeited unless a claim thereto is made before then in accordance with subsection (6).

[*10/2002*]

(6) A person asserting—

(a) that he is the owner of, or that he is entitled to, any item which has been seized under the provisions of this Act; and

(b) that the item is not liable to forfeiture, may, personally or by his agent authorised in writing, give written notice to the Director - General that he claims the item.

[*10/2002*]

(7) On receipt of a notice under subsection (6), the Director - General may direct that the item be released to the person who has given the notice or may refer the matter to a court for decision.

[*10/2002*]

(8) Where no claim is received on the expiration of 7 days from the date specified in the notice referred to in subsection (5), the item to which the notice relates shall be deemed to be forfeited.

[*10/2002*]

(9) Where the owner of any item seized under the provisions of this Act consents to its disposal, the item shall thereupon be deemed to be forfeited.

[*10/2002*]

(10) Any item forfeited or deemed to be forfeited under this section shall be delivered to an authorised officer and shall be disposed of in such manner as the Director - General thinks fit.

[*10/2002*]

(11) In this section, "item" means any animal, bird, carcase or any other article.

[*57*

[*10/2002*]

Presumptions

65. (1) Where the owner or person in charge of a diseased animal or bird is charged with an offence under this Act in respect of the disease, he shall be presumed to have known of the existence of the disease in the animal or bird until he shows to the satisfaction of the court before which he is charged that he had no such knowledge and could not with reasonable diligence have obtained such knowledge.

(2) Where there is any doubt regarding the ownership of any animal or bird, the person found in possession of the animal or bird, or the occupier of the premises frequented by it may be presumed to be the owner thereof until the contrary is proved.

[*58*

Offences committed by bodies corporate and by agents and servants

66. (1) Where an offence under this Act has been committed by a body corporate, a partnership or an unincorporated association of persons, any person who at the time of the commission of the offence was a director, manager, partner, secretary or other similar officer thereof, or was purporting to act in any such capacity shall be guilty of that offence unless he proves that—

(a) the offence was committed without his consent or connivance; and

(b) he had exercised all such diligence to prevent the commission of the offence as he ought to have exercised having regard to the nature of his functions in that capacity and to all the circumstances.

[*10/2002*]

(2) Where an offence under this Act is committed by any person acting as an agent or servant of another person, or being otherwise subject to the supervision or instruction of another person for the purposes of any employment in the course of which the offence was committed, that other person shall, without prejudice to the liability of the first - mentioned person, be liable under this Act in the same manner and to the same extent as if he

had personally committed the offence if it is proved that the act which constituted the offence was committed with his consent or connivance or that it was attributable to any neglect on his part.

[69D

[10/2002]

Jurisdiction of court

67. (1) Notwithstanding any provision to the contrary in the Criminal Procedure Code (Cap. 68), a District Court and a Magistrate's Court shall have jurisdiction to try any offence under this Act and shall have power to impose the full penalty or punishment in respect of any offence under this Act.

[10/2002]

(2) For the purpose of section 133 of the Criminal Procedure Code and notwithstanding subsections (1) and (2) thereof, a Magistrate may take cognizance of an offence under this Act upon receiving a complaint in writing and signed by the Director – General or an authorised officer.

[69I

[10/2002]

Evidence

68. (1) Subject to subsection (3) —

(a) a document or certificate purporting to be a report under the hand of the Director – General or an authorised officer upon any matter or thing in connection with the administration or enforcement of this Act or with any investigation carried out under this Act shall be admissible as evidence in any proceedings under this Act and shall be prima facie evidence of the facts stated therein; and

(b) a certificate of an authorised examiner stating that he has examined any animal or bird or any other matter and stating the result of his examination shall be admissible as evidence in any proceedings for an offence under this Act and shall be prima facie evidence of the facts stated therein and of the correctness of the result of the examination.

[10/2002]

(2) For the purposes of this section, a document purporting to be a certificate referred to in subsection (1) on its production by the prosecution shall, unless the contrary is proved, be presumed to be such a certificate.

[10/2002]

(3) A certificate referred to in subsection (1) shall not be received in evidence in pursuance of that subsection unless the person charged has been given—

(a) a copy of the certificate; and

(b) notice of the intention of the prosecution to produce the certificate as evidence in the proceedings, not less than 10 clear days before the date of commencement of the proceedings.

[10/2002]

(4) Where a certificate of the Director – General, an authorised officer or an authorised examiner is admitted in evidence under subsection (1), the person charged may require the Director – General, authorised officer or authorised examiner to be called as a witness for the prosecution and be cross – examined as if he had given evidence of the matters stated in the certificate.

[69J

[10/2002]

Composition of offences

69. (1) The Director – General or any officer authorised in writing in that behalf by the Authority may, in his discretion, compound any offence under this Act which is prescribed as a compoundable offence by collecting from a person reasonably suspected of having committed the offence a sum not exceeding $1,000.

[10/2002]

(2) On payment of such sum, no further proceedings shall be taken against such person in respect of the offence.

[69K

[10/2002]

Part X Miscellaneous provisions

Fees, etc., payable to Authority

70. All fees, charges, composition fines and moneys collected under this Act shall be paid to the Authority.

[59A

[16/2000]

Expenses

71. Any expense incurred by an authorised officer or other officer in the exercise of the powers conferred on him by this Act or any rule, order or direction made or given thereunder shall be charged against the owner, consignor, consignee or importer, as the case may be, of the animal, bird, carcase, article, building or conveyance concerned and may be recovered as a civil debt.

[60

[16/2000]

Action to be at risk and expense of owner

72. (1) Any action taken under the provisions of this Act or of any rule, order or direction made or given thereunder in respect of any animal, bird, carcase, article, building or conveyance shall be at the risk of the owner thereof.

(2) No liability shall attach to the Authority or to any officer thereof in respect of any expense, loss, damage or delay arising in or from the lawful exercise of the powers under this Act.

[61

[16/2000]

Powers of Director-General and authorised officer in cases of non-compliance with Act or any direction or order

73. (1) If a person to whom any of the provisions of this Act applies or to whom any direction or order is given under this Act fails to comply with such provision, direction or order, then, without prejudice to any proceedings that may be instituted against such person for such non-compliance, the Director-General or an authorised officer may perform any act or take any measure as is required by the provision, direction or order to be performed or taken and recover any costs and expenses reasonably incurred by him from that person.

[10/2002]

(2) In exercising the powers conferred by subsection (1), the Director-General or authorised officer may, without warrant, enter any premises, vehicle, ship or aircraft and, if the circumstances so warrant, may use such force as may be necessary to effect such entry.

[69B

[10/2002]

Power to require production of documents, etc.

74. (1) For the purpose of discharging his functions and duties under this Act, the Director – General or an authorised officer may at any time require any person—

(a) to produce to the Director – General or authorised officer for inspection or for the purpose of obtaining copies or extracts, or to provide the Director – General or authorised officer with copies or extracts of, any book, shipping bill, bill of lading or other document or record that the Director – General or authorized officer believes on reasonable grounds to contain any information relevant to the administration or enforcement of this Act; or

(b) to furnish any information as the Director – General or authorised officer may reasonably require.

[*10/2002*]

(2) The Director – General or an authorised officer may record any information furnished by any person under subsection (1)(b) as a statement which shall be admissible as evidence in any proceedings in connection with any offence under this Act.

[*10/2002*]

(3) Any person who fails to comply with any requirement made by the Director – General or an authorised officer under subsection (1)(a) or (b) shall be guilty of an offence and shall be liable on conviction to a fine not exceeding $5,000 or to imprisonment for a term not exceeding 6 months or to both.

[*69C*
[*10/2002*]

Form and authentication of notices, orders and other documents

75. (1) All notices, orders and other documents of whatsoever nature which the Director – General is empowered to give by this Act may be in such form as the Director – General may determine, and may be given by any authorised officer.

[*10/2002*]

(2) Where any such notice, order or document requires authentication—

(a) the signature of the Director – General or an authorised officer; or

(b) an official facsimile of such signature,

appended thereto shall be sufficient authentication.

[*69E*
[*10/2002*]

Inaccuracies in documents

76. (1) No misnomer or inaccurate description of any person, animal, bird, premises, building, street, place, vehicle, aircraft, ship or other conveyance named or described in any notice, order or document prepared, issued or served under or for the purposes of this Act shall in any way affect the operation of this Act as respects that person, animal, bird, premises, building, street, place, vehicle, aircraft, ship or other conveyance if that person, animal, bird, premises, building, street, place, vehicle, aircraft, ship or other conveyance is so designated in the notice, order or document as to be identifiable.

[*10/2002*]

(2) No proceedings taken under or by virtue of this Act shall be invalid for want of form.

[*69F*
[*10/2002*]

Service of documents

77. (1) Any notice, order or document required or authorised by this Act to be served on any person, and any summons issued by a court against any person in connection with any offence under this Act may be served on the person—

(a) by delivering it to the person or to some adult member or employee of his family or household at his usual or last known place of residence;

(b) by leaving it at his usual or last known place of residence or business in an envelope addressed to the person;

(c) by sending it by registered post addressed to the person at his usual or last known place of residence or business; or

(d) in the case of an incorporated company, a partnership or a body of persons—

(i) by delivering it to the secretary or other like officer of the company, partnership or body of persons at its registered office or principal place of business; or

(ii) by sending it by registered post addressed to the company, partnership or body of persons at its registered office or principal place of business.

[*10/2002*]

(2) Any notice, order, document or summons sent by registered post to any person in accordance with subsection (1) shall be deemed to be duly served on the person at the time when the notice, order, document or summons, as the case may be, would in the ordinary course of post be delivered and, in proving service of the notice, order, document or summons, it shall be sufficient to prove that the envelope containing the same was properly addressed, stamped and posted by registered post.

[*10/2002*]

(3) Any notice, order or document required or authorised by this Act to be served on the owner or occupier of any premises or any summons issued by a court against any such owner or occupier in connection with any offence under this Act may be served by delivering it or a true copy thereof to some adult person on the premises or, if there is no such person on the premises to whom it can with reasonable diligence be delivered, by affixing the notice, order, document or summons to some conspicuous part of the premises.

[*10/2002*]

(4) Any notice, order or document required or authorised by this Act to be served on the owner or occupier of any premises or any summons issued by a court against any such owner or occupier in connection with any offence under this Act shall be deemed to be properly addressed if addressed by the description of the owner or occupier of the premises without further name or description.

[*69G*

[*10/2002*]

Protection from liability

78. No suit or other legal proceedings shall lie against the Authority, the Director – General or any authorized officer, police officer, officer of customs or any other person acting under the direction of the Authority or Director – General for anything which is in good faith done in the execution or purported execution of this Act.

[*69H*

[*10/2002*]

Exemption

79. The Director – General may, subject to any general or special directions of the Minister, exempt any person, premises, animal or bird or any class of persons, premises, animals or birds from any of the provisions of this Act.

[*69L*

[*10/2002*]

Rules

80. (1) The Minister may make rules for carrying out the purposes of this Act and for any matter which is required under this Act to be prescribed.

[*10/2002*]

(2) Without prejudice to the generality of subsection (1), the Minister may make rules—

(a) to provide for the designation of an authorised examiner, the conditions to be complied with by an authorised examiner and the suspension or revocation of any such designation;

(b) to provide for the manner in which the quarantining, examination, treatment and certification of animals and birds are to be carried out;

(c) to regulate the import, export and transhipment of animals, birds or carcases;

(d) to provide for the prevention of the introduction and spread and for the control and eradication of diseases of animals and birds;

(e) to provide for the cleansing or disinfection of buildings, vehicles, aircraft or ships in which diseased animals, birds or carcases have been kept or carried;

(f) to provide for the disinfection of persons and the disinfection and treatment of animals, birds or articles that have been in contact with diseased animals, birds or carcases;

(g) to regulate and control the sale, marketing and distribution of animals and birds and their products;

(h) to provide for the licensing, control, supervision and inspection of places in which animals or birds are or may be kept in captivity for sale, export, exhibition, production, or any other purpose;

(i) to provide for the inspection of premises subject to this Act and of vehicles, aircraft or ships used for the carriage of animals and birds;

(j) to provide for the control of pollution caused by animals and the imposition of fees and charges for the purpose of such control together with the time, place and manner of collection;

(k) to provide for the control and improvement of animal or bird production in respect of breeding, nutrition, health, management, husbandry and method of production;

(l) to provide for the supply, collection and compilation of information and statistics of animals and birds and their products;

(m) to provide for the establishment and designation of quarantine stations;

(n) to regulate the management and maintenance of quarantine stations and veterinary centres;

(o) to prescribe the fees to be charged for the purposes of this Act; and

(p) to prescribe the offences which may be compounded under section 69 and the method and procedure by which such offences may be compounded.

[*10/2002*]

(3) The Minister may, in making any rules, provide that any contravention of, or failure or neglect to comply with, any provision of the rules or any directive issued by the Director – General pursuant to the rules shall be an offence punishable with a fine not exceeding $10,000 or with imprisonment for a term not exceeding 12 months or with both.

[*10/2002*]

(4) All rules made under this Act shall be presented to Parliament as soon as possible after publication in the *Gazette*.

[*70*

[*10/2002*]

Legislation history

1. Ordinance 3 of 1965—Animals and Birds Ordinance 1965

Date of First Reading : 19. 11. 64 (Bill No. 39/64 published on 12. 12. 64)
Date of Second and Third Readings : 16. 6. 65
Dates of commencement : 22. 10. 65 (except section 71)
: 20. 5. 66 (section 71)

2. Act 21 of 1973—Republic of Singapore (Miscellaneous Amendments) Act 1973

Date of First Reading : 7. 3. 73 (Bill No. 16/73 published on 9. 3. 73)
Date of Second and Third Readings : 20. 3. 73
Date of commencement : 6. 4. 73

3. Act 7 of 1996—Maritime and Port Authority of Singapore Act 1996

(Consequential Amendments made by)
Date of First Reading : 5. 12. 95 (Bill No. 46/95 published on 6. 12. 95)
Date of Second and Third Readings : 18. 1. 96
Date of commencement : 2. 2. 96

4. Act 7 of 1997—Statutes (Miscellaneous Amendments) Act 1997

Date of First Reading : 11. 7. 97 (Bill No. 6/97 published on 12. 7. 97)
Date of Second and Third Readings : 25. 8. 97
Dates of commencement : 1. 10. 97 (except section 3)
: 1. 9. 98 (section 3)

5. Act 16 of 2000—Agri - food and Veterinary Authority Act 2000

(Consequential Amendments made by)
Date of First Reading : 21. 2. 2000 (Bill No. 11/2000 published on 22. 2. 2000)
Date of Second and Third Readings : 17. 3. 2000
Date of commencement : 1. 4. 2000

6. Act 10 of 2002—Animals and Birds (Amendment) Act 2002

Date of First Reading : 3. 4. 2002 (Bill No. 2/2002 published on 4. 4. 2002)
Date of Second and Third Readings : 8. 7. 2002
Date of commencement : 15. 9. 2002

Comparative table

The following provisions in the 1985 Revised Edition of the Animals and Birds Act have been renumbered by the Law Revision Commissioners in this 2002 Revised Edition.

This Comparative Table is provided for the convenience of users. It is not part of the Animals and Birds Act.

(Delete)

动物与禽鸟进口规则

（动物及禽鸟法（第7章））

为践行动物与禽鸟法第7条（1)(b）款规定，国家发展部制定本规则：

引证和施行时间

1. 本规则可称为动物与禽鸟进口规则（2009版），并于2009年4月1日开始施行。

释义

2. 除非文中另有规定，在本规则中：

动物或禽鸟肢体及产品　　指动物尸体、精液、饲料、废弃物、动物或禽鸟的粪便或产品，或者可能携带或散播疫病的物品或材料。

转口　　指在车辆、飞机或船舶等运输工具间转移货物，用于出口。

进口禁令

3.（1）须遵循本条（2）款和第4条规定外，否则禁止从其他任何国家或地区向新加坡输入或转口动物或禽鸟以及其肢体或产品。

（2）附表第一栏所列动物或禽鸟肢体及产品，遵从于第四栏和局长认可的其他限制，可进口或转口的相关出口国或地区列于第二栏，进口或转口用途列于第三栏。

无条件进口

4. 局长可自行强加要求，同意满足条件的任何国家或地区的动物或禽鸟以及其肢体或产品（即使不列明于附表第一栏中）进口或转口至新加坡，且不论用途。

废止

5. 本规范施行开始起，废止执行动物与禽鸟进口规则（01版）。

保留规定

6. 依据已被废止的动物与禽鸟进口规则（01版）签署的进口证书或通行证，如果在本规范开始施行时仍有效的，将继续认可其符合本规则，可以使用直至有效期满。

附表

对应第 3 条（2）款和第 4 条

进口或转口动物或禽鸟肢体或产品进入新加坡

<table>
<tr><th>第一栏</th><th>第二栏</th><th>第三栏</th><th>第四栏</th></tr>
<tr><td>动物或禽鸟肢体及产品</td><td>进口或转口货物来源国家或地区</td><td>用途</td><td>限制</td></tr>
<tr><td>1. 动物精液</td><td>任何国家或地区</td><td>人工授精</td><td rowspan="5">（a）进口或转口这些物品前，须获得局长签发的每批货物的通行证。
（b）每次托运均要附带有：
（i）有相应能力的原产地政府兽医主管当局签发的检疫证书；或者
（ii）局长要求的其他文件。
（c）每批货物均要遵从局长决定开展的检查、采样和检测</td></tr>
<tr><td>2. 含动物源成分的肥料</td><td>任何国家或地区</td><td>肥料</td></tr>
<tr><td>3. 含动物源成分的饲料</td><td>任何国家或地区</td><td>饲料</td></tr>
<tr><td>4. 临床和病理标本</td><td>任何国家或地区</td><td>实验室诊断、检测或研究和技术开发</td></tr>
<tr><td>5. 动物尸体</td><td>任何国家或地区</td><td>任何用途</td></tr>
</table>

2009 年 3 月 9 日制定此规范。

TAN TEE HOW
常务秘书
新加坡国家发展部

Animals and birds (importation) order 2009

(Animals and birds ACT
(Chapter 7))

The Schedule

In exercise of the powers conferred by section 7 (1) (b) of the Animals and Birds Act, the Minister for National Development hereby makes the following Order:

Citation and commencement

1. This Order may be cited as the Animals and Birds (Importation) Order 2009 and shall come into operation on 1st April 2009.

Definitions

2. In this Order, unless the context otherwise requires—

animal or bird part or product means any carcase, semen, fodder, litter, dung or any product of animals or birds, or any article or substance that is likely to convey or spread any disease;

tranship means to remove goods from one vehicle, aircraft or ship to another for the purpose of export.

Prohibition of importation

3. (1) Except as provided in sub – paragraph (2) and paragraph 4, no person shall import or tranship any animal or bird part or product from any country or place.

(2) The animal or bird part or product specified in the first column of the Schedule may, subject to the restrictions specified in the fourth column and any other restrictions which the Director – General may think fit to impose, be imported or transhipped from the countries or places specified in the second column, for the purposes specified in the third column of that Schedule.

Discretionary imports

4. The Director – General may permit the importation or transhipment into Singapore of any animal or bird part or product (other than those specified in the first column of the Schedule) from any country or place for any purpose, subject to such conditions as he may think fit to impose.

Revocation

5. The Animals and Birds (Importation) Order (01) is revoked.

Savings

6. Any import certificate or import permit issued under the revoked Animals and Birds (Importation) Order and which is valid immediately before the date of commencement of this Order shall be deemed to be an import permit issued under this Order and shall subsist until its expiry.

The schedule

Paragraphs 3（2） and 4

Importaton or transhipment of animal or bird part or product into singapore

First column	*Second column*	*Third column*	*Fourth column*
Animal or bird part or product	*Country or place from which animal or bird part or product may be imported or transhipped*	*Purpose*	*Restrictions*
1. Animal semen	Any country or place	Artificial insemination	（a） Each consignment shall be in accordance with a permit issued by the Director – General, permitting the importation or transhipment of such animal or bird part or product. （b） Each consignment shall be accompanied by— （i） a certificate signed by a competent veterinary authority of the government of the country of origin attesting to the condition of the animal or bird part or product; or （ii） such other document as required by the Director – General. （c） Each consignment may be subjected to inspection, sampling and testing as the Director – General may determine
2. Fertiliser containing any animal product	Any country or place	Fertiliser	
3. Animal feed containing any animal product	Any country or place	Animal feed	
4. Clinical and pathological specimen	Any country or place	Laboratory diagnosis, tests, or research and development	
5. Carcase	Any country or place	Any purpose	

Made this 9th day of March 2009.

TAN TEE HOW
Permanent Secretary,
Ministry of National Development, Singapore.

动物与禽鸟疫病公告

（动物与禽鸟法第7章第2条“疫病”定义）

［2002年9月15日发布］

引证

1. 本公告可称为动物与禽鸟疫病公告。

公告的疫病

2. 附表中所列疫病现公告于此，用作动物与禽鸟法中疫病的定义。

附　　表

1. 非洲马瘟
2. 非洲猪瘟
3. 炭疽
4. 伪狂犬病
5. 禽传染性支气管炎
6. 禽传染性喉气管炎
7. 禽支原体感染，包括鸡毒支原体和滑液支原体
8. 禽鼻气管炎
9. 气肿疽（黑腿病）
10. 蓝舌病
11. 牛边虫病
12. 牛焦虫病
13. 牛布鲁氏杆菌病
14. 牛生殖道弯曲菌病
15. 牛恶性卡他
16. 牛海绵状脑病
17. 牛肺结核
18. 山羊关节炎－脑炎
19. 山羊/绵羊布鲁氏杆菌病
20. 传染性无乳症
21. 传染性牛胸膜肺炎
22. 传染性山羊胸膜肺炎
23. 传染性马子宫炎
24. 猪和猪源囊虫病
25. 嗜皮菌病
26. 马媾疫
27. 鸭病毒性肠炎（鸭瘟）
28. 鸭病毒性肝炎
29. 埃博拉病毒感染

30. 棘球蚴/包虫病
31. 流行性牛白血病
32. 流行性淋巴管炎
32A. 流行性溃疡综合征
33. 流行性脑脊髓炎
34. 马器质性脑病
35. 马传染性贫血
36. 马流感
37. 马焦虫病
38. 马病毒性流产
39. 马病毒性动脉炎
40. 埃希氏大肠杆菌 O157：H7 型
41. 口蹄疫
42. 禽霍乱
43. 真性鸡瘟（禽流感）
44. 禽痘
45. 禽伤寒（沙门氏菌感染）
46. 盖塔病毒感染
47. 马鼻疽（马慢性致命性放线菌病）
48. 多杀性巴氏杆菌病
49. 汉坦病毒病
50. 心水病
51. 亨德拉病毒感染
52. 马疥癣
53. 马痘
54. 传染性牛鼻气管炎
55. 传染性法氏囊病（甘波罗病）
56. 日本 B 型脑炎
56A. 鲤鱼疱疹病毒
57. 利什曼病
58. 细螺旋体病
59. 李氏杆菌病
60. 牛结节性皮疹
61. 莱姆病
62. 淋巴球性脉络丛脑膜炎病毒感染
63. 狂犬病毒脑炎
64. 梅迪 - 维斯纳病毒感染
65. 马尔堡病
66. 马立克氏病
67. 类鼻疽
68. 曼拉角病
69. 墨累山谷脑炎
70. 多发黏液瘤病

71. 内罗毕羊病
72. 新大陆螺旋蝇（食人蝇）
73. 新城疫
74. 尼帕病毒病
75. 旧大陆螺旋蝇蛆病（倍赞氏金蝇）
76. 绵羊肺腺瘤病
77. 副结核
78. 小反刍兽疫
79. 猪布鲁氏杆菌病
80. 鹦鹉热（鸟疫）
81. 鸡白痢
82. Q 热
83. 兔出血症
84. 狂犬病
84A. 真鲷虹彩病毒病
85. 裂谷热
86. 牛瘟
87. 牛流产沙门氏菌病
88. 沙门氏菌性肠炎
89. 羊痒病
90. 仙台病毒感染
91. 羊痘/山羊痘
92. 猴 B 病毒感染
92A. 鲤春病毒血症
93. 腺疫
94. 苏拉病
95. 猪丹毒
96. 猪瘟
97. 猪水疱病
98. 泰勒虫病
99. 弓形虫病
100. 传染性海绵状脑病
101. 旋毛虫病
102. 毛滴虫症
103. 锥虫病
104. 土拉菌病
105. 溃疡性淋巴炎
106. 水泡性口炎
106A. 白点病
107. 黄热病

［2002 年公告号：S 479］

Animals and birds (disease) notification

(Animals and birds ACT Chapter7, Definition of "disease" in section 2)

[15th September 2002]

Citation

1. This Notification may be cited as the Animals and Birds (Disease) Notification.

Declared diseases

2. The diseases set out in the Schedule are declared to be diseases within the meaning of the Act.

THE SCHEDULE

1. African horse sickness
2. African swine fever
3. Anthrax
4. Aujeszky's disease
5. Avian infectious bronchitis
6. Avian infectious laryngotracheitis
7. Avian mycoplasmosis caused by M gallisepticum and M synoviae
8. Avian tuberculosis
9. Black quarter (blackleg)
10. Bluetongue
11. Bovine anaplasmosis
12. Bovine babesiosis
13. Bovine brucellosis
14. Bovine genital campylobacteriosis
15. Bovine malignant catarrh
16. Bovine spongiform encephalopathy
17. Bovine tuberculosis
18. Caprine arthritis/encephalitis
19. Caprine/ovine brucellosis
20. Contagious agalactia
21. Contagious bovine pleuropneumonia
22. Contagious caprine pleuropneumonia
23. Contagious equine metritis
24. Cysticercosis of bovine and porcine origin
25. Dermatophilosis
26. Dourine
27. Duck virus enteritis (duck plague)

28. Duck virus hepatitis
29. Ebola disease
30. Echinococcosis/hydatidosis
31. Enzootic bovine leucosis
32. Epizootic lymphangitis
32A. Epizootic ulcerative syndrome
33. Equine encephalomyelitis
34. Equine encephalosis
35. Equine infectious anaemia
36. Equine influenza
37. Equine piroplasmosis
38. Equine rhinopneumonitis
39. Equine viral arteritis
40. Escherichia coli O157：H7
41. Foot – and – mouth disease
42. Fowl cholera
43. Fowl plague （avian influenza）
44. Fowl pox
45. Fowl typhoid （Salmonella gallinarum）
46. Getah virus disease
47. Glanders （Farcy）
48. Haemorrhagic septicaemia
49. Hanta virus disease
50. Heartwater
51. Hendra virus disease
52. Horse mange
53. Horse pox
54. Infectious bovine rhinotracheitis
55. Infectious bursal disease （Gumboro disease）
56. Japanese B encephalitis
56A. Koi herpesvirus
57. Leishmaniosis
58. Leptospirosis
59. Listeriosis
60. Lumpy skin disease
61. Lyme disease
62. Lymphocytic choriomenigitis
63. Lyssa encephalitis
64. Maedi – visna
65. Marburg disease
66. Marek's disease
67. Melioidosis
68. Menangle virus disease

69. Murray Valley Encephalitis
70. Myxomatosis
71. Nairobi sheep disease
72. New World screwworm (Cochliomyia hominivorax)
73. Newcastle disease
74. Nipah virus disease
75. Old World screwworm (Chrysomya bezziana)
76. Ovine pulmonary adenomatosis
77. Paratuberculosis
78. Peste des petits ruminants
79. Porcine brucellosis
80. Psittacosis (ornithosis)
81. Pullorum disease
82. Q fever
83. Rabbit haemorrhagic disease
84. Rabies
84A. Red sea bream iridoviral disease
85. Rift Valley fever
86. Rinderpest
87. Salmonellosis caused by S. abortusovis
88. Salmonellosis caused by Salmonella enteritidis
89. Scrapie
90. Sendai virus infection
91. Sheep pox/goat pox
92. Simian B Herpes virus
92A. Spring viraemia of carp
93. Strangles
94. Surra
95. Swine erysipelas
96. Swine fever
97. Swine vesicular disease
98. Theileriosis
99. Toxoplasmosis
100. Transmissible spongiform encephalopathies
101. Trichinellosis
102. Trichomonosis
103. Trypanosomiasis
104. Tularaemia
105. Ulcerative lyamphangitis
106. Vesicular stomatitis
106A. White spot disease
107. Yellow Fever.

[*G. N. No. S* 479/2002]

印度尼西亚

印度尼西亚进口新鲜蔬果采取植物检疫措施的条例

（2012 年第 42 号农业部条例
2012 年 6 月第 140 号植物类农业部长令）

鉴于：

a. 2006 年第 37 号农业部条例/2006 年 1 月第 60 号决定、2011 年第 89 号农业部条例/2011 年 12 月第 140 号植物类农业部长令、2012 年第 15 号农业部条例/2011 年 3 月第 140 号植物类农业部长令中已对印度尼西亚进口新鲜蔬果应具备的技术条件和采取的植物检疫措施进行了相应规定；

b. 随着植物有害生物检疫科学技术水平的发展，2006 年第 37 号农业部条例/2006 年 1 月第 60 号决定、2011 年第 89 号农业部条例/2011 年 12 月第 140 号植物类农业部长令和 2012 年第 15 号农业部条例/2011 年 3 月第 140 号植物类农业部长令中的部分条款已不再适用；

c. 根据上述两条所述，需要针对进口到印度尼西亚的新鲜蔬果出台新的植物检疫条例。

根据：

1. 1992 年第 16 号法令《动植物检疫法》，公布于 1992 年第 56 号国家公报，第 3482 号国家公报增补；

2. 1994 年第 7 号法令《关于世界贸易组织成立的决定》，公布于 1994 年第 57 号公报，印度尼西亚共和国第 35 号国家公报增补；

3. 1996 年第 7 号法令《粮食法》，公布于 1996 年第 99 号国家公报，印度尼西亚共和国第 3817 号国家公报增补；

4. 2010 年第 13 号法令《园艺法》，公布于 2010 年第 132 号国家公报，印度尼西亚共和国第 5170 号国家公报增补；

5. 2002 年第 14 号政府令《植物检疫令》，公布于 2002 年第 35 号国家公报，印度尼西亚共和国第 4196 号国家公报增补；

6. 2004 年第 28 号政府条例（食品的安全、质量与营养条例，公布于印度尼西亚共和国 2004 年第 107 号国家公报，印度尼西亚共和国第 4424 号国家公报增补）；

7. 1977 年第 2 号总统令和 1990 年第 45 号总统令（针对 1951 年国际植物保护大会的修改案）；

8. 1992 年第 58 号总统令（关于成立亚洲植物保护大会的决定）；

9. 2009 年第 47 号总统条例（关于国家部委的设立和组织机构的条例）；

10. 2009 年第 84 号总统令（建立统一的内阁二号令）；

11. 2010 年第 24 号总统条例（国家部委的地位、任务、功能、梯队建设和组织结构条例）；

12. 农业部第 22 号条例（农业检疫技术工具使用规范）/2008 年 4 月第 140 号植物类农业部长令；

13. 2009 年第 9 号农业部条例（关于对进入印度尼西亚的植物有害生物传播媒介的检疫措施的条例，公布于印度尼西亚共和国 2009 年第 35 号国家公报上）/2019 年 2 月第 140 号植物类农业部长令；

14. 2010 年第 61 号农业部条例（农业部组织机构条例）/2010 年 10 月第 140 号植物类农业部长令；

15. 2011 年第 88 号农业部条例（关于对植物类新鲜食品进出口安全管控的条例，公布于 2011 年第 842 号国家公报上）/2011 年 12 月第 340 号政府条例农业部长令；

16. 2011 年第 93 号农业部条例（植物有害生物种类条例，公布于印度尼西亚共和国 2012 年第 6 号国家公报上）/2011 年 12 月第 140 号植物类农业部长令；

17. 2011 年第 94 号农业部条例（关于植物有害生物传播媒介出现的地点的条例，公布于印度尼西亚共和国 2012 年第 7 号国家公报上）/2011 年 12 月第 140 号植物类农业部长令。

参照：

1. WTO 2005 年 5 月 18 日的通报 G/SPS/N/IDN/24；

2. WTO 2012 年 5 月 7 日的通报 G/SPS/N/IDN/46。

特决定：

制定：农业部条例（关于印度尼西亚进口新鲜蔬菜和水果所采取的植物检验检疫措施的条例）。

第一章 总　　则

第一条

下列术语在本条例中做如下定义：

1. 新鲜蔬菜和水果是指种植收获后的植物制品，制品尚未加工，且有可能成为植物有害生物的传播媒介。

2. 植物有害生物检疫是指针对印度尼西亚农业部确定的有害生物采取的防止进入印度尼西亚并传播有害生物的措施。

3. 植物检疫证书是指农产品出口国或者中转国当局出具的免检证书、符合条件证书以及说明其他有用信息的证书。

4. 进口港是指当局确认的为进口新鲜蔬果而设定的海港、河港、渡口、机场、邮局、路上边境口岸等，且这些港口有可能成为植物有害生物进入印度尼西亚的场所。

5. 植物检疫人员是指根据法律规定专职于植物检疫工作的国家公务人员。

6. 新鲜蔬果所有人或者代理人是指对新鲜蔬果进口承担责任的自然人或法人代表。

第二条

1. 此条例是新鲜蔬果进入印度尼西亚并进行相关检疫工作的依据。

2. 制定此条例是为了防止植物有害生物进入印度尼西亚，满足植物类食品的安全标准。

第三条

该条例的内容包含植物检疫措施和对进口口岸的确定。

第四条

1. 无论是植物有害生物疫区还是非疫区，均可从其地区进口新鲜蔬果。

2. 第四条第 1 款中所述的非疫区需由农业检疫局局长确定，并通过农业部条例的形式发布。

3. 第四条第 2 款中所述的非疫区的确定应按照法律规定办理。

第五条

1. 第四条中所述从非疫区进口新鲜蔬果必须满足相关技术条件。

2. 第五条第 1 款中所述的技术条件是指针对蔬菜和水果采取的相应检疫措施。

3. 第五条第 2 款中所述的措施是为了防止新鲜蔬果植物有害生物疫情的发生。

第六条

附件中提及的新鲜蔬果的种类、有害生物和措施等应视作本规定的一部分，不可分开。

第七条

1. 第四条所述的新鲜蔬果进口除应满足第五条所述的相关技术条件外，还应满足植物类新鲜蔬果食品安全要求。

2. 第七条第 1 款所述的植物类新鲜蔬果食品安全要求需要依据相关法律规定办理。

第二章 植物检疫措施

第八条

1. 新鲜蔬果进口印度尼西亚需满足下列条件：

a. 出具出口国和中转国的植物卫生证书。

b. 从政府确定的进口港进口。

c. 将进口情况报告给检疫人员，提交待进口货物，以满足植物检疫工作开展的需要。

2. 第八条第一款 a 中所述的植物卫生证书需表明下列情况之一：

a. 进口的新鲜蔬果来源于非疫区。

b. 出口国已对该产品进行植物检疫。

3. 如果出现第八条第 2 款 a 中的情况，即进口的新鲜蔬果来源于非疫区，此类情况需要在附件补充声明栏中体现出来。

4. 如果出现第八条第 2 款 b 中的情况，即进口的新鲜蔬果来源于有害生物疫区，此类情况则需要在检疫措施栏中体现出来。

第九条

1. 新鲜蔬果的所有人或代理人有义务在进口港向检疫人员打报告，并提交进口蔬果。

2. 第九条第一款中所述的报告需最晚于新鲜蔬果到达进口港时提交，并提供所需的相应文件。

第十条

1. 检疫人员对提交的报告进行行政检查，以保证报告信息的完整性、真实性和合法性。

2. 在对植物卫生证书进行第十条第一款所述的行政检查时，如出现下列情况之一，将不允许进口该批次的新鲜蔬果。

a. 声称产品来源于非疫区，但在提交的报告中没有附上出口国开具的非疫区情况说明。

b. 产品来源于疫区，但在提交的报告中没有附上已经进行过植物检疫的报告。

第十一条

在进行第十条所述的行政检查时，

1. 如果提交资料不齐全，则对进口产品进行扣押。

2. 如果提交资料完整、真实、合法，则可进行卫生检疫。

第十二条

1. 第十一条中所述的卫生检疫是指检查进口的新鲜蔬果的植物有害生物和产品情况。

2. 在进行第十一条第 1 款中所述的卫生检疫时。

a. 如发现产品有第一类植物有害生物、腐烂、损毁等情况，应对产品进行销毁。

b. 如发现产品有第二类植物有害生物，应根据情况采取响应措施。

c. 如没有发现产品有植物有害生物，则可进行通关。

3. 只有满足植物类食品安全相关的法律要求，才能对进口蔬果进行第十二条第 2 款 b 小点中所示之通关。

第十三条

第十一条和第十二条中所述的行政检查、卫生检疫、扣押、拒绝、措施、销毁和通关等行为，均需按照相关法律规定要求执行。

第三章 进境口岸

第十四条

1. 第八条第 1 款 b 小点中所述的进境口岸，是政府批准的进口新鲜蔬果的港口，包括有：

a. 泗水丹戎佩拉海港；

b. 棉兰巴拉湾机场；

c. 雅加达苏加诺－哈达机场；

d. 望加锡苏加诺－哈达海港。

2. 除了第十四条第一款中提及的进境口岸之外，根据相关法律规定，自由商业地区和自由港口地区也可作为进口新鲜蔬果的进境口岸。

3. 如果从第十四条第2款所述的自由商业地区和自由港口地区进口新鲜蔬果，则该新鲜蔬果只能用于当地内需，不允许将其在自由商业地区和自由港口地区之外的地方流通。

4. 从非疫区进口新鲜蔬果或者从与印度尼西亚采取相同食品安全体系的国家进口新鲜蔬果，不适用进境口岸相关规定。

第四章　变更条例

第十五条

本条例出台之前所确立的非疫区，只要与现行规定没有冲突，仍可视为非疫区。

第五章　最终条款

第十六条

在本条例实施之后，2006年第37号农业部条例/2006年1月第60号决定、2011年第89号农业部条例/2011年12月第140号植物类农业部长令和2012年第15号农业部条例/2011年3月第140号植物类农业部长令即刻废止。

第十七条

本条例自2012年6月19日开始实施。

为使本条例公之于众，本条例将通过印度尼西亚共和国国家公报公布。

2012年6月13日于雅加达制定

农业部部长：**苏西沃诺（SUSWONO）**

农业部条例附件①

编号：42/2012年6月/植物类第140号/农业部长令

日期：2012年6月13日

蔬果种类、有害生物传播地区及处理措施

编号	蔬果名称	植物有害生物	传播地区	处理措施
14	桔子 柑橘属	蜜柑大实蝇；双翅目：实蝇科；蜜柑大实蝇	亚洲：中国、日本、越南	1. 冷处理：2～3℃/16～18d或 2. 熏蒸法：使用纯溴甲烷4磅/1000立方英尺/21℃/2小时或是 3. 辐射灭菌法：150戈瑞

① （注：只翻译了与中国有关的部分内容）

续表

编号	蔬果名称	植物有害生物	传播地区	处理措施
22	南瓜 南瓜属	基尔基实蝇；双翅目：实蝇科；果蝇	亚洲：中国台湾、日本、朝鲜半岛	1. 冷处理：2～3℃/16～20d 或 2. 熏蒸法：使用纯溴甲烷 4 磅/1000 立方英尺/21℃/2 小时或 3. 辐射灭菌法：150 戈瑞
33	香蕉 芭蕉属	蜜柑大实蝇；双翅目：实蝇科；蜜柑大实蝇	亚洲：中国、日本、越南	1. 冷处理：2～3℃/16～20d 或 2. 熏蒸法：使用纯溴甲烷 4 磅/1000 立方英尺/21℃/2 小时或是 3. 蒸汽法：46℃/10 分钟或 4. 辐射灭菌法：150 戈瑞
40	黄瓜及其他葫芦科作物	瓜实蝇；双翅目：实蝇科；果蝇	亚洲：中国台湾、日本、朝鲜半岛	1. 冷处理：2～3℃/16～20d 或 2. 熏蒸法：使用纯溴甲烷 4 磅/1000 立方英尺/21℃/2 小时或 3. 蒸汽法：44℃/360 分钟或 4. 辐射灭菌法：150 戈瑞

Plant quarantine measures for importation of fresh fruits and fresh fruit vegetables into the territory of the Republic of Indonesia in the mercy of the great unity, god minister of Agriculture

(The regulation of minister of Agriculture number: 42/Permentan/OT. 140/6/2012)

Considering:

a. that under the Regulation of Minister of Agriculture Number: 37/Kpts/HK. 060/1/2006, the Regulation of Minister Number 89/Permentan/OT. 140/12/2011 and the Regulation of Minister of Agriculture Number 15/Permentan/OT. 140/3/2012, the technical requirements and Plant Quarantine Measures for importation of Fresh Fruits and/or vegetables into the Territory of the Republic of Indonesia have been established;

b. that in the development of science and technology in the sector of plant quarantine for treatment of the plant pest organism carriers which are free of fruitflies, then the Regulation of Minister of Agriculture Number 37/Kpts/HK. 060/1/2006, the Regulation of Minister of Agriculture Number 89/Permentan/OT. 140/12/2011 and the Regulation of Minister of Agriculture Number 15/Permentan/OT. 140/3/2012 shall be no longer appropriate;

c. that based on the aforesaid matters, it is necessary to regulate Plant Quarantine Measures for Importation of Fresh Fruits and Fresh Fruit Vegetables into the Territory of The Republic of Indonesia.

In view of:

1. The Laws Number 16 of 1992 on Animal, Fish and Plant Quarantines (The State Gazette of the Republic of Indonesia Number 56 of 1992, the Additional State Gazette of the Republic of Indonesia Number 3482);

2. The Laws Number 7 of 1994 on Ratification for Agreement of Establishing The World Trade Organization (The State Gazette of the Republic of Indonesia Number 57 of 1994, the Additional State Gazette of the Republic of Indonesia Number 35);

3. The Laws Number 7 of 1996 on Food (The State Gazette of the Republic of Indonesia Number 99 of 1996, the Additional State Gazette of the Republic of Indonesia Number: 3817);

4. The Laws Number 13 of 2010 on Horticulture (The State Gazette of the Republic of Indonesia Number 132 of 2010, the Additional State Gazette of the Republic of Indonesia Number: 5170);

5. The Laws Number 14 of 2002 on Plant Quarantine (The State Gazette of the Republic of Indonesia Number 35 of 2002, the Additional State Gazette of the Republic of Indonesia Number 4196);

6. The Government Regulation Number 28 of 2004 on Food Security, Quality and Nutrient (The State Gazette of the Republic of Indonesia Number 107 of 2004, the Additional State Gazette of the Republic of Indonesia Number 4424);

7. The Presidential Decree Number 2 of 1977 connected with the Presidential Decree Number 45 of 1990 on Ratification for International Plant Protection Convention 1951;

8. The Presidential Decree Number 58 of 1992 on Ratification for Asian Plant Protection Convention;

9. The Presidential Regulation Number 47 of 2009 on Formation and Organization of State Ministry;

10. The Presidential Decree Number 84/P of 2009 on Formation of United Indonesian Cabinet II;

11. The Presidential Regulation Number 24 of 2010 on Position, Rule and Function of State Ministry, and Organizational Structure, Rule and Function of Echelon I;

12. The Regulation of Minister of Agriculture Number 22/Permentan/OT. 140/OT. 140/4/2008 on Organization and Work System of Technical Executive Unit for Agricultural Quarantine;

13. The Regulation of Minister of Agriculture Number 09/Permentan/OT. 140/2/2009 on Requirement and Procedure of Plant Quarantine Measures for Importation of Quarantined Plant Pest Organism Carriers Into The Territory of The Republic of Indonesia (The State Gazette of the Republic of Indonesia Number 35 of 2009);

14. The Regulation of Minister of Agriculture Number 61/Permentan/OT. 140/10/2010 on Organization and Work System of the Ministry of Agriculture;

15. The Regulation of Minister of Agriculture Number 88/Permentan/PP. 340/12/2011 on Food Safety Control Against Importation and Exportation of Fresh Food of Plant Origin (The State Gazette of The Republic of Indonesia of 2011 Number 842);

16. The Regulation of Minister of Agriculture Number 93/Permentan/OT. 140/12/2011 on Type of Quarantined Plant Pest Organism (The State Gazette of the Republic of Indonesia Number 6 of 2012);

17. The Regulation of Minister of Agriculture Number 94/Permentan/OT. 140/12/2011 on Entry and Exit Points for Carriers of Quarantined Plant Pest Organism (The State Gazette of the Republic of Indonesia Number 7 of 2012).

Taking Note of:

1. WTO's Notification Number G/SPS/N/IDN/24 dated 18th May 2005;

2. WTO's Notification Number G/SPS/N/IDN/46 dated 7th May 2012.

Has decided:

To Stipulate: The regulation of minister of agriculture regarding plant quarantine measure for importation of fresh fruit and fresh fruit vegetable into the territory of the Republic of Indonesia.

Chapter I General term

Article 1

In this Regulation the following meanings:

1. Fresh Fruit or Fresh Fruit Vegetables is a fruit or vegetable crop in the form of fleshy fruit, either whole or its parts that have not been yet processed into manufactured materials, which are still potential as carriers of quarantined plant Pest Organisms.

2. Quarantined Plant Pest Organism, hereinafter referred to as OPTK, is all plant Pest Organisms specified by the Minister of Agriculture in order to be prevented for both their importation into and their spread within the territory of the Republic of Indonesia.

3. Phytosanitary certificates is a certificate issued by the competent authorities from the country of origin or country of transit stating Fresh Fruits or Fresh Fruit Vegetable are free of quarantined Plant Pest Organisms (OPTK) and have met the specified plant quarantine requirements and / or stating other necessary information.

4. Entry Points are seaports, river ports, crossing seaports, airports, post offices, border posts with other countries and other places as may be deemed necessary, designated as locations for importation of quarantined plant pest organism carriers.

5. Plant Quarantine Officer, hereinafter referred to as a Quarantine Officer, is a specific civil servant assigned to perform plant quarantine measures pursuant to the applicable laws and regulations.

6. Owner of Fresh Fruits and / or Fresh Fruit Vegetables or His Proxy, hereinafter referred to as the owner or his proxy, is a person or legal entity that owns and / or is responsible for importation of Fresh Fruits and / or Fresh Fruit Vegetables.

Article 2

1. This regulation is intended as a basis for importation of Fresh Fruits and Fresh Fruit Vegetables into the territory of the Republic of Indonesia and the Implementation of plant quarantine measures.

2. This regulation is aimed at preventing the entry of OPTK (Quarantined Plant Pest Organism), species of fruit flies into the territory of the Republic of Indonesia and complying with the fresh food safety of plant origin.

Article 3

The scope of this regulation shall include plant quarantine measures and entry points.

Article 4

1. The Fresh Fruits or Fresh Fruit Vegetables may be imported to the territory of the Republic of Indonesia from the production area in the country of origin that is free or not free of any fruit fly infestation.

2. The production area in the country of origin shall be free of any fruit fly infestation as referred to in paragraph (1), determined by the Chief of Agricultural Quarantine Agency on behalf of the Minister under a decree.

3. The procedure for the determination of a production area in the country of origin that is free of fruit fly infestation as referred to in paragraph (2) shall be made under the provisions of the applicable laws and regulation.

Article 5

1. In case, the importation of Fresh Fruits or Fresh Fruit Vegetables into the territory of the Republic of Indonesia as referred to in Article 4 is derived from the production area in the country of origin which is not free of fruit fly infestation, then it shall meet the technical requirements.

2. The technical requirements referred to in paragraph (1) shall be in the form of treatment measures according to the type of Fresh Fruits or Fresh Fruit Vegetables.

3. The treatment referred to in paragraph (2) is to prevent any infestation of fruit flies on Fresh Fruits or Fresh Fruit Vegetables.

Article 6

Types of Fresh Fruits or Fresh Fruit Vegetables, fruit flies, and treatment as listed in the appendix shall be as the inseparable parts of this Regulation.

Article 7

1. Importation of Fresh Fruits or Fresh Fruit Vegetables as defined in Article 4 in addition to meeting the technical requirements as referred to in Article 5 shall comply with the requirements of fresh food safety of plant origin.

2. The Food safety requirements referred to in paragraph (1) shall comply with the applicable laws and regulation on fresh food safety of plant origin.

Chapter Ⅱ Plant quarantine measures

Article 8

1. Any Fresh Fruit or Fresh Fruit Vegetable imported to the territory of the Republic of Indonesia shall:

a. be completed with a Phytosanitary Certificate issued by both the country of origin and the country of transit;

b. pass through the designated entry point; and

c. be reported and submitted to the Quarantine Officer at the entry point for purpose of a plant quarantine measure.

2. The Phytosanitary Certificate referred to in paragraph (1) letter a shall contain the following statements:

a. The Fresh Fruits or Fresh Fruit Vegetables are derived from the production area that is free of any fruit fly infestation, or

b. Treatment measures for Fresh Fruits or Fresh Fruit Vegetables have been already taken in the country of origin.

3. The statement referred to in paragraph (2) letter a, shall be obligated for importation of Fresh Fruits or Fresh Fruit Vegetables derived from the production area in the country of origin which is free of any fruit fly infestation, and shall be expressed in the additional declaration column.

4. The statement referred to in paragraph (2) letter b shall be obligated/mandatory for importation of the Fresh Fruits or Fresh Fruit Vegetables derived from the production area in the country of origin which is free of any fruit fly infestation, and shall be expressed in the treatment column.

Article 9

1. The owner or his proxy shall report and deliver the fresh fruits and / or Fresh Fruit Vegetables to the Quarantine Officer at the entry point.

2. The report referred to in paragraph (1) shall be made no later than the time when the Fresh Fruits and / or Fresh Fruit Vegetables arrive at the entry point, equipped with the required documents.

Article 10

1. The quarantine officer shall take an administrative examination on the required documents so as to find out the completeness, correctness and validity of document.

2. In case, the result of administrative examination on the Phytosanitary Certificate as referred to in paragraph (1), the Fresh Fruits or Fresh Fruit Vegetables are derived from the production area which is:

a. Free of, proven not to include a statement of which the products are from the production area in the country of origin which is free of any fruit fly infestation, or

b. not free of, proven not to include a statement of which a treatment measure has been taken;

It shall be rejected;

Article 11

In case, the result of administrative examination as referred to in Article 10 is proven:

a. incomplete, then a detention shall be made;

b. complete, valid and correct, a medical examination shall be taken.

Article 12

1. The medical examination referred to in Article 11 letter b shall be taken for detecting any possibility of pest organisms and to know the physical condition of Fresh Fruits or Fresh Fruit Vegetables.

2. In case, the result of medical examination referred to in paragraph (1) is proven:

a. Not free of clsss – I OPTK, rotten or damaged, the products shall be destroyed;

b. Not free of class – II, the products shall be treated; or

c. free of OPTK, deliverance shall be made.

3. The deliverance as referred to in paragraph (2) letter c, may be done if the Fresh Fruit or Fresh Fruit Vegetables have complied with the laws and regulations on fresh food safety of plant origin.

Article 13

The actions of administrative examination, medical examination, detention, denial, treatment, disposal and deliverance referred to in Article 10, Article 11 and Article 12

shall be carried out pursuant to the provisions of the applicable laws and regulations.

Chapter Ⅲ Entry points

Article 14

1. The Entry Points for Fresh Fruits and Fresh Fruit Vegetable referred to in Article 8 paragraph (1) letter b shall consist of:

a. Tanjung Perak Seaport, Surabaya;

b. Belawan Seaport, Medan;

c. Soekarno – Hatta Airport, Jakarta; and

d. Soekarno – Hatta Seaport, Makassar.

2. Besides the entry points referred to in paragraph (1), the entry points defined under the laws and regulations on Free Trade Zone and Free Port may be used as entry points for Fresh Fruits and Fresh Fruit Vegetables.

3. Importation of Fresh Fruits and Fresh Fruit Vegetables via the entry points referred to in paragraph (2) may be done only to meet the need of consumption and shall be prohibited from being distributed outside the Free Trade Zone and Free Ports.

4. The terms and conditions of entry point referred to in paragraph (1) shall not apply to any importation of the Fresh Fruits or Fresh Fruit Vegetables derived from the production area which is free of any fruit fly infestation in the country of origin as specified in Article 4, or in the countries whose food safety systems have been recognized.

Chapter Ⅳ Transitional provisions

Article 15

Any production area in the country of origin, which is free of any fruit fly infestation and has been defined before this Regulation is otherwise declared to remain applicable as long as it is not contrary to this Regulation.

Chapter Ⅴ Closing

Article 16

Upon enactment of this Regulation, then the Regulation of Minister of Agriculture No. 37/Kpts/HK. 060/1/2006, the Regulation of Minister of Agriculture No. 89/Permentan/OT. 140/12/2011 and the Regulation of Minister of Agriculture No. 15/Permentan/OT. 140/3 / 2012 shall be revoked and declared no longer effective.

Article 17

This Regulation shall take effect on 19th June 2012.

For public cognizance, this Ministerial Regulation shall be enacted by placing it in the State Gazette of the Republic of Indonesia.

Enacted in Jakarta
On 13th June 2012
MINISTER OF AGRICULTURE,
(Signed)
SUSWONO

Vegetable & Fruit species, pest spreading area and treatment measures

NO.	Vegetable and Fruit	Plant Pest	Spreading area	Treatment
14	(Orange), *Citrus* spp.	*Bactrocera tsuneonis* (Miyake); (= *Dacus cheni* = *D. tsuneonis* = *Tetradacus tsuneonis*); Diptera: Tephritidae; Japanese orange fly, citrus fruitfly	Asia: China, Japan, Vietnam	1. Cold Treatment: 2 ~ 3℃/16 ~ 18 days; or 2. Fumigation (CH3Br): 4 lb/1000 ft^3/21℃/2 hours; or 3. Irradiation: 150 gray
22	Pumpkin, *Cucurbita moschata*	*Bactrocera depressa* (Shiraki); (= *Bactrocera* (Paradacus) *depressa* = *B. depressus* = *Dacus depressus* = *Paradacus depressus* = *Zeugodacus depressus*); Diptera: Tephritidae; fruitfly	Asia: China Taiwan, Japan, Korea	1. Cold Treatment: 2 ~ 3℃/16 ~ 18 days; or 2. Fumigation (CH3Br): 4 lb/1000 ft^3/21℃/2 hours; or 3. Irradiation: 150 gray
33	(Banana) Musa spp.	*Bactrocera tsuneonis* (Miyake); (= *Dacus cheni* = *D. tsuneonis* = *Tetradacus tsuneonis*); Diptera: Tephritidae; Japanese orange fly, citrus fruitfly	Asia: China, Japan, Vietnam	1. Cold Treatment: 2 ~ 3℃/16 ~ 18 days; or 2. Fumigation (CH3Br): 4 lb/1000 ft^3/21℃/2 hours; or 3. Vapour Heat Treatment (VHT):46℃/10 minutes; 4. Irradiation: 150 gray
40	Mentimun dan kelompok Cucurbita lainnya Cucurbitaceae	*Bactrocera depressa* (Shiraki); (= *Bactrocera* (Paradacus) depressa = *B. depressus* = *Dacus depressus* = *Paradacus depressus* = *Zeugodacus* depressus); Diptera: Tephritidae; fruitfly	Asia: China Taiwan, Japan, Korea	1. Cold Treatment: 2 ~ 3℃/16 ~ 18 days; or 2. Fumigation (CH3Br): 4 lb/1000 ft^3/21℃/2 hours; or 3. Vapour Heat Treatment (VHT): 44℃/360 minutes; 4. Irradiation: 150 gray

印度尼西亚进口鳞茎类新鲜蔬菜采取检疫措施的条例

（第43号农业部条例，
2012年6月/植物类第140号/农业部长令）

鉴于：

1. 第18号农业部条例/2008年2月/植物类第140号/农业部长令，第90号农业部条例/2011年12月/植物类第140号/农业部长令和第16号农业部条例/2012年3月/植物类第140号/农业部长令已对印度尼西亚进口鳞茎类蔬菜的植物检疫条件和相应措施做出了规定；

2. 随着植物有害生物检疫科学技术水平的发展，第18号农业部条例/2008年2月/植物类第140号、第90号农业部条例/2011年12月/植物类第140号/农业部长令和第16号农业部条例/2012年3月/植物类第140号/农业部长令中的部分条款已不再适用；

3. 根据上述两条所述，需要针对进口到印度尼西亚的鳞茎类新鲜蔬菜出台新的植物检疫条例。

根据：

1. 1992年第16号法令《动植物检疫法》，公布于1992年第56号国家公报，第3482号国家公报增补；

2. 1994年第7号法令《关于世界贸易组织成立的决定》，公布于1994年第57号公报，印度尼西亚共和国第35号国家公报增补；

3. 1996年第7号法令《粮食法》，公布于1996年第99号国家公报，印度尼西亚共和国第3817号国家公报增补；

4. 2010年第13号法令《园艺法》，公布于2010年第132号国家公报，印度尼西亚共和国第5170号国家公报增补；

5. 2002年第14号政府令《植物检疫令》，公布于2002年第35号国家公报，印度尼西亚共和国第4196号国家公报增补；

6. 2004年第28号政府条例（食品的安全、质量与营养条例，公布于印度尼西亚共和国2004年第107号国家公报，印度尼西亚共和国第4424号国家公报增补；

7. 1977年第2号总统令和1990年第45号总统令（针对1951年国际植物保护大会的修改案）；

8. 1992年第58号总统令（关于成立亚洲植物保护大会的决定）；

9. 2009年第47号总统条例（关于国家部委的设立和组织机构的条例）；

10. 2009年第84号总统令（建立统一的内阁二号令）；

11. 2010年第24号总统条例（国家部委的地位、任务、功能、梯队建设和组织结构条例）；

12. 第22号农业部条例（农业检疫技术工具使用规范）/2008年4月/植物类第140号/农业部长令；

13. 第9号农业部条例（关于对进入印度尼西亚的植物有害生物传播媒介的检疫措施的条例，公布于印度尼西亚共和国2009年第35号国家公报上）/2009年2月/植物类第140号/农业部长令；

14. 第61号农业部条例（农业部组织机构条例）/2010年10月/植物类第140号/农业部长令；

15. 第88号农业部条例（关于对植物类新鲜食品进出口安全管控的条例，公布于2011年第842号国家公报上）/2011年12月/政府条例第340号/农业部长令；

16. 第93号农业部条例（植物有害生物种类条例，公布于印度尼西亚共和国2012年第6号国家公报上）/2011年12月/植物类第140号/农业部长令；

17. 第94号农业部条例（关于植物有害生物传播媒介出现的地点的条例，公布于印度尼西亚共和国2012年第7号国家公报上）/2011年12月/植物类第140号/农业部长令。

参照：

1. WTO 2007年10月26日的通报G/SPS/N/IDN/37；

2. WTO 2012年5月7日的通报G/SPS/N/IDN/47。

特决定

制定：第43号农业部条例（关于印度尼西亚进口鳞茎类新鲜蔬菜采取检疫措施的条例）

第一章　总　　则

下列术语在本条例中做如下释义：

1. 新鲜鳞茎类蔬菜（以下统称鳞茎类蔬菜）是指农作物有一部分为鳞茎形状的葱属植物，且该作物还未进行加工。

2. 植物有害生物检疫（即：OPTK）是指针对印度尼西亚农业部确定的有害生物进行的防止进入印度尼西亚并传播病虫害的措施。

3. 植物检疫证书（卫生证书）是指农产品出口国或者中转国官方出具的免检证书、符合条件证书以及说明其他有用信息的证书。

4. 进境口岸是指官方确认的为进口新鲜鳞茎类蔬菜而设定的海港、河港、渡口、机场、邮局、路上边境口岸等，且这些港口有可能成为植物有害生物进入印度尼西亚的场所。

5. 植物检疫人员是指根据法律规定专职于植物检疫工作的国家公务人员。

6. 鳞茎类植物所有人或者代理人是指对新鲜鳞茎类植物进口承担责任的自然人或法人代表。

第二条

1. 此条例为新鲜鳞茎类蔬菜进入印度尼西亚并进行相关检疫工作的依据。

2. 制定此条例是为了防止植物有害生物进入印度尼西亚，满足植物类食品安全标准。

第三条

该条例的内容包含植物检疫措施和对进境口岸的确定。

第二章　检疫条件

第四条

1. 无论是植物有害生物疫区还是非疫区，均可从其地区进口新鲜鳞茎类植物。

2. 第四条第一款所述的鳞茎类植物中不应掺杂其他物质，如植物的根、叶子、土块和肥料。

第五条

1. 第四条中所述的确定进口新鲜鳞茎类植物的非疫区必须经由检疫局局长同意，并以农业部条例的形式公布出来。

2. 第五条第一款中所述的非疫区的确立需按照法律相关规定执行。

第六条

1. 如第四条中所述的从疫区进口新鲜鳞茎类植物，应采用熏蒸法和辐射灭菌法进行处理。

2. 附件中提及的新鲜鳞茎类植物的种类、病虫害和措施等应视作本规定的一部分，不可随意分割。

第七条

1. 第四条和第六条中所述的进口新鲜鳞茎类植物需要满足植物类食品安全要求。

2. 第七条第一款中所述的满足植物类食品安全要求是指依据植物类食品安全相关法律要求执行。

第三章　植物检疫措施

第八条

1. 新鲜鳞茎类植物进口印度尼西亚需满足下列条件：

a. 出具出口国和中转国的植物卫生证书；

b. 从政府确定的进口港进口；

c. 将待进口货物情况报告并提交给检疫人员，以满足植物检疫工作开展的需要。

2. 第八条第一款 a 中所述的植物卫生证书需表明下列情况之一：

a. 进口的新鲜鳞茎类植物来源于非疫区；

b. 鳞茎类植物中不应掺杂其他物质，如植物的根、叶子、土块和肥料。

3. 如第八条第 1 款 a 中所述的从疫区进口新鲜鳞茎类植物，则需满足下列条件：

a. 已采用熏蒸法和辐射灭菌法进行处理；

b. 鳞茎类植物中不掺杂其他物质，如植物的根、叶子、土块和肥料。

4. 如出现第八条第 2 款和第八条第 3 款 b 中的情况，则需要在附件补充声明栏中体现出来。

5. 如果出现第八条第 3 款 a 中的情况，则需要在检疫措施栏中体现出来。

第九条

1. 新鲜鳞茎类植物的所有人或代理人有义务在进境口岸向检疫人员汇报，并提交鳞茎类植物。

2. 第九条第 1 款中所述的报告需最迟于新鲜鳞茎类植物到达进境口岸时提交，并提供所需的相应文件。

第十条

1. 检疫人员对提交的报告进行审查，以保证报告信息的完整性、真实性和合法性。

2. 在对植物卫生证书进行第十条第 1 款所述之行政检查时，如出现下列情况之一，将不允许进口该批次的新鲜鳞茎类植物。

a. 没有表明产品来源于非疫区，没有表明其不掺杂其他物质，如植物的根、叶子、土块和肥料；

b. 没有进行检疫措施，没有表明其不掺杂其他物质，如植物的根、叶子、土块和肥料。

第十一条

在进行第十条所述的行政检查时，

a. 如果提交资料不齐全，则对进口产品进行扣押；

b. 如果提交资料完整、真实、合法，则可进行卫生检疫

第十二条

1. 第十一条中所述的卫生检疫是指检查进口的新鲜鳞茎类植物的植物有害生物和产品情况。

2. 在进行第十一条第 1 款中所述的卫生检疫时，

a. 如发现产品有第一类植物有害生物、腐烂、损毁等情况，应对产品进行销毁；

b. 掺杂其他物质，如植物的根、叶子、土块和肥料，则不允许进口；

c. 如发现产品有第二类植物有害生物，应根据情况采取相应措施；

d. 如没有发现产品有植物有害生物，且不掺杂其他物质，如植物的根、叶子、土块和肥料，则可进行通关。

3. 只有满足植物类食品安全相关的法律要求，才能对进口鳞茎类植物进行第十二条第 2 款 d 中所示之通关。

第十三条

4. 第十条、第十一条和第十二条中所述的行政检查、卫生检疫、扣押、拒绝、措施、销毁和通关等行为，均需按照相关法律规定要求执行。

第四章 进 境 口 岸

第十四条

1. 第八条第 1 款 b 中所述的进境口岸是指政府批准的进口新鲜鳞茎类植物的港口，包括有：

a. 泗水丹戎佩拉海港；

b. 棉兰巴拉湾机场；

c. 雅加达苏加诺－哈达机场；

d. 望加锡苏加诺－哈达海港。

2. 除了第十四条第一款中提及的进境口岸之外，根据相关法律规定，自由商业地区和自由港口地区也可作为进口新鲜鳞茎类植物的进口港。

3. 如果从第十四条第 2 款所述之自由商业地区和自由港口地区进口新鲜鳞茎类植物，则该新鲜鳞茎类植物只能用于当地内需，不允许将其在自由商业地区和自由港口地区外的地方流通。

4. 从非疫区进口新鲜鳞茎类植物或者从与印度尼西亚采取相同食品安全体系的国家进口新鲜鳞茎类植物，不适用进境口岸相关规定。

第五章 最 终 条 款

第十五条

在本条例实施之后，第 18 号农业部条例/2008 年 2 月/植物类第 140 号/农业部长令、第 90 号农业部条例/2011 年 12 月/植物类第 140 号/农业部长令和第 16 号农业部条例/2012 年 3 月/植物类第 140 号/农业部长令即刻废止。

第十六条

本条例自 2012 年 6 月 19 日开始实施。

为使本条例公之于众，本条例将通过印度尼西亚共和国国家公报公布。

2012 年 6 月 13 日于雅加达制定

农业部部长：苏西沃诺（SUSWONO）

农业部条例附件[①]

编号：43/2012 年 6 月/ 植物类第 140 号/农业部长令

日期：2012 年 6 月 13 日

有害生物种类、鳞茎类植物、处理措施和来源国

I. 昆虫类

序号	有害生物种类	鳞茎类植物种类	处理措施	来源国
4	葱蝇；双翅目：花蝇科	洋葱、韭葱、大蒜和其他葱类	1. 熏蒸法：使用纯溴甲烷 a. $40g/m^3$/26～31℃/2h 或是 b. $32g/m^3$/32～35℃/2h 或是 c. $16g/m^3$/26～31℃/2h 或是 2. 辐射灭菌法：70 戈瑞	非洲：（略） 美洲：（略） 亚洲：亚美尼亚、中国、格鲁吉亚、印度、伊朗、伊拉克、以色列、日本、哈萨克斯坦、朝鲜半岛、蒙古、菲律宾、土耳其 欧洲：（略）

① （注：只翻译了与中国有关的部分内容。）

续表

序号	有害生物种类	鳞茎类植物种类	处理措施	来源国
5	疆夜蛾；鳞翅目：夜蛾科	洋葱	1. 熏蒸法：使用纯溴甲烷 a. $40g/m^3$/26 ~ 31℃/2h 或是 2. 辐射灭菌法：70 戈瑞	非洲：（略） 美洲：（略） 亚洲：亚美尼亚、中国、以色列、日本、斯里兰卡、叙利亚、土耳其 欧洲：（略）
Ⅱ. 线虫类				
1	芽叶线虫；滑刃线虫属：滑刃科	洋葱和大蒜	1. 熏蒸法：使用纯溴甲烷 a. $40g/m^3$/26 ~ 31℃/2h 或是 b. $32g/m^3$/32 ~ 35℃/2h 或是 c. $16g/m^3$/26 ~ 31℃/2h 或是 2. 辐射灭菌法：70 戈瑞	美洲：（略） 欧洲：（略） 亚洲：中国、印度、以色列、韩国、吉尔吉斯斯坦、日本、土耳其 大洋洲：（略）
3	马铃薯茎线虫	洋葱和大蒜	1. 熏蒸法：使用纯溴甲烷 a. $40g/m^3$/26 ~ 31℃/2h 或是 b. $32g/m^3$/32 ~ 35℃/2h 或是 c. $16g/m^3$/26 ~ 31℃/2h 或是 2. 辐射灭菌法：70 戈瑞	欧洲：（略） 亚洲：阿塞拜疆、中国、印度、伊朗、日本、哈萨克斯坦、韩国、吉尔吉斯斯坦、马来西亚、巴基斯坦、阿拉伯、塔吉克斯坦、土耳其 非洲：（略） 美洲：（略） 大洋洲：（略）
Ⅴ. 螨类				
1	麦长腿蜘蛛；叶螨科	大蒜和葱	1. 熏蒸法：使用纯溴甲烷 a. $40g/m^3$/26 ~ 31℃/2h 或是 b. $16g/m^3$/26 ~ 31℃/2h 或是 2. 辐射灭菌法：70 戈瑞	欧洲：（略） 亚洲：中国、印度、韩国 非洲：埃及 美洲：（略） 大洋洲：（略）

Plant quarantine measures for importation of fresh bulbs vegetables into the territory of the Republic of Indonesia

(Regulation of the Minister of Agriculture number 43/Permentan/OT. 140/6/2012)

By the grace of god almighty

The Minister of Agriculture of the Republic of Indonesia

Considering:

a. that Regulation of the Minister of Agriculture Number 18/Permentan/ OT. 140/2/2008 in conjunction with Regulation of the Minister of Agriculture Number 90/Permentan/OT. 140/12/2011 and Regulation of the Minister of Agriculture Number 16/Permentan/OT. 140/3/2012 established Technical Requirements and Plant Quarantine Measures for Importation of Products of Living Plants in the form of Fresh Bulbs into the Territory of the Republic of Indonesia;

b. that by development of science and technology in the plant quarantine field for treatment on the pest carrier of plants free from quarantine plant disturbing organism, Regulation of the Minister of Agriculture Number 18/Permentan/OT. 140/2/2008 in conjunction with Regulation of the Minister of Agriculture Number 90/Permentan/OT. 140/12/2011 and Regulation of the Minister of Agriculture Number 16/Permentan/OT. 140/3/2012 are no longer appropriate;

c. that based on above reasons, it is necessary to regulate Plant Quarantine Measures for the Entry of Fresh Bulbs into the Territory of the Republic of Indonesia.

In view of:

1. Law Number 16 Year 1992 concerning Animal, Fish and Plant Quarantine (State Gazette of the Republic of Indonesia Year 1992 Number 56, Addendum Number 3482);

2. Law Number 7 Year 1994 concerning Ratification of Agreement Establishing The World Trade Organization (State Gazette of the Republic of Indonesia Year 1994 Number 57, Addendum Number 35);

3. Law Number 7 Year 1996 concerning Food (State Gazette of the Republic of Indonesia Year 1996 Number 99, Addendum Number 3817);

4. Law Number 13 Year 2010 concerning Horticulture (State Gazette of the Republic of Indonesia Year 2010 Number 132, Addendum Number 5170);

5. Government Regulation Number 14 Year 2002 concerning Plant Quarantine (State Gazette of the Republic of Indonesia Year 2002 Number 35, Addendum Number 4196);

6. Government Regulation Number 28 Year 2004 concerning Food Safety, Quality and Nutrition (State Gazette of the Republic of Indonesia Year 2004 Number 107, Addendum Number 4424);

7. Presidential Decree Number 2 Year 1977 in conjunction with Presidential Decree Number 45 Year 1990 concerning Ratification of International Plant Protection Convention 1951;

8. Presidential Decree Number 58 Year 1992 concerning Ratification of Asian Plant Protection Convention;

9. Presidential Regulation Number 47 Year 2009 concerning Establishment and Organization of State Ministries;

10. Presidential Decree Number 84/P Year 2009 concerning Establishment of United Indonesia Cabinet II;

11. Presidential Regulation Number 24 Year 2010 concerning the Positions, Duties, and Functions of State Ministries, as well as Organization Structure, Tasks, and Function of Echelon I;

12. Regulation of the Minister of Agriculture Number 22/Permentan/OT. 140/4/2008 concerning Organization and Work Procedure of Technical Implementation Unit of Agriculture Quarantine;

13. Regulation of the Minister of Agriculture Number 09/Permentan/OT. 140/2/2009 concerning Requirements and Procedures of Plant Quarantine Action on Importation of Quarantine Plant Pest Carrier into Territory of the Republic of Indonesia (State Gazette of the Republic of Indonesia Year 2009 Number 35);

14. Regulation of the Minister of Agriculture Number 61/Permentan/OT. 140/10/2010 concerning Organization and Work Procedure of Ministry of Agriculture;

15. Regulation of the Minister of Agriculture Number 88/Permentan/PP. 340/12/2011 concerning Food Safety Control on the Importation and Exportation of Fresh Fruit of Plants Origin (State Gazette of the Republic of Indonesia Year 2011 Number 842);

16. Regulation of the Minister of Agriculture Number 93/Permentan/OT. 140/12/2011 concerning Types of Quarantine Plants Pest (State Gazette of the Republic of Indonesia Year 2012 Number 6);

17. Regulation of the Minister of Agriculture Number 94/Permentan/OT. 140/12/2011 concerning Importation and Exportation Points of Quarantine Plants Pest Carrier (State Gazette of the Republic of Indonesia Year 2012 Number 7).

Observing:

1. WTO Notification Number G/SPS/N/IDN/37 dated October 26, 2007;

2. WTO Notification Number G/SPS/N/IDN/47 dated May 7, 2012.

Decides:

To Stipulate: Regulation of the Minister of Agriculture concerning plant quarantine measures for the importation of fresh bulbs vegetables into territory of the Republic of Indonesia.

Chapter I General provision

Article 1

In this regulation what is meant by:

1. Fresh Bulbs Vegetables hereinafter called Bulbs are part of plants in the form of bulbs (bulb) include in the Alliums family, either whole or parts that have not been processed into processed materials.

2. Quarantine Plant Pests hereinafter called OPTK are all plant disturbing organisms stipulated by the Minister of Agriculture to be prevented of its entry into and spreading into the Territory of the Republic of Indonesia.

3. Plant Health Certificate (Phytosanitary Certificate) is a statement letter made by the authorized official from the country of origin or transiting country that state Bulbs are free from OPTK and had met requirements of stipulated Plant Quarantine and/or declaring other required information.

4. Importation Points are sea - ports, river - ports, ferry - ports, airports, post offices, border posts with other countries and other important places, stipulated as places for the entrance of carrier of plant pests.

5. Plant Quarantine Officials are certain Government employees assigned the duty to carry out Plant Quarantine measures based on prevailing legislations.

6. Bulbs owner or its proxy, hereinafter called Owner or Proxy are a person or legal entity owned and/or re-

sponsible on the entry of living plant products in the form of fresh bulbs vegetables.

Article 2

1. This Regulation is intended as a basis for the entry of Bulbs into the territory of the Republic of Indonesia and the implementation of Plant Quarantine Measure.

2. The purpose of this regulation is to prevent the entry of OPTK into the territory of the Republic of Indonesia and meet the safety of plant based fresh food.

Article 3

The scope of this regulation includes plant quarantine measure and Importation Point.

Chapter Ⅱ Quarantine requirements

Article 4

1. Entry of Bulbs into territory of the Republic of Indonesia can be derived from the production area in the country of origin that is free or not free from OPTK infestation.

2. Bulbs as intended in paragraph (1) must be free of roots, leaves, and particles of soil/compost.

Article 5

1. Production areas in country of origin are free from OPTK infestation as intended in Article 4 are determined by the Head of Agricultural Quarantine Agency on behalf of the Minister in the form of Decree.

2. The procedure for the determination of production areas in the country of origin that are free from OPTK infestation as intended in paragraph (2), is conducted under the regulating legislation.

Article 6

1. In case of importation of Bulbs from the production area in the country of origin that is not free from OPTK infestation as intended in Article 4, treatment action in the form of fumigation or irradiation is conducted.

2. Types of Bulbs, OPTK and treatment as intended in paragraph (1) are as listed in the attachment as an integral part of this Regulation.

Article 7

1. Entry of Fresh bulbs as intended in Article 4 and Article 6 shall meet the provision requirements of the safety of plant based fresh food.

2. Food safety requirements as intended in paragraph (1) are to comply with the regulating legislation in the field of safety of plant based fresh food.

Chapter Ⅲ Plant quarantine measure

Article 8

1. Fresh bulbs that are imported into the territory of the Republic of Indonesia, shall:

a. be equipped with Plant Health Certificate from the country of origin and transit country;

b. pass through designated Importation Point; and

c. be reported and submitted to the Quarantine Official in the Importation Point for the necessary plant quarantine measure.

2. Plant Health Certificate as intended in paragraph (1) letter a, for the importation of Bulbs from production areas in the country of origin free from OPTK infestation, shall include a statement that:

a. it originated from production area that is free from OPTK infestation; and

b. free of roots, leaves, and particles of soil/compost.

3. Plant Health Certificate as intended in paragraph (1) letter a, for Bulbs that are from production areas in the country of origin which are not free from OPTK infestation, shall include a statement that:

a. treatment measure in the form of fumigation or irradiation is already conducted; and

b. free of roots, leaves, and particles of soil/compost.

4. Statement as intended in paragraph (2) and paragraph (3) letter b is stated in additional information column (additional declaration).

5. Statement as intended in paragraph (3) letter a, is stated in treatment column.

Article 9

1. The owner or its proxy shall report and deliver Bulbs to the Quarantine Official at the Importation Point.

2. The report as intended in paragraph (1) is made no later than during the arrival of Bulbs at the Importation Point, equipped with the required documents.

Article 10

1. Quarantine official will conduct administrative inspection against the required documents to determine the completeness, correctness, and validity of the documents.

2. In case of administrative inspection as intended in paragraph (1) on the Plant Health Certificate, is proven not to include the statement:

a. derived from the production area in the country of origin is free from OPTK infestations, free of roots and leaves, and free from particles of soil/compost as intended in Article 8; or

b. treatment measures have been conducted, free of roots and leaves, and free of particles of soil/compost as intended in Article 8; rejection is enforced.

Article 11

In the case of administrative inspection result as intended in Article 10 is proven:

a. incomplete, detention is conducted;

b. complete, valid and correct, health examination is performed.

Article 12

1. The health examination as intended in Article 11 letter b is performed to detect the possible presence of OPTK and to know the physical condition of Bulbs.

2. In the case of health examination result as intended in paragraph (1), Bulbs are proven:

a. not free from group I OPTK, rotten or damaged, extermination is performed;

b. not free from roots, leaves, or particles of soil/compost, rejection is enforced;

c. not free from group II OPTK, treatment is performed, or

d. free of OPTK, roots, leaves, and particles of soil/compost, clearance is conducted.

3. Clearance as intended in paragraph (2) letter d, can be conducted if the Bulbs comply with provisions of the regulating legislation in the field of safety of plant based fresh food.

Article 13

Measures of administrative inspection, health examination, detention, rejection, treatment, extermination and clearance as intended in Article 10, Article 11 and Article 12 are carried out in accordance with provisions of the regulating legislation.

Chapter Ⅳ Entry places

Article 14

1. Importation Point of Bulbs as intended in Article 8 paragraph (1) b, consists of:

a. Port of Tanjung Perak, Surabaya;

b. Port of Belawan, Medan;

c. Soekarno – Hatta Airport, Jakarta, and;

d. Port of Soekarno – Hatta, Makassar.

2. In addition to Importation Points as intended in paragraph (1), Importation Points based on the regulating legislation in the area of Free Trade and Free Port Zone can be used as Importation Point for Bulbs.

3. Importation of Bulbs through Importation Point as intended in paragraph (2) can be done only to meet consumption needs and are prohibited for circulation outside the Free Trade and Free Port Zone.

4. Provision of the Importation Points as intended in paragraph (1) shall not apply on the importation of Bulbs from production areas that are free of OPTK infestation in its country of origin as intended in Article 5, or countries with recognized food safety system.

Chapter V Closing provision

Article 15

With the enactment of this Regulation, Regulation of the Minister of Agriculture No. 18/Permentan/OT. 140/2/2008 in conjunction with Regulation of the Minister of Agriculture No. 90/Permentan/OT. 140/12/2011 and Regulation of the Minister of Agriculture No. 16/Permentan/OT. 140/3/2012 shall be revoked and declared invalid.

Article 16

This Regulation shall come into effect on 19 June 2012.

For public cognizance, ordering the promulgation of this Ministerial Regulation by including it in the State Gazette of the Republic of Indonesia.

Stipulated in Jakarta on, 13 June 2012

THE MINISTER OF AGRICULTURE

SUSWONO

Pest species、bulbs plant、treatment measures and the origin country

No	Pest	Plant	Treatment	Country
I. INSECTS				
4	*Delia antiqua* (Meign.); (= *Anthomyia antique* = *A. ceparum* = *Chortophila antiqua Delia cepetorum* = *Hylemya antiqua* = *H. ceparum* = *Leptohylemyia antique* = *Pegomyia ceparum* = *P. cepetorum* = *Phorbia ceparum P. cepetorum* = *P. antiqua*); Diptera: *Anthomyiidae*; onion maggot, onion fly	*Allium ascalonicum*, *Allium porrum*, *Allium sativum*, *Allium* spp	1. Fumigation (CH_3Br): a. 40 gr/1000 ft^3/26 ~ 31℃/2 h; or b. 32 gr/m^3/32 ~ 35℃/2 h; or c. 16 gr/m^3/26 ~ 31℃/2 h; or 2. Irradiation: 70 gray	Afrika: (omitted) Amerika: (omitted) Asia: Armenia, China, Georgia, India, Iran, Iraq, Israel, Japan, Kazakhstan, Korea, Mongolia, Philippines, Turky Europe: (omitted)
5	*Peridroma saucia* (Hubner); (= *Agrotis angulifera* = *A. impacta* = *A. inermis* = *A. intecta* = *A. ortonii* = *A. saucia* = *Lycophotia margaritosa* = *L. ochronota* = *L. saucia* = *Noctua aequa* = *N. majuscula* = *N. margaritosa* = *N. saucia* = *Rhyacia margaritosa* = *R. saucia* = *Peridroma margaritosa*); Lepidoptera: Noctuidae variegated cutworm, pirly underwing moth	*Allium ascalonicum*	1. Fumigation (CH_3Br): 40 gr/m^3/26 ~ 31℃/2 h; or 2. Irradiation: 70 gray	Africa: (omitted) America: (omitted) Asia: Armenia, China, Israel, Japan, Sri Lanka, Syria, Turky Europe: (omitted)

Continue Table

No	Pest	Plant	Treatment	Country
II. NEMATODES				
1	*Aphelenchoides fragariae* (Chriestie); (= *Aphelenchoides olesistus* = *A. olesistus* var. *longicollis* = *A. pseudolesistus* = *Aphelenchus fragariae* = *A. olesistus* = *A. olesistus* var. *longicollis* = *A. pseudolesistus*); *Aphelenchoididae*; bud and leaf nematode	*Allium ascalonicum*, *Allium sativum*	1. Fumigation (CH_3Br): a. 40 gr/m^3/26 ~ 31℃/2 h; or b. 32 gr/m^3/32 ~ 35℃/2 h; or c. 16 gr/m^3/26 ~ 31℃/2 h; or 2. Irradiation: 70 gray	America: (omitted) Europe: (omitted) Asia: China, India, Israel, Korea Selatan, Kirgyztan, Japan, Turky Oceania: (omitted)
3	*Ditylenchus destructor* Thorne	*Allium ascalonicum*, *Allium sativum*	1. Fumigation (CH_3Br): a. 40 gr/m^3/26 ~ 31℃/2 h; or b. 32 gr/m^3/32 ~ 35℃/2 h; or c. 16 gr/m^3/26 ~ 31℃/2 h; or 2. Irradiation: 70 gray	Europe: (omitted) Asia: (omitted) Azerbaijan, China, India, Iran, Japan, Kazakhstan, Korea Selatan, Kirgistan, Malaysia, Pakistan, Saudi Arabia, Tajikistan, Turky, Uzbekistan Africa: (omitted) America: (omitted)
V. Mites				
1	*Petrobia lateens* (Tetranychidae) Brown Wheat Mite	*Allium sativum*, *Allium cepa*	1. Fumigation (CH_3Br): a. 40 gr/m^3/26 ~ 31℃/2 h; or b. 16 gr/m^3/26 ~ 31℃/2 h; or 2. Irradiation: 70 gray	Europe: (omitted) Asia: China, India, Republic of Korea Africa: (omitted) America: (omitted) Oceania: (omitted)

印度尼西亚动物、鱼类和植物检疫法

（1992 年 16 号）

第一章　总　　则

第 1 条　本法中名词定义

1. 检疫　指为防止寄生虫和疾病传入、传出国境及其在印度尼西亚境内传播所实施的隔离措施和隔离区。

2. 动物、鱼类和植物检疫　指为防止动物、鱼类和植物寄生虫和疾病传入、传出国境及其在印度尼西亚境内各地区间相互传播所采取的措施。

3. 有害生物和动植物及鱼类疫病　指所有能危害或潜在危害动物、鱼类和植物健康及可能引起动物、鱼类和植物死亡的所有生物。

4. 检疫性有害生物和动物疫病　指为防止其传入、传出或在印度尼西亚境内散播，由政府规定的有害生物及动物疫病种类。

5. 检疫性有害生物和鱼类及植物疫病　指为防止其传入或在印度尼西亚境内散播，由政府规定的有害生物和鱼类及植物疫病种类。

6. 检疫性有害生物和动植物及鱼类疫病的传播载体　指动物、动物原材料、动物源性产品、鱼类、植物及其产品，以及可能携带检疫性有害生物和动植物及鱼类疫病的其他物品。

7. 动物　指所有驯养的或野生的陆生动物。

8. 动物原材料　指取自动物的加工原材料。

9. 动物源性产品　指由动物源性材料加工而成的产品。

10. 鱼类　指所有完全或部分生活史处于水中的水生动植物，无论是否存活，并包括其肢体部分。

11. 植物　指所有种类的植物，包含活的、死的、加工或未加工的植物。

12. 进出境口岸　指动物、鱼类、植物寄生虫和疾病载体可以进出境的海港、河港、渡口、机场、邮局、边境港或其他必经地。

13. 动物、鱼类和植物检疫官　指按此法规实施和管理检疫任务的国家公务员。

第 2 条　动物、鱼类和植物检疫是建立在动物、鱼类和植物持续存在的基础上的。

第 3 条　动物、鱼类和植物检疫的目的是：

（a）防止检疫性有害生物和动植物及鱼类疫病传入印度尼西亚境内。

（b）防止检疫性有害生物和动植物及鱼类疫病在印度尼西亚境内各地区间传播。

（c）防止检疫性有害生物和动物疫病随出口动物传出印度尼西亚国境。

（d）防止进口国要求的有害生物和鱼类及植物疫病随出口鱼、植物传出印度尼西亚国境。

第 4 条　动物、鱼和植物检疫法范围包括：

（a）检疫要求。

（b）检疫措施。

（c）疫区。

（d）有害生物和疫病种类，及其传播载体。

（e）进出境口岸。

第二章 检疫要求

第5条 检疫性有害生物和动植物及鱼类疫病的传播载体进入印度尼西亚时需满足：

（a）随附由原产国或中转国签发的传播载体卫生证书，传播载体包括动物、动物原材料、动物源性产品、鱼类、植物及其产品，除非该物品未被归类为传播载体。

（b）从指定地点入境。

（c）通知并交由入境地检疫机关实施检疫。

第6条 检疫性有害生物和动植物及鱼类疫病的传播载体在境内运输应实施以下检疫：

（a）随附由产地签发的传播载体卫生证书，传播载体包括动物、动物原材料、动物源性产品、鱼类、植物及其产品，除非该物品未被归类为传播载体。

（b）通过指定地点进出。

（c）通知并交由指定进出点的检疫部门实施检疫。

第7条

（1）拟出口的检疫性有害生物和动物疫病的传播载体应满足：

（a）随附动物、动物原材料或动物源性产品的卫生证书，除非该物品未被归类为传播载体。

（b）从指定地点出境。

（c）通知并交由出境点检疫部门实施检疫。

（2）依据第7条（1）款规定对拟出口的检疫性有害生物和动物疫病的传播载体实施检疫时，依据进口国要求执行。

第8条 根据有害生物和动物、鱼类或植物疫病的特性，除参照第5条、第6条和第7条外，政府还可提出其他检疫要求。

第三章 检疫行为

第9条

（1）检疫性有害生物和动物疫病传播载体在进出印度尼西亚国境或在印度尼西亚境内转运时，必须进行检疫。

（2）检疫性有害生物和鱼类及植物疫病传播载体进入印度尼西亚国境或在印度尼西亚境内转运时，必须进行检疫。

（3）检疫性有害生物和鱼类及植物疫病传播载体在出境时，除非进口国要求的，否则不实施检疫。

第10条 检疫人员应实施以下检疫措施

（a）检查。

（b）隔离。

（c）观察。

（d）处理。

（e）扣留。

（f）拒绝。

（g）销毁。

（h）放行。

第11条

（1）第10条（a）是指检查是否随附必要文件，以及核对文件内容和检查是否携带检疫性有害生物和动植物及鱼类疫病。

（2）对于动物、动物源材料、动物原产品和鱼类的检查，可以与授权能处置影响人类健康的检疫性疾病的代理机构协作完成。

第 12 条 由于某种检疫性有害生物和动植物及鱼类疫病的特性，由于检测需要较长的时间、特殊的设施和特定的条件，为此，对第 11 款提到的有害生物和疫病传播载体可作进一步隔离观察。

第 13 条

（1）检疫性有害生物和动植物及鱼类疫病传播的载体应被处理直至不携带或感染检疫性有害生物和动植物及鱼类疫病。

（2）如果经检验或隔离观察，传播载体出现以下情况，应按条款（1）要求进行处理：

（a）携带/感染或可疑携带/感染了检疫性有害生物和动植物及鱼类疫病；

（b）存在或可疑存在检疫性有害生物和动植物及鱼类疫病。

第 14 条

（1）按第 11 条检查发现，检疫性有害生物和动植物及鱼类疫病传播载体在入境或在境内转运过程中，没有完全遵守相关法律要求的，应予扣留。

（2）出现本条（1）情形的，政府应规定其限期内达到相关法规要求。

第 15 条 检疫性有害生物和动植物及鱼类疫病传播载体在入境或境内转运时，如发现如下情况，将禁止入境：

（a）经运输工具上现场检疫发现，传播载体携带或感染了政府规定的检疫性有害生物和动植物及鱼类疫病，或逐渐腐烂变质，或属于国家明令禁止进口的物种。

（b）没有完全遵守本法第 5 条、第 6 条、第 8 条（相关检疫文件）要求的。

（c）适用第 14 条（1）后，在规定的隔离期限内没有完全符合要求的。

（d）在交通工具上经治疗处理后，仍存在检疫性有害生物和动植物及鱼类疫病的。

第 16 条 检疫性有害生物和动植物及鱼类疫病的传播载体在入境或境内转运时，发现以下情况的，应予销毁：

（1）检疫性有害生物和动植物及鱼类疫病的传播媒介在进口或境内转运中，当发生如下情况时，应当作销毁处理。

（a）从运载工具上卸载后，经检疫发现感染了政府规定的某种检疫性有害生物和动植物及鱼类疫病，或逐渐腐烂变质，或属于国家明令禁止的物种。

（b）根据第 15 条作出的不准入境处理后，但其货主没有在规定的时间内将其运出印度尼西亚共和国境内或其境内目的地区的。

（c）隔离观察后发现，传播载体携带或感染政府规定的某种检疫性有害生物和动植物及鱼类疫病的。

（d）卸离运载工具后，经处理后，仍存在检疫性有害生物和动植物及鱼类疫病的。

（2）政府依据本条（1）款规定销毁的检疫性有害生物和动植物及鱼类疫病的传播载体，其货主无权要求任何补偿。

第 17 条 输入印度尼西亚或在境内移动的检疫性有害生物和动植物及鱼类疫病传播载体如发现如下情况的，将予以放行：

（a）经第 11 条的检验，未发现载体携带或感染检疫性有害生物和动植物及鱼类疫病的。

（b）经第 12 条隔离检疫，未发现载体携带或感染检疫性有害生物和动植物及鱼类疫病的。

（c）按第 13 条处理后，载体不再携带或感染检疫性有害生物和动植物及鱼类疫病的。

（d）按第 14 条扣押的载体符合要求后。

第 18 条 参照第 6 条、第 7 条和第 8 条规定，输出印度尼西亚国境或在其境内运输的检疫性有害生物和动植物及鱼类疫病传播载体经检疫证明符合以下情况的准予放行：

（a）经第 11 条的检验，未发现载体携带或感染检疫性有害生物和动植物及鱼类疫病的。

（b）经第 12 条隔离检疫，未发现载体携带或感染检疫性有害生物和动植物及鱼类疫病的。

（c）按第 13 条处理后，载体不再携带或感染检疫性有害生物和动植物及鱼类疫病的。

第 19 条

(1) 按第 17 条放行的应出具放行证书。

(2) 按 18 条放行的应出具健康证书。

第 20 条

(1) 参照第 10 条规定检疫人员应在口岸进行现场检疫和实验室检验。

(2) 在特定情况下参照本条 (1) 可以在非口岸地实施现场检疫和实验室检验。

(3) 本条 (2) 在口岸以外实施检疫的法令由政府制定。

第 21 条 与第 9 条一致，携带或可能携带有检疫性有害生物和动植物及鱼类疫病的交通工具、设施、用水和包装由专人负责检疫。

第 22 条

(1) 任何利用政府提供的实施动物、鱼和植物检疫的设施和服务的个人或实体，要按规定交纳检疫费用及其他费用。

(2) 涉及本条 (1) 的收费办法应予以规范。

(3) 收费条款应列入政府规定中。

第四章 疫 区

第 23 条

(1) 如果某地区发生了原来本地区没有的检疫性有害生物和动植物及鱼类疫病，政府可以宣布此地区为疫区，直到另行通知为止。

(2) 疫区内动物、鱼类和植物等的出入将由政府管理。

第五章 寄生虫、疾病及其载体的种类

第 24 条 政府将指定：

a. 携带或感染检疫性有害生物和动植物及鱼类疫病的种类。

b. 携带或感染检疫性有害生物和动植物及鱼类疫病传播载体的种类。

c. 禁止进入印度尼西亚境内和在境内运输的检疫性有害生物和动植物及鱼类疫病传播载体的种类。

第 25 条 同一交通工具运输的其他载体在入口处卸离后，在检疫人员的监督下由货主自行销毁。

第六章 出入境口岸

第 26 条 动物、鱼类和植物等的出入境口岸由政府指定。

第 27 条 运输动物、鱼类和植物进入印度尼西亚境内的交通工具运输计划的条款由印度尼西亚规定。

第七章 检疫意识的培养

第 28 条 政府负责培养公众的动物、鱼类和植物的检疫意识。

第 29 条 政府将采取有效措施鼓励和指导民众参与动物、鱼类和植物检疫事务。

第八章 调 查 研 究

第 30 条

(1) 除印度尼西亚的警察外，负责动物、鱼类和植物的检疫官也有一定的特权，比如，参照 1981 年刑事诉讼程序法第 8 条，调查动物、鱼类和植物检疫领域的处罚行为。

(2) 参照本条 (1) 规定的权力不得消减 1985 年渔业法第 9 条和 1990 年自然生物资源和生态系统保护法所赋予调查员的权力。

（3）按照本条（1）调查员有如下权力：

（a）核实动物、鱼类和植物检疫领域的处罚实施方面的信息和报告。

（b）传唤动物、鱼类和植物检疫领域处罚行为的嫌疑人或证人。

（c）为动物、鱼类和植物检疫领域的处罚行为取证。

（d）要求与动物、鱼类和植物领域处罚实施有关的人员或实体提供信息和证据素材。

（e）起草和签署官方报告。

（f）当没有足够证据表明动物、鱼类和植物检疫领域的处罚行为可疑时终止调查。

（4）参照本条第一项，依据 1961 年刑事诉讼程序法第八章第 107 条，调查人通过公安机关通知原告调查开始。

第九章 处罚条款

第 31 条

（1）任何故意违反第 5 条、第 6 条、第 7 条、第 9 条、第 21 条和第 25 条法规的，处 3 年以下有期徒刑或拘役，并处以 150 亿卢比以下罚金。

（2）任何过失违反第 5 条、第 6 条、第 7 条、第 9 条、第 21 条和第 25 条法规的，处 1 年以下有期徒刑或拘役，并处以 50 亿卢比以下罚金。

（3）本条第一项处罚行为的构成犯罪，本条第二项处罚行为的构成犯法。

第十章 暂行条款

第 32 条 所有现行有效的在本法以下的关于动物、鱼类和植物检疫的法规，只要不违背本法的将继续生效。

第十一章 终止条款

第 33 条 自本法生效之日起，以下法规失效

（1）1912 年第 432 号政府公告《关于政府监督管理兽医事件和兽医局条款》修订版，就动物检疫方面的法令。

（2）1917 年第 9 号政府公告《关于政府监管荷兰—东西印度群岛的兽医事件和兽医局法规修正案》。

（3）1923 年第 289 号政府公告《关于政府监管荷兰—东西印度群岛兽医事件和兽医局法规修正案》。

（4）1936 年第 205 号政府公告《关于政府控制荷兰—东西印度群岛兽医事件和兽医局法规修正案》。

（5）1921 年第 532 号政府公告《关于禁止从西里伯斯岛（现苏拉威西岛）及万鸦老港运输香蕉的果实、植株、根茎及其他器官的法令》。

（6）1924 年第 439 号政府公告《关于防止咖啡豆螟虫（或蛀虫）传入西里伯斯岛（现苏拉威西岛）及万鸦老港、安汶岛、巴厘岛、龙目岛、Timor 及属地》。

（7）1924 年第 439 号政府公告《关于阻止 Sansihe 和 Talaud 岛的 Sexava 蝗虫传播的措施》。

（8）1925 年第 114 号政府公告《关于阻止马铃薯块茎霉烂病进一步传播的措施》。

（9）1926 年第 427 号政府公告《关于为阻止植物寄生虫和疾病传入荷兰—东西印度群岛摘要和修改进境活植物材料管理条例》。

（10）1926 年第 451 号政府公告《关于阻止和控制荷兰—东西印度群岛狂犬病的新条款》中关于动物检疫部分。

（11）1932 年第 523 号政府公告《1926 年第 427 号政府公告〈摘要和修改进境活植物材料管理条

例〉修正案》。

（12）1936 年第 715 号政府公告《关于修改 1912 年第 432 号政府公告〈关于政府监督管理兽医事件和兽医局条款修订版〉和 1926 年第 451 号政府公告〈关于阻止和控制荷兰—东西印度群岛狂犬病的新条款〉》中关于动物检疫部分。

（13）1938 年第 699 号政府公告《关于岛内运输马铃薯的法令》。

第 34 条 本法自发布之日起开始生效。

Law of the Republic of Indonesia No. 16 of 1992 concerning animal, fish, and plant quarantine

Chapter I General provisions

Article 1

As used in this law:

1. Quarantine means place of isolation and/or actions as the effort to prevent the introduction into, the dissemination from one area to another within, or the exportation from, the territory of the Republic of Indonesia of pests and diseases;

2. Animal, fish, and plant quarantine means actions in the effort to prevent the introduction into, the dissemination from one area to another within, or the exportation from, the territory of the Republic of Indonesia of pests and diseases of animals, fish, and plants;

3. Pests and diseases of animals, fish, and plants means all organisms capable of doing damage to, undermining the health of, or causing death of animals, fish, and plants;

4. Quarantine pests and diseases of animals means all pests and diseases of animals designated by the Government to be prevented from being introduced into, disseminated within, and exported from, the territory of the Republic of Indonesia;

5. Quarantine pests and diseases of fish and plants means all pests and diseases designated by the Government to be prevented from being introduced into and disseminated within, the territory of the Republic of Indonesia;

6. Carrier of quarantine pests and diseases of animals, fish, and plants means animal, material of animal origin, product of material of animal origin, fish, plant and parts thereof, and/or other article capable of carrying quarantine pests and diseases of animals, fish, and plants;

7. Animal means all terrestrial animals, both wild and cultivated;

8. Material of animal origin means material obtained from animal which can be processed further;

9. Product of material of animal origin means material of animal origin that has been processed;

10. Fish means all aquatic biota the life – cycle of which takes place wholly or partly in water, whether alive or dead, including parts thereof;

11. Plant means all species of plants, whether living or dead, both unprocessed and processed;

12. Place of entry and place of export means seaport, river port, ferry port, airport, post office, border post, or any other place deemed necessary which has been designated as the place entry and export of carriers of pests and diseases of animals, fish, and plants;

13. Animal, fish, and plant quarantine officers means certain government employees charged with the task of carrying out quarantine actions under this law.

Article 2

Animal, fish, and plant quarantine is based on the principle of continuous existence of animal, fish and plant biotic natural resources.

Article 3

The objectives of animal, fish, and plant quarantine are:

a. to prevent the introduction of quarantine pests and diseases of animals, fish, and plants into the territory of the Republic of Indonesia;

b. to prevent the dissemination of quarantine pests and diseases on animals, fish, and plants from one area to another within the territory of the Republic of Indonesia;

c. to prevent the concomitant exportation of quarantine pests and diseases of animals from the territory of the Republic of Indonesia;

d. to prevent the concomitant exportation of certain pests and diseases of fish and plants from the territory of the Republic of Indonesia if so required by the country of destination.

Article 4

The scope of animal, fish, and plant quarantine regulations includes:

a. quarantine requirements;

b. quarantine actions;

c. quarantine area;

d. kinds of pests and diseases, and carriers thereof;

e. places of entry and export.

Chapter Ⅱ　Quarantine requirements

Article 5

Any carrier of quarantine pests and diseases of animals, fish, and plants imported into the territory of the Republic of Indonesia shall be:

a. accompanied by a health certificate from the country of origin and the country in which the carrier was landed and from which it was later re-consigned, for animal, material of animal origin, product of material of animal origin, fish, plant, or part of plant, except carrier classified as other article;

b. through the designated place of entry;

c. notified and presented to the quarantine officer at the place of entry for quarantine actions.

Article 6

Any carrier of quarantine pests and diseases of animals, fish, and plants to be moved from one area to another within the territory of the Republic of Indonesia shall be:

a. accompanied by a health certificate from the area of origin for animal, material of animal origin, product of material of animal origin, fish, plant, or parts of plants, except carrier classified as other article;

b. through the designated place of entry and place of exit;

c. notified and presented to the quarantine officer at the places of entry and exit for quarantine actions.

Article 7

(1) Any carrier of quarantine pests and diseases of animals to be exported from the territory of the Republic of Indonesia shall be:

a. accompanied by a health certificate for animal, material of animal origin, or product of material of animal origin, except carrier classified as other article;

b. through the designated place of export;

c. notified and presented to the quarantine officer at the place of export for quarantine actions.

(2) The requirements referred to in Section (1) shall apply to carrier of pests and diseases of fish and plants to be exported from the territory of the Republic of Indonesia if so required by the country of destination.

Article 8

In certain cases, owing to the nature of the pests and diseases of animals, fish, or plants, the Government may impose other requirements in addition to those referred to in Article 5, Article 6, and Article 7.

Chapter Ⅲ Quarantine actions

Article 9

(1) Any carrier of quarantine pests and diseases of animals imported into, or to be moved from one area to another within, or to be exported from, the territory of the Republic of Indonesia shall be subjected to quarantine actions;

(2) Any carrier of quarantine pests and diseases of fish or plants imported into, or to be moved from one area to another within, the territory of the Republic of Indonesia shall be subjected to quarantine actions;

(3) Carrier of quarantine pests and diseases of fish or plants to be exported from the territory of the Republic of Indonesia shall not be subjected to quarantine actions unless required by the country of destination.

Article 10

Quarantine actions performed by the quarantine officers shall be:

a. inspection;

b. isolation;

c. observation;

d. treatment;

e. detention;

f. refusal;

g. destruction;

h. release.

Article 11

(1) The inspection referred to in Article 10 letter a shall be performed to determine the presence of required documents, to verify the particulars given therein, and to detect quarantine pests and diseases of animals, fish, and plants;

(2) Inspection of animals, material of animal origin, products of material of animal origin, andfish can be performed coordinately with the agency authorized to deal with quarantine diseases that affect human health.

Article 12

For further detection of certain quarantine pests and diseases of animals, fish, and plants which, due to their nature, requires an indefinitely long period, special facilities, and controlled environmental conditions, the carrier of pests and diseases that has been inspected as mentioned in Article II may be kept in isolation for observation.

Article 13

(1) Carrier of quarantine pests and diseases of animals, fish, and plants shall be treated to free it from infestation or infection by quarantine pests and diseases of animals, fish, and plants;

(2) The treatment referred to in Section (1) shall be performed if after inspection or solation for observation it becomes evident that the carrier:

a. is infested/infected or suspected of being infested/infected by quarantine pests and diseases of animals, fish, and plants, or

b. is not free or suspected of being not free from quarantine pests and diseases of animals, fish, and plants.

Article 14

(1) Carrier of quarantine pests and diseases of animals, fish, and plants shall be detained if after inspection as mentioned in Article 11, it becomes evident that the requirements for the importation into, or for the

movement from an area to another within the territory of the Republic of Indonesia, have not been fully complied with.

(2) The Government shall stipulate the period within which the requirements referred to in Section (1) shall be complied with.

Article 15

Carrier of quarantine pests and diseases of animals, fish, and plants imported into, or moved from an area to another within the territory of the Republic of Indonesia, shall be refused entry if it becomes evident that:

a. after inspection on board the means of conveyance, the carrier is infested or infected by certain quarantine pests and diseases of animals, fish, and plants designated by the Government, or is in a decaying condition or damage, or belong to those species the importation of which is prohibited, or

b. the requirements referred to in Article 5, Article 6, and Article 8 have not been fully complied with, or

c. after detention referred to in Article 14 Section (1), the requirements cannot be fully complied with within the stipulated period.

d. after treatment on board the means of conveyance, the carrier cannot be freed from infestation or infection by quarantine pests and diseases of animals, fish, and plants.

Article 16

(1) Carrier of quarantine pests and diseases of animals, fish, and plants imported into, or moved from an area to another within the territory of the Republic of Indonesia shall be destroyed if it becomes evident that:

a. after discharge from the means of conveyance and subsequent inspection, the carrier is infected by certain quarantine pests and diseases of animals, fish, and plants designated by the Government, or is in a decaying condition or damage, or belongs to those species the introduction of which is prohibited, or

b. after refusal of entry as mentioned in Article 15, the carrier is not moved out of the territory of the Republic of Indonesia or area of destination by its owner within the stipulated period, or

c. after observation in isolation, the carrier is not free from infestation of infection by certain quarantine pests and diseases of animals, fish, and plants designated by the Government, or

d. after discharge from the means of conveyance and subsequent treatment, the carrier cannot be freed from infestation or infection by quarantine pests and diseases of animals, fish, and plants.

(2) In case of destruction as mentioned in Section (1) the owner of the carrier of quarantine pests and diseases of animals, fish, and plants shall not be entitled to any compensation.

Article 17

Carrier of quarantine pests and diseases of animals, fish, and plants imported into, or moved from an area to another within the territory of the Republic of Indonesia shall be released if it becomes evident that:

a. after inspection as mentioned in Article 11, the carrier is free from infestation or infection by quarantine pests and diseases of animals, fish, and plants;

b. after observation in isolation as mentioned in Article 12, the carrier is free from infestation or infection by quarantine pests and diseases of animals, fish, and plants;

c. after treatment as mentioned in Article 13, the carrier can be free from infestation or infection by quarantine pests and diseases of animals, fish, and plants; or

d. after detention as mentioned in Article 14, the requirements have been fully complied with.

Article 18

Subject to the provisions referred to in Article 6, Article 7, and Article 8, carrier of quarantine pests and diseases of animals, fish, and plants to be exported from, or to be moved from an area to another within the territory of the Republic of Indonesia shall be released if it becomes evident that:

a. after having been inspected as mentioned in Article 11, the carrier is free from infestation or infection by quarantine pests and diseases of animals, fish, and plants; or infection by quarantine pests and diseases of animals, fish, and plants; or

b. after having been observed in isolation as mentioned in Article 12, the carrier is free from infestation or infection by quarantine pests and diseases of animals, fish, and plants; or

c. after having been treated as mentioned in Article 13, the carrier can be freed from infestation or infection by quarantine pests and diseases of animals, fish, and plants.

Article 19

(1) The release referred to in Article 17 shall be accompanied by the grant of a certificate of release.

(2) The release referred to in Article 18 shall be accompanied by the grant of a health certificate.

Article 20

(1) The quarantine actions referred to in Article 10 shall be performed by the quarantine officers at the place of entry and export, either inside or outside the quarantine establishments.

(2) In certain cases the quarantine actions referred to in Section (1) may be performed outside the place of entry and export, either inside or outside the quarantine establishments.

(3) Regulations regarding the quarantine actions outside the places of entry and export referred to in Section (2) shall be set forth by the Government.

Article 21

Consistent with the provision referred to in Article 9 quarantine actions may be imposed on persons, means of conveyance, equipment, water, or packing which is found to carry or suspected of carrying quarantine pests and diseases of animals, fish, and plants.

Article 22

(1) Any person or body making use of the services provided or facilities made available by the Government in the performance of quarantine actions may be required to pay quarantine fees and charges.

(2) Regulation regarding the collection of quarantine fees and charges referred to in Section(1).

(3) shall be set forth in Government Regulation.

Chapter Ⅳ Quarantine area

Article 23

In case a quarantine pest or disease of animal, fish, and plant is found to be present or suspected of being present in an area previously known to be free from such a pest or disease, the Government may proclaim such an area to be a quarantine area until further notice.

Chapter Ⅴ Kinds of pests and diseases and carries thereof

Article 24

The Government shall designate:

a. the kinds of quarantine pests and diseases of animals, fish, and plants;

b. the kinds of carriers of quarantine pests and diseases of animals, fish, and plants;

c. the kinds of carriers of quarantine pests and diseases of animals, fish, and plants, the importation of which into, or the movement of which from an area to another within, the territory of the Republic of Indonesia is prohibited.

Article 25

Other carriers transported by a means of conveyance and discharged at the place of entry shall be destroyed by the owner of the means of conveyance under the supervision of a quarantine officer.

Chapter Ⅵ Places of entry and export

Article 26

The Government shall designate the places of entry and export of carriers of quarantine pests and diseases of animals, fish, and plants.

Article 27

Regulations regarding means of conveyance that brings carriers of quarantine pests and diseases of animals, fish, and plants into the territory of the Republic of Indonesia on a transit scheme shall be set forth in Government Regulation.

Chapter Ⅶ Development of quarantine mindedness

Article 28

The Government is responsible for generating the awareness of the public concerning animal, fish, and plant quarantine.

Article 29

The participation of the public in animal, fish, and plant quarantine shall be encouraged and directed by the Government through various efficient and effective activities.

Chapter Ⅷ Investigation

Article 30

(1) In addition to the officers of the Police of the Republic of Indonesia, certain government employees of the ministry responsible for animal, fish, and plant quarantine may be given such special authority as that of the investigators referred to in Law No. 8 of 1981concerning Procedure for Criminal Justice to investigate punishable acts in the field of animal, fish, and plant quarantine;

(2) The authority of the investigators referred to in Section (1) shall not diminish the authorityof the investigators referred to in Law No. 9 of 1985 concerning Fisheries and Law No. 5 of 1990 concerning Conservation of Biotic Natural Resources and Their Ecosystem;

(3) The investigators referred to in Section (1) shall be authorized:

a. to verify reports or information on punishable acts in the field animal, fish, and plant quarantine;

b. to summon a person for investigation, whether as a suspect or as a witness in a punishable act in the field of animal, fish, and plant quarantine;

c. to search and seize any object that serves as proof of a punishable act in the field of animal, fish, and plant quarantine;

d. to demand information and evidence material from a person or body in connection with a punishable act in the field of animal, fish, and plant quarantine;

e. to draw up and sign an official report;

f. to discontinue an investigation when no sufficient evidence is found concerning a suspected punishable act in the field of animal, fish, and plant quarantine.

(4) The investigators referred to in Section (1) shall inform the public prosecutor of the commencement of an investigation through the investigators of the Police of the Republic of Indonesia in accordance with the provi-

sion of Article 107 of Law No. 8 of 1981 concerning Procedure for Criminal Justice.

Chapter Ⅸ Penalty provision

Article 31

(1) Any person who willfully violate the provisions referred to in Article 5, Article 6, Article 7, Article 9, Article 21, and Article 25, shall be punishable by a maximum imprisonment of 3 (three) years in addition to a maximum fine of Rp. 150,000,000 (one hundred and fifty million rupiahs); LAW 16/92/p. 12 of 21.

(2) Any person due to negligence violate the provisions of Article 5, Article 6, Article 7, Article 9, Article 21, and Article 25, shall be punishable by both maximum imprisonment of 1 (one) year in addition to a maximum fine of Rp. 50,000,000 (fifty million rupiahs);

(3) The punishable act referred to in Section (1) shall be a crime, and the punishable act referred to in Section (2) shall be an offense.

Chapter Ⅹ Temporary provision

Article 32

All existing executive regulations under the laws regarding animal quarantine, fish quarantine, and plant quarantine, so long as they are not in contravention of this Law, shall remain in force pending the issuance of new executive regulations under this Law.

Chapter Ⅺ Final provision

Article 33

At the time this Law comes into effect, the following shall be invalid:

1. Ordinance regarding Revision of the Provision relating to Government Supervision in Veterinary Affairs and the Veterinary Police, Government Gazette of 1912 No. 432, as far as animal quarantine is concerned;

2. Ordinance regarding Amendment and addition to the Regulation concerning GovernmentSupervision in Veterinary Affairs and the Veterinary Police in Netherlands Indies, Government Gazette of 1913 No. 598;

3. Ordinance regarding Further Addition and Amendment to the Regulation concerning Government Supervision in Veterinary Affairs and the Veterinary Police in Netherlands Indies, Government Gazette of 1917 No. 9;

4. Ordinance regarding Further Addition and Amendment to the Regulation concerning Government Supervision in Veterinary Affairs and the Veterinary Police in Netherlands Indies, Government Gazette of 1923 No. 289;

5. Ordinance regarding Amendment and Addition to the Regulation concerning Government Supervision in Veterinary Affairs and the Veterinary Police in Netherlands Indies, Government Gazette of 1936 No. 205; 6. Ordinance regarding Prohibition on the Transportation of Banana Fruit, Banana Plants, Banana Suckers or Parts Thereof from Sulawesi and Its Dependencies, Manado, Government Gazette of 1921 No. 532;

6. Ordinance regarding Measures for the Prevention of Introduction of Coffee Berry Borer into the Islands of Sulawesi and its Dependencies, Manado, Bali and Lombok, Timor and its Dependencies (Maatregelen ter Voorkoming van de Invoer van de offiebessenboeboek op de Eilanden behorende tot Celebes en Onderhorigheden, Manado, Amboina, Bali en Lombok, Timor en Onderhorigheden), Government Gazette of 1924 No. 439;

7. Ordinance regarding Measures for the Prevention of Dissemination of Sexava Grasshopper Existing in Sangihe and Talaud Islands, Government Gazette of 1924 No. 571;

8. Ordinance regarding Measures for the Prevention of Further Spread of the Potato Tuber Moth, Government Gazette of 1925 No. 114;

9. Ordinance regarding Summary and Revision of the Rules Governing the Importation of Living Plant Material to Prevent the Introduction of Plant Pests and Diseases into the Netherlands Indies, Government Gazette of 1926 No. 427;

10. Ordinance regarding New Provisions for the Prevention and Control of Rabies in Netherlands – Indies, Government Gazette of 1926 No. 451. as far as animal quarantine is concerned;

11. Ordinance regarding Amendment to the Ordinance in Government Gazette of 1926 No. 427 Concerning Summary and Revision of the Rules Governing the Importation of Living Plant Material, Government Gazette of 1932 No. 523;

12. Ordinance regarding Amendment to the Regulation Governing Revision of the Provision Regarding Government Control in Veterinary Affairs, and Veterinary Police in Government Gazette of 1912 No. 432, and to the Ordinance on New Provisions Regarding LAW 16/92/p. 14 of 21 Prevention and Control of Rabies in Government Gazette of 1926 No. 451, Government Gazette of 1936 No. 715, as far as animal quarantine is concerned;

13. Ordinance regarding Inter – island Movement of Potatoes, Government Gazette of 1938 No. 699.

Article 34

This Law shall come into effect on the day of publication.

In order that everybody may take cognizance of it, this Law shall be published in the Government Gazette of the Republic of Indonesia.

动物、鱼类和植物检疫法释义

（印度尼西亚共和国1992年第16号）

总　　则

印度尼西亚动物、鱼类和植物等物产丰富，国家赖以发展，居民赖以生存。自然生物资源可持续性发展的威胁之一就是病虫害的侵袭，病虫害危害了动物、鱼类和植物，给国家和人民都造成了巨大的损失，降低了动物、鱼类和植物产品的产量和质量，也可能引起某些珍贵的动物、鱼类和具有很高经济和科学价值的植物绝种，甚至某些动物和鱼类的疾病还可能危害公众的健康。

印度尼西亚共和国国土还没有被不同种类的外来动物、鱼类和植物病虫害侵袭。印度尼西亚共和国是由成千上万个岛屿组成的，这个地理环境是一个优势，群岛周围的海域是阻挡动物、鱼类和植物病虫害蔓延的天然屏障。随着人和货物越来越频繁地流动和有限的控制、预防和保护能力，病虫害传入和蔓延的可能性越来越大。

这将危害到自然生物资源的可持续性发展和国家经济。因此，为了预防病虫害的传入和蔓延，必须提前做准备和保持高度警惕。

政府通过对动物、鱼类和植物实施检疫来阻止病虫害在印度尼西亚境内各个地区间传播蔓延。遵照国际惯例，印度尼西亚也有义务阻止印度尼西亚国内的动物、鱼类和植物病虫害传出国境。因此，动物、鱼类和植物检疫的实施也是履行国际义务的一个表现。

动物、鱼类和植物检疫是非常重要的，它的执行必须建立在一个清晰、稳固和全面的法律基础上。

一些现有的动物检疫、鱼类检疫和植物检疫条例是殖民地政府时期留下来的，现在已经过时了。而且，现在国家使用的动物、鱼类和植物检疫基础法律条例：1961年2号关于植物和植物性原材料进出口法律、1967年6号法律关于动物管理和动物健康基本规定和1985年9号关于渔业法律，这些法律中关于动物检疫、鱼类检疫和植物检疫的科目都是不完全和不清楚的。因此，这些法律是不能解决动物、鱼类和植物检疫中出现的各种问题。

综上所述，建立一个全面完整的动物、鱼类和植物检疫法律是非常必要的。

释　　义

第1条　第六点“其他能携带动物、鱼类和植物病虫害的物体”是指有病变的材料、生物产品、鱼饲料、牛或鱼饲料的原材料、生物控制媒介、培养的生物组织、土壤、混合肥料或其他在发育的媒介和携带者等。

第七点“动物”包括受保护动物，同其他现行的法律中提到的一样。

第八点“动物原材料”包括肉、牛奶、鸡蛋、毛发、角、蹄、兽皮、精液等。

第九点“动物产品”包括在水中煮沸过的肉、干燥过的肉、制革兽皮的半成品、埋于地下的尸骨、骨头、血液、动物毛发、角蹄、内脏、动物肥料、动物器官、腺体、组织和体液。

第十点“鱼类”包括：

a. 鳍鱼（鱼纲）；

b. 虾、蟹等（甲壳类）；

c. 贝类、介壳类、墨鱼、乌贼、章鱼、蜗牛和与之类似的（软体动物类）；

d. 水母、海蛰和与之类似的（腔肠动物类）；

e. 海黄瓜、海胆和与之类似的（棘皮动物类）；

f. 青蛙和与之类似的（两栖动物类）；

g. 鳄鱼、海龟、陆龟、蜥蜴、水蛇和与之类似的（爬行动物类）；

h. 鲸、海豚、海牛（象）和与之类似的（哺乳动物类）；

i. 海草和其他的水生植物（藻类）；

j. 其他的和上面提到的种类相关的水生生物和被保护的鱼类。

第十一点“植物”是指除海草和其他水生植物（藻类）之外的所有被保护植物；

第2条 始终坚持动物、鱼类和植物的自然生物资源可持续性发展的原则，动物、鱼类和植物检疫法的唯一目标就是保护自然资源，使它们免受病虫害的侵害。

第3条 B：“地区”是指印度尼西亚共和国境内某个岛的一部分、或整个岛屿、或群岛，根据病虫害的传播情况来设定。

健康证是由被授权的官方机构签发的证书。

如果应检物调离检疫实施地，或者在境内自由地运送，就可认为应检物被输入到印度尼西亚共和国境内了。

第6条 如果应检物调离检疫实施地，或者在境内目的地自由地运送，就可认为应检物从印度尼西亚共和国境内的一个地区被带进另一个地区。如果应检物在出口的地方被包装运输到印度尼西亚共和国境内的另一个地区，就可认为应检物调离印度尼西亚共和国境内的一个地区，进入另一个地区。

第7条 第（1）部分 如果应检物在出境口岸被包装好后运输到印度尼西亚共和国境外的另一个地方，就可认为应检物是被输出到印度尼西亚共和国境外。

第8条 政府强制的附加要求如下：

a. 在病虫害源头国家对携带者实施除害处理；

b. 在第三国家强迫实施检疫；

c. 如果应检物的运输工具停靠在一个国家的港口，而这个国家的应检物被输入到印度尼西亚，禁止在这个国家的港口卸货；

d. 输入某些携带者，必须持有专门的证书。

第9条 第（2）部分 这部分提到的检疫措施应该在初步检查后实施，初检的货物档案应该遵循动物、鱼类和植物检疫病虫害咨询目录建立。

第10条 D：在这部分提到的除害处理就是利用物理的、化学的、生物的或者其他的一些方法对动物、鱼类和植物携带者进行除害和消毒处理。物理的除害方法包括照射、加热、冷却；化学的除害处理方法包括使用杀虫剂、抗生素和化学疗法；生物的除害处理方法包括注射免疫血清和疫苗。

H：放行作为一个检疫措施，是指应检物在出口、进口或在印度尼西亚共和国境内给地区间的调运中都被放行。出口和在境内各地区间的调运需要持有健康证书，进口放行需持有放行证书。

第11条 第（2）部分 在1962年的第1号法律关于海港检疫和1962年的第2号法律关于空港检疫中列出的危及人类健康的检疫传染病如下：

a. 瘟疫；

b. 霍乱；

c. 黄热病；

d. 天花；

e. 虱传斑疹伤寒；

f. 虱传播回归热。

如果在检验携带者的过程中发现上面提到的疫病，检疫官必须和口岸的医师一起采取行动。

第14条 第（1）部分 如果在出货运输时没有提供健康证书或一些附加的证书，就表示没有完全满足检疫要求。

第 16 条 第（2）部分 这个规定使政府部门或者政府官员免除了承担合法实施了检疫的动物、鱼类和植物被破坏的责任。

第 19 条 第（1）部分 放行证书是由属于其相关领域的检疫官员签发，而动物检疫方面的放行证书只能由兽医检疫官签发。

第（2）部分 健康证书是由属于其相关领域的检疫官员签发，而动物检疫方面的健康证书只能由兽医检疫官签发。

第 20 条 第（1）部分 在检疫机构外的进出境地点进行检疫是指在牛圈、马厩、仓库、货主接受的地方、在运输工具上、在海港、河港、渡口的码头上、在机场、在邮局、或在边境站进行检疫。

第 22 条 第（1）部分 动物、鱼类和植物检疫的管理和实施需要相当多的资金，因此，政府要求使用了服务和设施的人应当承担一部分检疫费用。

第 25 条 “其他应检物”包括来源于动物原材料、鱼类和植物的食品废弃物、动物饲料的废料和家畜粪便。

Explanatory memorandum on law of the Republic of Indonesia No. 16 of 1992 concerning animal, fish, and plant quarantine

General provisions

Indonesia is endowed by Almighty God with rich biotic natural resources comprising various kinds of animals, fish, and plants. These biotic natural resources constitute a basic wealth for national development which is important in the effort to raise the standard of living, prosperity and welfare of the people, and need, therefore, to be preserved and protected. One of the menaces to the continuous existence of the biotic natural resources is the incursion of pests and diseases which do damage to animals, fish, and plants. The damage inflicts severe losses on the people and government, since it reduces the animal, fish, and plant production in terms of quantity as well as quality, or it may cause extinction of certain species of animals, fish, and plants of high economic or scientific value. Certain diseases of animals, and fish may even affect public health.

The territory of the Republic of Indonesia is still free from different kinds of exotic pests and diseases of animals, fish, and plants. The geographical condition of the territory of the Republic of Indonesia, which is an archipelago consisting of thousands of islands, is an advantage in the effort to prevent the introduction and dissemination of pests and diseases of animals, fish, and plants, since the sea around the archipelago and among the islands serves as a natural barrier. With the ever – increasing movement of people and goods, which are likely to carry pests and diseases of animals, fish, and plants, and the limited capability to exercise control, prevention, and safeguard, the chance for the introduction and dissemination of pests and diseases becomes greater.

This may endanger the continuous existence of biotic natural resources and the national economy. It is, therefore, necessary to be highly anticipatory and vigilant, in order that the introduction and dissemination of pests and diseases may be prevented.

The endeavor to prevent the introduction into, and the dissemination from one area to another within, the territory of the Republic of Indonesia of pests and diseases of animals, fish, and plants is effectuated by the government through animal, fish, and plant quarantine.

Conformable to international convention Indonesia is also obligated to prevent the concomitant exportation of pests and diseases in the exportation of animals, fish, and plants from the territory of the Republic of Indonesia. The effectuation of animal, fish, and plant quarantine is, therefore, a manifestation of the fulfillment of such international obligation. The important role of animal, fish, and plant quarantine requires for its execution a clear, firm, and comprehensive legal foundation in the form of a law.

Some existing ordinances regarding animal quarantine, fish quarantine, and plant quarantine left behind by the colonial government are considered to be out of date. Moreover, in the national laws that are being used as the basis for animal quarantine, fish quarantine, and plant quarantine regulation, namely Law No. 2 of 1961 concerning Exportation and Importation of Plants and Planting Materials, Law No. 6 of 1967 concerning Basic Provision for Animal Husbandry and Animal Health, and Law No. 9 of 1985 concerning Fisheries, the subjects of animal quarantine, fish quarantine, and plant quarantine are not adequately or explicitly. Covered. Consequently these laws are unable to deal with various problem arising in the field of animal, fish, and plant quarantine. In view of the above – mentioned facts, it is deemed necessary to establish a law dealing with an overall subject on animal, fish, and plant quarantine.

Article by article elucidation

Article 1

Numeral 6

"Other articles" means pathogenic material, biological products, fish feed, material for the preparation of cattle and/or fish feed, biological control agents, cultures of organism, soil, compost or other growing media, vector, etc.

Numeral 7

"Animals" includes protected animal, as referred to in other existing laws.

Numeral 8

"Materials of animal origin" includes meat, milk, egg, hair, horn, hoof, hide, semen, etc.

Numeral 9

"Products of materials of animal origin" includes meat that has been boiled in water, dried meat, semi processed tanned hide, ground bones, bones, blood, animal hair, hoof and horn, intestines, animal manure, animal organs, glands, tissue, and body fluid.

Numeral 10

"Fish" includes:

a. finned fish (Pisces);

b. shrimp, crab, and the like (Crustacean);

c. shell – fish, cuttlefish, octopus, snails and the like (Mollusk);

d. jelly – fish and the like (Coelenterate);

e. sea – cucumber, sea urchin, and the like (Echinoderm);

f. frogs and the like (Amphibian);

g. crocodile, turtle, tortoise, lizard, water snake and the like (Reptile);

h. whale, dolphin, sea – cow, and the like (Mammalian);

i. sea – weed and other aquatic plants (Algae);

j. other aquatic biota related to the above – mentioned species and protected fish.

Numeral 11 "Plants" includes protected plants, except sea – weed and other aquatic plants (Algae);

Article 2

Adherence to the principle of continuity – in – existence of biotic natural resources of animal, fish and plants, means that animal, fish and plant quarantine shall have as its only objective the protection of biotic natural resources against the attack of pests and disease of animal, fish and plants, and shall have no other objectives.

Article 3

Character b "Area" means part of an island, or entire island, or group of island, within the territory of the Republic of Indonesia, which term is related to the prevention of dissemination of pests and diseases. Certificates of health are issued by authorized officials. It is considered to have been imported into the territory of the Republic of Indonesia, if the carrier has been removed from the place of quarantine actions or has been moved in free traffic within the territory of the Republic of Indonesia.

Article 6

It is considered to have been brought into an area from another within the territory of the Republic of Indonesia, if the carrier has been removed from the place of quarantine actions or has been moved in free traffic in the area of destination within the territory of the Republic of Indonesia .

It is considered to have been moved out of an area to another within the territory of the Republic of Indonesia, if the carrier has been loaded into a means of conveyance at the place of exit to be transported to another area within the territory of the Republic of Indonesia.

Article 7

Section (1)

It is considered to have been exported from the territory of the Republic of Indonesia, if the carrier has been loaded into a means of conveyance at the place of export to be shipped to another place outside the territory of the Republic of Indonesia.

Article 8

Additional requirements imposed by the Government are among others:

a. application of certain treatment to carrier of pests and diseases of animals, fish, or plants in the country of origin; or

b. imposition of quarantine actions in a third country; or

c. prohibition on the unloading in a certain country of carrier of animal, fish or plant pests and diseases being imported into the territory of the Republic of Indonesia, if the means of conveyance of such carrier calls at a port in that country.

d. obligation that certain imported carrier be accompanied by special certificates.

Article 9

Section (2)

The quarantine action mentioned in this Section shall be performed after preliminary examination has been done of the documents of goods followed by consultation of the list of quarantine pests and diseases of animals, fish, or plants.

Article 10

Character d

The treatment mentioned in this Section is the act of disinfesting or disinfecting carriers of pests and diseases of animals, fish, and plants by physical, chemical, biological, or any other method. Treatment by physical method includes among others: irradiation, application of heat, and refrigeration; chemical treatment includes among others: application of pesticides, antibiotics, and chemotherapy; biological treatment includes among others serum and vaccine injection.

Character h

Release as a quarantine actions means release in connection with exportation from, importation into, or movement from one area to another within, the territory of the Republic of Indonesia of carriers of quarantine pests and diseases of animals, fish, and plants. Release in connection with exportation or movement from one area to another is accompanied by a health certificate, while release in connection with importation is accompanied by a certificate of release.

Article 11

Section (2)

Quarantine diseases that endanger human health are among others those quarantine diseases specified in Law No. 1 of 1962 concerning Sea Quarantine, and Law No. 2 of 1962 concerning Air Quarantine, namely:

a. plague,

b. cholera,

c. yellow fever,

d. small – pox,

e. typhus exanthematicus infectiosa (louse – borne typhus)

f. louse – borne relapsing fever.

If in the course of inspection the carriers of the above mentioned diseases are detected, the quarantine officer must act coordinately with the port health physician.

Article 14

Section (1)

Quarantine requirements have not been fully complied with, if for example the shipment has not yet been provided with a health certificate or a certain additional certificate.

Article 16

Section (2)

This provision confirms that the execution of destruction exempts the ministry or the official responsible for animal, fish, and plant quarantine from all legal actions.

Article 19

Section (1)

Certificate of release are issued by quarantine officers belonging to their respective fields. As for the issuance of certificates of release in the field of animal quarantine, this is performed by the quarantine veterinarian only.

Section (2)

Certificates of health are issued by quarantine officers belonging to their respective fields. As for the issuance of certificates of health in the field of animal quarantine, this is performed by the quarantine veterinarian only.

Article 20

Section (1)

Quarantine actions at the places of entry and export outside the quarantine establishments are performed among others in the cow – sheds, stables, warehouses, owners go downs, on board the means of conveyance, at the wharves of seaports, river ports, ferry ports, at airports, in the post offices, and at border posts.

Article 22

Section (1)

Animal, fish, and plant quarantine administration and operations require considerable funds, and therefore it is deemed necessary that the persons who make use of the services rendered and the facilities made available by the Government be required to take a share in the funding of quarantine activities.

Article 25

The term "other carrier" includes garbage which consist of among others food wastes derived from material of animal origin, fish, plants, wastes of animal feed, and drug.

越　南

越南植物检疫和植物保护法

（第 36/2001/PL－UBTVQH10 号法令，2001 年 7 月 25 日）

为加强国家管理效力，提高植物有害生物的防治效果，促进现代农业生产的发展，保障人民群众的身体健康，保护生态环境，维持生态平衡，根据 1992 年《越南社会主义共和国宪法》以及 2001 年越南十届国会第八次会议关于制定法律法令计划的决议，制定《越南社会主义共和国植物检疫和植物保护法》，全文如下：

第一章　总　　则

第 1 条

本法所称的植物检疫和植物保护是指对植物有害生物进行防治、实施植物检疫和植物保护。

第 2 条

本法适用于在越南境生产、经营和使用植物资源及其他与植物资源、植物检疫、植物保护活动有关的越南及境外组织机构和个人，但越南签署或参加的国际条约中有相关规定的，则服从其规定。

第 3 条　本法中各种定义如下：

1. 植物资源　包括有益的植物和植物产品。

2. 有害生物　指对植物资源能够造成危害的微生物、害虫、杂草、鼠等各种生物体。

3. 外来生物侵害　指尚未得到科学确认或在越南国内尚未发现的有害生物对植物资源造成的侵害。

4. 有益生物　指各种对生物侵害有限制作用的昆虫、动物和其他生物体。

5. 检疫对象　指能在一定区域内对植物资源造成严重危害，在越南国内没有分布或分布区域很小的存在潜在危害的生物体。

6. 检疫物　指植物、植物产品及用于生产、储藏、运输或可能携带检疫对象的物体。

7. 植物资源所有者　指对植物资源有使用权、所有权的单位或个人。

8. 物主　即“货主”，是指对植物检疫物拥有所有权、使用权或直接进行管理的组织或个人。

9. 植物保护药剂　指来源于化学物质、植物体、动物体、微生物或其他物体的可用于防治植物有害生物的加工品。

10. 树种　包括种子、核、树的一部分或其他可供种植的繁殖类材料。

11. 树种引进　指从国外进口树种在国内作科研和种植。

第 4 条　植物检疫和保护工作须遵循以下原则：

1. 以防为主，及时发现，彻底根除；既保证防治效果，又确保对人体健康无害；防止污染环境，保持生态平衡。

2. 当前利益与长远利益相结合，保障社会公共利益。

3. 运用先进的科学技术，将现代科学技术同先进的经验相结合。

第 5 条

国家为投资参与此项防治工作的国内外组织及个人创造有利条件。

国家鼓励研究、生产、经营及使用对其他生物无害的植物防治药剂的投资活动。

第 6 条

所有国家机关、经济、政治或社会团体、社会组织、社会－专业组织、人民武装力量及个人均应遵守本法之规定。

越南祖国阵线及其成员单位在自己职权范围内有责任向社会宣传本法并对本法的实施进行监督。

第7条

严禁各种破坏植物资源、环境资源、生态资源，危害人体健康和生态平衡的行为。

第二章 植物有害生物的防治

第8条

要长期坚持植物保护和防治工作，及时研究各种措施，保证试验、生产、开发、创造、保管、买卖、使用、出口、进口、转口、过境和其他关系到植物资源安全的活动顺利进行。

第9条 植物保护和防治工作包括：

1. 调查、发现、预测和通报发生危害植物资源事件的可能性、时间、分布范围、危害程度等。
2. 制定并指导防治工作。
3. 运用先进的科学技术指导防治工作。

第10条 植物资源主的权利和义务

1. 要求具有植物检疫和保护权限的国家机关通报植物资源危害状况，并接受这些机构的指导意见进行防治工作。
2. 主动制定和落实防治计划。
3. 发生危害植物资源的事件时，及时向植物检疫和保护机关报告。
4. 采取各项力所能及的措施对危害植物资源的事件进行有效控制，以免使植物有害生物扩散至其他地方。
5. 按照具有植物检疫和保护权限的国家机关的要求及时采取各项措施保护植物资源免受侵害。

第11条

1. 当信息显示有害生物侵害可能发展成疫情时，国家植物检疫机关应及时予以确认，并指导植物资源主进行预防。
2. 当某省内的有害生物侵害发展速度快、密度高、面积广，传播蔓延趋于形成危机时，由直属中央的省级人民委员会主席决定采取预防措施、检查落实情况和公布疫情，并负责向农业与农村发展部报告。疫情属于两省范围内的，由农业与农村发展部决定采取预防措施、检查落实情况和公布疫情，并报告政府总理。

第12条 如有疫情公布，国家机关、组织和个人的责任如下：

1. 农业和农村发展部指导迅速控制、扑灭疫区疫情，防止其扩散；并根据疫情的严重程度决定或建议政府总理决定采取相应措施。
2. 疫区的各级人民委员会主席负责组织有关机构与各社会团体配合，带领人民群众采取有效措施控制和彻底扑灭疫情。疫区的各级人民委员会主席根据疫情的严重程度、扩散程度，负责直接向上级领导汇报，以采取及时、有效措施扑灭疫情、消除影响，防止疫情的再次传播。
3. 疫区植物资源主、有关组织及个人应当采取相应措施在有关机构的指导下及时控制和扑灭疫情。

疫情结束后，有关权力机构负责人应当公布疫情解除的有关决定。

第13条 严禁以下行为：

1. 采取可能危害人体、动植物健康的措施进行植物防治的。
2. 有能力采取措施而未采取，致使危害行为发展成疫情，严重危害植物资源的。
3. 投放过期的库存防治药剂到市场上的。
4. 进口、出口、生产、运输、储藏、买卖、使用被病虫害污染或危害的树种。

第三章 植物检疫

第14条

1. 植物检疫工作应当及时、迅速，确保发现植物有害生物，并做出正确鉴定结论。

2. 植物检疫工作包括：

（1）采用各种检疫方法或手段对检疫物实施植物检疫；

（2）按照操作程序，选择控制检疫对象的有效方法处理检疫物；

（3）监督、检查各种处理办法的执行情况；

（4）对引进植物和仓储植物产品实施病虫害监督管理；

（5）普及植物检疫知识，认清检疫对象，按照植物检疫流程实施检疫工作。

3. 植物检疫机关应配备开展业务所必需的各种现代化技术装备，确保植物检疫工作的顺利开展。

第 15 条

按照各个时期的发展需要，由农业与农村发展部研究、调整检疫对象名录，并由部长签发。

第 16 条

物主（货主）要清楚自己的检疫物受生物侵害的状况，在发现或怀疑检疫物受已公布的检疫对象或其他生物侵害时，要有针对性地采取各种除害处理办法进行处理，防止疫情传播蔓延，同时，报告国家植物保护和植物检疫机关以及就近的地方政府。

第 17 条

1. 当检疫发现已公布的检疫对象时，国家植物检疫机关有权要求物主（货主）立即执行国家规定的各种处理办法，消除有害生物的危害。

2. 检疫对象或其他有害生物已经传播蔓延，造成危害的，物主（货主）要及时向国家植物保护和植物检疫机关以及就近的地方政府报告，并按照本法第 11 条的规定执行。

第 18 条

1. 所有进口、出口、进口加工后再出口或出口加工后再进口的检疫物都应当实施植物检疫。

2. 经检疫发现检疫对象时应对检疫物作以下处理：

（1）检出在越南境内尚无分布的检疫对象，不准其入境，作退回或销毁处理；

（2）检出在越南境内有局部分布的检疫对象，由国家植物检疫机关实施除害处理后，再决定是否准予其入境。

3. 在条件不允许和对检疫对象的危害情况难以做出准确结论时，应将检疫物封存在指定的地点，严格保管，同时，报请国家植物检疫机关作进一步的检疫，并出具检疫报告，做出允许使用检疫物或按有关规定处理或按本法第 2 条执行的决定。

第 19 条

1. 进口到内地的种子或可能做种用的有益生物、植物资源，由国家植物检疫机关实施检疫、监督管理，依本法的规定执行。

2. 进口到内地的种子或可能做种用的有益生物、植物资源，当需要从一地调运到另一地时，应将有益生物、植物资源的来源地等有关情况报告国家植物检疫机关，经同意后，由国家植物检疫机关监督调运。

3. 首次进口的新树种（苗），应先种植在国家植物检疫机关指定的地点，由国家植物检疫机关经过一段时间的观察和调查，做出检疫结论后，方可在越南境内进行种植。

第 20 条

1. 出口植物的检疫，按照越南已签署的国际条约和贸易合同中规定的检疫要求实施检疫。

2. 经检疫发现有害生物时，应当实施除害处理，未达到检疫标准的，国家植物检疫机关不得签发植物检疫证书。

第 21 条

单位或个人运输检疫物过境之前，应事先报经国家植物检疫机关同意，并保证在各种有害生物不会造成传播蔓延的情况下，运输过境。当造成传播蔓延时，物主（货主）应及时向国家植物检疫机关报告，由国家植物检疫机关按照越南法律规定实施严格检疫和执行各种保护措施。

第 22 条

1. 单位或个人经营（的）检疫物属于进口、出口、进口加工后再出口、出口加工后再进口或转口的，按第 18 条第（1）款、第 20 条第（1）款和第 21 条的规定，应向驻守在公路口岸、火车站、渡口、港口、机场、邮局的国家植物检疫机关报检，办理植物检疫手续，领取植物检疫证书。

2. 国家植物检疫机关接到报检单后，根据货物性质、数量、类型和存货地点，及时检疫。

3. 在货物到达国家植物检疫机关规定的地点后马上进行检疫。

4. 出口、进口、过境、转口的检疫物，按照政府规定的具体检疫制度、检疫标准实施检疫。

第 23 条

发现有散落、被遗弃或非法引入到越南境内的外来检疫物时，货主或发现者应及时报告就近的国家植物检疫机关进行处理。

第 24 条

单位或个人从事植物检疫和除害处理工作的，应有政府签发的专业证书。

第 25 条

实施植物检疫业务时，公务人员应身着制服，佩戴徽章，出示政府颁发的检疫证件。

第 26 条

按照政府的规定办理植物检疫手续，缴纳植物检疫费或植物保护费。

第 27 条 严禁下列物体入境：

1. 已公布的检疫对象。

2. 越南国内尚未发现有分布的有害生物。

3. 其他有害生物、土壤。

第四章 农药管理

第 28 条

植物用农药是限制经营类药剂。国家根据有关法律统一管理此类药剂的生产、出口、进口、保管、储存、运输、买卖及使用。

国家对于此类药剂的无害化研究、投资、生产、经营活动采取优惠政策。

第 29 条 农业和农村发展部有如下职责：

1. 检验和登记越南境内的新型防治药剂进行。

2. 对此类新药剂检验合格后给其颁发许可证。

3. 每年公布允许使用、禁止使用的此类药剂名录。

第 30 条

1. 此类药剂的生产、加工、包装、储存、保管、运输、买卖、使用及销毁都应当保证人体、植物、牲畜及环境的安全。

2. 如此类药剂流散，直接管理机关应当根据有关法律规定及时采取措施进行处理；如大量流散，可能造成严重后果的，应当立即向植物检疫和保护机关、当地政府或有关机构报告，并根据法律规定承担相应责任。

3. 发现此类药剂流散的个人也应立即向国家管理机关或最近的当地人民委员会报告。

第 31 条

1. 此类药剂生产、加工、包装、买卖等活动的直接管理和经营者须具有专业证照及其他政府应求具备的资质。

2. 核发生产、加工、包装、买卖此类药剂外国投资许可证应当有农业和农村发展部的书面意见。

3. 进口未列入名录的药剂用于实验目的或其他限制使用地区或领域的须有农业和农村发展部的批准书。

第 32 条

1. 进口、生产、加工、包装、买卖此类药剂的组织和个人应当具备国家管理机关所规定的标准。

2. 使用此类药剂的组织和个人应当严格按照规定的对象、种类、用量、浓度、时间、期限、时间间隔及使用范围使用。

3. 使用此类药剂的组织和个人应当保证人体、植物、牲畜和生态环境的安全，并为因未按本条第 2 款之规定使用而承担责任。

第 33 条

1. 应销毁或退回原产地的药剂包括：

（1）越南禁止使用的药剂名录中所列药剂；

（2）假冒药剂；

（3）无使用价值的过期药剂；

（4）产地不明的药剂；

（5）不在越南允许使用药剂名录所列范围的药剂。

政府对各类应当销毁或退回原产地的药剂作具体规定。

2. 销毁药剂及包装应当严格按照政府规定办理，并须经国家植物检疫和保护部门、环境保护机构、当地政府监督和确认。

3. 需销毁和退回药剂的，由药剂的进口商、生产商及销售商承担因此而产生的费用。

第 34 条　储存药剂应遵守以下规定：

1. 中央应当建立国家药剂储备库。

2. 省、直辖市应当有地区级药剂储备库。

建立药剂储备库、管理和使用药剂的有关事宜由政府作统一规定。

第 35 条　严禁如下行为：

1. 生产、加工、包装、进口、储存、运输、买卖及使用列入禁止使用药剂名录中的药剂、假冒药剂、产地不明药剂、无商标或商标不合规定的药剂、列入用于特殊场合或限制使用药剂名录的药剂（如需使用此类药剂需遵循本法第 31 条第（3）款之规定）。

2. 进口、买卖、使用过期药剂。

3. 对禁止使用、限制使用、不再允许使用药剂名录之列的药剂进行广告宣传。

第五章　国家植物检疫和植物保护管理机构

第 36 条　国家植物检疫和植物保护管理机构的职责包括：

1. 制定植物检疫和植物保护规划、计划并指导具体实施和落实。

2. 颁布并组织实施各项植物检疫和植物保护法律。

3. 组织跟踪监管，发现、确认危害植物资源的有害生物，并指导开展保护植物资源的除害工作，阻止病虫害传播蔓延，负责公布和撤销疫情。

4. 组织实施植物检疫工作。

5. 组织登记、鉴定、检验农药。

6. 签发、收回新农药检验许可证、进口农药限制使用和未列入允许使用药剂名录的许可证、植物检疫证书、农药登记证书、农药经营行业许可证、熏蒸证书。

7. 组织植物检疫和植物保护科研开发，培训植物检疫和植物保护专业人才。

8. 宣传、普及法律，提高植物检疫和植物保护知识。

9. 监督和处理植物检疫和植物保护领域中各种违法行为，受理申诉、控诉和投诉案件。

10. 搞好植物检疫和植物保护工作中的国际合作。

第 37 条

1. 政府统一管理全国范围内的国家植物检疫和植物保护工作。

2. 农业与农村发展部负责管理全国范围内的国家植物检疫和植物保护机构。

3. 干部、国家直属机构，在规定的业务范围内，行使管理国家植物检疫和植物保护的职责。

4. 各级地方人民委员会结合地方政府范围内的劝农工作，执行、管理和指导植物检疫和植物保护工作。

5. 植物检疫和植物保护系统可以规定从中央到地方政府，各植物检疫和植物保护专业部门具体的组织机构、业务范围和权限。

第 38 条

实行专业监察员制度。植物检疫和植物保护专业监察员，负责监督检查法律执行情况，消除植物资源有害生物的情况，植物检疫、农药管理和各种预防措施的落实情况。防止发生各种违反植物检疫和植物保护法律的行为。

植物检疫和植物保护行业的督察工作由政府规定。

第 39 条

单位和个人有权向国家职权管理机关申诉各种违反法律的行为。

个人有权向国家职权管理机关控诉各种违反法律的行为。

解决申诉、控诉违反法律的行为可依照申诉、控诉的法律规定执行。

第六章　奖励和处罚

第 40 条

在保护植物资源、防治危害事件中取得成绩或在发现、阻止与植物检疫和保护有关违法行为发生中作出贡献的团体和个人可根据法律给予相应奖励。

第 41 条

如有违反本法的行为，伪造植物检疫和保护领域专用许可证、证明、专业资格证或违反其他有关植物检疫和保护法律的，依照违法性质、违法情节对其进行行政处罚或追究其法律责任。

第 42 条

在颁发、收回植物检疫和保护领域各类许可证、证明、专业资格证过程中如有人利用职务、权力之便或滥用职权，缺乏责任感；或在执行有关植物检疫和保护法律过程中滥用职权，包庇违法或犯罪分子，则应依照情节轻重、违反程度对其进行行政处分或依照法律追究其刑事责任。

第 43 条

违反植物检疫和保护有关法律规定，给国家、组织、个人造成损失的，除按本法第 41 条或第 42 条追究法律责任外，还应根据法律规定赔偿受损害一方的损失。

第七章　执 行 条 款

第 44 条

本法从 2002 年 1 月 1 日起施行，1993 年 2 月 4 日国会常务委员会讨论通过的植物检疫和植物保护法同时废止。本法施行前制定的与本法相抵触的其他法律条款全部废止。

第 45 条

由政府对本法进行解释，并指导本法的执行。

Ordinance on the plant protection and quarantine

(No. 36/2001/PL – UBTVQH10 of July 25, 2001)

In order to enhance the State management effect, to raise the effectiveness of the prevention and elimination of organisms harmful to plant resources, contributing to developing the modern and sustainable agricultural production, protecting the people's health, conserving the environment and maintaining the ecological balance;

Pursuant to the 1992 *Constitution of the Socialist Republic of Vietnam;*

Pursuant to the Resolution of the Xth *National Assembly, eighth session, on the* 2001 *law – and ordinance – making program;*

This Ordinance prescribes the plant protection and quarantine.

Chapter I　General provisions

Article 1　The plant protection and quarantine prescribed in this Ordinance cover the prevention and elimination of organisms harmful to plant resources, the plant quarantine and the management of plant protection drugs.

Article 2　This Ordinance is applicable to Vietnamese and foreign organizations and individuals engaged in the production of, trading in, and use of plant resources, and in other activities related to the plant protection and/or quarantine on the Vietnamese territory, except for cases otherwise provided for by international agreements which the Socialist Republic of Vietnam has signed or acceded.

Article 3　In this Ordinance, the following words and phrases are construed as follows:

1. Plant resources　include useful plants and products thereof.

2. Harmful organisms　include microorganisms, pests, weeds, mice and other organisms harmful to plant resources.

3. Alien harmful organisms　mean harmful organisms not yet identified scientifically and not yet ever discovered at home.

4. Useful organisms　include funguses, insects, animals and other organisms that have the effect on limiting the harms caused by harmful organisms to plant resources.

5. Plant quarantine objects　are species of harmful organisms which are likely to cause serious damage to plant resources in areas where they have not yet appeared or have appeared on a narrow scale.

6. Plant quarantine – liable articles　are plants, plant products, means of production, preservation and transport, or other articles capable of carrying plant quarantine objects.

7. Plant resource owners　are organizations and individuals having the right to own, to use or directly manage plant resources.

8. Owners of plant quarantine – liable articles　are organizations and individuals having the right to own, to use or directly manage such articles.

9. Plant protection drugs　are preparations originating from chemicals, plants, animals, microorganisms and other preparations used to prevent and eliminate organisms harmful to plant resources.

10. Plant varieties　include seeds, tubers, saplings, tree parts or other biological substances used for breeding.

11. Imported plant varieties are plant varieties imported from abroad for domestic research and/or cultivation.

Article 4 Plant protection and quarantine shall be carried out on the following principles:

1. Prevention is most important. Detection and elimination must be timely and thorough, ensuring the effective prevention and elimination of harmful organisms, safety for the people's health; limiting environmental pollution and maintaining ecological balance.

2. Combination of immediate and long term benefits, ensuring common benefits of the entire society.

3. Application of scientific and technological advances, combination of modern sciences and technologies and the population's experiences.

Article 5 The State creates conditions for domestic and foreign organizations and individuals to invest in preventing and eliminating organisms harmful to plant resources.

The State encourages the investment and research in the production of, trading in and use of plant protection drugs of biological origin and less toxicity, as well as integrated preventive and eliminative measures.

Article 6 State agencies, economic organizations, political organizations, socio – political organizations, social organizations, socio – professional organizations, armed force units and all individuals shall have to abide by the provisions of this Ordinance.

The Vietnam Fatherland Front Committee and the Front's member organizations shall, within the ambit of their tasks and powers, have to propagate and mobilize people to abide by, and supervise the implementation of, the law provisions on plant protection and quarantine.

Article 7 All acts of causing harms to the plant resources, people's health, environment and ecological system shall be strictly prohibited.

Chapter Ⅱ Prevention and elimination of organisms harmful to plant resources

Article 8 The prevention and elimination of organisms harmful to plant resources must be carried out regularly, synchronously and timely through studying, experimenting, producing, exploiting, processing, preserving, trading, using, exporting, importing, temporarily importing for reexport, temporarily exporting for reimport, transiting and other activities related to plant resources.

Article 9 The prevention and elimination of organisms harmful to plant resources cover:

1. Investigation, detection, projection, forecasting and notification of the possibility, time of emergence, distribution area and extent of harm caused by harmful organisms.

2. Decision and guidance on the application of measures to prevent and eliminate harmful organisms.

3. Guidance on the application of scientific and technological advances to the prevention and elimination of harmful organisms.

Article 10 Plant resource owners shall have the following rights and obligations:

1. To request the competent State bodies in charge of plant protection and quarantine to notify the situation of harmful organisms in the areas and provide guidance on the application of preventive and eliminative measures.

2. To take initiative in making and implementing plans to prevent and eliminate harmful organisms.

3. To report to competent State bodies in charge of plant protection and quarantine upon the detection of harmful organisms capable of causing serious damage to plant resources.

4. To apply measures suited to their capability to effectively prevent and eliminate organisms harmful to plant resources, not to let them spread and destroy plant resources of other persons.

5. To apply preventive and eliminative measures in time in order to protect plant resources at the requests of the competent State bodies in charge of plant protection and quarantine.

Article 11

1. Where there are signs that harmful organisms may develop into a plague, the competent State bodies in charge of plant protection and quarantine must quickly determine and guide plant resource owners to promptly take preventive and eliminative measures.

2. When harmful organisms grow quickly and densely on a large scale, posing a danger of seriously damaging plant resources on the area of a province or centrally – run city, the president of the People's Committee of such province or city shall consider and decide to declare the plague, then report it to the Minister of Agriculture and Rural Development. Where the plague occurs in an area covering two or more provinces, the Minister of Agriculture and Rural Development shall consider and decide to declare the plague, then report it to the Prime Minister.

Article 12 Responsibilities of State bodies, organizations and individuals when there are plague declaration decisions:

1. The Minister of Agriculture and Rural Development shall guide and direct the localities where plagues occur to quickly stamp them out and prevent them from spreading to other areas; base himself/herself on the gravity of the plagues to decide or propose the Prime Minister to decide to apply necessary measures to stamp them out.

2. The presidents of the People's Committees at all levels of the places where plagues outbreak must organize and direct concerned agencies to coordinate with social organizations, mobilize the people in these plague – stricken places to immediately take effective measures to stamp out the plagues and prevent them from spreading to other areas. Basing themselves on the danger and the contagiousness of the plagues, the presidents of the People's Committees of the plague – stricken places shall report to their immediate superiors for the application of necessary measures to stamp out the plagues, overcome their consequences and prevent their possible reoccurrence.

3. Concerned plant resource owners, organizations and individuals in the plague – stricken places must apply measures to stamp out plagues under the guidance of the competent bodies.

When plagues are completely stamped out, the competent persons who have issued plague declaration decisions shall cancel such decisions.

Article 13 The following acts are strictly forbidden:

1. Applying plant protection measures likely to pose danger to men, useful organisms and destroy the environment and ecological system.

2. Failing to apply preventive measures though being so capable of, thus letting harmful organisms develop into a plague and destroy plant resources.

3. Putting in trading and use products with residual volumes of plant protection drugs exceeding the permitted limits.

4. Importing, exporting, producing, transporting, stockpiling, trading in, and using plant varieties heavily infected with pests or carrying dangerous pests.

Chapter Ⅲ Plant quarantine

Article 14

1. The plant quarantine work must ensure accurate, quick and timely detection and conclusion of the situation on plant quarantine – liable articles infected with plant quarantine objects

2. The plant quarantine work includes:

a. Applying measures to examine plant quarantine - liable articles;

b. Deciding appropriate measures to handle articles infected with plant quarantine objects;

c. Overseeing and certifying the application of handling measures;

d. Investigating, monitoring and supervising the situation of harmful organisms on imported plant varieties and plant products kept in warehouses;

e. Popularizing and guiding the methods of detecting and identifying plant quarantine objects, plant quarantine rules and measures.

3. The plant protection and quarantine agencies shall be furnished with necessary and modern equipment to discharge their assigned tasks.

Article 15 For each period, the Minister of Agriculture and Rural Development shall determine and publicize the list of plant quarantine objects and the list of plant quarantine - liable articles

Article 16 Owners of plant quarantine - liable articles must monitor the harmful organism - infection status of their plant quarantine - liable articles.

When detecting or doubting that there are plant quarantine objects which are on the publicized list or alien harmful organisms, the owners of the carrying articles must apply necessary measures to kill them and prevent their spread and at the same time immediately inform the competent State bodies in charge of plant protection and quarantine or the nearest local administrations thereof.

Article 17

1. When detecting plant quarantine objects which are on the publicized list or alien harmful organisms, the competent State bodies in charge of plant protection and quarantine must decide on measures to encircle and eliminate such objects and request the owners of the carrying articles to immediately apply these measures.

2. Where plant quarantine objects or alien harmful organisms have developed into a plague, the competent State bodies in charge of plant protection and quarantine shall have to immediately report such to competent bodies for decision to declare the plague under the provisions of Article 11 of this Ordinance.

Article 18

1. Plant quarantine shall apply to all plant quarantine - liable articles, which are imported, temporarily imported for re - export or temporarily exported for re - import.

2. Where plant quarantine objects are detected, they shall be handled as follows:

a. If the articles are infected with plant quarantine objects which have not yet appeared on the Vietnamese territory but are on Vietnam's list of plant quarantine objects, they shall be either banned from import and returned to their origin place or destroyed.

b. If the articles are infected with plant quarantine objects which are distributed on a narrow scale on the Vietnamese territory and on Vietnam's list of plant quarantine objects or other alien harmful organisms, before being transported inland, thorough handling measures decided by the competent State bodies in charge of plant protection and quarantine must be applied.

3. Where there are not enough grounds to make conclusions on the state of plant quarantine - liable articles being affected with plant quarantine objects, such articles must be put under strict preservation at a designated place. Within the time limit stipulated by the Government, competent State bodies in charge of plant protection and quarantine shall have to make conclusion so that such articles may be used or handled according to the provisions of Point a or Point b, Clause 2 of this Article.

Article 19

1. Useful organisms and plant resources which are imported for breeding or with possible use for breeding

must be examined, supervised and closely monitored by the competent State bodies in charge of plant protection and quarantine according to the law provisions on plant protection and quarantine.

2. When transporting useful organisms or plant resources imported for breeding or with possible use for breeding from one locality to another, the article owners must notify the competent State bodies in charge of plant protection and quarantine of the destination localities for monitoring and supervision.

3. New plant varieties, which are imported for the first time, must be grown in mandated places to facilitate the monitoring of the situation of harmful organisms and can be put into production only after the competent State bodies in charge of plant protection and quarantine conclude that they carry no plant quarantine objects.

Article 20

1. The plant quarantine shall apply to exported plant quarantine – liable articles if the purchase and sale contracts or international agreements that the Socialist Republic of Vietnam has signed or acceded to stipulate that they must be quarantined.

2. Where plant quarantine – liable articles against which handling measures have been applied fail to meet plant quarantine standards, the competent State bodies in charge of plant protection and quarantine shall not grant plant quarantine certificates.

Article 21 Organizations and individuals, before transiting plant quarantine – liable articles on the Vietnamese territory, must obtain the consent of the competent State bodies in charge of plant protection and quarantine and apply measures to prevent harmful organisms on such articles from spreading into Vietnam. In case of a spread, the article owners shall have to immediately report thereon to Vietnam's nearest competent State bodies in charge of plant protection and quarantine and must apply protective measures and plant quarantine as provided for by Vietnamese laws.

Article 22 Organizations and individuals, when importing, exporting, temporarily importing for re – export, temporarily exporting for re – import or transiting plant quarantine – liable articles in the cases specified in Clause 1, Article 18, Clause 1, Article 20, and Article 21 of this Law, shall have to declare such to the competent Vietnamese State bodies in charge of plant protection and quarantine at Vietnam's land road, railway, river way, seaway, airway and postal border – gates and must obtain plant quarantine certificates granted by these bodies.

2. The competent State bodies in charge of plant protection and quarantine shall, upon receiving such written declarations, base themselves on the character, quantity and category of the goods to decide on, and notify the article owners of, the quarantine time and place.

3. The plant quarantine must be carried out right after the plant quarantine – liable articles arrive at the places designated by competent State bodies in charge of plant protection and quarantine.

4. The Government shall specify the plant protection and quarantine regime and standards for plant quarantine – liable articles which are exported, imported, temporarily imported for reexport, temporarily exported for re – import or transited.

Article 23 Where foreign – originated plant quarantine – liable articles are scattered, abandoned in or illegally introduced into Vietnam, their owners or detectors must immediately report such to the competent Vietnamese State bodies in charge of plant protection and quarantine in the nearest places for handling.

Article 24 Organizations and individuals that handle plant quarantine – liable articles by sterile steaming method must have practicing certificates and meet other conditions prescribed by the Government.

Article 25 When performing quarantine tasks, State employees must wear uniform, badges, insignia and quarantine cards as prescribed by the Government.

Article 26 Owners of plant quarantine – liable articles must pay plant protection and quarantine charges and fees according to law provisions.

Article 27 It is strictly forbidden to bring into Vietnam or spread from one region to another in the country:

1. Plant quarantine objects on the publicized list.
2. Alien harmful organisms.
3. Soil containing harmful organisms.

Chapter Ⅳ Management of plant protection drugs

Article 28 Plant protection drugs are goods subject to restricted and conditional business. The State performs the unified management over the production, export, import, preservation, stockpiling, transportation of, trading in, and use of plant protection drugs according to law provisions.

The State adopts preferential policies for research and investment in, production of, trading in, and use of plant protection drugs having biological origin and causing less toxicity.

Article 29 The Ministry of Agriculture and Rural Development shall have to:

1. Provide for the assay and registration of new plant protection drugs for circulation in Vietnam.
2. Grant permits for the assay of new plant protection drugs, certificates of registration of plant protection drugs in Vietnam.
3. Annually publicize the detailed lists of plant protection drugs permitted for use, plant protection drugs for restricted use, and plant protection drugs banned from use, in Vietnam.

Article 30

1. The production, processing, bottling, packing, reservation, preservation, transportation of, trading in, use and destruction of plant protection drugs must ensure safety for human beings, plants, livestock and the environment.
2. Where plant protection drugs are scattered or leaked, the causers or their direct managers must promptly apply handling measures according to law provisions; if drugs are scattered or leaked in large quantities, thus possibly causing serious consequences, they must immediately report such to the competent State bodies in charge of plant protection and quarantine, environmental protection bodies, local administrations or concerned bodies for handling and must bear responsibility therefor according to law provisions.
3. Those who detect scattered or leaked plant protection drugs must immediately report such to State bodies in charge of plant protection and quarantine or the nearest People's Committees.

Article 31

1. Those who personally manage and/or trade in plant protection drugs in the fields of production, processing, bottling, packing and trading must have practicing certificates and satisfy other conditions prescribed by the Government.
2. The licensing of foreign investment in the fields of plant protection drug production, processing, bottling and packing in Vietnam must be approved in writing by the Ministry of Agriculture and Rural Development.
3. The importation of plant protection drugs not on the lists of plant protection drugs permitted for use for assay and for use in foreign – invested projects which are permitted to use these drugs, and of plant protection drugs on the list of those subject to restricted use, must be permitted in writing by the Ministry of Agriculture and Rural Development.

Article 32

1. Organizations and individuals that import, produce, process, bottle, pack and/or trade in plant protection drugs must ensure the quality standards already registered with the competent State bodies in charge of plant

protection and quarantine and their marks and labels be inscribed according to law provisions.

2. Organizations and individuals that use plant protection drugs must ensure the right objects, kinds, dosages and concentrations as prescribed, the right time, use duration, isolation duration and permitted scale.

3. Organizations and individuals that use plant protection drugs must ensure safety for human beings, plants, livestock, food quality and hygiene as well as environment and bear responsibility for the use of plant protection drugs at variance with the provisions of Clause 2 of this Article.

Article 33

1. Plant protection drugs that may be destroyed or returned to the places of their origin include:

a. Plant protection drugs on the list of those banned from use in Vietnam;

b. Fake plant protection drugs;

c. Expired plant protection drugs which no longer have use value;

d. Plant protection drugs of unidentified origin;

e. Plant protection drugs outside the lists of those permitted for use in Vietnam.

The Government shall specify kinds of drug to be destroyed or returned back to their origin places.

2. The destruction of plant protection drugs and their packages must comply with the Government's stipulations, be supervised and certified by the competent State bodies in charge of plant protection and quarantine, environmental protection bodies and local administrations.

3. For plant protection drugs which have been handled with measures of destruction or returning back to their places of origin, organizations and individuals that have imported, produced and/or traded in such plant protection drugs must incur all expenses therefor.

Article 34 The reservation of plant protection drugs is prescribed as follows:

1. At the central level, there shall be the national reserve of plant protection drugs.

2. In provinces and centrally - run cities, there shall be local reserves of plant protection drugs.

The setting up of the reserves of plant protection drugs, the management and use of reserve plant protection drugs shall be stipulated by the Government.

Article 35 All the following acts are strictly forbidden:

1. Producing, processing, bottling, packing, importing, stockpiling, transporting, trading in and using plant protection drugs on the list of those banned from use; fake plant protection drugs, plant protection drugs of unidentified origin; plant protection drugs having marks or labels at variance with law provisions; plant protection drugs outside the lists of those restricted from use and permitted for use in Vietnam, except for cases where they are permitted under the provisions of Clause 3, Article 31 of this Ordinance.

2. Importing, trading in and using expired plant protection drugs.

3. Advertising plant protection drugs which are banned, or restricted from use, or outside the list of those permitted for use, or at variance with their registered contents.

Chapter V State management over plant protection and quarantine

Article 36 Contents of the State management over plant protection and quarantine include:

1. Elaborating and directing the implementation of, plannings and plans on plant protection and quarantine.

2. Promulgating and organizing the implementation of, legal documents on plant protection and quarantine.

3. Organizing the monitoring, detection and identification of organisms harmful to plant resources; directing the prevention and stamping out of plagues damaging plant resources; issuing plague declaration decisions and annulling such decisions.

4. Organizing the implementation of the plant quarantine work.

5. Organizing the registration, examination and assay of plant protection drugs.

6. Granting and withdrawing permits for assay of new plant protection drugs, permits for import of plant protection drugs subject to restricted use or not on the list of those permitted for use, plant quarantine certificates, certificates of registration of plant protection drugs, practicing certificates of trading in plant protection drugs and practicing certificates of sterile steaming.

7. Organizing scientific research, professional training and fostering in plant protection and quarantine.

8. Propagating and popularizing the legislation on and knowledge about plant protection and quarantine.

9. Supervising, inspecting, handling violations and settling complaints and denunciations in the field of plant protection and quarantine.

10. Effecting international cooperation in the field of plant protection and quarantine.

Article 37

1. The Government shall perform the unified State management over plant protection and quarantine nationwide.

2. The Ministry of Agriculture and Rural Development shall take responsibility to the Government for performing the State management over plant protection and quarantine nationwide.

3. The ministries, ministerial – level agencies and agencies attached to the Government shall, within the ambit of their respective tasks and powers, perform the State management over plant protection and quarantine.

4. The People's Committees at all levels shall perform the State management over and direct plant protection and quarantine activities in combination with agricultural promotion activities in their respective localities according to the responsibility assignment by the Government.

5. The specialized plant protection and quarantine network shall be organized from the central to local level. The Government shall specify the organizational structure, tasks and powers of the specialized plant protection and quarantine agencies.

Article 38 The plant protection and quarantine inspectorate is a specialized inspectorate.

The specialized plant protection and quarantine inspectorate shall have to inspect the observance of the legislation on prevention and elimination of organisms harmful to plant resources, the plant quarantine and management of plant protection drugs as well as propose measures to prevent and stop acts of violating the legislation on plant protection and quarantine.

The organization and operation of the specialized plant protection and quarantine inspectorate shall be stipulated by the Government.

Article 39 Organizations and individuals shall be entitled to complain about acts of violating the legislation on plant protection and quarantine to the competent State bodies.

Individuals shall be entitled to denounce acts of violating the legislation on plant protection and quarantine to competent State bodies.

The settlement of complaints and denunciations against acts of violating the legislation on plant protection and quarantine shall comply with the law provisions on complaints and denunciations.

Chapter Ⅵ Commendation and handling of violations

Article 40 Organizations and individuals that record achievements in the protection of plant resources, the prevention of harmful organisms or make merits in the detection and stop of acts of violating the legislation on plant protection and quarantine shall be commended and/or rewarded according to law provisions.

Article 41 Those who violate the provisions of this Ordinance, forge permits, certificates and practicing certificates in the field of plant protection and quarantine or violate other law provisions on plant protection and quarantine shall, depending on the nature and seriousness of their violations, be administratively sanctioned or examined for penal liability according to law provisions.

Article 42 Those who take advantage of their positions and powers or abuse their powers in the granting or withdrawal of permits, certificates and practicing certificates in the field of plant protection and quarantine in contravention of law; show irresponsibility or abuse their positions and powers in the enforcement of the legislation on plant protection and quarantine; cover up violators or violate other law provisions on plant protection and quarantine shall, depending on the nature and seriousness of their violations, be disciplined or examined for penal liability according to law provisions.

Article 43 Those who violate the legislation on plant protection and quarantine, thus causing damage to the State, organizations and/or individuals, shall not only be handled according to the provisions of Article 41 or 42 of this Ordinance but also have to pay compensation therefor according to law provisions.

Chapter Ⅶ Implementation provisions

Article 44 This Ordinance takes effect as from January 1, 2002.

This Ordinance replaces the Ordinance on the Plant Protection and Quarantine passed by the Standing Committee of the National Assembly on February 4, 1993.

All previous provisions contrary to this Ordinance are hereby annulled.

Article 45 The Government shall specify and guide the implementation of this Ordinance.

越南植物检疫条例

依据2001年12月25日《政府组织法规》、2001年7月25日《植物检疫和植物保护法》、农业与农村发展部部长的建议，兹颁布：

第一章　总　　则

第一条　目的

本条例规定了出入境、临时出入境、过境和境内植物检疫相关工作以及对应检物的处理。

第二条　适用范围

本条例适用于越南境内任何涉及到植物检疫活动的越南及外国组织和/或个人，但越南签署或缔结的国际公约中另有规定的除外。

第三条　定义

本条例中涉及的术语作如下解释：

1. 有害生物　任何对植物或植物产品有害的动物、植物、病原体的种、株或型，包括：昆虫、真菌、细菌、病毒、植原体、杂草、鼠以及其他对植物资源有害的生物体。

2. 检疫性有害生物　具有潜在的重要经济影响，但并未在某地区发生，或者虽然已经发生，但未广泛分布，并且已受到官方控制的有害生物。

3. 限定的非检疫性有害生物　某种存在于植物中会对植物的用途产生不可接受的经济影响，因此在输入国受到管制的非检疫性有害生物。

4. 限定性有害生物　检疫性有害生物或限定的非检疫性有害生物。

5. 有害生物新种　在本国未经科学鉴定或之前从未发现的有害生物。

6. 有益生物　任何能够帮助减少有害生物对植物和植物产品的损害的病毒、细菌、线虫、菌类、昆虫、动物或其他生物。

7. 应检物　指植物、植物产品、储存地、包装、运输工具、容器、土壤以及任何其他可能携带植物检疫对象的生物、物品或材料。

8. 染疫情况　货物感染有害生物的程度和特征。

9. 货物查验　包括通过调查、观察、监测、抽样、测试、鉴定和研究以确定感染状况。

10. 消毒　彻底消灭货物中的有害生物的官方程序。

11. 熏蒸　使用完全或基本气态的化学试剂对物品进行处理的方法。

12. 疫点　存在检疫性有害生物名录或限定的非检疫性有害生物名录中所列的一种或几种有害生物的地方。

13. 疫区　检疫机构认定的检疫性有害生物发生区域。

14. 货物批次　具有相似的结构和易感病条件的一定数量的货物。

15. 检疫场所　应施检疫物卸离前进行检查的地方。

16. 有害生物风险分析　对有害生物进行生物、其他科学及经济评估的过程，以确定是否应对此生物进行管制或采取植物检疫措施以及应采取的力度。

17. 非疫区　有科学证据证明某种有害生物在该地区并未发生，且这种情况正由官方所维持。

18. 等效措施　使用不同的植物检疫措施但达到相似的效果。

19. 监控　通过调查、监测或其他手段收集、记录有害生物的发生与否的官方过程。

20. 植物检疫措施一致性　不同国家基于共同的标准建立、认可及应用的植物检疫措施。

21. 植物　活的植物或其部分，包括种子和胚质。

22. 植物产品　未加工的植物材料以及因其性质或加工过程可能造成有害生物的引入或扩散的植物制成品。

23. 新引进的种子　任何未出现在允许生产和销售种类名录上的种子。

24. 植物检疫措施　旨在防止或限制有经济影响的限定的非检疫性有害生物传入和/或扩散的任何法律、法规或官方程序。

25. 原产地　植物最初生长或出现的地方。

26. 检疫设施　官方划定的与周围环境相对隔离，用于种植植物或对植物产品进行检疫的场所。

27. 进口许可　根据具体植物检疫要求，准予物品进口的官方文件。

第四条　货主的责任

1. 对有害生物进行监控，根据植物检疫法规对染疫的、不符合进出口标准的或从疫区输出的货物实施处理。

不同货主的染疫货物必须同时处理时，若货主未能对处理措施达成一致意见，则植物检疫机构将做出决定，货主必须遵循。

2. 对其所有或直接控制的货物定期开展植物有害生物监测。

对于从疫区转运或输出的进境货物经常集中的地区，在做以上监测时须依据国家植物保护和检疫机构的要求和指导进行。

3. 当检出或怀疑检出名录中的应检有害生物或陌生的有害生物体时，货主或发现者必须采取有效措施消灭或阻止有害生物的扩散，同时向就近的国家植物保护和检疫机关或当地相关行政部门报告。

4. 按照植物保护和检疫机关的规定对货物实施处理。

5. 承担植物检疫和货物处理的全部费用。对于找不到货主的货物，运输工具所有者、货物运输或储存的相关负责人必须执行植物检疫法规的规定，并承担货物处理的全部费用。

6. 向越南相关植物保护和检疫机关提供必要的信息，包括：植物和植物产品的产地、栽培方式、有害生物名单、包装工序、出口计划和政策以及任何其他相关的文件。

7. 协助植物检疫人员工作，包括开关运输工具、储存设施或货物包装，提供人员进行检查和抽样。

第五条　植物检疫机关的责任

1. 指导、监督、证明相关检测、控制和处理措施的实施。如果染疫货物必须马上处理但货主无法实施，植物检疫机构应采取处理措施。

2. 查验货物并签发植物检疫证书。

3. 根据《实施卫生与植物卫生措施协定》（《SPS 协定》）和《国际植物保护公约》（IPPC）的规定向输入国提供充分的植物保护和检疫信息。

4. 根据相关国家标准建立并维持非疫区。

5. 评估和了解其他国家对进出境货物的植物检疫措施。

6. 按照农业和农村发展部的规定，在必要时采取紧急行动预防有害生物的引入和扩散。

7. 依据 IPPC 的标准、指导方针和建议统一植物检疫措施。

8. 在适当时与输出国的植物检疫机构合作，在输出国家进出境货物实施查验和处理。

第六条　植物检疫人员的责任及权力

植物检疫人员应负以下责任：

1. 根据《植物保护和检疫》法规的规定实施植物检疫查验；

2. 穿着制服，佩戴徽章和植物检疫证件；

3. 有权进入应检物存放地点；

4. 在限制区域及其他特殊场所执行公务时，应由这些场所的权力部门允许和指引，以满足保密性和植物检疫的要求。

第七条　其他政府机构、人民委员会的责任

1. 农业与农村发展部应定期确定并公布：

a）限定性有害生物名录；

b）进境前应实施有害生物风险分析的应检物名录。

2. 海关应在对货物查验和监管时与植物检疫机关合作，应检物必须在完成所有植物检疫程序后才能办理海关程序。植物检疫申报的内容应在进出境申报单上体现。

植物检疫机构必须将要求转口或销毁或经过植物检疫后确定允许进出境的货物通知货物进出境口岸的海关。海关及其他相关机构应与植物检疫机关协作处理植物检疫的相关问题。

2. 国家运输机关、海关、邮政、公共安全、边防、市场监督及其他相关单位有责任协助植物检疫机关检查、预防和/或处理违反植物检疫法规的情况。

3. 各级人民委员会应指导当地相关机构依法实施植物检疫。

第八条　植物检疫程序

1. 货主或货主委托人必须：

a. 至少提前24小时向就近的植物检疫机关作进出口货物检疫申报；

b. 手提行李或旅客随身携带行李中含有应检物品的，须在出入境申报处填表申报，行李应接受植物检疫机关的检查；

c. 若进境物品是随其他进境货物（手提行李和旅客随身携带行李除外）包装进境的，货主在做清关手续时须提供越南植物检疫机关签发的植物检疫证书或卫生证书；

d. 若出境物品是随其他出境货物（手提行李和旅客随身携带行李除外）包装出境的，如果输入国要求，货主在做清关手续时须提供越南植物检疫机关签发的卫生证书。

2. 植物检疫机关应对货物进行检验检疫，并在查验后24小时内做出结论。超过24小时的，应告知货主。

3. 应检货物的查验和建档应按照农业与农村发展部的规定采用全国统一的形式。

第九条　严禁以下行为

1. 将本条例第七条1. a）名录中所列的任何应检有害生物或任一生长阶段的活的新的有害生物带入越南境内。

2. 将本条例第七条1. a）名录中所列的任何活的限定性有害生物带入非疫区。

3. 将本条例第七条1. b）名录中所列的任何应进行有害生物风险分析的物品带入非疫区。

4. 以任何形式向越南境内输入带有土壤的植物。

第二章　入境植物检疫

第十条　入境植物检疫要求

入境货物必须符合以下要求：

1. 具有输出国植物检疫机关签发的植物检疫证书；

2. 不含本条例第七条1. a）名录中所列的限定性有害生物或新有害生物；如果已受感染，必须经过彻底处理；

3. 货物入境前，植物保护部门必须在风险分析的前提下签发进境植物检疫许可证；

4. 进口木质包装材料必须经过适当的检疫措施。

第十一条　入境植物检疫许可证签发程序

1. 组织和/或个人按照规定的形式申请进境检疫许可。

2. 组织和/或个人按照本条例第四条第6款及农业与农村发展部的规定，向植物保护部门提供充分的入境货物相关信息。

3. 植物保护部门应对入境货物实施有害生物风险分析。

4. 依据有害生物风险分析的结果，植物保护部门可决定是否向相关组织和/或个人签发进口植物检疫许可证明。

第十二条　进口植物检疫

1. 当入境货物到达第一个口岸时，货主必须按照本条例第八条的规定完成植物检疫程序。

2. 植物检疫机构应在入境口岸实施检疫。如有特殊情况，植物检疫可以在其他相关法律规定的植物检疫场所实施。

3. 当载有应检货物的船舶到达越南领海时，船舶运营商应进行植物检疫申报；经检疫，若未发现检疫性有害生物，该船舶允许进入港口；否则，必须对货物及船舶进行彻底处理。

4. 暂时出入境货物必须和出入境货物一样进行植物检疫。

第十三条　植物种子和有益生物进口

1. 进口植物种子和有益生物的组织和/或个人必须符合本条例第十条的要求，并满足以下条件：

a）植物种子应在相关植物检疫机构指定的口岸进行植物检疫。

b）列于允许种植和贸易名单上的植物种子，应运抵已向植物检疫机关注册的隔离圃进行隔离种植。上述组织和/个人应向当地植物保护和检疫机关报告，以便进一步对有害生物状态进行监测和检查。

c）为了进行有害生物的监控，首次进口的植物新品种只能在植物检疫机关指定的地点种植。

d）在某些特殊情况下，需要农业与农村发展部的允许。

2. 进口栽培植物和有益生物的组织和/或个人应依法保证不同种类植物的隔离监测时间。

3. 具体的植物种类和有益生物的监测时间以及检疫设施的标准应遵守农业与农村发展部的规定。

第十四条　进口货物的监测、流动、储存和使用

1. 从货物进入越南境内时起，植物检疫机关即有权对该货物进行检疫监管。

2. 货主必须持有越南植物检疫机关签发的植物检疫证书，且在货物运输、储存和使用过程中执行证书中规定的所有检疫措施。

第三章　出境植物检疫

第十五条　出境植物检疫情况

植物检疫机关仅在下述情况下对出境物品实施植物检疫：

1. 贸易合同或国际协议要求植物检疫；

2. 货主要求出具植物检疫证书的。

第十六条　出口植物检疫

1. 出境货物到达最后一个港口或离境口岸时，货主必须提前通知就近的植物检疫机构，并按照本条例第八条实施植物检疫措施。

2. 植物检疫机关应在指定口岸实施检疫查验。若已在产地、启运地或储存地进行植物检疫的，货主应在离境口岸提供植物检疫证书。

第十七条　出境货物监管

1. 从货物检验、植物检疫证书签发到货物离开越南，植物检疫机构都有权对其进行监管。

2. 运输过程中，货主应执行植物检疫证书上规定的所有措施。

第四章　过境植物检疫

第十八条　货物过境条件

1. 必须持有原产国相关机构签发的植物检疫证书。

2. 货物过境越南或使用越南境内的仓储设施，必须经过越南植物检疫机关的同意。

3. 为了避免运输和储存过程中有害生物的扩散，过境货物必须按照货物的不同特性进行包装。

第十九条　过境货物植物检疫

1. 在过境货物到达越南第一个入境口岸时，货主必须向就近的植物检疫机关申报，并出示原产国植物检疫证书。

2. 越南植物检疫机关有权对过境货物进行监管，检查运输工具和货物外包装。

3. 如果货物在过境越南时，被检测出越南检疫性有害生物、未按货物特性包装或者不具备原产国植物检疫证书，则越南植物检疫机关有责任对货物和运输工具进行检查或暂停货物转运，直到货物按要求重新包装为止。植物检疫机关应对这些情况进行监管、检查以便签发过境检疫证书。

第五章　境内植物检疫

第二十条　境内植物检疫内容

1. 管理越南境内的限定性有害生物和有益生物；

2. 当发现疫情爆发时，对疫点进行控制和处理；

3. 对入境种子和储存的植物产品中存在的限定性有害生物开展监控，并对有害生物进行调查、记录。

第二十一条　境内植物检疫程序

1. 境内植物检疫的申报、检测、处理及检疫证书的签发应符合本条例第八条的规定。

2. 境内生产的、既非来自疫区也非经疫区运输的植物种子在境内流动的过程不需要进行植物检疫。

第二十二条　境内植物检疫监测

1. 对入境的植物种子和仓储的植物产品定期进行有害生物状态检查、监控；

2. 如果引进的植物种子和/或有益生物是用于种植或释放的，当地相关植物保护和检疫机构必须：

a）核对植物种子和/或有益生物的相关记录；

b）对其种植或释放的地点进行监测和管理；

c）如果货主未能按照规定履行检疫程序，当地相关植物检疫机构应依法采取检疫措施。

3. 明确疫区边界，确定从疫区输出货物的植物检疫地点，签发国内植物检疫证书，监管货物从疫区的输出。

4. 核查植物检疫证书，监管从疫区输入当地的货物。

5. 确定对染疫货物的处理措施；指导、监督货主实施处理。

6. 当疫情扩散时，当地相关植物检疫机构应按照《植物保护和检疫法》第十一条的规定将情况立即上报负责发布疫情公告的机构。

第六章　应检物处理

第二十三条　应检物处理

1. 货物处理措施包括加工、挑选、分类、清洗、除虫、退运、废弃及其他消灭限定性有害生物的措施。

2. 植物检疫处理必须按照相关植物保护和检疫机关的法律规定实施。

第二十四条　进境货物处理

1. 感染限定性有害生物的货物应采取以下处理措施：

a）如果货物感染了未在越南境内发生的限定性有害生物或新的有害生物，则该货物不得入境，且必须作退运或销毁处理。如果有可行的彻底处理的办法也可以采用。

b）如果货物感染了未在越南境内广泛分布的限定性有害生物，或者是越南规定的限定的非检疫性有害生物名录上的一种有害生物，则植物检疫机关应确定要采取的处理措施。如果在越南境内无法采取措施，则货物必须作退运或销毁处理。

2. 植物检疫机关有责任协助当地政府及其他相关部门对从国外漂流、坠落、丢弃或泄漏到越南境内的应检物进行处理。

第二十五条　出境、过境及国内流动货物处理

1. 出境货物处理应按照货主、输入国植物检疫或贸易合同的要求进行。

2. 如果检出越南规定的检疫性有害生物或发现货物没有按照其特性进行包装，则货主应用适当方式对货物实施处理或重新包装。

3. 境内植物检疫活动中对感染有害生物的货物的处理措施应按照相关检疫机构的决议进行。

第二十六条　熏蒸处理

熏蒸处理机构应完全满足以下要求：

1. 其管理者或操作者必须具有《熏蒸执业证书》；

2. 直接从事熏蒸处理的工人必须持有《熏蒸资格证》；

3. 具有开展熏蒸活动的技术规程、设施和设备，保证人、家畜的安全；

4. 按照相关机构的法律规定，确保环境卫生、工作安全和防火；

5. 熏蒸处理的工作场所、储存场所和化学品必须取得相关部门的书面批准。

农业与农村发展部应根据规定签发《熏蒸执业证书》、《熏蒸资格证》以及《达到熏蒸要求证书》。

第二十七条　签发《熏蒸执业证书》的条件

1. 申请者必须取得化学或植物保护专业的大学或大学以上学历；

2. 具有至少 3 年的熏蒸工作经验；

3. 具有县级或县级以上医疗机构签发的健康证明。

第二十八条　签发《熏蒸资格证》的条件

1. 申请者必须经过一定时间的熏蒸处理的培训，并通过相关植物保护部门的技能考试。

2. 具有县级或县级以上医疗机构签发的健康证明。

第二十九条　熏蒸处理机构的权利和义务

1. 从事熏蒸处理的机构和/或个人必须完全符合本条例第二十六条的规定，并在整个操作过程中严格遵守这些要求；

2. 有权签发熏蒸处理证书；

3. 对染疫货物实施熏蒸处理时，必须在植物检疫机构的指导和监督下进行；

4. 采用的熏蒸处理措施不能影响货物的质量及商业价值，并对熏蒸结果负责。

第七章　执行条款

第三十条　生效时间

本条例在政府公报上发布 15 日后生效。本条例将取代 2002 年 6 月 3 日政府发布的、编号 58 / 2002/ ND – CP《关于植物保护条例法令》的附件《植物检疫条例》和《农药管理条例》。与本条例产生冲突的之前的所有法规均废止。

第三十一条　实施责任

农业与农村发展部有责任指导本条例的实施。

中央政府下属各部级部长、负责人、政府部门负责人、省、市人民委员会主席必须贯彻实施本条例。

代表政府

总理

阮晋勇

Decree on plant quarantine

Pursuant to the December 25, 2001 Law on Organization of the Government;

Pursuant to the July 25, 2001 Ordinance on Plant Protection and Quarantine;

At the proposal of the Minister of Agriculture and Rural Development.

Chapter I General provisions

Article 1 Purpose

This Decree prescribes the plant quarantine activities related to import, export, temporary import, temporary export, transit, domestic quarantine and treatments of regulated articles.

Article 2 Scope of application

This Decree shall apply to any Vietnamese and foreign organizations and/or individuals that are involved in plant quarantine activities carried out in the territory of Viet Nam, except otherwise stipulated in international treaties to which Viet Nam is a signatory or a contracting party.

Article 3 Definitions

In this Decree, the following terms shall have the meanings hereunder assigned to them:

1. *Pest*: any species, strain or biotype of plant, animal or pathogenic agent injurious to plants or plant products, including: insects, fungi, bacteria, virus, phytoplasma, weeds, mouse and other organisms harmful to plant resources.

2. *Quarantine pest*: a pest of potential economic importance to the area endangered thereby and not yet present there, or present but not widely distributed and being officially controlled.

3. *Regulated non - quarantine pest*: a non - quarantine pest whose presence in plants for planting affects the intended use of those plants with an economically unacceptable impact and which is therefore regulated within the territory of the importing country.

4. *Regulated pest*: a quarantine pest or a regulated non - quarantine pest.

5. *New pest*: any pest that has not been identified on the basis of scientific evidence and not found previously in the country.

6. *Beneficial organism*: any virus, bacterium, nematode, fungus, insect, animal or any other organism which helps reduce damage to plants and plant products due to pests.

7. *Regulated article*: any plant, plant product, storage place, packaging, conveyance, container, soil and any other organism, object or material capable of harboring regulated pests.

8. *Pest infestation status*: level and characteristics of pest present in a commodity.

9. *Inspection of articles*: involves survey, observation, monitoring, sampling, testing, identification and research to determine infestation status.

10. *Disinfestation*: official procedure for the absolute killing of pests on articles.

11. *Fumigation*: treatment with a chemical agent that reaches the commodity wholly or primarily in a gaseous state.

12. *Epidemic focus*: is a place where exist one or several kinds of harmful organisms on the promulgated lists of quarantine pests or regulated non - quarantin pests.

13. *Outbreak area*: an area with a quarantine pest defined by a competent quarantine authority.

14. *Lot of articles*: a quantity of articles, identifiable by its homogeneity of composition and potential of infestation.

15. *Place of quarantine inspection*: a premise where inspection is conducted before moving the articles.

16. *Pest risk analysis*: the process of evaluating biological or other scientific and economic evidence to determine whether a pest should be regulated and the strength of any phytosanitary measures to be taken against it.

17. *Pest free area*: An area in which a specific pest does not occur as demonstrated by scientific evidence and in which, where appropriate, this condition is being officially maintained.

18. *Equivalence*: the use of different phytosanitary measures while achieving similar effects.

19. *Surveillance*: an official process which collects and records data on pest occurrence or absence by survey, monitoring or other procedures.

20. *Harmonization of phytosanitary measures*: the establishment, recognition and application by different countries of phytosanitary measures based on common standards.

21. *Plant*: living plants and parts thereof, including seeds and germplasm.

22. *Plant products*: unmanufactured material of plant origin and those manufactured products that, by their nature or that of their processing, may create a risk for the introduction and spread of pests.

23. *Newly imported seed*: any seed which has not appeared as in the list of varieties permitted for production and sale.

24. *Phytosanitary measure*: Any legislation, regulation or official procedure having the purpose to prevent the introduction and/or spread of quarantine pests, or to limit the economic impact of regulated non – quarantine pests.

25. *Place of origin*: a place where the plants were grown or initate the infested status.

26. *Quarantine facility*: official station for growing plants or holding plant products in quarantine which is isolated from the environment.

27. *Import permit*: official document authorizing importation of a commodity in accordance with specified phytosanitary requirements.

Article 4　Responsibilities of article owner

1. Monitoring and control pests, treatment of infested articles, non – compliance articles for import or export, and movement of articles from a outbreak area in accordance with phytosanitary regulations.

In cases where infested articles of various owners must be treated simultaneously while the article owners cannot reach agreement on the treatment thereof, the plant quarantine authority shall make decisions with which the articles owners must comply.

2. Regularly monitoring the pest status harmful to plant resources under ownership or directly handle.

At places where import articles are often gathered, transited or brought from outbreak areas, the above – mentioned monitoring must be effected upon requests and under the guidance of the competent plant protection and quarantine State bodies.

3. Upon detecting or doubting the existence of regulated pests on the promulgated list or strange harmful organisms, the articles owners or the detectors shall have to apply necessary measures to eliminate and stop their spread, and at the same time to immediately report to the nearest competent plant protection and quarantine State bodies or local administration thereon.

4. To apply article – treating measures decided by the competent plant protection and quarantine State bodies.

5. Payment of plant quarantine charge and costs of treatment of articles as prescribed. Where the articles

owners are not available, the owners of conveyance or those responsible for transport or storage of the articles must comply with relevant phytosanitary regulations and bear all expenses for the treatment of articles.

6. Provision of necessary information on plant protection and quarantine to relevant competent authorities of Viet Nam, including: information about plants and plant products such as production areas, cultivated methods, pest lists, packing procedures, export programs and policies, and any other relating documents.

7. Facilitating plant quarantine officers to perform their duties by opening and closing conveyance, storage facilities or commodity packages, supplying personnel for inspection and sampling.

Article 5 Responsibilities of plant quarantine authority

1. Guiding, monitoring and certifying the implementation of inspection, control and treatment measures. In cases where the infested articles must be urgently treated while the articles owners are incapable of doing so, the plant quarantine authorities shall conduct treatments.

2. Inspecting articles and issuing phytosanitary certificates.

3. Providing sufficient information on plant protection and quarantine to importing countries in accordance with the Agreement on the Application and Sanitary and Phytosanitary Measures (SPS Agreement) and International Plant Protection Convention (IPPC).

4. Establishing and maintaining pest free areas according to the related National Standard.

5. Reviewing and recognizing phytosanitary measures of other countries applied to import or export articles as equivalence.

6. Taking emergency actions as specified by the Ministry of Agriculture and Rural Development to prevent the introduction and spread of pests, when necessary.

7. Harmonizing phytosanitary measures on the basis of IPPC standards, guidelines and recommendations.

8. Coordinating with the quarantine authorities of the exporting country, where appropriate, to conduct inspection and treatment of imported and exported articles in the exporting country.

Article 6 Responsibilities and powers of plant quarantine officer

The plant quarantine officers on duty shall take responsibilities to:

1. Conduct quarantine inspection in compliance with legislative provisions on Plant Protection and Quarantine;

2. Wear uniform, badges and quarantine identity card;

3. Have right to access the premises where regulated articles exist;

4. When performing tasks in restricted areas and in other special cases, plant quarantine officers shall be accepted and guided by the competent authorities of those areas in order to satisfy requirements of both confidentiality and plant quarantine.

Article 7 Responsibilities of other government agencies, people's committees

1. Periodically, the Minister of Agriculture and Rural Development shall determine and issue:

a) The list of regulated pest;

b) The list of regulated articles and the list of articles subject to PRA prior to import.

2. The Customs shall coordinate with the plant quarantine authorities in inspecting and monitoring regulated articles. The customs procedures will be completed for regulated articles only after the completion of all plant quarantine procedures. The contents of plant quarantine declaration are reflected in the entry/exit form.

For articles which are required to re-export or destroy, or which, after quarantine inspection, are allowed for export or import, the plant quarantine authorities shall notify such to the Customs offices at the border ports through which such articles are exported or imported. The Customs and other relevant agencies shall collaborate with plant quarantine authorities in handling related matters at the request of the plant quarantine authorities.

3. The concerned State bodies of Transport, Customs, Post Office, Public Security, Border Guard, Market Control and other relevant agencies shall have responsibilities to coordinate with the plant quarantine authorities in inspecting, preventing and/or handling violations of the plant quarantine regulations.

4. People's Committees at all levels shall guide local concerned agencies to implement plant quarantine activities in accordance with legislative provisions.

Article 8　Plant quarantine procedures

1. The articles owners or persons authorized by the articles owners shall:

a. Make declarations at least 24 hours in advance to the nearest plant quarantine office before import or export of articles;

b. For hand luggage or accompanied luggage which contains regulated articles, declaration shall be made in the entry/exit form and the luggage shall be subject to phytosanitary inspection.

c. For imported articles being packed together with other imports (except hand luggage and accompanied luggage), the owner, when submitting the customs dossiers for customs clearance, must have the quarantine application form or phytosanitary certificate issued by Viet Nam plant quarantine authority.

d. For exported articles being packed together with other exports (except hand luggage and accompanied luggage), the owner, when submitting dossiers for customs clearance, must have phytosanitary certificate issued by Viet Nam plant quarantine authority if it is required by the importing country.

2. The plant quarantine authorities shall inspect, verify and make results available within 24 hours after inspection of the consignment. Where it is longer than 24 hours, the articles owners shall be notified.

3. The inspection and documentation of regulated articles shall be undertaken uniformly nationwide in compliance with legislative provisions of the Ministry of Agriculture and Rural Development.

Article 9　Prohibitions

1. Bringing into Viet Nam any regulated pests under the lists referred to in paragraph 1. a of Article 7 of this Decree, or any living new pests at any development stage.

2. Bringing any living regulated pests under the lists prescribed in paragraph 1. a of Article 7 of this Decree into non – infested areas.

3. Bringing any subjected to PRA prescribed in paragraph 1. b of Article 7 of this Decree into non – infested areas.

4. Bringing plants with soil into Viet Nam in any form.

Chapter Ⅱ　Import plant quarantine

Article 10　Import plant quarantine requirements

The imported consignment shall meet the following requirements:

1. A phytosanitary certificate issued by the competent authority of the exporting country.

2. Free from regulated pests in the lists referred to in paragraph 1. a of Article 7 of this Decree and new pests; if infested, complete treatments must be made.

3. Import plant quarantine permit issued by the Plant Protection Department is required for articles subject to PRA before importing into Viet Nam.

4. Imported wood packaging materials must undergo appropriate phytosanitary treatments.

Article 11　Procedure for issuing import plant quarantine permit

1. Organizations and/or individuals file the request for import quarantine permit according to specified form.

2. Providing sufficient information relating to imported articles to The Plant Protection Department in ac-

cordance with Paragraph 6 of Article 4 of this Decree and regulations of the Ministry of Agriculture and Rural Development.

3. The Plant Protection Department shall conduct PRA for imported articles.

4. Depending on PRA results, the Plant Protection Department may or may not grant import plant quarantine permit to the organizations and/or individuals concerned.

Article 12 Import quarantine inspection

1. When the imported articles arrive at the first point of entry, the articles owners have responsibility to complete plant quarantine procedures in accordance with Article 8 of this Decree.

2. Plant quarantine office which will carry out the procedures at the point of entry. In special cases, the plant quarantine procedures may be carried out at other places with quarantine facilities in compliance with legislative provisions.

3. When vessels carrying regulated articles and reaching the water territory of Viet Nam, the vessel operator shall make declaration for phytosanitary inspection; if no quarantine pest is found, such vessel will be allowed to accommodate the water port; if a regulated pest is detected, they must undergo complete treatment.

4. Articles temporarily imported or temporarily exported must go through plant quarantine procedures like the imported articles.

Article 13 Importation of plant seeds and beneficial organisms

1. Organizations and/or individuals that import plant seeds and beneficial organisms shall satisfy the requirements as specified in Article 10 of this Decree and meet the following conditions:

a) Plant seeds shall undergo quarantine procedures at the point of entry designated by the competent quarantine authority.

b) As for plant seeds in the list permitted for growing and trading, they shall be transported to and grown at the sites that have been registered with the plant quarantine authority. The said organizations and/or individuals shall report to the local plant protection and quarantine agencies for further monitoring and checking pest status;

c) As for new plant varieties imported for the first time, they may be grown only at a quarantine facility which is designated by the plant quarantine authorities for pest screening.

d) In some special cases, permission of the Minister of Agriculture and Rural Development is required.

2. Orginizations and/or individuals import plant for planting and beneficial organisms shall satisty the monitoring duration for specific group of plant varieties prescribed in legislative regulations.

3. The monitoring duration for specific groups of plant varieties and beneficial organisms as well as specifications of a standard quarantine facility shall comply with provisions of the Ministry of Agriculture and Rural Development.

Article 14 Monitoring, movement, storage and use of imported articles

1. The plant quarantine authorities are empowered to supervise quarantine of imported articles as from the time such articles are brought into the Vietnamese territory.

2. The articles owners must have the phytosanitary certificate granted by Vietnamese plant quarantine authorities and implement all measures described in such certificate during the process of transport, storage and use of the articles.

Chapter Ⅲ Export plant quarantine

Article 15 Export plant quarantine basements

The plant quarantine authority shall only conduct phytosanitary inspection on exported articles in cases where:

1. The commercial contract or international agreements require quarantine procedures;

2. The articles owners request plant quarantine certification.

Article 16　Export quarantine inspection

1. When the exported articles arrive at the final port or export terminal, the article owners must notify in advance the nearest and carry out quarantine inspection according with Article 8 of this Decree.

2. The plant quarantine authority shall carry out quarantine inspection at the designated port. When inspection is conducted at the production site, departure site or storage facility, the owner shall present the phytosanitary certificate at the export terminal.

Article 17　Monitoring of exported articles

1. The quarantine authorities shall have the right to supervise the plant quarantine of export articles from the time the articles are inspected and granted with phytosanitary certificate until they are transported out of the territory of Viet Nam;

2. During the process of shipment, the articles owners shall fully implement all measures that have been specified in the phytosanitary certificate.

Chapter Ⅳ　Transit plant quarantine

Article 18　Conditions for consignments in transit.

1. A phytosanitary certificate issued by the competent authority of the country of origin.

2. The consignment in transit or using storage facilities in the territory of Viet Nam shall be agreed by the Vietnamese plant quarantine authorities.

3. The articles in transit must be packed with specific commodity configurations in order to prevent the spread of pests in the process of transportation and storage.

Article 19　Quarantine inspection of consignments in transit

1. When the articles in transit arrive at the first point of entry of Viet Nam, the article owners shall inform the nearest plant quarantine office and present the phytosanitary certificate of the country of origin;

2. The plant quarantine authorities of Viet Nam shall have the right to supervise such articles, inspect the conveyance and the outside of the consignment.

3. If the articles transiting Vietnam are found with Vietnam's plant quarantine objects or packed improperly under the commodity specifications, without phytosanitary certificate of origin country, the plant quarantine bodies have reposibility to inspect the articles and transport means or suspend the movement until re – packing meet the requirements. The Plant quarantine authorities monitor and inspect these cases for issuance of phytosanitary transit certificates.

Chapter Ⅴ　Domestic plant quarantine

Article 20　Contents of domestic plant quarantine

1. Management of regulated pests and beneficial organisms in Viet Nam;

2. Management and implementation of treatment measures once pest outbreaks are detected.

3. Development and implementation of effective pest record surveys, surveillance and control programmes of regulated pests on imported seeds and stored plant products.

Article 21　Procedure for domestic plant quarantine

1. The declaration, inspection, treatment and granting of domestic phytosanitary certificates shall comply with Article 8 of this Decree.

2. Domestically produced seeds that neither come from nor move through outbreak areas shall not be subject to quarantine procedures in the process of domestic movement.

Article 22　Monitoring domestic quarantine

1. Undertake regular observations, surveillance and monitoring of pest status on imported plant seeds and

stored plant products;

2. When plant seeds and/or beneficial organisms are introduced for growing or release, the local competent plant protection and quarantine agencies shall:

a) Check records associated with plant seeds and/or beneficial organisms;

b) Monitor and supervise places of growing and/or release;

c) If the owners of imported articles fail to comply with the provisions, the local competent agencies shall take phytosanitary measures in accordance with legislative provisions;

3. Establish the boundaries of pest outbreak area, determine places for domestic quarantine inspection of articles transported from the outbreak area, issue domestic phytosanitary certificates, supervise the movement of regulated articles out of the outbreak area;

4. Check phytosanitary certificates and supervise consignments brought from the outbreak area to local fields;

5. Determine measures for treatment of articles infested with regulated pests; provide guidance and supervise the articles owners in the implementation of treatments;

6. When pest outbreak becomes spreading, the local competent agency shall immediately report thereof to the authority responsible for declaring the outbreak as provided for in Article 11 of the Ordinance on Plant Protection and Quarantine.

Chapter Ⅵ Treatment of regulated articles

Article 23 Treatment of regulated articles

1. Treatment of articles involves such measures as processing, selection, sorting, cleaning, disinfestation, return to the place of origin, disposal and other measures for the purpose of eradication of regulated pests.

2. The phytosanitary treatments must be applied in accordance with legislative provisions of competent plant protection and quarantine authorities.

Article 24 Treatment of imported articles

1. The treatment of articles infested with regulated pests shall be conducted as follows:

a) If the articles infested with a pest in the list of regulated pests but not present in the territory of Viet Nam, or with a new pest, such articles shall not be allowed for import and must be returned to the place of origin or be destroyed. Where absolute treatments are available, such measures may be applied;

b) If the articles infested with a pest in the list of regulated pests but not widely distributed in the territory in Viet Nam, or infested with a pest appeared in the list of regulated non – quarantine pests of Viet Nam, absolute treatment measures shall be decided by the plant quarantine authority. Where treatments are not feasible in Viet Nam, the consignment shall be returned to the place of origin or destroyed.

2. The plant quarantine authority is responsible for, in coordination with local governments and other agencies concerned, the treatment of foreign articles adrift, dropped, discarded or leaked into Viet Nam.

Article 25 Treatment of export, in transit and domestic movement articles

1. The treatment of exported articles shall be conducted at the request of the article owners or in accordance with phytosanitary requirements of the importing countries or commercial contracts.

2. If a quarantine pest of Viet Nam is intercepted or the articles are not packed with specific commodity configurations, the owner shall conduct treatment or repack the articles in an appropriate manner.

3. Treatment of infested articles in domestic phytosanitary activities shall be conducted by the decisions of competent quarantine authorities

Article 26 Fumigation

the fumigation organizations shall fully meet the following requirements:

1. The manager or operator of the facility must obtain Fumigation Practice Certificate;

2. The workers directly involved in fumigation must have Fumigation Cards;

3. Having technical process, facilities and equipment in service of fumigation activities, ensuring safety for human and livestock ;

4. Ensuring environment hygiene, working safety, fire prevention in accordance with legislative provisions of competent authorities;

5. Working sites, storage facility and chemicals must be approved in writing by competent authorities.

The Minister of Agriculture and Rural Development shall adopt provisions for issuing the Fumigation Practice Certificate, the Fumigation Cards and the Certificate of Satisfaction of Fumigation Requirements.

Article 27 Conditions for granting the Fumigation Practice Certificate

1. The applicant should achieve university or higher degree major in chemists or plant protection;

2. At least 3 years of experience in fumigation;

3. Health certificate issued by the health clinic at the district or higher levels.

Article 28 Conditions for granting the Fumigation Card

1. The applicant must undergo a training course on fumigation and a skill test by the competent regulatory agency.

2. Health certificate issued by the health clinic at the district or higher levels.

Article 29 Rights and obligations of organization operating fumigation

1. Organizations and individuals engaged in fumigation activities only conduct the fumigation as from the time they fully meet the conditions prescribed in Article 26 of this Decree and commit to strictly observing those conditions throughout their operation process;

2. Eligible for issuing Fumigation Certificate for regulated articles;

3. The fumigation of articles infested with quarantine pests shall be designated and supervised by the plant quarantine authorities;

4. Fumigation methods taken will not affect the quality of goods, articles and community wealthy. Responsible for results of fumigation.

Chapter Ⅶ Implementation provision

Article 30 Effect

This Decree takes effect in 15 days from the date being registered in the Official Gazette. This Decree replaces the Plant Quarantine Regulation which was attached with the June 03, 2002 Decree No 58/2002/ND – CP of the Government promulgating the Plant Protection Regulation, the Plant Quarantine Regulation and Pesticide Management Regulation. All previous provisions contrary to this Ordinance shall be annulled.

Article 31 Implementation responsibilities

The Minister of Agriculture and Rural Development takes responsibility to guide the implementation of this Decree.

Ministers, Heads of ministerial level agencies, Directors of government agencies, Presidents of People's Committees of provinces and cities under the Central Government are responsible for the implementation of this Decree.

ON BEHALF OF GOVERNMENT

PRIMER MINISTER

(*Signed*)

Nguyen Tan Dung

越南引进植物品种和有益生物的植物检疫规定

（2002 年 10 月 8 日与农业与农村发展部
2002 年第 89 号决定一同颁布）

第 1 条　实施范围和对象

1. 本规定适用于全国的植物检疫。

2. 本规定适用于作为植物品种和有益生物引进的应施检疫物。

第 2 条　名词及术语解释

本规定中下列名词及术语应作如下解释：

1. 植物品种包括种子、块茎、茎秆和植株的部分、其他原生质体（组织、胚胎、细胞）等作为种质资源的材料。

2. 允许进口的植物品种指列入农业与农村发展部公布的允许进口植物品种名单的品种。

3. 首次进口的新植物品种指未列入农业与农村发展部公布的允许进口植物品种名单，且首次引进越南的品种。

4. 有益生物指真菌、昆虫、动物以及其他对植物资源有益或能限制有害生物的破坏作用的生物。

第 3 条　植物品种和有益生物进境前检疫的规定

1. 允许进境的植物品种

引进植物品种的组织和个人必须至少提前 3 天向植物保护部申报。

2. 首次引进的新植物品种

1）引进植物品种的组织和个人必须服从农业与农村发展部或其他授权允许进口部门的行政人员的调遣；至少提前 10 天将品种的学名、品种的归属、品种的产地、品种可能携带的虫害、品种的计划用途、品种试种地点及其他相关情况书面报告（如果可能的话）植物保护部。

2）植物保护部应指定地点，提前 5 天进行播种或栽培，以监控害虫情况，并将情况报告货主及进境口岸植物检疫部门。

3. 引进有益生物

1）引进有益生物的组织和个人必须服从农业与农村发展部或其他授权允许进口部门的行政人员的调遣，至少提前 10 天将该物种的地理分布、生物学和生态学特性、使用目的、生长繁殖地点及其他相关情况书面报告（如果可能的话）植物保护部。

2）植物保护部应至少提前 5 天通知货主，并将该上述有害生物情况报告进境口岸植物检疫部门。

第 4 条　口岸植物品种和有益生物植物检疫规定

1. 查验单证

——进境植物检疫许可证；

——输出国植物检疫证书；

——其他相关材料（如果有的话）；

——植物检疫注册登记材料（根据 2002 年第 82 号决定）。

2. 检验、抽样

1）方法

——植物品种为块茎、果实：根据部门标准 No. 10 TCN 336 – 98：植物检疫　进出境或过境块茎、果实检验方法

——植物品种为种子：根据部门标准 No. 10 TCN 337 - 98：植物检疫　进出境或过境各类种子检验方法

——植物品种为植株、枝条、幼芽：根据部门标准 No. 10 TCN 338 - 98：植物检疫　进出境或过境植物检验方法

2）样品处理

——允许进境植物品种的样品，经检验和专家鉴定受害虫为害的，必须把一部分留存在口岸，其余部分应送交进境后植物检疫中心，在隔离的植物检疫场地内进行播种和种植。整批货物应在登记的地点种植。

——初次引进的新植物品种，经检验和专家鉴定受害虫为害的，必须送交进境后植物检疫中心，在隔离的植物检疫场地内进行播种和种植。整批货物应在植物保护部指定的地点种植。

——其他原生质体：

口岸实行批批查验，不在现场抽取样品。整批货物应当运往指定地点。

——有益生物：

口岸实行批批查验，不在现场抽取样品。整批货物应当运往指定地点进行增殖培养。

3. 操作规程

1）经检验、分析、专家鉴定，该植物品种符合进口的所有条件，口岸植物检疫部门应当签发进境、过境、境内转运植物检疫证书（根据农业与农村发展部2000年11月20日第118号决定第10条）。

2）送达植物检疫通知书：签发进境、过境、境内转运植物检疫证书后，口岸植物检疫部门应送达植物检疫通知书：

——植物品种允许进境：送达植物保护部、进境后植物检疫中心和该植物品种进行播种、种植地的省植物保护部门。

——初次引进的新植物品种：送达植物保护部、进境后植物检疫中心、直属的植物检疫部门和该植物品种指定播种、种植地的省植物保护部门。

——有益生物：送达植物保护部、对该有益生物的增殖培养进行监管的进境后植物检疫中心。

4. 对引进植物品种和有益生物的管理就执行现行规定。

第5条　植物品种和有益生物的邮寄 - 进境植物检疫规定

1. 允许进境的植物品种

——在隔离条件下对隐藏病害进行监管。

——在种植地点对害虫情况进行监管。

2. 初次引进的新植物品种

——在隔离条件下对隐藏病害进行监管。

——在指定隔离地点对邮寄 - 进境害虫进行监管。

——监管结束后，植物检疫部门应就该品种能否投入使用给予答复。

3. 有益生物

——在指定的增殖培养机构对有益生物的生长情况进行监管；

——评估其影响及定殖范围；

——监管期（见第6条）结束后，植物检疫部门应就该生物能否广泛使用给予答复。

第6条　对初次引进的新植物品种和有益生物监管期的规定

序号	受监管植物、生物	监管时间
1	多年生果树的种子	1 ~ 2 年
2	果树的嫁接苗	1 ~ 2 年
3	林业树种	1 ~ 2 年
4	短期产业化树种、草药	3 ~ 6 个月

5	多年生产业化树种、药用树种	1～2 年
6	粮食作物	6 个月
7	蔬菜和次要粮食作物	3 个月
8	管状植物	1 个生长周期
9	花卉植物、装饰植物	6～12 个月
10	草及绿色铺地植物	6 个月
11	其他原生质体	3 个月
12	有益生物	1 年

第 7 条 补充条款

在执行过程中出现任何问题或新情况，有关组织和个人应立即报告植物保护部，并由其汇总上报农业与农村发展部，以便对解决、改正和/或补充。

The regulation on plant quarantine for imported plant varieties and useful organisms

(Issued together with Decision No. 89/2002/DQ – BNN of October 8, 2002 of the Minister of Agriculture and Rural Development)

Article 1 Application scope and objects

1. This Regulation applies to plant quarantine nationwide.

2. This Regulation applies to plant quarantine – liable objects being imported plant varieties and useful organisms.

Article 2 Interpretation of terms and phrases

In this Regulation, the following terms and phrases shall be construed as follows:

1. *Plant varieties* mean seeds, tubers, stems and parts of plants, other plasma (tissue, embryo, cell), which are used as varieties.

2. *Plant varieties permitted for import* mean those on the list of plant varieties allowed for import, which are prescribed by the Ministry of Agriculture and Rural Development.

3. *New plant varieties*, *imported for the first time*, mean those not on the list of plant varieties allowed for import, which are prescribed by the Ministry of Agriculture and Rural Development and imported for the first time into Vietnam.

4. *Useful organisms* means fungi, insects, animals and other organisms, which exert positive effect on plants or restrict harms caused by harmful organisms to plant resources.

Article 3 Provisions on plant quarantine for plant varieties and useful organisms before they are imported

1. For plant varieties allowed for import

Organizations and individuals, that import plant varieties, must declare with the Plant Protection Department at least three days in advance.

2. For new plant varieties imported for the first time

a) Organizations and individuals, that import plant varieties, must submit the official dispatches of the Ministry of Agriculture and Rural Development (MARD) or the official dispatches with the Ministry's authorization permitting the import; the scientific names of the varieties; the files on varieties; the origins of varieties; pest components on varieties; plans on use of varieties; places for experimentation and other relevant papers (if any) to the Plant Protection Department at least 10 days in advance.

b) The Plant Protection Department shall prescribe places for sowing or cultivation to monitor harmful pests and notify such to the object owners and plant quarantine offices at the import border gates at least 5 days in advance.

3. For imported useful organisms

a) Organizations and individuals, that import useful organisms, must submit the official dispatches of the MARD or the official dispatches with the Ministry's authorization permitting the import, the information on geographical distribution, biological and ecological characteristics, use purposes, places for multiplication growing and other relevant papers (if any) to the Plant Protection Department at least 10 days in advance.

b) The Plant Protection Department shall notify the object owners and import border – gate quarantine offices of the import of the above – said useful organisms at least 5 days in advance.

Article 4 Provisions on plant quarantine for plant varieties and useful organisms at border – gates.

1. Checking dossiers

—The import plant quarantine permit;

—The plant quarantine certificate of the exporting country;

—Other relevant papers (if any);

—The plant quarantine registration paper (according to the set form in Decision No. 82/2002/QD – BNN).

2. Inspection, sampling

a) Methods:

—For plant varieties being tubers, fruits: To comply with branch standard No. 10 TCN 336 – 98: Plant quarantine – Methods of examining tubers and fruits on export, import or transit.

—For plant varieties being seeds: To comply with the branch standard No. 10 TCN 337 – 98: Plant quarantine – Methods of examining assorted seeds on export, import or transit.

—For plant varieties being plants, branches, sprouts: To comply with the branch standard No. 10 TCN 338 – 98: Plant quarantine – Methods of examining plants on export, import or transit.

b) Sample treatment:

—Samples of plant varieties allowed for import, after being analyzed and expertised in term of pest components, must be partly kept at the border – gates; the remainder shall be sent to the post – import Plant Quarantine Center for sowing and growing in isolated plant quarantine areas. The entire lots of objects shall be brought to the registered places of cultivation.

—New plant varieties imported for the first time, after being analyzed and expertised in term of pest components, must be sent to the post – import Plant Quarantine Center for sowing and growing in isolated plant quarantine areas. The entire lots of objects shall be brought to places prescribed by the Plant Protection Department.

—For other plasma:

Inspecting at the border – gates 100% of the lots of objects. Not taking samples at border – gates. The entire lots of objects shall be brought to prescribed places.

—For useful organisms:

Inspecting at the border – gates 100% of the lots of objects. Not taking samples. The entire object lots shall be brought to prescribed places for multiplication culture.

3. Completing procedures

a) After the inspection, analysis and expertise, if the plant varieties meet all conditions for import, the plant quarantine offices at the border – gates shall grant plant quarantine certificates for import, export, transit and inland transportation (according to Form No. 10 of Decision No. 118/2000/QD – BNN – BVTV of November 20, 2000 of the Minister of Agriculture and Rural Development).

b) Sending plant quarantine notices: After granting plant quarantine certificates for import, transit and inland transportation, the border – gate plant quarantine offices must send the plant quarantine notices:

—For plant varieties allowed for import: To the Plant Protection Department, Post – Import Plant Quarantine Center, Plant Protection Sub – Departments of the provinces where such plant varieties are sown or grown.

—For new plant varieties imported for the first time: To the Plant Protection Department, the Post – Import Plant Quarantine Center, the Plant Quarantine Sub – Departments of regions under management, Plant Protection Sub – Departments of the provinces with places prescribed for sowing or growing such plant varieties.

—For useful organisms: To the Plant Protection Department, the Post – Import Plant Quarantine Center for monitoring and supervision in the course of multiplication culture of useful organisms.

4. Plant quarantine charges for imported plant varieties and useful organisms shall comply with the current regulations.

Article 5 Provisions on post - import plant quarantine for plant varieties and useful organisms

1. For plant varieties permitted for import

—Monitoring diseases hidden under isolation conditions.

—Monitoring pest situation at the cultivation places.

2. For new varieties imported for the first time

—Monitoring diseases hidden under isolation conditions

—Post - import monitoring pests at the prescribed isolation places.

—After the period of monitoring, the plant quarantine offices shall have to reply whether such varieties can be put into production or not.

3. For useful organisms

—Monitoring the situation on the development of useful organisms at the prescribed multiplication culture establishments;

—Evaluating the effects and registered spectrum;

—After the monitoring duration (prescribed in Article 6), the plant quarantine offices shall have to reply whether such organisms can be used on a large scale or not.

Article 6 The provisions on duration for monitoring pests causing harms to groups of new plant varieties, imported for the first time and imported useful organisms

Ordinal number	Groups of monitored plants, organisms	Monitoring duration
1	Seeds of perennial fruit trees	1 to 2 years
2	Grafted stems, grafted branches of fruit trees	1 to 2 years
3	Forestrial trees	1 to 2 years
4	Short - day industrial plants, pharmaceutical herbs	3 to 6 months
5	Perennial industrial trees, pharmaceutical trees	1 to 2 years
6	Food crops	6 months
7	Vegetable and subsidiary food crops	3 months
8	Tubular plants	1 growth cycle
9	Flower plants, ornamental plants	6 to 12 months
10	Grass, plants for green coverage	6 months
11	Other plasma	3 months
12	Useful organisms	1 year

Article 7 Implementation provisions

If in the course of implementation any problems or new matters arise, organizations and individuals should promptly report them to the Plant Protection Department for synthesization and report to the MARD for settlement, appropriate amendment and/or supplementation to the Regulation.

越南社会主义共和国植物检疫对象名录

（2005 年 11 月 14 日越南农业和农村发展部
（QD－BNN）2005 第 73 号决定）

Ⅰ类：未在越南境内发生，但对植物资源有重要的潜在经济影响的有害生物。

A. 昆虫：

序号	中 文 名	学 名
1	南美实蝇	*Anastrepha fraterculus*（Wiedemann）
2	墨西哥实蝇	*Anastrepha ludens*（Loew）
3	地中海实蝇	*Ceratitis capitata*（Wiedemann）
4	昆士兰实蝇	*Bactrocera tryoni*（Froggratt）
5	蜜柑大实蝇	*Bactrocera tsuneonis*（Miyake）
6	纳塔尔小条实蝇	*Ceratitis rosa* Karsch
7	苍白豆象	*Pachymerus pallidus* Olivier
8	美国白蛾	*Hyphantria cunea*（Drury）
9	日本金龟子	*Popillia japonica* Newman
10	欧洲阔喙谷象	*Caulophilus latinasus* Say
11	谷斑皮蠹	*Trogoderma granarium* Everts
12	肾斑皮蠹	*Trogoderma inclusum* LeConte
13	墨西哥棉铃象	*Anthonomus grandis* Boheman
14	南非桔蓟马	*Scirtothrips aurentii* Faure
15	马铃薯甲虫	*Leptinotarsa decemlineata* Say
16	谷象	*Sitophilus granarius*（Linnaeus）
17	大谷蠹	*Prostephanus truncatus* Horn
18	巴西豆象	*Zabrotes subfasciatus*（Boheman）
19	梨圆盾蚧	*Quadraspidiotus pernicious*（Comstock）
20	白缘象	*Graphognathus leucoloma*（Boheman）
21	美洲稻飞虱（传播水稻白叶病毒）	*Tagosodes orizicolus* Muir
22	古巴稻飞虱（传播水稻白叶病毒）	*Tagosodes cubanus* D. L. Crawford

B. 病害：

序号	中 文 名	学 名
23	柠檬梢枯病菌	*Phoma tracheiphila* Petri，Kantachveli & Gikachvili
24	棉花根腐病菌	*Phymatotrichopsis omnivora*（Duggar）Hennebert

续表

序号	中 文 名	学 名
25	橡胶南美叶疫病菌	*Microcyclus ulei* (P. Henn.) V. Arx
26	马铃薯癌肿病菌	*Synchytrium endobioticum* (Schilb.) Perciva
27	小麦印度腥黑穗病菌	*Tilletia indica* Mitra
28	咖啡细菌性凋萎病菌	*Pseudomonas garcae* Amaral Teixeira & Pinheiro
29	水稻白叶病毒	Rice hoja blanca virus
30	咖啡环斑病毒	Coffee ring spot virus
31	棉枯黄萎病菌	*Verticillium albo – atrum* Reinke & Berthold
32	美洲咖啡叶斑病菌	*Mycena citricolor* (Berk. & Curtis) Sacc
33	番茄溃疡病菌	*Clavibacter michiganensis* subsp. *Michiganensis* (Smith) Davis

C. 线虫：

序号	中 文 名	学 名
34	马铃薯根腐茎线虫	*Ditylenchus destructor* Thorne
35	马铃薯白线虫	*Globodera pallida* (Stone) Mulvey & Stone
36	马铃薯金线虫	*Globodera rostochiensis* (Wollenweber) Mulvey & Stone
37	椰子红环腐线虫	*Rhadinaphelenchus cocophilus* (Cobb) Goodey
38	松材线虫	*Bursaphelenchus xylophilus* (Steiner & Burher) Nickle

D. 杂草：

序号	中 文 名	学 名
39	弯叶独脚金	*Striga hermonthica* (Del.) Bentham
40	密花独脚金	*Striga densiflora* (Benth.) Bentham
41	田蓟	*Cirsium arvense* (L.) Scop.
42	锯齿列当	*Orobanche crenata* Forskal
43	欧亚列当	*Orobanche cernua* Loefl.
44	分枝列当（大麻列当）	*Orobanche ramosa* L.
45	瓜列当（埃及列当）	*Orobanche aegyptiaca* Pers.

Ⅱ类：越南境内未广泛发生，且具有重要潜在经济影响的有害生物

A. 昆虫：

序号	中 文 名	学 名
46	马铃薯块茎蛾	*Phthorimaea operculella* (Zeller)
47	玉米跳甲（传播玉米细菌性枯萎病菌）	*Chaetocnema pulicaria* (Melcheimer)
48	松褐天牛（传播松材线虫）	*Monochamus alternatus* Hope

B. 病害：

序号	中 文 名	学 名
49	瘤座菌属	*Balansia oryzae – sativae* Hashioka
50	花生条纹病毒	Peanut stripe virus
51	斯氏泛菌	*Pantoea stewartii*（Smith 1898）Mergaert

C. 线虫：

序号	中 文 名	学 名
52	香蕉穿孔线虫	*Radopholus similis*（Cobb）Thorne
53	鳞球茎茎线虫	*Ditylenchus dipsaci*（Kuhn）Filipjev

D. 杂草：

序号	中 文 名	学 名
54	窄叶独脚金	*Striga angustifolia*（Don.）C. J. Saldanha
55	独脚金	*Striga asiatica*（L.）Kuntze
56	南方菟丝子	*Cuscuta australis* R. Br.
57	中国菟丝子	*Cuscuta chinensis* Lam.

The list of plant quarantine pests of Socialist Republic of Vietnam

(Enacted by decision No: 73/2005/QD – BNN dated November 14th, 2005 of Minister of Agriculture and Rural Development)

GROUP I: Pests of potential economic importance to the vegetation resourses and not yet presented in territory of Socialist Republic of Vietnam

A/Insect:

1. South American Fruit fly	*Anastrepha fraterculus* (Wiedemann)
2. Mexico fruit fly	*Anastrepha ludens* (Loew)
3. Mediterranean fruit fly	*Ceratitis capitata* (Wiedemann)
4. Queensland fruit fly	*Bactrocera tryoni* (Froggatt)
5. Chinensis citrus fly	*Bactrocera tsuneonis* (Miyake)
6. Natal fruit fly	*Ceratitis rosa* Karsch
7. Grounut borer	*Pachymerus pallidus* (Olivier)
8. American white moth	*Hyphantria cunea* (Drury)
9. Japanese beetle	*Popillia japonica* (Newmann)
10. Broad – nosed grain weevil	*Caulophilus oryzae* Say
11. Khapra beetle	*Trogoderma granarium* Everts
12. Trogoderma beetle	*Trogoderma inclusum* LeConte
13. Boll weevil	*Anthonomus grandis* Boheman
14. South African citrus thrips	*Scirtothrip aurantii* Faure
15. Colorado potato beetle	*Leptinotarsa decemlineata* Say
16. Granary weevil	*Sitophilus granarius* (Linnaeus)
17. Larger grain borer	*Prostephanus truncatus* Horn
18. Mexico bean weevil	*Zabrotes subfasciatus* (Boheman)
19. California scale	*Quadraspidiotus perniciosus* (Comstock)
20. White fringed beetle	*Graphognathus leucoloma* (Boheman)
21. Rice leaf hopper	*Tagosodes orizicolus* Muir
	(Vector transmitsed chlorosis of rice – Rice hoja blanca virus)
22. Paddy plant hopper	*Tagosodes cubanus* D. L. Crawford
	(Vector transmitsed chlorosis of rice – Rice hoja blanca virus)

B/Diseaes:

23. Citrus mal secco	*Phoma tracheiphila* Petri, Kantachveli & Gikachvili
24. Taxas root rot of cotton	*Phymatotrichopsis omnivora* (Duggar) Hennebert
25. South American leaf blight	*Microcyclus ulei* (Henn.) Arx
26. Wart diseases of potato	*Synchytrium endobioticum* (Schilb.) Percival
27. Karnal bunt	*Tilletia indica* Mitra

28. Coffee bacterial leaf spot	*Pseudomonas garcae* Amaral, Teixeira & Pinheiro
29. Chlorosis of rice	Rice hoja blanca virus
30. Coffee ring spot virus	Coffee ringspot virus
31. Verticillium wilt	*Verticullium albo – atrum* Reinke & Berthold
32. American leaf spot of coffee	*Mycena citricolor* (Berk. & Curtis) Sacc
33. Bacterial canker of tomato	*Clavibacter michiganensis* subsp. *michiganensis* (Smith 1910) Davis

C/Nematodes:

34. Potato rot nematode	*Ditylenchus destructor* Thorne
35. Pale potato cyst nematode	*Globodera pallida* (Stone) Behrens
36. Yellow potato cyst nematode	*Globodera rostochiensis* (Wollenweber) Behrens
37. Red ring nematode	*Rhadinaphelenchus cocophilus* (Cobb) Goodey
38. Pine wood nematode	*Bursaphelenchus xylophilus* (Steiner & Burher) Nickle

D/Weeds:

39. Purple witchweed	*Striga hermonthica* (Del.) Benth.
40. Witchweed	*Striga densiflora* (Benth.) Benth.
41. Creeping thistle	*Cirsium arvense* (L.) Scop.
42. Scalloped broomrape	*Orobanche crenata* Forskal
43. Broomrape cernua	*Orobanche cernua* Loefl.
44. Broomrape ramo	*Orobanche ramosa* L.
45. Broomrape aegyp	*Orobanche aegyptiaca* Pers.

GROUP Ⅱ: Pests of potential economic importance to the vegetation resourses and not widely

A/Insects:

46. Potato moth	*Phthorimaea operculella* (Zeller)
47. Corn flea beetle	*Chaetocnema pulicaria* (Melsheimer) (Vector transmitsed bacterial leaf blight of maize – *Pantoea stewartii*)
48. Japanese pine sawyer	*Monochamus alternatus* Hope (Vector transmitsed Pine wood nematode – *Bursaphelenchus xylophilus*)

B/Diseases:

49. Black choke	*Balansia oryzae – sativae Hashioka*
50. Groundnut stripe disease	Peanut stripe virus
51. Bacterial leaf blight of maize	*Pantoea stewartii* (Smith 1898) Mergaert

C/Nematodes:

52. Burrowing nematode	*Radopholus similis* (Cobb) Thorne
53. Brown ring disease of hyacinth	*Ditylenchus dipsaci* (Kuhn) Filipjev

D/Weeds:

54. Witchweed S. a	*Striga angustifolia* (Don.) Saldanha
55. Witchweed S. I	*Striga asiatica* (L.) Kuntze
56. Australis dodder	*Cuscuta australis* R. Br.
57. Chinensis dodder	*Cuscuta chinensis* Lam.

关于发布《越南社会主义共和国应检物名录》的决议

（农业与农村发展部编号 72/2005/QD – BNN
2005 年 11 月 14 日，河内）

农业与农村发展部（MARD）部长依据 2003 年 7 月 18 日、编号为 86/2003/ND – CP，关于农业与农村发展部的任务、权力以及组织结构规定的政府法令；依据 2001 年《植物保护及检疫条例》的规定；依据植物保护部部长要求，兹决定：

第一条 公布《越南社会主义共和国应检物名单》，包括：

1. 植物：用于繁殖或其他目的的活的植物及植物机体。

2. 植物产品：

a）块茎/球茎、果实、种子、淀粉（面粉）、纤维，干花；

b）碎米、糠、蘑菇、干植物油饼、药用植物；

c）烟草的叶、茎或纤维；啤酒或酒精酵母菌、饲料酵母、茶叶、棉花、椰壳纤维、木薯干片、藤条、竹、莎草垫、稻草、禾草、水葫芦和海藻（水草）；

d）木材和木制品（不包括经过化学浸泡或高压热处理的木材和木制品）；

e）植物制成的艺术品和手工艺品；

f）植物制成的包装

g）植物制成的饲料

3. 鱼粉、蚕茧、蚕蛹、羽毛、皮革、骨头、角、指甲和紫梗原胶。

4. 用于诊断、培养、生物防治和研究的昆虫、蜘蛛/螨类、真菌、线虫、细菌、病毒、杂草和植物标本。

5. 运输、生产或储藏应检物及其他有可能携带检疫性有害生物的物品的工具。

第二条 在 2002 年 6 月 3 日编号为 58/2002/ND – CP 的政府法令中颁布的《植物检疫管理条例》第 18 条中述及的出口的应检物，植物检疫仅在出口商有要求或根据越南签署或遵守的国际公约规定应执行植物检疫条例时进行。

第三条 本决议将在政府公报发布 15 日后生效；并替代农业与农村发展部于 2001 年5 月 23 日编号为 56/2001/BNN – BVTV 的政府法令决议中公布的《越南社会主义共和国货物进出境、进境加工后再出口、出境加工后再进口或过境时应检物名单》。

第四条 MARD 秘书处主任、植物保护部部长、相关组织的负责人及个人有责任执行本决议。

Decision
Regarding the issuance of the List of Regulated Articles of the Socialist Republic of Vietnam Minister of Ministry of Agriculture and Rural Development

(No: 72/2005/QD - BNN Hanoi, Nov 14th 2005)

Based on the Decree No: 86/2003/ND - CP of July 18th 2003 of the Government on stipulating the mission, authority and organizational structure of Ministry of Agriculture and Rural Development.

Based on the Ordinance on Plant Protection and Quarantine in 2001;

According to the Request of Director General of the Plant Protection Department,

Decided:

Article 1 Promulgating the List of Regulated Articles of the Socialist Republic of Vietnam, including:

1. Plant:

Live plant and plant parts used for propagation and other objectives.

2. Plant products:

a) Tuber/bulb, fruit, seed, starch (flour), fibre, dried flowers;

b) Broken rice, bran, mushroom, dried plant oil cake, plants for medicine;

c) Leaf, stem or fibre of tobaco, beer or alcohol yeast, feed yeast, tea, cotton, coconut fibre, casava slice, rattan, bamboos, sedge mat, straw, grass, water hyacinth and sea plant (aquatic plants);

d) Wood and wooden products (exemption for wood and wooden products treated by chemical soak or heat treatment with high pressure);

e) Arts or handicralf made from plant;

f) Packages made from plant.

g) Feedstuff made from plant .

3. Fish meal, silkworm cocoon, silkworm cocoon without silk, feather, leather, bone, horn, nail and sticklac.

4. Insects, spiders/mites, fungus, nematodes, bacteria, virus, weeds and plant specimen for diagnostics, training, biological control and research.

5. Means of conveyance, production, storage of regulated articles and other objects capable of harbouring quarantine pests.

Article 2 For the exporting regulated articles described in the Article 18 of Regulation on Plant quarantine promulgated with the Decree No: 58/2002/ND - CP of June 03rd 2002 of the Government, the Plant quarantine inspection should be implemented only as requirements of exporters or international treaties that Vietnam signed or adhered to implement regulations on plant quarantine.

Article 3 This Decision will enter into effect after 15 days published by official gazette of the Government; and replacing the Decision No: 56/2001/BNN - BVTV of May 23 rd 2001 of Minister of Agriculture and Rural Development on promulgating the List of Regulated Articles for import, export, temporary export & re - import , transit in the Socialist Republic of Vietnam.

Article 4 Chief of the Secretariat of MARD, Director General of Plant Protection Department and Chief of relevant organizations and individuals shall be responsible for implementing this Decision.

发布进口越南之前应进行植物检疫及有害生物风险分析的应检物名录的决议

农业与农村发展部

（编号 34/2007/QD－BNN　2007 年 4 月 23 日，河内）

依据 2003 年 7 月 18 日编号为 86/2003/ND－CP 的、关于农业与农村发展部的任务、权力以及组织结构规定的政府法令；依据 2001 年《植物保护及检疫条例》的规定；依据 2007 年 1 月 5 日 No. 02/2007/ND－CP 政府法令关于植物检疫的规定；依据植物保护部门负责人的要求，兹决定：

第一条　公布进境到越南之前应进行植物检疫及有害生物风险分析的应检物名录，包括：

1. 植物以及植物产品

a）植物品种和繁殖材料；

b）新鲜果实。

2. 植物保护范畴内的活有机体

a）生物防治媒介；

b）其他活有机体。

3. 在某个时期极可能携带有害生物的其他应检物。

第二条　若上述进境应检物属于以下情况之一，则应开展有害生物风险分析或对之前的有害生物风险分析结果重新审核：

1. 首次进口到越南境内；

2. 来自新的产地；

3. 有事实以及科学依据证明出口国爆发的疫情是由越南的限定性有害生物引起的；

4. 检出某种限定性有害生物。

第三条　本决议在越南政府公报公布 15 天后生效。本决议应根据进境物品植物检疫的实际情况，随时对名录进行修正或补充；

第四条　农业与农村发展部、植物保护部以及相关组织的负责人以及相关个人应贯彻执行本决议。

农业与农村发展部代表

副部长　**裴白蓬（Bui Ba Bong）**

Decision
Promulgating a list of articles subject to plant quarantine and pest risk analysis before they are imported into Vietnam

The Ministry of Agriculture and Rural Development
(No. 34/2007/QD – BNN   Hanoi, April 23, 2007)

Pursuant to the Government's Decree No. 86/2003/ND – CP dated July 18, 2003 defining the functions, tasks, powers and organizational structure of the Ministry of Agriculture and Rural Development;

Pursuant to the 2001 Ordinance on Plant Protection and Quarantine;

Pursuant to the Government's Decree No. 02/2007/ND – CP dated January 5, 2007 on plant quarantine;

At the proposal of the Director of Plant Protection Department,

Decides:

Article 1

To promulgate a list of articles subject to plant quarantine and pest risk analysis before they are imported into Vietnam, including:

1. Plants and plant products

a) Plant varieties and breeding materials;

b) Fresh fruits.

2. Living organisms in the plant protection field.

a) Biological prevention agents.

b) Other living organisms.

3. Other articles at high risk of carrying harmful organisms shall be determined and added in each period.

Article 2

The above – mentioned articles, when imported, may only be subject to pest risk analysis or reconsideration of the result of earlier pest risk analyses if they fall in one of following cases:

1. Being imported into Vietnam for the first time;

2. Being of a new origin;

3. There are factual and scientific evidences on the outbreak of an epidemic subject to Vietnam's regulation on articles in the exporting country;

4. A pest subject to regulation is detected.

Article 3

This Decision takes effect 15 days after its publication in CONG BAO. In each period, this Decision shall be amended or supplemented to suit the actual situation of the import of articles subject to plant quarantine.

Article 4

The director of the Ministry's Office, the director of the Plant Protection Department, heads of relevant organizations, and concerned individuals shall implement this Decision.

FOR THE MINISTER OF AGRICULTURE AND RURAL DEVELOPMENT

VICE MINISTER

Bui Ba Bong

动物及动物产品的检疫、屠宰控制及兽医卫生检验法

（根据1993年11月27日　政府93/CP号法令发布）

第一章　总　　则

第1条　本法的适用范围

1. 动物等同于兽医服务法规第二条的规定。

2. 动物产品是指肉类和动物源性产品，包括生料、半成品及制成品。

3. 食品和家畜的动物性饲料。

4. 用于家畜生产的动物性材料、加工动物产品所用的水。

5. 圈舍、设备、仪器和屠宰方法、加工包装贮存、贸易、分销和动物及动物产品的运输。

6. 屠宰动物的废弃物，动物产品的加工、包装、贮存、贸易、流通、运输。

第2条　禁止违反动物检疫法规，伪造营业执照和检疫证明，抵制动物和动物产品的检疫、屠宰控制及兽医卫生监督，销售染疫或不符合标准的肉类和其他动物产品等行为。

禁止一切诱发和传播危害人类健康的疾病的行为。

第二章　动物及动物产品检疫

第3条　兽医服务法令第二十条所列的动物、动物产品和其他物品，经检疫并获得检疫证书后，都可以在越南境内运输、进出口或经越南中转。

农业食品产业部可临时规定对一些国内流通商品免于检疫。

第4条　只有符合以下条件的动物、动物产品才可以运输和销售：

1. 来自于非疫区、健康没有感染或携带严重疫病病原的、经检疫或注射疫苗免疫及接受其他预防措施后仍在免疫保护期内的动物。

2. 动物产品必须来自于健康、未感染或未携带严重疫病病原的动物，产品的加工、包装和储存必须符合兽医卫生标准。

3. 运输船舶、装载牲畜产品的器械和运输动物产品车辆必须符合本法规第33条的要求，在运输前后须进行清洁和消毒，并取得由兽医服务机构出具的兽医卫生证明。

第5条　转运家养和捕获野生的动物和动物产品的检疫要求如下：

1. 任何组织、个人在转运驯养或野生的动物、动物产品或其他需要检疫的货物时，在发货前，须向动物卫生分支局（SDAH）申报（如果是在省际之间转运）或向当地兽医服务机构申报（如果在省内转运），并支付相应的检疫费。兽医服务机构会根据货物特性和数量及时通知货主检疫的时间和地点。

2. 动物卫生分支局或检疫站将对符合兽医卫生标准的货物签发检验证书，并界定好运输方式、转运前收购点、运输路线以及其他在运输过程中须采取的必要防护措施。

3. 如果货物低于兽医卫生标准要求，兽医服务机构将不能签发检疫证明并要求货主整改。

4. 货主或其代理人负责看管和保护动物和动物产品，遵从兽医服务机构的检疫和整改指令，并交纳相应的法定费用。

第6条　收购、装载和运输动物必须遵照《动物疫病预防和控制法规》的第11条，货主或其代理

在出发之前必须把兽医服务机构签发的检疫证明出示给沿途的动物检疫站及目的地的兽医服务机构。

第 7 条 在陆路、铁路、江河及海运、空运、边境和邮政的检疫点，应设置动物检疫区，其设施设备应满足兽医卫生检查以及染疫动物及动物产品的清洁、消毒和处理。

第 8 条 在海关公布开放口岸实施进境、出境或转口的动物、动物产品及其他产品均需要检疫。

货主应向口岸检疫员出示出示必要的资料，并服从检疫员对运输工具、装载容器、包装物、动物产品、动物和其他检疫名录内商品、采样、技术处理、清洁和消毒的检疫要求。

第 9 条 动物、动物产品出口的检疫程序：

1. 任何组织和个人，在出口动物、动物产品和其他应检物前 30 天，必须向动物卫生局下属的地区动物卫生中心或者口岸动物检疫点提出申报，并交纳检疫费用。

2. 在提交书面申报后的 7 个工作日内，地区动物卫生中心和口岸动物检疫站必须根据货物的特性和数量，通知货主有关检疫时间、期限和地点。

第 10 条 动物出口检疫程序如下：

1. 出口的动物必须健康，来自无世界动物卫生组织（OIE）规定 A 类疫病或进口国规定疫病的企业。动物必须经疫苗免疫或其他预防措施，并且仍然在免疫保护期内，免疫标记应清晰可辨。

2. 在“边界动物检疫站”的检疫点，经隔离期达到出口标准的动物必须转运到已消毒的运输工具上。不允许动物在运输途中停留或者接触其他动物。

当“区域动物健康中心”或者“边界动物检疫站”在出发点实施检疫时，货主或其代理必须依据法规和进出口国家签署的协议收购、装载、运输动物并在沿途动物检疫站以及出境口岸检疫站出示检疫证明。

3. 在运输之前的 24 小时内，由地区动物卫生中心或者口岸动物检疫站负责给符合兽医卫生标准的动物、动物产品签发检疫证明。

动物卫生中心或者口岸动物检疫站不能给那些低于出口标准的动物出具证书，并要求货主或其代理处理这些动物。

4. 在检疫、装载和运输期间，货主应该严格遵守兽医服务机构的各项指令饲养动物并依法实施处理措施，提供隔离费用、采取正确的措施。

第 11 条 动物产品出口检疫程序如下：

1. 出口动物产品原料动物必须来自动物卫生局规定无疫病区域和无 A 类疫病或进口国规定其他疫病的流行区域。产品的包装必须满足进口国家的要求，符合兽医卫生标准。

2. 地区动物健康中心 或者口岸动物检疫站负责规定出口产品的检疫地点。检疫期过后，符合出口标准的动物产品才允许通过清洁和消毒好的运输工具装载到装货地。

3. 在装载前的 24 小时内，地区动物卫生中心 或者口岸动物检疫站负责给那些符合兽医卫生标准的出口动物和运输工具出具检疫证明。

4. 货主或其代理提交事项同第 10 条 4 款规定。

第 12 条 动物、动物产品的进口检疫：

1. 任何进口动物、动物产品或其他应检商品的组织和个人必须向动物卫生局申请办理许可证。获许可证的货主或其代理在商品到达口岸的 30 天前，需向地区兽医卫生中心或者边界动物检疫站申报并支付检疫费用。

2. 根据货物预定的入境日期、越南口岸、商品的特性、数量和种类、运输方式，地区兽医卫生中心 或者口岸动物检疫站将通知货主有关检疫的时间和地点。

第 13 条 以下为禁止进口的动物和动物产品：

1. 明令进口的动物、动物产品及物品；从疫区来的动物、动物产品和其他应检物；转运自存在危及越南家畜疫病的动物及动物产品。

2. 经检疫发现感染或怀疑感染传染病的动物以及不符合兽医卫生标准的动物产品。

3. 动物尸体。

4. 没有检疫证明或者提供不合法证明的动物、动物产品。

第 14 条　载运须检疫的动物、动物产品及其他物品抵境时，货主或其代理必须向进口国口岸动物检疫点提交由出口国兽医服务机构签发的检疫证书和其他相关材料。

只有获得动物检疫局许可，货主或其代理才能将货物从运输工具或装载容器上卸离。

第 15 条　动物进口检疫程序如下：

1. 边界动物检疫站负责执行口岸检疫，并给直接接触动物的人员以卫生方面的指导，这些人员负责清洁、消毒仪器，装御设备，运输工具，容器以及与此相关的其他物品。动物应搬运至检疫地点。

2. 在隔离期间以及运输、装载、饲养动物过程中，货主及其代理必须遵守兽医服务机构的指导方针并支付检疫、处理、清洁、消毒的费用。

第 16 条　只有动物、动物产品和明文规定应检疫的物品符合兽医卫生标准要求，并随附有出口国签发的合法检疫证明，口岸动物检疫站才会签发进口检疫证书。

海关凭进口检疫证书办理清关手续。动物、动物产品以及明文规定应检疫的物品必须运抵检疫地点。口岸动物检疫站应将检疫地点通知海关以便于其办理清关手续。

第 17 条　口岸动物检疫站不得允许进口不符合兽医卫生标准或不随附合法的出口国检疫证书的动物、动物产品及其他应检物入境，并可采取以下必要措施：

1. 携带国家农业与食品产业部禁止入境疾病的动物须退运至最后离境地原产国，若该动物是经由第三方国中转入境的，则销毁处理。

2. 携带国家农业与食品产业部非禁止入境疾病的动物可退运至原产国，或者销毁染疫动物并对未染病的动物进行隔离检疫或屠杀处理。

3. 不符合兽医卫生标准的或没有出口国出具的卫生检疫证书的动物产品必须退回或销毁，必要时需通知出口国以便于复检。

第 18 条　少量或旅客携带的入境动物及动物产品的检疫规定如下：

1. 持有者必须申报并出示出口国出具的检疫证书：

a. 该动物是产于非疫区的健康动物，并已预防接种或进行了有效预防性措施。

b. 非食用性动物产品的原料来自未感染传染性疾病的健康动物，该动物产品不携带病原体。

c. 动物源性饲料和其他应检物不得带有病原体。

2. 以下情况，持有人可以不申报及出具检疫证书：

a. 兽医卫生合格的、不用作销售且在海关许可名单中列出的动物源性食品。

b. 经工业加工处理非食用性的动物产品。

3. 接到申报后，边境动物检疫签证处须实施检疫并检查相关材料。检查证书符合法律要求且进口动物商品符合兽医卫生标准后，方可签发进口检疫证书。若该商品不符合兽医卫生标准或不在检疫名单中且检疫证书不符合法律要求的，依法对其进行处理。

第 19 条　邮寄的动物及动物产品的检疫程序如下：

1. 任何组织或个人通过邮局以包裹形式进出口的动物、动物产品及其他应检物必须向动物检疫官员申报检疫。

2. 若经检疫，该邮包符合兽医卫生标准和相关规定的，动物检疫部门方可签发检疫证书。若进口商品不符合要求或不能达到要求的，该商品将退还持有人或将其销毁。

3. 国内邮件中的应检物由 SDAHs 负责检疫，进出口邮件中的应检物由地区兽医卫生中心和口岸动物检疫站负责检疫。

第 20 条　交通工具、包装物的兽医卫生和灭菌消毒方面的规定：

1. 交通工具、包装物的兽医卫生和灭菌消毒方面的具体规定见于动物疾病预防和控制法令第 12 条。

2. 边界动物检疫站检查到达口岸的运输交通工具和集装箱的同时，须指导完成对运输交通工具和集装箱、运输中泄漏的水和动物排泄物的消毒杀菌。

如果在交通工具和集装箱中发现有公告列有的传染病病原，检疫站必须严格按规定采取一切消毒灭菌措施，以预防和控制疾病。

第 21 条 进口标本、生物制品和疫苗的管理规定：

1. 经越南 DAH 签发了证书的标本和生物制品方能入境，相反，不符合规定要求的标本和生物制品则将被退回最后离境的原产国的相关部门。

2. 供兽医部门用的进口疫苗须附有出口国签发的检测证书和检验证书。此类物品的进口须按兽医药品管理条例的规定来办理。

第 22 条 越南过境动物及动物产品的检疫规定：

1. 携带动物、动物产品及其他应检物通过越南境内的任何组织或个人都必须征得越南 DAH 的许可。在许可后，货主必须在入境 7 天前，向地区兽医卫生中心或边境动物检疫站申报并交纳相应检疫费。

2. 根据过境货物的数量、种类、运输方式、贮藏条件，地区兽医卫生中心或口岸动物检疫站会通知货主相应的送货时间、进出口地点、运输线路、运输材料和其他要求。

第 23 条 禁止过境物

1. 经过有传染性疾病发生的国家和地区运输，或途经带有对越南牲畜构成威胁性疾病的地区的动物、动物产品及其他应施检疫物。

2. 检疫证书不符合法律要求或根本没有检疫证书的货物。

3. 经检验，发现已感染或怀疑感染的动物及不符合兽医卫生标准的动物产品。

4. 不完全符合越南动物检疫部门预先规定的贮藏条件的货物。

第 24 条 过境动物及动物产品的管理规定：

1. 运输动物、动物产品或其他应检货物的交通工具抵达口岸时，货主或代理人必须向过境货物经过的边境动物检疫站出示出口国签发的检疫证书及其他有关文件。

2. 货主申报货物或过境时，边境动物检疫站应检查货物检疫证书、兽医卫生状况和运输方式是否符合规定的要求，以上条件都符合方能签发过境检疫证书。

3. 任何组织和个人必须严格遵守过境口岸动物检疫部门的所有规定：

a. 未经动物检疫部门允许，不得私卸货物或改变运输方式；

b. 必须保证交通工具的技术性辅助设备的安全，禁止废弃物外泄；

c. 不得擅自改变运输路线或随意停靠；

d. 在检疫机构的监督下，可在越南境内为过境动物提供食物和水或经许可进行的特殊处理，但应防止与国内的动物接触。

e. 动物尸体、废弃物、用于牲畜的铺垫物、饲料残留物、动物产品的包装物及其他运输中产生的废物都必须在动物检疫机构的指导下在指定地点销毁。

第 25 条 处理过境动物及动物产品的规定：

1. 动物、动物产品或其他应检物不符合兽医卫生标准的，检疫证书不符合法律规定的，或感染了检疫名录中列出的传染性疾病的动物，边境动物检疫站不得允许其过境，且根据具体情况采取相应措施。

a. 退回至原产国的相关部门

b. 若将货物退回至原产国可能引起疾病传播或环境污染，动物及动物产品则必须在指定或专门的地方销毁。所有运输材料、排泄物和铺垫物都必须灭菌消毒。

c. 若检疫证书不符合法律规定，必须及时通知出口国的兽医部门修改证书或按照本节第一部分的 a 和 b 款中的规定进行处理。

2. 货主或代理人必须按照动物检疫机构的指示完成过境动物及动物产品的消毒灭菌处理，并支付相应费用。

第 26 条　用集装箱或其他密封设备运载动物、动物产品或其他检疫名录中列出的物品过境时，边境动物检疫站应检查其出口国签发的检疫证书，运输材料和过境许可证是否符合要求，发现有异常情况，检查站可以要求货主开柜进行检疫查验。

第 27 条　越南境内临时停靠运输工具的管理办法：

1. 无论过境交通工具临时停靠在检查站或是口岸，货主或代理人不得私卸或让动物及其产品着陆，更不得将残留物或排泄物抛弃在口岸或检查站。

2. 运输动物及动物产品的飞机、火车或船只因紧急情况必须在检查站或口岸停留的，货主或代理人必须按照边境动物检疫站的要求处理。

3. 若运输工具未按指定路线行驶或停靠在指定的地点，货主不得接触货物，并应当通知最近的兽医部门，在对该运输工具进行处理后方能继续使用。

第 28 条　动物及动物产品的临时进口和再出口的管理规定：

1. 任何需要临时进口或转口动物及动物产品的组织或个人必须申请办理 动物卫生局许可，经获得许可证后，货主应在入境 7 天前向地区兽医卫生中心或口岸动物检疫站提出申报，申报经批准后通知货主检疫货物的时间和地点。

2. 动物及动物产品的临时进口或转口须遵照以上规定办理。

第 29 条　动物和动物产品收购、交易及展览场所的管理：

1. 动物卫生分支局鼓励当地政府建立专门用于收购、交易及展览动物及动物产品的场所，并负责活动期间的兽医卫生指导和监督。

2. 任何组织或个人在运送动物及动物产品至收购、交易和展览场所时，必须遵守以下规定：

a. 国内动物及动物产品必须持有动物卫生分支局签发的检疫证书。

b. 国外动物及动物产品必须持有口岸动物检疫站或地区兽医卫生中心签发的进口检疫证书；

c. 在集散点、市场或展览期间必须遵守动物卫生分支局的所有规定和指示。

3. 集散点、市场或展览结束后，动物卫生分支局负责检查场地内所有动物及动物产品的兽医卫生状况，并进行消毒灭菌。

a. 符合兽医卫生标准的动物及动物产品，由动物卫生分支局签发国内使用的检疫证书。

交易或展览的动物和动物产品需要带出境外的，货主必须按照进出口动物检疫规程来办理。

b. 不符合兽医卫生标准的动物及动物产品必须按照以上规定予以销毁。

第三章　动物源食品的兽医卫生检验和动物屠宰控制

第 30 条　动物屠宰的一般规定：

1. 猪、水牛、黄牛、山羊、马、家禽和兔子等用于食用、工业材料和动物饲养的动物，用于屠宰的动物必须保证其健康并来自非传染疾病疫区。

2. 禁止屠宰已感染或怀疑感染了国家农业与食品产业部规定疫病的动物。

3. 动物屠宰检疫时，若兽医或技术人员检测出或怀疑感染了农业和食品产业部规定疫病，必须立即向当地兽医部门报告。

4. 出现以下情况，必须在动物卫生分支局指定地点进行动物尸体剖检：

a. 怀疑感染了检疫名单中的一种传染性疾病的动物，除已感染或怀疑感染了禁止解剖的疾病的动物，如炭疽病等。

b. 因其他原因必须进行解剖检验的。

第 31 条　用于出口和商业性动物屠宰的控制规定：

1. 商业性动物屠宰必须有当地畜牧局和部门的认可，经当地人民委员会许可后，在专门的屠宰点进行。当地兽医部门应实施屠宰管理并进行兽医卫生检验，在省、市、县内，动物屠宰必须按照规定在屠宰点进行。

2. 用于出口的动物屠宰场/点经动物卫生分支局和当地相关部门的许可，并报经中央政府管辖下的省/市的人民委员会批准。由地区动物卫生中心负责对屠宰和屠宰场兽医卫生条件进行监督。

3. 离屠宰场/点较远的地区，若屠宰动物不用作买卖时，货主可要求当地兽医部门进行现场卫生检验。

4. 任何开设动物屠宰场或屠宰点的组织或个人，都必须符合动物疾病预防和控制法令第 13 条中规定的兽医卫生要求。

第 32 条 运送动物至屠宰场/点的程序：

1. 任何组织或个人将大量动物运送至屠宰场/点的都必须持有当地兽医部门签发的检疫证书。

2. 任何组织或个人将用于出口的动物运到屠宰场/点时必须持有动物卫生分支局原产地检疫证书。每一种动物必须在屠宰前的 12 至 24 小时内被集中带到屠宰场/点待宰。

3. 负责屠宰控制的兽医和技术人员必须核实检疫证书，运输材料，将动物分类并指导运输材料的消毒灭菌。健康动物则送至屠宰场屠宰，带病或怀疑带病的动物必须按规定移送隔离屠宰区。

第 33 条 动物屠宰过程中，肉制品及其他产品的卫生检疫和处理规定：

1. 动物屠宰和每种动物肉制品及其他产品的卫生检疫程序由国家农业和食品产业部依法制定。

肉制品及其他动物产品符合兽医卫生标准，兽医和技术人员方可签发卫生检疫证书。

2. 按规定处理不符合兽医卫生标准的动物肉制品、内脏或其他副产品。

适于食用的动物产品需进行动物产品质量检验，符合食品标准的，方可签发正式证书，且该证书不同于本节第一段中所指的证书，若该产品不符合食品标准，它们将经加工处理或作为动物饲料或销毁处理。

3. 任何运送动物至屠宰场/点的组织或个人都必须遵照兽医屠宰和检验的指示并支付相关费用。若屠宰后，兽医和技术人员发现动物产品不符合卫生标准，应实施销毁并对屠宰区进行消毒灭菌处理，货主应支付相关处理费用。

第 34 条 若货主对兽医和技术人员的建议有异议而提出复检，畜牧局主管人员可以进行复检。进行复检后的兽医意见具有法定效力。

若复检结果确认初检无误，货主将承担复检费用。反之，由检验方赔偿相应损失并支付一切费用。

第 35 条 贮存和运送动物产品的规定：

1. 未加工或待售肉制品、尸体及其副产品在贮存前必须符合兽医卫生要求并保持产品的质量。贮藏肉、尸体和副产品必须与外界隔离。

2. 运载待售动物产品的工具必须符合兽医卫生标准，运载前后都应进行消毒杀菌处理，并保证不污染动物产品或对消费者产生危害。

城乡运送动物产品必须使用畜牧局专门制定并授权的运输设备。

3. 待售的动物肉制品和其他产品必须有卫生检疫标记或持有卫生检疫证书。兽医和技术人员负责在市场内检查肉制品和其他产品的兽医卫生情况。

第 36 条 经加工的动物产品的兽医卫生检验规定：

1. 动物产品加工企业的建造和运作都必须符合动物疾病预防和控制法令第 13 条有关的兽医卫生要求。

2. 这些企业的动物原材料加工必须使用来自屠宰场/点且符合兽医卫生要求的动物和动物产品 。

3. 兽医和技术人员在企业检查和监督动物产品的加工过程，根据法律规定可以取样并进行试验室检测。

第 37 条 签发加工动物产品卫生许可证的规定：

1. 国内销售的符合卫生标准的加工动物产品的兽医卫生证书由动物卫生分支局签发。

地区动物健康中心签发进出口和过境的符合兽医卫生标准的加工动物产品卫生检疫证书。

2. 不符合兽医卫生标准的加工动物产品将按规定处理。

3. 加工过程中货主应遵照畜牧局的指示并支付检疫和处理的所有费用。

4. 对加工动物产品的兽医卫生检疫结果存有异议并要求复检的，按照本法第 34 条的相关规定处理。

第 38 条　动物源性食品的市场管理规定：

1. 各种动物源食品在推向市场前，必须依据兽医卫生标准进行各项指标检验，如表征，理化性质，微生物和食物中的残留物，如重金属、抗生素和激素等。达到兽医卫生标准的食品将被标记盖戳或获得合格证书，表明该食品完全符合兽医卫生标准，才准许上市出售。

进出口和过境动物源性食品的兽医卫生检验标准由动物卫生局负责制定。只在当地销售的动物源性食品的兽医卫生检验标准由动物卫生分支局负责制定。农业与食品工业部制定检验标准和内容。

2. 畜牧局负责监督本地加工、贮藏、贸易、运输和销售动物源食品企业的兽医卫生检疫规定的执行情况。

3. 货主应遵照畜牧局的指示进行检疫处理并依法支付相应的检疫、消毒灭菌费用。

农业与食品产业部部长控制兽医卫生检疫制度，签发检疫证书，盖兽医卫生印章，必要时有临时免除动物源食品兽医卫生检查的权力。

第 39 条　只有符合卫生部制定的健康标准的人员才能在动物屠宰场/点和动物产品加工、贮藏和销售企业工作，在屠宰、贮藏和加工过程中，这些员工在接触动物和动物产品时必须穿隔离防护服。

第 40 条　动物卫生局直接检查和监督动物屠宰场/点的动物及加工和贮藏出口动物产品企业的兽医卫生状况。

本地动物屠宰场/点和国内动物产品加工、贮藏、销售和运输的贸易公司的兽医卫生条件由当地畜牧局提供指导，负责检疫和检测。

第 41 条　受法律保护并按农业与食品工业部有关规定，兽医和技术人员在从事检疫、屠宰管理和动物与动物产品的兽医卫生检验工作时必须穿工作服、佩带执法肩章、徽章、检疫工作卡或检验卡。

第四章　动物检疫、屠宰控制和动物源性食品的兽医卫生检验的国家管理办法

第 42 条　动物检疫、屠宰控制和动物源性食品的兽医卫生检验的国家管理办法的具体内容见畜牧法的第 41 条。

农业与食品产业部负责执行和指导国家动物及动物产品的检疫、屠宰控制、动物源食品的兽医卫生检疫，主要包括：

a. 向政府提交或制定有关动物及动物产品的检疫、屠宰控制和兽医卫生检疫法规的议案；

b. 制定检疫、屠宰控制和兽医卫生检验的实施方案；

c. 监督检疫查验、屠宰控制和兽医卫生检验的执行情况，处理纠纷、投诉和诉讼；

d. 签发或起草各种动物及动物产品检疫、屠宰控制和兽医卫生检验证书和合格证；

e. 定期公布检疫名单；

f. 培训、教育宣传检疫、屠宰控制和兽医卫生检验知识；

g. 开展检疫、屠宰控制和兽医卫生方面的国际间合作。

第 43 条　中央政府省/市人民委员会主席有以下权力：

1. 依照农业和食品工业部指令，在所辖区域内指导检疫、屠宰控制、兽医卫生检验，指导当地兽医服务机构有效运行。

2. 在辖区内发布检疫、屠宰控制、兽医卫生检验的公文。

3. 发布与检疫、屠宰控制、兽医卫生检验有关的执照、许可证的签发与撤销的相关文件。

4. 与国家上级兽医服务机构联合实施检查、检验及处理违反检疫、屠宰控制、兽医卫生检验法令的案例。

5. 受理关于检疫、屠宰控制、兽医卫生检验相关的申述，或向相关部门移交。

第44条 兽医服务机构移交动物性食品的动物检疫、屠宰控制、兽医卫生检验。

1. 动物卫生局局长向农业和食品工业部部长负责，依照本法令第四十二条行使国家检疫、屠宰控制、兽医卫生检验权力。

2. 动物卫生局下属的地区动物卫生中心和兽医卫生检验中心按动物卫生局的委派负责实施进出口及境内动物运输、动物生产过程的检疫、屠宰控制和兽医卫生检验。

3. 动物卫生局各分支机构支持中央政府下属省市人民委员会在各自辖区内实施境内动物和动物产品的检疫、屠宰控制和兽医卫生检验。

第五章　特殊动物和动物产品的检疫、屠宰控制、兽医卫生检验

第45条 特殊的动物和动物产品的检疫、屠宰控制、兽医卫生检验必须依法执行，并应采取有效措施防止违法行为发生。

动物卫生局和各分支局局长负责组织和实施辖区内动物和动物产品的检验检疫、屠宰控制和兽医卫生检验。

第46条 动物和动物产品的检疫、屠宰控制、兽医卫生检验的具体内容包括：

1. 检查组织和个人遵守动物和动物产品的检疫、屠宰控制、兽医卫生检验相关法律的执行情况。

2. 检查动物和动物产品的检疫、屠宰控制、兽医卫生检验情况。

3. 检查动物和动物产品的检疫、屠宰控制、兽医卫生检验相关法律的立法情况。

第47条 动物和动物产品的检疫、屠宰控制、兽医卫生检验应依照农业和食品工业部发布的兽医服务条令、兽医检验规程实施。

第六章　补 充 条 款

第48条 农业和食品产业部单独或与相关部门联合执行本法令。

部长、部门办公室领导、政府管理的代理机构领导、中央下属省市人民委员会主席在各自职权范围内负责组织本法令的执行。

本法令自签发之日起实施，同时取代以前的相关规定。

On quarantine, slaughter control and veterinary hygiene inspection of animals and animal products

(Issued under Decree 93/CP of the Government on 27 November 1993)

Chapter Ⅰ General provisions

Article 1 Application of the Rule:

1. Animals as stipulated at Article 2 of the Ordinance on Veterinary Services;

2. Anima products are meat and other products of animal origin in the forms of raw materials, half – processed and processed;

3. Food and livestock feed of animal origin;

4. Materials of animal origin for livestock production, water for processing animal products;

5. Housing, equipment, implements and means used for slaughter, processing, package storage, trade, distribution and transport of animals and animal products;

6. Waste discharged from slaughter, processing, package, storage, trade, circulation and transport of animals and animal products.

Article 2 All acts which violate the regulations on animal quarantine, forgery of licences, quarantine certificates, opposition against quarantine, slaughter control, veterinary hygiene inspection of animals and animal products, selling meat and other animal products either carrying the agents of serious infectious diseases or being sub – standard in veterinary hygiene are strictly forbidden.

All actions that produce and spread diseases and cause harm to human health are strictly forbidden.

Chapter Ⅱ Quarantine of animals and animal products

Article 3 Animals, animal products and other articles listed to be subjects of quarantine as stipulated at Article 20 of the Ordinance on Veterinary Services can be transported between areas, exported from, imported to and transited through Vietnam only after having been quarantined and granted quarantine certificates to do so.

The Minister of Agriculture and Food Industry is to stipulate temporary exemption from quarantine for some cases of domestic marketing.

Article 4 Transport and marketing of animals and animal products can only be conducted on the following conditions:

1. Animals that leave disease free zones and are healthy and not affected with or carrying agents of dangerous diseases that must be inspected for or vaccinated against or subjected to other preventive measures and are within the period of immunity.

2. Animal products from healthy animals that are not affected with or do not carry agents of serious diseases, that are processed, packaged and preserved in accordance with stipulations and that meet the veterinary hygiene standards.

3. Transport vehicles, equipment for livestock production and carriage of animal products must meet the requirements of Article 35 of this Rule and be cleaned and disinfected prior to and after transportation and granted

certificates of veterinary hygiene by the Veterinary Service.

Article 5 The requirement for the quarantine of domesticated and captured animals and animal products in transit is as below:

1. Every organization or individual who transports domesticated and captured animals and animal products or other commodities required to be quarantined must declare to the SDAH at departure if the transport is between provinces and to district Veterinary Services if the transport is within one province and pay the quarantine fee.

Based on the characteristics and quantity of the commodities, the Veterinary Service make will give notice of the location and time of quarantine to the commodity owner.

2. SDAH or the Veterinary Station will grant quarantine certificates for the inspected commodity if the standard of veterinary hygiene is satisfied and will give to the owner instruction on the means of transport and collection point prior to transport, the route and other necessary guidance during transport.

3. If the commodities are found sub-standard in veterinary hygiene, the Veterinary Service will not issue quarantine certificates and will ask the owner to carry out necessary measures.

4. The owner or the representative is in charge of caring for and protecting the animals and animal products and obeying all instructions given by the Veterinary Service during quarantine and the application of corrective measures and paying for costs as stipulated by the law.

Article 6 The collection, loading and transport of animals are carried as stipulated at Article 11 of the Rules on Animal Disease Prevention and Control. The owner or the representative has to show quarantine certificates issued by the Veterinary Service at departure to the Animal Quarantine Stations on the route and to the Veterinary Service at the destination as stated in the licence.

Article 7 The levels and services involved have remits to facilitate the Veterinary Service, which posses animal quarantine area, to inspect veterinary hygiene, carry out cleaning and disinfection and deal with diseased animals and animal products at transport checkpoints of land road, railway, river and sea routes, air ways and at frontiers and post offices.

Article 8 Animals, animal products and other commodities required to be quarantined in export, import and transit at the border gates are parts of the Custom declaration.

The owner must produce the necessary papers to quarantine inspectors at the border and follow all directions given by the inspector in checking the means of transport, stores, packages, animal products, animals and other commodities on the list required to be quarantined, sampling, technical treatment, cleaning and disinfection.

Article 9 Procedures of quarantine for the export of animals and animal products:

1. Every organization and individual who exports animals, animal products and other commodities required to be quarantined must make a declaration to the Regional Animal Health Centre or border Animal Quarantine Stations under DAH at least 30 days in advance and pay for the quarantine fees.

2. In 7 days, after the declaration in a printed form has been submitted, the Regional Animal Health Centre or border Animal Quarantine Station must inform the owner about the time, time limit and location for quarantine, depending on characteristics and quantity of the commodities.

Article 10 The quarantine process for the export of animals is set as below:

1. Animals for export must be healthy and taken from disease free enterprises in which there is no circulation of diseases in List A as stipulated by the O. I. E or of other diseases listed by the importing country and animals which are vaccinated or to which other preventive measures have been applied and are within the period of immunity and marked for easy identification.

2. After an isolation period at the quarantine site of the border Animal Quarantine Station, animals that are

of export standard must be transported to the loading location by a disinfected vehicle. Animals are not allowed to stop on the transport route or to have contact with other animals.

When the Regional Animal Health Centre or border Animal Quarantine Station carries out quarantine at the place of departure, the owner or representative must conduct collection, loading and transport of animals in accordance with the regulations and agreements made between exporting and importing countries. The Owner has to show the quarantine certificate to the Animal Quarantine Stations on the route and to the border quarantine station at the destination.

3. The Regional Animal Health Centre or border Animal Quarantine Station issues quarantine certificates for animals and animal products, which meet the veterinary hygiene standard, in 24 hours prior to transport.

The Regional Animal Health Centre or border Animal Quarantine Station will not issue certificates to animals, which are below export standard and will request the owner or the representative to deal with the animals.

4. The owner is to take care of the animals and abide by every instruction given by the Veterinary Service during the quarantine process, loading and transport. The owner is also to implement handling measures and pay for quarantine and corrective measures as stipulated by law.

Article 11 The quarantine process for the export of animal products is stipulated as follows:

1. Animal products for export must be from animals that are taken from disease free zones pointed by DAH and are not affected with diseases in List A and or with other diseases listed by the importing country. The products must be packaged in compliance with the requirements of the importing country and meet the standard of veterinary hygiene.

2. The Regional Animal Health Centre or border Animal Quarantine Station is to regulate the quarantine site for the export of animal products.

After the quarantine period, animal products of export standard are allowed to be moved to the loading place by a cleaned and disinfected vehicle.

3. The Regional Animal Health Centre or border Animal Quarantine Station issues quarantine certificate for export only to animals and means of transport which meet the veterinary hygiene standard in 24 hours prior to loading.

4. The remits of the owner or the representative of the commodities are stipulated at paragraph 4, Article 10.

Article 12 Quarantine procedures for the import of animals and animal products:

1. Every organization and individual who imports animals, animal products and commodities required to be quarantined must apply to DAH for a permit. After being permitted by DAH, the owner or representative makes a declaration to the Regional Veterinary Centre or border Animal Quarantine Station at least 30 days prior to arrival of the commodities at the port and pays for the quarantine fees.

2. Based on the proposed date and port of arrival in Vietnam and on the characteristics, quantity and type of commodities and means of transport, the Regional Veterinary Centre or border Animal Quarantine Station inform the owner about the time and location of the quarantine.

Article 13 It is forbidden to import in the following cases:

1. Animals, animal products and articles in the list of prohibitions from import; animals, animal products and other subjects of quarantine from disease areas or transited through an area of a disease that is dangerous for Vietnamese livestock.

2. At quarantine, animals are found affected or suspected of being affected with infectious disease and animal products are found not meet the standard of veterinary hygiene.

3. Carcases of animals.

4. Animals and animal products without quarantine certificates or if the accompanying certificates are not legal.

Article 14 On animal of the transport vehicle for animals, animal products and other subjects of quarantine at the port, the owner or the representative must produce quarantine certificates issued by Veterinary Service of exporting country and other relevant papers to the border Animal Quarantine Station of importing country.

The owner or the representative can unload the vehicle/container only when permitted by the Animal Quarantine Office.

Article 15 The quarantine process for the import of animals is as follows:

1. The Border Animal Quarantine Station must conduct quarantine at the port and give instructions on hygiene to persons with direct contact with animals, who do cleaning and disinfection of equipment, facilities for loading and unloading, means of transport, animal containers and related objects. Animals will be moved to the quarantine site.

2. During transport, loading and taking care of animals, during the isolation period in the quarantine site, the owner or representative must obey all guidelines from the Veterinary Service and pay for quarantine, handling, cleaning and disinfection.

Article 16 The border Animal Quarantine Station grants import quarantine certificates only to animals, animal products and other articles listed as subjects of quarantine which meet the veterinary hygiene standard and for which the accompanying quarantine certificates issued by exporting country are legal.

The Custom Office makes use of the import quarantine certificates to carry out customs procedures.

Animals, animal products and other subjects in the list to be quarantined must be brought to the quarantine site. The border Animal Quarantine Station notifies the location of quarantine site to Custom office to carry out the procedures.

Article 17 The border Animal Quarantine Station should not allow the import of animals, animal products and other subjects of quarantine which are below the of veterinary hygiene standard or for which the accompanying quarantine certificates issued by the exporting country are not legal and take necessary procedures according to the situation.

1. Animals carrying diseases in the list forbidden to be imported as stipulated by the Ministry of Agriculture and Food Industry will be returned to the originating country of departure or will be destroyed if the animals would have to be transited through a third country.

2. Animals carrying diseases which are not listed as forbidden to be imported by the Ministry of Agriculture and Food Industry will be returned to the originating country of departure or affected animals will be destroyed and healthy animals will be isolated for quarantine or be slaughtered and disposed of.

3. Animal products that do not meet the veterinary hygiene standard or for which the quarantine certificates issued by exporting country are not legal can be returned or disposed of, but it is necessary to inform the exporting country in order to allow re – inspection.

Article 18 The quarantine of animals and animal products in small numbers or in hand luggage at the frontier is stipulated as the followings:

1. The owner must make a declaration and show quarantine certificates issued by the exporting country to confirm that:

a. The animals are healthy and originate in disease free zones and have been vaccinated or had have prophylatic measures applied.

b. Animal products, which are not for use as food, are from healthy animals not infected with infectious diseases and the products do not carry disease agents.

c. Livestock feed of animal origin and other subjects of quarantine do not contain disease agents.

2. In the following cases, the owner does not have to declare and show quarantine certificates:

a. Food of animal origin that has been treated for veterinary hygiene, will not be offered for sale and is in the list allowed by the Customs;

b. Animal products that are industrially processed and not for use as food.

3. Upon receipt of the declaration, the border Animal Quarantine Certificate conducts quarantine and inspects relevant papers. If the certificates are legal and the commodities meet the veterinary hygiene standard, it is to issue quarantine certificates for import.

If the commodities are do not meet the veterinary hygiene standard or are not listed as subjects of quarantine and if the certificates are not legal, it is to deal with them as stipulated by the law.

Article 19 Quarantine procedures for animals and animal products transported by post are stipulated as below:

1. Every organization and individual who exports or imports animals and animal products or other subjects of quarantine by post in the form of parcels or packages must make a declaration to animal quarantine office for inspection.

2. The animal quarantine agency will issue quarantine certificates if inspection shows that the veterinary hygiene standard is met and the packages comply with the stipulations.

If import commodities do not satisfy the requirements or cannot be made to comply with the requirements, the commodities will be returned to the owner or destroyed.

3. SDAHs inspect subjects of quarantine transported by domestic post. Regional Veterinary Centres and border Animal Quarantine Stations inspect subjects of quarantine transported by post for import and export.

Article 20 Regulations on veterinary hygiene, cleaning and disinfection of vehicles/containers for transport are as follows:

1. Veterinary hygiene and cleaning and disinfection of vehicles/containers for transport are conducted as stipulated at Article 12 of the Rules on Animal Disease Prevention and Control.

2. The Border Animal Quarantine Station inspects the vehicles/containers for transport upon arrival at the port and at the same time, provides directions on cleaning and disinfection of vehicles/containers for transport, water and animal waste from the transport.

If the vehicle/container is found to carry agents of infectious diseases listed as notifiable, the Station must utilize all measures to clean and disinfect and strictly block according to stipulations on disease prevention and control.

Article 21 Stipulations on the import of samples, biological products and vaccines:

1. Samples and bio-products can be imported only after DAH Vientnam has issued certificates for import. Otherwise, samples and biological products that do not satisfy stipulated requirements will be returned to the originating country of departure.

2. Vaccines to be imported for use in veterinary services must be enclosed with certificates of tests and inspection issued by the exporting country. This kind of import should be conducted according to the Rules on Veterinary Drugs Management.

Article 22 Quarantine procedures for animals and animal products in transit through Vietnam are set as below:

1. Every organization and individual who transit animals and animal products or other subjects of quarantine through Vietnam must apply DAH Vietnam for permission. After being permitted by DAH, the owner of the commodities must make a declaration to the Regional Veterinary Centre or the border Animal Quarantine Station sev-

en days prior to transit and pay for the quarantine fees.

2. Based on the quantity, type of commodities, means of transport and conditions for preservation of the transit goods, the Regional Veterinary Centre or the border Animal Quarantine Station will inform the owner about the time, port of entry, port of exit, route, means of transport and other concerned stipulations.

Article 23 The following cases are forbidden from transiting through Vietnam:

1. Animals and animal products or other subjects of quarantine leaving a disease infected country/region or transiting through an area with a disease that is a risk for Vietnamese livestock.

2. The accompanying quarantine certificates are not legal or there is no accompanying certificate.

3. By inspection, the animals are found to be affected or suspected of being affected and animal products are found to be below veterinary hygiene standard.

4. Conditions notified in advance by the Animal Quarantine Agency of Vietnam have not been fully implemented.

Article 24 Stipulations on transiting of animals and animal products through Vietnam:

1. On arrival of the vehicle carrying the animals, animal products or other commodities listed for quarantine at the port, the owner or the representative must produce quarantine certificates issued by the exporting country and other relevant documents to Animal Quarantine Station at the border through which the commodities will be transited.

2. The border Animal Quarantine Station inspects the quarantine certificates, veterinary hygiene status of the commodities and means of transport and compliance with the requirements notified to the owner at the time of application for transit. If all the conditions are satisfied, the Station grants quarantine certificates for transit.

3. Every organization and individual allowed to transit through Vietnam must abide by all the regulations of the animal quarantine agency at transit port:

a. It is not allowed to unload the commodity or dismantle the means of transport unless permitted by the animal quarantine agency;

b. The technical accessories of the vehicle must be safe and wastes must not drop on road.

c. It is not allowed to change the route or to stop at unspecified places.

d. Animals in transit can be released on the territory of Vietnam to get feed and water or in special cases only when permitted and supervised by the quarantine authority to prevent these animals from contact with domestic animals.

e. Carcases, waste matter, materials used as bedding for livestock, leftovers of feed, packages of animal products and other wastes of transport must be disposed of at appointed sites in accordance with the instructions from the animal quarantine agency.

Article 25 Stipulations on dealing with animals and animal products in transit through Vietnam:

1. The border Animal Quarantine Station does not allow animals and animal products or the subjects of quarantine to transit through if they do not satisfy the veterinary hygiene standard, if the quarantine certificates are not legal or if the animals display signs of infectious diseases listed as notifiable. The Station will take necessary measures according to the situation:

a. To return to the originating country of departure;

b. If return of the commodities to the originating country might cause disease spread or environment contamination, the animals and animal products must be disposed of on the spot or at a specified place. All means of transport, wastes and materials used as bedding must be cleaned and disinfected;

c. If the quarantine certificates are not legal, it is necessary to inform the National Veterinary Service of the exporting country to rectify or take action as stipulated at points a and b, Paragraph 1 of this Article.

2. The owner or the representative must follow every instruction given by the animal quarantine authority on handling, cleaning and disinfection and pay for those works.

Article 26 For animals and animal products or other articles listed as subjects of quarantine transiting through Vietnam in containers or other closed facilities, the border Animal Quarantine Station inspects the quarantine certificates issued by the exporting country and the means of transport and grants a permit for transit if all the requirement are met. If there are some unusual signs, the Station is allowed to request the owner to open the container for hygiene inspection.

Article 27 Stipulations on temporary stopping or parking vehicles on the territory of Vietnam:

1. Wherever a vehicle in transit through Vietnam stops/parks temporarily at stations, on ports, the owner or the representative is not permitted to unload or land animals and animal products. It is also not allowed to discharge leftovers or wastes at the stations and ports.

2. If in emergency cases, planes, trains or ships transporting animals and animal products have to stop at stations or ports, the owner or the representative must abide by all instructions given by the border Animal Quarantine Station.

3. If vehicles do not follow the set route or park/stop on stipulated places, the owner must leave the commodities untouched and inform the nearest veterinary authority. The transport can be continued only after having been dealt with by the veterinary authority.

Article 28 Stipulations on temporary import and re – export of animals and animal products

1. Every organization and individual who require temporary import – re – export of animals and animal products must apply to DAH for permission. After having been permitted by DAH, the owner must make a declaration to the Regional Veterinary Centre or border Animal Quarantine Station at least 7 days before. After the declaration has been submitted the Regional Animal Health Centre or border Animal Quarantine Station give notice of the quarantine time and location.

2. Temporary import and re – export of animals and animal products must be conducted according to this Rule.

Article 29 Stipulations on location for collection points, fairs and exhibitions of animals and animal products:

1. SDAH supports the local People's Committee to specify location for collection points, fairs and exhibitions of animals and animal products and is in charge of supervising and providing guidance on veterinary hygiene during the collection, fair and exhibition period.

2. Every Organization and individual has to abide by the following stipulations when moving animals and animal product to collection points, fairs and exhibition places.

a. Domestic animals and animal products must be accompanied by quarantine certificates issued by SDAH of departure;

b. Animals and animal products from other countries must be enclosed with quarantine certificates for import issued by border Animal Quarantine Station or Regional Veterinary Centre;

c. To abide by all stipulations and instructions given by the SDAH during the collection, fair or exhibition period.

3. After the collection, fair or exhibition is finished, the SDAH inspects veterinary hygiene of all the animals and animal products and cleans and disinfects the whole area.

a. SDAH issues quarantine certificates to animals and animal products which meet the veterinary hygiene standard for domestic use.

If animals and animal products brought in for a fair or exhibition need to be brought out of Vietnam, the owner must follow the quarantine procedures for export;

b. Animals and animal products, which do not satisfy the veterinary hygiene standard, will be disposed in accordance with this Rule.

Chapter Ⅲ Animal slaughter control and veterinary hygiene inspection of food of animal origin

Article 30 General provisions on animal slaughter:

1. Animals destined for slaughter include pigs, buffaloes, cattle, goats, horses, poultry and rabbits etc. for use food, industrial materials and livestock feed.

Animal intended for slaughter must be healthy and taken from infectious disease free zones.

2. It is forbidden to slaughter animals affected or suspected of being affected with infectious diseases listed to be excluded from slaughter by the Ministry of Agriculture and Food Industry.

3. During animal slaughter inspection, if veterinary surgeons or technicians detect or suspect the existence of listed infectious notifiable diseases issued by the Ministry of Agriculture and Food Industry, it is necessary to report to the local veterinary authority immediately.

4. Opening animals for post mortem must be carried out at locations specified by SDAH in the following cases:

a. Animals suspected of being affected with one of the listed infectious notifiable diseases, except animals affected or suspected of being infected with one of the diseases prohibited from being opened, such as Anthrax etc..

b. They have to be opened for inspection because of other reasons.

Article 31 Stipulations on slaughtering animals for sales and export:

1. Slaughtering animals for sales must be carried out at slaughterhouses/points permitted by the local People's Committee after the local Veterinary Service and authorities concerned have agreed. The local Veterinary Authority is to carry out slaughter control and veterinary hygiene inspection of these establishments. In cities, provincial towns and district towns, slaughtering animals must be done at slaughterhouses/points as stipulated.

2. Slaughtering animals for export must be conducted at slaughterhouses/points for export permitted by the People's Committees of provinces/cities under the Central Government after DAH and local concerned institutions have agreed. The Regional Animal Health Centre is in charge of supervising slaughter and inspecting the veterinary hygiene of these enterprises.

3. In remote areas where are far from slaughterhouses/slaughterpoints, the livestock owner requests the local Veterinary Service for hygiene inspection on the spot if animals are slaughtered other than for sale.

4. Every organization and individual who has an animal slaughterhouse /slaughterpoint must comply with the requirements for veterinary hygiene as stipulated at Article 13 of the Rules on Animal Disease Prevention and Control.

Article 32 Procedures for taking animals to slaughterhouses/points:

1. Any organization and individual who brings animals in large numbers to the slaughterhouses/points must have quarantine certificates issued by the local Veterinary Service.

2. Any organization and individual who takes animals to the slaughterhouses /points for export purpose must have quarantine certificates issued by the SDAH at the place of origin.

Animals must be gathered at the slaughterhouse/slaughterpoints at least from 12 to 24 hours prior to slaughter depending on each animal species.

3. Veterinary surgeons and technicians in charge of slaughter control must inspect quarantine certificates,

the means of transport, classify the animals and provide instructions on cleaning and disinfection of the means of transport.

Healthy animals will be moved to slaughterhouse lairage for slaughter.

Animals that are sick or suspected of being diseased must be moved to a separate slaughter area as stipulated.

Article 33 Stipulations on veterinary hygiene inspection and treatment of meat and other products during the slaughtering process:

1. The process of animal slaughter and veterinary hygiene inspection of meat and other products of each animal species is conducted as stipulated by the Ministry of Agriculture and Food Industry.

Veterinary surgeons and technician affix seal or issue a hygiene certificate for meat and other animal products if the standard of veterinary hygiene is met.

2. If animal meat, viscera or by – products are below the veterinary hygiene standard, they must be treated in accordance with the stipulations.

Depending on the quality of the products after being treated, it is to affix seals and issue certificates in forms that are different from seals and certificates referred to Paragraph 1 of this Article if the products are of the standard for use as food. If the products do not satisfy the standard for food they will be industrially processed or used for livestock feed or destroyed.

3. Every organization and individual who brings animals to a slaughterhouse /slaughterpoint must follow the instructions of veterinarians in slaughter, inspection and pay for those services. If after slaughter, the animal products are below the hygiene standard, the veterinary surgeons and technicians have to dispose of the products, clean and disinfect the slaughter area and the livestock owner has to pay the costs.

Article 34 If the organization or individual complains against the decision of a veterinary surgeon and technician or requests re – inspection, the direct superior of the Veterinary Service will conduct the re – inspection. The decision of the veterinary surgeon in charge of re – inspection shall be effective.

If the re – inspection confirms the decision of the first inspection, the organization/individual must bear all costs of the re – inspection. Otherwise, the inspectors must pay the compensation and all costs.

Article 35 Stipulations on the storage and transport of animal products:

1. Premises for storage of meat, viscera and by – products before processing and trade must meet the requirements of veterinary hygiene and maintain product quality.

Stored meat, viscera and by – products must be kept separate.

2. Facilities and equipment for the transport and carriage of animal products for sale must meet the veterinary hygiene standard, be cleaned and disinfected prior to and after transport and not contaminate animal products or be harmful to the consumer.

The transport of animal products in cities/towns must be carried out by special facilities and authorised by the Veterinary Service.

3. Animal meat and other products for sale must have a hygiene stamp on the carcases or have been granted hygiene certificates.

Veterinary surgeons and technicians inspect the veterinary hygiene of meat and other animal products in markets.

Article 36 Stipulations on the veterinary hygiene of processed animal products:

1. The construction and operation of animal product processing enterprises must meet requirements for veterinary hygiene as stipulated at Article 13 of the Rules on Animal Disease Prevention and Control.

2. Raw material of animal origin for processing at these enterprises must be from animals and animal prod-

ucts that meet the requirements for veterinary hygiene and are produced in slaughterhouses/slaughterpoints.

3. Veterinary surgeons and technicians inspect and supervise animal product processing in the enterprises and are allowed to take samples for laboratory tests as stipulated by the law.

Article 37 Stipulations on the issuing of hygiene certificates for processed animal products:

1. SDAHs issue veterinary hygiene certificates for processed animal products which satisfy the hygiene standard for domestic consumption.

The Regional Animal Health Centres issue certificates for processed animal products that satisfy the veterinary hygiene standard for export, import and transit.

2. If processed animal products do not satisfy the veterinary hygiene standard, they should be treated as stipulated.

3. The owner of commodities should obey all instructions given by the Veterinary Service during processing, inspection or treatment and must pay all costs.

4. Complaints and re – examination of decisions of the veterinary hygiene inspection of processed animal products are conducted as stipulated at Article 34 of this Rule.

Article 38 Stipulations on the marketing of food of animal origin:

1. Various kinds of food of animal origin must be inspected for veterinary hygiene criteria before being put on the market, i. e. perceptible measures, physical and chemical characteristics, microorganisms and residues remaining in food such as heavy metals, antibiotics, hormones etc. Foods that meet the veterinary hygiene standard will be sealed or stamped on or issued certificates and can be sold at shops and stands which satisfy veterinary hygiene standards

DAH is responsible for the inspection of the veterinary hygiene criteria for food of animal origin for export, import and transit.

SDAHs are responsible for the inspection of the veterinary hygiene criteria for food of animal origin for local consumption.

The Ministry of Agriculture and Food Industry stipulates the inspection standard and contents.

2. The Veterinary Service supervises veterinary hygiene implementation in enterprises for processing, preservation, trade, transport and marketing of food of animal origin in their own area.

3. The owner of commodities should follow every instruction given by the Veterinary Service in inspection and treatment and must pay for inspection, cleaning and disinfection as stipulated by the law.

The Minister of Agriculture and Food Industry regulates regimes of veterinary hygiene inspection, issuing of certificates and stamps of veterinary hygiene and temporary exceptions from the veterinary hygiene inspection of food of animal origin in some cases.

Article 39 Only persons who satisfy the health standard issued by the Ministry of Health are allowed to work at animal slaughterhouses/slaughterpoints and animal products processing, preservation and trading enterprises. Those persons must use protective clothing wherever they contact with animals and animal products during the process of slaughter, preservation and processing.

Article 40 The DAH directly inspects and supervises veterinary hygiene at animal slaughterhouses/points and animal product processing and preservation enterprises for export.

In its own area, the local Veterinary Service provides instructions, and inspects and monitors veterinary hygiene compliance with at animal slaughterhouses/points, animal product processing, preservation, marketing, transport and trading enterprises for domestic consumption.

Article 41 Veterinary surgeons and technicians in charge of quarantine, slaughter control and veterinary hygiene inspection of animals and animal products must wear uniforms, epaulettes, insignia, quarantine cards or inspection cards as stipulated by the Ministry of Agriculture and Food Industry and be protected by law.

Chapter Ⅳ　State management on animal quarantine and slaughter control and veterinary hygiene inspection of food of animal origin

Article 42　The contents of the State management of animal quarantine and slaughter control and veterinary hygiene inspection of food of animal origin are set at Article 41 of the Ordinance on Veterinary Services.

Minister of Agriculture and Food Industry is responsible for implementing and giving guidance on quarantine of animals and animal products, slaughter control and veterinary hygiene inspection of food of animal origin through the country, including:

a. To submit proposals to the Government to promulgate or promulgate legislation papers on quarantine, slaughter control and veterinary hygiene inspection of animals and animal products;

b. To work out plans on quarantine, slaughter control and veterinary hygiene inspection;

c. To carry out inspection and examination of quarantine, slaughter control and veterinary hygiene inspection. To deal with disputes, complaints and petitions relating to veterinary services;

d. To regulate the issuing or withdrawal of various kinds of certificates and licenses relating to quarantine, slaughter control and veterinary hygiene inspection of animals and animal products;

e. To publish lists of subjects of quarantine periodically;

f. To train, educate and disseminate knowledge of quarantine, slaughter control and veterinary hygiene inspection.

g. To cooperate internationally in quarantine, slaughter control and veterinary hygiene.

Article 43　Chairpersons of the People's Committees of provinces/cities under the Central Government have the following remits:

1. To direct quarantine, slaughter control and veterinary hygiene inspection in their own areas in compliance with instructions from the Ministry of Agriculture and Food Industry. To direct the local Veterinary Service to operate effectively.

2. To issue subordinate texts on quarantine, slaughter control and veterinary hygiene inspection in their own areas.

3. To issue stipulations on the issuing or withdrawal of certificates and licenses relating to quarantine, slaughter control and veterinary hygiene as stipulated by law.

4. To cooperate with superior State management offices on veterinary services to check, inspect and settle violations of the legislation on quarantine, slaughter control and veterinary hygiene inspection.

5. To receive and deal with complaints and petitions about quarantine, slaughter control and veterinary hygiene inspection or convey the cases to the authorized bodies.

Article 44　Remits of the Veterinary Services on animal quarantine and slaughter control and veterinary hygiene inspection of food of animal origin:

1. The Director of DAH is responsible to the Ministry of Agriculture and Food Industry for conducting State management on quarantine, slaughter control and veterinary hygiene inspection as stipulated at Article 42 of this Rule.

2. The Regional Animal Heal Centres and Centres for Veterinary Hygiene Inspection under DAH take responsibility for carrying out duties of quarantine, slaughter control and veterinary hygiene inspection of export, import and transit animals and animal products as allocated by DAH.

3. SDAHs support the People's Committees of provinces and cities under the Central Government to conduct

State management on quarantine, slaughter control and veterinary hygiene inspection of animals and animal products for domestic use in their own areas.

Chapter V Special inspection of quarantine, slaughter control and veterinary hygiene inspection of animals and animal products

Article 45 Special inspection of quarantine, slaughter control and veterinary hygiene inspection of animals and animal products is to check on the implementation of the veterinary legislation and to propose measures to prevent violations of the legislation on quarantine, slaughter control and veterinary hygiene inspection of animals and animal products.

The Director of DAH and Directors of SDAHs are in charge of organizing and carrying out inspection of quarantine, slaughter control and veterinary hygiene inspection of animals and animal products within roles assigned.

Article 46 Content of special inspection of quarantine, slaughter control and veterinary hygiene inspection of animals and animal products includes:

1. To inspect implementation of regulations on quarantine, slaughter control and veterinary hygiene of organizations and individuals who carry out activities relating to the veterinary services.

2. To inspect quarantine, slaughter control and veterinary hygiene inspection.

3. To inspect activities relating to legislation on quarantine, slaughter control and veterinary hygiene inspection of animals and animal products.

Article 47 Inspection of quarantine, slaughter control and veterinary hygiene inspection of animals and animal products is as stipulations on inspection in the Regulations on implementation of the Ordinance on Veterinary Services and the Rule on Veterinary Inspection issued by the Ministry of Agriculture and Food Industry.

Chapter VI Implementing provisions

Article 48 The Minister of Agriculture and Food Industry provides instructions, alone or in cooperation with concerned bodies, on implementation of this Rule.

The Minister, Heads of ministerial ranking offices, Heads of agencies under the Government and Chairpersons of the People's Committees of provinces and cities under the Central Government, within their own powers and responsibilities must organize the implementation of this Rule.

The Rule takes effects from the date of signing and replaces previously issued regulations.

兽医法实施细则

政府依据1992年9月30日国家基本法、1993年2月15日兽医法、农业和食品产业部部长提议，颁布：

第1条 该实施细则与以下法令联合发布：

1. 兽医服务法
2. 动物疾病防预与控制法
3. 检疫、屠宰控制及动物和动物产品的兽医卫生检疫法
4. 兽医药品管理法
5. 兽医处罚法

第2条 中央以下各部委领导、各级政府部门首长、各级省、市人民政府委员会主席有责任执行本法。

第3条 本法令自颁布之日起生效，同时废止之前与此相抵触的旧法令。

动物疫病预防与控制法

（1993年11月27日 政府93/CP号）

第一章 总 则

第1条 任何在越南从事兽医相关工作的国内外组织和个人必须遵守本法及其他相关法律。

第2条 所有服务机构、标准、经济组织、社会组织、人民军队和所有公民有责任监督、支持兽医服务以预防控制动物疾病。

第3条 禁止所有引起疾病传播，从而对动物、公众健康、环境卫生产生危害的行为。强制执行必要的免疫及预防措施。

第二章 动物疾病预防

第4条 动物疫病预防控制的一般条款：

1. 任何饲养动物的组织和个人，必须采取适当的措施预防动物疫病。
2. 规模化养殖动物的要求：

a. 动物饲养圈舍必须符合相应的兽医卫生标准；

b. 规模化养殖场地必须有排泄物储存场所、垫料储存场所、剩余饲料储存场所、病畜隔离场所、开放性尸体储存场所、检查和埋葬动物尸体的场所；

c. 凡进出规模化养殖场所的人员和交通工具必须经过消毒。

3. 一旦有家畜出现疾病症状，畜主应立即隔离病畜，并及时向当地兽医主管部门上报，再向上报告。病畜严禁屠宰食用、出售或随意丢弃。

第5条 饲料确保对动物无害，饲料的生产、加工、储存必须满足以下要求：

1. 有毒化学物品必须远离饲料生产、加工、储存场所。
2. 采取有效的方法根除啮齿类、有害昆虫。

在动物卫生局和其分支局管辖动物卫生分支局的范围内，对饲料实行兽医卫生检疫，建立饲料的生产、贸易、使用体系，限制不符合标准的饲料生产、贸易。农业和食品产业部负责规范饲料的兽医卫生检疫、生产、贸易。

第 6 条 非食用动物屠宰后，动物产品、动物性食品，用做动物的饲料的在使用前需经过兽医卫生检疫，假如处理后仍不符合饲料使用标准的，予以销毁。

第 7 条 关于动物饮用水、饲料、牧草、排泄物的规定如下：

1. 饮用和处理饲料的水必须清洁，不引起动物感染疾病，不允许使用未经处理、不适宜动物饮用的工业废水。

2. 只有未感染疾病的动物允许在牧场放牧。

3. 不允许使用可能染有疾病传染原的畜舍、排泄池。

4. 使用过杀虫剂、消毒剂的牧场，在杀虫剂、消毒剂分解前不允许放牧。

第 8 条 各级人民委员会给家畜贸易、家畜产品贸易划定专门区域。

只有无疾病症状，未携带疾病病原体的、符合各项相关标准的家畜产品才允许上市。

地方兽医部门在家畜、家畜产品交易市场实施监督和兽医卫生检疫。

第 9 条 关于新进动物的隔离、进口规定：

1. 规模化家畜生产单位必须建立检疫隔离区域，从别处新进动物必须在检疫隔离区内做相应兽医检查，确保健康以后才能合群。

2. 进口动物必须在地方动物健康中心或边境动物检疫站指定地点隔离，该隔离场所必须远离居住区、水源，这些隔离的动物必须远离当地原有家畜。

3. 检疫场所必须配备相应的人员和设备。

4. 各疾病的检疫隔离期最短为 45 天 。

第 10 条 畜主必须对其家畜进行一定的免疫接种及其他的疾病预防措施。

农业和食品产业部定期公布严重疾病名录，对不同地区，不同动物建立强制的免疫程序及其他的预防措施。

各级人民委员会负责指导辖区内强制免疫，动物卫生分支局每年组织强制免疫及其他必要的预防措施。

第 11 条 关于大宗动物、动物产品的运输规定：

1. 大宗动物、动物产品的铁路、水路、海运、空运只能经由指定车站、港口、机场进行。

车站、港口、机场必须配备相应的设备，以实施动物检疫、隔离病畜、储存动物产品和消毒。

2. 动物运输需消毒，运载车辆的地板要求密封，以防运输过程中排泄物滴漏。

3. 国家兽医管理部门官员负责动物运输的兽医卫生检疫：

a. 运输动物装载前必须检疫。水牛、牛、猪、羊和其他可疑染疫家畜要求逐个检查，其他动物可以群体观察。只有经过检疫的动物才签发检疫合格证。

b. 动物在运输过程、装载或卸载时都要检疫。

c. 监督动物的装载和卸载。

d. 运输前检查检疫证书。

有染疫可疑情况或不符合兽医卫生检疫标准时，检疫人员有权决定停止或暂缓运输，并依法对他们的决定负责。

第 12 条 关于运输动物的交通工具及其他用具的清洗消毒规定如下：

1. 用于运输动物、动物产品的车辆、工具须清洗消毒，接触、处理动物的人员在以下情况要求消毒：

a. 运输动物和动物产品之前。

b. 卸载动物和动物产品后、处理垫褥及排泄物后。

2. 兽医服务当局监督清洗消毒过程，以防这些工作引起运输中的动物、动物产品、精液、受精卵、饲料、人员、车辆、设备污染。

畜主或法人代表、车主及人员必须遵守兽医服务机构的指导，并且为运输动物和动物产品的车辆、设备的清洗消毒支付费用。

a. 动物卫生分支局为辖区内动物和动物产品的国内运输车辆和工具清洗消毒进行指导，签发卫生检疫证书。

b. 地方动物健康中心或边境动物检疫站为指定区域内动物和动物产品的进口、出口及过境运输车辆和工具清洗消毒进行指导，签发卫生检疫证书。

第 13 条　关于动物的屠宰、动物产品的处理、包装、储存的规定如下：

1. 凡有家畜屠宰场、产品、处理、包装、储存单位的组织和个人，须遵守如下约定：

a. 场地、建筑布局、单位的经营必须符合兽医卫生检疫、公共健康和环境卫生的标准。

b. 用水、废水排放、人员通道、车辆、储存及运输必须符合兽医卫生检疫标准。

c. 仪器和工具的材料必须是符合兽医卫生检疫标准的，在动物产品的生产、储存、处理、包装过程中不改变其质量。

d. 饲料的生产、储存必须按照兽医卫生检疫标准执行。

e. 必须有远离工作场所的，供放牧人员使用的洗手间、卫生间。

f. 必须执行啮齿动物的根除计划。

g. 必须坚持执行日常的清洁和消毒。

h. 所有国家的兽医卫生检疫规定、检测、处理、清洁、消毒必须完全实施到位，收费所得全部用于相应服务。

2. 兽医、健康、环境部门商议以后，由各级人民委员会负责动物产品生产、储存、处理、包装的检查和发证。

3. 国家兽医管理部门指导、检查兽医卫生检疫规定的实施，对相关单位的清洁、消毒给予说明指导。

第三章　动物疾病的控制

第 14 条　动物疾病控制的总则

1. 所有动物生产单位的畜主、运输单位的车主或者员工，任何时候发现有动物发病或不明原因死亡的，应及时向最近的兽医机构报告，并且不允许出售、屠宰病死畜作为肉用或私自处理。

2. 接到疫情报告后，兽医机构应立即作出反应，诊断原因，给予妥善处理。

一旦疫情确定，兽医机构应立即向同级人民委员会报告并尽快上报给上级主管部门。

3. 疾病一旦确诊，畜主、车主及员工必须按照要求接受隔离、诊断、药物治疗、预防，并支付相应费用。

第 15 条　疫情爆发时，如果动物卫生分支局诊断疾病不属于或可疑属于公布的名录，动物卫生分支局应向中央领导下的省、市人民委员会上报疫情，以控制动物及动物产品的流通，同时向动物卫生局报告。如动物卫生分支局不能确定疾病原因，应向动物卫生局送样确诊。禁止隔离区内的动物接触易感动物，禁止携带病原体的动物产品进出隔离区。

第 16 条　当严重的疾病在越南边境爆发，当地动物卫生分支局必须向省、市人民委员会报告，以通报疫情，确定该地区成为疫区，以采取以下措施：

1. 边境上进出口的动物数量和种类应严格遵守名录规定。

2. 禁止从感染危险区运输易感动物和携带病原体的动物产品进入越南。

3. 对通过边境的人员和车辆进行清洁消毒。

4. 按本规定第二十二条建立一个 10km 范围的免疫保护带，此范围内同样实行隔离区的措施。

第 17 条 关于疾病公布的权限规定如下：

1. 某区域爆发危险疾病时，省、市人民委员会主席签署决议在以下情况公布疫情：

a. 疾病确实存在于动物体内并造成传播。

b. 下级人民委员会已经递交了疾病情况书面报告。

c. 该疾病确定在动物卫生分支局或动物卫生局规定的必须公布的疾病名录范围内。

确定公布疾病后，省、市人民委员会主席应立即向农业和食品工业部部长、国家总理报告，报告中须清楚说明疾病的名称和爆发地点。

2. 当疾病在 2 个省以上范围同时爆发，以下情况由农业和食品工业部部长签署决议并公布疫情：

a. 传染病日益传播，对家畜及人民健康引起严重的危害。

b. 省、市的疫情报告已经提交。

c. 严重的疾病必须公布时，由动物卫生局递交疫情公告。当决定公布疫情时，农业和食品工业部部长必须向国家总理报告。由农业和食品工业部公布需周期性公布的严重疾病的名录。

第 18 条 关于疾病预防机构的规定：

1. 制定疾病方面的通知时，疾病出现地中央政府下属的省市人民委员会主席命令所有服务部门和机构协同社会各界，动员全社会的人力、财力、物力以法律形式确保相关疾病预防措施的执行。

中央政府下属的省市人民委员会确定疫区和保护带范围，并通告下级相关单位以引起关注。

2. 动物卫生分支局 有权力和义务指导当地兽医部门对抗疾病，负责疾病的预防和控制技术，同时负责每 10 天向中央政府下属的省市人民委员会及动物卫生局汇报疫情直至疾病完全得到控制。

第 19 条 疫情通报指的疫区，必须切实执行以下规定：

1. 建立由警察和兽医组成的警戒带，以指导、检查、监督动物的转运；在疫区发布通告；限制动物和动物产品的运输；给患病动物及污染的环境接触、使用过的畜舍、排泄物清洁消毒。

2. 兽医服务机构负责检查和列明动物名录，按名录划定应隔离动物范围，采用相应兽医卫生处理。

第 20 条 关于疫区内动物隔离的规定

1. 对疫区的动物要求如下：

a. 所有已经感染、疑似感染或正存在感染可能的动物在治疗期间要求隔离并不允许放牧。

b. 保障患病动物治疗和隔离需要的人员和设备。所有接触患畜、剩余饲料、排泄物、垃圾等的设备、材料必须坚持清洁和消毒直至疫情结束。

c. 无关人员禁止进入有动物染疫或死亡的地区。

2. 兽医服务机构监督患畜的隔离和治疗，监督畜主对无法治愈或已经死亡的动物进行处理。

第 21 条 关于疫区内限制动物和动物产品的运输及开展兽医卫生控制规定如下：

1. 严禁将已感染或可疑感染了需通报疾病的易感动物和动物产品及污染的饲料、排泄物、垫料、设备带入或带出疫区，除了带去隔离或必须的屠宰之外。

2. 经过疫区运输易感动物、饲料、废气物，运输工具必须按照规定的路线行驶，中途不允许停车。

3. 禁止在疫区市场交易易感的动物和动物产品，以免引起疾病的传播，禁止在疫区举办参观或展览。禁止在疫区屠宰或运输易感动物和动物产品。

第 22 条 以下是关于感染疾病 30km 范围内，即保护带（受威胁区）的规定：

1. 限制市场易感动物、动物产品的转移、运输、贸易和交流。

2. 兽医服务机构必须加强对动物和动物产品的运输的控制、检查以及时发现感染动物。

第 23 条 关于在疫区及保护带范围对易感动物实施强制免疫的规定如下：

1. 动物卫生分支局规定疫区和保护带内必须实施强制免疫的易感动物名录并指导强制免疫的实施。

2. 对于某些特定疾病，动物卫生分支局 必须得到动物卫生局的许可才能实施强制免疫。

第 24 条 关于感染和可疑动物的强制屠宰规定：

1. 为了控制疾病的传播，由动物卫生分支局向省人民委员会提议对感染及可疑感染不能治愈的疾病的动物实施强制屠宰。

疫区内强制屠宰必须在指定的屠宰点实施，由兽医服务机构指导，并确保相应兽医卫生措施的实施。

2. 运输强制屠宰动物的交通工具必须密封，以防止废弃物在运输过程中滴漏。

3. 处理屠宰动物和动物产品的用水必须符合要求。

4. 在肉和下水移走后，动物宰杀和动物产品处理地点必须经过清洁消毒处理。

5. 未经治疗强制屠宰的动物畜体不能使用，只能按兽医卫生规定处理；不能使用的二级产品及其他产品按本法令第二十五条规定处理。

兽医服务机构负责监督、控制动物屠宰的运输、宰杀、处理、清洁消毒。兽医服务机构同样按兽医卫生要求监督屠宰，并许可动物产品的使用。

第 25 条　患传染病的动物的畜体处理规定如下：

1. 感染或者疑似感染疾病的、必须强制宰杀的、不适宜再使用的动物尸体及动物产品，应当与家畜垫料、排泄物一起深埋于两层适当的消毒剂之间。埋葬地点必须远离生活区、饮用及畜用、放牧水源。

2. 感染危险性疾病如口蹄疫、炭疽的动物尸体、垫料、排泄物必须在兽医机构的监督和证明下焚烧。

3. 对于炭疽，各级人民委员会必须提供详细清单，列出以往死亡动物的埋葬地点、封闭埋葬坑的情况；只有在中央领导下的省、市人民委员会同意并签发许可证以后，特定代理人才能实施埋葬坑的所有处理工作。动物卫生分支局负责指导代理人对埋葬坑内埋葬物的消毒、销毁工作，代理人承担所有相关费用。

第 26 条　疫区内动物畜舍、工具、排泄物、牧草、运输工具、宰杀场地以及动物死亡的场地必须按兽医机构的规定程序用适当的浓缩化学消毒药品进行清洁、消毒处理。清洁、消毒必须对人体、动物健康无害。动物卫生分支局对相应疫区内的清洁消毒负责指导、监督。

第 27 条　满足以下条件可以给予疫情解除的通报：

1. 定期对疫区及保护带内所有易感动物进行预防性免疫接种，以防止疫情传播。

2. 根据不同疾病的特点，在最后一头动物死亡、恢复或者强制屠宰实施后 15 ~ 30 天内没有新的病例出现。

3. 按兽医卫生要求对疾病爆发后实施清洁消毒。

向动物卫生局上报以后，动物卫生分支局的主管领导可以要求政府下属省、市人民委员会签发通报，解除一定区域的疫情。2 个省以上范围内疫情的解除，由动物卫生局主管领导向农业与食品工业部提出签发疫情解除通报的请求。

第 28 条　一旦疫情难以控制，中央下属省市人民委员会、农业及食品工业部应当请求政府动用国库资金保证兽医药品的供应。

第 29 条　越南境内一旦出现新的动物疫情，疾病出现地区所在的中央下属省市人民委员会应调动兽医及其他相关部门严格封锁疫区。

各级兽医机构应迅速确诊疾病并向农业和食品工业部报告，及时采取有效的措施阻止疫情传播。

第四章　动物疫病预防与控制的国家管理

第 30 条　关于动物疾病控制国家管理责任的划分如下：

1. 动物疫病预防控制的国家管理要求在兽医服务条例第四十一条里有具体规定。

2. 农业和食品工业部负责组织执行和指导全国动物疾病的预防控制工作，具体如下：

a. 向政府立法机构提供动物疾病预防和控制的文案；在权限范围内发布动物疾病预防控制的文件；

指导各部委、部委下属的办公室、政府各级机关、各地方人民委员会、外国驻越南的机构和个人执行兽医法规。

b. 起草疾病的预防控制计划，负责向所有机构和各部门解释并指导计划的执行细节。

c. 对疾病预防控制各方面起协调作用，管理资金的使用。

d. 检查疾病的预防控制，对疾病的预防控制进行释疑。

e. 管理与疾病预防控制相关的国内或国外组织及个人证书的签发或撤消。

f. 发表通告，公布那些需要定期检疫、定期强制免疫的疾病名录。公布或解除 2 个以上省范围的疫情。

g. 组织培训，宣传疾病预防控制的知识、动员群众参与疾病预防控制。

h. 加强国际合作，组织参加国际间关于疾病预防控制的合作与会议。

3. 中央政府下属各省市人民委员会主席负责执行和制导疾病预防控制，具体如下：

a. 管理和指导当地兽医服务机构按农业和食品工业部的每个指令执行疾病预防控制的具体有效的措施。

b. 在所辖范围内发布疾病预防控制指导文件。

c. 在权限范围内，签发或撤消与疾病预防控制有关的证书与执照。

d. 在所辖范围内发布或撤消疫情通告，严重的疫情爆发时，与农业和食品工业部一起向政府建议动用国库资金用于购买兽医药品。

e. 与国家兽医管理部门合作，控制、检查、处理违反动物疫病预防控制法令的行为。

f. 在责任范围内受理有关疾病预防控制的争端、申诉或者代为移交给相关部门。

第 31 条 物疫病预防控制机构的权限：

1. 动物卫生局负责人向农业和食品工业部负责，与动物疫病预防控制有关的具体见第三十条。

2. 动物卫生分支局 负责人向中央政府下属各省市人民委员会主席负责，在其管理区域内的与动物疫病预防控制有关的具体见第 30 条第 3 款。

农业和食品工业部负责兽医卫生检疫机构的设立，功能、责任、权利的划分。

第五章 动物疫病预防控制的其他特殊规定

第 32 条 动物疫病预防控制的特殊检疫就是指检查是否与动物疫病预防控制相关法令相符合，是否与预防疾病原则相违背，是否与预防控制疾病的法令有违反。

动物卫生局及动物卫生分支局的各负责人各按其功能、职责、权力负责组织执行动物疾病预防控制。

第 33 条 动物疫病的预防控制的检疫具体内容包括：

1. 检查组织及个人是否按兽医卫生和动物疫病预防控制的要求执行兽医机构的职责。

2. 检查中央及各级地方兽医卫生官员及兽医诊断官员的动物疾病预防控制工作。

3. 检查其他动物疾病预防控制相关行为。

第 34 条 动物疫病预防控制的其他行为检查参照兽医服务条令及农业和食品工业部的兽医检疫规则有具体规定。

第六章 补 充 条 款

第 35 条 农业和食品生产部，单独或者与代理机构合作，应该为法令的实施提供指导。部长、部门负责人、政府领导下的代理机构领导、中央政府下属各省市人民委员会主席应各司其职，组织执行相关法律。

本法令自签发之日起生效，同时废止之前与之相抵触的其他规定。

兽医违法处罚条例

第 1 条　违反动物疫病预防控制的规定：

1. 给予警告或最低 10000 最高 50000 越南盾罚款。如果造成了严重的危害，符合以下情形的，可给予 100000 越南盾罚款：

a. 对于农业和食品工业部公布的名录上列出的严重疾病，畜主没有申请强制免疫或实施其他预防措施的；

b. 出售或处理感染了严重疾病的动物尸体而引起疾病传播的；

c. 携带必须申报的疾病的动物或携带有病原体的动物产品进出 限制区域的；出售有正在流行疾病的动物或动物产品的；携带易感动物接触已感染了需通报疾病的动物的；按要求不允许停留而在感染区域内卸载动物的；

d. 不按规定执行相应的预防措施，比如对动物畜舍、排泄物清洁、消毒、处理的。

2. 对以下情形处以 50000 至 200000 越南盾罚款，危害严重的可罚款 500000 越南盾：

a. 疫区和保护带内未按规定进行口蹄疫、炭疽、猪瘟强制免疫的；

对其他危害严重的疾病，农业和食品工业部应按具体需要制定规定；

b. 未按兽医服务规定采取兽医卫生措施处理猪瘟或按规定焚烧因口蹄疫、炭疽死亡的动物尸体的；

c. 所有养殖行业、饲料行业未按规定对畜舍、饲料、深加工用品、屠宰、处理、包装、贮存和贸易过程进行周期性兽医卫生检验的。

第 2 条　违反动物屠宰检疫和兽医卫生检验规定的：

1. 处以 20000 至 50000 越南盾罚款，符合以下情形有足够证据表明造成了严重危害的，可处以 100000 越南盾罚款：

a. 在运输过程或在采样点、市场、展览检疫名录上列明的动物和动物产品时被发现没有检疫证书，或者是非法的检疫证书的；

b. 进出口或运输过程中，检疫名录中的动物和动物产品、兽药逃避兽医卫生检验的；

c. 出售没有屠宰检疫的水牛肉、黄牛肉、马肉、猪肉的，商店、售卖点没有兽医服务机构签发的证书或签章而出售动物产品的，不符合卫生标准的；

d. 在非法定屠宰场私宰商业用动物的；

e. 屠宰场的清洁、消毒、动物和动物产品、饲料、药品及原材料的的处理、保存不符合规定的；

f. 屠宰的出口动物不能提供动物卫生局的证书，证明动物来源于指定的非疫区。

2. 处以 50000 至 500000 越南盾罚款，符合以下情形，危害严重的，可处以 2000000 越南盾罚款：

a. 进口或运输动物、动物产品、兽医药品未按规定申报或预先申报的；

b. 进口或运输动物、动物产品、兽医药品未得到越南当局有关部门批准的；

c. 虚假的动物产品检疫，或未经许可随意更改兽医检验部门已检验的动物产品包装的；

d. 不经检疫进口动物、动物产品或尚在检疫期间即使用的；

e. 不在动物卫生局签发执照的许可范围内使用进口动物、动物产品的；

f. 屠宰、出售感染炭疽、口蹄疫的动物、动物产品的。

3. 违反本条规定第二款 f 项的，同时并处没收动物产品。

第 3 条　违反动物药品管理规定的：

1. 符合以下情形的，处以 100000 至 500000 越南盾罚款，证据确凿，危害严重的，可处以 2000000 越南盾罚款，同时吊销兽药营业执照：

a. 无证或在执照许可范围之外生产、经营兽药的，或者未在兽医服务机构取得执照编码的；

b. 生产假药，比如：与注册的质量不相符的、配方、含量与注册的不完全一致的、商标未注册的；

c. 无证经营原始材料、售卖假药 、劣质药、农业和食品工业部未公布许可的药品、兽医服务机构未签发注册编码的药品的；

d. 未经批准进口药品原材料或成药的；

e. 进口药材原材料包装随意更改的；

f. 经营农业和食品工业部未公布的进口药品的；

g. 进出口假药或任何形式经营伪劣药品原材料的；

h. 未经许可或不按动物卫生局规定试用新药的；

i. 不按动物卫生局许可范围使用进口药品的；

j. 未经动物卫生局许可使用微生物制作兽药的。

2. 违反本条第 1 项 b、d、e 、f、g、k 款的，同时并处没收兽药或其原材料；

除以上的处罚，在造成严重危害的情形下，根据危害的程度，可限期或无限期取消试用执照或新药试用执照。

第 4 条　违反兽医经营管理规定的：

1. 以下情形下处以 50000 至 200000 越南盾罚款，造成严重危害的，可处以罚款 500000 越南盾：

a. 更改、涂改或伪造免疫证、兽医卫生检验、检疫、兽医药品检验、生产注册、兽医经营、兽药实验等证件以及兽医检验章；

b. 未经兽医服务机构当局批准，私自从事兽医经营的；

c. 转借营业执照、从业资格证或许可证的；

d. 滥用兽医服务机构人员制服、肩章、徽章假冒的兽医的。

2. 以下情形处以 100000 至 500000 越南盾罚款，证据确凿，造成严重危害的可处以 2000000 越南盾罚款：

a. 虚假申报或制造假材料申请兽医从业许可证的；

b. 阻挠干扰兽医实行其职责的。

第 5 条　违反兽药及其标签的宣传规定的：

1. 以下情形处以 100000 至 500000 越南盾罚款，证据确凿，造成严重危害的，可处以 2000000 越南盾罚款，同时撤消其生产执照、从业许可证：

a. 不按兽药的实际质量和效果做虚假广告、宣传的；

b. 未得到兽医主管当局许可或者不按样品标签随意流通兽药的；

c. 伪造或仿造兽药；

d. 标签未注明“仅用于兽药”或未以其他方式标明兽药专用的。

2. 违反本条 a、b 款规定，有证据表明危害严重的，吊销兽药执照。

3. 违反本条 b、c 款规定的，药品和标签予以没收。

违法处罚的权限和程序

第 6 条　关于违法处罚的权限和程序规定：

1. 各级兽医服务机构对违法管理的权限规定如下：

a. 执行兽医卫生检验、动物和动物产品的检疫、屠宰控制、兽医药品检验的兽医师和技术人员有权对管辖区内的违法行为做出 100000 越南盾以下的罚款；

b. 地区兽医站站长或副站长、动物卫生分支局下属兽医检疫队或检疫官的副职有权处以 500000 越南盾以内的罚款，应当吊销实习资格证或其他许可证时，应及时向上级部门备案；

c. 边境动物检疫站或铁路检查点、邮政检查点领导及代理有权处以 1000000 越南盾罚款，应当吊销实习资格证或其他许可证时，应及时向上级部门备案；

d. 地区动物健康中心主任、副主任，动物卫生局检查官员，动物卫生分支局首席检查员，各动物卫生分支局的正副局长，有权处以 2000000 越南盾以内罚款，并视情节严重程度处以其他规定的措施；

e. 动物卫生局首席检查员、正、副局长有权依照本法令有关规定实施其他处罚。

2. 依照本法令第 17、19 条规定，有权实施处罚的国家机构和个人行使处罚权的时候受第 18 条约束。

第 7 条　兽医服务违法处罚程序如下：

1. 简单程序：

警告及 100000 越南盾以内的罚款可以现场执行，但必须出具收条，没有开具收条时，被处罚人可以拒绝接受处罚。

2. 处罚决定：

罚款在 100000 越南盾以上，必须按第 21 条的规定记录在档案，记录 15 天内，必须按第 18 条的规定向被处罚人下达书面的处罚决定 。

3. 所有罚款所得资金必须直接上缴国库。

4. 处罚决定下达后 5 天，被处罚单位或个人不执行的，按第 32 条，由决定下达单位强制执行。

被处罚的机构、组织、法人单位必须依法执行处罚决定。

第 8 条　许可证的吊销：

1. 任何单位或个人实施兽医服务时有违反法律的行为时，都应依法吊销执照、许可证（一般统称执照）。

2. 限期吊销在经过严肃调查确认可以继续经营后可再恢复经营。

3. 限期吊销在以下情形实施：

a. 执照的签发单位不具备签发能力；

b. 执照的内容违反法律规定；

c. 出现了严重违法的经营行为不能继续经营。

4. 本法第 6 条所指行使兽医服务违法处罚权的机关和个人，有权向发证机关提议吊销执照。

第 9 条　其他管理措施的实施程序：

1. 本法第 6 条规定的的机构和个人必须遵守本法，凡因决议不当引起的损失适用罚则处理，决议人对其决议负责。

2. 其他管理行为必须有书面决议时才能实施，该书面决议与处罚决定书一起送达受罚的组织和个人。

3. 刑事处罚 5 日内执行。

4. 检疫隔离、兽医药品销毁必须立即执行，并做好记录，记录上要求被处罚人、执法人、目击证人签字证明。如果销毁不能立即执行，封条要完整，并出具书面材料授权代理执行。

5. 限期内处罚没有被实施的组织和个人，必须强制执行，并承担其费用。

第 10 条　被行使兽医处罚的组织、个人对处罚决议不满时允许申诉，对申述的处理依照本法第 36、37 条执行。

第 11 条　实施处罚权的国家机构或个人在执法过程有触犯法规或强行处罚等行为的，依法追究刑事责任或处罚，给国家造成损失的要负责赔偿 。

第 12 条　凡对兽医管理有杰出贡献的个人，或产生了巨大积极效应的官员依照本法第 39 条给予奖励。

补 充 条 款

第 13 条　在越南的外国机构、个人和投资企业违反了兽医法令的，依照本法第 3、5 条处罚。

第 14 条　农业和食品工业部负责指导、监督本法的实施：档案记录、处罚决议等，财政部负责管理、印发、控制罚款收据凭条。

第 15 条 部门领导、首长，政府机构领导、中央政府下属各省、市人民委员会主席在各自职权范围内组织本法的实施。

本法自签发之日起执行，之前与之相违背的法令同时废止。

兽医服务条例

为了加强国家管理，改善预防措施，防止疫病扩散，促进畜牧业的发展，为了给国内、外市场提供高质量的家畜及畜产品，保障人民健康和生态环境，特制定本条例。

根据越南社会主义共和国宪法第 91 条。

本条例为兽医服务而制定。

第一章 总 则

第 1 条 本条令所提及的服务包括动物疫病的预防和控制、隔离封锁动物及其产品、动物屠宰的控制，动物源性食物的兽医监测，用于兽医的药品及微生物的管理。

第 2 条 本条令所用的术语应做以下理解：

1－1 本条令指的动物包括兽类、禽类、爬行动物、甲壳动物、软体动物和各种鱼类、蜜蜂、蚕、受精卵、精液和动物胚胎。

2－2 动物产品包括肉类和其他动物源性产品。

3－3 兽医药物是指动物源性产品、植物和化学物质、疫苗和其他用于兽医的生化物质。

4－4 微生物是指细菌、病毒、寄生虫、真菌和一些用于动物疫病诊断、预防和治疗其他种类以及为了预防和控制动物疫病而进行研究、生产和检测的药品。

5－5 兽医卫生标准的满意程度是指保护和发展畜牧业、避免影响人类健康及造成生态环境污染的能力。

6－6 动物屠宰的控制是指动物宰前宰后兽医卫生标准的监测和家畜生产、屠宰和动物产品加工处理、贮存、销售、运输和消费的监测。

第 3 条 通过结合现代科学与传统实验，国家集中管理兽医服务以确保整个社会的利益。

国家要遵守越南社会主义人民共和国已签署或参与的有关国际兽医服务协议。

第 4 条 国家鼓励国内外组织和个人在越南境内以多种形式投资兽医领域。

第 5 条 所有国家机构、金融公司、社会组织、人民军队和公民必须服从本兽医条例。

任何海外组织和个人在越南领土内从事家畜和畜产品的生产和贸易或其他与兽医服务有关活动的都必须遵从本条例，除了越南社会主义共和国特别签署或已接受的有关国际协议之外。

第 6 条 各级人民议会和委员会、其他国家机构、全国各口岸及各机构组织都有责任监控兽医法规的实施。

第 7 条 所有对动物保护和发展，人民健康或生态环境有害的行为都应该禁止。

第二章 动物疫病的预防和控制

第 8 条 动物疫病预防和控制目的是：

1. 确保家畜生产、饲养过程和动物加工处理过程的兽医卫生而设立一个合理的卫生标准。
2. 履行疫病预防（预防疫病的）措施，诊断、控制和消除疫病。
3. 鉴定和预防疫病扩散、确保消费者的安全而实施动物、动物产品的隔离、屠宰控制和动物源性食品的兽医卫生监测。

第 9 条　家畜生产禁止接触污染的环境

农场、家畜圈舍、养殖水域、材料和用于家畜生产的设施和动物饮水都应该符合兽医卫生标准。

农业和食品工业部应该制定一个养殖动物和家畜生产场所的兽医卫生标准。为了家畜生产和饲养过程，各级兽医机构在其辖区内都有责任指导、监督兽医法规的实施。

第 10 条　畜主必须制定强制性免疫措施或利用强制性预防疫病措施避免动物疫病传染人类，防止严重动物疫病的发生。

本条例所提及的严重动物疫病清单由农业和食品工业部制定。

第 11 条　在动物运输途中为了不引起环境污染，如果畜主、运输业主或随从人员发现患病、死亡的动物应禁止销售、屠宰或丢弃。当地主管部门应立即报告最近的兽医当局。

接到此类报告后兽医当局必须尽快查处。一旦确定疫病爆发，兽医服务机构应提供解决指导方案并给直接向兽医监督机构和与前者同级别的人民议会递送紧急报告。

在疫病诊断、治疗和预防时，畜主、搬运工和随从人员必须遵从兽医服务机构人员的询问。此项工作开支由政府支付。

第 12 条　当有严重疫病症状出现时，各级兽医当局应立即鉴定疫病，给畜主提供指导方案以制定隔离和兽医卫生措施。

当确定有严重疫病存在时，当地兽医服务机构应报告同级人民议会并由其颁布一份限制动物、动物产品流通的申明，同时呈报直管兽医监督当局。禁止运输那些易于感染、携带病原的动物和动物产品进出封锁限制区。

第 13 条　当越南境内或与越南比邻的边界地区爆发严重疫病时，该流行地区或面临该疫病威胁的省级兽医服务机构请求省人民议会颁布疫病通告。

省级人民委员会主席决定颁布或撤消该地区的疫病通告并报告省政府。

农业与食品工业部决定颁布或撤消两个省以上的疫病通告。

农业与食品工业部应定期颁布制定疫病清单。

政府制定颁布和撤消疫病通告决议的标准和方式。

第 14 条　当颁布疫病通告时，有疫病存在的省级人民委员会应该组织各分支机构提供指导方针和协调当地社会组织采取以下措施：

1. 证实和公布有疫病存在的地区，控制感染地区周围的保护区，设立公告和检测点，为该地区的运输业提供指导路线。

2. 严禁人们进入患病或有动物死亡的地区进行商业行为。严禁兽医卫生监察文件规定的任何形式的运输工具进出该疫区；严禁在该地区屠宰动物、销售明文规定为易感动物的产品、严禁明文规定的易感动物进入该地区。

3. 在感染地区和保护区组织紧急免疫或给明文规定对该病易感的各类动物提供保护措施。患病动物必须根据兽医机构的有关规定进行治疗。

4. 清理、消毒患病动物的圈舍和牧场、养殖家畜所使用的设施以及废弃物。在遵照农业与食品工业部法规的前提下，在该地区制定另一套切实可行的卫生措施。

5. 如有新的严重危害疫病出现，应及时报告政府以便及时采取特殊措施阻止疫病流行，应该采取的措施已在本条例中标明，阻止疫病爆发。

第 15 条　有关撤消疫病通告的决议规定如下：

1. 在感染地区或在保护区中易感动物都应进行疫苗免疫或采用其他预防措施。

2. 在最后一头动物死亡或康复以后的 15 到 30 天内实施，直至证明不再出现感染动物或动物死亡。

3. 清理和消毒与疫病有关的物品。

第 16 条　农业与食品工业部根据疫病爆发位置、疫病特点、动物种类，在疫区内制定一个强制免疫或强制预防措施实施的时间界限。

第 17 条 各级人民委员会要负责给辖区提供有关疫病预防和控制的指导方案，也有权力依法动员人力、物力援助以实施预防。

如有严重疫病流行，省人民委员会、农业与食品工业部可以请求政府动用国库资金采购兽医药品，如第 18 条所述。

第 18 条 为控制和消除主要疫病，政府和省人民委员会应该划拨适当比例的财政资金用于动物健康福利。在部级建立国家储备资金采购兽药；在省级建立地方资金采购兽药；兽药资金的设立、管理、使用由政府统一调控。

第三章 动物的检疫与屠宰控制

第 19 条 动物检疫措施有：监测和鉴定那些已在流行或尚没有传入越南境内的动物传染病和寄生虫病以及那些国际检疫关注的传染病和寄生虫病；检查和发现那些与外国合作伙伴进行买卖、交换和签署援助协议上列明需要检查的疫病以及对人类或动物有害的有毒物质、激素和抗生素。

农业与食品工业部应定期出版一些需要监测的疫病和有毒物质的清单。

第 20 条 动物检疫主要对象包括：

1. 动物和动物产品。

2. 家畜饲养和生产环境；

3. 明确规定的动物和动物产品的生产、屠宰、加工、贮存和运输；在屠宰、加工过程中所使用的设备、仪器和材料；动物、动物产品包装、装纳、流通和运输。

4. 应检物清单由农业与食品工业部颁发。

第 21 条 需异地转运时，应检物清单中提及的家养、狩猎、捕获的动物和动物产品必须检疫，检疫证书由兽医官方授权的机构颁发。

商品物主、运输者或搬运工必须出示检疫证书给兽医人员以便掌握其行程或目的地。

农业与食品工业部负责制定检疫要求、检疫证书的颁发和豁免检疫的条件。

第 22 条 只有符合以下条件才能运输和销售动物、动物产品。

1. 动物必须来自非疫区、健康、已免疫或已采取其他预防措施且在免疫有效期内。

2. 动物产品必须由健康、没有感染或携带烈性传染病病原的动物加工制造；包装应该符合卫生管理条理，产品必须到达卫生标准。

3. 在运输前后，运输工具、饲养家畜的设备和动物产品的容器必须清理、消毒。

第 23 条 由公路、铁路、河流、海洋或飞机运输大量动物时必须指明规定的车站和码头切实落实兽医卫生措施。

在收购、运输动物时，物主、搬运者或随从人员需要提高动物福利待遇，确保运载动物的环境符合兽医法规的要求。

第 24 条 在公路、铁路、河流和海洋和国家边界和邮局检测点，有关人员必须协助兽医机构检疫动物、动物产品以便履行其职责。

第 25 条 应检物清单中标明的进出口或通过越南转运的动物、动物产品都由越南兽医官方检查，如果符合兽医卫生标准将颁发检疫证书。

在越南兽医当局检查之前，进口或通过越南转运的动物及动物产品，商品物主或代理人应出示由出口国兽医机构签发的动物检疫证书。

农业与食品工业部负责规定检疫职责、制定为了公共安全、国家防御、科学研究或其他目的而进出口的动物的检疫证书的样式。

第 26 条 任何组织个人出口动物、动物产品必须给兽医官方服务机构递交一份申明。当兽医服务机构收到申明时要做出决定并通知商品物主有关隔离检疫的时间、地点。

对达到兽医卫生标准的动物、动物产品由兽医当局的服务机构签发检疫证书。

假如动物、动物产品达不到卫生标准，兽医服务机构不能签发检疫证书并要求商品物主采取必要处理措施。

第 27 条　任何组织、个人在越南境内进口动物、动物产品必须给越南兽医当局的服务机构递交一份申明。兽医当局的服务机构收到申明之后要根据商品的性质、数量和类型，作出决议并通知商品物主检查商品的时间、地点。

在越南兽医当局指定的隔离地点实施动物、动物产品的隔离检疫，对动物产品的隔离检疫期不超过七天；而于活动物的隔离检疫期由农业与食品工业部制定。

越南兽医当局对符合兽医卫生标准的动物、动物产品签发检疫证书，对于不符合卫生标准的动物、动物产品不允许进口。这些产品应该退回货主或根据越南兽医法规处理。

Decree of the governmenton guidelines for the implementation of the ordinance on veterinary services

The governemnt

Pursuant to the Law on Organization of the Government issued on 30 September 1992;

Pursuant to the Ordinance on Veterinary Services published on 15 February 1993;

At the proposal of the Minister of the Agriculture and Food Industry.

Hereby decrees:

Article 1 To issue in conjunction with this Decree the following texts:

Regulation on the implementation of the Ordinance on Veterinary Services;

Regulations on the prevention and control of animal diseases;

Regulations on the quarantine, slaughter control and veterinary hygiene inspection of animals and animal products;

Regulations on veterinary drug management;

Regulations on the settlement of administrative violations in the veterinary services.

Article 2 The Ministers, Heads of ministerial ranking bodies, Heads of bodies under the Government, Chairpersons of the People's Committees of Provinces and Cities under the central Government have responsibilities for implementing this Decree.

Article 3 This Decree takes effect from the date of signing and replaces previous regulations that are contrary to this Decree.

Regulations on prevention and control of animal diseases

(Issued under the Decree 93/CP of the Government dated 27 November 1993)

Chapter Ⅰ General provisions

Article 1 Every domestic and foreign organization and individual whose business relates to the veterinary services in Vietnam must abide by the stipulations of the Rules and other relevant legislative documents.

Article 2 All services and levels, economic organizations, social organizations, the People's armed forces and all citizens take responsibility for supervising and supporting the Veterinary Service in preventing and controlling of animal diseases.

Article 3 Every action that causes the spread of diseases which are harmful to animals, public health and the ecological environment is forbidden. It is not allowed to avoid compulsory vaccination and other preventive measures.

Chapter Ⅱ Animal disease prevention

Article 4 Below are general provisions on animal disease prevention and control:

1. Every organization and individual raising animals must carry out measures of animal disease preventive hygiene.

2. Intensive livestock production establishments must fulfil the following requirements:

a) The housing and the grazing environment must comply with the veterinary hygiene standard;

b) For intensive livestock production housing, it is required to have areas for faeces storage, for the treatment of bedding materials or leftovers of feed, for isolation of sick animals, for opening carcases for post mortem examinations and burying dead animals;

c) At entry to and exit from for the intensive farm, disinfection should be used for people and means of transport passing through.

3. A livestock owner must isolate animals which display signs of disease from other animals and at the same time inform the local Veterinary Service and follow instructions given by the Veterinary Authority. It is not allowed to slaughter sick animals for food and for sales or to abandon them.

Article 5 Feed must not be harmful to animals. Places for feed production, processing and storage must satisfy the following requirements:

1. Toxic chemicals must be kept away from the feed production, processing and storage areas;

2. Measures must be taken to eradicate rodents and to destroy pests.

The DAH and SDAHs, within their area, carry out veterinary hygiene inspection of feed and or establishments of feed production, trade and use and are entitled to suspend the production, trade and use of feed that is sub - standard of veterinary hygiene.

The Ministry of Agriculture and Food Industry is to issue regulations on the veterinary hygiene inspection of feed and establishments for feed production, trade and use.

Article 6 If animals intended for slaughter, animal products or food that are unfit for use as human's food are to be used for livestock feed, they should be treated for veterinary hygiene before use as stipulated. After being treated, if those things are still sub - standard for feed they must be destroyed.

Article 7 Rules on livestock drinking water, feed, grazing pastures and faeces are as below:

1. Water for drinking and processing feed must be clean and not cause infection to animals. It is not allowed to use industrial wastewater that has not been treated for livestock.

2. Only animals, which are not infected with infectious diseases, can be grazed at pasture.

3. It is not allowed to use livestock carcases, faeces containing agents of infectious diseases unless they have just been treated.

4. When insecticides and disinfectants are applied on the pasture, it is not allowed to graze animals on the pasture during degradation period of the insecticides/disinfectants.

Article 8 The People's Committees at all levels must locate separate areas for livestock trading and areas for trading in livestock products at markets in the area.

Only livestock showing no signs of infectious diseases and livestock products showing no signs of carrying infectious disease agents or being sub - standard are allowed to be put on the market.

The local Veterinary Service is to supervise and inspect veterinary hygiene at livestock and livestock product trading places.

Article 9 Rules on the isolation of new animals in a herd and of imported animals:

1. Intensive livestock production units are required to have a quarantine area. Animals transported in from

other places must be kept in the quarantine area for the Veterinary Service to check. When animals are confirmed to be healthy, they are allowed to enter the herd.

2. Imported animals must be kept in a quarantine area as specified by the Regional Animal Health Centre or border Animal Quarantine Stations. This area must distance from the residential area and water sources and these animals must be prevented from contact with local livestock.

3. The quarantine area must have its own personnel and implements.

4. The minimum quarantine period is 45 days depending on each specific disease.

Article 10 The livestock owner must carry out compulsory vaccination or other prophylactic measures on his livestock.

Periodically, the Ministry of Agriculture and Food Industry will publish lists of serious infectious diseases and set up procedures of compulsory vaccination or other compulsory preventive measures for each area and for each species of animal.

The People's Committees of all levels are in charge of giving instructions on compulsory vaccination in their own management area. The SDAH will organize the implementation of periodic compulsory vaccination or preventive measures annually.

Article 11 Regulations on transport of animals and animal products in large quantity:

1. Transport of animals and animal products in large quantity by railway, waterway, sea and by air can only be carried out at approved stations, ports and airports.

In these stations, ports and airport there must be the necessary facilities for animal inspection, isolation of diseased animals, storage of animal products and disinfection.

2. Animals can be transported only by disinfected means. The flooring of the transport vehicle must be sealed in order to prevent animal waste materials from dripping during transportation.

3. The State veterinary management bodies have remits to carry out veterinary hygiene inspection for transport of animals as below:

a. To inspect animals before loading. For buffaloes, cattle, horses, pigs, goats and other livestock suspected of being affected, it is required to check every animal individually. Other animals can be inspected by observation. After carrying out the inspection, certificates are to be granted;

b. To check the veterinary hygiene of means of transport, loading and unloading of animals;

c. To supervise the loading and unloading of animals;

d. To check quarantine certificates before transportation.

Quarantine inspectors can stop or temporarily suspend the transport to consult for decisions of the superior if there are signs of infectious diseases or sub - standard of veterinary hygiene and take responsibility to the law for their decisions.

Article 12 Regulations on cleaning and disinfection of vehicles and implements used in the transport of animals are as follows:

1. Cleaning and disinfection of vehicles and equipment used in the transport of animals or animal products, and caring for and treating the animals must be carried out:

a. Before transporting animals or animal products.

b. Immediately after unloading the animals or animal products and disposing of the bedding and waste materials.

2. The authorized Veterinary Service is to supervise cleaning and disinfection in order that these works will not cause adverse effects to animals, animal products, semen, breeding eggs, feed, attendants, vehicles and equipment used in the transport.

The livestock owner or representative, the owner of the vehicle and the attendant must obey all instructions given by the Veterinary Service and pay for cleaning and disinfection of vehicles and equipment used in the transport of animals and animal products.

a. The SDAH give guidance on cleaning and disinfection and issues a hygiene certificate vehicles and equipment used for domestic transport of animals and animal products in its area as stipulated.

b. Regional Veterinary Centres and border Animal Quarantine Stations provide guidance for cleaning and disinfection of and issue certificates for vehicles and equipment used in the transport of animals and animal products to be exported from, imported to and transited through Vietnam.

Article 13 Regulations on the slaughter of animals, processing, packaging and preservation of animal products are as below:

1. Every organization and individual owning livestock slaughterhouses, production, processing, packaging and preservation units has to abide by the following stipulations:

a. Construction location, building structure and operation of the units must be up to the standard of veterinary hygiene, public health and the environment.

b. Water for use, the wastewater drainage system, passages for people and vehicles, storage and means of transport must be up to veterinary hygiene standard.

c. Equipment and implements must be made from materials that do not change the quality of animal products during production, storage, processing and packing.

d. By products for feed must be contained and preserved according to stipulations on veterinary hygiene.

e. There must be a toilet and a rest – room for the herdsmen separated from working place.

f. Disinfection and rodent eradication must be carried out.

g. Routine cleaning and disinfection must be carried out regularly.

h. All stipulations of the State on veterinary hygiene inspection, tests, handling, cleansing and disinfection must be fulfilled and payment must be made for those services.

2. The People's Committees at all levels take responsibility to for considering and granting licenses to set up production, storage, processing and packing establishments for animal products after consulting the veterinary service and the health and environment offices.

3. The State veterinary management office guides and inspects those establishments in implementing veterinary hygiene regulations for setting up and operating, and give instruction on cleaning and disinfection of these units.

Chapter Ⅲ Animal disease control

Article 14 General stipulations on animal disease control:

1. Where a livestock owner, the owner of a vehicle or attendants, either at the production unit or on transport, find animals sick or dead suddenly without a clear reason, it is necessary to inform the nearest Veterinary Service and it is not permitted to sell, slaughter for meat or dispose of such an animal.

2. On receiving such information, the Veterinary Service must quickly identify the cause and carry out treatment or deal with the situation.

If a disease is suspected, the Veterinary Service must immediately inform the People's Committee at the same level and the superior management body.

3. If existence of the disease is confirmed, the livestock owner, vehicle owner or attendant must follow instructions on isolation, diagnosis, curative treatment and prevention of the disease given by the Veterinary Service and pay for those services.

Article 15 When an outbreak of disease occurs, if the SDAH diagnoses that the disease does not belong or is suspected of belonging to the list to be published, the SDAH reports to the People's Committee of the province/city under the Central Government to notify the restrictions on the movement of animals and animal products and at the same time report to the DAH.

If the SDAH is still doubtful about the cause of the disease, the SDAH should send samples to DAH to identify the disease.

It is forbidden to bring animals susceptible to infection or animal products carrying disease agents into or out of the restricted area.

Article 16 When an outbreak of a dangerous disease occurs in an area near the border of Vietnam with neighbouring, the local SDAH must report to the People's Committees of the provinces/cities under the Government to make notice that the area is under threat of disease and the following measures must be applied for that area:

1. To specify border entries and the number and species of animals allowed to pass through the frontiers.

2. It is forbidden to transport animals susceptible to infection with the disease and animal products carrying the agents of the disease in to Vietnam.

3. To carry out cleaning and disinfection for persons and vehicles passing the through the frontiers.

4. To establish a protective belt in a radius of 10 km from the border and to carry out the same measures there as for an area under threat of disease stipulated at Article 22 of the Rules.

Article 17 Jurisdiction over disease notification is set as follows:

1. When an outbreak of dangerous notifiable animal disease occurs in the area, the Chairperson of the People's Committees of the provinces/cities under the Government make a decision on disease notification on the following conditions:

a. Disease is present in animals and is spreading.

b. Written reports on the disease situation from the lower People's Committees are submitted;

c. The disease is is confirmed as being on the list for which disease notification is required and it is requested to make disease notification in writing by SDAH or DAH.

When deciding on the issuing of a disease notification, the Chairperson of the People's Committees of the provinces/cities under the Government has to report immediately to the Minister of Agriculture and Food Industry and the Prime Minister of the Government. The name and location of the disease should be given clearly in the notification.

2. When a disease occurs seriously in an area of at least 2 provinces, the Minister of Agriculture and Food Industry makes a decision on the disease notification on the following conditions:

a. The epidemic is increasingly spreading and is causing serious losses to livestock or infection to humans.

b. A report on the disease situation in writing by the People's Committees of the provinces/cities under the Government is available.

c. It is concluded that there is an occurrence of a serious notifiable disease a request for the issuing of a disease notification is submitted by DAH.

When deciding to make a disease notification, the Minister of Agriculture and Food Industry must report to the Prime Minister.

The list of serious diseases for which disease notifications are to be made periodically is stipulated by the Minister of Agriculture and Food Industry.

Article 18 Regulations on the organization of disease prevention:

1. When a decision on disease notification is made, the Chairperson of the People's Committee of the prov-

ince/city under the central Government in which the disease is present, instructs all Services and Levels to cooperate with local social organizations and to mobilize human resources and materials as stipulated by the law to carry out the disease preventive measures.

The People's Committees of the provinces/cities under the Central Government is to determine the boundaries of the infected area and the protective belt and to inform the lower level and bodies concerned.

2. Within the duties and powers designated, the SDAH gives instructions to the local veterinary services to fight against the disease and is responsible for veterinary expertise in disease prevention and control. At the same time, it is to report on the disease situation and results every 10 days to the People's Committees of the provinces/cities under the Government and DAH until the outbreak is eradicated.

Article 19 In the infected area as announced in the disease notification, it is essential that the following requirements are fulfilled:

1. To set up guard posts with police and veterinarians to guide, check and supervise the transport of animals; to set up notices of the infected area; to restrict movement of animals and animal products; to clean and disinfect animal stables, materials used for livestock rearing, waste material from diseased animals and contaminated environments.

2. The Veterinary Service examines and specifies animals susceptible to the notified disease to isolate animals and to apply other veterinary hygienic measures.

Article 20 Regulations on the isolation of animals in the infected area:

1. Animal isolation in the infected area is required as follows:

a. All animals affected, suspected of being affected, infected or suspected of being infected must be kept separately during the treatment period and not grazed at pasture.

b. Persons to take care for and separate implements for sick animals are required. All implements, materials for sick livestock, leftovers of feed, faeces and rubbish etc. must be cleaned and disinfected until the disease comes to an end;

c. Persons having no duty there are prohibited from entering the area there are affected animals or animals that have died of the disease.

2. The Veterinary Services supervises the isolation and treatment of sick animals.

The Service instructs the livestock keeper to carry out necessary measures if the animals can not be cured or if they die.

Article 21 Restrictions on the movement of animals and animal products and subjects of veterinary hygiene control infected area are as follows:

1. It is prohibited to bring livestock or livestock products susceptible to infection with the notified disease, various kinds of feed, faeces, materials used as bedding for livestock, or equipment which can spread the disease in to or out of the infected area, with the exception of the transport of animals to a place for isolation or compulsory slaughter.

2. In the case of transport of animals susceptible to infection, feed or waste materials through the infected area being requested, the vehicle should follow stipulated routes and should not stop on the way.

3. It is prohibited to hold markets for trading animals or animal products susceptible to infection with the notified disease. It is also forbidden to organize visits and exhibition in the infected area.

Slaughter and movement of livestock and livestock products susceptible to infection in the infected are banned.

Article 22 The following provisions must be carried out in the protective belt (area under threat) in the radius of 30 km depending on each disease from the infected area:

1. Movement, transport, trade and exchange of animals and animal products susceptible to infection in markets in the regions should be restricted.

2. The Veterinary Service should strengthen control of transport of animals and animals products and inspection to find out affected animals in time.

Article 23 To urgently organize compulsory vaccination or to carry out other preventive measures on susceptible animals in infected area and protective belt as stipulated below:

1. The SDAH specifies which species of animal are to be vaccinated and provides instructions on compulsory vaccination for animals in the protective belt and infected area.

2. For some specified diseases, the SDAH can carry out compulsory vaccination in the infected area only when permitted by DAH.

Article 24 Stipulations on compulsory slaughter of animals affected or suspected of being affected:

1. To limit disease spread, the SDAH has to make a proposal to the provincial People's Committee that it decides compulsory slaughter of animals affected or suspected of being affected with incurable diseases.

The slaughter must be carried at slaughterpoints as instructed by the Veterinary Service and the same veterinary hygienic measures must be fully implemented at these points as in the infected area.

2. Vehicles for the transport of animals intended for compulsory slaughter must have sealed flooring in order not to allow waste materials to drip during movement.

3. It is required to treat water used for slaughtering animals and handling animal products.

4. After the meat and offal have been removed, it is necessary to clean and disinfect the places where animals were slaughtered and the animal products and waste were handled.

5. Carcasses of animals compulsorily slaughtered can not be used untreated. They must be treated by veterinary hygiene methods as stipulated. Secondary products and other products that can not be used must be dealt with as per Article 25 of the Rules.

The Veterinary Service is in charge of supervising and controlling transport, slaughter, handling, cleaning and disinfection of animals being slaughtered. The Veterinary Service also supervises the slaughterpoints and grants permits for the use of animal products which meat the veterinary hygiene standard.

Article 25 Handling carcases of animals affected with infectious diseases is as below:

1. Carcases of animals affected or suspected of being affected, products of animals compulsorily slaughtered that are unfit for use along with materials used as bedding for livestock and livestock wastes must be buried deeply between 2 layers of appropriate disinfectant. The burial place must be distance resident areas, sources of drinking water or livestock farms and pastures.

2. Carcases of animals affected with a dangerous disease such as FMD and Anthrax, bedding and wastes must be burnt under the supervision and witness of the Veterinary Service.

3. For Anthrax, People's Committees at all levels require an inventory to be made of the graves of all previous animal cases and the capping of these graves with concrete.

Should any work have to be carried out on the graves, the contractor can do the job only after having been granted written permission by the People's Committees of the provinces/cities under the central Government.

The SDAH is responsible for instructing the contractor to excavate and destroy all things contained in the graves and to clean and disinfect the area. The contractor is responsible for the payment of all the costs of these activities.

Article 26 Animal housings, husbandry implements, wastes, pastures, means of transport, slaughter places and places in which animals had died in the infected area must be cleaned and disinfected with necessary properly – concentrated chemicals in accordance with procedures laid down by the veterinary service.

The cleaning and disinfection must not be harmful to humans and animals.

The relevant SDAH is responsible for providing instructions and supervising the cleaning and disinfection activitites in infected area.

Article 27 The Decision on disease notification is withdrawn on the following conditions:

1. Vaccination or preventive measures have been applied to all animals susceptible to infection in the infected area and the protective belt as stated and they are immunized against infection.

2. In 15 to 30 days, depending on each disease, following the death or recovery of the last animal or following compulsory slaughter, there has been no more animal illness or death due to the notified disease.

3. All outbreaks of disease has been cleaned and disinfected as required by veterinary hygiene.

After reporting to DAH and agreement by DAH, the Director of SDAH requests the People's Committee of the province/city under the Government to decides on withdrawal of the disease notification in its area.

The Director of DAH requests the Minister of Agriculture and Food Industry to decide on withdrawal of the disease notification in the scope of at least 2 provinces.

Article 28 If an outbreak of disease cannot be controlled, the People's Committee of the province/city under the Central Government and Ministry of Agriculture and Food Industry will request the Government for the use of the State fund for veterinary drugs as stipulated.

Article 29 When a new disease dangerous to animals is introduced in Vietnam, the People's Committee of the provinces/cities under the Government, where the disease is detected, should instruct the Veterinary Service and concerned bodies to strictly block the infected area.

The Veterinary Services at all levels must quickly identify the disease and report to the Ministry of Agriculture and Food Industry so that specific measures to stop the disease may be carried out.

Chapter Ⅳ State management of animal disease prevention and control

Article 30 Decentralization of state management on animal disease control is stipulated as below:

1. Requirements of the State management of animal disease prevention and control are set out at Article 41 of the Ordinance on Veterinary Services.

2. The Minister of Agriculture and Food Industry is responsible for organizing the implementation of and guiding animal disease prevention and control throughout the country as follows:

a. To submit to the Government legislative texts on animal disease prevention and control; issue papers on disease prevention and control within his jurisdiction; provide guidance to and inspect Ministries, ministerial ranking offices, offices under the Government, the local People's Committees and foreign organizations and individuals in Vietnam in implementing veterinary legislation.

b. To draft plans, organize and give instructions to all Services and Levels on carrying out disease prevention and control.

c. To coordinate with concerned bodies to establish and manage funding scheme for disease prevention and control.

d. To inspect and check disease prevention and control. To settle disputes, claims and complaints relating to disease prevention and control.

e. To regulate issuing or withdrawal of certificates and licenses relating to disease prevention and control for domestic and foreign organizations and individuals.

f. To publish lists of diseases for which notification, periodic inspection and compulsory vaccination are required periodically. To make decisions on the issuing and withdrawal of disease notification for at least 2 provinces.

g. To organize training in disease prevention and control. To disseminate awareness and mobilize the masses to take part in disease prevention and control.

h. To establish international cooperation, organize and attend international workshops and conferences on disease prevention and control.

3. Chairpersons of the People's Committees of provinces/cities under the Central Government are in charge of implementing and providing guidelines on disease prevention and control as follows:

a. To manage and direct the local Veterinary Service to carry out effective disease prevention and control in their area as per instructions by Ministry of Agriculture and Food Industry.

b. To issue guidance papers on disease prevention and control in their own area.

c. To grant or withdraw certificates and licenses relating to disease prevention and control within their jurisdiction.

d. To make decisions on the issuing and withdrawal of disease notification in their area. Together with Ministry of Agriculture and Food Industry to make proposals to the Government for the use of the State fund for veterinary drugs when a serious outbreak of diseases occurs.

e. To cooperate with the State veterinary management office to control, inspect and deal with violations of the legislation on animal disease prevention and control.

f. To receive and settle disputes, complaints and petitions about disease prevention and control within assigned roles or pass them to authorized bodies.

Article 31 The designation of institutions to be in charge of state management on animal disease prevention and control is stipulated as below:

1. The Director of DAH is to support the Minister of Agriculture and Food Industry in implementing State management on animal disease prevention and control as regulated at Article 30 of the Rules.

2. The Director of SDAH is to support the Chairperson of the People's Committee of the province/city under the Central Government in implementing state management on animal disease prevention and control in his area as stipulated at paragraph 3, Article 30 of the Rules.

The Ministry of Agriculture and Food Industry is to regulate the organizational setup, functions, duties and rights of the veterinary hygiene inspection agencies.

Chapter V Special inspection on animal disease prevention and control

Article 32 Special inspection on animal disease prevention and control is to check compliance with implementation of the legislation on animal disease prevention and control and to propose measures to prevent and stop violations of the legislation on disease prevention and control.

The Director of DAH and the Directors of SDAHs are responsible for organizing and carrying out checks on animal disease prevention and control as assigned functions, duties and rights.

Article 33 The content of the inspection of animal disease prevention and control includes:

1. To inspect organizations and individuals carrying out duties relating to the veterinary services in implementing veterinary hygiene and disease prevention and control.

2. To inspect veterinary hygiene inspection bodies and veterinary diagnostic bodies at central and local levels in animal disease prevention and control.

3. To inspect other activities relating to legislation on animal disease prevention and control.

Article 34 Activities of the inspection of animal disease prevention and control are stipulated in the Regulation on the implementation of the Ordinance on Veterinary Services and Rules on Veterinary Inspection of Ministry of Agriculture and Food Industry.

Chapter Ⅵ　Implementing provisions

Article 35　The Ministry of Agriculture and Food Industry, either alone or in cooperation with agencies involved, shall provide guidance on executing the Rules.

Ministers, Heads of ministerial ranking bodies, Heads of agencies under the Government, and Chairpersons of the People's Committees of provinces/cities under the Central Government, within their roles, shall organize implementation of the Rules.

The Rules take effect from the date of signing and replace all previous Regulations which are against the Rules.

Regulations
On settlement of administrative violations in the veterinary services

(Issued under Decree 93/CP of the Government on 27 November 1993)

Forms and levels of penalty on administrative violations in the veterinary services

Article 1　Violations of regulations on animal disease prevention and control:

1. Punishment may be a warning or a fine from VND 10,000 to VND 50,000. If there are evidences of serious violations, the fine can be of VND 100,000 for the following cases:

a. The livestock owner does not apply compulsory vaccination or other preventive measures against the diseases listed as serious animal diseases published by the Ministry of Agriculture and Food Industry;

b. Offering the dressed carcas of an animal which has died of infectious disease for sale or disposing of them in such a way as to cause disease spread.

c. To bring animals sick of a notifiable disease or animal products containing such disease agents into or out of an area where movements are restricted. To sell such animals and animal products during an existing outbreak of disease. To bring into an existing outbreak animals susceptible to infection of the notified disease. To unload animals in an infected area from transport when requested to go straight through without stopping.

d. Required preventive measures such as cleaning and disinfection of an animal house, the waste from sick animals or disposal of carcass are not carried out.

2. To fine from VND 50,000 to VND 200,000 and if there is evidence of serious violations, the fine can be VND 500,000 for the following violations:

a. Required vaccinations and preventive measures against FMD, Anthrax, Classical Swine Fever are not implemented in the infected area and protective belt as stipulated in the Decision on disease notification.

For some other serious infectious diseases the Minister of Agriculture and Food Industry may issue more stipulations as required.

b. Stipulations on veterinary hygiene treatment for animals affected with Classical Swine Fever or the burning of carcases of animals which have died of Anthrax, FMD are not fulfilled as stipulated by the Veterinary Service.

c. Periodic veterinary hygiene inspection in livestock breeding, intensive production and slaughter enterprises; processing, packaging, preservation and trade enterprises of livestock products and feedstuff are not implemented as stipulated.

Article 2 Violations of regulations on animal quarantine slaughter control and veterinary hygiene inspection:

1. To warn or fine from VND 20,000 to VND 50,000 and if there is evidence of serious violations, the fine can be of VND 100,000 for the following cases:

a. There is no accompanying quarantine certificate when transporting animals or animal products listed as subjects of quarantine between regions or to collection points, markets and exhibition, or the quarantine certificates are not legal.

b. To avoid veterinary hygiene inspection of animals and animal products listed as subjects of quarantine and veterinary drugs in export, import and transit.

c. To sell buffalo meat, beef; horse meat and pork without the seal of "slaughter control" on the carcasses. To sell animal products without certificates or stamps from the veterinary services and shops and stands do not satisfy the hygiene standard.

d. Animals are slaughtered for sale not in slaughterhouses/points as permitted by the authorised agency.

e. Cleaning and disinfection at animal slaughterhouses/points, processing, preservation of animal products, feed, drugs and raw materials for drug production are not implemented as stipulated.

f. Animals are slaughtered for export without certificates proving that the animals are from disease free zones as stipulated by DAH.

2. To fine from VND 50,000 to VND 500,000 and if there are circumstances of serious violations, the fine can be of VND 2,000,000 for the following cases:

a. Declaration or advance declaration is not made when importing and transiting animals, animal products and veterinary drugs as stipulated.

b. There is no legal permit issued by authorised body when importing to and transiting through Vietnam animals, animal products or veterinary drugs.

c. To make fraudulent substitution for quarantined animal products or change packages of animal products inspected for veterinary hygiene without asking for permission.

d. Imported animals and animal products that have not been quarantined or put into use during the quarantine period.

e. Imported animals and animal products are used for the purpose that is different from stipulations in the license issued by DAH.

f. To slaughter and trade animals and animal products infected with Anthrax and FMD.

3. Animal products are confiscated in settlement of for violations as stipulated at Point f, Paragraph 2 of this Article.

Article 3 Violations of stipulations on veterinary drug management:

1. To fine from VND 100,000 to VND 500,000 and if there is evidence of serious violations, the fine can be of VND 2,000,000 and the practice license for veterinary drugs is withdrawn for the cases as below:

a. To produce, or process drugs without a license or stipulations in the licence are not followed, or there is no registration number from authorised Veterinary Service.

b. To produce fraudulent drugs, i. e. registered quality is not matched, the approved formula is not followed or the content as notified in the label and trademark is not ensured.

c. Trade in raw materials without certificate, or in fraudulent drugs, low quality drugs, drugs that are not in the list published by the Ministry of Agriculture and Food Industry, drugs without a control number or registration number issued by the authorised Veterinary Service.

d. Raw materials or drugs are imported without a licence issued by the authorised Agency.

e. Packages of imported raw materials are not in original condition.

f. Drugs are not in the list for import as published by the Ministry of Agriculture and Food Industry.

g. Export or import fraudulent drugs and raw material in any forms.

h. Test of new drug without a permit or failure to comply with stipulations stated in the license issued by DAH.

i. Imported drugs are used for a purpose different from that stipulated in the permit granted by DAH.

j. Microorganisms are used for the production of livestock drugs without permit by DAH.

2. Veterinary drugs or raw materials are confiscated in the case of violations at Point b, d, e, f, g and k, Paragraph 1 of this Article.

In addition to the fines mentioned above, if there are circumstances of serious violations, depending on the level of violations, practice licences or permit for testing veterinary drugs can be withdrawn for a limited or unlimited period.

Article 4 Violations of stipulations on veterinary administrative management and practice:

1. To warn or fine from VND 50,000 to VND 200,000 and if there is evidence of serious violations, the fine can be of VND 500,000 for the following cases:

a. To alter, erase or counterfeit certificates of vaccination, veterinary hygiene, quarantine, veterinary drug inspection etc, or the registration of production, permit for veterinary practice, test of veterinary drugs and veterinary hygiene stamps.

b. To practise veterinary services without a permit issued by the authorised veterinary service.

c. To use the practice licence, professional degrees or certificates of another person.

d. To use the uniform, epaulettes and insignia of the veterinary services as stipulated by the State to pretend to be a veterinarian.

2. To fine from VND 100,000 to VND 500,000, and if there is evidence of serious violations, the fine can be of VND 2,000,000 for the following cases:

a. To make a false declaration, to make counterfeit of or to alter a document in order to obtain a permit or registration for veterinary activities.

b. To prevent or impede a veterinarian in carrying out his/her duty.

Article 5 Violations of stipulations on information and advertisement of drugs and labels:

1. To fine from VND 100,000 to VND 500,000 and if there circumstances of serious violations, the fine can be of VND 2,000,000 and production licences, practice licences can be withdrawn for the following cases:

a. To release information or advertisements that are different from the quality and effects of the veterinary drugs.

b. To circulate veterinary drugs which are not allowed by the Veterinary Authority or to have labels printed that are different from the approved samples.

c. To make counterfeits of registered drugs that are in circulation.

d. On the label, there is no wording "for use in veterinary services only" or no indication of use in veterinary services only.

2. For violations at Points a, b, Paragraph 1 of this Article, if there are circumstances of serious violations, the licence for the veterinary drug practice will be withdrawn.

3. The drugs and labels referred to at Points b, c Paragraph 1 of this Article will be confiscated.

Jurisdiction and procedures of settlement of administrative violations in the veterinary services

Article 6 Stipulations on jurisdiction over punishment for administrative violations in the veterinary services:

1. Jurisdiction of the Veterinary Services at all levels over punishments for administrative violations are stipulated as follows:

a. Veterinary surgeons and technicians carrying out duties of veterinary hygiene inspection, quarantine of animals and animal products, animal slaughter control, and veterinary drugs inspection are entitled to give warnings and make fines up to VND 100,000 for administrative violations of professional aspects and in their administrative area.

b. Heads and Deputy Heads of District Veterinary Stations; Heads and Deputy Heads of Animal Quarantine Teams and inspectors under SDAH are entitled to make fines up to VND 500,000. If it is necessary to withdraw practice licences or other veterinary certificates, documents must be submitted to the immediately higher level to be dealt with.

c. Heads and Deputy Heads of the border Animal Quarantine Stations or Checkpoints at transit checkpoints and post offices are entitled to make fines up to VND 1,000,000. If it is necessary to withdraw practice licences or other veterinary certificates, documents must be submitted to the immediately higher level to be dealt with.

d. Directors, Vice Directors of Regional Animal Health Centres; Inspectors under DAH, Chief Inspectors under SDAH; Directors and Vice Directors of SDAHs are entitled to make fines up to VND 2,000,000 and to apply various punishments and other administrative measures as stipulated in this Regulation.

e. The Chief Inspector, Director and Vice Directors of DAH are entitled to apply all kinds of punishments and administrative measures as stipulated in the Ordinance on Settlement of Administrative Violations and this Rule.

2. State Institutions and persons having jurisdiction over the punishment of administrative violations set at Articles 17 & 19 of the Ordinance on the Settlement of Administrative Violations are entitled to punish administrative violations in the veterinary services but it is required to abide by the stipulations at Article 18 of the Ordinance.

Article 7 Procedures for administrative violations in veterinary services are as below:

1. Simple procedures:

If the punishment is a warning or a fine up to VND 100,000, the authorised person can impose penalty on the spot. The person fined must make payment and receive a receipt. The person fined should not make payment if there is no receipt.

2. Decision on penalties

If the fine is over VND 100,000, the authorised person must make a record as stipulated at Article 21 of the Ordinance on the settlement of administrative violations. Within 15 days of making the record, the authorised agency or person must decides on the penalty and send the Decision to the fined organization/individual fined as stipulated at Article 18 of the Ordinance on the settlement of administrative violations.

3. The authorised agency or person should collect the fine directly and deliver it to a financial institution as stipulated by the State.

4. If, within 5 days from the date the decision on the penalty takes effect, the fined organization or individual has not complied with it, the decision making agency enforces implementation as stipulated at Article 32, the Ordinance on Settlement of Administrative Violations.

Institutions, organizations and legal representative of the person fined are responsible for implementing strictly the enforcement of the decision making agency.

Article 8 Withdrawal of licences:

1. All kinds of licences and certificates (generally called licences) granted by the authorised Veterinary Service to organizations/individuals to perform veterinary services can be withdrawn if there are administrative violations directly relating to stipulations on the use of such licences.

2. Licences can be withdrawn for a limited period for violations until verification of the nature and seriousness of the violation shows that the practice can be continued.

3. Withdrawal of licences for a limited period can be applied in the following cases:

a. The licence is issued under the wrong competence;

b. The content of the licence is against the regulations of the law;

c. Serious violations have occurred so that the practice can not be continued.

4. Authorised agencies or persons impose penalties for administrative violations in the veterinary services, as stipulated at Article 46 of this Rule, are entitled to make proposals to the licensing agency to make decisions on the withdrawal of the licences.

Article 9 Procedures for the application of other administrative measures:

1. Authorised bodies or persons, as stipulated at Article 6 of this Regulation, must take account of the stipulations of the law and actual losses caused by the violations to make decisions on the application of other administrative measures and be responsible for their own decisions.

2. Other administrative measures can be applied only when there is a written decision. This Decision should be sent to organization/individual who commits administrative violations together with the decision on punishment.

3. Organizations/individuals who are penalised by administrative measures must implement the penalty within 5 days.

4. In case of subjects of quarantine and veterinary drugs that must be destroyed immediately, a record must be made and signed by the person fined, the person implementing the penalty and witnesses. If the articles have not yet been destroyed, request is made to seal the material evidence and to set up Handling Commission to destroy them.

5. Organizations or individuals punished for administrative violations will be compelled to implement the penalty if they do not follow the set time limit. The penalised organizations or individuals will pay for costs of enforcement.

Article 10 The organizations or individuals are allowed to make complaints about decisions on penalty for administrative violations in the veterinary services.

The making and handling of complaints are carried out according to Articles 36 & 37 of the Ordinance on Settlement of Administrative Violations.

Article 11 State institutions and persons authorised to impose penalties for administrative violations in the veterinary services who break the stipulations on the settlement of administrative violations or impose penalties in the wrong competence will be penalised either by administrative measures or charged with criminal responsibility. The organization or citizen has to make compensation for the loss to the State if any.

Article 12 Anyone who has made a valuable contribution to the discovery of administrative violations and any person on official duty who has produced successful results will be appraised and rewarded as stipulated at Article 39, the Ordinance on Settlement of Administrative Violations.

Implementing provisions

Article 13 Foreign organizations and individuals, and foreign investment enterprises in Vietnam who commit administrative violations in the veterinary services in Vietnam will be penalised as stipulated at Articles 3 & 5, the Ordinance on the Settlement of Administrative violations.

Article 14 The Ministry of Agriculture and Food Industry provides instructions and supervision on the implementation of this Regulation and regulates the forms of record and decisions on penalty in every aspect of the veterinary services. Ministry of Finance regulates the forms of receipt of fines, and issues and controls the receipts.

Article 15 The Minister, Heads of ministerial ranking offices, Heads of Governmental Institutions and Chairpersons of the People's Committees of provinces, cities under the Central Government, within their own roles, organize the implementation of this Regulation.

This Regulation takes effect from the date of signing. Other previous Regulations contrary to this Regulation will be revoked.

Ordinance On veterinary services

In order to strengthen State management, to improve prophylaxis and the prevention of disease spread for the protection and development of livestock, to supply high quality livestock and livestock products to the domestic and export markets and to protect human health and the ecological environment.

Pursuant to Article 91 of the Constitution of the Socialist Republic of Vietnam.

This Ordinance is to regulate the veterinary services.

Chapter Ⅰ General provisions

Article 1 The Veterinary Services regulated in this Ordinance are animal disease prevention and control, quarantine of animals and animal products, animal slaughter control and veterinary hygiene inspection of food of animal origin, management of drugs and microorganisms for veterinary use.

Article 2 The terms used in this Ordinance should be understood as follows:

1. Animals consist of beasts, birds, reptiles, crustaceans, molluscs and various species of fish, bees, silkworms, breeding eggs, semen and animal embryos.

2. Animal products include meat and other products of animal origin.

3. Veterinary drugs are products of animal origin, plant and chemical products, vaccines and other biological products for veterinary use.

4. Microorganisms are bacteria, viruses, parasites, fungi and some other species used for the diagnosis, prevention and treatment of animal diseases, research, production and tests of drugs for animal disease prevention and control.

5. Satisfaction of the veterinary hygiene standard is the capability to protect and develop livestock to avoid affecting human health and causing ecological environmental pollution.

6. Animal slaughter control is inspection of the veterinary hygiene standard of animals before and after being slaughtered, inspection of the conditions of livestock production and slaughter, processing, storage, marketing, transportation and consumption of animal products.

Article 3 The State is to centralize management of the veterinary services through a combination of advanced science and traditional experience to ensure the benefit of the entire society.

The State is to fulfil international agreements on veterinary services which the Socialist Republic of Vietnam has signed or takes part in.

Article 4 The State encourages domestic and overseas organizations and individuals to invest in the veterinary field in Vietnam under various forms.

Article 5 All institutions of the State, economic establishments, social organizations, the people's armed forces and citizens must abide by the veterinary legislation.

Any overseas organizations and individuals practising production and trade of livestock and livestock products or other activities concerning the veterinary services within Vietnamese territory must abide by the veterinary legislation, unless it has otherwise been stipulated by international agreements signed or accepted by the Socialist Republic of Vietnam.

Article 6 The People's Councils and Committees at all levels, other State institutions, the Fatherland Front and its member organizations, within their roles, have responsibilities for controlling and supervising the implementation of the veterinary legislation.

Article 7 All actions which adversely affect animal protection and development, human health or the ecological environment are forbidden.

Chapter Ⅱ Animal disease prevention and control

Article 8 Animal disease prevention and control is:

1. To ensure that the veterinary hygiene of livestock production, feed processing and animal processing establishments is of a satisfactory standard.

2. To implement disease preventive (prophylactic) measures, diagnose, control and eradicate diseases;

3. To conduct quarantine of animals and animal products, slaughter control and veterinary hygiene inspection of food of animal origin in order to identify and prevent disease spread and ensure the safety of the consumer.

Article 9 Livestock production is not allowed to pollute the environment.

Farms, livestock housing, aquacultural areas, materials and equipment used in livestock production and water for animals should meet the veterinary hygiene standard.

The Ministry of Agriculture and Food Industry is to establish the standard for breeding animals and the standard of veterinary hygiene for livestock production farms.

Veterinary institutions at all levels, within their area, are responsible for directing, supervising the implementation of the veterinary legislation for livestock production and for feed processing establishments.

Article 10 Livestock owners have to carry out compulsory vaccination or utilize compulsory prophylactic measures in order not to affect humans and to prevent serious diseases of animals.

The List of serious animal diseases mentioned at this Article is stipulated by the Ministry of Agriculture and Food Industry.

Article 11 During transport of animals, if livestock owners, transport owners or attendants find sick or dead animals, it is not allowed to sell, slaughter or dispose of those animals in order not to cause environmental pollution, and the situation must immediately be reported to the nearest Veterinary Authority.

On receiving such a report, the Veterinary Authority have to make a quick check. If an outbreak of disease is confirmed, the Veterinary service should provide guidance on solutions and make an immediate report to the directly superior veterinary authority and the People's Committee at the same level as the former.

Livestock owners, conveyors and attendants must comply with requests by the Veterinary Service in disease diagnosis, treatment and prevention. Payment of costs for those works is stipulated by the Government.

Article 12 When symptoms of a serious disease appear, the Veterinary Authorities at all levels should immediately identify the disease and give instructions to the livestock owner to carry out isolation and veterinary hygiene measures.

When the existence of a dangerous disease is confirmed, the local veterinary services should report to the People's Committee at the same level for a declaration of restrictions on the movement of animals and animal products and at the same time report to the directly superior authority.

It is forbidden to transport animals and animal products which are easily infected or which are carrying the disease agents into or out of the restricted area.

Article 13 When an outbreak of a serious disease occurs within Vietnam's territory or in the area of a country bordering on Vietnam, the provincial Veterinary Service of the area in which the epizootic exists or which is under threat, requests the provincial People's Committee to decide on the issuing of disease notification.

The Chairperson of the provincial People's Committee decides on the issuing or withdrawal of the disease notification in his area and reports to the Government.

Minister of Agriculture and Food Industry decides on the issuing or withdrawal of the disease notification for at least 2 provinces.

Ministry of Agriculture and Food Industry issues a List of diseases for which disease notification should be made periodically.

The Government is to stipulate criteria and the manner in which decisions should be made on the issuing or withdrawal of disease notifications.

Article 14 When a disease notification is issued, the People's Committee of the province where disease exists is to organize and provide instructions to all branches and coordinate with local social organizations to take the following measures:

1. To confirm and publicize the existence of disease in the area, to regulate the protection zone surrounding the infected area, to erect notices and checkpoints and to provide guidelines on transportation in the area.

2. To prohibit entry to the area where there are sick or dead animals to people having no business there; to forbid transport of whatever listed to be subject for veterinary hygiene inspection out of and into the area; to ban the slaughter of animals and the marketing of animal products that are susceptible to the disease notified and the movement of animals that are susceptible to the infection with the disease notified into the area.

3. To organize immediate vaccination or apply other preventive measures to all types of animal, which are susceptible to the notified disease in the infected area and the protection zone. Sick animals must be treated according to regulations by the Veterinary Service.

4. To clean and disinfect housing and pastures for sick animals, facilities used in livestock production and waste materials; to carry out other necessary hygiene measures in the area in compliance with the regulations of the Ministry of Agriculture and Food Industry.

5. To report to the Government without delay in order that the Government can take specific measures to stop the epidemic if a new dangerous disease should occur or if, having carried out measures as indicated in this Article, the outbreak has not been halted.

Article 15 A decision on the withdrawal of a disease notification is made when:

1. Animals in the infected area or in the protection zone which are susceptible to the disease notified have been vaccinated or treated with other preventive measures.

2. In 15 to 30 days after the last animal has died or recovered, there have been no more animals infected or died due to the disease notified.

3. Cleaning and disinfection for the disease concerned have been carried.

Article 16 Depending on the location, characteristics of each disease and every species of animal, the Ministry of Agriculture and Food Industry sets a time limit for compulsory vaccination or application of compulsory preventive measures in the infected area.

Article 17 Th People's Committees at all levels are responsible for providing guidance on disease prevention and control in their own area and have powers to mobilize human resources and materials according to the provisions of the law to implement preventive measures.

If there is a serious epidemic, the provincial People's Committees and the Ministry of Agriculture and Food Industry can request the Government for use of the State Fund for veterinary drugs as in Article 18 of this Ordinance.

Article 18 The Government and the Provincial People's Committees have charge of the proper financing of the animal health services to control and eradicate major diseases.

At the central level, it is to establish the State Fund for veterinary drugs.

At the provincial level, it is to establish a local fund for veterinary drugs.

The establishment, management and use of the fund for veterinary drugs are regulated by the Government.

Chapter Ⅲ Animal quarantine and slaughter control

Article 19 Animal quarantine consists of measures to inspect and identify animal infectious diseases and parasites which are now in circulation or which have not yet been introduced into Vietnam, infectious diseases and parasites which are subjects of international quarantine; to inspect and discover diseases to be inspected which are listed in agreements of purchase, exchange and aid signed by Vietnam and foreign partners, toxic substances, hormones and antibiotics which have adverse effects on humans or animals.

Periodically, the Ministry of Agriculture and Food Industry will publish a list of diseases and toxic substances to be inspected for.

Article 20 Subjects of animal quarantine are:

1. Animals and animal products.

2. Livestock feed and production environments.

3. Establishments involved in the production, slaughter, processing, storage and circulation of animals and animal products; equipment, facilities and materials used in the slaughtering process and for packaging, containing, circulating and transporting animals and animal products.

4. A List of subjects for quarantine is issued by the Ministry of Agriculture and Food Industry.

Article 21 Domestic, hunted and captured animals and animal products listed as subjects of quarantine must be quarantined and issued with quarantine certificates by the authorized veterinary agency when being transported from one area to the other.

The owner of such commodities, the owner of the means of transport or the conveyor have to show quarantine certificates to the Veterinary Service in places through which journeys are undertaken or at places of destination.

The Ministry of Agriculture and Food Industry is to stipulate the conditions of quarantine, the issuing of quarantine certificates and exemptions from quarantines.

Article 22 Transport and marketing of animals and animal products can only be implemented when the following conditions are met with:

1. The animals originate from an area where there is no outbreak of disease and are healthy and have been vaccinated or had other preventive measures and immunity is still effective.

2. Animal products must be manufactured from animals that are healthy, not infected or do not carry agents of serious diseases. Packages should comply with the regulations. The products must be up to hygiene standard.

3. Means of transport, equipment for livestock raising and containers for animal products must be cleaned and disinfected prior to and after transport.

Article 23 Transport of a large number of animals by road, railway, river, sea or air should be conducted at regulated stations and ports. Veterinary hygiene measures must be fully taken.

During the collection and transport of animals, the owners or conveyors and/or attendants are required to provide health care to the animals and ensure that the environment is as stipulated by the veterinary legislation.

Article 24 Concerned bodies have to help the veterinary agency to perform its duties in quarantine of animals and animal products at checkpoints on road, railway, river and sea routes and airways and at international frontiers and post offices.

Article 25 Animals and animal products listed as subjects of quarantine which are imported from, exported to or transited through Vietnam should be inspected by the authorized veterinary agency of Vietnam. They will be granted quarantine certificates if the veterinary hygiene standard is matched.

For animals and animal products to be imported into or transited through Vietnam, the owner of the commodities or authorized personnel should show certificates granted by the animal quarantine institution of the exporting country prior to inspection by authorized veterinary agency of Vietnam.

The Ministry of Agriculture and Food Industry stipulates the quarantine duties and the issuing of quarantine certificates to animals which are exported from, imported to and transited for sports, public security, national defense, scientific research or other purposes.

Article 26 Organizations and individuals who export animals and animal products must make a declaration to the authorized veterinary service. When the Veterinary Service has received the declaration, depending on the nature, quantity and types of commodities, it will make a decision and inform the commodity owner about the time and location of the quarantine inspection.

The authorized veterinary service issues quarantine certificates only to animals and animal products which are up to the veterinary hygiene standard.

If animals and animals products are found to be sub - standard, the veterinary service is not allowed to issue quarantine certificates and should ask the owners of the commodities to take the necessary measures.

Article 27 Organizations and individuals who import animals or animal products into Vietnam have to make a declaration to the authorized veterinary service of Vietnam. The veterinary service receives the declaration, depending on the nature, quantity and type of commodities, makes a decision and informs the owners of the commodity of the location and time of inspection.

The quarantine inspection will be carried out only after the animals and animal products are gathered at the quarantine site as stipulated by the Veterinary Authority of Vietnam. For animal products, the inspection period should not be longer than 7 days. For live animals, the inspection period is set by the Ministry of Agriculture and Food Industry.

The authorized veterinary service of Vietnam will issue quarantine certificates only to animals and animal products for which veterinary hygiene standard is met. Animals and animal products which are sub - standard are not allowed to be imported. Depending on the status of the commodities, they will be returned to the owners or handled according to the veterinary legislation of Vietnam.

财政部、农业与农村发展部、水产资源部联合通报

2003 年第 17 号

（2003 年 3 月 14 日）

2003 年 3 月 14 日财政部、农业与农村发展部、水产资源部 2003 年第 17 号联合通报，用于指导进出境动植物、水产品等需检疫货物的监督管理。

根据 2001 年 6 月 29 日越南社会主义共和国第 10 届人民代表大会 2001 第 29 号颁布的海关法；

根据 1989 年 4 月 25 日的植物保护和水产资源发展法；

根据 1993 年 2 月 15 日的兽医法；

根据 2001 年 7 月 25 日越南社会主义共和国第 10 届人民代表大会常务委员会第 36 号颁布的植物保护和检疫法；

财政部、农业与农村发展部和水产资源部据此协作指挥进出境动植物、水产品等需检疫货物（本通报中指从越南运到国外或从国外运到越南的境内的各种货物）的监管，包括：

第一章　总　　则

1. 仅对列入农业与农村发展部公布的应施动植物检疫物名单或列入水产资源部公布的应施水产品检疫物名单的货物应实施检疫程序。

2. 有权限签发上面第 1 款中所述货物检疫证书或对上述货物进行注册登记的单位（以下统称检疫机构）应是农业与农村发展部部长或水产资源部部长的决定中授权的单位（见本通报附录 1，他们是检疫的执行机构）。

3. 出入境旅客、外交大使和国际组织出于消费和日常生活需要的目的携带物品从非商业渠道进出境（非商业目的），海关官员可不要求出具注册登记证或检疫证书而直接办理通关程序，检疫机构在特定时间宣布对某一类特殊货物实行强制检疫的除外。

4. 如果空运或海运的货物不在港口装卸货的，则不适用本通报的规定。

5. 入境货物检疫应按先申报后施检的模式进行，具体如下：

——在办理海关程序前，货主必须先向检疫机构报检。

——检疫机构可以在海关查验货物的同时实施检疫，也可以在货物办完海关程序后，在报检单上确定的地点施检（见本通报附录 2）。

第二章　特 殊 条 款

1. 货主的责任：

1.1　出境货物：

货物出境前，为了实施检疫，并签发应施检疫物检疫证书，货主必须向检疫机构注册或申报。

1.2　入境货物：

办理海关程序前，货主必须填写报检单（格式见附录 2，一式三份）向检疫机构报检。

1.2.1　在办理海关程序时，根据海关档案管理的规定，货主必须提交已由检疫机构签字的报检单。

1.2.2　完成报检后，如果货物没有入境，货主必须将报检单的两联交回检疫机构（制作单证处）。

如果已完成入境程序，如果海关确认货物是不允许输入越南的，货主必须将报检单（货主联）连同海关出具的不允许入境原因证明交给检疫机构。

1.2.3 已完成海关程序和检疫程序的货物：

——已完成海关程序的货物必须按照报检单上登记的时间运达指定地点。

——如有紧急情况使货物不能按照报检单上登记的时间运达指定地点的，必须向检疫机构解释。

1.2.4 货主必须严格履行以下义务：

——只有在检疫机构签发检疫证书后才能将货物投入流通领域。

——服从检疫机构对货物的处理决定（如果需要的话）。

——那些经过检疫不能进口且必须退运的货物，在退运过程中，必须将入境通关单、检疫机构强制退运决定、货物向原来办理入境程序处的海关出示。

2. 检疫机构的责任：

2.1 完成报检登记和三联报检单的制作，其中两联给货主，一联作档案保存。

2.2 确认报检后，按法律规定对货物监管、实施检疫并签发检疫证书或实施处理。

2.3 已完成通关程序的货物，实施检疫前，应将货主申报的货物与通关单上填写的货物进行比较。如果出现任何的不一致，在做好记录的基础上立即按法律规定对货物进行处理。

2.4 实施检疫后，如果货物必须销毁，其销毁必须按法律执行；如果货物要退运，必须发布强制退运决定，清楚说明退运时间，并将一份复印件交货主以便执行，一份交海关（货物完成入境程序办理处）以便联合行动；对货物监控直至货物全部退运完；对不严格执行强制退运决定的货主进行处理。

2.5 迅速将那些不严格遵守报检登记时承诺事项的组织和个人报告省/自治区海关部门，要求随后的货物办理强制海关程序。

2.6 当组织或个人对执行了处理决定时，要求办理强制海关程序的检疫机构应签发证书并提交海关，以便取消对企业的强制程序，清楚说明编号、日期、违规行为、处理方式等几点情况。

3. 海关的职责

3.1 出境货物：

海关应根据法律规定只要求提交应施检疫货物的检疫证书。

3.2 入境货物：

3.2.1 当接到报关时，要求货主提交一份经检疫机构确认的报检单原件，并按法律规定完成通关程序。

3.2.2 对已完成通关程序但检疫机构作出退运出境决定的入境货物，货物完成通关程序地口岸的海关应将入境报关单上的货物与实际货物作比较，如果确认一致，可办理其退运出境程序。否则，将在作好记录的基础上立即通知作出强制退运出境决定的检疫机构，以便其根据法律规定作出处理。

3.2.3 已进行入境检疫申报但因违反出入境管理政策不允许出入境的货物，办理程序地的海关应作出证明，并在报检单（货主联）上签注原因。

3.2.4 违反报检登记时承诺的检疫规定的，根据检疫机构的要求，对组织或个人的进出境货物执行强制的海关程序。

3.2.5 如果组织或个人能提交检疫机构出具的关于处理决定已执行的证明的正本和副本，则可取消强制要求。组织的副本必须有证明、签名和印章，而个人的可以是复印件。

4. 合作关系：

4.1 如果检疫机构要求在货物办理海关程续前完成检疫程序，则这两个相关机构必须互相密切协作，海关应在检疫机构作出认定后再作出清关决定。

4.2 每年，海关应承担组织与相关的检疫机构会晤的责任，从而探讨在对物联合检验和监管时如何运用经验。如果有必要，可以根据海关或检疫机构的要求召开专门会议。

第三章　补 充 条 款

1. 本通报自2003年4月1日起生效。取消1995年8月31日农业与食品工业部、海关总署发布的第7号联合通报和1997年3月25日农业与农村发展部和海关总署发布的第3号联合通报。

2. 海关总署、兽医部、植物保护部和水产资源保护部必须指导本通报的实施。

3. 实施期间，如果出现问题，检疫机构和口岸各级海关部门应迅速提出处理建议，并将其报告上级机构。

附录 1

有权限办理出入境货物动物检疫登记和签发检疫证书的单位名单

Ⅰ. 河内兽医中心（The veterinary center of Hanoi region）

——地址: 63B Phuong Mai, Dong Da, Hanoi

——电话: 04. 8692627

——传真: 04. 8685390

——E - mail: tttyv@ fpt. vn

——管辖范围: Hannoi, Ha Tay, Hoa Binh, Ha Nam, Nam Dinh, Ninh Binh, Phu Tho, Vinh Phuc, Lao Cai, Son La, Lai Chau and Yen Bai.

Ⅱ. 海防兽医中心（The veterinary center of Hai Phong region）

——地址: 23 Da Nang street, Ngo Quyen district, Hai Phong city

——电话: 031. 836511

——传真: 031. 551698

——E - mail: ttytvhp@ hn. vnn. vn

——管辖范围: Hai Phong, Thai Binh, Quang Ninh, Lang Son, Cao Bang, Ha Giang, Tuyen Quang, Bac Can, Thai Nguyen, Bac Giang, Bac Ninh, Hai Duong and Hung Yen

——口岸局: Cat Bi airport and Hai Phong port.

Ⅲ. 荣市兽医中心（The veterinary center of Vinh region）

——地址: 51 Nguyen Sinh Sac street, Vinh city, Nghe An

——电话: 038. 842786

——传真: 038. 841571

——E - mail: tyvvinh@ hn. vnn. vn

——管辖范围: Thanh Hoa, Nghe An, Ha Tinh, Quang Binh, Quang Tri and Thua Thien - Hue.

——口岸局: Lao Bao and Cau Treo.

Ⅳ. 岘港兽医中心（The veterinary center of Da Nang region）

——地址: 12 Tran Quy Cap street, Hai Chau district, Da Nang city

——电话: 0511. 822515

——传真: 0511. 826926

——E - mail: tttyvdn@ dn. vnn. vn

——管辖范围: Da Nang, Quang Nam, Quang Ngai, Binh Dinh, Gia Lai, Kon Tum, Dak Lak, Phu Yen and Khanh Hoa

——口岸局: Da Nang airport and Tien Sa port.

Ⅴ. 胡志明市兽医中心（The veterinary center of Ho Chi Minh City region）

——地址: 124 - 126 Pham The Hien street, District 8, Ho Chi Minh City

——电话: 08. 8568886; 08. 8568887

——传真: 08. 8569050

——E - mail: rahhcm@ hcm. fpt. vn

——管辖范围: Ho Chi Minh City, Lam Dong, Ninh Thuan, Binh Thuan, Dong Nai, Ba Ria - Vung Tau, Binh Duong, Binh Phuoc, Tay Ninh, Long An, Tien Giang and Ben Tre.

——口岸局: Tan Son Nhat airport, Sai Gon port and Moc Bai station.

Ⅵ. 芹苴兽医中心（The veterinary center of Can Tho region）

——地址：Cach Mang Thang Tam road，Can Tho city，Can Tho province

——电话：071. 820203

——传真：071. 823386

——管辖范围：Can Tho，Vinh Long，Tra Vinh，Dong Thap，An Giang，Soc Trang，Kien Giang，Bac Lieu and Ca Mau

——口岸局：Can Tho port.

Ⅶ. 兽医部口岸动物检疫局（The border - gate animal quarantine stations under the Veterinary Department）

1. 内排机场动物检疫局（Noi Bai Airport Animal Quarantine Station）

——地址：Noi Bai International Airport

——电话：04. 8840120

2. 同登动物检疫局（Dong Dang Animal Quarantine Station）

——地址：39 Dong Dang Railway Station Zone，Dong Dang township，Lang Son

——电话：025. 851275

——传真：025. 812536

口岸局：Dong Dang station，Huu Nghi，Coc Nam，Tan Thanh and Chi Ma

3. 老街动物检疫局（Lao Cai Animal Quarantine Station）

——地址：Lao Cai provincial capital，Lao Cai province

——电话：020. 830260

4. 芒街动物检疫局（Mong Cai Animal Quarantine Station）

——地址：Mong Cai town，Quang Ninh

——Tel：033. 881502

——Fax：033. 881502

——口岸局：Mong Cai and Bac Phong Sinh.

说明：

* 出入境货物接受动物检疫应遵照 1994 年 6 月 9 日农业与食品工业部（现称农业与农村发展部）的第 607 号决定。

* 经兽医部授权，省、自治区兽医局可以在辖区口岸实施检疫工作。

附录 2

办理出入境货物植物检疫登记和签发检疫证书的单位名单

1. The Plant Quarantine Sub - Department of Region I:

地址: 2 Tran Quang Khai street, Hai Phong city

电话: 031. 842104 - 031. 823366

传真: 031. 821839　E - mail: kdtv1hp@ hn. vnn. vn

管辖范围: Thai Binh, Hai Duong, Hung Yen, Hai Phong and Quang Ninh

口岸局: Hai Phong port; Mong Cai; and Binh Lieu

地址: 28 Mac Dinh Chi street, District 1, Ho Chi Minh City

电话: 08. 8251401 - 0808. 8238948　传真: 08. 8293266

E - mail: kdtv2@ hcmc. netnam. vn

管辖范围: Ninh Thuan, Binh Thuan, Lam Dong, Binh Duong, Binh Phuoc, Tay Ninh, Dong Nai, Ho Chi Minh City, Long An, Tien Giang, Dong Thap and Ba Ria - Vung Tau

口岸局: Sai Gon port; Moc Bai; Vung Tau; Tan Son Nhat airport; Binh Hiep; Tho Mo; Hung Dien A; Xa Mat; Ka Tum; Phuoc Tan; Hoa Lu; Hoang Dieu; Thuong Phuoc; Dong Thap post office; Ba Ria Vung Tau post office; and Dong Nai post office.

3. The Plant Quarantine Sub - Department of Region III:

地址: 146 Hoang Dieu street, Da Nang city

电话: 0511. 821622

传真: 0511. 826863

E - mail: lethinghanh@ dng. vnn. vn

管辖范围: Quang Tri, Thua Thien Hue, Quang Nam, Da Nang and Quang Ngai

口岸局: Da Nang port; Hue city; and Lao Bao.

4. The Plant Quarantine Sub - Department of Region IV:

地址: 66 Le Hong Phong street, Quy Nhon, Binh Dinh

电话: 056. 822964 - 056. 823538

传真: 056. 822964 (823538)

E - mail: cckdtv4@ dng. vnn. vn

管辖范围: Binh Dinh, Phu Yen, Khanh Hoa, Kon Tum, Gia Lai and Dac Lac.

口岸局: Nha Trang; Bo Y; Duc Co; Buprang; and Dac Bo.

5. The Plant Quarantine Sub - Department of Region V:

地址: 149 Ho Dac Di street, Dong Da, Hanoi

电话: 04. 8513500

传真: 04. 5330043

E - mail: kdtv5 - hn@ fpt. vn

管辖范围: Bac Giang, Bac Ninh, Phu Tho, Vinh Phuc, Ha Tay, Ninh Binh, Nam Dinh, Ha Nam, Hanoi, and Hoa Binh

口岸局: Hanoi city; and Noi Bai airport.

6. The Plant Quarantine Sub - Department of Region VI:

地址: 28 Tran Phu street, Vinh city, Nghe An

电话: 038. 842992

E－mail：cckdtvv6@ hn. vnn. vn

管辖范围：Thanh Hoa，Nghe An，Ha Tinh，and Quang Binh

口岸局：Cau Treo and Chalo.

7. The Plant Quarantine Sub－Department of Region VII：

地址：98B Ngo Quyen street，Dong Kinh ward，Lang Son provincial capital

电话：025. 875797－025. 875798 传真：025. 872941

管辖范围：Lang Son，Cao Bang，Bac Kan，and Thai Nguyen

口岸局：Huu Nghi；Dong Dang；Tan Thanh；Chi Ma；Cong Trang；Ta Lung；Tra Linh；Ha Quang；and Soc Giang.

8. The Plant Quarantine Sub－Department of Region VIII：

地址：Lao Cai provincial capital

电话：020. 830503－020. 830097

传真：020. 830503 E－mail：tuankd8lc@ hn. vnn. vn

管辖范围：Ha Giang，Tuyen Quang，Yen Bai，Lao Cai，Lai Chau，and Son La

口岸局：Lao Cai；Lao Cai railway station；Bat Sat；Muong Khuong；

地址：386B Cach Mang Thang Tam road，Can Tho city

电话：071. 826709－071. 883551

传真：071. 828408

E－mail：kdtvv9@ hcm. vnn. vn

管辖范围：Can Tho，An Giang，Kien Giang，Ca Mau，Bac Lieu，Tra Vinh，Soc Trang，Vinh Long，Ben Tre

口岸局：My Thoi port；Tinh Bien；Vinh Hoi Dong；Vinh Xuong；and Khanh Binh.

说明：

1. 出入境货物应检物名单遵照 2001 年 5 月 23 日农业与农村发展部第 56 号决定。

2. 成立新的检疫局时，植物检疫机构应就此通知口岸海关，以便合作。

3. 经植物保护部的授权，省、自治区植物检疫部门允许在辖区内口岸实施检疫工作。

附录 3

办理出入境货物水产品检疫登记和签发检疫证书的单位名单

水产资源保护部 - 水产资源部

地址：10 Nguyen Cong Hoan street，Ba Dinh，Hanoi

电话：04. 8345953 - 04. 7718298 - 04. 351759

传真：04. 8353363

管辖范围：全国

说明：

1. 在设有办理出入境货物检疫登记或签发检疫证书的口岸的地方，水产资源保护部可授权省级水产资源保护部实施水产品检疫。

2. 未设立水产品检疫局的口岸，应联系水产资源保护部进行指导。

3. 水产动物及其产品检疫对象名单（根据 1994 年 6 月 25 日水产资源部第 2 号联合通报）：

——鱼、甲壳类动物、软体动物、棘皮动物、海藻类、两栖动物及其卵；哺乳动物。

——可能携带水产动物病原物的鲜活产品、初加工产品（冰冻、半干燥、盐渍等）。

The Ministry of Finance
The Ministry of Agriculture and Rural Development
The ministry of Aquatic Resources

(17/2003/TTLT/BTC 2003. 3. 14)

JOINT CIRCULAR NO. 17/2003/TTLT/BTC - BNNPTNT - BTS OF MARCH 14, 2003 GUIDING THE INSPECTION AND SUPERVISION OF IMPORT/EXPORT GOODS SUBJECT TO ANIMAL, PLANT OR AQUATIC PRODUCT QUARANTINE

Pursuant to Customs Law No. 29/2001/QH10 of June 29, 2001;

Pursuant to the Ordinance on the Protection and Development of Aquatic Resources of Aprial 25, 1989;

Pursuant to the Veterinary Ordinance of February 15, 1993;

Pursuant to Plant Protection and Quarantine Ordinance No. 36/2001/PL - UBTVQH10 of July 25, 2001;

The Ministry of Finance, the Ministry of Agriculture and Rural Development and the Ministry of Aquatic Resources hereby jointly agree to guide the inspection and supervision of import/export goods (which, in this Circular, are construed as assorted goods brought from Vietnam to foreign countries and from foreign countries into the Vietnamese territory), which are subject to animal, plant or aquatic product quarantine, as follows:

I. General provisions

1. Only goods on the list of import/export goods subject to animal or plant quarantine, announced by the Minister of Agriculture and Rural Development, or on the list of goods subject to aquatic product quarantine, announced by the Minister of Aquatic Resources, are subject to quarantine procedures.

2. Units competent to grant quarantine certificates or certify written quarantine registration for the goods prescribed at Point 1 above (hereinafter referred collectively to as the quarantine agencies) shall be the units assigned the tasks by decisions of the Minister of Agriculture and Rural Development or the Minister of Aquatic Resources (according to Appendix No. 1 to this Circular, they are the quarantine agencies performing the tasks).

3. For goods imported and/or exported through non - commercial channel (not for the business purposes) in service of consumption and daily - life demands of passengers on entry and/or exit, diplomatic missions and international organizations, the customs offices shall effect the customs clearance without requesting the submission of written quarantine registration or quarantine certificates, except for cases where the quarantine agencies announce the compulsory quarantine for each specific goods item at each specific time.

4. This Circular's provisions shall not apply to goods transited by air or sea in cases where goods are neither loaded nor unloaded at ports.

5. The quarantine of import goods shall be conducted by mode of registration first and inspection later, concretely as follows:

—Before carrying out customs procedures, the goods owners must register the quarantine with the quarantine agencies.

—The quarantine agencies may conduct the quarantine simultaneously with the goods inspection by the customs offices or after the completion of customs procedures for goods at the time and places determined in the written quarantine registration (according to the form in Appendix No. 2 to this Circular).

Ⅱ. Specific provisions

1. Responsibilities of the goods owners:

1. 1 For export goods:

Before exporting goods, the goods owners must register and declare with the quarantine agencies for carrying out inspection procedures and granting of quarantine certificates for quarantine – liable goods according to law provisions or at the requests of the purchasers.

1. 2 For import goods:

Before carrying out customs procedures, the goods owners must make the quarantine registration (in 3 copies made according to the form in Appendix No. 2) with the quarantine agencies.

1. 2. 1 When carrying out customs procedures, apart from the dossier set prescribed by the customs offices, they must submit written quarantine registration already certified by the quarantine agencies.

1. 2. 2 After making the quarantine registration, if failing to import goods, they must return 2 copies of written quarantine registration to the quarantine agencies (where certification is made). When carrying out import procedures, if the customs offices determine that goods are not allowed for import into Vietnam, the goods owners must return the written quarantine registration (the goods owners' copies) to the quarantine agencies (where certification is made), with the customs offices' certification of the reasons for not allowing the import.

1. 2. 3 For goods with the quarantine procedures being carried out after the completion of customs procedures:

—Goods having gone through the customs procedures must be brought in status quo to the right places and at the right time already registered in the written quarantine registration.

—In case of *force majeure* where goods cannot be brought to the right places and at the right time already registered for quarantine, such must be explained to the quarantine agencies.

1. 2. 4 They must strictly perform the following obligations:

—To put goods into circulation only after the quarantine agencies have granted quarantine certificates.

—To observe the quarantine agencies' decisions on handling of goods lots (if any).

—For those goods lots which are quarantined and not qualified for import and must be re – exported, when carrying out export procedures, the import customs dossiers, the quarantine agencies' decisions on forcible re – export, and goods must be produced to the customs offices where import procedures for the goods lots have been carried out.

2. Responsibilities of the quarantine agencies:

2. 1 To effect the registration and make certification in 3 copies of written quarantine registration, 2 of them to be returned to the goods owners and 1 to be kept.

2. 2 After certifying the written quarantine registration, to monitor, conduct the quarantine and grant quarantine certificates or handle the cases according to regulations.

2. 3 For those goods lots having completely gone through the customs procedures, before conducting the quarantine, to compare goods with the goods owners' declaration and the customs dossier set. If there appears any disparity, to make records thereon and handle them according to law provisions.

2. 4 After conducting the quarantine, if goods must be destroyed, the destruction thereof must comply with law provisions; if goods must be re – exported, the decisions on forcible re – export must be issued, clearly stating the time of re – export, 1 copy to be handed to goods owners for implementation, and 1 copy to be sent to the customs office (where import procedures for the goods lots were carried out) for implementation coordination; to monitor the goods lots until they are actually re – exported; and handle violations for those goods owners who

fail to strictly abide by the decisions on forcible re – export.

2. 5　To promptly inform the provincial/municipal Customs Departments of those individuals and organizations that fail to strictly abide by the commitments on the quarantine already registered, and request the coercive customs procedures for the subsequent goods lots.

2. 6　Upon the implementation of the handling decisions by organizations or individuals, the quarantine agencies (which request the coercive customs procedures) shall grant written certifications to be submitted to the customs offices for canceling the coercive procedures, clearly stating the notices (number, date, violation acts, forms of handling), under which the enterprises are coerced.

3. Responsibilities of the customs offices:

3. 1　For export goods:

The customs offices shall only request the submission of quarantine certificates for quarantine – liable goods according to law provisions.

3. 2　For import goods:

3. 2. 1　When receiving the registration of customs dossiers, to request the goods owners to submit 1 copy of written quarantine registration (the original) already certified by the quarantine agencies, and carry out procedures according to regulations.

3. 2. 2　For import goods which have completely gone through the customs procedures but must be re – exported under the quarantine agencies' decisions, the border – gate customs offices (where the import procedures for the goods lots have been carried out) shall compare the goods lots' import dossiers with the actual goods, if they are found compatible, they shall carry out procedures for re – export thereof, if not, they shall make records thereon and notify such to the quarantine agencies (which issue decisions on forcible re – export) for handling according to law provisions.

3. 2. 3　For import goods lots which have already been registered for quarantine, but are not allowed for import due to violations of the import and export management policies, the customs offices where procedures are carried out shall certify and clearly inscribe the reasons therefor in the written quarantine registration (the goods owners' copies).

3. 2. 4　To impose coercive customs procedures on goods imported and/or exported by organizations or individuals at the requests of the quarantine agencies due to the violation of the legislation on quarantine for import goods which have already been registered for quarantine.

3. 2. 5　To cancel the coercion when organizations or individuals submit copies and produce the originals of the documents of the quarantine agencies (which request the coercion) which certify that the handling decisions have been executed. Organizations' copies must be certified, signed and stamped, while individuals' copies are those photocopied.

4. Coordination relations:

4. 1　In cases where the quarantine agencies request the completion of quarantine of the goods lots before the customs procedures are completed, the two concerned agencies must closely coordinate with each other therein, and the customs offices shall decide on the customs clearance only after the quarantine agencies' conclusions are made.

4. 2　Annually, the Customs Sub – Departments shall assume the prime responsibility in meeting with the concerned quarantine agencies to draw experiences on the coordination in the inspection and supervision of quarantine – liable goods. In case of necessity, extraordinary meetings may be convened at the requests of the customs offices or the quarantine agencies.

Ⅲ. Implementation provisions

1. This Circular takes effect as from April 1, 2003. To annul Joint Circular No. 07/TTLN of August 31, 1995 of the Ministry of Agriculture and Foodstuff Industry and the General Department of Customs and Joint Circular No. 03/TTLT of March 25, 1997 of the Ministry of Agriculture and Rural Development and the General Department of Customs.

2. The General Department of Customs, the Veterinary Department, the Plant Protection Department and the Department for the Protection of Aquatic Resources shall have to guide the implementation of this Circular.

3. In the course of implementation, if any problems arise, the quarantine agencies and the border – gate Customs Sub – Departments should promptly propose measures to handle them and report thereon to their immediate superior agencies for prompt direction and settlement.

Appendix No. Ⅰ

List of units competent to certify written quarantine registration or grant quarantine certificates for import/export goods subject to animal quarantine

Ⅰ. The veterinary center of Hanoi region

—Address: 63B Phuong Mai, Dong Da, Hanoi

—Tel: 04. 8692627

—Fax: 04. 8685390

—E - mail: tttyv@ fpt. vn

—Localities under management: Hanoi, Ha Tay, Hoa Binh, Ha Nam, Nam Dinh, Ninh Binh, Phu Tho, Vinh Phuc, Lao Cai, Son La, Lai Chau and Yen Bai.

II. The veterinary center of Hai Phong region

—Address: 23 Da Nang street, Ngo Quyen district, Hai Phong city

—Tel: 031. 836511

—Fax: 031. 551698

—E - mail: ttytvhp@ hn. vnn. vn

—Localities under management: Hai Phong, Thai Binh, Quang Ninh, Lang Son, Cao Bang, Ha Giang, Tuyen Quang, Bac Can, Thai Nguyen, Bac Giang, Bac Ninh, Hai Duong and Hung Yen

—Border - gate stations: Cat Bi airport and Hai Phong port.

III. The veterinary center of Vinh region

—Address: 51 Nguyen Sinh Sac street, Vinh city, Nghe An

—Tel: 038. 842786

—Fax: 038. 841571

—E - mail: tyvvinh@ hn. vnn. vn

—Localities under management: Thanh Hoa, Nghe An, Ha Tinh, Quang Binh, Quang Tri and Thua Thien - Hue.

—Border - gate stations: Lao Bao and Cau Treo.

IV. The veterinary center of Da Nang region

—Address: 12 Tran Quy Cap street, Hai Chau district, Da Nang city

—Tel: 0511. 822515

—Fax: 0511. 826926

—Border gate stations: Dong Dang station, Huu Nghi, Coc Nam, Tan Thanh and Chi Ma.

—E - mail: tttyvdn@ dn. vnn. vn

—Localities under management: Da Nang, Quang Nam, Quang Ngai, Binh Dinh, Gia Lai, Kon Tum, Dak Lak, Phu Yen and Khanh Hoa

—Border - gate stations: Da Nang airport and Tien Sa port.

V. The veterinary center of Ho Chi Minh City region

—Address: 124 - 126 Pham The Hien street, District 8, Ho Chi Minh City

—Tel: 08. 8568886; 08. 8568887

—Fax: 08. 8569050

—E – mail: rahhcm@ hcm. fpt. vn

—Localities under management: Ho Chi Minh City, Lam Dong, Ninh Thuan, Binh Thuan, Dong Nai, Ba Ria – Vung Tau, Binh Duong, Binh Phuoc, Tay Ninh, Long An, Tien Giang and Ben Tre.

—Border – gate stations: Tan Son Nhat airport, Sai Gon port and Moc Bai station.

VI. The veterinary center of Can Tho region

—Address: Cach Mang Thang Tam road, Can Tho city, Can Tho province

—Tel: 071. 820203

—Fax: 071. 823386

—E – mail:

—Localities under management: Can Tho, Vinh Long, Tra Vinh, Dong Thap, An Giang, Soc Trang, Kien Giang, Bac Lieu and Ca Mau

—Border – gate station: Can Tho port.

VII. The border – gate animal quarantine stations under the Veterinary Department

1. Noi Bai Airport Animal Quarantine Station

—Address: Noi Bai International Airport

—Tel: 04. 8840120

2. Dong Dang Animal Quarantine Station

– Address: 39 Dong Dang Railway Station Zone, Dong Dang township, Lang Son

—Tel: 025. 851275

—Fax: 025. 812536

3. Lao Cai Animal Quarantine Station

—Address: Lao Cai provincial capital, Lao Cai province

—Tel: 020. 830260

4. Mong Cai Animal Quarantine Station

—Address: Mong Cai town, Quang Ninh

—Tel: 033. 881502

—Fax: 033. 881502

—Border gate stations: Mong Cai and Bac Phong Sinh.

Notes:

* Import/export goods subject to animal quarantine shall comply with Decision No. 607 NN – TY/QD of June 9, 1994 of the Ministry of Agriculture and Foodstuff Industry (now the Ministry of Agriculture and Rural Development)

* The provincial/municipal Veterinary Sub – Departments may, under the authorization of the Veterinary Department, perform the quarantine work at border gates within the authorized scope.

Appendix No. Ⅱ

List of units competent to certify written quarantine registration or grant quarantine certificates for import/export goods (articles) subject to plant quarantine

1. The Plant Quarantine Sub - Department of Region I:
Address: 2 Tran Quang Khai street, Hai Phong city
Tel: 031. 842104 - 031. 823366
—Fax: 031. 821839
E - mail: kdtv1hp@ hn. vnn. vn
Localities under management: Thai Binh, Hai Duong, Hung Yen, Hai Phong and Quang Ninh
Border - gate stations: Hai Phong port; Mong Cai; and Binh Lieu.
2. The Plant Quarantine Sub - Department of Region II:
Address: 28 Mac Dinh Chi street, District 1, Ho Chi Minh City
Tel: 08. 8251401 - 0808. 8238948
Fax: 08. 8293266
E - mail: kdtv2@ hcmc. netnam. vn

Localities under management: Ninh Thuan, Binh Thuan, Lam Dong, Binh Duong, Binh Phuoc, Tay Ninh, Dong Nai, Ho Chi Minh City, Long An, Tien Giang, Dong Thap and Ba Ria - Vung Tau

Border - gate stations: Sai Gon port; Moc Bai; Vung Tau; Tan Son Nhat airport; Binh Hiep; Tho Mo; Hung Dien A; Xa Mat; Ka Tum; Phuoc Tan; Hoa Lu; Hoang Dieu; Thuong Phuoc; Dong Thap post office; Ba Ria Vung Tau post office; and Dong Nai post office.

3. The Plant Quarantine Sub - Department of Region III:
Address: 146 Hoang Dieu street, Da Nang city
Tel: 0511. 821622
Fax: 0511. 826863
E - mail: lethinghanh@ dng. vnn. vn
Localities under management: Quang Tri, Thua Thien Hue, Quang Nam, Da Nang and Quang Ngai
Border - gate stations: Da Nang port; Hue city; and Lao Bao.
4. The Plant Quarantine Sub - Department of Region IV:
Address: 66 Le Hong Phong street, Quy Nhon, Binh Dinh
Tel: 056. 822964 - 056. 823538
Fax: 056. 822964 (823538)
E - mail: cckdtv4@ dng. vnn. vn
Localities under management: Binh Dinh, Phu Yen, Khanh Hoa, Kon Tum, Gia Lai and Dac Lac.
Border - gate stations: Nha Trang; Bo Y; Duc Co; Buprang; and Dac Bo.
5. The Plant Quarantine Sub - Department of Region V:
Address: 149 Ho Dac Di street, Dong Da, Hanoi
Tel: 04. 8513500
Fax: 04. 5330043

E - mail: kdtv5 - hn@ fpt. vn

Localities under management: Bac Giang, Bac Ninh, Phu Tho, Vinh Phuc, Ha Tay, Ninh Binh, Nam Dinh, Ha Nam, Hanoi, and Hoa Binh

Border - gate stations: Hanoi city; and Noi Bai airport.

6. The Plant Quarantine Sub - Department of Region VI:

Address: 28 Tran Phu street, Vinh city, Nghe An

Tel: 038. 842992

Fax:

E - mail: cckdtvv6@ hn. vnn. vn

Localities under management: Thanh Hoa, Nghe An, Ha Tinh, and Quang Binh

Border - gate stations: Cau Treo and Chalo.

7. The Plant Quarantine Sub - Department of Region VII:

Address: 98B Ngo Quyen street, Dong Kinh ward, Lang Son provincial capital

Tel: 025. 875797 - 025. 875798

Fax: 025. 872941

E - mail:

Localities under management: Lang Son, Cao Bang, Bac Kan, and Thai Nguyen

Border - gate stations: Huu Nghi; Dong Dang; Tan Thanh; Chi Ma; Cong Trang; Ta Lung; Tra Linh; Ha Quang; and Soc Giang.

8. The Plant Quarantine Sub - Department of Region VIII:

Address: Lao Cai provincial capital

Tel: 020. 830503 - 020. 830097

Fax: 020. 830503

E - mail: tuankd8lc@ hn. vnn. vn

Localities under management: Ha Giang, Tuyen Quang, Yen Bai, Lao Cai, Lai Chau, and Son La

Border - gate stations: Lao Cai; Lao Cai railway station; Bat Sat; Muong Khuong;

Quang Kim; Luc Cau; Km6; Thanh Thuy; Ma Lu Thang; Pay Chang; Chieng Khoi; Si Ma Cai; and Tay Trang.

9. The Plant Quarantine Station of Region IX:

Address: 386B Cach Mang Thang Tam road, Can Tho city

Tel: 071. 826709 - 071. 883551

Fax: 071. 828408

E - mail: kdtvv9@ hcm. vnn. vn

Localities under management: Can Tho, An Giang, Kien Giang, Ca Mau, Bac Lieu, Tra Vinh, Soc Trang, Vinh Long, Ben Tre

Border - gate stations: My Thoi port; Tinh Bien; Vinh Hoi Dong; Vinh Xuong; and Khanh Binh.

Notes:

1. List of import/export goods (articles) subject to plant quarantine shall comply with Decision No. 56/2001/QD/BNN - BVTV of May 23, 2001 of the Ministry of Agriculture and Rural Development.

2. When new quarantine stations are put into operation, the plant quarantine agencies shall notify thereof to the border - gate Customs Sub - Departments for coordination.

3. The provincial/municipal Plant Protection Sub - Departments shall, under the Plant Protection Department's authorization, be permitted to perform the quarantine work at border gates within the authorized scope.

Appendix No. Ⅲ

Agencies competent to certify written quarantine registration or grant quarantine certificates for import/export goods subject to aquatic product quarantine

The Department for the Protection of Aquatic Resources – The Ministry of Aquatic Resources

Address: 10 Nguyen Cong Hoan street, Ba Dinh, Hanoi

Tel: 04. 8345953 – 04. 7718298 – 04. 351759

Fax: 04. 8353363

Localities under management: Nationwide.

Notes:

1. The Department for the Protection of Aquatic Resources may authorize the Sub – Departments for the Protection of Aquatic Resources of the provinces where border gates exist to certify written quarantine registration or grant quarantine certificates for import/export goods subject to aquatic product quarantine.

2. For border gates where aquatic product quarantine stations do not exist, they should contact the Department for the Protection of Aquatic Resources for guidance.

3. List of quarantine objects with regard to aquatic animals and products thereof (under Circular No. 02/TS – TT of June 25, 1994 of the Ministry of Aquatic Resources):

—Fish, crustaceans, molluscs, pelmatozoan, sponges, corollaceous sinus, amphibians and their eggs; and mammals.

—Fresh and live products, treated or preliminarily processed products (frozen, dried for half – done, salted, ...) which may carry agents causing diseases to aquatic animals.

老　挝

植物保护法

（首都万象 2008 年 12 月 9 日　No 06/NA）

第1章　总　　则

第1条　宗旨

为了防止有害生物在国内蔓延，传入、传出国境，植物保护法明确了法律法规以及与植物保护相关的检查、管理和机构等措施。目的是保护人类、动物和植物卫生和环境安全；确保植物生长，产品质量和数量能满足老挝人民日常生活需要；促进对外经济和贸易发展，为可持续的社会和经济发展做出贡献。

第2条　植物保护

根据本法和国际植物保护公约，植物保护是对原产地植物、植物产品和限定物品调运到另一地区的检查和控制措施，目的是限制和防止有害生物在老挝人民民主共和国境内蔓延、传入和传出。

第3条　定义

在本法中使用的术语具有下列含义：

1. 植物系指活的植物及其部分，包括水果、谷物、种子和繁殖材料；

2. 有害生物指对植物或植物产品和环境有害的任何物种、菌株或生物型、昆虫和微生物或病原体，如细菌、真菌、病毒等；

3. 有害植物指杂草或植物；

4. 植物产品指未经加工的植物原料和已加工的产品，其加工过程可能产生有害生物传入和扩散的风险，如大米、白米、玉米、咖啡、玉米面、木薯；

5. 限定物品指用于植物研究的物品、植物废料、土壤、植物介质，以及包装材料，如集装箱、托盘、垫木、板条箱、填塞块、袋子、篮筐；

6. 病毒系指仅通过电子显微镜能见的，对植物、动物和人类有害的微生物；

7. 细菌系指仅通过体视显微镜能见的，对植物、动物和人类有害的多属微生物；

8. 寄生系指依附在植物、动物和人类等较大生物体上，并取食为生的生物体；

9. 孢子系指带有外壳、具有传染性的、非常小的分散繁殖体；

10. 公约系指老挝 1995 年 2 月 28 日为缔约方，并于 2006 年 12 月 24 日加入的国际植物保护公约；

11. 植物保护授权系指植物保护局官方指定的技术人员，依据法律法规，在边境检查站或有害生物爆发区开展植物检查工作。

12. 植物保护边境检查站系指植物保护授权的工作区域或场所。

13. 植物检疫证书系指进出口植物、植物产品和其他物品，未携带管制性有害生物的证明文件。

14. 原产地证书系指植物、植物产品和管制物品产地、产区或国家的证明文件。

15. 植物检疫处理系指有害生物灭杀、灭活或剔除，或使有害生物不育或失活的官方程序；

16. 货主系指进出口植物、植物产品和限定物品的人员，包括从事植物检疫业务的人员；

17. 投诉权系指向管理机构投诉、向人民法院诉讼和要求国会进行公平听证。

第4条　关于植物保护的政府政策

为了促进国内社会和经济向国际一体化方面发展，国家将制定相关扶持政策、法律、法规，以及有关税收、义务、信贷、技术和工艺方面的规定，支持国内外个体、家庭和机构更好执行植物保护工作。

第5条 关于植物保护的一般原则

植物保护应当根据下列原则执行：

1. 确保整个国家集中统一管理。

2. 国家、社会、家庭，以及国内外企业家的安全利益。

3. 为获取短期和长期的社会效益，更加关注植物、人与动物的健康和安全以及生态系统的重要性。

4. 执行植物保护应当与促进农业生产和维持农林发展统筹协调。

5. 实施植物保护应考虑老挝人民民主共和国的指令、政策、法律、法规和法规，以及老挝作为国际协定或公约缔约方承担的义务和权力。

第6条 范围

本法适用于控制有害生物在国内扩散；进出口和过境各类植物的管理和检查，以确保植物、人类和动物的安全和卫生。

本法未涵盖植物保护中农药使用引起的农残问题。

第7条 国际合作

国家支持与国外、区域或国际组织开展合作与联系。通过交流经验和教训、信息和资讯；开展科学和技术研究，开发人力资源；履行国际协定和公约缔约方的义务和权力，更好实施和完善植物保护工作。

第2章 植物保护活动

第8条 活动的目标

本法第9条规定了活动的目标，比如，应依照技术规定对进口、出口和过境环节进行严格管控和检查，也应在国内对管控疫区实施限制调运措施。

第9条 有关植物保护的活动和业务

○ 植物保护活动如下：

■ 国内植物保护

■ 进口植物检疫

■ 出口植物检疫

■ 过境植物检疫

■ 旅客携带和邮寄物品检疫

■ 车辆检疫

○ 植物保护业务

第1部分 国内植物保护

第10条 国内植物的管控

为防止限定性有害生物从原产地传到另一地区，应依照技术规定和法律、规则和法规，对国内调运植物进行检查和限制。

第11条 有害生物报告

任何个人、家庭和机构对截获或在某个地区爆发的有害生物，应及时向国家农业和林业办公室或当地有关的管理机构报告。

第12条 疫区通报

政府和地方管理机构应依据植物保护管理机构的建议按照下列要求公布疫区：

1. 如果在某个行政区或城市爆发疫情，该行政区的主要领导或市长公布疫区；

2. 如果在某个省的多个行政区或城市爆发疫情，应由该省省长和主管市长公布疫区；

3. 如果在多个省爆发疫情，应由总理公布疫区。

第 13 条　有害生物爆发的控制措施

农业与林业部应协同地方管理当局应当在适当的时间，根据下列要求公布控制有害生物爆发的措施：

1. 采用适当和有效的措施，控制有害生物的爆发。

2. 在某一地区或全国范围，采用必要措施，预防、控制和根除有害生物的爆发，防止有害生物广泛扩散。

3. 及时依规对感染有害生物或病原菌的植物、植物产品和物品进行销毁和处理。

4. 对生态因素有利于有害生物定殖的疑似区域开展监测和调查。

第 2 部分　进口植物检疫

第 14 条　植物的进口

任何以贸易、外国援助形式进口的植物、植物产品、限定物品的个人和家庭，应当遵循老挝人民民主共和国的政策、法律、规则、法规以及老挝作为国际协定和公约缔约方的职责和义务。

第 15 条　进口植物的许可

任何个人或家庭拟进口植物种子，或从疫区进口老挝人民民主共和国受控有害生物名录所列的品种和植物产品，应依据现行的法律、法规和规则，事先向国家农业和林业办公室申请办理进口许可手续。

第 16 条　报检

进口植物、植物产品和限定物品的任何个人、家庭和货主，应当向植物保护边境检查站报检，提交相关的文件，如植物检疫证书、出口国或原产国签发的其他相关文件。

第 17 条　植物商品的检验

以贸易方式进口的植物、植物产品和限定物品，应当接受检查，并符合技术法规的要求。如果未发现有害生物，可允许货物入境。

如果国外爆发有害生物，并可能扩散到本国的情况下，植物保护机构有权在入境口岸，对进境限定物品进行扣留、检疫、监测、检查和测试。

如果在从进口物品中发现管控的有害生物，植物保护当局应当通知货主，由植物保护机构采取强制性的处理措施。如果在老挝人民民主共和国不能处理，该批货物应当退回原产地或作销毁处理。

进口物品涉及有关处理、退回或销毁中的费用或损失应当由货主承担。

第 18 条　禁止物品的进口

因社会、经济、环境发展以及科研、教育活动，需要进口植物、植物产品和限定物品的任何个人、家庭和货主，应事先向农业与林业部办理特许手续，并在严格的控制条件下进口。

第 3 部分　出口植物检疫

第 19 条　植物检查申报

出口植物、植物产品和限定物品的任何个人、家庭和货主，应当根据进口国的要求，向农林主管部门申请植物检疫。

第 20 条　植物复验申请

根据下列情况，任何个人、家庭和企业家，有权向农林主管部门对出口的植物、植物产品和限定物品申请复验：

1. 来自进口国的通告

2. 包装材料的改变或泄漏

3. 植物检疫证书超过有效期

第 21 条 出口植物证书

出口的植物、植物产品和限定物品，应当由农林主管部门根据相关规定进行检查，并签发植物检疫证书。

第 4 部分 过境植物检疫

第 22 条 植物过境和检疫

运输植物、植物产品和限定物品从老挝过境的任何个人、家庭和货主，必须遵循老挝人民民主共和国的政策、法律、法规、规则，以及老挝作为国际协定和公约缔约方的职责和权力。

植物保护机构应当检查植物、植物产品和限定物品的运输车辆，查看是否携带植物检疫证书、证书的有效性，鉴别证书真伪，核实货证的一致性、货物的完整性和安全性。

如果怀疑过境植物携带疫情，应依据老挝人民民主共和国的技术规定、法规和法律实施植物检疫的现场检查。如果截获到管制名单所列的有害生物，应当按照本法第 17 条第三款和第四款规定的措施实施处理。

第 23 条 运输工具装载

过境的植物、植物产品和限定物品，在其过境期间需包装密闭，未经农林主管部门许可不得从运输工具上装卸。

第 5 部分 旅客携带和邮寄植物的检疫

第 24 条 旅客携带或邮寄植物的进口

携带或邮寄植物种子、幼苗或其他繁殖材料进入老挝人民民主共和国的个人、家庭和货主，根据相关规定必须事先在指定的进出境边境检查站或邮局申报，办理检查手续。

如果在进口物品中发现管制的有害生物，植物保护机构应当通知货主，由植物保护局采取强制性的处理措施。如果在老挝人民民主共和国内不能进行处理，该批货物应当退回原产国或销毁处理。对进口物品处理、退回或销毁中发生的费用或损失由货主承担。

以销售或繁殖为目的的进口植物，应依据相关法律法规，事先向农林主管部门申请进口许可证。

第 25 条 旅客携带或邮寄植物的检疫

旅客携带或邮寄植物到老挝，需在植物检疫合格后方可进入。

第 6 部分 运输工具的检疫

第 26 条 运输工具

依据技术规程、法规和法律，所有的运输工具必须清洁、无有害生物。

第 27 条 来自有害生物疫区的运输工具

来自有害生物疫区的船舶、飞机或卡车需经植物保护局检查。如果发现管制性有害生物，应依据技术规程对货物进行消毒除害处理。

第 28 条 植物运输工具

运载进出口植物、植物产品和限定物品的运输工具，应当符合技术规定、双边或老挝作为国际协定和公约缔约方承担的职责和义务。

第 29 条 植物运输工具上的废弃物处理

通过运输工具进入老挝的植物废弃物、植物产品和限定物品，应依据相关规定，在指定场所进行清洁或消毒除害处理 。

第 30 条 废旧设备和包装材料的进口

进口到老挝的废旧设备和包装材料，如果怀疑携带有害生物，应接受植物保护局的检查。如果检疫发现有害生物，应依据技术规程，对货物进行消毒除害处理。

第 7 部分　植物检疫业务

第 31 条　植物检疫业务

国内外的个人、家庭和团体，如需开展植物检疫业务，应遵循相关的技术标准、法规和法律。

第 32 条　植物检疫业务的类型

植物检疫业务包括下列内容：

1. 有害生物统计
2. 植物检疫除害处理

第 33 条　有害生物预防和控制业务

有害生物统计业务包含有害生物监测；评估对生态系统，植物、动物、人类的卫生影响；为相关实体或机构开发有害生物爆发的预防和控制措施提供必要的指南。

第 34 条　植物检疫除害处理业务

依据技术标准和规程，植物检疫处理业务涉及有害生物控制和对植物、植物产品和限定物品的植物检疫除害处理，方法包括：

1. 在种植区、仓储及其他场所的有害生物管理服务。
2. 使用蒸汽热处理、热空气或冷处理、熏蒸、辐照及其他方法对植物、植物产品和限定物品实施的植物检疫处理服务。

第 3 章　植物保护当局和货主的权利、职责和义务

第 35 条　植物保护官员和机构的权利、职责和义务

- 植物保护官员和机构具有以下权利和义务：

1. 在执行植物保护的法律、法规和规则中，向社会提供宣传和建议。
2. 检查和核实植物检疫证书和相关文件。
3. 对检疫合格的植物、植物产品和限定物品入境。
4. 对来自疫区的植物、植物产品和限定物品进行扣留和检疫。
5. 依据规定，通知货主对受感染的植物、植物产品和限定物品到指定场所进行除害、退回或销毁处理。
6. 依据植物保护法律和法规，在其职责范围内对违法行为采取措施，包括查封商品、限制违法者，以及向相关部门提交诉讼文件。
7. 在履职期间，协调其他相关部门和地方管理机构。
8. 评估并定期向上级主管部门报告植物保护活动的执行情况。

- 植物保护官员和机构具有下列义务

1. 执行规则、法规和法律，包括老挝人民民主共和国作为协定和国际公约缔约方的义务；
2. 在紧急情况下，协助和监控疫区的有害生物根除项目；
3. 严格按照法律和法规要求，促进有关植物、植物产品和限定物品的贸易；
4. 根据法律和法规，收取和转交植物保护服务费和其他手续费。

第 36 条　货主的权利和义务

货主具有以下权利和义务：

1. 严格遵照技术标准、法律和法规，在授权范围内经营其业务；
2. 全力协助有害生物的预防、控制、处理和根除，并采取必要的预防措施，解决有害生物可能随疫区植物、植物产品和限定物品进出口造成扩散的问题；
3. 根据法律和法规，向有关机构投诉植物保护官员和机构的违法行为；

4. 通过损赠资金或人力，协助植物检疫工作的发展；
5. 配合、支持公职人员工作，并提供必要的信息；
6. 对检出或疑似检出有害生物蔓延的事件或实例，应向有关机构和地方管理机构报告；
7. 根据法规和法律的规定，支付手续费、服务费以及其他义务。

第 37 条 公民的权利和义务

1. 全力监测有害生物，控制其发生率。
2. 向主管部门和地方管理机构报告有害生物的发生情况。
3. 在植物保护工作中，配合植物保护官员和机构开展工作。
4. 向相关的机构投诉货主、植物保护官员和机构的违法行为。

第4章 禁 止

第 38 条 一般禁止

禁止任何个人、家庭和其他实体，包括国内外企业家从事下列活动：

1. 进口对国家经济发展有潜在影响，对老挝人民民主共和国的植物、动物和人类健康有害的植物、植物产品和限定物品。
2. 将疫区的植物、植物产品和限定物品运到国内其他地区。
3. 出口、转口和过境感染危害性有害生物的植物、植物产品和限定物品。
4. 未经许可，进口、出口、移动和卸载植物、植物产品和限定物品。
5. 贿赂植物保护官员和机构，伪造文件和假冒植物保护印章。
6. 威胁、延误或妨碍植物保护官员和机构执行公务。
7. 从事违反植物保护法的其他活动。

第 39 条 植物保护官员和机构的禁令

除本法第 38 条禁令外，禁止植物保护官员和机构违反下列条款：

1. 使用武力威胁、强迫、施压等方式滥用职权，以及收受可能导致损害国家、集体和个人利益的贿赂；
2. 透露公共或官方机密事项；延误和伪造证件；在执行植物保护活动中不负责任；
3. 在检查植物、植物产品和限定物品时，不按法规和规则操作，不依据技术规程解决问题；
4. 未经许可，擅自增加或减少检疫费和服务费，并用于个人利益。

第5章 争端解决

第 40 条 争端解决的方式

应依据下列条款解决有关植物保护的争端：

1. 双方协商解决。
2. 由农林部官员协调其他相关部门解决。
3. 由经济争端调解委员会裁决。
4. 由人民法院裁决。

第 41 条 国际争端解决

老挝与外国企业之间，老挝境内外国企业之间，或外国企业与老挝国家机构之间有关植物保护的争端，应由国内的、国外的和国际经济争端调解委员会裁决。

涉及有关国际植物保护措施争端，应当根据老挝人民民主共和国作为合同和条约缔约方所承担的责任和义务来解决。

第 6 章　管理和检查

第 1 部分　管　　理

第 42 条　管理机构

政府授权农业与林业部成立植物保护管理机构，统一管理全国的植保工作；协调产业和商务部、公共卫生部、地方管理机构等相关部门行使管理职能。

植物保护管理机构的组成：

1. 农业部；
2. 省/直辖市/地区/县农业和林业官员；
3. 区/镇农业和林业官员；
4. 植物保护边境检查站。

第 43 条　农业与林业部的权利和义务

在植物保护活动的管理中，农业与林业部具有下列权利和义务：

1. 为了管理和实施全国各地的植物保护活动，作为政府的秘书处对政策指南、战略、政策计划，以及相关政策的实施计划、法律、规则和法规进行研究和执行；
2. 在全国范围宣传有关植物保护的政策、法律、规则和法规；
3. 通过全国的垂直机构，指导、监控和评估植物保护措施的执行情况；
4. 与其他相关部门和地方机构协调，加强能力建设和业务培训，任命、调任或解聘植物保护官员，设立或撤销检疫机构；
5. 与其他相关部门和地方机构协调，授权建立植物保护边境检查站和实验室；
6. 授权开始或结束植物检疫业务的运作；
7. 在国内外为植物保护的发展筹集资金；
8. 为执行好植物保护的法规法规，向植物保护机构、官员和企业家发放的决议、指令、通告和操作手册，解决争端；
9. 为了确定全部有害生物或管制性有害生物名单中的某种有害生物的控制区域，应协同其他相关机构和地方机构共同执行植物保护活动，包括有害生物监测工作；
10. 管理签发植物进出口许可证、植物检疫证书和其他相关文件；
11. 与国外进行植物检疫方面的交流和合作；
12. 定期总结和向政府报告有关植物检疫（如有害生物发生率）的执行情况。

第 44 条　省和首都万象农业和林业办公室的权利和义务

在管理植物保护活动中，省和首都万象的农业和林业办公室具有下列权利和义务：

1. 将有关植物保护工作的政策、策略、协定、指令和法规转换成详细的计划和项目，以便在职责范围内执行；
2. 提高公众意识，加强法律法规的宣传，开展植物保护工作的信息交流，严格执行法律和法规；
3. 对行政区和直辖市农业和林业办公室的植物保护执行情况进行指导、监控和评估；
4. 与相关部门和地方机构协调，签发或吊销植物检疫业务的运营许可证；
5. 根据上级部门授权职责，管理签发植物检疫证书及其他文件；
6. 管理和制定受控有害生物名单，确定检疫区域；
7. 根据上级部门授权职责或在职责范围内，在国内外为植物保护的发展筹集资金；
8. 在职责范围内，与其他地方机构和部门协调，共同做好植物保护工作；
9. 总结并定期向农业与林业部、省和首都万象政府报告植物检疫工作（如有害生物发生率）的执行情况。

第 45 条 行政区和直辖市农业和林业办公室的权利和义务

在管理植物保护活动中，行政区和直辖市的农业和林业办公室具有下列权利和义务：

1. 执行工作计划、项目、决议、指令、通报和上级部门的工作指南；

2. 宣传植物保护法律和法规，扩大公众意识，并严格执行法律法规；

3. 参与管理，制定禁止植物有害生物名单，划定植物有害生物疫区；

4. 参与管理，制定受控有害生物名单，确定检疫区；

5. 解决争端，向省和首都万象农业和林业办公室建议签发或吊销植物检疫业务运营许可证；

6. 与地方机构和相关部门协调，在行政区和直辖市内共同执行植物检疫工作；

7. 总结和定期向省和首都万象的农业和林业办公室报告植物检疫工作（如行政区和直辖市内有害生物发生率）的执行情况；

第 46 条 植物保护边境检查站的权利和义务

植物保护边境检查站具有下列权利和义务：

1. 在职责范围内执行有关植物保护的工作计划、政策、法律、规则和法规；

2. 按照技术原则和操作规程，严格、准确和快捷的履行工作职责；

3. 阻止任何形式的违反植物保护法律、规则和法规的活动在检查站发生，向相关部门起诉违法者；

4. 根据法律和法规规定，公正快捷促进植物、植物产品和限定物品的进出口贸易；

5. 与边境检查站的其他相关部门和地方机构协调，确保执法工作的一致性；

6. 扣留、隔离和样品鉴定，通知企业家对受感染的植物、植物产品和限定物品进行处理、退回或销毁；

7. 根据法律和法规收取技术服务费；

8. 总结和定期向农业和林业部门报告边境检查站有关植物、植物产品和限定物品的进出口数据和检疫情况。

第 47 条 其他部门的权利和义务

根据植物保护法律法规，包括地方机构在内的任何部门，如果发现或收到有害生物流行和违法行为的报告，应及时通知植物保护机构，按照相关单位的职责，共同合作、协同做好工作。

第 2 部分　检　　查

第 48 条 检查机构

检查机构的组成：

- 内部检查机构相当于本法第 42 条中确定的植物保护管理机构，由农业部、农业办公室和当地农业与林业部门的代表组成；
- 外部检查机构包括国会、国家检查机构、公共检察当局。

第 49 条 检查机构的权利和义务

植物、植物产品及其他材料的检查机构具有下列权利和义务：

1. 检查植物保护法律法规的执行情况；

2. 检查植物检疫业务的运作情况；

3. 检查有关进出口植物、植物产品和限定物品在边境检查的检疫情况，包括签发植物检疫证书和其他文件，是否依据法律法规取样检测；

4. 与调查机构合作，提供违法者违反植物保护法律法规的违法行为及相关信息；

5. 委派工作人员开展监测、检查、收集信息，包括指挥预防有害生物疫情扩散；

6. 根据植物保护的法律法规，对违法行为采取必要措施，如在发现进出口植物、植物产品及其他限定物品感染有害生物时，发布命令停止与植物保护有关的业务活动；

7. 配合并协调中央和当地相关部门，行使自身权利和义务；

8. 总结和定期对下级机构进行工作检查。

第 50 条　检查形式

检查包括以下三种形式：

1. 定期检查；
2. 预先通知检查；
3. 紧急检查。

定期检查是根据不同管理层的职责、权利和义务，在规定时间内进行的常规检查；

预先通知检查是针对某项任务设定的专项检查；

紧急检查是不事先通知的特殊检查。

第 7 章　制服、徽章和印章

第 51 条　制服和徽章

由农业与林业部授权，边境检查站的植物保护官员配有制服、徽章和工牌号。植物保护机构和边境检查站的植物保护官员应穿着制服、佩戴徽章和工牌号。

第 52 条　印章

由农业与林业部授权，植物检疫官员在开展植物检疫工作时可以使用官方边境植物检疫印章。

第 8 章　奖励和处罚

第 53 条　奖励

对在管理、检查、控制和根除等执行活动中，表现出色的个人或团体，应依法给予奖励和表彰。

第 54 条　处罚

对违法行的个人或团体，按照违法程度进行再教育、纪律处分、罚款、惩处、民事处分和犯罪指控等处罚。

第 55 条　再教育措施

根据植物保护法、法规和禁令，犯有较轻的民事违法行为，造成损害不到 50 万基普，倘若违法者做出诚实的报告承认其的错误行为并返还所获的所有不义财产，应当受到警告和再教育。

第 56 条　惩戒措施

根据植物检疫法、法规和禁令，政府工作人员和植物保护机构及官员犯有较轻的民事违法行为，造成损害不到 50 万基普，但做出诚实的报告并尽量避免其错误行为所带来影响的，应当取决于罪行的严重程度受到下列惩罚：

1. 批评，受到记入个人档案的警告；
2. 延迟提升、任何加薪和/或任何奖励；
3. 降职或调往较低的职位；
4. 立即开除公职。

第 57 条　处罚措施

根据植物检疫法、法规和禁令，任何个人或团体犯有本法中确定的违法行为，应当处以与被植物有害生物感染的植物价值相等的罚款。

如果违法者第二次违法或多次屡犯，罚款应当是被植物有害生物感染的植物价值的两倍，而且植物、植物产品和限定物品应当被没收并根据法律和法规处理。

第 58 条　民事违法行为措施

未能遵守植物检疫，并且因此对其他人造成损害的个人和团体，应当根据法律和法规，对所造成的损失承担责任。

第 59 条　刑事违法行为措施

根据植物保护法和法规，犯有刑事犯罪的个人或团体，应当根据处罚法，取决于犯罪的严重程度论处，并且根据民事法处以罚金。

第 60 条 进一步处罚措施

除第 59 条确定的处罚之外，根据进一步处罚措施，违者可能面临进一步地处罚，如暂停或取消植物保护和植物检疫业务活动的经营许可。

第9章 最终条款

第 61 条 实施

本法应当由老挝人民民主共和国政府实施。

第 62 条 有效性

本法在老挝人民民主共和国主席令颁布之日起九十天生效。

任何与本法相矛盾的规定和法规应当全部废除。

国会主席

通邢 塔马冯

Law on plant protection

(Vientiane Capital, 9 December 2008 No 06/NA)

Chapter Ⅰ General Provisions

Article 1 Objectives

Plant Protection Law defines rules, regulations related and measures related to organization, management and inspection of plant protection in order to prevent pest from spreading within, into and out of the country. Its objectives are: to protect human, animal and plant health and safe environment; to ensure growing of plant and plant's product in quantity and quality response to domestic demand which contributes to develop livelihoods of Lao people and promote the development of foreign economic relations and trade and to participate and contributes to sustainable social and economic development.

Article 2 Plant Protection

Plant Protection, according to this law and in comply with International Plant Protection Convention, is the control and inspection of plant, plant's product and regulated article which are moving from its originate area to another area with the aim to restrict and prevent pest from spreading within, into and out of Lao People's Democracy Republic's territory.

Article 3 Definitions

The terms used in this law have the following meaning:

1. Plant refers to living plants and parts thereof, including fruits, grains, seeds, and germplasm.

2. Pest refers to any species, strain or biotype of plant, insect and microorganism or pathogenic agent such as bacteria, fungi, virus etc. . . injurious to plants or plant products and environment.

3. Injuries plant refers to weed or plant that.

4. Plant product refers to unmanufactured material of plant origin and those manufactured products that, by their nature or that of their processing, may create a risk for the introduction and spread of pests such as rice, milled rice, maize, coffee, corn flour, cassava.

5. Regulated articles refers to objectives used for plant research, waste of plant, soil, plant medium as well as packaging material such as container, pallets, dunnage, crating, packing blocks, sag, basket.

6. Virus refers to a microorganism injurious to plant, animal and human and only visible by with electron microscope.

7. Bacteria refers to a microorganism with many genus injurious to plant, animal and human which is only visible by stereo microscope.

8. Parasite refers to an organism which lives on or in a larger organism such as plant, animal and human, feeding upon it.

9. A spore refers a very small dispersal reproductive unit with an outer covering and that may be infectious.

10. Convention refers to International Plant Protection Convention which Lao is contracting party in 28 February, 1995 and deposited in 24 December, 2006.

11. Plant protection authority refers to technical staff who is officially assigned by plant protection administrative office to facilitate and conduct plant inspection at border check point or in the pest outbreak area in ac-

cordance with the laws and regulations.

12. Plant Protection border check point refers to working area or location for plant protection authority.

13. Phytosanitary certificate refers to a document certifying that plants, plant products and other materials for export or import are free from regulated pest.

14. Place of origin certificate refers to document certifying production place, country, region, area or site where is the origin of plant, plant's product and regulated article.

15. Phytosanitary treatment refers to official procedure for the killing, inactivation or removal of pests, or for rendering pests infertile or for devitalization.

16. Entrepreneur refers to person who export, import, produce plant, plant's product and regulated article and includes individuals engaged in phytosanitary businesses.

17. Right to complain means the right to make a complaint to the administration, to institute court proceedings in the People's Court and to request the National Assembly for a fair hearing.

Article 4　Government policies on Plant Protection

The state promotes plant protection through development of supportive policy, law, regulation and provisions on tax, duty, credit, technique and technology that is favorable to facilitate individuals, families and organization, both domestic and foreign in implementation of plant protection in order to response to national social and economic development in term of international integration.

Article 5　General principle on Plant Protection

Plant Protection shall be implemented based on following principles:

1. Ensure centralized and harmonized management throughout the country.

2. Safe interests of state, community, family and entrepreneur both domestic and foreign.

3. bearing in mind the importance of eco-systems, health and safety of plants, people and animals for achieving the short and long term benefit of society.

4. Plant protection shall be implemented in harmony with promoting agricultural production and sustain agriculture and forestry development.

5. Plant protection shall be implemented together with directives, policies, laws, rules and regulations of Lao PDR. and the relevant international agreements or conventions of which Lao is the contracting party.

Article 6　Scope

This Law applies to control pest from spreading within the county; to manage and inspect import, export and transit of all type of plant to ensure safety and sanitary of plant, human and animal.

The issue of chemical used for plant protection, residue in plant is not covered in the scope of this law

Article 7　International Cooperation

The state promotes links and cooperation with foreign country, region, international including international organization to implement and improve plant protection through exchanging lessons, experiences, information, news; conduct scientific and technology researches; development of human resource; following the implementation of the international agreement and convention of which Lao is the contracting party.

Chapter Ⅱ　Plant protection activities

Article 8　Target of Activities

Target of activities defined in the Article 9 of this law such as import, export and transit shall be strictly regulated and inspected in accordance with technical provision. Regarding to activities within the country, regulating infested area and restricting movement shall be applied.

Article 9　Activities and business related to Plant Protection

○ Plant protection activities are as follows:

■ Domestic plant protection

■ Import plant inspection

■ Export plant inspection

■ Transient plant inspection

■ Inspection of articles carried by passenger and sent by post.

■ Vehicle inspection

○ Plant Protection business

Session 1　Domestic plant protection

Article 10　Regulating plant within the country

Regulating plant within the country shall be conducted in accordance with technical provision and law, rule and regulation through inspection, containment and restriction movement of the regulated pest from its original area to another area.

Article 11　Pest reporting

Individual, family or organization who intercepts pest infestation or outbreak in an area shall urgently report to state agriculture and forestry office or relevant local administrative authority.

Article 12　Declaration of epidemic area

Government and local administrative authority shall declare epidemic area as proposed by Plant protection administration organization by the following:

1. If the outbreak occurs within one district or municipality, the chief of the district or mayor of municipality declare epidemic zone;

2. If the outbreak occurs in more than one district or municipality, but within on province or municipality, the government and mayor of the municipality shall make the declaration;

3. If the outbreak occurs more than one province, the prime minister will make the declaration.

Article 13　Control measure on pest out break

Ministry of Agriculture and Forestry in coordinate with local administrative authority shall announce the measure to control the outbreak of pest in appropriate time as follows:

1. Imply appropriate and effective measure to control the outbreak of pest.

2. Imply necessary measure in specific area or whole country to prevent, control and eradicate pest out break and to restrict pest widely distribution.

3. Destruct and dispose pest, plant, plant products and articles that is infest, contaminate or harbored pathogen in time and provisions.

4. Monitor and survey infested area or suspected area where ecological factors favor the establishment of a pest.

Session 2　Import plant inspection

Article 14　Import of plant

Individuals, families who intend to import plant , plant product, regulated article in form of trade, foreign assistance shall follow policy, law, rule, regulation of Lao PDR, international agreement and convention of which Lao is the contracting party.

Article 15 Permission for importing plant

Individuals, families whose intend to import plant seed, variety and its part specified in the list of regulated pest of Lao PDR. or from exporting country where is reported to be infested area shall apply for import permit from state agriculture and forestry office and follow the existing law, rules and regulation.

Article 16 Declaration of Document

Individuals, families and entrepreneur who import plant, plant product and regulated articles shall presented relevant document to plant protection border check point such as phytosanitary certificate and another relevant document issued by exporting country or country of origin.

Article 17 Inspection of Plant commodity

Plant, plant product and regulated articles imported for trade shall be inspected in consistence with technical provision. If no pest intercepted, the consignment should be allowed to enter the country.

In the event that serious pest occur abroad and is reliable to spread into the country, Plant protection authority with its right shall detain imported regulated article in post entry quarantine for monitoring, inspection and testing.

In the circumstance that regulated pest is intercepted from imported article, plant protection authority shall notify to the owner and absolute treatment measures shall be decided by the plant protection authority. Where treatments are not feasible in Lao PDR, the consignment shall be returned to the place of origin or destroyed.

The required expense or the losses incurred in the treatment, returning or destruction for the imported articles shall be borne by the owner.

Articles 18 Import of prohibited articles

Individuals, families and entrepreneur who intend to import plant, plant product and regulated articles in the propose of research, education and activities that benefits to develop society, economy and environment shall have special authorization from Ministry of Agriculture and forestry under strictly specific control.

Session 3 Export plant inspection

Article 19 Application of plant inspection

Individuals, families and entrepreneur who intend to export plant, plant product and regulated articles shall apply to competence agriculture and forestry authority for phytosanitary inspection according to the requirement of importing country.

Article 20 Application of plant re – inspection

Individuals, families and entrepreneurs have right to apply to competence agriculture and forestry authority for conducting re – inspection of plant, plant product and regulated articles as following circumstances:

1. Notification from importing country
2. Change or leakage of packaging material
3. The validity period of phytosanitary certificate is expired

Article 21 Export plant certification

Plants, plant products and regulated articles exported to foreign country shall be inspected and certified on phytosanitary from competence agricultural and forestry authority according to the defined regulation.

Session 4 Transit plant inspection

Article 22 transit and inspection of plant

Individuals, families and entrepreneurs who intend to transport plant, plant product and regulated article through the Lao territory is required to follow policy, law, rule, regulation of Lao PDR, international agreement and convention of which Lao is the contracting party.

Plant protection authority shall inspect phytosanitary certificate, transporting vehicle of plant, plant product and regulated articles to examine validity and not fraudulent certificates; verify the identity, integrity and safely of consignment.

In case the infestation is suspected or there is epidemic information evidence from the original place of transit plant, phytosanytary visual inspecting for detection of pest shall be implied according to technical provision, regulation and Law of Lao PDR and if the pest or harmful organism specified in the list of regulated pest is intercepted, the measure stipulated in paragraph three and fourth of Article 17. of this Law shall be enforced.

Article 23　loading from the mean of transport

Plant, plant product and regulated article, in the course of their transit may not be unpacked or loading from the means of transport without the approval of competence agricultural and forestry authority.

Session 5　Inspection of plant carried by passenger or by post

Article 24　Importation of Plant Carried by Passenger or by Post

Individuals, families and entrepreneurs who intend to carry or post plant seeds, seedlings or other propagating materials into Lao PDR. must declare in advance and go through the formalities for inspection at the designed entry - export border check point or post office according to defined regulation.

In case that regulated pest is intercepted from imported article, plant protection authority shall notify to the owner and absolute treatment measures shall be decided by the plant protection authority. Where treatments are not feasible in Lao PDR. , the plant shall be returned to the place of origin or destroyed. The required expense or the losses incurred in the treatment, returning or destruction for the imported articles shall be borne by the owner.

Importation of plant with the propose of marketing or propagation is required import license from the competence agriculture and forestry authority and follow the relevant rule, regulation and law.

Article 25　Inspection of plant carried by passenger or by post

The plant carried by passenger or by post into Lao PDR should be allowed to enter the country after approval of the phytosanitary examination.

Session 6　Inspection of means of transport

Article 26　Means of Transport

All mean of transport must be cleaned and disinfestations according to technical provision, regulation and Law.

Article 27　Means of transport from pest epidemic area

Ship, airplanes or truck from the pest epidemic area requires inspection from plant protection authority. In case if the pest or harmful organism specified in the list of regulated pest is intercepted, the cargoes shall be subjected to such treatment as disinfestations according to the technical provision.

Article 28　Means of plant transport

Means of transport carrying import - export plant, plant product and regulated articles shall conform to the technical provision, bilateral or international agreement and convention of which Lao is the contracting party.

Article 29　Deposal of waste on means of plant transport

The wastes of plant nature, plan product and regulated articles on the means of transport entering Lao territory shall be disposed and disinfested such as cleaning in designed place in accordance with the regulation.

Article 30　Importation of used equipment and packing material

Importation of used equipment and packing material into Lao territory, it is suspected to be investigation shall be inspected by plant protection authority. In case if the pest or harmful organism pest is intercepted, the cargoes shall be subjected to such treatment as disinfestations according to the technical provision.

Session 7 Phytosanitary Business

Article 31 Phytosanitary business

Domestic and foreign Individuals, families and entities who intend to conduct a phytosanitary business shall follow relevant technical standard, regulation and Law.

Article 32 Type of phytosanitary business

Phytosanitary business comprises the following:

1. Pest inventory business

2. Phytosanitary treatment service business

Article 33 Pest prevention and control businesses

Pest inventory business involves pest surveillance; evaluation of impact on ecosystem, sanitary of plant; human and animal to provide necessary guideline to relevant entity or organization for developing prevent and control measure on pest outbreak.

Article 34 Phytosanitary treatment service business

Phytosanitary treatment service business involves pest control and phytosanitary treatment on plant, plant product and regulated articles according to the technical standard and provision as following methodologies:

1. Pest management serviced in the cultivation areas, storage and others.

2. Phytosanitary treatment service for plant, plant product and regulated articles using vapor heat treatment, hot air or cold treatment, fumigation, irradiation and others.

Chapter Ⅲ Rights, duties and obligations of plant protection authority and entrepreneurs

Article 35 Rights, Duties and Obligations of Plant protection officers and Authorities

- Plant protection officers and Authorities have the follow primary right and duties:

1. To disseminate, propagate and provide recommendation to society in implementation of the laws, rules and regulations on plant protection

2. To inspect and verify the phytosanitary certification and relevant document

3. To permit the entry of plant, plant product and regulated article after the result of inspection shown non infestation

4. To detain and quarantine plant, plant product and regulated article known coming from epidemic area

5. To notify the owner on the designed treatment or return or destruction of infested plant, plant product and regulated article according to the regulation.

6. To take measure against violation under plant protection law and regulations wihin the areas of their responsibilities including seizes goods, propose to confine violator and present he case file to the relevant sector for prosecution.

7. Coordinate with others relevant sectors and local administrative authority during the perform of their duty.

8. Evaluate and regularly report the performance of plant protection activity to higher levels of authority.

- Plant Protection Officers and Authorities have the following obligations:

1. To implement the rule, regulation and Law including agreement and international convention to which the Lao PDR. is the contracting party;

2. To assist and monitor pest eradication program in epidermic area or in the case of emergency.

3. To facilitate business operations involving plants, plant products and regulated articles in strict accordance with the laws and regulations;

4. To collect and forward the fee and other charge on plant protection service in under the laws and regulations.

Article 36 Rights and Obligations of Entrepreneurs

Entrepreneurs have the rights and obligations as follows:

1. To operate their businesses as authorised strictly following the technical standards and the laws and regulations;

2. To take ownership in preventing, controlling, treating and eradicating pests as well as using all available measures for prevention and solving problem caused spreading of pest by export and import plant, plant product and regulate article from the infested area.

3. To complain to the relevant organisation about offences under the laws and regulations committed by plant protection officials and authority;

4. To assist contribute the development of plant quarantine work by donating funds or labour;

5. To cooperate with public officers, facilitates the work of officials and provide necessary information;

6. To inform or report situation, event or case of pest detected or suspected to be spread out to relevant authority and local administrative authority.

7. To pay charge and fees service and others obligations as prescribed under regulations and laws.

Article 37 Rights and Obligations of Citizens

1. To take ownership in monitoring and controlling pest incident in their properties.

2. To report pest incident in their properties to the competence authority and local administrative authority.

3. To cooperate with plant protection officers and authorities in performing plant protection works.

4. To appeal to relevant organization on activities of entrepreneurs, plant protection officers and authorities against violation of plant protection law.

Chapter Ⅳ Prohibitions

Articles 38 General prohibition

Individuals, families and other entities including domestic and foreign entrepreneurs are prohibited from committing the following:

1. To Import plant, plant product and regulated articles that causes potential impact to national economic development and harms to health of plants, animals and humans in the Lao People Democratic Republic.

2. To move plant, plant product and regulated articles from infested area to others area within the country.

3. To export, re - export and transit of plant, plant product and regulated article that infested with harmful pest.

4. Import, export, movement and unload of plant, plant product and regulated articles without permission.

5. Bribing of plant protection officers and authorities, forging of document and falsification of seal on plant protection.

6. Threatening, delaying or impeding the performance of plant protection officers and authorities.

7. Performing other activities against violation of plant protection law.

Article 39 Prohibition of Plant protection officers and authorities

In addition to the prohibitions identified in article 38 of this Law, the following are prohibited for plant protection officers and authorities:

1. To abuse his/her powers and duty by forcing or threatening, coercing, pressurising and accepting bribes that may lead to damage to interests of state, collective and individual.

2. To disclose public or official confidential items; delays or forge document; acting irresponsibly in the given tasks on plant protection activities.

3. To ignore the regulation and rule on inspection of plant, plant product and regulated articles, solving problem inconsistence with technical procedure.

4. To increase or reduce charge and service fee and use collated fee for their personal benefit without permission.

Chapter V Conflict resolution

Article 40 Form of Conflict resolution

Conflict relating to plant protection shall be resolved according to the following:

1. Resolution by compromise among 2 parties.

2. Resolution by Administration of Agriculture and Forestry office in coordination with others relevant sectors.

3. Resolution by the Economic Conflict Resolution Committee;

4. Resolution by the People's Court.

Article 41 International Conflict Resolution

Conflict on plan protection between Lao and foreign entrepreneur; foreign and between foreign entrepreneur in Lao PDR. or foreign entrepreneur and Lao state organization shall be solved by domestic, foreign and international Economic Conflict Resolution Committee.

Conflict relating to plant protection practices that are international in nature shall be based on the contract and treaties to which Lao PDR. is a party and related international regulation.

Chapter Ⅵ Administration and inspection

Session 1 Administration

Article 42 Administrative Organization

The Government administers activities in plant protection matters in harmony by a centralized system and gives authority to the Ministry of Agriculture and Forestry to act as coordinate central along with other sectors concerns such as Industry and Commerce, Public health and local administrative authority.

The Plant protection administration organization comprises:

1. The ministry of Agriculture;

2. Provincial/Municipality/prefecture/city Agriculture and Forestry officers;

3. District/Town Agriculture and Forestry offices;

4. Plant Protection border check point.

Article 43 Rights and Duties of the Ministry of Agriculture and Forestry

In the administration of plant protection activities, the Ministry of Agriculture and forestry has the following right and duties:

1. To serve as secretariat for government in study and transform policy guideline, strategy, policy plans and other policies into detail programs, projects, laws, rules, and regulation in order to administrates and manage activities of plant protection throughout the country.

2. To disseminate policies, laws, rule and regulations related to plant protection countrywide.

3. To guide, monitor and evaluate the implementation of plant protection measures by vertical line agencies countrywide.

4. To build capacity, provide training, appoint, transfer or dismiss plant protection officials and authority in coordination with other relevant sectors and local authorities.

5. To authorise the establishment of plant protection border checkpoints and laboratories in coordination with other relevant sectors and local authorities.

6. To authorise the opening or closing down of phytosanitary business operations.

7. To raise and mobilize funds from both domestic and international sources for plant protection development.

8. To resolve conflicts, issue decisions, ordinances, notifications and instructions to plant protection and officer, entrepreneurs for the implementation of plant protection law, rules and regulations.

9. To coordinate with other concerns sectors and local authorities in implementing plant protection activities such as pest surveillance in order to determine areas for control of all pests or of specific pests including those on the list of regulated pests.

10. To manage issuing of permissions for plant import and export, and of phytosanitary certificate and other relevant documents with its area responsibility.

11. To communicate and cooperate with foreign countries in plant quarantine.

12. To regularly summarise and report on performance of plant quarantine such as pest incidence to the government.

Article 44 Rights and Duties of the Provincial and Vientiane Capital Agriculture and Forestry Offices

In the administration of plant protection activities, the Provincial and Vientiane Capital Agriculture and Forestry Offices have the following right and duties:

1. To transform policies, strategies, agreements, directives and regulations for plant protection work into detail programs and projects in order to implement within its own areas of responsibility.

2. To propose, publicise and disseminate laws and regulations, and information related to development of the plant protection work for public understanding and awareness, and strictly implementation them.

3. To guide, monitor and evaluate results of the implementation of plant protection of the District and Municipality Agriculture and Forestry Offices.

4. To propose the issue or cancel permission to operate a phyto – sanitary business in coordination with the relevant sectors and local authorities.

5. To manage the issuing of phyosanitary certificates and other documents in accordance with those responsibilities as assigned by higher authorities.

6. To manage and establish the list of regulated pests and determine quarantine area.

7. To raise and mobilize funds from both domestic and international sources for plant protection development within their own areas of responsibility or in accordance with those responsibilities as assigned by higher authorities.

8. To coordinate with other local authorities and sectors in the performance of plant protection work within their own areas of responsibility.

9. To summarise and regularly report on the implementation of plant quarantine work such as pest incidence in the provinces and Vientiane Capital to the Ministry of Agriculture and Forestry and the provincial and Vientiane Capital authorities.

Article 45 Rights and Duties of the District and Municipality Agriculture and Forestry Offices

In the administration of plant protection activities, the District and Municipality Agriculture and Forestry Offices have the following right and duties:

1. To implement the work plans, projects, decisions, ordinance, notification and guidance from higher authorities.

2. To disseminate plant protection laws and regulations for enhancing the public's understanding and strictly implement them.

3. To participate in the management, establish the list of prohibited plant pests and determining areas of plant infestation epidemics.

4. To participate in managing and establishing of the list of regulated pests and determining of quarantine area.

5. To resolve conflicts, propose the issue or cancel the permission of phytosanitary business operation to Provincial and Vientiane Capital Agriculture and Forestry Offices for consideration.

6. To coordinate with local authorities and the relevant sectors in district and municipality on the plant quarantine work.

7. To summarise and regularly report on the implementation of the plant quarantine work such as pest incidence within the districts and municipality to the Provincial and Vientiane Capital Agriculture and Forestry offices and the district and municipality administrative authorities.

Article 46 Rights and Duties of Plant protection border check point

Plant protection border check points have the following Rights and Duties:

1. To implement work plans, policies, Law, rules and regulations on plant protection within their own areas of responsibility.

2. To strictly, correctly and promptly perform their work duties in accordance with their roles and technical principles.

3. To repress activities in any forms to curve the law, rules and regulation on plant protection occurred at the check point and inform relevant sectors to prosecute violators.

4. To facilitate import - export of plants, plant products and regulated articles be fast, transparency and correct in line with the laws and regulations.

5. To coordinate with other relevant sectors at the border check point and local authorities to ensure the uniformity of implementation of work.

6. To detain, isolate and send samples for identification, inform entrepreneurs to carry out treatment, return or destruct infected plants, plant products and regulated articles.

7. To technical services collect charge and fees in line with the laws and regulations;

8. To summarise and regularly report on import - export data on plants, plant products and regulated articles at their own border check point to the agricultural and forestry sectors.

Article 47 Rights and Duties of Other Sectors

If any sections including the local authorities find or receive a report of pest epidemic and an offence under plant protection laws and regulations they must urgently inform Plant protection authority and cooperate and coordinate with the work of those authorities as determined by their own roles.

Section 2 Inspection

Article 48 Inspection organisation

Inspection organisation comprises:

• The Internal inspections organisation is equivalence to the management organisations of Plant protection as determined in Article 42 of this Law by Department of Agriculture, agriculture offices and agriculture units acting as representatives of the Agriculture and Forestry sector within their own areas of responsibility;

• The external inspections authorities are the National Assembly, the State Inspection authority, the National Inspection authority and the Public Prosecutor's authority.

Artcle 49. Rights and Duties of the Inspection Organisation

The organisations for the inspection of plants, plant products and other materials have the following rights and duties –:

1. To inspect the implementation of plant protection laws and regulations.
2. To inspect activities and operations of phytosanitary businesses.
3. To inspect phytosanitary certificates and other documents related to import – export plants, plant products and regulated through border check point including the collection of samples for testing and certification in accordance with the laws and regulations.
4. To cooperate in the provision of information for a criminal investigation related to a plant protection offence.
5. To appoint their own staff to monitor, inspect, collect information including as well as lead prevention of pest epidemic.
6. To use necessary measures for offences under plant protection laws and regulations or such as issuing orders to quit those activities related to plant protection when the import – export plants, plant products and other regulated articles found to be infected with pest.
7. To cooperate and coordinate with relevant sectors at the central and local levels for the exercise of their own rights and duties.
8. To summarise and regularly report on periodic work inspections to the next level of authority.

Article 50 Forms of Inspections

Inspections consist of three forms as follow:

1. Regular Inspections.
2. Inspections with advance notification.
3. Urgent inspections.

Regular inspections are inspections which are routine carried out in a prescribed times in accordance with the roles, rights and duties of the various management levels.

Inspections with advance notification are inspections that are deemed necessary and for which advance notification is given to the subject.

Urgent inspections are special inspections that are deemed necessary to be conducted urgently and for which no advance notification is given.

Chapter Ⅶ Uniforms, insignia and seal

Article 51 Uniforms and insignia

A Plant protection Official has uniforms, insignia and identity cards for a specific border check point which are authorised by the Ministry of Agriculture and Forestry. The plant protection authority shall wear a uniform with a insignia and carry an identity card for a specific border check point.

Article 52 Seal

Plant Quarantine Officials may use the official Border Plant Quarantine seal as authorised by the Ministry of

Agriculture and Forestry for the conduct of the official work of plant protection.

Chapter Ⅷ Rewards and penalties

Article 53 Rewards

Individuals or organisations that perform outstandingly in implementing this Law for example in regulation, inspection, control and eradication work, shall receive a award and other form of recognition in accordance with the regulations.

Article 54 Penalties

Individuals or organisations committing offences under this Law shall be subject to the following sanction: Re – educated, disciplinary sanctions, fined, penalty, civil sanctions and crime charges under the law depending on the severity of the offence.

Article 55 Re – educated Measures

Individuals or organisations that commit minor civil offences under the plant protection laws and regulations and prohibitions that result in damages of less than 500,000 kip, and provided that the offender makes an honest report recognising their wrong – doing and makes restitution of any property so gained – shall be warned and re – educated.

Article 56 Disciplinary Measures

Government staff and Plant protection authorities and officials that commit minor civil offences under the plant quarantine laws and regulations and prohibitions that result in damages of less than 500,000 kip but that make a dishonest report and try to avoid the repercussions of their wrong – doing, shall be disciplined, depending on the severity of the offence:

1. be criticised, receive a warning – that is recorded in the individual's personal biography;
2. have their promotion, any salary increase and/or presentation of any award delayed;
3. be demoted or transferred to a lower position;
4. be summarily dismissed from government service.

Article 57 Penalty Measures

Any indivuals or organisations committing offences under the plant protection laws and regulations and prohibitions as determined in this Law shall be fined that equal to the value of the plants infected by plant pests.

If the offender commits a second offence or re – offends many times the fine shall be double the value of the plants infected by plant pests, and the plants, plant products and regulated articles shall be confiscated and dealt with under the laws and regulations.

Article 58 Measures for Civil Offences

Individuals or organisations failing to observe plant quarantine and so causing damage to other persons shall be held responsible for the damage caused under the laws and regulations.

Article 59 Measures for Criminal Offences

Individuals or organisations committing criminal offences under plant protection laws and regulations shall be punished in accordance with the Penal Law depending on the severity of the offence and fined under the Civil Law.

Article 60 Measures for Further Punishment

In addition to punishments as determined in Article 59, offenders may face further punishment in accordance with the measures for further punishment such as suspension or cancellation of permission for the operation of plant protection and phytosanitary business activities.

Chapter Ⅸ　Final provisions

Article 61　Implementation

This Law shall be implemented by the Government of the Lao People's Democratic Republic.

Article 62　Effectiveness

This Law enters into force ninety days after the date of the promulgation of the Decree of the President of the Lao People's Democratic Republic.

Any provisions and regulation which are in contradiction to this Law shall be all abolished.

President of the National Assembly

Thongsing THAMMAVONG